IDEAS OF HUMAN NATURE
From the Bhagavad Gita to Sociobiology

David P. Barash

University of Washington

PRENTICE HALL, Upper Saddle River, New Jersey 07458

Library of Congress Cataloging-in-Publication Data

Barash, David P.
   Ideas of human nature : from the Bhagavad Gita to sociobiology /
David P. Barash.
     p. cm.
   Includes bibliographical references.
   ISBN 0-13-647587-6
   1. Philosophical anthropology. I. Title.
BD450.B288   1998
128—dc21   97-36775
                                     CIP

Editorial Director: Charlyce Jones Owen
Acquisitions Editor: Karita France
Assistant Editor: Emsal Hasan
Editorial Assistant: Jennifer Ackerman
Managing Editor: Jan Stephan
Project Manager: Karen Trost/ComCom
Project Liaison: Fran Russello
Manufacturing Manager: Nick Sklitsis
Prepress and Manufacturing Buyer: Tricia Kenny
Cover Director: Jayne Conte
Cover Designer: Bruce Kenselaar
Marketing Manager: Chris Johnson

This book was set in 10/12 Helvetica by ComCom
and printed and bound by Courier Companies, Inc.
The cover was printed by Phoenix Color Corp.

Acknowledgments appear on pp. 292–294, which constitute a continuation of this copyright page.

 © 1998 by Prentice-Hall, Inc.
Simon & Schuster/A Viacom Company
Upper Saddle River, NJ 07458

Printed in the United States of America

10   9   8   7   6   5   4   3   2   1

ISBN 0-13-647587-6

Prentice-Hall International (UK) Limited, *London*
Prentice-Hall of Australia Pty. Limited, *Sydney*
Prentice-Hall Canada Inc., *Toronto*
Prentice-Hall Hispanoamericana, S.A., *Mexico*
Prentice-Hall of India Private Limited, *New Delhi*
Prentice-Hall of Japan, Inc., *Tokyo*
Simon & Schuster Asian Pte. Ltd., *Singapore*
Editora Prentice-Hall do Brasil, Ltda., *Rio de Janeiro*

PART III   THE SOCIAL SETTING   126

Contents

18. UNIQUELY HUMAN?   279

CREDITS   292

Introduction: The Idea of *Ideas of Human Nature*

"Self-contemplation is a curse," wrote the poet Theodore Roethke, "that makes an old confusion worse." Maybe so, but self-contemplation has long been a human preoccupation, nonetheless. Socrates urged each student to "know thyself," and Alexander Pope echoed, "Know then thyself, presume not God to scan; the proper study of mankind is man" (to which we happily add, "and woman"). And yet, although people have been struggling to understand themselves for thousands of years, it cannot be said that human nature is currently "known," nor does it seem likely to be fully understood any time soon, if ever. Such efforts have been rewarding, however, and that is where *Ideas of Human Nature* comes in.

In this volume I have tried to gather some of the most renowned and stimulating attempts at humanity's self-contemplation. (I have not been shy about including some fiction as well—poetry and prose—since there is no reason to think that philosophers and scientists have a monopoly on understanding or depicting human nature.) This book, then, is a sampling of great thoughts by great thinkers, most of which have already stood the test of time. Ethicists sometimes say that we should steer by the light of the stars and not by that of each passing ship; my goal in this book has been to provide a survey of the stars, when it comes to the nature of human nature.

Such an enterprise has built-in disadvantages. Of necessity, *Ideas of Human Nature* treads lightly on any one perspective. This is the downside of whatever benefit comes from covering so many diverse points of view. (Mark Twain said that it was easy to stop smoking: he had done it hundreds of times! Similarly, it is easy to understand human nature; many people have "done" it!) But perhaps the brevity of each treatment can itself become an asset, if students and instructors use *Ideas of Human Nature* as a plate of hors d'oeuvres, a tasty introduction that whets their appetite for more nourishing fare. This book will therefore be especially successful if it makes itself obsolete, if it inspires readers to experience the originals—and other works—in their entirety.

Even then, no one should be under any illusion that he or she is likely to catch and pin human nature, like a prize insect, in a collector's box. The human species may very well be too complex for easy—or even difficult!—generalization. In his "Essay on Man," Alexander Pope lamented that

He hangs between, in doubt to act, or rest,
In doubt to deem himself a God, or beast;
In doubt his mind or body to prefer;
Born but to die, and reasoning but to err.

Pope concluded that we are creatures of preeminent paradox:

Created half to rise and half to fall;
Great lord of all things, yet a prey to all;
Sole judge of truth, in endless error hurled:
The glory, jest, and riddle of the world!

Perhaps this, too, is an idea of human nature: that *Homo sapiens* is paradoxical, maybe even unknowable. But it is nonetheless worth a try, if only because it makes for such great sport.

Although I have designed *Ideas of Human Nature* to survey various theories of human nature rather than to suggest definitive answers, I, like just about everyone else, have my own bias as to what human nature is "really about," and I encourage instructors to indulge their own preferences and inclinations and to supplement *Ideas of Human Nature* with texts of their own choosing. Each chapter includes some study questions intended to help stimulate discussion, and/or serve as the basis for paper topics, essay exams, bull sessions, and so on. I also conclude each chapter with a small number of suggested additional readings. Just as it was difficult to choose among so much excellent primary material in putting this book together, it was also frustrating to recommend a handful of such readings amid the immense array of excellent material. . . . Sort of like selecting your favorite stars among a glittering nighttime array.

Two other things. First, it is sometimes unfair to the authors when a small segment of their work is reprinted as part of what I, as editor, chose to illustrate a particular perspective on human nature. My goal has not been to present a rounded sample of each person's work but to focus on aspects that illuminate a particular approach to human nature. Plato, for example, didn't concern himself only with the nature of the human soul, nor did Locke restrict himself to the role of experience in giving rise to thought. Moreover, even the limited selections reprinted here often concern themselves with things other than the topic of each particular chapter in which they are placed. Pigeonholing may be intellectually satisfying, but it can be misleading to students, and—like the unfortunate victims of Procrustes, that mythical highwayman who used to stretch or amputate his prey to fit his iron bed—it generally does violence to those forced to undergo the procedure. My apologies to everyone thus victimized.

Second, although ideas of human nature are in no way limited to Western thought, *Ideas of Human Nature* pretty much is. For this, I accept full responsibility and offer no excuses other than my personal limitations, including, perhaps, my own nature, complete with its share of human failings.

If this is a good book—and I would like to think it is!—then the credit must be shared. Most of all, I thank those thinkers and writers whose ideas of human nature, herein captured, have made *Ideas of Human Nature* possible. Particular thanks also goes to Angie Stone, for seeing merit in the initial concept; Karita France, for seeing it through to completion; Karen Trost, for attending so beautifully to its many details; and to the reviewers of the text: Andrew Beedle, Trinity College (Connecticut); Daniel Conway, Pennsylvania State University; Suzanne Cunningham, Loyola University (Chicago); and Dale Jacquette, Pennsylvania State University. I am grateful, as well, to my honors students at the University of Washington, for serving as willing, helpful, and creative guinea pigs, as I kept searching for the best possible mix of "ideas." And to my family, who remind me in so many ways (most of them delightful) that "human nature" is not merely a theoretical construct.

David P. Barash

PART ONE
RELIGIOUS VIEWS

People look at themselves, and at the problem of who and what they are, in many ways. In some cases, truth or falsity can be demonstrated, as when images of human nature involve specific statements of fact: details of evolution, for example, or about the information-processing capacity of the human brain. In others, however, the truth of any given idea of human nature is more debatable, perhaps even beyond evidence. This is especially so when it comes to religious ideas about human nature. Our task in such cases is to try to understand these approaches or, failing that, at least to glimpse their diversity (and sometimes, their underlying similarity).

CHAPTER ONE

In the Beginning: Views of Creation and Being

There are very many creation stories, describing how human beings came to be; indeed, such accounts can be identified for virtually every human culture, including perhaps the smallest tribal group. Beliefs about human origin are widely catalogued in the world's folktales and mythologies. In this chapter, we are not especially concerned with the specifics: whether, for example, a particular tradition holds that the first human beings were formed from mud, or the stars, or a particular body part of an animal, or of God. Rather, we consider samples from some of the major religious approaches to what human beings *are* (which often merges imperceptibly into what they ought to be, or to do). Debate often swirls around whether any given account is to be taken literally or as metaphor. In addition, although it is generally possible to identify an orthodox perspective within any tradition, we must note that all of the world's predominant religions contain various contending sects, each of which makes use of its own interpretations.

HINDU (THE *BHAGAVAD GITA*)

Hinduism is the world's oldest living religion. It employs many sacred writings, including the ancient Vedas and numerous other texts, as well as a lengthy epic, the *Mahabharata.* Part of the *Mahabharata,* in turn, is the *Bhagavad Gita,* considered by most Hindus to contain the core of their belief. In the "Gita," the warrior Arjuna is instructed by his charioteer, Krishna (who is really an incarnation of the god Vishnu), about his responsibility as a human being, which in this case is to participate in a dreadful battle. But the Gita is far more concerned with an interior battle, that of human beings in search of their deeper selves.

According to Hinduism—and to many other religious traditions—there is timeless reality to human existence beneath the superficial world of change and appearances. This deeper self, the Atman, transcends our immediate concerns. In the following selections, Krishna speaks both as God and as the Atman.

The wise grieve neither for the living nor for the dead. There has never been a time when you and I and the kings gathered here have not existed, nor will there be a time when we will cease to exist. As the same person inhabits the body through childhood, youth, and old age, so too at the time of death he attains another body. The wise are not deluded by these changes.

When the senses contact sense objects, a person experiences cold or heat, pleasure or pain. These experiences are fleeting; they come and go. Bear them patiently, Arjuna. Those who are not affected by these changes, who are the same in pleasure and pain, are truly wise and fit for immortality. Assert your strength and realize this!

The impermanent has no reality; reality lies in the eternal. Those who have seen the boundary between these two have attained the end of all knowledge. Realize that which pervades the universe and is indestructible; no power can affect this unchanging, imperishable reality. The body is mortal, but he who dwells in the body is immortal and immeasurable. Therefore, Arjuna, fight in this battle.

One man believes he is the slayer, another believes he is the slain. Both are ignorant; there is neither slayer nor slain. You were never born; you will never die. You have never changed; you can never change. Unborn, eternal, immutable, immemorial, you do not die when the body dies. Realizing that which is indestructible, eternal, unborn, and unchanging, how can you slay or cause another to slay?

As a man abandons worn-out clothes and acquires new ones, so when the body is worn out a new one is acquired by the Self, who lives within.

The Self cannot be pierced by weapons or burned by fire; water cannot wet it, nor can the wind dry it. The Self cannot be pierced or burned, made wet or dry. It is everlasting and infinite, standing on the motionless foundations of eternity. The Self is unmanifested, beyond all thought, beyond all change. Knowing this, you should not grieve.

O mighty Arjuna, even if you believe the Self to be subject to birth and death, you should not grieve. Death is inevitable for the living; birth is inevitable for the dead. Since these are unavoidable, you should not sorrow. Every creature is unmanifested at first and then attains manifestation. When its end has come, it once again becomes unmanifested. What is there to lament in this?

The glory of the Self is beheld by a few, and a few describe it; a few listen, but many without understanding. The Self of all beings, living within the body, is eternal and cannot be harmed. Therefore, do not grieve. . . .

They live in wisdom who see themselves in all and all in them, who have renounced every selfish desire and sense craving tormenting the heart.

Neither agitated by grief nor hankering after pleasure, they live free from lust and fear and anger. Established in meditation, they are truly wise. Fettered no more by selfish attachments, they are neither elated by good fortune nor depressed by bad. Such are the seers.

Even as a tortoise draws in its limbs, the wise can draw in their senses at will. Aspirants abstain from sense pleasures, but they still crave for them. These cravings all disappear when they see the highest goal. Even of those who tread the path, the stormy senses can sweep off the mind. They live in wisdom who subdue their senses and keep their minds ever absorbed in me.

When you keep thinking about sense objects, attachment comes. Attachment breeds desire, the lust of possession that burns to anger. Anger clouds the judgment; you can no longer learn from past mistakes. Lost is the power to choose between what is wise and what is unwise, and your life is utter waste. But when you move amidst the world of sense, free from attachment and aversion alike, there comes the peace in which all sorrows end, and you live in the wisdom of the Self.

The disunited mind is far from wise; how can it meditate? How be at peace? When you know no peace, how can you know joy? When you let your mind follow the call of the senses, they carry away your better judgment as storms drive a boat off its charted course on the sea.

Use all your power to free the senses from attachment and aversion alike, and live in the full wisdom of the Self. Such a sage awakes to light in the night of all creatures. That which the world calls day is the night of ignorance to the wise.

As rivers flow into the ocean but cannot make the vast ocean overflow, so flow the streams of the sense-world into the sea of peace that is the sage. But this is not so with the desirer of desires.

They are forever free who renounce all selfish desires and break away from the ego-cage of "I," "me," and "mine" to be united with the Lord. This is the supreme state. Attain to this, and pass from death to immortality.*

---

*From *Bhagavad Gita* (1985). (E. Easwaran, Trans.). Petaluma, CA: Nilgiri Press.

The Gita succinctly expresses the closest that Hinduism comes to an explicit taxonomy of human nature: the three *gunas*. These are primordial mixtures of energy and matter, which have no translations into English. In a sense, *tamas,* the lowest, can be seen as stability, or, more negatively, inertia, darkness, sloth, and ignorance. It is also equivalent to a specieswide unconscious. *Rajas,* or activity, is ambition, enthusiasm, will, or, more negatively, passion, greed, or hatred. It is the goad to action but also the vigorous play of the mind. The highest of the three gunas, *sattva,* indicates harmony; it is serene, detached, and unruffled. All states of mind and matter—and thus, all human personalities—involve different proportions of *tamas, rajas,* and *sattva.* Even *sattva,* however, for all its seeming perfection, must eventually be overcome if the self is to attain final peace and liberation.

It is the three gunas born of prakriti—sattva, rajas, and tamas—that bind the immortal Self to the body. Sattva—pure, luminous, and free from sorrow—binds us with attachment to happiness and wisdom. Rajas is passion, arising from selfish desire and attachment. These bind the Self with compulsive action. Tamas, born of ignorance, deludes all creatures through heedlessness, indolence, and sleep.

Sattva binds us to happiness; rajas binds us to action. Tamas, distorting our understanding, binds us to delusion.

Sattva predominates when rajas and tamas are transformed. Rajas prevails when sattva is weak and tamas overcome. Tamas prevails when rajas and sattva are dormant.

When sattva predominates, the light of wisdom shines through every gate of the body. When rajas predominates, a person runs about pursuing selfish and greedy ends, driven by restlessness and desire. When tamas is dominant a person lives in darkness—slothful, confused, and easily infatuated.

Those dying in the state of sattva attain the pure worlds of the wise. Those dying in rajas are reborn among people driven by work. But those who die in tamas are conceived in the wombs of the ignorant.

The fruit of good deeds is pure and sattvic. The fruit of rajas is suffering. The fruit of tamas is ignorance and insensitivity.

From sattva comes understanding; from rajas, greed. But the outcome of tamas is confusion, infatuation, and ignorance.

Those who live in sattva go upwards; those in rajas remain where they are. But those immersed in tamas sink downwards.

The wise see clearly that all action is the work of the gunas. Knowing that which is above the gunas, they enter into union with me.*

*From *Bhagavad Gita* (1985). (E. Easwaran, Trans.). Petaluma, CA: Nilgiri Press.

BUDDHIST (THE *PRAJÑAPARAMITA SUTRA*)

Buddhism was founded in India about 500 BCE by Siddhartha Guatama (the title *Buddha* means Enlightened One). Legend has it that the Buddha was deeply troubled by the pain and suffering of life and resolved to obtain freedom from it. After unsuccessfully seeking enlightenment by extreme self-denial, he eventually achieved wisdom and peace. There are many doctrines, numerous schools of thought and practice, and an abundance of lengthy and difficult texts in Buddhism (as in all of the major world religions); the *Prajñaparamita* or *Heart Sutra,* however, is widely regarded as the essence of Buddhist teaching. It is concerned as much with the nature of being as with the nature of human beings. This is significant because, according to Buddhism, human beings are inseparably connected to the rest of the world.

The *Prajñaparamita Sutra* was taught by Avalokitisvara, one of the most beloved *bodhisattvas,* or Buddhas who devote themselves to bringing peace and enlightenment to others. Westerners seeking to "penetrate" this brief, dense, paradoxical teaching will profit from the following glossary:

> Avalokita—Avalokitisvara
> bodhi—awake
> bodhisattva—an awakened being
> dharma—path or way (in the *Prajnaparamita Sutra* it refers to things generally)
> the five skandhas—the five major components of human beings (body, feelings, perceptions, thoughts, and consciousness)
> gate (pronounced "gah-tay"), gate, paragate parasamgate bodhi svaha,—[the concluding mantra, loosely translated as "gone, gone, gone far beyond, all gone together, oh what an awakening, hallelujah!"
> mantra—a repeated phrase or sequence that is—or becomes—especially meaningful
> nirvana—a state of perfect peace
> prajñaparamita—perfect understanding
> sattva—living being

Zen master Thich Nhat Hanh provides some useful clues for interpreting the *Prajñaparamitra Sutra.* He emphasizes, for example, that the key concept is "inter-being," by which he means that nothing exists by itself. All things are connected, composed of energy and matter that is shared: a sheet of paper, for example, literally contains within it a cloud (moisture), soil, sunlight, trees, a logger, the logger's parents, and so on. Similarly for people. When Avalokita says that all things are "empty," he means that they are empty of an isolated, independent existence. Moreover, all things are impermanent: At heart, they were never really created, nor can they ever be destroyed, and thus, "The Prajñaparamita gives us solid ground for making peace with ourselves, for transcending the fear of birth and death, the duality of this and that. In the light of emptiness, everything is everything else, we inter-are, everyone is responsible for everything that happens in life."

It would probably be best to read the *Prajñaparamita Sutra* more than once, giving it more attention than its brevity and paradox might seem to warrant.

The Heart of the Prajñaparamita

The Bodhisattva Avalokita, while moving in the deep course of Perfect Understanding, shed light on the five skandhas and found them equally empty. After this penetration, he overcame all pain.

"Listen, Shariputra, form is emptiness, emptiness is form, form does not differ from emptiness, emptiness does not differ from form. The same is true with feelings, perceptions, mental formations, and consciousness.

"Hear, Shariputra, all dharmas are marked with emptiness; they are neither produced nor destroyed, neither defiled nor immaculate, neither increasing nor decreasing. Therefore, in emptiness there is neither form, nor feeling, nor perception, nor mental formations, nor consciousness; no eye, or ear, or nose, or tongue, or body, or mind, no form, no sound, no smell, no taste, no touch, no object of mind; no realms of elements (from eyes to mind-consciousness); no interdependent origins and no extinction of them (from ignorance to death and decay); no suffering, no origination of suffering, no extinction of suffering, no path; no understanding, no attainment.

"Because there is no attainment, the bodhisattvas, supported by the Perfection of Understanding, find no obstacles for their minds. Having no obstacles, they overcome fear, liberating themselves forever from illusion and realizing perfect Nirvana. All Buddhas in the past, present, and future, thanks to this Perfect Understanding, arrive at full, right, and universal Enlightenment.

"Therefore, one should know that Perfect Understanding is a great mantra, is the highest mantra, is the unequalled mantra, the destroyer of all suffering, the incorruptible truth. A mantra of Prajñaparamita should therefore be proclaimed. This is the mantra:

"Gate gate paragate parasamgate bodhi svaha."*

TAOIST (THE *TAO TE CHING*)

Chinese religious tradition has long been closely akin to philosophy. True to form, Taoism (pronounced "dow-ism") has both a philosophical and a religious component; both are joined in the renowned *Tao Te Ching.* This mixture of prose, poetry, philosophy, and political advice is believed to have been written between the fifth and first centuries BCE; its authorship is

*From *Prajñaparamita Sutra* (1988). (Thich Nat Hanh, Trans.). Berkeley, CA: Parallax Press.

equally uncertain, although it is widely attributed to the Chinese sage, Lao tsu. Taoism stands in contrast to an even older Chinese tradition, the teachings of Confucius, and may have developed in reaction to it. Thus, whereas Confucius taught the importance of submission to rigid sociocultural tradition and authority, Taoism celebrated nature, and the free, spontaneous human spirit. Although "the Tao" is generally translated "the Way" (as in, "the Way of perfect peace,") it is often employed by Taoists to signify "the way" of human nature, such that happiness and a fulfilling life can best be achieved by behaving in accord with "one's Tao."

Tao can be talked about, but not the Eternal Tao.
Names can be named, but not the Eternal Name.
As the origin of heaven-and-earth, it is nameless:
As "the Mother" of all things, it is nameable.
So, as ever hidden, we should look at its inner essence:
As always manifest, we should look at its outer aspects.
There two flow from the same source, though differently named;
And both are called mysteries.
The Mystery of mysteries is the Door of all essence. . . .

Heaven-and-Earth is not sentimental;
It treats all things as straw-dogs. . . .
Between Heaven and Earth, There seems to be a Bellows:
It is empty, and yet it is inexhaustible;
The more it works, the more comes out of it.
No amount of words can fathom it: Better look for it within you. . . .

It lies in the nature of Grand Virtue
To follow the Tao and the Tao alone.
Now what is the Tao?
It is Something elusive and evasive. Evasive and elusive!
And yet It contains within Itself a Form. Elusive and evasive!
Any yet It contains within Itself a Substance. Shadowy and dim!
And yet it contains within Itself a Core of Vitality.
The Core of Vitality is very real,
It contains within Itself an unfailing Sincerity.
Throughout the ages Its Name has been preserved
In order to recall the Beginning of all things.
How do I know the ways of all things at the Beginning?
By what is within me. . . .

He who knows men is clever; He who knows himself has insight.
He who conquers men has force; He who conquers himself is truly strong. . . .

When a man is living, he is soft and supple,
When he is dead, he becomes hard and rigid.
When a plant is living, it is soft and tender.
When it is dead, it becomes withered and dry.
Hence, the hard and rigid belongs to the company of the dead:
The soft and supple belongs to the company of the living.
Therefore, a mighty army tends to fall by its own weight,
Just as dry wood is ready for the axe. . . .

Nothing in the world is softer and weaker than water;
But, for attacking the hard and strong, there is nothing like it!
For nothing can take its place.*

JUDEO-CHRISTIAN (THE OLD TESTAMENT)

The Bible is overwhelmingly concerned with describing the relationship between God and people. It contains relatively little that speaks directly to the question of human nature; this is true of both the Old and New Testaments. It is nonetheless possible to infer a Jewish and Christian idea of human beings, although like so much in the Bible, there is abundant material to support a variety of interpretations.

Much of the Old Testament is taken up with detailing the covenant between God and the Israelites, although perspectives on human nature can readily be gleaned from the books of Job and Ecclesiastes, as well as specific depictions of identifiable personalities. A review of the Ten Commandments also leads to conclusions about the Judaic view of human nature, if only because we can assume there would be no need to prohibit behavior that people did not find tempting!

To explore the richest Old Testament source, however, we begin, literally, with The Beginning.

Genesis 1–4:16

IN THE BEGINNING GOD CREATED the heavens and the earth. The earth was without form and void, and darkness was upon the face of the deep; and the Spirit of God was moving over the face of the waters.

And God said, "Let there be light"; and there was light. And God saw that the light was good; and God separated the light from the darkness. God called the light Day, and the darkness he called Night. And there was evening and there was morning, one day.

And God said, "Let there be a firmament in the midst of the waters, and let it separate the waters from the waters." And God made the firmament and separated the waters which were under the firmament

---

*From *Tao Te Ching* (1961). (John C. H. Wu, Trans.). New York, NY: St. John's University Press.

from the waters which were above the firmament. And it was so. And God called the firmament Heaven. And there was evening and there was morning, a second day.

And God said, "Let the waters under the heavens be gathered together into one place, and let the dry land appear." And it was so. God called the dry land Earth, and the waters that were gathered together he called Seas. And God saw that it was good. And God said, "Let the earth put forth vegetation, plants yielding seed, and fruit trees bearing fruit in which is their seed, each according to its kind, upon the earth." And it was so. The earth brought forth vegetation, plants yielding seed according to their own kinds, and trees bearing fruit in which is their seed, each according to its kind. And God saw that it was good. And there was evening and there was morning, a third day.

And God said, "Let there be lights in the firmament of the heavens to separate the day from the night; and let them be for signs and for seasons and for days and years, and let them be lights in the firmament of the heavens to give light upon the earth." And it was so. And God made the two great lights, the greater light to rule the day, and the lesser light to rule the night; he made the stars also. And God set them in the firmament of the heavens to give light upon the earth, to rule over the day and over the night, and to separate the light from the darkness. And God saw that it was good. And there was evening and there was morning, a fourth day.

And God said, "Let the waters bring forth swarms of living creatures, and let birds fly above the earth across the firmament of the heavens." So God created the great sea monsters and every living creature that moves, with which the waters swarm, according to their kinds, and every winged bird according to its kind. And God saw that it was good. And God blessed them, saying, "Be fruitful and multiply and fill the waters in the seas, and let birds multiply on the earth." And there was evening and there was morning, a fifth day.

And God said, "Let the earth bring forth living creatures according to their kinds: cattle and creeping things and beasts of the earth according to their kinds." And it was so. And God made the beasts of the earth according to their kinds and the cattle according to their kinds, and everything that creeps upon the ground according to its kind. And God saw that it was good.

Then God said, "Let us make man in our image, after our likeness; and let them have dominion over the fish of the sea, and over the birds of the air, and over the cattle, and over all the earth, and over every creeping thing that creeps upon the earth." So God created man in his own image, in the image of God he created him; male and female he created them. And God blessed them, and God said to them, "Be fruitful and multiply, and fill the earth and subdue it; and have dominion over the fish of the sea and over the birds of the air and over every living thing that moves upon the earth." And God said, "Behold, I have given you every plant yielding seed which is upon the face of all the earth, and every tree with seed in its fruit; you shall have them for food. And to every beast of the earth, and to every bird of the air, and to everything that creeps on the earth, everything that has the breath of life, I have given every green plant for food." And it was so. And God saw everything that he had made, and behold, it was very good. And there was evening and there was morning, a sixth day.

Thus the heavens and the earth were finished, and all the host of them. And on the seventh day God finished his work which he had done, and he rested on the seventh day from all his work which he had done. So God blessed the seventh day and hallowed it, because on it God rested from all his work which he had done in creation.

These are the generations of the heavens and the earth when they were created.

In the day that the LORD God made the earth and the heavens, when no plant of the field was yet in the earth and no herb of the field had yet sprung up—for the LORD God had not caused it to rain upon the earth, and there was no man to till the ground; but a mist went up from the earth and watered the whole face of the ground— then the LORD God formed man of dust from the ground, and breathed into his nostrils the breath of life; and man became a living being. And the LORD God planted a garden in Eden, in the east; and there he put the man whom he had formed. And out of the ground the LORD God made to grow every tree that is pleasant to the sight and good for food, the tree of life also in the midst of the garden, and the tree of the knowledge of good and evil. . . .

The LORD God took the man and put him in the garden of Eden to till it and keep it. And the LORD God commanded the man, saying, "You may freely eat of every tree of the garden; but of the tree of the knowledge of good and evil you shall not eat, for in the day that you eat of it you shall die."

Then the LORD God said, "It is not good that the man should be alone; I will make him a helper fit for him." So out of the ground the LORD God formed every beast of the field and every bird of the air, and brought them to the man to see what he would call them; and whatever the man called every living creature, that was its name. The man gave names to all cattle, and to the birds of the air, and to every beast of the field; but for the man there was not found a helper fit for him. So the LORD God caused a deep sleep to fall upon the man, and while he slept took one of his ribs and closed up its place with flesh; and the rib which the LORD God had taken from the man he made into a woman and brought her to the man. Then the man said, "This at last is bone of my bones and flesh of my flesh; she shall be called Woman, because she was taken out of Man." Therefore a man leaves his father and his mother and cleaves to his wife, and they become one flesh. And the man and his wife were both naked, and were not ashamed.

Now the serpent was more subtle than any other wild creature that the LORD God had made. He said to the woman, "Did God say, 'You shall not eat of any tree of the garden'?" And the woman said to the serpent, "We may eat of the fruit of the trees of the garden; but God said, 'You shall not eat of the fruit of the tree which is in the midst of the garden, neither shall you touch it, lest you die.' " But the serpent said to the woman, "You will not die. For God knows that when you eat of it your eyes will be opened, and you will be like God, knowing good and evil." So when the woman saw that the tree was good for food, and that it was a delight to the eyes, and that the tree was to be desired to make one wise, she took of its fruit and ate; and she also gave some to her husband, and he ate. Then the eyes of both were opened, and they knew that they were naked; and they sewed fig leaves together and made themselves aprons.

And they heard the sound of the LORD God walking in the garden in the cool of the day, and the man and his wife hid themselves from the presence of the LORD God among the trees of the garden. But the LORD God called to the man, and said to him, "Where are you?" And he said, "I heard the sound of thee in the garden, and I was afraid, because I was naked; and I hid myself." He said, "Who told you that you were naked? Have you eaten of the tree of which I commanded you not to eat?" The man said, "The woman whom thou gavest to be with me, she gave me fruit of the tree, and I ate." Then the LORD God said to the woman, "What is this that you have done?" The woman said, "The serpent beguiled me, and I ate." The LORD God said to the serpent, "Because you have done this, cursed are you above all cattle, and above all wild animals; upon your belly you shall go, and dust you shall eat all the days of your life. I will put enmity between you and the woman, and between your seed and her seed; he shall bruise your head, and you shall bruise his heel."

To the woman he said, "I will greatly multiply your pain in childbearing; in pain you shall bring forth children, yet your desire shall be for your husband, and he shall rule over you."

And to Adam he said, "Because you have listened to the voice of your wife, and have eaten of the tree of which I commanded you, 'You shall not eat of it,' cursed is the ground because of you; in toil you shall eat of it all the days of your life; thorns and thistles it shall bring forth to you; and you shall eat the plants of the field. In the sweat of your face you shall eat bread till you return to the ground, for out of it you were taken; you are dust, and to dust you shall return."

The man called his wife's name Eve, because she was the mother of all living. And the LORD God made for Adam and for his wife garments of skins, and clothed them.

Then the LORD God said, "Behold, the man has become like one of us, knowing good and evil; and now, lest he put forth his hand and take also of the tree of life, and eat, and live for ever"— therefore the LORD God sent him forth from the garden of Eden, to till the ground from which he was taken. He drove out the man; and at the east of the garden of Eden he placed the cherubim, and a flaming sword which turned every way, to guard the way to the tree of life.

Now Adam knew Eve his wife, and she conceived and bore Cain, saying, "I have gotten a man with the help of the Lord." And again, she bore his brother Abel. Now Abel was a keeper of sheep, and Cain a tiller of the ground. In the course of time Cain brought to the Lord an offering of the fruit of the ground, and Abel brought of the firstlings of his flock and of their fat portions. And the Lord had regard for Abel and his offering, but for Cain and his offering he had no regard. So Cain was very angry, and his countenance fell. The Lord said to Cain, "Why are you angry, and why has your countenance fallen? If you do well, will you not be accepted? And if you do not do well, sin is couching at the door; its desire is for you, but you must master it."

Cain said to Abel his brother, "Let us go out to the field." And when they were in the field, Cain rose up against his brother Abel, and killed him. Then the LORD said to Cain, "Where is Abel your brother?" He said, "I do not know; am I my brother's keeper?" And the LORD said, "What have you done? The voice of your brother's blood is crying to me from the ground. And now you are cursed from the ground, which has opened its mouth to receive your brother's blood from your hand. When you till the ground, it shall no longer yield to you its strength; you shall be a fugitive and a wanderer on the earth." Cain said to the LORD, "My punishment is greater than I can bear. Behold, thou hast driven me this day away from the ground; and from thy face I shall be hidden; and I shall be a fugitive and a wanderer on the earth, and whoever finds me will slay me." Then the LORD said to him, "Not so! If any one slays Cain, vengeance shall be taken on him sevenfold." And the LORD put a mark on Cain, lest any who came upon him should kill him. Then Cain went away from the presence of the LORD, and dwelt in the land of Nod, east of Eden.*

CHRISTIAN (THE NEW TESTAMENT)

The New Testament is concerned with the life and teachings of Jesus of Nazareth. From the many parables, sermons, and exhortations, it is once again possible to abstract a Christian view of human nature, but as with the Old Testament—and perhaps even more so—the result

*From the Revised Standard Version.

is largely a synthesis on the part of the reader, rather than an explicit picture offered by the Scripture. Our selections from the New Testament emphasize two pervasive themes: love and resurrection. The first selection is from the Sermon on the Mount (Matthew 5); the second, from 1 Corinthians 13; and the third from 1 Corinthians 15.

Matthew 5:3–10

"Blessed are the poor in spirit, for theirs is the kingdom of heaven.

"Blessed are those who mourn, for they shall be comforted.

"Blessed are the meek, for they shall inherit the earth.

"Blessed are those who hunger and thirst for righteousness, for they shall be satisfied.

"Blessed are the merciful, for they shall obtain mercy.

"Blessed are the pure in heart, for they shall see God.

"Blessed are the peacemakers, for they shall be called sons of God.

"Blessed are those who are persecuted for righteousness' sake, for theirs is the kingdom of heaven. . . .

1 Corinthians 13:1–13

If I speak in the tongues of men and of angels, but have not love, I am a noisy gong or a clanging cymbal. And if I have prophetic powers, and understand all mysteries and all knowledge, and if I have all faith, so as to remove mountains, but have not love, I am nothing. If I give away all I have, and if I deliver my body to be burned, but have not love, I gain nothing.

Love is patient and kind; love is not jealous or boastful; it is not arrogant or rude. Love does not insist on its own way; it is not irritable or resentful; it does not rejoice at wrong, but rejoices in the right. Love bears all things, believes all things, hopes all things, endures all things.

Love never ends; as for prophecies, they will pass away; as for tongues, they will cease; as for knowledge, it will pass away. For our knowledge is imperfect and our prophecy is imperfect; but when the perfect comes, the imperfect will pass away. When I was a child, I spoke like a child, I thought like a child, I reasoned like a child; when I became a man, I gave up childish ways. For now we see in a mirror dimly, but then face to face. Now I know in part; then I shall understand fully, even as I have been fully understood. So faith, hope, love abide, these three; but the greatest of these is love. . . .

1 Corinthians 15: 35–58

But some one will ask, "How are the dead raised? With what kind of body do they come?" You foolish man! What you sow does not come to life unless it dies. And what you sow is not the body which is to be, but a bare kernel, perhaps of wheat or of some other grain. But God gives it a body as he has chosen, and to each kind of seed its own body. For not all flesh is alike, but there is one kind for men, another for animals, another for birds, and another for fish. There are celestial bodies and there are terrestrial bodies; but the glory of the celestial is one, and the glory of the terrestrial is another. There is one glory of the sun, and another glory of the moon, and another glory of the stars; for star differs from star in glory.

So is it with the resurrection of the dead. What is sown is perishable, what is raised is imperishable. It is sown in dishonor, it is raised in glory. It is sown in weakness, it is raised in power. It is sown a physical body, it is raised a spiritual body. If there is a physical body, there is also a spiritual body. Thus it is written, "The first man Adam became a living being"; the last Adam became a life-giving spirit. But it is not the spiritual which is first but the physical, and then the spiritual. The first man was from the earth, a man of dust; the second man is from heaven. As was the man of dust, so are those who are of the dust; and as is the man of heaven, so are those who are of heaven. Just as we have borne the image of the man of dust, we shall also bear the image of the man of heaven. I tell you this, brethren: flesh and blood cannot inherit the kingdom of God, nor does the perishable inherit the imperishable.

Lo! I tell you a mystery. We shall not all sleep, but we shall all be changed, in a moment, in the twinkling of an eye, at the last trumpet. For the trumpet will sound, and the dead will be raised imperishable, and we shall be changed. For this perishable nature must put on the imperishable, and this mortal nature must put on immortality. When the perishable puts on the imperishable, and the mortal puts on immortality, then shall come to pass the saying that is written: "Death is swallowed up in victory." "O death, where is thy victory? O death, where is thy sting?"

The sting of death is sin, and the power of sin is the law. But thanks be to God, who gives us the victory through our Lord Jesus Christ.

Therefore, my beloved brethren, be steadfast, immovable, always abounding in the work of the Lord, knowing that in the Lord your labor is not in vain.*

MUSLIM (THE KORAN OR QUR'AN)

For Muslims, the Koran (or Qur'an) is the infallible word of God (Allah), revealed to the Prophet Mohammed (A.D. 570?–632) by the angel Gabriel. Islam is determinedly monotheistic: Islam means "submission," and the primary message of the Koran is the need for human beings to submit to the will of the one God, along with a recitation of precisely what God demands (i.e., detailed rules concerning marriage, prayer, inheritance, eating, conducting business, etc.). According to the Koran, human beings are endowed with great potential but are also prone to evil; in particular, they often insist on functioning without reference to God's will. The cardinal human sin is thus a kind of pride, a refusal to acknowledge one's debt to God, and one's obligation to obey His laws.

In a sense, Islam is more inclusive and tolerant than either Judaism or Christianity (something that may surprise many Americans!). Thus, the Koran accepts many aspects of the Old and New Testaments (recognizing, for example, Abraham, Moses, and Jesus as important prophets). To Islam, human beings are not endowed with original sin. Instead, people are seen as directly responsible for their actions; in particular, whether they choose to obey God. At the same time, God is described as not only omniscient but also fully in control of human

*From the Revised Standard Version.

history. The resulting ambiguity provides room for differing Islamic interpretations of the nature of human nature, and of the human condition.

Although many Muslims believe that the Koran cannot be translated literally from its original Arabic without necessarily being misrepresented, the following selection is presented in the hope that even a brief, inadequate portrayal is better than none at all.

IN THE NAME OF ALLAH THE COMPASSIONATE, THE MERCIFUL, Praise be to Allah, Lord of the Creation, the Compassionate, the Merciful, King of Judgement-day! You alone we worship, and to You alone we pray for help. Guide us to the straight path, the path of those whom You have favoured, not of those who have incurred Your wrath, not of those who have gone astray. . . . When Earth is rocked in her last convulsion; when Earth shakes off her burdens and man asks "What may this mean?"—on that day she will proclaim her tidings, for your Lord will have inspired her.

On that day mankind will come in broken bands to be shown their labours. Whoever has done an atom's weight of good shall see it, and whoever has done an atom's weight of evil shall see it also. . . . When the sky is rent asunder; when the stars scatter and the oceans roll together; when the graves are hurled about; each soul shall know what it has done and what it has failed to do.

Oh man! What evil has enticed you from your gracious Lord, who created and proportioned you, and moulded your body to His will? Yes, you deny the Last Judgement. Yet there are guardians watching over you, noble recorders who know of all your actions. The righteous shall surely dwell in bliss. But the wicked shall burn in Hell-fire upon the Judgement-day: they shall not escape. . . . This is an admonition to all men: to those among you that have the will to be upright. . . .

Does there not pass over man a space of time when his life is a blank? We have created man from the union of the two sexes so that We may put him to the proof. We have endowed him with sight and hearing and, be he thankful or oblivious of Our favours, We have shown him the right path. . . .

We have made known to you the Koran by gradual revelation; therefore wait with patience the judgement of your Lord and do not yield to the wicked and the unbelieving. Remember the name of your Lord morning and evening. . . . The unbelievers love this fleeting life too well, and thus prepare for themselves a heavy day of doom. We created them, and endowed their limbs and joints with strength; but if We please We can replace them by other men. This is indeed an admonition. Let him that will, take the right path to his Lord. Yet you cannot will, except by the will of Allah. Allah is wise and all-knowing. . . .

It is the Merciful who has taught you the Koran. He created man and taught him articulate speech. The sun and the moon pursue their ordered course. The plants and the trees bow down in adoration. He raised the heaven on high and set the balance of all things, that you might not transgress it. Give just weight and full measure. He laid the earth for His creatures, with all its fruits and blossom-bearing palm, chaff-covered grain and scented herbs. Which of your Lord's blessings would you deny? He created man from potter's clay. . . . Which of your Lord's blessings would you deny? . . .

Recite in the name of your Lord, the Creator, who created man from clots of blood! Recite! Your Lord is the Most Bountiful One, who by the pen has taught mankind things they did not know. Indeed, man transgresses in thinking himself his own master: for to your Lord all things return. . . .

Your hearts are taken up with worldly gain from the cradle to the grave. But you shall know. . . . I swear by the declining day that perdition shall be the lot of man, except for those who have faith and do good works and exhort each other to justice and fortitude. . . .

We created man to try him with afflictions. Does he think that none has power over him? . . . Have We not given him two eyes, a tongue, and two lips, and shown him the two paths?* Yet he would not scale the Height. . . . Would that you knew what the Height is! It is the freeing of a bondsman; the feeding, in the day of famine, of an orphaned relation or a needy man in distress; to have faith and to enjoin fortitude and mercy. . . .

It is He who has subdued the earth to you. Walk about its regions and eat of that which He has given you. . . . Who will provide for you if He witholds His sustenance? Yet they persist in arrogance and in rebellion. . . . It is He who has created you and given you ears and eyes and hearts. Yet you are seldom thankful. . . .

When evil befalls man, he prays to his Lord and turns to Him in repentance; yet no sooner does He bestow on him His favour than he forgets that for which he had prayed before and worships other gods. . . . Whatever of good befalleth thee (O man) it is from Allah, and whatever of ill befalleth thee it is from thyself. . . .

Surely We created man of the best stature; then We reduced him to the lowest of the low. . . .

We first created man from an essence of clay; then placed him, a living germ, in a safe enclosure.†

The germ We made a clot of blood and the clot a lump of flesh. This We fashioned into bones, then clothed the bones with flesh, thus bringing forth another creation. Blessed be Allah, the noblest of creators!‡

STUDY QUESTIONS

1. What connection(s), if any, exists between these famous lines from John Donne and the material of this chapter?

No man is an island, entire of itself; every man is a piece of the continent, a part of the main; if a clod be washed away by the sea, Europe is the less; . . . any man's death diminishes me, because I am involved in mankind; and therefore never send to know for whom the bell tolls, it tolls for thee. . . .

2. Describe some important differences between the various religions depicted in this chapter, and some similarities.

3. What implication(s) for human nature derives from the different conceptions of the relationship of people to God? What implications might be derived from an atheistic conception?

4. Jewish and Christian theologians have devoted considerable attention to "theodicy," the attempt to reconcile God's goodness with the presence of evil and suffering in the world. How do the various approaches in this chapter differ with respect to theodicy? What implications might theodicy have for ideas of human nature, and vice versa?

SOME ADDITIONAL READINGS

Deshpande, V. W. (1996). *The Impact of Ancient Indian Thought on Christianity.* New Delhi, India: APH Publishing Corp.

Hick, John (1983). *Philosophy of Religion.* Englewood Cliffs, N.J.: Prentice-Hall.

*Editor's note: of right and wrong.
†Editor's note: inside the womb.
‡From *The Koran* (1910). (E. H. Palmer, Trans.). London: P. F. Collier.

Maspero, Henri (1981). *Taoism and Chinese Religion.* Amherst, Mass.: University of Massachusetts Press.

Rippin, Andrew, ed. (1988). *Approaches to the History of the Interpretation of the Quran.* New York: Oxford University Press.

Sharma, Arvind (1995). *The Philosophy of Religion: A Buddhist Perspective.* New York: Oxford University Press.

CHAPTER TWO

Body and Soul

For many, the concept of human nature is inextricably connected to something else, namely, the soul. Although definitions differ widely, there is a basic commonality; human beings are widely thought to consist of something beyond their mere material substance, something that is transcendent, immortal, and that connects them to the divine.

PLATO

It has been said that all of Western philosophy is a footnote to Plato (427?–347? B.C.E.). Plato's thought, combined with that of Socrates, whose ideas he developed and presented, touches significantly on questions of human nature. In his renowned parable of the cave, for example, Plato maintains that most people are unenlightened, like prisoners chained within a cave and with a large fire behind them, able only to see shadows reflected on the cave wall rather than reality as it truly is. Consistent with this notion of absolute, unchanging "Forms," Plato also believes in the immortality of the soul. Not surprisingly, he was much taken with mathematics because of its absolute, unchanging truth. At one point in the *Meno,* Plato demonstrates that even an uneducated shepherd understands basic geometry without having to be given any information not already in his head. Plato concludes that such "fore-knowledge" shows that the human soul must have existed before birth, later recalling what it had previously learned in the world of Forms.

In this selection from the *Phaedo,* Plato assumes the existence of eternal Forms (e.g., the Form of the triangle, of which, say, any particular slice of pizza temporarily "participates"), and of the soul's preexistence. He proceeds to argue that the soul is immortal.

Then may we not say, Simmias, that if, as we are always repeating, there is an absolute beauty, and goodness, and essence in general, and to this, which is now discovered to be a previous condition of our being, we refer all our sensations, and with this compare them—assuming this to have a prior existence, then our souls must have had a prior existence, but if not, there would be no force in the argument. There can be no doubt that if these absolute ideas existed before we were born, then our souls must have existed before we were born, and if not the ideas, then not the souls.

Yes, Socrates; I am convinced that there is precisely the same necessity for the existence of the soul before birth, and of the essence of which you are speaking: and the argument arrives at a result which happily agrees with my own notion. For there is nothing which to my mind is so evident as that beauty, good, and other notions of which you were just now speaking have a most real and absolute existence; and I am satisfied with the proof.

Well, but is Cebes equally satisfied? for I must convince him too.

I think, said Simmias, that Cebes is satisfied: although he is the most incredulous of mortals, yet I believe that he is convinced of the existence of the soul before birth. But that after death the soul will continue to exist is not yet proven even to my own satisfaction. I cannot get rid of the feeling of the many to which Cebes was referring—the feeling that when the man dies the soul may be scattered, and that this may be the end of her. For admitting that she may be generated and created in some other place, and may have existed before entering the human body, why after having entered in and gone out again may she not herself be destroyed and come to an end?

Very true, Simmias, said Cebes; that our soul existed before we were born was the first half of the argument, and this appears to have been proven; that the soul will exist after death as well as before birth is the other half of which the proof is still wanting, and has to be supplied.

But that proof, Simmias and Cebes, has been already given said Socrates, if you put the two arguments together—I mean this and the former one, in which we admitted that everything living is born of the dead. For if the soul existed before birth, and in coming to life and being born can be born only from death and dying, must she not after death continue to exist, since she has to be born again? surely the proof which your desire has been already furnished. Still I suspect that you and Simmias would be glad to probe the argument further; like children, you are haunted with a fear that when the soul leaves the body, the wind may really blow her away and scatter her; especially if a man should happen to die in stormy weather and not when the sky is calm.

Cebes answered with a smile: Then, Socrates, you must argue us out of our fears—and yet, strictly speaking, they are not our fears, but there is a child within us to whom death is a sort of hobgoblin; him too we must persuade not to be afraid when he is alone with him in the dark.

Socrates said: Let the voice of the charmer be applied daily until you have charmed him away.

And where shall we find a good charmer of our fears, Socrates, when you are gone?

Hellas, he replied, is a large place, Cebes, and has many good men, and there are barbarous races not a few: seek for him among them all, far and wide, sparing neither pains nor money; for there is no better way of using your money. And you must not forget to seek for him among yourselves too; for he is nowhere more likely to be found.

The search, replied Cebes, shall certainly be made. And now, if you please, let us return to the point of the argument at which we digressed.

By all means, replied Socrates; what else should I please?

Very good, he said.

Must we not, said Socrates, ask ourselves some question of this sort?—What is that which, as we imagine, is liable to be scattered away, and about which we fear? and what again is that about which we have no fear? And then we may proceed to inquire whether that which suffers dispersion is or is not of the nature of soul—our hopes and fears as to our own souls will turn upon that.

That is true, he said.

Now the compound or composite may be supposed to be naturally capable of being dissolved in like manner as of being compounded; but that which is uncompounded, and that only, must be, if anything is, indissoluble.

Yes; that is what I should imagine, said Cebes.

And the uncompounded may be assumed to be the same and unchanging, where the compound is always changing and never the same?

That I also think, he said.

Then now let us return to the previous discussion. Is that idea or essence, which in the dialectical process we define as essence of true existence—whether essence of equality, beauty, or anything else: are these essences, I say, liable at times to some degree of change? or are they each of them always what they are, having the same simple, self-existent and unchanging forms, and not admitting of variation at all, or in any way, or at any time?

They must be always the same, Socrates, replied Cebes.

And what would you say of the many beautiful—whether men or horses or garments or any other things which may be called equal or beautiful—are they all unchanging and the same always, or quite the reverse? May they not rather be described as almost always changing and hardly ever the same either with themselves or with one another?

The latter, replied Cebes; they are always in a state of change.

And these you can touch and see and perceive with the senses, but the unchanging things you can only perceive with the mind—they are invisible and are not seen?

That is very true, he said.

Well, then, he added, let us suppose that there are two sorts of existences, one seen, the other unseen.

Let us suppose them.

The seen is the changing, and the unseen is the unchanging.

That may be also supposed.

And, further, is not one part of us body, and the rest of us soul?

To be sure.

And to which class may we say that the body is more alike and akin?

Clearly to the seen: no one can doubt that.

And is the soul seen or not seen?

Not by man, Socrates.

And by "seen" and "not seen" is meant by us that which is or is not visible to the eye of man?

Yes, to the eye of man.

And what do we say of the soul? is that seen or not seen?

Not seen.

Unseen then?

Yes.

Then the soul is more like to the unseen, and the body to the seen?

That is most certain, Socrates.

And were we not saying long ago that the soul when using the body as an instrument of perception, that is to say, when using the sense of sight or hearing or some other sense (for the meaning of perceiving through the body is perceiving through the senses)—were we not saying that the soul too is then dragged by the body into the region of the changeable, and wanders and is confused; the world spins round her, and she is like a drunkard when under their influence?

Very true.

But when returning into herself she reflects; then she passes into the realm of purity, and eternity, and immortality, and unchangeableness, which are her kindred, and with them she ever lives, when she is by herself and is not let or hindered; then she ceases from her erring ways, and being in communion with the unchanging is unchanging. And this state of the soul is called wisdom?

That is well and truly said, Socrates, he replied.

And to which class is the soul more nearly alike and akin, as far as may be inferred from this argument, as well as from the preceding one?

I think, Socrates, that, in the opinion of every one who follows the argument, the soul will be infinitely more like the unchangeable—even the most stupid person will not deny that.

And the body is more like the changing?

Yes.

Yet once more consider the matter in this light: When the soul and the body are united, then nature orders the soul to rule and govern, and the body to obey and serve.

Now which of these two functions is akin to the divine? and which to the mortal? Does not the divine appear to you to be that which naturally orders and rules, and the mortal that which is subject and servant?

True.

And which does the soul resemble?

The soul resembles the divine and the body the mortal—there can be no doubt of that, Socrates.

Then reflect, Cebes: is not the conclusion of the whole matter this—that the soul is in the very likeness of the divine, and immortal, and intelligible, and uniform, and indissoluble, and unchangeable; and the body is in the very likeness of the human, and mortal, and unintelligible, and multiform, and dissoluble, and changeable. Can this, my dear Cebes, be denied?

No, indeed.

But if this is true, then is not the body liable to speedy dissolution? and is not the soul almost or altogether indissoluble?

Certainly.

And do you further observe, that after a man is dead, the body, which is the visible part of man, and has a visible framework, which is called a corpse, and which would naturally be dissolved and decomposed and dissipated, is not dissolved or decomposed at once, but may remain for a good while, if the constitution be sound at the time of death, and the season of the year favorable? For the body when shrunk and embalmed, as is the custom in Egypt, may remain almost entire through infinite ages; and even in decay, still there are some portions, such as the bones and ligaments, which are practically indestructible. You allow that?

Yes.

And are we to suppose that the soul, which is invisible, in passing to the true Hades, which like her is invisible, and pure, and noble, and on her way to the good and wise God, whither, if God will, my soul is also soon to go—that the soul, I repeat, if this be her nature and origin, is blown away and perishes immediately on quitting the body as the many say? That can never be, dear Simmias and Cebes. The truth rather is that the soul which is pure at departing draws after her no bodily taint, having never voluntarily had connection with the body, which she is ever avoiding, herself gathered into herself (for such abstraction has been the study of her life). And what does this mean but that she has been a true disciple of philosophy and has practised how to die easily? And is not philosophy the practice of death?

Certainly.

That soul, I say, herself invisible, departs to the invisible world—to the divine and immortal and rational: thither arriving, she lives in bliss and is released from the error and folly of men, their fears and wild passions and all other human ills, and forever dwells, as they say of the initiated, in company with the gods.*

*From *Phaedo* (1909). *Dialogues of Plato.* (B. Jowett, Trans.). London: Collier.

AUGUSTINE

The work of Saint Augustine (A.D. 354–430) is fundamental to much of Catholicism, and to Christian doctrine more generally. His early influences included the works of Plato and the neo-Platonists (notably Plotinus), as well as Manicheanism, which saw the world as compounded of warring elements of good and evil, with the human soul an element of light entangled in darkness. Augustine's conversion to orthodox Christianity ("Give me chastity," he once prayed, "but not yet!") is portrayed in his *Confessions.* Its first lines summarize Augustine's message: "Thou hast created us for Thyself, and our hearts know no rest until they repose in Thee."

For our purposes, Augustine's theology of human nature is important in several respects. For one, it involves a revived conviction—as taught in the New Testament by Saint Paul—that human beings possess a heavy dose of original sin, from which they can be relieved only by God's grace (see Chapter 9). Augustine also venerates faith over intellect: "Seek not to understand that you may believe, but believe that you may understand." And finally, he carries into Christianity a Platonic belief in the soul as ideal and perfect, "eternal and changeless," forever distinct from and superior to the human body.

Augustine's *The City of God* juxtaposes two invisible communities, the saved and the damned, or, symbolically, the spirit and the flesh. He concerns himself with various details of the body/soul connection, such as the exact bodily form to be assumed by resurrected people. Although partly intended to explain why Christianity as such was not to blame for the sacking of Rome by the Visigoths, *The City of God* also presents a powerful philosophy of human predestination and of redemption via faith.

Book 12

23. OF THE NATURE OF THE HUMAN SOUL CREATED IN THE IMAGE OF GOD

God, then, made man in His own image. For He created for him a soul endowed with reason and intelligence, so that he might excel all the creatures of earth, air, and sea, which were not so gifted. And when He had formed the man out of the dust of the earth, and had willed that his soul should be such as I have said—whether He had already made it, and now by breathing imparted it to man, or rather made it by breathing, so that that breath which God made by breathing (for what else is "to breathe" than to make breath?) is the soul,—He made also a wife for him, to aid him in the work of generating his kind, and her He formed of a bone taken out of the man's side, working in a divine manner. For we are not to conceive of this work in a carnal fashion, as if God wrought as we commonly see artisans, who use their hands, and material furnished to them, that by their artistic skill they may fashion some material object. God's hand is God's power; and He, working invisibly, effects visible results. But this seems fabulous rather than true to men, who measure by customary and everyday works the power and wisdom of God, whereby He understands and produces without seeds even seeds themselves; and because they cannot understand the things which at the beginning were created, they are sceptical regarding them—as if the very things which they do know about human propagation, conceptions and births, would seem less incredible if told to those who had no experience of them; though these very things, too, are attributed by many rather to physical and natural causes than to the work of the divine mind. . . .

Book 13

1. OF THE FALL OF THE FIRST MAN, THROUGH WHICH MORTALITY HAS BEEN CONTRACTED

Having disposed of the very difficult questions concerning the origin of our world and the beginning of the human race, the natural order requires that we now discuss the fall of the first man (we may say of the first men), and of the origin and propagation of human death. For God had not made man like the angels, in such a condition that, even though they had sinned, they could none the more die. He had so made them, that if they discharged the obligations of obedience, an angelic immortality and a blessed eternity might ensue, without the intervention of death; but if they disobeyed, death should be visited on them with just sentence—which, too, has been spoken to in the preceding book.

2. OF THAT DEATH WHICH CAN AFFECT AN IMMORTAL SOUL, AND OF THAT TO WHICH THE BODY IS SUBJECT

But I see I must speak a little more carefully of the nature of death. For although the human soul is truly affirmed to be immortal, yet it also has a certain death of its own. For it is therefore called immortal, because, in a sense, it does not cease to live and to feel; while the body is called mortal, because it can be forsaken of all life, and cannot by itself live at all. The death, then, of the soul takes place when God forsakes it, as the death of the body when the soul forsakes it. Therefore the death of both—that is, of the whole man—occurs when the soul, forsaken by God, forsakes the body. For, in this case, neither is God the life of the soul, nor the soul the life of the body. And this death of the whole man is followed by that which, on the authority of the divine oracles, we call the second death. . . .

Book 14

28. OF THE NATURE OF THE TWO CITIES, THE EARTHLY AND THE HEAVENLY

Accordingly, two cities have been formed by two loves: the earthly by the love of self, even to the contempt of God; the heavenly by the love of God, even to the contempt of self. The former, in a word, glories in itself, the latter in the Lord. For the one seeks glory from men; but the greatest glory of the other is God, the witness of conscience. The one lifts up its head in its own glory; the other says to its God, "Thou art my glory, and the lifter up of mine head." In the one, the princes and the nations it subdues are ruled by the love of ruling; in the other, the princes and the subjects serve one another in love, the latter obeying, while the former take thought for all. The one delights in its own strength, represented in the persons of its rulers; the other says to its God, "I will love Thee, O Lord, my strength." And therefore the wise men of the one city, living according to man, have sought for profit to their own bodies or souls, or both, and those who have known God "glorified Him not as God, neither were thankful, but became vain in their imaginations, and their foolish heart was darkened; professing themselves to be wise"—that is, glorying in their own wisdom, and being possessed by pride—"they became fools, and changed the glory of the incorruptible God into an image made like to corruptible man, and to birds, and four-footed beasts, and creeping things." For they were either leaders or followers of the people in adoring images, "and worshipped and served the creature more than the Creator, who is blessed for ever." But in the other city there is no human wisdom, but only godliness, which offers due worship to the true God, and looks for its reward in the society of the saints, of holy angels as well as holy men, "that God may be all in all." . . .

Book 22

4. AGAINST THE WISE MEN OF THE WORLD, WHO FANCY THAT THE EARTHLY BODIES OF MEN CANNOT BE TRANSFERRED TO A HEAVENLY HABITATION

But men who use their learning and intellectual ability to resist the force of that great authority which, in fulfilment of what was so long before predicted, has converted all races of men to faith and hope in its promises, seem to themselves to argue acutely against the resurrection of the body while they cite what Cicero mentions in the third book *De Republica*. For when he was asserting the apotheosis of Hercules and Romulus, he says: "Whose bodies were not taken up into heaven; for nature would not permit a body of earth to exist anywhere except upon earth." This, forsooth, is the profound reasoning of the wise men, whose thoughts God knows that they are vain. For if we were only souls, that is, spirits without any body, and if we dwelt in heaven and had no knowledge of earthly animals, and were told that we should be bound to earthly bodies by some wonderful bond of union, and should animate them, should we not much more vigorously refuse to believe this, and maintain that nature would not permit an incorporeal substance to be held by a corporeal bond? And yet the earth is full of living spirits, to which terrestrial bodies are bound, and with which they are in a wonderful way implicated. If, then, the same God who has created such beings wills this also, what is to hinder the earthly body from being raised to a heavenly body, since a spirit, which is more excellent than all bodies, and consequently than even a heavenly body, has been tied to an earthly body? If so small an earthly particle has been able to hold in union with itself something better than a heavenly body, so as to receive sensation and life, will heaven disdain to receive, or at least to retain, this sentient and living particle, which derives its life and sensation from a substance more excellent than any heavenly body? If this does not happen now, it is because the time is not yet come which has been determined by Him who has already done a much more marvelous thing than that which these men refuse to believe. For why do we not more intensely wonder that incorporeal souls, which are of higher rank than heavenly bodies, are bound to earthly bodies, rather than that bodies, although earthly, are exalted to an abode which, though heavenly, is yet corporeal, except because we have been accustomed to see this, and indeed are this, while we are not as yet that other marvel, nor have as yet ever seen it? Certainly, if we consult sober reason, the more wonderful of the two divine works is found to be to attach somehow corporeal things to incorporeal, and not to connect earthly things with heavenly, which, though diverse, are yet both of them corporeal. . . .

20. THAT, IN THE RESURRECTION, THE SUBSTANCE OF OUR BODIES, HOWEVER DISINTEGRATED, SHALL BE ENTIRELY REUNITED

Far be it from us to fear that the omnipotence of the Creator cannot, for the resuscitation and reanimation of our bodies, recall all the portions which have been consumed by beasts or fire, or have been dissolved into dust or ashes, or have decomposed into water, or evaporated into the air. Far from us be the thought, that anything which escapes our observation in any most hidden recess of nature either evades the knowledge or transcends the power of the Creator of all things. Cicero, the great authority of our adversaries, wishing to define God as accurately as possible, says, "God is a mind free and independent, without materiality, perceiving and moving all things, and itself endowed with eternal movement." This he found in the systems of the greatest philosophers. Let me ask, then, in their own language, how anything can either lie hid from Him who perceives all things, or irrevocably escape Him who moves all things?

This leads me to reply to that question which seems the most difficult of all—To whom, in the resurrection, will belong the flesh of a dead man which has become the flesh of a living man? For if some one, famishing for want and pressed with hunger, use human flesh as food—an extremity not unknown, as both ancient history and the unhappy experience of our own days have taught us—can it be contended, with any show of reason, that all the flesh eaten has been evacuated, and that none of it has been assimilated to the substance of the eater, though the very emaciation which existed before, and has now disappeared, sufficiently indicates what large deficiencies have been filled up with this food? But I have already made some remarks which will suffice for the solution of this difficulty also. For all the flesh which hunger has consumed finds its way into the air by evaporation, whence, as we have said, God Almighty can recall it. That flesh, therefore, shall be restored to the man in whom it first became human flesh. For it must be looked upon as borrowed by the other person, and, like a pecuniary loan, must be returned to the lender. His own flesh, however, which he lost by famine, shall be restored to him by Him who can recover even what has evaporated. And though it had been absolutely annihilated, so that no part of its substance remained in any secret spot of nature, the Almighty could restore it by such means as He saw fit. For this sentence, uttered by the Truth, "Not a hair of your head shall perish," forbids us to suppose that, though no hair of a man's head can perish, yet the large portions of his flesh eaten and consumed by the famishing can perish.

From all that we have thus considered, and discussed with such poor ability as we can command, we gather this conclusion, that in the resurrection of the flesh the body shall be of that size which it either had attained or should have attained in the flower of its youth, and shall enjoy the beauty that arises from preserving symmetry and proportion in all its members. And it is reasonable to suppose that, for the preservation of this beauty, any part of the body's substance, which, if placed in one spot, would produce a deformity, shall be distributed through the whole of it, so that neither any part, nor the symmetry of the whole, may be lost, but only the general stature of the body somewhat increased by the distribution in all the parts of that which, in one place, would have been unsightly. Or if it is contended that each will rise with the same stature as that of the body he died in, we shall not obstinately dispute this, provided only there be no deformity, no infirmity, no languor, no corruption—nothing of any kind which would ill become that kingdom in which the children of the resurrection and of the promise shall be equal to the angels of God, if not in body and age, at least in happiness.

21. OF THE NEW SPIRITUAL BODY INTO WHICH THE FLESH OF THE SAINTS SHALL BE TRANSFORMED

Whatever, therefore, has been taken from the body, either during life or after death, shall be restored to it, and, in conjunction with what has remained in the grave, shall rise again, transformed from the oldness of the animal body into the newness of the spiritual body, and clothed in incorruption and immortality. But even though the body has been all quite ground to powder by some severe accident, or by the ruthlessness of enemies, and though it has been so diligently scattered to the winds, or into the water, that there is no trace of it left, yet it shall not be beyond the omnipotence of the Creator—no, not a hair of its head shall perish. The flesh shall then be spiritual, and subject to the spirit, but still flesh, not spirit, as the spirit itself, when subject to the flesh, was fleshly, but still spirit and not flesh. . . .

It is He, then, who has given to the human soul a mind, in which reason and understanding lie as it were asleep during infancy, and as if they were not, destined, however, to be awakened and exercised as years increase, so as to become capable of knowledge and of receiving instruction, fit to understand what is true and to love what is good. It is by this capacity the soul drinks in wisdom, and becomes endowed with those virtues by which, in prudence, fortitude, temperance, and righteousness, it makes war upon error and the other inborn vices, and conquers them by fixing its desires upon no other object than the supreme and unchangeable Good. . . .

30. Of the eternal felicity of the city of God, and of the perpetual Sabbath

How great shall be that felicity, which shall be tainted with no evil, which shall lack no good, and which shall afford leisure for the praises of God, who shall be all in all! For I know not what other employment there can be where no lassitude shall slacken activity, nor any want stimulate to labour. I am admonished also by the sacred song, in which I read or hear the words, "Blessed are they that dwell in Thy house, O Lord; they will be still praising Thee." All the members and organs of the incorruptible body, which now we see to be suited to various necessary uses, shall contribute to the praises of God; for in that life necessity shall have no place, but full, certain, secure, everlasting felicity. For all those parts of the bodily harmony, which are distributed through the whole body, within and without, and of which I have just been saying that they at present elude our observation, shall then be discerned; and, along with the other great and marvellous discoveries which shall then kindle rational minds in praise of the great Artificer, there shall be the enjoyment of a beauty which appeals to the reason. What power of movement such bodies shall possess, I have not the audacity rashly to define, as I have not the ability to conceive. Nevertheless I will say that in any case, both in motion and at rest, they shall be, as in their appearance, seemly; for into that state nothing which is unseemly shall be admitted. One thing is certain, the body shall forthwith be wherever the spirit wills, and the spirit shall will nothing which is unbecoming either to the spirit or to the body. True honour shall be there, for it shall be denied to none who is worthy, nor yielded to any unworthy; neither shall any unworthy person so much as sue for it, for none but the worthy shall be there. True peace shall be there, where no one shall suffer opposition either from himself or any other. God Himself, who is the Author of virtue, shall there be its reward; for, as there is nothing greater or better, He has promised Himself. What else was meant by His word through the prophet, "I will be your God, and ye shall be my people," than, I shall be their satisfaction, I shall be all that men honourably desire—life, and health, and nourishment, and plenty, and glory, and honour, and peace, and all good things? This, too, is the right interpretation of the saying of the apostle, "That God may be all in all." He shall be the end of our desires who shall be seen without end, loved without cloy, praised without weariness. This outgoing of affection, this employment, shall certainly be, like eternal life itself, common to all. . . .

There we shall rest and see, see and love, love and praise. This is what shall be in the end without end. For what other end do we propose to ourselves than to attain to the kingdom of which there is no end?*

LUCRETIUS

For a very different, entirely un-Platonic and un-Augustinian view of the soul, we turn to the Roman philosopher Lucretius (first century B.C.E.), whose masterpiece bears the immodest title *On the Nature of Things.* Lucretius worked in the tradition of the early Greek materialists, Democritus and especially Epicurus (fifth and fourth centuries B.C.E.), who maintain that the soul was altogether dependent on the body (see the "mind/body problem," Chapter 7).

Here is Lucretius on the material nature of the soul, followed by his opinion as to whether the soul is immortal.

*From *The City of God* (1871). (M. Dods, Trans.). Edinburgh: T and T Clark.

Now I say that mind and soul are held in union one with the other, and form of themselves a single nature, but that the head, as it were, and lord in the whole body is the reason, which we call mind or understanding, and it is firmly seated in the middle region of the breast. For there it is that fear and terror throb, around these parts are soothing joys; here then is the understanding and the mind. The rest of the soul, spread abroad throughout the body, obeys and is moved at the will and inclination of the understanding. The mind alone by itself has understanding for itself and rejoices for itself, when no single thing stirs either soul or body. And just as, when head or eye hurts within us at the attack of pain, we are not tortured at the same time in all our body; so the mind sometimes feels pain by itself or waxes strong with joy, when all the rest of the soul through the limbs and frame is not roused by any fresh feeling. Nevertheless, when the understanding is stirred by some stronger fear, we see that the whole soul feels with it throughout the limbs, and then sweat and pallor break out over all the body, and the tongue is crippled and the voice is choked, the eyes grow misty, the ears ring, the limbs give way beneath us, and indeed we often see men fall down through the terror in their mind; so that any one may easily learn from this that the soul is linked in union with the mind; for when it is smitten by the force of the mind, straightway it strikes the body and pushes it on.

This same reasoning shows that the nature of mind and soul is bodily. For when it is seen to push on the limbs, to pluck the body from sleep, to change the countenance, and to guide and turn the whole man—none of which things we see can come to pass without touch, nor touch in its turn without body—must we not allow that mind and soul are formed of bodily nature? Moreover, you see that our mind suffers along with the body, and shares its feelings together in the body. If the shuddering shock of a weapon, driven within and laying bare bones and sinews, does not reach the life, yet faintness follows, and a pleasant swooning to the ground, and a turmoil of mind which comes to pass on the ground, and from time to time, as it were, a hesitating will to rise. Therefore it must needs be that the nature of the mind is bodily, since it is distressed by the blow of bodily weapons.

Now of what kind of body this mind is, and of what parts it is formed, I will go on to give account to you in my discourse. First of all I say that it is very fine in texture, and is made and formed of very tiny particles. That this is so, if you give attention, you may be able to learn from this. Nothing is seen to come to pass so swiftly as what the mind pictures to itself coming to pass and starts to do itself. Therefore the mind bestirs itself more quickly than any of the things whose nature is manifest for all to see. But because it is so very nimble, it is bound to be formed of exceeding round and exceeding tiny seeds, so that its particles may be able to move when smitten by a little impulse. For so water moves and oscillates at the slightest impulse, seeing it is formed of little particles, quick to roll. But, on the other hand, the nature of honey is more stable, its fluid more sluggish, and its movement more hesitating; for the whole mass of its matter clings more together, because, we may be sure, it is not formed of bodies so smooth, nor so fine and round. For a light trembling breath can constrain a high heap of poppy-seed to scatter from top to bottom before your eyes: but, on the other hand, a pile of stones or corn-ears it can by no means separate. Therefore, in proportion as bodies are tinier and smoother, so they are gifted with nimbleness. But, on the other hand, all things that are found to be of greater weight or more spiky, the more firm set they are. Now, therefore, since the nature of the mind has been found nimble beyond the rest, it must needs be formed of bodies exceeding small and smooth and round. And this truth, when known to you, will in many things, good friend, prove useful, and will be reckoned of service. This fact, too, declares the nature of the mind, of how thin a texture it is formed, and in how small a place it might be contained, could it be gathered in a mass; that as soon as the unruffled peace of death has laid hold on a man, and the nature of mind and soul has passed away, you could discern nothing there, that sight or weight can test, stolen from the entire body; death preserves all save the feeling of life, and some warm heat. And so it must needs be that the whole soul is made of very tiny seeds, and is linked on throughout veins, flesh, and sinews; inasmuch as, when it is all already gone from the whole body, yet the outer contour of the limbs is preserved unbroken, nor is a jot of weight wanting. Even so it is, when the flavour of wine has passed away or when the sweet breath of a perfume is scattered to the air, or when its savour is gone from some body; still the thing itself seems not a whit smaller to the eyes on that account, nor does anything seem withdrawn from its weight, because, we may be sure, many tiny seeds go to make flavours and scent in the whole body of things. Wherefore once and again you may know that the nature of the understanding and the soul is formed of exceeding tiny seeds, since when it flees away it carries with it no jot of weight. . . .

I continue to speak of the soul, proving that it is mortal, suppose that I speak of mind as well, inasmuch as they are at one each with the other and compose a single thing. First of all, since I have shown that it is finely made of tiny bodies and of first-beginnings far smaller than the liquid moisture of water or cloud or smoke—for it far surpasses them in speed of motion, and is more prone to move when smitten by some slender cause; for indeed it is moved by images of smoke and cloud: even as when slumbering in sleep we see altars breathing steam on high, and sending up their smoke; for beyond all doubt these are idols that are borne to us:—now therefore, since, when vessels are shattered, you behold the water flowing away on every side, and the liquid parting this way and that, and since cloud and smoke part asunder into air, you must believe that the soul too is scattered and passes away far more swiftly, and is dissolved more quickly into its first-bodies, when once it is withdrawn from a man's limbs, and has departed. For indeed, since the body, which was, as it were, the vessel of the soul, cannot hold it together, when by some chance it is shattered and made rare, since the blood is withdrawn from the veins, how could you believe that the soul could be held together by any air, which is more rare than our body?

Moreover, we feel that the understanding is begotten along with the body, and grows together with it, and along with it comes to old age. For as children totter with feeble and tender body, so a weak judgement of mind goes with it. Then when their years are ripe and their strength hardened, greater is their sense and increased their force of mind. Afterward, when now the body is shattered by the stern strength of time, and the frame has sunk with its force dulled, then the reason is maimed, the tongue raves, the mind stumbles, all things give way and fail at once. And so it is natural that all the nature of the mind should also be dissolved, even as is smoke, into the high breezes of the air; inasmuch as we see that it is born with the body, grows with it, and, as I have shown, at the same time becomes weary and worn with age.

Then follows this that we see that, just as the body itself suffers wasting diseases and poignant pain, so the mind too has its biting cares and grief and fear; wherefore it is natural that it should also share in death. Nay more, during the diseases of the body the mind often wanders astray; for it loses its reason and speaks raving words, and sometimes in a heavy lethargy is carried off into a deep unending sleep, when eyes and head fall nodding, in which it hears not voices, nor can know the faces of those who stand round, summoning it back to life, bedewing face and cheeks with their tears. Therefore you must needs admit that the mind too is dissolved, inasmuch as the contagion of disease pierces into it. For both pain and disease are alike fashioners of death, as we have been taught ere now by many a man's decease. Again, when the stinging strength of wine has entered into a man, and its heat has spread abroad throughout his veins, why is it that there follows a heaviness in the limbs, his legs are entangled as he staggers, his tongue is sluggish, and his mind heavy, his eyes swim, shouting, sobbing, quarrelling grows apace, and then all the other signs of this sort that go along with them; why does this come to pass, except that the mastering might of the wine is wont to confound the soul even within the body? But whenever things can be so confounded and entangled, they testify that, if a cause a whit stronger shall have made its way within, they must needs perish, robbed of any further life.

When mind and soul then even within the body are tossed by such great maladies, and in wretched plight are rent asunder and distressed, why do you believe that without the body in the open air they can continue life amid the warring winds? And since we perceive that the mind is cured, just like the sick body, and we see that it can be changed by medicine, this too forewarns us that the mind has a mortal life. For whosoever attempts and essays to alter the mind, or seeks to change any other nature, must indeed add parts to it or transfer them from their order, or take away some small whit at least from the whole. But what is immortal does not permit its parts to be transposed, nor that any whit should be added or depart from it. For whenever a thing changes and passes out of its own limits, straightway this is the death of that which was before. And so whether the mind is sick, it gives signs of its mortality as I have proved, or whether it is changed by medicine. So surely is true fact seen to run counter to false reasoning, and to shut off retreat from him who flees, and with double-edged refutation to prove the falsehood.*

AQUINAS

The influence of Saint Thomas Aquinas (1224–1274) upon Catholic, and more generally, Christian, thought regarding the soul has been roughly comparable to that of Saint Augustine— that is, immense. Writing nearly one thousand years after Augustine, Aquinas succeeded in moving Church doctrine somewhat away from the Augustinian tradition and toward a view of religious faith that more readily accommodated reason as well.

In a sense, Plato (and subsequently, Augustine) represent one extreme on the question of the human soul, and Lucretius, the other. Bestriding the middle, as he bestrode much of Western thought, is Aristotle (384–322 B.C.E.). (We excerpted Lucretius rather than Aristotle because, frankly, Aristotle is much more difficult!) Aristotle maintained that the soul was neither an incomprehensible incorporeal entity, nor a physical thing, but rather the "qualities" of a living body. In *de Anima,* Aristotle wrote that

> If, then, we have to give a general formula applicable to all kinds of soul, we must describe it as the first grade of actuality of a natural organized body. That is why we can wholly dismiss as unnecessary the question whether the soul and body are one: it is as meaningless as to ask whether the wax and the shape given to it by the stamp are one, or generally the matter of a thing and that of which it is the matter.

For Aristotle, then, all living things possess a kind of soul, the nature of which defines the different forms of life: plants merely grow and reproduce, animals also experience sensations along with the power to move, and human beings additionally possess the ability to *reason* (see Chapter 5). Aristotle demurs in his empirical approach, however, in this last case:

> We have no evidence as yet about mind or the power to think; it seems to be a widely different kind of soul, differing as what is eternal from what is perishable; it alone is capable of existence in isolation from all other psychic powers. All the other parts of soul . . . are . . . incapable of separate existence.

We begin this commentary on Aquinas with a discussion of Aristotle because with respect to the "nature of human nature," Aquinas's major contribution was to introduce Aris-

*From *On the Nature of Things* (1910). (C. Bailey, Trans.). Oxford: Oxford University Press.

totelian thinking (so-called Scholasticism) into Church doctrine. Aristotle's works had been lost to the Christian West until the late Middle Ages when they were reintroduced via Arab scholarship. They became immensely influential, particularly because of Aquinas, who used Aristotle's acceptance of the independent mind to argue for the eventual resurrection of individual human beings, claiming that particular souls and particular bodies can be reconnected.

Aquinas argues that soul and body are one, that matter is not a "barbarian enemy" to humanity or to God, and that the Platonic and Augustinian emphasis on abstract essences is misleading because human beings, although composed of both soul and body, have nonetheless one nature. The soul is the "substantial form" of the body, giving existence and vitality to the matter that constitutes human beings. If this is paradoxical, it is no more paradoxical than human nature itself.

The assertion, *the soul is a man*, can be taken in two senses. First, that man is a soul, though this particular man (Socrates, for instance) is not a soul, but composed of soul and body. I say this, because some held that the form alone belongs to the species, while matter is part of the individual, and not of the species. This cannot be true, for to the nature of the species belongs what the definition signifies, and in natural things the definition does not signify the form only, but the form and the matter. Hence, in natural things the matter is part of the species; not, indeed, signate matter, which is the principle of individuation, but common matter. For just as it belongs to the nature of this particular man to be composed of this soul, of this flesh, and of these bones, so it belongs to the nature of man to be composed of soul, flesh, and bones; for whatever belongs in common to the substance of all the individuals contained under a given species must belong also to the substance of the species.

That *the soul is a man* may also be understood in this sense, namely, that this soul is this man. Now this could be held if it were supposed that the operation of the sensitive soul were proper to it without the body; because in that case all the operations which are attributed to man would belong only to the soul. But each thing is that which performs its own operations, and consequently that is man which performs the operations of a man. But it has been shown above that sensation is not the operation of the soul alone. Since, then, sensation is an operation of man, but not proper to the soul, it is clear that man is not only a soul, but something composed of soul and body.—Plato, through supposing that sensation was proper to the soul, could maintain man to be *a soul making use of a body.* . . .

The difference which constitutes man is *rational*, which is said of man because of his intellectual principle. Therefore the intellectual principle is the form of man.

I answer that, We must assert that the intellect which is the principle of intellectual operation is the form of the human body. For that whereby primarily anything acts is a form of the thing to which the act is attributed. For instance, that whereby a body is primarily healed is health, and that whereby the soul knows primarily is knowledge; hence health is a form of the body, and knowledge is a form of the soul. The reason for this is that nothing acts except so far as it is in act; and so, a thing acts by that whereby it is in act. Now it is clear that the first thing by which the body lives is the soul. And as life appears through various operations in different degrees of living things, that whereby we primarily perform each of all these vital actions is the soul. For the soul is the primary principle of our nourishment, sensation, and local movement; and likewise of our understanding. Therefore this principle by which primarily we understand, whether it be called the intellect or the intellectual soul, is the form of the body. This is the demonstration used by Aristotle.

But if anyone say that the intellectual soul is not the form of the body, he must explain how it is that this action of understanding is the action of this particular man; for each one is conscious that it is he himself who understands. Now an action may be attributed to anyone in three ways, as is clear from the Philosopher. For a thing is said to move or act, either by virtue of its whole self, for instance, as a physician heals; or by virtue of a part, as a man sees by his eye, or through an accidental quality, as when we say that something that is white builds, because it is accidental to the builder to be white. So when we say that Socrates or Plato understands, it is clear that this is not attributed to him accidentally, since it is ascribed to him as man, which is predicated of him essentially. We must therefore say either that Socrates understands by virtue of his whole self, as Plato maintained, holding that man is an intellectual soul, or that the intellect is a part of Socrates. The first cannot stand, as was shown above, because it is one and the same man who is conscious both that he understands and that he senses. But one cannot sense without out a body, and therefore the body must be some part of man. It follows therefore that the intellect by which Socrates understands is a part of Socrates, so that it is in some way united to the body of Socrates.

As to this union, the Commentator held that it is through the intelligible species, as having a double subject, namely, the possible intellect and the phantasms which are in the corporeal organs. Thus, through the intelligible species, the possible intellect *is linked* to the body of this or that particular man. But this link or union does not sufficiently explain the fact that the act of the intellect is the act of Socrates. This can be clearly seen from comparison with the sensitive power, from which Aristotle proceeds to consider things relating to the intellect. For the relation of phantasms to the intellect is like the relation of colors to the sense of sight, as he says *De Anima* iii. Therefore, just as the species of colors are in the sight, so the species of phantasms are in the possible intellect. Now it is clear that because the colors, the likenesses of which are in the sight, are on a wall, the action of seeing is not attributed to the wall; for we do not say that the wall sees, but rather that it is seen. Therefore, from the fact that the species of phantasms are in the possible intellect, it does not follow that Socrates, in whom are the phantasms, understands, but that he or his phantasms are understood.

Some, however, have tried to maintain that the intellect is united to the body as its mover, and hence that the intellect and body form one thing in such a way that the act of the intellect could be attributed to the whole. This is, however, absurd for many reasons. First, because the intellect does not move the body except through the appetite, whose movement presupposes the operation of the intellect. The reason therefore why Socrates understands is not because he is moved by his intellect, but rather, contrariwise, he is moved by his intellect because he understands.—Secondly, because, since Socrates is an individual in a nature of one essence composed of matter and form, if the intellect be not the form, it follows that it must be outside the essence, and then the intellect is to the whole Socrates as a motor to the thing moved. But to understand is an action that remains in the agent, and does not pass into something else, as does the action of heating. Therefore the action of understanding cannot be attributed to Socrates for the reason that he is moved by his intellect.—Thirdly, because the action of a mover is never attributed to the thing moved, except as to an instrument, just as the action of a carpenter is attributed to a saw. Therefore, if understanding is attributed to Socrates as the action of his mover, it follows that it is attributed to him as to an instrument. This is contrary to the teaching of the Philosopher, who holds that understanding is not possible through a corporeal instrument.—Fourthly, because, although the action of a part be attributed to the whole, as the action of the eye is attributed to a man, yet it is never attributed to another part, except perhaps accidentally; for we do not say that the hand sees because the eye sees. Therefore, if the intellect and Socrates are united in the above manner, the action of the intellect cannot be attributed to Socrates. If, however, Socrates be a whole composed of a union of the intellect with whatever else belongs to Socrates, but with the supposition that the intellect is united to the other parts of Socrates only as a mover, it follows that Socrates is not one absolutely, and consequently neither a being absolutely, for a thing is a being according as it is one.

There remains, therefore, no other explanation than that given by Aristotle—namely, that this particular man understands because the intellectual principle is his form. Thus from the very operation of the intellect it is made clear that the intellectual principle is united to the body as its form.

The same can be clearly shown from the nature of the human species. For the nature of each thing is shown by its operation. Now the proper operation of man as man is to understand, for it is in this that he surpasses all animals. Whence Aristotle concludes that the ultimate happiness of man must consist in this operation as properly belonging to him. Man must therefore derive his species from that which is the principle of this operation. But the species of each thing is derived from its form. It follows therefore that the intellectual principle is the proper form of man.

But we must observe that the nobler a form is, the more it rises above corporeal matter, the less it is subject to matter, and the more it excels matter by its power and its operation. Hence we find that the form of a mixed body has an operation not caused by its elemental qualities. And the higher we advance in the nobility of forms, the more we find that the power of the form excels the elementary matter; as the vegetative soul excels the form of the metal, and the sensitive soul excels the vegetative soul. Now the human soul is the highest and noblest of forms. Therefore, in its power it excels corporeal matter by the fact that it has an operation and a power in which corporeal matter has no share whatever. This power is called the intellect.

It is well to remark, furthermore, that if anyone held that the soul is composed of matter and form, it would follow that in no way could the soul be the form of the body. For since form is an act, and matter is being only in potentiality, that which is composed of matter and form cannot in its entirety be the form of another. But if it is a form by virtue of some part of itself, then that part which is the form we call the soul, and that of which it is the form we call the *primary animate,* as was said above.*

Saint Thomas Aquinas pursues an Aristotelian approach (hierarchical and influenced by biology), suggesting that the soul has five faculties, more or less in order of increasing complexity: vegetative, sensitive, appetitive, locomotive, and culminating in the intellectual, which is the trademark of human beings:

[T]he various souls are distinguished according as the operation of the soul transcends the operation of the corporeal nature in various ways; for the whole corporeal nature is subject to the soul, and is related to it as its matter and instrument. There exists, therefore, an operation of the soul which so far exceeds the corporeal nature that it is not even performed by any corporeal organ; and such is the operation of the *rational soul.* Below this, there is another operation of the soul, which is indeed performed through a corporeal organ, but not through a corporeal quality, and this is the operation of the *sensitive soul.* For though hot and cold, wet and dry, and other such corporeal qualities are required for the work of the senses, yet they are not required in such a way that the operation of the senses takes place by the power of such qualities; but only for the proper disposition of the organ. The lowest of the operations of the soul is that which is performed by a corporeal organ and by the power of a corporeal quality. Yet this transcends the operation of the corporeal nature; because the movements of bodies are caused by an extrinsic principle, while these operations are from an intrinsic principle. For this is common to all the operations of the soul, since every animate thing, in some way, moves itself. Such is the operation of the *vegetative soul;* for digestion, and what follows, is caused instrumentally by the action of heat, as the Philosopher says.

*From *Summa Theologica* (1896). (J. Rickaby, Trans.). London: Burns and Oates.

Now the powers of the soul are distinguished generically by their objects. For the higher a power is, the more universal is the object to which it extends, as we have said above. But the object of the soul's operation may be considered in a triple order. For in the soul there is a power whose object is only the body that is united to that soul; and the powers of this genus are called *vegetative*, for the vegetative power acts only on the body to which the soul is united. There is another genus in the powers of the soul which regards a more universal object—namely, every sensible body, and not only the body to which the soul is united. And there is yet another genus in the powers of the soul which regards a still more universal object—namely, not only the sensible body, but universally all being. Therefore it is evident that the latter two genera of the soul's powers have an operation in regard not merely to that which is united to them, but also to something extrinsic. Now, since whatever operates must in some way be united to the object in relation to which it operates, it follows of necessity that this something extrinsic, which is the object of the soul's operation, must be related to the soul in a twofold manner. First, inasmuch as this something extrinsic has a natural aptitude to be united to the soul, and to be by its likeness in the soul. In this way there are two kinds of powers—namely, the *sensitive*, in regard to the less common object, the sensible body; and the *intellectual*, in regard to the most common object, universal being. Secondly, inasmuch as the soul itself has an inclination and tendency to the external thing. And in this way there are again two kinds of powers in the soul: one—*the appetitive*—according to which the soul is referred to something extrinsic as to an end, which is first in the intention; the other—the *locomotive* power—according to which the soul is referred to something extrinsic as to the term of its operation and movement; for every animal is moved for the purpose of realizing its desires and intentions.

The modes of living, on the other hand, are distinguished according to the degrees of living things. There are some living things in which there exists only vegetative power, as plants. There are others in which along with the vegetative there exists also the sensitive, but not the locomotive, power; and such are immovable animals, as shellfish. There are others which, besides this, have locomotive powers, as do the perfect animals, which require many things for their life, and consequently need movement to seek necessaries of life from a distance. And there are some living things which along with these have intellectual power   namely, men. But the appetitive power does not constitute a degree of living things; because *wherever there is sense there is also appetite.**

Aquinas also proclaims that all things act for an end, that this end is goodness, and that for the human soul, this goodness consists in residing ultimately with God.

From the fact that they acquire the divine goodness, creatures are made like unto God. Therefore, if all things tend to God as their last end, so as to acquire His goodness, it follows that the last end of things is to become like unto God.

Moreover. The agent is said to be the end of the effect in so far as the effect tends to be like the agent; and hence it is that *the form of the generator is the end of the act of generation*. Now God is the end of things in such wise as to be also their first producing cause. Therefore all things tend to a likeness to God, as their last end.

Again. Things give evidence that *they naturally desire to be;* so that if any are corruptible, they naturally resist corruptives, and tend to where they can be safeguarded, as the fire tends upwards and earth downwards. Now all things have being in so far as they are like God, Who is self-subsistent being, since they are all beings only by participation. Therefore all things desire as their last end to be like God.

*From *Summa Theologica* (1896). (J. Rickaby, Trans.). London: Burns and Oates.

Further. All creatures are images of the first agent, namely God, since *the agent produces its like.* Now the perfection of an image consists in representing the original by a likeness to it, for this is why an image is made. Therefore all things exist for the purpose of acquiring a likeness to God, as for their last end.

Again. Each thing by its movement or action tends to some good as its end, as was proved above. Now a thing partakes of good in so far as it is like to the first goodness, which is God. Therefore all things, by their movements and actions tend to a likeness to God as to their last end. . . .

Again. Man's last end is the term of his natural appetite, so that when he has obtained it, he desires nothing more; because if he still has a movement towards something, he has not yet reached an end wherein to be at rest. Now this cannot happen in this life, since the more man understands, the more is the desire to understand increased in him (for this is natural to man), unless perhaps there be someone who understands all things. Now in this life this never did nor can happen to anyone that was a mere man, seeing that in this life we are unable to know separate substances which in themselves are most intelligible, as we have proved. Therefore man's ultimate happiness cannot possibly be in this life.

Besides. Whatever is in motion towards an end has a natural desire to be established and at rest therein. Hence a body does not move away from the place towards which it has a natural movement, except by a violent movement which is contrary to that appetite. Now happiness is the last end which man naturally desires. Therefore it is his natural desire to be established in happiness. Consequently, unless together with happiness he acquires a state of immobility, he is not yet happy, since his natural desire is not yet at rest. When, therefore, a man acquires happiness, he also acquires stability and rest; so that all agree in conceiving stability as a necessary condition of happiness. Hence the Philosopher says: *We do not look upon the happy man as a kind of chameleon.* Now in this life there is no sure stability, since, however happy a man may be, sickness and misfortune may come upon him, so that he is hindered in the operation, whatever it be, in which happiness consists. Therefore man's ultimate happiness cannot be in this life.

Moreover. It would seem unfitting and unreasonable for a thing to take a long time in becoming, and to have but a short time in being; for it would follow that for a longer duration of time nature would be deprived of its end. Hence we see that animals which live but a short time are perfected in a short time. But if happiness consists in a perfect operation according to perfect virtue, whether intellectual or moral, it cannot possibly come to man except after a long time. This is most evident in speculative matters, wherein man's ultimate happiness consists, as we have proved; for hardly is man able to arrive at perfection in the speculations of science, even though he reach the last stage of life, and then, in the majority of cases, but a short space of life remains to him. Therefore man's ultimate happiness cannot be in this life.

Further. All admit that happiness is a perfect good, or else it would not bring rest to the appetite. Now perfect good is that which is wholly free from any admixture of evil; just as that which is perfectly white is that which is entirely free from any admixture of black. But man cannot be wholly free from evils in this state of life, and not only from evils of the body, such as hunger, thirst, heat, cold and the like, but also from evils of the soul. For there is no one who at times is not disturbed by inordinate passions; who sometimes does not go beyond the mean, wherein virtue consists, either in excess or in deficiency; who is not deceived in some thing or another; or who at least is not ignorant of what he would wish to know, or does not feel doubtful about an opinion of which he would like to be certain. Therefore no man is happy in this life.

Again. Man naturally shuns death, and is sad about it, not only shunning it at the moment when he feels its presence, but also when he thinks about it. But man, in this life, cannot obtain not to die. Therefore it is not possible for man to be happy in this life.

Besides. Ultimate happiness consists, not in a habit, but in an operation, since habits are for the sake of actions. But in this life it is impossible to perform any action continuously. Therefore man cannot be entirely happy in this life.

Further. The more a thing is desired and loved, the more does its loss bring sorrow and pain. Now happiness is most desired and loved. Therefore its loss brings the greatest sorrow. But if there be ultimate happiness in this life, it will certainly be lost, at least by death. Nor is it certain that it will last till death, since it is possible for every man in this life to encounter sickness, whereby he is wholly hindered from the operation of virtue, *e.g.,* madness and the like, which hinder the use of reason. Such happiness therefore always has sorrow naturally connected with it, and consequently it will not be perfect happiness.

But someone might say that, since happiness is a good of the intellectual nature, perfect and true happiness is for those in whom the intellectual nature is perfect, namely, in separate substances, and that in man it is imperfect, and by a kind of participation. For man can arrive at a full understanding of the truth only by a sort of movement of inquiry; and he fails entirely to understand things that are by nature most intelligible, as we have proved. Therefore neither is happiness, in its perfect nature, possible to man; but he has a certain participation of it, even in this life. This seems to have been Aristotle's opinion about happiness. Hence, inquiring whether misfortunes destroy happiness, he shows that happiness seems especially to consist in deeds of virtue, which seem to be most stable in this life, and concludes that those who in this life attain to this perfection are happy *as men*, as though not attaining to happiness absolutely, but in a human way.

We must now show that this explanation does not remove the foregoing arguments. For although man is below the separate substances according to the order of nature, he is above irrational creatures, and so he attains his ultimate end in a more perfect way than they. Now these attain their last end so perfectly that they seek nothing further. Thus a heavy body rests when it is in its own proper place, and when an animal enjoys sensible pleasure, its natural desire is at rest. Much more, therefore, when man has obtained his last end, must his natural desire be at rest. But this cannot happen in this life. Therefore in this life, man does not obtain happiness considered as his proper end, as we have proved. Therefore he must obtain it after this life.

Again. Natural desire cannot be empty, since *nature does nothing in vain*. But nature's desire would be empty if it could never be fulfilled. Therefore man's natural desire can be fulfilled. But not in this life, as we have shown. Therefore it must be fulfilled after this life. Therefore man's ultimate happiness is after this life.

Besides. As long as a thing is in motion towards perfection, it has not reached its last end. Now in the knowledge of truth all men are always in motion and tending towards perfection; because those who follow make discoveries in addition to those made by their predecessors, as is also stated in *Metaph.* ii. Therefore in the knowledge of truth man is not situated as though he had arrived at his last end. Since, then, as Aristotle himself shows, man's ultimate happiness in this life consists apparently in speculation, whereby he seeks the knowledge of truth, we cannot possibly allow that man obtains his last end in this life.

Moreover. Whatever is in potentiality tends to become actual, so that as long as it is not wholly actual, it has not reached its last end. Now our intellect is in potentiality to the knowledge of all the forms of things, and it becomes actual when it knows any one of them. Consequently, it will not be wholly actual, nor in possession of its last end, except when it knows all things, at least all these material things. But man cannot obtain this through the speculative sciences, by which we know truth in this life. Therefore man's ultimate happiness cannot be in this life.

For these and like reasons, Alexander and Averroes held that man's ultimate happiness does not consist in that human knowledge obtained through the speculative sciences, but in that which results from a union with a separate substance, which union they deemed possible to man in this life. But as Aristotle realized that man has no knowledge in this life other than that which he obtains through the speculative sciences, he maintained that man attains to a happiness which is not perfect, but a human one.

Hence it becomes sufficiently clear how these great minds suffered from being so straitened on every side. We, however, shall be freed from these straits if we hold, in accordance with the foregoing arguments, that man is able to reach perfect happiness after this life, since man has an immortal soul; and that in that state his soul will understand in the same way as separate substances understand, as we proved in the Second Book.

Therefore man's ultimate happiness will consist in that knowledge of God which the human mind possesses after this life.*

STUDY QUESTIONS

1. How was Augustine more "Platonic" and Aquinas more "Aristotelian"?

2. According to the Roman Catholic catechism, the soul is "a living being without a body, having reason and free will." Discuss the importance of each of these qualities. Could the views of Lucretius be reconciled with Christian theology?

3. What did Augustine mean by the "City of God," and what does this have to do with ideas of human nature?

4. Imagine that a "living fossil," such as *Australopithecus* or *Homo erectus,* was just discovered, and that you were a theologian forced to confront the question of whether or not such a being possessed a soul. How would you proceed?

SOME ADDITIONAL READINGS

Ellis, William (1940). *The Idea of the Soul in Western Philosophy and Science.* London: Allen and Unwin Ltd.

Flew, Antony, ed. (1964). *Body, Mind, and Death.* New York: Macmillan.

Frank, S. L. (1993). *Man's Soul: An Introductory Essay in Philosophical Psychology.* Athens, Ohio: Ohio University Press.

Hartman, Edwin (1977). *Substance, Body, and Soul: Aristotelian Investigations.* Princeton, N.J.: Princeton University Press.

Swinburne, Richard (1986). *The Evolution of the Soul.* New York: Oxford University Press.

*From *Summa Contra Gentiles* (1915). (A. Pegis, Trans.). New York: Collier.

PART TWO
THE MIND

Looked at objectively, that is, in terms of their anatomy or physiology, human beings are not really very extraordinary. Aside from the question of their souls, what distinguishes human beings and what therefore must be crucial to any consideration of human nature, is their minds. Accordingly, in this section, we turn to various aspects of the human mind.

CHAPTER THREE

The Imprint of Experience

Is the mind like a furnished apartment, already equipped with basic appliances? Or is it unfurnished, primordially bare and vacant, ready to be filled with whatever the tenant happens to move in? This question—at the heart of what philosophers mean by *epistemology,* the study of the sources of human knowledge—is also fundamental to human nature. This is because if the mind is somehow prewired, prestocked, already furnished (choose your own metaphor), then this existing structure, whatever it is, comprises much of our human nature. On the other hand, if the mind comes to us essentially empty, then human nature is a bit like Gertrude Stein's renowned (and admittedly unfair) observation about Oakland, California: "There is no *there* there."

LOCKE

John Locke (1632–1704) was one of the initiators of the European Enlightenment. Although Locke presumably did not invent common sense, he may have been the first to think and write about it in an organized way. For our purposes, Locke could be excerpted in Chapter 4, which considers the role of reason in human life, or in Chapter 10, as an influential voice on behalf of humanity's fundamental goodness. Locke also influenced Thomas Jefferson's thought in writing the Declaration of Independence, with his argument that governments serve a specific and limited end, and must be freely chosen by their subjects.

Locke's concern for moderation and tolerance led him to oppose what he saw as the immoderate, intolerant attitude of many Church leaders of his day. There was, at the time, a widespread theological view that people possessed an innate knowledge of morality and of

God. Locke felt that such certainty led to intolerance, and in *An Essay Concerning Human Understanding,* he sets about demonstrating that human beings are literally "open-minded" in that their information comes from experience. Locke lived long before psychology existed as an organized discipline, and he was a pioneer in attempts to understand the workings of the human mind.

1. *An inquiry into the understanding, pleasant and useful.*—Since it is the *understanding* that sets man above the rest of sensible beings, and gives him all the advantage and dominion which he has over them, it is certainly a subject, even for its nobleness, worth our labor to inquire into. The understanding, like the eye, whilst it makes us see and perceive all other things, takes no notice of itself; and it requires art and pains to set it at a distance, and make it its own object. But whatever be the difficulties that lie in the way of this inquiry, whatever it be that keeps us so much in the dark to ourselves, sure I am that all the light we can let in upon our own minds, all the acquaintance we can make with our own understandings, will not only be very pleasant, but bring us great advantage in directing our thoughts in the search of other things.

2. *Design.*—This, therefore, being my purpose, to inquire into the original, certainty, and extent of *human knowledge,* together with the grounds and degrees of *belief, opinion,* and *assent,* I shall not at present meddle with the physical consideration of the mind, or trouble myself to examine wherein its essence consists or by what motions of our spirits, or alteration of our bodies, we come to have any sensation by our organs, or any *ideas* in our understandings; and whether those ideas do, in their formation, any or all of them, depend on matter or not. These are speculations which, however curious and entertaining, I shall decline, as lying out of my way in the design I am now upon. . . .

1. *Idea is the object of thinking.*—Every man being conscious to himself that he thinks, and that which his mind is applied about whilst thinking being the ideas that are there, it is past doubt that men have in their mind several ideas, such as are those expressed by the words whiteness, hardness, sweetness, thinking, motion, man, elephant, army, drunkenness, and others: it is in the first place then to be inquired, How he comes by them? I know it is a received doctrine, that men have native ideas and original characters stamped upon their minds in their very first being. This opinion I have at large examined already; and, I suppose, what I have said in the foregoing book will be much more easily admitted, when I have shown whence the understanding may get all the ideas it has, and by what ways and degrees they may come into the mind; for which I shall appeal to everyone's own observation and experience.

2. *All ideas come from sensation or reflection.*—Let us then suppose the mind to be, as we say, white paper, void of all characters, without any ideas; how comes it to be furnished? Whence comes it by that vast store, which the busy and boundless fancy of man has painted on it with an almost endless variety? Whence has it all the materials of reason and knowledge? To this I answer, in one word, from experience. In that all our knowledge is founded, and from that it ultimately derives itself. Our observation, employed either about external sensible objects, or about the internal operations of our minds, perceived and reflected on by ourselves, is that which supplies our understandings with all the materials of thinking. These two are the fountains of knowledge, from whence all the ideas we have, or can naturally have, do spring.

3. *The object of sensation one source of ideas.*—First, our senses, conversant about particular sensible objects, do convey into the mind several distinct perceptions of things, according to those various ways wherein those objects do affect them; and thus we come by those ideas we have of yellow, white, heat, cold, soft, hard, bitter, sweet, and all those which we call sensible qualities; which when I say the senses convey into the mind, I mean, they from external objects convey into the mind what produces there those

perceptions. This great source of most of the ideas we have, depending wholly upon our senses, and derived by them to the understanding, I call *sensation*.

4. *The operations of our minds the other source of them.*—Secondly, the other fountain, from which experience furnisheth the understanding with ideas, is the perception of the operations of our own mind within us, as it is employed about the ideas it has got; which operations when the soul comes to reflect on and consider, do furnish the understanding with another set of ideas which could not be had from things without; and such are perception, thinking, doubting, believing, reasoning, knowing, willing, and all the different actings of our own minds; which we, being conscious of, and observing in ourselves, do from these receive into our understandings as distinct ideas, as we do from bodies affecting our senses. This source of ideas every man has wholly in himself; and though it be not sense as having nothing to do with external objects, yet it is very like it, and might properly enough be called *internal sense*. But as I call the other sensation, so I call this *reflection*, the ideas it affords being such only as the mind gets by reflecting on its own operations within itself. By reflection, then, in the following part of this discourse, I would be understood to mean that notice which the mind takes of its own operations, and the manner of them, by reason whereof there come to be ideas of these operations in the understanding. These two, I say, viz., external material things as the object of sensation, and the operations of our own minds within as the objects of reflection, are, to me, the only originals from whence all our ideas take their beginnings. The term *operations* here, I use in a large sense, as comprehending not barely the actions of the mind about its ideas, but some sort of passions arising sometimes from them, such as is the satisfaction or uneasiness arising from any thought.

5. *All our ideas are of the one or the other of these.*—The understanding seems to me not to have the least glimmering of any ideas which it doth not receive from one of these two. *External objects* furnish the mind with the ideas of sensible qualities, which are all those different perceptions they produce in us; and *the mind* furnishes the understanding with ideas of its own operations.

These, when we have taken a full survey of them, and their several modes, [combinations, and relations,] we shall find to contain all our whole stock of ideas; and that we have nothing in our minds which did not come in one of these two ways. Let anyone examine his own thoughts, and thoroughly search into his understanding, and then let him tell me, whether all the original ideas he has there, are any other than of the objects of his senses, or of the operations of his mind considered as objects of his reflection; and how great a mass of knowledge soever he imagines to be lodged there, he will, upon taking a strict view, see that he has not any idea in his mind but what one of these two have imprinted, though perhaps with infinite variety compounded and enlarged by the understanding, as we shall see hereafter.

6. *Observable in children.*—He that attentively considers the state of a child at his first coming into the world, will have little reason to think him stored with plenty of ideas that are to be the matter of his future knowledge. It is by degrees he comes to be furnished with them; and though the ideas of obvious and familiar qualities imprint themselves before the memory begins to keep a register of time or order, yet it is often so late before some unusual qualities come in the way, that there are few men that cannot recollect the beginning of their acquaintance with them: and, if it were worth while, no doubt a child might be so ordered as to have but a very few even of the ordinary ideas till he were grown up to a man. But all that are born into the world being surrounded with bodies that perpetually and diversely affect them, variety of ideas, whether care be taken about it or not, are imprinted on the minds of children. Light and colors are busy at hand everywhere when the eye is but open; sounds and some tangible qualities fail not to solicit their proper senses, and force an entrance to the mind; but yet I think it will be granted easily, that if a child were kept in a place where he never saw any other but black and white till

he were a man, he would have no more ideas of scarlet or green than he that from his childhood never tasted an oyster or a pineapple has of those particular relishes. . . .

1. *Uncompounded appearances.*—The better to understand the nature, manner, and extent of our knowledge, one thing is carefully to be observed concerning the ideas we have; and that is, that some of them are *simple*, and some *complex*.

Though the qualities that affect our senses are, in the things themselves, so united and blended that there is no separation, no distance between them; yet it is plain the ideas they produce in the mind enter by the senses simple and unmixed. For though the sight and touch often take in from the same object, at the same time, different ideas—as a man sees at once motion and color, the hand feels softness and warmth in the same piece of wax—yet the simple ideas thus united in the same subject are as perfectly distinct as those that come in by different senses; the coldness and hardness which a man feels in a piece of ice being as distinct ideas in the mind as the smell and whiteness of a lily, or as the taste of sugar and smell of a rose: and there is nothing can be plainer to a man than the clear and distinct perception he has of those simple ideas; which, being each in itself uncompounded, contains in it nothing but *one uniform appearance or conception in the mind,* and is not distinguishable into different ideas.

2. *The mind can neither make nor destroy them.*—These simple ideas, the materials of all our knowledge, are suggested and furnished to the mind only by those two ways above mentioned, viz., sensation and reflection. When the understanding is once stored with these simple ideas, it has the power to repeat, compare, and unite them, even to an almost infinite variety, and so can make at pleasure new complex ideas. But it is not in the power of the most exalted wit or enlarged understanding, by any quickness or variety of thought, to *invent* or *frame* one new simple idea in the mind, not taken in by the ways before mentioned; nor can any force of the understanding *destroy* those that are there: the dominion of man in this little world of his own understanding, being much-what the same as it is in the great world of visible things; wherein his power, however managed by art and skill, reaches no farther than to compound and divide the materials that are made to his hand but can do nothing towards the making the least particle of new matter, or destroying one atom of what is already in being. The same inability will everyone find in himself, who shall go about to fashion in his understanding any simple idea not received in by his senses from external objects, or by reflection from the operations of his own mind about them. I would have anyone try to fancy any taste which had never affected his palate, or frame the idea of a scent he had never smelt; and when he can do this, I will also conclude that a blind man hath *ideas* of colors, and a deaf man true, distinct notions of sounds.

3. *Only the qualities that affect the senses are imaginable.*—This is the reason why, though we cannot believe it impossible to God to make a creature with other organs, and more ways to convey into the understanding the notice of corporeal things than those five as they are usually counted, which He has given to man; yet I think it is not possible for anyone to imagine any other qualities in bodies, howsoever constituted, whereby they can be taken notice of, besides sounds, tastes, smells, visible and tangible qualities. And had mankind been made with but four senses, the qualities then which are the objects of the fifth sense had been as far from our notice, imagination, and conception, as now any belonging to a sixth, seventh, or eighth sense can possibly be; which, whether yet some other creatures, in some other parts of this vast and stupendous universe, may not have, will be a great presumption to deny. He that will not set himself proudly at the top of all things, but will consider the immensity of this fabric, and the great variety that is to be found in this little and inconsiderable part of it which he has to do with, may be apt

to think, that in other mansions of it there may be other and different intelligible beings, of whose faculties he has as little knowledge or apprehension, as a worm shut up in one drawer of a cabinet hath of the senses or understanding of a man; such variety and excellency being suitable to the wisdom and power of the Maker. I have here followed the common opinion of man's having but five senses, though perhaps there may be justly counted more; but either supposition serves equally to my present purpose.*

HUME

David Hume (1711–1776) turned a devastating, if good natured, skepticism on religion, morality, history, even the foundation of science, namely cause-and-effect. In *A Treatise on Human Nature,* Hume attempts to establish psychology as the empirical science of human nature. He analyzes, in turn, sensation (which he calls "impression"), perception, memory, imagination, thought, reason, and belief. Ever the skeptic, Hume takes Locke's emphasis on sense experience as the foundation of the human mind, pushes it somewhat further, and comes up with a remarkable result: that "mind," as such, does not really exist at all! Rather, it is simply the temporary, eddying swirl of the various mental states—sensations, perceptions, memories, and so on—that comprise human consciousness at any given time.

"That which we call mind," he writes, "is nothing but a heap or collection of different perceptions, united together by different relations, and supposed, though falsely, to be endowed with a perfect . . . identity." (A side note: After Locke called attention to mental experience, Bishop Berkeley carried Locke one step beyond, arguing that for all we know, mental experience is the only reality; the material world can only be asserted, not proved. When Hume then proceeded to abolish mind, hard on the heels of Berkeley's discounting of matter, philosophy's disconnection from the real world seemed complete, reflected in the waggish dismissal: "No matter, never mind!")

The following selections are from Hume's *A Treatise on Human Nature.*

There are some philosophers, who imagine we are every moment intimately conscious of what we call our SELF; that we feel its existence and its continuance in existence; and are certain, beyond the evidence of a demonstration, both of its perfect identity and simplicity. The strongest sensation, the most violent passion, say they, instead of distracting us from this view, only fix it the more intensely, and make us consider their influence on *self* either by their pain or pleasure. To attempt a farther proof of this were to weaken its evidence; since no proof can be deriv'd from any fact, of which we are so intimately conscious; nor is there any thing, of which we can be certain, if we doubt of this.

Unluckily all these positive assertions are contrary to that very experience, which is pleaded for them, nor have we any idea of *self,* after the manner it is here explain'd. For from what impression cou'd this idea be deriv'd? This question 'tis impossible to answer without a manifest contradiction and absurdity; and yet 'tis a question, which must necessarily be answer'd, if we wou'd have the idea of self pass for clear and intelligible. It must be some one impression, that gives rise to every real idea. But self or person is not any one impression, but that to which our several impressions and ideas are suppos'd to have a reference. If any impression gives rise to the idea of self, that impression must continue invariably the same, thro' the whole course of our lives; since self is suppos'd to exist after that manner. But there is no im-

*From *An Essay Concerning Human Understanding* (1690; 1939). New York: The Modern Library.

pression constant and invariable. Pain and pleasure, grief and joy, passions and sensations succeed each other, and never all exist at the same time. It cannot, therefore, be from any of these impressions, or from any other, that the idea of self is deriv'd; and consequently there is no such idea.

But farther, what must become of all our particular perceptions upon this hypothesis? All these are different, and distinguishable, and separable from each other, and may be separately consider'd, and may exist separately, and have no need of any thing to support their existence. After what manner, therefore, do they belong to self; and how are they connected with it? For my part, when I enter most intimately into what I call *myself*, I always stumble on some particular perception or other, of heat or cold, light or shade, love or hatred, pain or pleasure. I never can catch *myself* at any time without a perception, and never can observe any thing but the perception. When my perceptions are remov'd for any time, as by sound sleep; so long am I sensible of *myself*, and may truly be said not to exist. And were all my perceptions remov'd by death, and cou'd I neither think, nor feel, nor see, nor love, nor hate after the dissolution of my body, I shou'd be entirely annihilated, nor do I conceive what is farther requisite to make me a perfect non-entity. . . .

I may venture to affirm of the rest of mankind, that they are nothing but a bundle or collection of different perceptions, which succeed each other with an inconceivable rapidity, and are in a perpetual flux and movement. Our eyes cannot turn in their sockets without varying our perceptions. Our thought is still more variable than our sight; and all our other senses and faculties contribute to this change; nor is there any single power of the soul, which remains unalterably the same, perhaps for one moment. The mind is a kind of theatre, where several perceptions successively make their appearance; pass, re-pass, glide away, and mingle in an infinite variety of postures and situations. . . . The comparison of the theatre must not mislead us. They are the successive perceptions only, that constitute the mind; nor have we the most distant notion of the place, where these scenes are represented, or of the materials, of which it is compos'd.

What then gives us so great a propension to ascribe an identity to these successive perceptions, and to suppose ourselves possest of an invariable and uninterrupted existence thro' the whole course of our lives? . . .

We have a distinct idea of an object, that remains invariable and uninterrupted thro' a suppos'd variation of time; and this idea we call that of *identity* or *sameness*. We have also a distinct idea of several different objects existing in succession, and connected together by a close relation; and this to an accurate view affords as perfect a notion of *diversity*, as if there was no manner of relation among the objects. But tho' these two ideas of identity, and a succession of related objects be in themselves perfectly distinct, and even contrary, yet 'tis certain, that in our common way of thinking they are generally confounded with each other. That action of the imagination, by which we consider the uninterrupted and invariable object, and that by which we reflect on the succession of related objects, are almost the same to the feeling, nor is there much more effort of thought requir'd in the latter case than in the former. The relation facilitates the transition of the mind from one object to another, and renders its passage as smooth as if it contemplated one continu'd object. This resemblance is the cause of the confusion and mistake, and makes us substitute the notion of identity, instead of that of related objects. However at one instant we may consider the related succession as variable or interrupted, we are sure the next to ascribe to it a perfect identity, and regard it as invariable and uninterrupted. Our propensity to this mistake is so great from the resemblance above-mention'd, that we fall into it before we are aware; and tho' we incessantly correct ourselves by reflexion, and return to a more accurate method of thinking, yet we cannot long sustain our philosophy, or take off this biass from the imagination. Our last resource is to yield to it, and boldly assert that these different related objects are in effect the same, however interrupted and variable. In order to justify to ourselves this absurdity, we often feign some new and unintelligible principle, that connects the objects together, and prevents their interruption or variation. Thus we feign the continu'd existence of the perceptions of our senses, to remove the interruption; and run into the notion of a *soul,* and *self,* and *substance,* to disguise the variation. But we may farther observe, that where we do not give rise to such a fiction, our propension to confound identity with relation is so great, that we are apt to imagine something unknown and mysterious, connecting the parts, beside their relation; and this I take to be the case with regard to the identity we ascribe to plants and vegetables. And even when this does not take place, we still feel a propensity to confound these ideas, tho' we are not able fully to satisfy ourselves in that particular, nor find any thing invariable and uninterrupted to justify our notion of identity.

Thus the controversy concerning identity is not merely a dispute of words. For when we attribute identity, in an improper sense, to variable or interrupted objects, our mistake is not confin'd to the expression, but is commonly attended with a fiction, either of something invariable and uninterrupted, or of something mysterious and inexplicable, or at least with a propensity to such fictions. . . .

We now proceed to explain the nature of *personal identity,* which has become so great a question in philosophy, especially of late years in *England,* where all the abstruser sciences are study'd with a peculiar ardour and application. . . .

'Tis evident, that the identity, which we attribute to the human mind, however perfect we may imagine it to be, is not able to run the several different perceptions into one, and make them lose their characters of distinction and difference, which are essential to them. . . .

When we talk of *self* or *substance,* we must have an idea annex'd to these terms, otherwise they are altogether unintelligible. Every idea is deriv'd from preceding impressions; and we have no impression of self or substance, as something simple and individual. We have, therefore, no idea of them in that sense.

Whatever is distinct, is distinguishable; and whatever is distinguishable, is separable by the thought or imagination. All perceptions are distinct. They are, therefore, distinguishable, and separable, and may be conceiv'd as separately existent, and may exist separately, without any contradiction or absurdity.

When I view this table and that chimney, nothing is present to me but particular perceptions, which are of a like nature with all the other perceptions. This is the doctrine of philosophers. But this table, which is present to me, and that chimney, may and do exist separately. This is the doctrine of the vulgar, and implies no contradiction. There is no contradiction, therefore, in extending the same doctrine to all the perceptions.

In general, the following reasoning seems satisfactory. All ideas are borrow'd from preceding perceptions. Our ideas of objects, therefore, are deriv'd from that source. Consequently no proposition can be intelligible or consistent with regard to objects, which is not so with regard to perceptions. But 'tis intelligible and consistent to say, that objects exist distinct and independent, without any common *simple* substance or subject of inhesion. This proposition, therefore, can never be absurd with regard to perceptions.

When I turn my reflexion on *myself,* I never can perceive this *self* without some one or more perceptions; nor can I ever perceive any thing but the perceptions. 'Tis the composition of these, therefore, which forms the self.

We can conceive a thinking being to have either many or few perceptions. Suppose the mind to be reduc'd even below the life of an oyster. Suppose it to have only one perception, as of thirst or hunger. Consider it in that situation. Do you conceive any thing but merely that perception? Have you any notion of *self* or *substance?* If not, the addition of other perceptions can never give you that notion.

The annihilation, which some people suppose to follow upon death, and which entirely destroys this self, is nothing but an extinction of all particular perceptions; love and hatred, pain and pleasure, thought and sensation. These therefore must be the same with self; since the one cannot survive the other.

Is *self* the same with *substance?* If it be, how can that question have place, concerning the subsistence of self, under a change of substance? If they be distinct, what is the difference betwixt them? For my part, I have a notion of neither, when conceiv'd distinct from particular perceptions.

Philosophers begin to be reconcil'd to the principle, *that we have no idea of external substance, distinct from the ideas of particular qualities.* This must pave the way for a like principle with regard to the mind, *that we have no notion of it, distinct from the particular perceptions.*

So far I seem to be attended with sufficient evidence. But having thus loosen'd all our particular perceptions, when I proceed to explain the principle of connexion, which binds them together, and makes us attribute to them a real simplicity and identity; I am sensible, that my account is very defective, and that nothing but the seeming evidence of the precedent reasonings cou'd have induc'd me to receive it. If perceptions are distinct existences, they form a whole only by being connected together. But no connexions among distinct existences are ever discoverable by human understanding. We only *feel* a connexion or determination of the thought, to pass from one object to another. It follows, therefore, that the thought alone finds personal identity, when reflecting on the train of past perceptions, that compose a mind, the ideas of them are felt to be connected together, and naturally introduce each other. However extraordinary this conclusion may seem, it need not surprize us. Most philosophers seem inclin'd to think, that personal identity *arises* from consciousness; and consciousness is nothing but a reflected thought or perception. The present philosophy, therefore, has so far a promising aspect. But all my hopes vanish, when I come to explain the principles, that unite our successive perceptions in our thought or consciousness. I cannot discover any theory, which gives me satisfaction on this head.*

KANT

Many say that Immanuel Kant (1724–1804) was the greatest thinker Germany ever produced. He was certainly among the most wide-ranging, prolific, and obscure. Kant wrote on subjects as diverse as physics, cosmology, world peace, aesthetics, morality, and metaphysics. As the founder of the German Enlightenment, his work was immensely influential. His magnum opus, the *Critique of Pure Reason,* contains something for (and against) most basic positions on free will, materialism, theology, and the relative primacy of reason as opposed to feeling. According to Kant, it was the earlier work of David Hume that awakened him from a "dogmatic slumber" and inspired him to write nothing less than an all-embracing natural history of human thought which sought in particular to reestablish the role of the human mind as something more than a passive recipient of experience and sensation (à la Locke) or a disconnected array of perceptions and ideas (à la Hume). In the *Critique* (which is really a critical analysis, not a criticism as such), Kant also sought to demonstrate that the mind contains certain "a priori" notions, independent of experience, with which it orders and makes sense of the information it receives from "outside."

Concepts are a priori if they arise first (or "prior to") direct experience. Kant distinguished between human knowledge that is "analytic"—true by logic alone, and thus not especially informative—and "synthetic," true because our experience tells us it is so. He concerned himself in particular with what he called "synthetic a priori," prior truths which are known to human beings because of the very structure of their minds, but which are not mere tautologies. He listed space and time among these, quickly followed by causation.

*From *A Treatise on Human Nature* (1739; 1939). New York: The Modern Library.

Kant's work is pretty much restricted to the attention of philosophers, and yet, his contribution is central to an increasingly important perspective on human nature: that the mind is neither a blank paper nor passive wax, to be written upon or imprinted, willy-nilly, by the force of experience. Rather, "perceptions without conceptions are blind." According to Kant, Locke was wrong in stating that "there is nothing in the intellect except what was first in the senses," (and Leibnitz was correct when he added "nothing, except the intellect itself"). Just as we can learn a great deal about the nature of air by examining a bird's wing, and just as the fin of a fish speaks eloquently about the properties of water, Kant's crucial contribution, for our purposes, is that the human mind, via our a priori concepts, is not simply a passive recipient. The mind brings something to the arena of existence; it is pretuned to reality.

Kant himself claimed, somewhat immodestly, that he produced a Copernican revolution in what passed at the time for scientific psychology. Whereas previously it was thought that the mind (the sun) revolved around the sensations it received, he put the mind in the center of things, with the phenomenal world revolving around it.

Hitherto it has been supposed that all our knowledge must conform to the objects: but, under that supposition, all attempts to establish anything about them *a priori*, by means of concepts, and thus to enlarge our knowledge, have come to nothing. The experiment therefore ought to be made, whether we should not succeed better with the problems of metaphysic, by assuming that the objects must conform to our mode of cognition, for this would better agree with the demanded possibility of an *a priori* knowledge of them, which is to settle something about objects, before they are given us. We have here the same case as with the first thought of Copernicus, who, not being able to get on in the explanation of the movements of the heavenly bodies, as long as he assumed that all the stars turned round the spectator, tried, whether he could not succeed better, by assuming the spectator to be turning round, and the stars to be at rest. A similar experiment may be tried in metaphysic, so far as the *intuition* of objects is concerned. If the intuition had to conform to the constitution of objects, I do not see how we could know anything of it *a priori*, but if the object (as an object of the senses) conforms to the constitution of our faculty of intuition, I can very well conceive such a possibility. As, however, I cannot rest in these intuitions, if they are to become knowledge, but have to refer them, as representations, to something as their object, and must determine that object by them, I have the choice of admitting, either that the *concepts*, by which I carry out that determination, conform to the object, being then again in the same perplexity on account of the manner how I can know anything about it *a priori;* or that the objects, or what is the same, the experience in which alone they are known (as given objects), must conform to those concepts. In the latter case, the solution becomes more easy, because experience, as a kind of knowledge, requires understanding, and I must therefore, even before objects are given to me, presuppose the rules of the understanding as existing within me *a priori*, these rules being expressed in concepts *a priori*, to which all objects of experience must necessarily conform, and with which they must agree. . . .

That all our knowledge begins with experience there can be no doubt. For how should the faculty of knowledge be called into activity, if not by objects which affect our senses, and which either produce representations by themselves, or rouse the activity of our understanding to compare, to connect, or to separate them; and thus to convert the raw material of our sensuous impressions into a knowledge of objects, which we call experience? In respect of time, therefore, no knowledge within us is antecedent to experience, but all knowledge begins with it.

But although all our knowledge begins with experience, it does not follow that it arises from experience. For it is quite possible that even our empirical experience is a compound of that which we receive through impressions, and of that which our own faculty of knowledge (incited only by sensuous impressions), supplies from itself, a supplement which we do not distinguish from that raw material, until long practice has roused our attention and rendered us capable of separating one from the other.

It is therefore a question which deserves at least closer investigation, and cannot be disposed of at first sight, whether there exists a knowledge independent of experience, and even of all impressions of the senses? Such *knowledge* is called *a priori*, and distinguished from *empirical* knowledge, which has its sources *a posteriori*, that is, in experience.

This term *a priori*, however, is not yet definite enough to indicate the full meaning of our question. For people are wont to say, even with regard to knowledge derived from experience, that we have it, or might have it, *a priori*, because we derive it from experience, not *immediately*, but from a general rule, which, however, has itself been derived from experience. Thus one would say of a person who undermines the foundations of his house, that he might have known *a priori* that it would tumble down, that is, that he need not wait for the experience of its really tumbling down. But still he could not know this entirely *a priori*, because he had first to learn from experience that bodies are heavy, and will fall when their supports are taken away.

We shall therefore, in what follows, understand by knowledge *a priori* knowledge which is *absolutely* independent of all experience, and not of this or that experience only. Opposed to this is empirical knowledge, or such as is possible *a posteriori* only, that is, by experience. Knowlledge *a priori*, if mixed up with nothing empirical, is called *pure*. Thus the proposition, for example, that every change has its cause, is a proposition *a priori*, but not pure: because change is a concept which can only be derived from experience.

II. We are in Possession of Certain Cognitions *a priori*, and even the Ordinary Understanding is never without them

All depends here on a criterion, by which we may safely distinguish between pure and empirical knowledge. Now experience teaches us, no doubt, that something is so or so, but not that it cannot be different. *First*, then, if we have a proposition, which is thought, together with its necessity, we have a judgment *a priori;* and if, besides, it is not derived from any proposition, except such as is itself again considered as necessary, we have an absolutely *a priori* judgment. *Secondly*, experience never imparts to its judgments true or strict, but only assumed or relative universality (by means of induction), so that we ought always to say, so far as we have observed hitherto, there is no exception to this or that rule. If, therefore, a judgment is thought with strict universality, so that no exception is admitted as possible, it is not derived from experience, but valid absolutely *a priori*. Empirical universality, therefore, is only an arbitrary extension of a validity which applies to most cases, to one that applies to all: as, for instance, in the proposition, all bodies are heavy. If, on the contrary, strict universality is essential to a judgment, this always points to a special source of knowledge, namely, a faculty of knowledge *a priori*. Necessity, therefore, and strict universality are safe criteria of knowledge *a priori*, and are inseparable one from the other. As, however, in the use of these criteria, it is sometimes easier to show the contingency than the empirical limitation of judgments, and as it is sometimes more convincing to prove the unlimited universality which we attribute to a judgment than its necessity, it is advisable to use both criteria separately, each being by itself infallible.

That there really exist in our knowledge such necessary, and in the strictest sense universal, and therefore pure judgments *a priori*, is easy to show. If we want a scientific example, we have only to look to any of the propositions of mathematics; if we want one from the sphere of the ordinary understanding, such a proposition as that each change must have a cause, will answer the purpose; nay, in the latter case, even the concept of cause contains so clearly the concept of the necessity of its connection with an effect, and of the strict universality of the rule, that it would be destroyed altogether if we attempted to derive it, as Hume does, from the frequent concomitancy of that which happens with that which precedes, and from a habit arising thence (therefore from a purely subjective necessity), of connecting representations. It is possible even, without having recourse to such examples in proof of the reality of pure propositions *a priori* within our knowledge, to prove their indispensability for the possibility of experience itself, thus proving it *a priori*. For whence should experience take its certainty, if all the rules which it follows were always again and again empirical, and therefore contingent and hardly fit to serve as first principles? For the present, however, we may be satisfied for having shown the pure employment of the faculty of our knowledge as a matter of fact, with the criteria of it. . . .

How far we can advance independent of all experience in *a priori* knowledge is shown by the brilliant example of mathematics. It is true they deal with objects and knowledge so far only as they can be represented in intuition. But this is easily overlooked, because that intuition itself may be given *a priori*, and be difficult to distinguish from a pure concept. Thus inspirited by a splendid proof of the power of reason, the desire of enlarging our knowledge sees no limits. The light dove, piercing in her easy flight the air and perceiving its resistance, imagines that flight would be easier still in empty space. It was thus that Plato left the world of sense, as opposing so many hindrances to our understanding, and ventured beyond on the wings of his ideas into the empty space of pure understanding. He did not perceive that he was making no progress by these endeavours, because he had no resistance as a fulcrum on which to rest or to apply his powers, in order to cause the understanding to advance. It is indeed a very common fate of human reason first of all to finish its speculative edifice as soon as possible, and then only to enquire whether the foundation be sure. Then all sorts of excuses are made in order to assure us as to its solidity, or to decline altogether such a late and dangerous enquiry. The reason why during the time of building we feel free from all anxiety and suspicion and believe in the apparent solidity of our foundation, is this:—A great, perhaps the greatest portion of what our reason finds to do consists in the analysis of our concepts of objects. This gives us a great deal of knowledge which, though it consists in no more than in simplifications and explanation of what is comprehended in our concepts (though in a confused manner), is yet considered as equal, at least in form, to new knowledge. It only separates and arranges our concepts, it does not enlarge them in matter or contents. As by this process we gain a kind of real knowledge *a priori*, which progresses safely and usefully, it happens that our reason, without being aware of it, appropriates under that pretence propositions of a totally different character, adding to given concepts new and strange ones *a priori*, without knowing whence they come, nay without even thinking of such a question. . . .

Space is a necessary representation *a priori*, forming the very foundation of all external intuitions. It is impossible to imagine that there should be no space, though one might very well imagine that there should be space without objects to fill it. Space is therefore regarded as a condition of the possibility of phenomena, not as a determination produced by them; it is a representation *a priori* which necessarily precedes all external phenomena. . . .

Time is not an empirical concept deduced from any experience, for neither coexistence nor succession would enter into our perception, if the representation of time were not given *a priori*. Only when this representation *a priori* is given, can we imagine that certain things happen at the same time (simultaneously) or at different times (successively).

Time is a necessary representation on which all intuitions depend. We cannot take away time from phenomena in general, though we can well take away phenomena out of time. Time therefore is given *a priori*. In time alone is reality of phenomena possible. All phenomena may vanish, but time itself (as the general condition of their possibility) cannot be done away with. . . .

c. Time is the formal condition, *a priori*, of all phenomena whatsoever. Space, as the pure form of all external intuition, is a condition, *a priori*, of external phenomena only. But, as all representations, whether they have for their objects external things or not, belong by themselves, as determinations of the mind, to our inner state, and as this inner state falls under the formal conditions of internal intuition, and therefore of time, time is a condition, *a priori*, of all phenomena whatsoever, and is so directly as a condition of internal phenomena (of our mind) and thereby indirectly of external phenomena also. If I am able to say, *a priori*, that all external phenomena are in space, and are determined, *a priori*, according to the relations of space, I can, according to the principle of the internal sense, make the general assertion that all phenomena, that is, all objects of the senses, are in time, and stand necessarily in relations of time. . . .

We have seen that the understanding possesses everything which it draws from itself, without borrowing from experience, for no other purpose but for experience. The principles of the pure understanding, whether constitutive *a priori* (as the mathematical) or simply relative (as the dynamical), contain nothing but, as it were, the pure schema of possible experience; for that experience derives its unity from that synthetical unity alone which the understanding originally and spontaneously imparts to the synthesis of imagination, with reference to apperception, and to which all phenomena, as data of a possible knowledge, must conform *a priori*. But although these rules of the understanding are not only true *a priori*, but [are] the very source of all truth, that is, of the agreement of our knowledge with objects, because . . . [they contain] the conditions of the possibility of experience, as the complete sphere of all knowledge in which objects can be given to us. . . .*

Kant's other major contribution to the idea of human nature comes in his *Critique of Practical Reason,* which develops a theory of morality. As does his analysis of "Pure Reason," Kant's view of "Practical Reason" focuses on the presence of a preexisting mental construct, which, in his view, is neither produced nor refuted by experience. Rather, it is universally valid, a "categorical imperative." This imperative is, for Kant, a source of continuing religious awe; in fact, he reverses the common practice of deriving moral rules from God, seeking instead to derive the existence of God from the presence within the human mind of these moral rules. "Two things fill my mind with ever new and increasing admiration and awe," he wrote in the *Critique of Practical Reason,* "the starry heavens above, and the moral law within."

Kant's moral law, his "categorical imperative," is, in short, that one should always treat other people as ends rather than means, or to put it another way, you can evaluate the morality of your actions by asking whether you would be content to have that pattern become a general one for all humanity. (For example, are you tempted to lie? How would you feel if everyone became a liar?) For Kant, the fact that people are so equipped—with such morality within their minds—is a demonstration of the divine.

Act so that the maxim of your will can be valid at the same time as a principle of universal legislation. . . .

Pure geometry has postulates which are practical propositions, but which contain nothing more than the assumption that we *can* do something if it is required that we *should* do it; these are the only geometrical propositions that concern existence. They are practical rules under a problematical condition of the will. But the rule [contained in the above law] says that we must absolutely proceed in a certain, definite manner. Therefore this practical rule is unconditional and is conceived *a priori* as a categorical, practical proposition by which the will is objectively determined, absolutely and immediately. . . . For pure reason, which is practical in itself and by itself, is directly legislative in this case. The will is thought of as independent of empirical conditions and therefore it is thought of as pure will determined by the *mere*

*From *Critique of Pure Reason* (1881). (J. H. Stirling, Trans.). Edinburgh: Oliver and Boyd.

form of the law; this principle of determination is regarded as the supreme condition of all maxims. The thing is very strange and has no parallel in all the rest of our practical knowledge. . . .

The rule of judgment according to laws of pure practical reason is this: If the action you propose were to take place by a law of the system of nature of which you are a part yourself, ask yourself whether you could regard it as a possible result of your own will. Everyone does, in fact, decide by this rule as to whether actions are good or evil. Thus people say: Suppose *everyone* permitted himself to deceive when he thought it to his advantage; or thought himself justified in shortening his life as soon as he was thoroughly weary of it; or looked with perfect indifference on the needs of others; if you belonged to such an order of things would you assent to it of your own free will? Now everyone knows well that if he secretly allows himself to deceive, it does not follow that everyone else does the same, or if, unobserved, he is destitute of compassion, others would not necessarily be the same to him. Hence this comparison of the maxim of his actions with a general law of nature is not the determining principle of his will. Nevertheless a law is a *type* of judgment concerning a maxim based on moral principles. If the maxim of the action is not such that it can stand the test of the form of a general law of nature, then it is morally inadmissible. This is also the judgment of common sense; for its ordinary judgments, even those of experience, are always based on the law of nature. Therefore common sense will always use this kind of judgment. . . .

Two things fill the mind with ever new and increasing awe and admiration the more frequently and continuously reflection is occupied with them; the starred heaven above me and the moral law within me. I ought not to seek either outside my field of vision, as though they were either shrouded in obscurity or were visionary. I see them confronting me and link them immediately with the consciousness of my existence. The first [the wonder of the starred heaven] begins with the place I occupy in the external world of sense, and expands the connection in which I find myself into the incalculable vastness of worlds upon worlds, of systems within systems, over endless ages of their periodic motion, their beginnings and perpetuation. The second [the wonder of the moral law within] starts from my invisible self, from my personality, and depicts me as in a world possessing true infinitude which can be sensed only by the intellect. With this I recognize myself to be in a necessary and general connection, not just accidentally as appears to be the case with the external world. Through this recognition I also see myself linked with all visible worlds. The first view of a numberless quantity of worlds destroys my importance, so to speak, since I am an *animal-like being* who must return its matter from whence it came to the planet (a mere speck in the universe), after having been endowed with vital energy for a short time, one does not know how. The second view raises my value infinitely, as an *intelligence,* through my personality; for in this personality the moral law reveals a life independent of animality and even of the entire world of sense. This is true at least as far as one can infer from the purposeful determination of my existence according to this law. This [determination] is not restricted to the conditions and limits of this life, but radiates into the infinite.*

Kant's admiration of duty as an innate human trait led to one of his few poetical and nearly emotional outbursts.

Duty! Sublime and mighty name that embraces nothing charming or insinuating but requires submission, and yet does not seek to move the will by threatening anything that would arouse natural aversion or terror in the mind but only holds forth a law that of itself finds entry into the mind and yet gains reluctant

*From *Critique of Practical Reason* (1909). (T. K. Abbott, Trans.). London: Longmans, Green.

reverence (though not always obedience), a law before which all inclinations are dumb, even though they secretly work against it; what origin is there worthy of you, and where is to be found the root of your noble descent which proudly rejects all kinship with the inclinations, descent from which is the indispensable condition of that worth which human beings alone can give themselves?*

STUDY QUESTIONS

1. Compare Locke and Kant with regard to the source(s) of information available to human beings.

2. Hume once said that whenever he became overwrought over the question of whether his mind really existed as a continuous and meaningful entity, he would go play some billiards or have a good meal, after which he felt much better! Comment on this.

3. Kant is often considered to have been exceedingly rational. Can you identify any irrational components to his thought?

4. Locke is often considered to have been exceedingly open-minded. Can you identify any close-minded components to his thought?

SOME ADDITIONAL READINGS

BonJour, Laurence (1985). *The Structure of Empirical Knowledge.* Cambridge, Mass.: Harvard University Press.

Carruther, Peter (1992). *Human Knowledge and Human Nature: a New Introduction to an Ancient Debate.* New York: Oxford University Press.

Law, Jules David (1993). *The Rhetoric of Empiricism: Language and Perception from Locke to I. A. Richards.* Ithaca, N.Y.: Cornell University Press.

Thomas, Keith, ed. (1992). *British Empiricists.* New York: Oxford University Press.

Turner, Merle B. (1967). *Philosophy and the Science of Behavior.* New York: Appleton-Century-Crofts.

*From *Critique of Practical Reason* (1996). (M. J. Gregor, Trans.). New York: Cambridge University Press.

CHAPTER FOUR

The Role of Reason

It is an interesting question whether a trait must be unique to human beings in order to be considered part of human nature. It is also an interesting, and unanswered, question whether human beings are unique among living things in being capable of reason. But it is nonetheless clear that the ability to reason is one of the most important of human characteristics. It seems likely, in fact, that people have been proud of their rationality for about as long as they have been aware of themselves as human. And often, they have equated the one with the other.

Shakespeare's Hamlet exults "What a piece of work is a man! How noble in reason! How infinite in faculty! In form and moving how express and admirable! In action how like an angel! In apprehension how like a god!" And the Roman poet Virgil spoke for many when he extolled the pleasure of using one's head: "Happy he who has been able to know the causes of things." In the West, the exaltation of reason was especially characteristic of Classical (Greek and Roman) civilization, after which it slumbered during the Dark Ages of the Medieval period, to be resurrected once again with the Renaissance. Isaac Newton and the birth of physics played a powerful role in this resuscitation of reason, not only by showing how the physical world could be understood, but also by bestowing dignity on rationality itself (Berlin, 1956):

Nature and Nature's Laws lay hid in Night:
God said, Let Newton be! and all was Light.

Reason was especially enshrined during the French Enlightenment (in the eighteenth century), with Diderot's *Encyclopedia,* which literally sought to summarize all of human knowledge, confident that human beings would make good—that is, rational—use of their "highest" faculties. Although the so-called Age of Reason coincided with a decline in the power of unquestioned religious faith, reason and faith have not always been in opposition. Thus, "of all human pursuits," wrote Saint Thomas Acquinas: "the pursuit of wisdom is the most perfect, the most sublime, the most profitable, the most delightful." Some renowned rationalists, such as France's Voltaire and the American patriot Tom Paine, found that their admiration of reason placed them at odds with organized religion. Nonetheless, Aquinas suggested that "the proper operation of man is to understand."

PLATO

The Greek mind in general, and Plato in particular, are both nearly synonymous with valuing the intellect. In *The Republic,* Plato proposes that a well-run city requires harmony among three components: guardians (philosopher-kings), soldiers, and tradesmen. In the following selection, Plato extends this to a three-part theory of human nature, made up of reason, will, and appetite, in descending order of merit (analogous in his system to gold, silver, and bronze). For Plato, "justice" within a city requires balance in its government, with reason (the philosopher-kings) in charge. He argues that analogously, individual well-being—a kind of personalized "justice"—requires an appropriate internal balance among these qualities. Note that this does not involve equality of the three; just as a platonic human relationship is widely considered to be one in which the sexual is dominated by the cerebral, a Platonic view of human nature celebrates the rational over the irrational, and mind over matter.

The following selection is from *The Republic.* ("I" refers to Socrates.)

First let us complete the old investigation, which we began, as you remember, under the impression that, if we could previously examine justice on the larger scale, there would be less difficulty in discerning her in the individual. That larger example appeared to be the State, and accordingly we constructed as good a one as we could, knowing well that in the good State justice would be found. Let the discovery which we made be now applied to the individual—if they agree, we shall be satisfied; or, if there be a difference in the individual, we will come back to the State and have another trial of the theory. The friction of the two when rubbed together may possibly strike a light in which justice will shine forth, and the vision which is then revealed we will fix in our souls.

That will be in regular course; let us do as you say.

I proceeded to ask: When two things, a greater and less, are called by the same name, are they like or unlike in so far as they are called the same?

Like, he replied.

The just man then, if we regard the idea of justice only, will be like the just State?

He will.

And a State was thought by us to be just when the three classes in the State severally did their own business; and also thought to be temperate and valiant and wise by reason of certain other affections and qualities of these same classes?

True, he said.

And so of the individual; we may assume that he has the same three principles in his own soul which are found in the State; and he may be rightly described in the same terms, because he is affected in the same manner?

Certainly, he said.

Once more then, O my friend, we have alighted upon an easy question—whether the soul has these three principles or not? . . .

[M]ight a man be thirsty, and yet unwilling to drink?

Yes, he said, it constantly happens.

And in such a case what is one to say? Would you not say that there was something in the soul bidding a man to drink, and something else forbidding him, which is other and stronger than the principle which bids him?

I should say so.

And the forbidding principle is derived from reason, and that which bids and attracts proceeds from passion and disease?

Clearly.

Then we may fairly assume that they are two, and that they differ from one another; the one with which a man reasons, we may call the rational principle of the soul, the other, with which he loves and hungers and thirsts and feels the flutterings of any other desire, may be termed the irrational or appetitive, the ally of sundry pleasures and satisfactions?

Yes, he said, we may fairly assume them to be different.

Then let us finally determine that there are two principles existing in the soul. And what of passion, or spirit? Is it a third, or akin to one of the preceding?

I should be inclined to say—akin to desire.

Well, I said, there is a story which I remember to have heard, and in which I put faith. The story is, that Leontius, the son of Aglaion, coming up one day from the Piraeus, under the north wall on the outside, observed some dead bodies lying on the ground at the place of execution. He felt a desire to see them, and also a dread and abhorrence of them; for a time he struggled and covered his eyes but at length the desire got the better of him; and forcing them open, he ran up to the dead bodies, saying, Look, ye wretches, take your fill of the fair sight.

I have heard the story myself, he said.

The moral of the tale is, that anger at times goes to war with desire, as though they were two distinct things.

Yes; that is the meaning, he said.

And are there not many other cases in which we observe that when a man's desires violently prevail over his reason, he reviles himself, and is angry at the violence within him, and that in this struggle, which is like the struggle of factions in a State, his spirit is on the side of his reason;—but for the passionate or spirited element to take part with the desires when reason decides that she should not be opposed[1], is a sort of thing which I believe that you never observed occurring in yourself, nor, as I should imagine, in any one else?

Certainly not.

Suppose that a man thinks he has done a wrong to another, the nobler he is the less able is he to feel indignant at any suffering, such as hunger, or cold, or any other pain which the injured person may inflict upon him—these he deems to be just, and, as I say, his anger refuses to be excited by them.

True, he said.

But when he thinks that he is the sufferer of the wrong, then he boils and chafes, and is on the side of what he believes to be justice; and because he suffers hunger or cold or other pain he is only the more determined to persevere and conquer. His noble spirit will not be quelled until he either slays or is slain; or until he hears the voice of the shepherd, that is, reason, bidding his dog bark no more.

The illustration is perfect, he replied; and in our State, as we were saying, the auxiliaries were to be dogs, and to hear the voice of the rulers, who are their shepherds.

I perceive, I said, that you quite understand me; there is, however, a further point which I wish you to consider.

What point?

You remember that passion or spirit appeared at first sight to be a kind of desire, but now we should say quite the contrary; for in the conflict of the soul spirit is arrayed on the side of the rational principle.

Most assuredly.

But a further question arises: Is passion different from reason also, or only a kind of reason; in which latter case, instead of three principles in the soul, there will only be two, the rational and the concupiscent; or rather, as the State was composed of three classes, traders, auxiliaries, counsellors, so may there not be in the individual soul a third element which is passion or spirit, and when not corrupted by bad education is the natural auxiliary of reason?

Yes, he said, there must be a third.

Yes, I replied, if passion, which has already been shown to be different from desire, turn out also to be different from reason.

But that is easily proved:—We may observe even in young children that they are full of spirit almost as soon as they are born, whereas some of them never seem to attain to the use of reason, and most of them late enough.

Excellent, I said, and you may see passion equally in brute animals, which is a further proof of the truth of what you are saying. And we may once more appeal to the words of Homer, which have been already quoted by us,

> He smote his breast, and thus rebuked his soul;

for in this verse Homer has clearly supposed the power which reasons about the better and worse to be different from the unreasoning anger which is rebuked by it.

Very true, he said.

And so, after much tossing, we have reached land, and are fairly agreed that the same principles which exist in the State exist also in the individual, and that they are three in number.

Exactly.

Must we not then infer that the individual is wise in the same way, and in virtue of the same quality which makes the State wise?

Certainly.

Also that the same quality which constitutes courage in the State constitutes courage in the individual, and that both the State and the individual bear the same relation to all the other virtues?

Assuredly.

And the individual will be acknowledged by us to be just in the same way in which the State is just?

That follows of course.

We cannot but remember that the justice of the State consisted in each of the three classes doing the work of its own class?

We are not very likely to have forgotten, he said.

We must recollect that the individual in whom the several qualities of his nature do their own work will be just, and will do his own work?

Yes, he said, we must remember that too.

And ought not the rational principle, which is wise, and has the care of the whole soul, to rule, and the passionate or spirited principle to be the subject and ally?

Certainly.

And, as we were saying, the united influence of music and gymnastic will bring them into accord, nerving and sustaining the reason with noble words and lessons, and moderating and soothing and civilizing the wildness of passion by harmony and rhythm?

Quite true, he said.

And these two, thus nurtured and educated, and having learned truly to know their own functions, will rule over the concupiscent, which in each of us is the largest part of the soul and by nature most insatiable of gain; over this they will keep guard, lest, waxing great and strong with the fullness of bodily pleasures, as they are termed, the concupiscent soul, no longer confined to her own sphere, should attempt to enslave and rule those who are not her natural-born subjects, and overturn the whole life of man?

Very true, he said.

Both together will they not be the best defenders of the whole soul and the whole body against attacks from without; the one counselling, and the other fighting under his leader, and courageously executing his commands and counsels?

True.

And he is to be deemed courageous whose spirit retains in pleasure and in pain the commands of reason about what he ought or ought not to fear?

Right, he replied.

And him we call wise who has in him that little part which rules, and which proclaims these commands; that part too being supposed to have a knowledge of what is for the interest of each of the three parts and of the whole?

Assuredly.

And would you not say that he is temperate who has these same elements in friendly harmony, in whom the one ruling principle of reason, and the two subject ones of spirit and desire are equally agreed that reason ought to rule, and do not rebel?

Certainly, he said, that is the true account of temperance whether in the State or individual. . . .

But in reality justice was such as we were describing, being concerned however, not with the outward man, but with the inward, which is the true self and concernment of man: for the just man does not permit the several elements within him to interfere with one another, or any of them to do the work of others,—he sets in order his own inner life, and is his own master and his own law, and at peace with himself; and when he has bound together the three principles within him, which may be compared to the higher, lower, and middle notes of the scale, and the intermediate intervals—when he has bound all these together, and is no longer many, but has become one entirely temperate and perfectly adjusted nature, then he proceeds to act, if he has to act, whether in a matter of property, or in the treatment of the body, or in some affair of politics or private business; always thinking and calling that which preserves and co-operates with this harmonious condition, just and good action, and the knowledge which presides over it, wisdom, and that which at any time impairs this condition, he will call unjust action, and the opinion which presides over it ignorance.

You have said the exact truth, Socrates.

Very good; and if we were to affirm that we had discovered the just man and the just State, and the nature of justice in each of them, we should not be telling a falsehood?

Most certainly not.

May we say so, then?

Let us say so.

And now, I said, injustice has to be considered.

Clearly.

Must not injustice be a strife which arises among the three principles—a meddlesomeness, and interference, and rising up of a part of the soul against the whole, an assertion of unlawful authority, which is made by a rebellious subject against a true prince, of whom he is the natural vassal,—what is all this confusion and delusion but injustice, and intemperance and cowardice and ignorance, and every form of vice?

Exactly so.

And if the nature of justice and injustice be known, then the meaning of acting unjustly and being unjust, or, again, of acting justly, will also be perfectly clear?

What do you mean? he said.

Why, I said, they are like disease and health; being in the soul just what disease and health are in the body.

How so? he said.

Why, I said, that which is healthy causes health, and that which is unhealthy causes disease.

Yes.

And just actions cause justice, and unjust actions cause injustice?

That is certain.

And the creation of health is the institution of a natural order and government of one by another in the parts of the body; and the creation of disease is the production of a state of things at variance with this natural order?

True.

And is not the creation of justice the institution of a natural order and government of one by another in the parts of the soul, and the creation of injustice the production of a state of things at variance with the natural order?

Exactly so, he said.

Then virtue is the health and beauty and well-being of the soul, and vice the disease and weakness and deformity of the same?

True.*

Plato's imagery is often colorful and poetic, as in this selection from the *Phaedrus,* which further develops his theory of the tripartite soul using the now-famous image of a charioteer and his horses. Look for parallels with Freud's concept of the id, ego, and superego, discussed in Chapter 8.

At the beginning of this tale, I divided each soul into three parts—two having the form of horses and the third being like a charioteer; the division may remain. I have said that one horse was good, the other bad, but I have not yet explained in what the goodness or badness of either consists, and to that I will now proceed. The right-hand horse is upright and cleanly made; he has a lofty neck and an aquiline nose; his colour is white, and his eyes dark; he is one who loves honour with modesty and temperance, and the follower of true opinion; he needs no touch of the whip, but is guided by word and admonition only. The other is a crooked, lumbering animal, put together anyhow; he has a short, thick neck; he is flat-faced and of a dark colour, with grey eyes and blood-red complexion; the mate of insolence and pride, shag-eared and deaf, hardly yielding to whip and spur. Now when the charioteer beholds the vision of love, and has his soul warmed through sense, and is full of the prickings and ticklings of desire, the obedient steed, then as always under the government of shame, refrains from leaping on the beloved; but the other, heedless of the pricks and of the blows of the whip, plunges and runs away, giving all manner of trouble to his companion and the charioteer, whom he forces to approach the beloved and to remember the joys of love. They at first indignantly oppose him and will not be urged on to do terrible and unlawful deeds; but at last, when he persists in plaguing them, they yield and agree to do as he bids them. And now they are at the spot and behold the flashing beauty of the beloved; which when the charioteer sees, his memory is carried to the true beauty, whom he beholds in company with Modesty like an image placed upon a holy pedestal. He sees her, but he is afraid and falls backwards in adoration, and by his fall is compelled to pull back the reins with such violence as to bring both the steeds on their haunches, the one willing and unresisting, the unruly one very unwilling; and when they have gone back a little,

*From *The Republic* (1871). (B. Jowett, Trans.). Oxford: Oxford University Press.

the one is overcome with shame and wonder, and his whole soul is bathed in perspiration; the other, when the pain is over which the bridle and the fall had given, having with difficulty taken breath, is full of wrath and reproaches, which he heaps upon the charioteer and his fellow steed, for want of courage and manhood, declaring that they have been false to their agreement and guilty of desertion. Again they refuse, and again he urges them on, and will scarce yield to their prayer that he would wait until another time. When the appointed hour comes, they make as if they had forgotten, and he reminds them, fighting and neighing and dragging them on, until at length he, on the same thoughts intent, forces them to draw near again. And when they are near he stoops his head and puts up his tail, and takes the bit in his teeth and pulls shamelessly. Then the charioteer is worse off than ever; he falls back like a racer at the barrier, and with a still more violent wrench drags the bit out of the teeth of the wild steed and covers his abusive tongue and jaws with blood, and forces his legs and haunches to the ground and punishes him sorely. And when this has happened several times and the villain has ceased from his wanton way, he is tamed and humbled, and follows the will of the charioteer, and when he sees the beautiful one he is ready to die of fear. And from that time forward the soul of the lover follows the beloved in modesty and holy fear.*

ARISTOTLE

Aristotle (384–322 B.C.E.) was Plato's most renowned pupil (just as Plato was Socrates'). He was one of the most influential figures of Western history, as philosopher, teacher, ethicist, literary theorist, early scientist, and master systematizer of human knowledge. Aquinas called Aristotle simply "The Philosopher," and Dante referred to him as "master of those who know."

Compared to Plato, Aristotle's approach is much more grounded in the material world. The two agree, however, on the importance of reason to human life. Consistent with his "this worldly" approach, Aristotle maintains that happiness (not truth or justice or communion with God) is the ultimate goal of human life, and that happiness, in turn, comes from the use of our reason, since that is the glory and power of human beings. For Aristotle, reason is the faculty that distinguishes us from all other living things, and the life of reason is the greatest good to which human beings can aspire. The following selection is from *The Nicomachean Ethics*.

But leaving this subject for the present let us revert to the good of which we are in quest and consider what its nature may be. For it is clearly different in different actions or arts; it is one thing in medicine, another in strategy, and so on. What then is the good in each of these instances? It is presumably that for the sake of which all else is done. This in medicine is health, in strategy, victory, in domestic architecture, a house, and so on. But in every action and purpose it is the end, as it is for the sake of the end that people all do everything else. If then there is a certain end of all action, it will be this which is the practicable good, and if there are several such ends it will be these.

Our argument has arrived by a different path at the same conclusion as before; but we must endeavour to elucidate it still further. As it appears that there are more ends than one and some of these, e.g. wealth, flutes, and instruments generally we desire as means to something else, it is evident that they are not all final ends. But the highest good is clearly something final. Hence if there is only one final end, this will be the object of which we are in search, and if there are more than one, it will be the most final of them.

*From *Phaedrus* (1871). (B. Jowett, Trans.). Oxford: Oxford University Press.

We speak of that which is sought after for its own sake as more final than that which is sought after as a means to something else; we speak of that which is never desired as a means to something else as more final than the things which are desired both in themselves and as means to something else; and we speak of a thing as absolutely final, if it is always desired in itself and never as a means to something else.

It seems that happiness preeminently answers to this description, as we always desire happiness for its own sake and never as a means to something else, whereas we desire honour, pleasure, intellect, and every virtue, partly for their own sakes (for we should desire them independently of what might result from them) but partly also as being means to happiness, because we suppose they will prove the instruments of happiness. Happiness, on the other hand, nobody desires for the sake of these things, nor indeed as a means to anything else at all.

We come to the same conclusion if we start from the consideration of self-sufficiency, if it may be assumed that the final good is self-sufficient. But when we speak of self-sufficiency, we do not mean that a person leads a solitary life all by himself, but that he has parents, children, wife, and friends, and fellow-citizens in general, as man is naturally a social being. But here it is necessary to prescribe some limit; for if the circle be extended so as to include parents, descendants, and friends' friends, it will go on indefinitely. Leaving this point, however, for future investigation, we define the self-sufficient as that which, taken by itself, makes life desirable, and wholly free from want, and this is our conception of happiness.

Again, we conceive happiness to be the most desirable of all things, and that not merely as one among other good things. If it were one among other good things, the addition of the smallest good would increase its desirableness; for the accession makes a superiority of goods, and the greater of two goods is always the more desirable. It appears then that happiness is something final and self-sufficient, being the end of all action.

Perhaps, however, it seems a truth which is generally admitted, that happiness is the supreme good; what is wanted is to define its nature a little more clearly. The best way of arriving at such a definition will probably be to ascertain the function of Man. For, as with a flute-player, a statuary, or any artisan, or in fact anybody who has a definite function and action, his goodness, or excellence seems to lie in his function, so it would seem to be with Man, if indeed he has a definite function. Can it be said then that, while a carpenter and a cobbler have definite functions and actions, Man, unlike them, is naturally functionless? The reasonable view is that, as the eye, the hand, the foot, and similarly each several part of the body has a definite function, so Man may be regarded as having a definite function apart from all these. What then, can this function be? It is not life; for life is apparently something which man shares with the plants; and it is something peculiar to him that we are looking for. We must exclude therefore the life of nutrition and increase. There is next what may be called the life of sensation. But this too, is apparently shared by Man with horses, cattle, and all other animals. There remains what I may call the practical life of the rational part *of Man's being.* But the rational part is twofold; it is rational partly in the sense of being obedient to reason, and partly in the sense of possessing reason and intelligence. The practical life too may be conceived of in two ways, *viz., either as a moral state, or as a moral activity:* but we must understand by it the life of activity, as this seems to be the truer form of the conception.

The function of Man then is an activity of soul in accordance with reason, or not independently of reason. Again the functions of a person of a certain kind, and of such a person who is good of his kind e.g. of a harpist and a good harpist, are in our view generically the same, and this view is true of people of all kinds without exception, the superior excellence being only an addition to the function; for it is the function of a harpist to play the harp, and of a good harpist to play the harp well. This being so, if we define the function of Man as a kind of life, and this life as an activity of soul, or a course of action in conformity with reason, if the function of a good man is such activity or action of a good and noble kind, and if everything is successfully performed when it is performed in accordance with its proper excellence, it follows that the good of Man is an activity of soul in accordance with virtue or, if there are more virtues than one, in accordance with the best and most complete virtue. But it is necessary to add the words "in a complete life." For as one swallow or one day does not make a spring, so one day or a short time does not make a fortunate or happy man.*

SMITH

In some ways, the most powerful testimony on behalf of human reason comes not from those who extol it directly, but who simply *use* it: scientists, for example, or people just "using their heads" to solve the problems of everyday life. Adam Smith (1723–1790) wrote little about the importance of reason as such, but the economic system he championed—liberal capitalism— is fundamentally based on the deep, unstated assumption that human beings are primarily moved by rational considerations. More specifically, Smith, and generations of economists that followed him, developed a model of human nature that is sometimes called "Homo economicus," under which people are considered to be "rational utility maximizers," which, in plain English, means that if left to their own devices, they will choose whatever yields as much benefit (especially profit or income) as possible, at the lowest cost (in money, time, or pain).

Second only to David Hume, Smith is the greatest figure of the Scottish Enlightenment. He wrote a notable treatise, *Theory of Moral Sentiments,* in which he argued that morality derives from social instincts, by which people learn to apply the same evaluations to themselves that they naturally apply to others. But Adam Smith's most important contribution, by far, is his *Inquiry into the Nature and Causes of the Wealth of Nations* (1776) (best known as simply *The Wealth of Nations*) which is the cornerstone of modern Western economics. It is primarily concerned with the division of labor. In the following selection, however, note how rational, utility-maximizing *Homo economicus* pervades the discussion. Smith's metaphor of the pin factory, incidentally, is one of the classic images of economic thought.

The greatest improvement in the productive powers of labour, and the greater part of the skill, dexterity, and judgment with which it is anywhere directed, or applied, seem to have been the effects of the division of labour. . . .

To take an example, therefore, from a very trifling manufacture; but one in which the division of labour has been very often taken notice of, the trade of the pin maker; a workman not educated to this business (which the division of labour has rendered a distinct trade), nor acquainted with the use of the machinery employed in it (to the invention of which the same division of labour has probably given occasion), could scarce, perhaps, with his utmost industry, make one pin in a day, and certainly could not make twenty. But in the way in which this business is now carried on, not only the whole work is a peculiar trade, but it is divided into a number of branches, of which the greater part are likewise peculiar trades. One man draws out the wire, another straightens it, a third cuts it, a fourth points it, a fifth grinds it at the top for receiving the head; to make the head requires two or three distinct operations; to put it on, is a peculiar business, to whiten the pins is another; it is even a trade by itself to put them into the paper; and the important business of making a pin is, in this manner, divided into about eighteen distinct operations, which, in some manufactories, are all performed by distinct hands, though in others the same man will sometimes perform two or three of them. I have seen a small manufactory of this kind

*From *The Nicomachean Ethics* (1920). (J. E. C. Welldon, Trans.). New York: Macmillan and Co.

where ten men only were employed, and where some of them consequently performed two or three distinct operations. But though they were very poor, and therefore but indifferently accommodated with the necessary machinery, they could, when they exerted themselves, make among them about twelve pounds of pins in a day. There are in a pound upwards of four thousand pins of a middling size. Those ten persons, therefore, could make among them upwards of forty-eight thousand pins in a day. Each person, therefore, making a tenth part of forty-eight thousand pins, might be considered as making four thousand eight hundred pins in a day. But if they had all wrought separately and independently, and without any of them having been educated to this peculiar business, they certainly could not each of them have made twenty, perhaps not one pin in a day; that is, certainly not the two hundred and fortieth, perhaps not the four thousand eight hundredth part of what they are at present capable of performing, in consequence of a proper division and combination of their different operations. . . .

This great increase of the quantity of work, which, in consequence of the division of labour, the same number of people are capable of performing, is owing to three different circumstances; first, to the increase of dexterity in every particular workman; secondly, to the saving of the time which is commonly lost in passing from one species of work to another; and lastly, to the invention of a great number of machines which facilitate and abridge labour, and enable one man to do the work of many. . . .

It is the great multiplication of the productions of all the different arts, in consequence of the division of labour, which occasions, in a well-governed society, that universal opulence which extends itself to the lowest ranks of the people. Every workman has a great quantity of his own work to dispose of beyond what he himself has occasion for; and every other workman being exactly in the same situation, he is enabled to exchange a great quantity of his own goods for a great quantity, or, what comes to the same thing, for the price of a great quantity of theirs. He supplies them abundantly with what they have occasion for, and they accommodate him as amply with what he has occasion for, and a general plenty diffuses itself through all the different ranks of the society. . . .

This division of labour, from which so many advantages are derived, is not originally the effect of any human wisdom, which foresees and intends that general opulence to which it gives occasion. It is the necessary, though very slow and gradual consequence of a certain propensity in human nature which has in view no such extensive utility; the propensity to truck, barter, and exchange one thing for another.

Whether this propensity be one of those original principles in human nature, of which no further account can be given; or whether, as seems more probable, it be the necessary consequence of the faculties of reason and speech, it belongs not to our present subject to enquire. It is common to all men, and to be found in no other race of animals, which seem to know neither this nor any other species of contracts. Two greyhounds, in running down the same hare, have sometimes the appearance of acting in some sort of concert. Each turns her towards his companion, or endeavours to intercept her when his companion turns her towards himself.

This, however, is not the effect of any contract, but of the accidental concurrence of their passions in the same object at that particular time. Nobody ever saw a dog make a fair and deliberate exchange of one bone for another with another dog. Nobody ever saw one animal by its gestures and natural cries signify to another, this is mine, that yours; I am willing to give this for that. When an animal wants to obtain something either of a man or of another animal, it has no other means of persuasion but to gain the favour of those whose service it requires. A puppy fawns upon its dam, and a spaniel endeavours by a thousand attractions to engage the attention of its master who is at dinner, when it wants to be fed by him. Man sometimes uses the same arts with his brethren, and when he has no other means of engaging them to act according to his inclinations, endeavours by every servile and fawning attention to obtain their good will. He has not time, however, to do this upon every occasion. In civilised society he stands at all times in need of the cooperation and assistance of great multitudes, while his whole life is scarce sufficient to gain the friendship of a few persons.

In almost every other race of animals each individual, when it is grown up to maturity, is entirely independent, and in its natural state has occasion for the assistance of no other living creature. But man has almost constant occasion for the help of his brethren, and it is in vain for him to expect it from their benevolence only. He will be more likely to prevail if he can interest their self-love in his favour, and show them that it is for their own advantage to do for him what he requires of them. Whoever offers to another a bargain of any kind, proposes to do this. Give me that which I want, and you shall have this which you want, is the meaning of every such offer; and it is in this manner that we obtain from one another the far greater part of those good offices which we stand in need of. It is not from the benevolence of the butcher, the brewer, or the baker, that we expect our dinner, but from their regard to their own interest. We address ourselves, not to their humanity but to their self-love, and never talk to them of our own necessities but of their advantages. Nobody but a beggar chooses to depend chiefly upon the benevolence of his fellow-citizens. Even a beggar does not depend upon it entirely. The charity of well-disposed people, indeed, supplies him with the whole fund of his subsistence. But though this principle ultimately provides him with all the necessaries of life which he has occasion for, it neither does nor can provide him with them as he has occasion for them. The greater part of his occasional wants are supplied in the same manner as those of other people, by treaty, by barter, and by purchase. With the money which one man gives him he purchases food. The old clothes which another bestows upon him he exchanges for other old clothes which suit him better, or for lodging, or for food, or for money, with which he can buy either food, clothes, or lodging, as he has occasion.

As it is by treaty, by barter, and by purchase, that we obtain from one another the greater part of those mutual good offices which we stand in need of, so it is this same trucking disposition which originally gives occasion to the division of labour. In a tribe of hunters or shepherds a particular person makes bows and arrows, for example, with more readiness and dexterity than any other. He frequently exchanges them for cattle or for venison with his companions; and he finds at last that he can in this manner get more cattle and venison, than if he himself went to the field to catch them. From a regard to his own interest, therefore, the making of bows and arrows grows to be his chief business, and he becomes a sort of armourer. Another excels in making the frames and covers of their little huts or moveable houses. He is accustomed to be of use in this way to his neighbours, who reward him in the same manner with cattle and with venison, till at last he finds it his interest to dedicate himself entirely to this employment, and to become a sort of house-carpenter. In the same manner a third becomes a smith or a brazier, a fourth a tanner or dresser of hides or skins, the principal part of the clothing of savages. And thus the certainty of being able to exchange all that surplus part of the produce of his own labour, which is over and above his own consumption, for such parts of the produce of other men's labour as he may have occasion for, encourages every man to apply himself to a particular occupation, and to cultivate and bring to perfection whatever talent or genius he may possess for that particular species of business.

The difference of natural talents in different men is, in reality, much less than we are aware of; and the very different genius which appears to distinguish men of different professions, when grown up to maturity, is not upon many occasions so much the cause, as the effect of the division of labour. The difference between the most dissimilar characters, between a philosopher and a common street porter, for example, seems to arise not so much from nature, as from habit, custom, and education. When they came into the world, and for the first six or eight years of their existence, they were, perhaps, very much alike, and neither their parents nor play-fellows could perceive any remarkable difference. About that age, or soon after, they come to be employed in very different occupations. The difference of talents comes then to be taken notice of, and widens by degrees, till at last the vanity of the philosopher is willing to acknowledge scarce any resemblance. But without the disposition to truck, barter, and exchange, every man must have procured to himself every necessary and convenience of life which he wanted. All must have had the same duties to perform, and the same work to do, and there could have been no such difference of employment as could alone give occasion to any great difference of talents.

As it is this disposition which forms that difference of talents, so remarkable among men of different professions, so it is this same disposition which renders that difference useful. Many tribes of animals acknowledged to be all of the same species, derive from nature a much more remarkable distinction of genius, than what, antecedent to custom and education, appears to take place among men. By nature a philosopher is not in genius and disposition half so different from a street porter, as a mastiff is from a greyhound, or a greyhound from a spaniel, or this last from a shepherd's dog. Those different tribes of animals, however, though all of the same species, are of scarce any use to one another. The strength of the mastiff is not, in the least, supported either by the swiftness of the greyhound, or by the sagacity of the spaniel, or by the docility of the shepherd's dog. The effects of those different geniuses and talents, for want of the power or disposition to barter and exchange, cannot be brought into a common stock, and do not in the least contribute to the better accommodation and convenience of the species. Each animal is still obliged to support and defend itself, separately and independently, and derives no sort of advantage from that variety of talents with which nature has distinguished its fellows. Among men, on the contrary, the most dissimilar geniuses are of use to one another; the different produces of their respective talents, by the general disposition to truck, barter, and exchange, being brought, as it were, into a common stock, where every man may purchase whatever part of the produce of other men's talents he has occasion for. . . .

As it is the power of exchanging that gives occasion to the division of labour, so the extent of this division must always be limited by the extent of that power, or, in other words, by the extent of the market. When the market is very small, no person can have any encouragement to dedicate himself entirely to one employment, for want of the power to exchange all that surplus part of the produce of his own labour, which is over and above his own consumption, for such parts of the produce of other men's labour as he has occasion for.

There are some sorts of industry, even of the lowest kind, which can be carried on nowhere but in a great town. A porter, for example, can find employment and subsistence in no other place. A village is by much too narrow a sphere for him; even an ordinary market town is scarce large enough to afford him constant occupation. In the lone houses and very small villages which are scattered about in so desert a country as the Highlands of Scotland, every farmer must be butcher, baker and brewer for his own family. In such situations we can scarce expect to find even a smith, a carpenter, or a mason, within less than twenty miles of another of the same trade. The scattered families that live at eight or ten miles distance from the nearest of them, must learn to perform themselves a great number of little pieces of work, for which, in more populous countries, they would call in the assistance of those workmen.*

DOYLE

There have been many nonfiction accounts of human reason; in fact, virtually all nonfiction uses reason in one way or another, even when not directly extolling it. It is interesting, however, that enthusiastic depictions of reason in fiction are relatively rare. Exceptions include Daniel Defoe's *Adventures of Robinson Crusoe* and the novels of Jane Austen. But even in these cases, whereas reason and the value of rationality pervades the work, it is not typically

*From *The Wealth of Nations* (1776; 1986). New York: Norton.

acknowledged or celebrated as such. So-called detective fiction is different, however, and no one did it like Arthur Conan Doyle (1859–1930), whose famed creation, Sherlock Holmes, is the epitome of self-congratulatory, if idiosyncratic, rationality. Whenever Holmes announces, "Elementary, my dear Watson," we get a whiff of the seemingly unassailable power of reason—along with some insufferable vanity. (Ironically, after Doyle's son was killed in World War I, Doyle devoted himself to spiritualism: Does this tell us something about human nature?)

The following selection is from the first Sherlock Holmes novella, *A Study in Scarlet* (1887). As we intrude, Dr. Watson, Holmes's good-hearted but somewhat obtuse sidekick, has recently been introduced to the renowned detective.

We met next day as he had arranged, and inspected the rooms at No. 221B, Baker Street, of which he had spoken at our meeting. They consisted of a couple of comfortable bedrooms and a single large airy sitting-room, cheerfully furnished, and illuminated by two broad windows. So desirable in every way were the apartments, and so moderate did the terms seem when divided between us, that the bargain was concluded upon the spot, and we at once entered into possession. That very evening I moved my things round from the hotel, and on the following morning Sherlock Holmes followed me with several boxes and portmanteaus. For a day or two we were busily employed in unpacking and laying out our property to the best advantage. That done, we gradually began to settle down and to accommodate ourselves to our new surroundings.

Holmes was certainly not a difficult man to live with. He was quiet in his ways, and his habits were regular. It was rare for him to be up after ten at night, and he had invariably breakfasted and gone out before I rose in the morning. Sometimes he spent his day at the chemical laboratory, sometimes in the dissecting-rooms, and occasionally in long walks, which appeared to take him into the lowest portions of the city. Nothing could exceed his energy when the working fit was upon him; but now and again a reaction would seize him, and for days on end he would lie upon the sofa in the sitting-room, hardly uttering a word or moving a muscle from morning to night. On these occasions I have noticed such a dreamy, vacant expression in his eyes, that I might have suspected him of being addicted to the use of some narcotic, had not the temperance and cleanliness of his whole life forbidden such a notion.

As the weeks went by, my interest in him and my curiosity as to his aims in life gradually deepened and increased. His very person and appearance were such as to strike the attention of the most casual observer. In height he was rather over six feet, and so excessively lean that he seemed to be considerably taller. His eyes were sharp and piercing, save during those intervals of torpor to which I have alluded; and his thin, hawk-like nose gave his whole expression an air of alertness and decision. His chin, too, had the prominence and squareness which mark the man of determination. His hands were invariably blotted with ink and stained with chemicals, yet he was possessed of extraordinary delicacy of touch, as I frequently had occasion to observe when I watched him manipulating his fragile philosophical instruments.

The reader may set me down as a hopeless busybody, when I confess how much this man stimulated my curiosity, and how often I endeavoured to break through the reticence which he showed on all that concerned himself. Before pronouncing judgment, however, be it remembered how objectless was my life, and how little there was to engage my attention. My health forbade me from venturing out unless the weather was exceptionally genial, and I had no friends who would call upon me and break the monotony of my daily existence. Under these circumstances, I eagerly hailed the little mystery which hung around my companion, and spent much of my time in endeavouring to unravel it.

He was not studying medicine. He had himself, in reply to a question, confirmed Stamford's opinion upon that point. Neither did he appear to have pursued any course of reading which might fit him for a degree in science or any other recognized portal which would give him an entrance into the learned world. Yet his zeal for certain studies was remarkable, and within eccentric limits his knowledge was so extraordinarily ample and minute that his observations have fairly astounded me. Surely no man would work so hard or attain such precise information unless he had some definite end in view. Desultory readers are seldom remarkable for the exactness of their learning. No man burdens his mind with small matters unless he has some very good reason for doing so.

His ignorance was as remarkable as his knowledge. Of contemporary literature, philosophy and politics he appeared to know next to nothing. Upon my quoting Thomas Carlyle, he inquired in the naïvest way who he might be and what he had done. My surprise reached a climax, however, when I found incidentally that he was ignorant of the Copernican Theory and of the composition of the Solar System. That any civilized human being in this nineteenth century should not be aware that the earth travelled round the sun appeared to me to be such an extraordinary fact that I could hardly realize it.

"You appear to be astonished," he said, smiling at my expression of surprise. "Now that I do know it I shall do my best to forget it."

"To forget it!"

"You see," he explained, "I consider that a man's brain originally is like a little empty attic, and you have to stock it with such furniture as you choose. A fool takes in all the lumber of every sort that he comes across, so that the knowledge which might be useful to him gets crowded out, or at best is jumbled up with a lot of other things, so that he has a difficulty in laying his hands upon it. Now the skilful workman is very careful indeed as to what he takes into his brain-attic. He will have nothing but the tools which may help him in doing his work, but of these he has a large assortment, and all in the most perfect order. It is a mistake to think that that little room has elastic walls and can distend to any extent. Depend upon it there comes a time when for every addition of knowledge you forget something that you knew before. It is of the highest importance, therefore, not to have useless facts elbowing out the useful ones."

"But the Solar System!" I protested.

"What the deuce is it to me?" he interrupted impatiently: "you say that we go round the sun. If we went round the moon it would not make a pennyworth of difference to me or to my work."

I was on the point of asking him what that work might be, but something in his manner showed me that the question would be an unwelcome one. . . .

During the first week or so we had no callers, and I had begun to think that my companion was as friendless a man as I was myself. Presently, however, I found that he had many acquaintances, and those in the most different classes of society. There was one little sallow, rat-faced, dark-eyed fellow, who was introduced to me as Mr. Lestrade, and who came three or four times in a single week. One morning a young girl called, fashionably dressed, and stayed for half an hour or more. . . . When any of these nondescript individuals put in an appearance, Sherlock Holmes used to beg for the use of the sitting-room, and I would retire to my bedroom. He always apologized to me for putting me to this inconvenience. "I have to use this room as a place of business," he said, "and these people are my clients." Again I had an opportunity of asking him a point-blank question, and again my delicacy prevented me from forcing another man to confide in me. I imagined at the time that he had some strong reason for not alluding to it, but he soon dispelled the idea by coming round to the subject of his own accord.

It was upon the 4th of March, as I have good reason to remember, that I rose somewhat earlier than usual, and found that Sherlock Holmes had not yet finished his breakfast. The landlady had become so accustomed to my late habits that my place had not been laid nor my coffee prepared. With the unreasonable petulance of mankind I rang the bell and gave a curt intimation that I was ready. Then I picked up a magazine from the table and attempted to while away the time with it, while my companion munched silently at his toast. One of the articles had a pencil mark at the heading, and I naturally began to run my eye through it.

Its somewhat ambitious title was "The Book of Life," and it attempted to show how much an observant man might learn by an accurate and systematic examination of all that came in his way. It struck me as being a remarkable mixture of shrewdness and of absurdity. The reasoning was close and intense, but the deductions appeared to me to be far fetched and exaggerated. The writer claimed by a momentary expression, a twitch of a muscle or a glance of an eye, to fathom a man's inmost thoughts. Deceit, according to him, was an impossibility in the case of one trained to observation and analysis. His conclusions were as infallible as so many propositions of Euclid. So startling would his results appear to the uninitiated that until they learned the processes by which he had arrived at them they might well consider him as a necromancer.

"From a drop of water," said the writer, "a logician could infer the possibility of an Atlantic or a Niagara without having seen or heard of one or the other. So all life is a great chain, the nature of which is known whenever we are shown a single link of it. Like all other arts, the Science of Deduction and Analysis is one which can only be acquired by long and patient study, nor is life long enough to allow any mortal to attain the highest possible perfection in it. Before turning to those moral and mental aspects of the matter which present the greatest difficulties, let the inquirer begin by mastering more elementary problems. Let him, on meeting a fellow-mortal, learn at a glance to distinguish the history of the man, and the trade or profession to which he belongs. Puerile as such an exercise may seem, it sharpens the faculties of observation, and teaches one where to look and what to look for. By a man's finger-nails, by his coat-sleeve, by his boots, by his trouser-knees, by the callosities of his forefinger and thumb, by his expression, by his shirt-cuffs—by each of these things a man's calling is plainly revealed. That all united should fail to enlighten the competent inquirer in any case is almost inconceivable."

"What ineffable twaddle!" I cried, slapping the magazine down on the table; "I never read such rubbish in my life."

"What is it?" asked Sherlock Holmes.

"Why, this article," I said, pointing at it with my eggspoon as I sat down to my breakfast. "I see that you have read it since you have marked it. I don't deny that it is smartly written. It irritates me, though. It is evidently the theory of some armchair lounger who evolves all these neat little paradoxes in the seclusion of his own study. It is not practical. I should like to see him clapped down in a third-class carriage on the Underground, and asked to give the trades of all his fellow-travellers. I would lay a thousand to one against him."

"You would lose your money," Holmes remarked calmly. "As for the article, I wrote it myself."

"You!"

"Yes; I have a turn both for observation and for deduction. The theories which I have expressed there, and which appear to you to be so chimerical, are really extremely practical—so practical that I depend upon them for my bread and cheese."

"And how?" I asked involuntarily.

"Well, I have a trade of my own. I suppose I am the only one in the world. I'm a consulting detective, if you can understand what that is. Here in London we have lots of government detectives and lots of private ones. When these fellows are at fault, they come to me, and I manage to put them on the right scent. They lay all the evidence before me, and I am generally able, by the help of my knowledge of the history of crime, to set them straight. There is a strong family resemblance about misdeeds, and if you have all the details of a thousand at your finger ends, it is odd if you can't unravel the thousand and first. Lestrade is a well-known detective. He got himself into a fog recently over a forgery case, and that was what brought him here."

"And these other people?"

"They are mostly sent on by private inquiry agencies. They are all people who are in trouble about something and want a little enlightening. I listen to their story, they listen to my comments, and then I pocket my fee."

"But do you mean to say," I said, "that without leaving your room you can unravel some knot which other men can make nothing of, although they have seen every detail for themselves?"

"Quite so. I have a kind of intuition that way. Now and again a case turns up which is a little more complex. Then I have to bustle about and see things with my own eyes. You see I have a lot of special knowledge which I apply to the problem, and which facilitates matters wonderfully. Those rules of deduction laid down in that article which aroused your scorn are invaluable to me in practical work. Observation with me is second nature. You appeared to be surprised when I told you, on our first meeting, that you had come from Afghanistan."

"You were told, no doubt."

"Nothing of the sort. I *knew* you came from Afghanistan. From long habit the train of thoughts ran so swiftly through my mind that I arrived at the conclusion without being conscious of intermediate steps. There were such steps, however. The train of reasoning ran, 'Here is a gentleman of a medical type, but with the air of a military man. Clearly an army doctor, then. He has just come from the tropics, for his face is dark, and that is not the natural tint of his skin, for his wrists are fair. He has undergone hardship and sickness, as his haggard face says clearly. His left arm has been injured. He holds it in a stiff and unnatural manner. Where in the tropics could an English army doctor have seen much hardship and got his arm wounded? Clearly in Afghanistan.' The whole train of thought did not occupy a second. I then remarked that you came from Afghanistan, and you were astonished."

"It is simple enough as you explain it," I said, smiling. "You remind me of Edgar Allan Poe's Dupin. I had no idea that such individuals did exist outside of stories."

Sherlock Holmes rose and lit his pipe. "No doubt you think that you are complimenting me in comparing me to Dupin," he observed. "Now, in my opinion, Dupin was a very inferior fellow. That trick of his of breaking in on his friends' thoughts with an apropos remark after a quarter of an hour's silence is really very showy and superficial. He had some analytical genius, no doubt; but he was by no means such a phenomenon as Poe appeared to imagine."

"Have you read Gaboriau's works?" I asked. "Does Lecoq come up to your idea of a detective?"

Sherlock Holmes sniffed sardonically. "Lecoq was a miserable bungler," he said, in an angry voice; "he had only one thing to recommend him, and that was his energy. That book made me positively ill. The question was how to identify an unknown prisoner. I could have done it in twenty-four hours. Lecoq took six months or so. It might be made a textbook for detectives to teach them what to avoid."

I felt rather indignant at having two characters whom I had admired treated in this cavalier style. I walked over to the window and stood looking out into the busy street. "This fellow may be very clever," I said to myself, "but he is certainly very conceited."

"There are no crimes and no criminals in these days," he said, querulously. "What is the use of having brains in our profession? I know well that I have it in me to make my name famous. No man lives or has ever lived who has brought the same amount of study and of natural talent to the detection of crime which I have done. And what is the result? There is no crime to detect, or, at most, some bungling villainy with a motive so transparent that even a Scotland Yard official can see through it."

I was still annoyed at his bumptious style of conversation. I thought it best to change the topic.

"I wonder what that fellow is looking for?" I asked, pointing to a stalwart, plainly dressed individual who was walking slowly down the other side of the street, looking anxiously at the numbers. He had a large blue envelope in his hand, and was evidently the bearer of a message.

"You mean the retired sergeant of Marines," said Sherlock Holmes.

"Brag and bounce!" thought I to myself. "He knows that I cannot verify his guess."

The thought had hardly passed through my mind when the man whom we were watching caught sight of the number on our door, and ran rapidly across the roadway. We heard a loud knock, a deep voice below, and heavy steps ascending the stair.

"For Mr. Sherlock Holmes," he said, stepping into the room and handing my friend the letter.

Here was an opportunity of taking the conceit out of him. He little thought of this when he made that random shot. "May I ask, my lad," I said, in the blandest voice, "what your trade may be?"

"Commissionaire, sir," he said, gruffly. "Uniform away for repairs."

"And you were?" I asked, with a slightly malicious glance at my companion.

"A sergeant, sir, Royal Marine Light Infantry, sir. No answer? Right, sir."

He clicked his heels together, raised his hand in salute, and was gone.*

STUDY QUESTIONS

1. What is the evidence for asserting that human beings are *fundamentally* rational?

2. What basis—if any—exists for valuing reason as a positive good, as opposed to simply acknowledging its existence?

3. What would you say to someone who argued that human happiness comes from denying reason and behaving in accord with "instinct"?

4. Are people with poorly developed reasoning abilities "less human" as a result? If so, then the ethical and legal problems are obvious; if not, then what about gorillas, for example, or chimpanzees, whose ability to reason is probably greater than that of severely retarded human beings?

SOME ADDITIONAL READINGS

Beiser, Frederick C. (1996). *The Sovereignty of Reason: The Defense of Rationality in the Early English Enlightenment.* Princeton, N.J.: Princeton University Press.

Berlin, Isaiah (1956). *The Age of Enlightenment.* New York: Mentor.

Mandelbaum, Maurice (1971). *History, Man, and Reason: A Study in Nineteenth-Century Thought.* Baltimore, Md.: Johns Hopkins University Press.

Rescher, Nicholas (1988). *Rationality: A Philosophical Inquiry into the Nature and the Rationale of Reason.* New York: Oxford University Press.

Stein, Edward (1996). *Without Good Reason: The Rationality Debate in Philosophy and Cognitive Science.* New York: Oxford University Press.

Toulmin, Stephen (1972). *Human Understanding.* Princeton, N.J.: Princeton University Press.

*From *A Study in Scarlet* (1887). New York: Doubleday.

CHAPTER FIVE

The Limits of Reason

Not everyone admires reason. Religious mystics have long distrusted it. Pascal, who abandoned his brilliant study of mathematics to pursue religious contemplation, urged that "the heart has its reasons that reason does not understand." In Jonathan Swift's *Gulliver's Travels,* our hero journeys to Laputa, whose (male) inhabitants are utterly devoted to their intellects: one eye focuses inward and the other upon the stars; neither looks straight ahead. These people are so cerebral that they cannot hold a normal conversation because their minds wander off into sheer contemplation; hence, they require servants who swat them with special instruments about the mouth and ears, reminding them to speak or listen as needed. Laputans concern themselves only with pure mathematics and equally pure music; appropriately, they inhabit an island that floats above the earth. Laputan women, however, are unhappy and regularly cuckold their husbands, who do not notice. The prime minister's wife, for example, repeatedly runs away, preferring to live down on earth with a drunk who beats her.

Montaigne (1533–1592) devoted many of his essays to a skeptical denunciation of the human ability to know anything with certainty. Undoubtedly the most influential of reason's opponents, however, was Jean-Jacques Rousseau (see Chapter 10) who claimed that "the man who meditates is a depraved animal," and thereby spoke for what came to be known as the Romantic movement. (Did he mean, incidentally, that a "feeling" person is therefore a healthy animal? And if so, does this suggest that the ideal person is one who is as animallike as possible?) Even before the advent of Romanticism, many thinkers, even those who employed reason in its most exquisitely theoretical precision, had been inclined to put reason "in its place." David Hume, for example, proclaimed that "Reason is, and ought to be, the slave of the passions, and can never pretend to any other office than to serve and obey them." Furthermore, when reason turns against the deeper needs of people, Hume argued, people will turn against reason.

In any event, the most pronounced turning against reason occurred during the Romantic movement, which embodied a rejection of what had seemed a sterile, dry, deadening exaltation of rationality as the distinguishing human trait. According to historians Will and Ariel Durant (*Rousseau and Revolution,* 1967, Macmillan), the Romantic movement constituted

> the rebellion . . . of sentiment against judgment, of the subject against the object, of subjectivism against objectivity, of solitude against society, of imagination against reality, of myth and legend against history, of religion against science, of mysticism against ritual, of poetry and poetic prose against prose and prosaic poetry, of neo-gothic against neoclassical art, of the feminine against the masculine, of romantic love against the marriage of convenience, of "Nature" and the "natural" against civilization and artifice, of emotional expression against conventional restraints, of individual freedom against social order, of youth against authority, of democracy against aristocracy, of man versus the state. . . .

But most importantly it embodied the rebellion of feeling against reason, of instinct against intellect. It is an approach to the meaning of being human that was reflected in the music of Schubert, Mendelssohn, Schumann, Wagner, Chopin and—the first great musical Romantic—Beethoven. Also the painting of Delacroix, Constable, and Turner, as well as the poetry of Coleridge, Keats, Shelley, Byron, and especially Wordsworth. More recently, modernism and post-modernism can be seen as yet another revolt against the seemingly sterile (and often downright destructive) triumphs of reason, especially in the form of mass society and increasingly lethal technology.

DOSTOYEVSKY

Probably the most articulate, not to mention downright angry, denunciation of human reason is found in the work of Fyodor Dostoyevsky (1821–1881). In his novels, notably *Crime and Punishment, The Brothers Karamazov, The Possessed,* and *The Idiot,* Dostoyevsky explores the darker side of human nature and the prospect of redemption. Dostoyevsky's dissatisfaction with rationality is consistent with his stance as a "Slavophile," part of a centuries-old schism in Russian thinking between the "Westernizers," who looked to Western Europe (and hence, to science, reason, and "modernity") and the Slavophiles, who favored a Romantic, near-mystical belief in Russian greatness as well as in the power of history, religion, irrationality, the peasantry, and the land. (It is a dichotomy that can be identified in twentieth-century Russia, to the present day.)

In his short novel *Notes from Underground,* Dostoyevsky depicts a nameless anti-hero: unattractive, unappealing, and irrational (although intelligent). The novel's writing was stimulated by the publication of a utopian, socialist novel titled *What Is To Be Done?,* in which the author, Nicolai Chernyshevsky, had argued for enlightened self-interest as the key to human happiness:

> A man does evil only because he does not know his real interests, and if he is enlightened and . . . understands what will really benefit him he will see his own best interest in virtue. . . . [I]t is well known that no man can knowingly act against his best interests.

This view is consistent with the utilitarian approach of nineteenth-century British social philosophers, notably Jeremy Bentham and John Stuart Mill, who sought to orchestrate human behavior by appealing to a rational calculus: "the greatest good for the greatest number." In recent decades, it has also been the foundation of much economic theory (so-called rational choice models in which people are thought to maximize their "utility," or benefits from a given act) as well as evolutionary biology (in which living things are seen as maximizing their "fitness").

Dostoyevsky would have none of it. In the longer part of *Notes from Underground,* his anti-hero recounts various willfully painful and irrational experiences he has undergone. The following selection is from the first part, a bitter, jeering monologue in which the Underground Man declaims against the notion that human nature could ever be encompassed within a "Crystal Palace" of rationality.

I am a sick man. . . . I am a spiteful man. I am a most unpleasant man. I think my liver is diseased. Then again, I don't know a thing about my illness; I'm not even sure what hurts. I'm not being treated and never have been, though I respect both medicine and doctors. Besides, I'm extremely superstitious—well at least enough to respect medicine. (I'm sufficiently educated not to be superstitious; but I am, anyway.) No, gentlemen, it's out of spite that I don't wish to be treated. Now then, that's something you proba-bly won't understand. Well, I do. Of course, I won't really be able to explain to you precisely who will be hurt by my spite in this case; I know perfectly well that I can't possibly "get even" with doctors by re-fusing their treatment; I know better than anyone that all this is going to hurt me alone, and no one else. Even so, if I refuse to be treated, it's out of spite. My liver hurts? Good, let it hurt even more!

I've been living this way for some time—about twenty years. I'm forty now. I used to be in the civil ser-vice. But no more. I was a nasty official. I was rude and took pleasure in it. After all, since I didn't accept bribes, at least I had to reward myself in some way. (That's a poor joke, but I won't cross it out. I wrote it thinking that it would be very witty; but now, having realized that I merely wanted to show off disgrace-fully, I'll make a point of not crossing it out!) When petitioners used to approach my desk for information, I'd gnash my teeth and feel unending pleasure if I succeeded in causing someone distress. I almost always succeeded. For the most part they were all timid people: naturally, since they were petitioners. But among the dandies there was a certain officer whom I particularly couldn't bear. He simply refused to be humble, and he clanged his saber in a loathsome manner. I waged war with him over that saber for about a year and a half. At last I prevailed. He stopped clanging. All this, however, happened a long time ago, during my youth. But do you know, gentlemen, what the main component of my spite really was? Why, the whole point, the most disgusting thing, was the fact that I was shamefully aware at every moment, even at the mo-ment of my greatest bitterness, that not only was I not a spiteful man, I was not even an embittered one, and that I was merely scaring sparrows to no effect and consoling myself by doing so. I was foaming at the mouth—but just bring me some trinket to play with, just serve me a nice cup of tea with sugar, and I'd prob-ably have calmed down. My heart might even have been touched, although I'd probably have gnashed my teeth out of shame and then suffered from insomnia for several months afterward. That's just my usual way.

I was lying about myself just now when I said that I was a nasty official. I lied out of spite. I was merely having some fun at the expense of both the petitioners and that officer, but I could never really become spiteful. At all times I was aware of a great many elements in me that were just the opposite of that. I felt how they swarmed inside me, these contradictory elements. I knew that they had been swarming in-side me my whole life and were begging to be let out; but I wouldn't let them out, I wouldn't, I deliber-ately wouldn't let them out. They tormented me to the point of shame; they drove me to convulsions and—and finally I got fed up with them, oh how fed up! Perhaps it seems to you, gentlemen, that I'm repenting about something, that I'm asking your forgiveness for something? I'm sure that's how it seems to you. . . . But really, I can assure you, I don't care if that's how it seems. . . .

I'll proceed calmly about people with strong nerves who don't understand certain refinements of pleasure. For example, although under particular circumstances these gentlemen may bellow like bulls as loudly as possible, and although, let's suppose, this behavior bestows on them the greatest honor, yet, as I've already said, when confronted with impossibility, they submit immediately. Impossibility—does that mean a stone wall? What kind of stone wall? Why, of course, the laws of nature, the conclusions of natural science and mathematics. As soon as they prove to you, for example, that it's from a monkey you're descended, there's no reason to make faces; just accept it as it is. As soon as they prove to you that in truth one drop of your own fat is dearer to you than the lives of one hundred thousand of your fel-low creatures and that this will finally put an end to all the so-called virtues, obligations, and other such similar ravings and prejudices, just accept that too; there's nothing more to do, since two times two is a fact of mathematics. Just you try to object.

"For goodness sake," they'll shout at you, "it's impossible to protest: it's two times two makes four! Nature doesn't ask for your opinion; it doesn't care about your desires or whether you like or dislike its laws. You're obliged to accept it as it is, and consequently, all its conclusions. A wall, you see, is a wall . . . etc. etc." Good Lord, what do I care about the laws of nature and arithmetic when for some reason I dislike all these laws and I dislike the fact that two times two makes four? Of course, I won't break through that wall with my head if I really don't have the strength to do so, nor will I reconcile myself to it just because I'm faced with such a stone wall and lack the strength.

As though such a stone wall actually offered some consolation and contained some real word of conciliation, for the sole reason that it means two times two makes four. Oh, absurdity of absurdities! How much better it is to understand it all, to be aware of everything, all the impossibilities and stone walls; not to be reconciled with any of those impossibilities or stone walls if it so disgusts you; to reach, by using the most inevitable logical combinations, the most revolting conclusions on the eternal theme that you are somehow or other to blame even for that stone wall, even though it's absolutely clear once again that you're in no way to blame, and, as a result of all this, while silently and impotently gnashing your teeth, you sink voluptuously into inertia, musing on the fact that, as it turns out, there's no one to be angry with; that an object cannot be found, and perhaps never will be; that there's been a substitution, some sleight of hand, a bit of cheating, and that it's all a mess—you can't tell who's who or what's what; but in spite of all these uncertainties and sleights-of-hand, it hurts you just the same, and the more you don't know, the more it hurts!

"Ha, ha, ha! Why, you'll be finding enjoyment in a toothache next!" you cry out with a laugh.

"Well, what of it? There is some enjoyment even in a toothache," I reply. "I've had a toothache for a whole month; I know what's what. In this instance, of course, people don't rage in silence; they moan. But these moans are insincere; they're malicious, and malice is the whole point. These moans express the sufferer's enjoyment; if he didn't enjoy it, he would never have begun to moan. This is a good example, gentlemen, and I'll develop it. In the first place, these moans express all the aimlessness of the pain which consciousness finds so humiliating, the whole system of natural laws about which you really don't give a damn, but as a result of which you're suffering nonetheless, while nature isn't. They express the consciousness that while there's no real enemy to be identified, the pain exists nonetheless; the awareness that, in spite of all possible Wagenheims, you're still a complete slave to your teeth; that if someone so wishes, your teeth will stop aching, but that if he doesn't so wish, they'll go on aching for three more months; and finally, that if you still disagree and protest, all there's left to do for consolation is flagellate yourself or beat your fist against the wall as hard as you can, and absolutely nothing else. Well, then, it's these bloody insults, these jeers coming from nowhere, that finally generate enjoyment that can sometimes reach the highest degree of voluptuousness. I beseech you, gentlemen, to listen to the moans of an educated man of the nineteenth century who's suffering from a toothache, especially on the second or third day of his distress, when he begins to moan in a very different way than he did on the first day, that is, not simply because his tooth aches; not the way some coarse peasant moans, but as a man affected by progress and European civilization, a man "who's renounced both the soil and the common people," as they say nowadays. His moans become somehow nasty, despicably spiteful, and they go on for days and nights. Yet he himself knows that his moans do him no good; he knows better than anyone else that he's merely irritating himself and others in vain; he knows that the audience for whom he's trying so hard, and his whole family, have now begun to listen to him with loathing; they don't believe him for a second, and they realize full well that he could moan in a different, much simpler way, without all the flourishes and affectation, and that he's only indulging himself out of spite and malice. Well, it's precisely in this awareness and shame that the voluptuousness resides. "It seems I'm disturbing you, tearing at your heart, preventing anyone in the house from getting any sleep. Well, then, you won't sleep; you too must be aware at all times that I have a toothache. I'm no longer the hero I wanted to pass for earlier, but simply a nasty little man, a rogue. So be it! I'm delighted that you've seen through me. Does it make you feel bad to hear my wretched little moans? Well, then, feel bad. Now let me add an even nastier flourish. . . ." You still don't understand, gentlemen? No, it's clear that one has to develop further and become even more conscious in order to understand all the nuances of this voluptuousness! Are you laughing? I'm delighted. Of course my jokes are in bad taste, gentlemen; they're uneven, contradictory, and lacking in self-assurance. But that's because I have no respect for myself. Can a man possessing consciousness ever really respect himself? . . .

But these are all golden dreams. Oh, tell me who was first to announce, first to proclaim that man does nasty things simply because he doesn't know his own true interest; and that if he were to be enlightened, if his eyes were to be opened to his true, normal interests, he would stop doing nasty things at once and would immediately become good and noble, because, being so enlightened and understanding his real advantage, he would realize that his own advantage really did lie in the good; and that it's well known that there's not a single man capable of acting knowingly against his own interest; consequently, he would, so to speak, begin to do good out of necessity. Oh, the child! Oh, the pure, innocent babe! Well, in the first place, when was it during all these millennia, that man has ever acted only in his own self interest? What does one do with the millions of facts bearing witness to the one fact that people knowingly, that is, possessing full knowledge of their own true interests, have relegated them to the background and have rushed down a different path, that of risk and chance, compelled by no one and nothing, but merely as if they didn't want to follow the beaten track, and so they stubbornly, willfully forged another way, a difficult and absurd one, searching for it almost in the darkness? Why, then, this means that stubbornness and willfulness were really more pleasing to them than any kind of advantage. . . . Advantage! What is advantage? Will you take it upon yourself to define with absolute precision what constitutes man's advantage? And what if it turns out that man's advantage sometimes not only may, but even must in certain circumstances, consist precisely in his desiring something harmful to himself instead of something advantageous? And if this is so, if this can ever occur, then the whole theory falls to pieces. What do you think, can such a thing happen? You're laughing; laugh, gentlemen, but answer me: have man's advantages ever been calculated with absolute certainty? Aren't there some which don't fit, can't be made to fit into any classification? Why, as far as I know, you gentlemen have derived your list of human advantages from averages of statistical data and from scientific-economic formulas. But your advantages are prosperity, wealth, freedom, peace, and so on and so forth; so that a man who, for example, expressly and knowingly acts in opposition to this whole list, would be, in your opinion, and in mine, too, of course, either an obscurantist or a complete madman, wouldn't he? But now here's what's astonishing: why is it that when all these statisticians, sages, and lovers of humanity enumerate man's advantages, they invariably leave one out? They don't even take it into consideration in the form in which it should be considered, although the entire calculation depends upon it. There would be no great harm in considering it, this advantage, and adding it to the list. But the whole point is that this particular advantage doesn't fit into any classification and can't be found on any list. I have a friend, for instance. . . . But gentlemen! Why, he's your friend, too! In fact, he's everyone's friend! When he's preparing to do something, this gentleman straight away explains to you eloquently and clearly just how he must act according to the laws of nature and truth. And that's not all: with excitement and passion he'll tell you all about genuine, normal human interests; with scorn he'll reproach the shortsighted fools who understand neither their own advantage nor the real meaning of virtue; and then—exactly a quarter of an hour later, without any sudden outside cause, but precisely because of something internal that's stronger than all his interests—he does a complete about-face; that is, he does something which clearly contradicts what he's been saying: it goes against the laws of reason and his own advantage, in a word, against everything. . . . I warn you that my friend is a collective personage; therefore it's rather difficult to blame only him. That's just it, gentlemen; in fact, isn't there something dearer to every man than his own best advantage, or (so as not to violate the rules of logic) isn't there one more advantageous advantage (exactly the one omitted, the one we mentioned before), which is more important and more advantageous than all others and, on behalf of which, a man will, if necessary, go against all laws, that is, against reason, honor, peace, and prosperity—in a word, against all those splendid and useful things, merely in order to attain this fundamental, most advantageous advantage which is dearer to him than everything else?

"Well, it's advantage all the same," you say, interrupting me. Be so kind as to allow me to explain further; besides, the point is not my pun, but the fact that this advantage is remarkable precisely because it destroys all our classifications and constantly demolishes all systems devised by lovers of humanity for the happiness of mankind. In a word, it interferes with everything. But, before I name this advantage, I want to compromise myself personally; therefore I boldly declare that all these splendid systems, all these theories to explain to mankind its real, normal interests so that, by necessarily striving to achieve them, it would immediately become good and noble—are, for the time being, in my opinion, nothing more than logical exercises! Yes, sir, logical exercises! Why, even to maintain a theory of mankind's regeneration through a system of its own advantages, why, in my opinion, that's almost the same as . . . well, claiming, for instance, following Buckle, that man has become kinder as a result of civilization; consequently, he's becoming less bloodthirsty and less inclined to war. Why, logically it all even seems to follow. But man is so partial to systems and abstract conclusions that he's ready to distort the truth intentionally, ready to deny everything that he himself has ever seen and heard, merely in order to justify his own logic. That's why I take this example, because it's such a glaring one. Just look around: rivers of blood are being spilt, and in the most cheerful way, as if it were champagne. Take this entire nineteenth century of ours during which even Buckle lived. Take Napoleon—both the great and the present one. Take North America—that eternal union. Take, finally, that ridiculous Schleswig-Holstein. . . . What is it that civilization makes kinder in us? Civilization merely promotes a wider variety of sensations in man and . . . absolutely nothing else. And through the development of this variety man may even reach the point where he takes pleasure in spilling blood. Why, that's even happened to him already. Haven't you noticed that the most refined bloodshedders are almost always the most civilized gentlemen to whom all these Attila the Huns and Stenka Razins are scarcely fit to hold a candle; and if they're not as conspicuous as Attila and Stenka Razin, it's precisely because they're too common and have become too familiar to us. At least if man hasn't become more bloodthirsty as a result of civilization, surely he's become bloodthirsty in a nastier, more repulsive way than before. Previously man saw justice in bloodshed and exterminated whomever he wished with a clear conscience; whereas now, though we consider bloodshed to be abominable, we nevertheless engage in this abomination even more than before. Which is worse? Decide for yourselves. They say that Cleopatra (forgive an example from Roman history) loved to stick gold pins into the breasts of her slave girls and take pleasure in their screams and writhing. You'll say that this took place, relatively speaking, in barbaric times; that these are barbaric times too, because (also comparatively speaking), gold pins are used even now; that even now, although man has learned on occasion to see more clearly than in barbaric times, *he's still far from having learned* how to act in accordance with the dictates of reason and science. Nevertheless, you're still absolutely convinced that he will learn how to do so, as soon as he gets rid of some bad, old habits and as soon as common sense and science have completely re-educated human nature and have turned it in the proper direction. You're convinced that then man will voluntarily stop committing blunders, and that he will, so to speak, never willingly set his own will in opposition to his own normal interests. More than that: then, you say, science itself will teach man (though, in my opinion, that's already a luxury) that in fact he possesses neither a will nor any whim of his own, that he never did, and that he himself is nothing more than a kind of piano key or an organ stop; that, moreover, there still exist laws of nature, so that everything he's done has been not in accordance with his own desire, but in and of itself, according to the laws of nature. Consequently, we need only discover these laws of nature, and man will no longer have to answer for his own actions and will find it extremely easy to live. All human actions, it goes without saying, will then be tabulated according to these laws, mathematically, like tables of logarithms up to 108,000, and will be entered on a schedule; or even better, certain edifying works will be published, like our contemporary encyclopedic dictionaries, in which everything will be accurately calculated and specified so that there'll be no more actions or adventures left on earth.

At that time, it's still you speaking, new economic relations will be established, all ready-made, also calculated with mathematical precision, so that all possible questions will disappear in a single instant, simply because all possible answers will have been provided. Then the crystal palace will be built. And then . . . Well, in a word, those will be our halcyon days. Of course, there's no way to guarantee (now this is me talking) that it won't be, for instance, terribly boring then (because there won't be anything left to do, once everything has been calculated according to tables); on the other hand, everything will be extremely rational. Of course, what don't people think up out of boredom! Why, even gold pins get stuck into other people out of boredom, but that wouldn't matter. What's really bad (this is me talking again) is that for all I know, people might even be grateful for those gold pins. For man is stupid, phenomenally stupid. That is, although he's not really stupid at all, he's really so ungrateful that it's hard to find another being quite like him. Why, I, for example, wouldn't be surprised in the least, if, suddenly, for no reason at all, in the midst of this future, universal rationalism, some gentleman with an offensive, rather, a retrograde and derisive expression on his face were to stand up, put his hands on his hips, and declare to us all: "How about it, gentlemen, what if we knock over all this rationalism with one swift kick for the sole purpose of sending all these logarithms to hell, so that once again we can live according to our own stupid will!" But that wouldn't matter either; what's so annoying is that he would undoubtedly find some followers; such is the way man is made. And all because of the most foolish reason, which, it seems, is hardly worth mentioning: namely, that man, always and everywhere, whoever he is, has preferred to act as he wished, and not at all as reason and advantage have dictated; one might even desire something opposed to one's own advantage, and sometimes (this is now my idea) one *positively must do so.* One's very own free, unfettered desire, one's own whim, no matter how wild, one's own fantasy, even though sometimes roused to the point of madness—all this constitutes precisely that previously omitted, most advantageous advantage which isn't included under any classification and because of which all systems and theories are constantly smashed to smithereens. Where did these sages ever get the idea that man needs any normal, virtuous desire? How did they ever imagine that man needs any kind of rational, advantageous desire? Man needs only one thing—his own *independent* desire, whatever that independence might cost and wherever it might lead. And as far as desire goes, the devil only knows. . . .

"Ha, ha, ha! But in reality even this desire, if I may say so, doesn't exist!" you interrupt me with a laugh. "Why science has already managed to dissect man so now we know that desire and so-called free choice are nothing more than . . ."

"Wait, gentlemen, I myself wanted to begin like that. I must confess that even I got frightened. I was just about to declare that the devil only knows what desire depends on and perhaps we should be grateful for that, but then I remembered about science and I . . . stopped short. But now you've gone and brought it up. Well, after all, what if someday they really do discover the formula for all our desires and whims, that is, the thing that governs them, precise laws that produce them, how exactly they're applied, where they lead in each and every case, and so on and so forth, that is, the genuine mathematical formula—why, then all at once man might stop desiring, yes, indeed, he probably would. Who would want to desire according to some table? And that's not all: he would immediately be transformed from a person into an organ stop or something of that sort; because what is man without desire, without will, and without wishes if not a stop in an organ pipe? What do you think? Let's consider the probabilities—can this really happen or not?"

"Hmmm . . . ," you decide, "our desires are mistaken for the most part because of an erroneous view of our own advantage. Consequently, we sometimes desire pure rubbish because, in our own stupidity, we consider it the easiest way to achieve some previously assumed advantage. Well, and when all this has been analyzed, calculated on paper (that's entirely possible, since it's repugnant and senseless to assume in advance that man will never come to understand the laws of nature) then, of course, all so-called desires will no longer exist. For if someday desires are completely reconciled with reason, we'll follow reason instead of desire simply because it would be impossible, for example, while retaining one's reason, to *desire* rubbish, and thus knowingly oppose one's reason, and desire something harmful to oneself. . . . And, since all desires and reasons can really be tabulated, since someday the laws of our so-called free choice are sure to be discovered, then, all joking aside, it may be possible to establish something like a table, so that we could actually desire according to it. If, for example, someday they calculate and demonstrate to me that I made a rude gesture because I couldn't possibly refrain from it, that I had to make precisely that gesture, well, in that case, what sort of *free choice* would there be, especially if I'm a learned man and have completed a course of study somewhere? Why, then I'd be able to calculate in advance my entire life for the next thirty years; in a word, if such a table were to be drawn up, there'd be nothing left for us to do; we'd simply have to accept it. In general, we should be repeating endlessly to ourselves that at such a time and in such circumstances nature certainly won't ask our opinion; that we must accept it as is, and not as we fantasize it, and that if we really aspire to prepare a table, a schedule, and, well . . . well, even a laboratory test tube, there's nothing to be done—one must even accept the test tube! If not, it'll be accepted even without you. . . .

"Yes, but that's just where I hit a snag! Gentlemen, you'll excuse me for all this philosophizing; it's a result of my forty years in the underground! Allow me to fantasize. Don't you see: reason is a fine thing, gentlemen, there's no doubt about it, but it's only reason, and it satisfies only man's rational faculty, whereas desire is a manifestation of all life, that is, of all human life, which includes both reason, as well as all of life's itches and scratches. And although in this manifestation life often turns out to be fairly worthless, it's life all the same, and not merely the extraction of square roots. Why, take me, for instance; I quite naturally want to live in order to satisfy all my faculties of life, not merely my rational faculty, that is, some one-twentieth of all my faculties. What does reason know? Reason knows only what it's managed to learn. (Some things it may never learn; while this offers no comfort, why not admit it openly?) But human nature acts as a whole, with all that it contains, consciously and unconsciously; and although it may tell lies, it's still alive. I suspect, gentlemen, that you're looking at me with compassion; you repeat that an enlightened and cultured man, in a word, man as he will be in the future, cannot knowingly desire something disadvantageous to himself, and that this is pure mathematics. I agree with you: it really is mathematics. But I repeat for the one-hundredth time, there is one case, only one, when a man may intentionally, consciously desire even something harmful to himself, something stupid, even very stupid, namely: in order *to have the right* to desire something even very stupid and not be bound by an obligation to desire only what's smart. After all, this very stupid thing, one's own whim, gentlemen, may in fact be the most advantageous thing on earth for people like me, especially in certain cases. In particular, it may be more advantageous than any other advantage, even in a case where it causes obvious harm and contradicts the most sensible conclusions of reason about advantage—because in any case it preserves for us what's most important and precious, that is, our personality and our individuality. There are some people who maintain that in fact this is more precious to man than anything else; of course, desire can, if it so chooses, coincide with reason, especially if it doesn't abuse this option, and chooses to coincide in moderation; this is useful and sometimes even commendable. But very often, even most of the time, desire absolutely and stubbornly disagrees with reason and . . . and . . . and, do you know, sometimes this is also useful and even very commendable? Let's assume, gentlemen, that man isn't stupid. (And really, this can't possibly be said about him at all, if only because if he's stupid, then who on earth is smart?) But even if he's not stupid, he is, nevertheless, monstrously ungrateful. Phenomenally ungrateful. I even believe that the best definition of man is this: a creature who walks on two legs and is ungrateful. But that's still not all; that's still not his main defect. His main defect is his perpetual misbehavior, perpetual from the time of the Great Flood. . . . Now I ask you: what can one expect from man as a creature endowed with such strange qualities? Why, shower him with all sorts of earthly blessings, submerge him in happiness over his head so that only little bubbles appear on the surface of this happiness, as if on water, give him such economic prosperity that he'll have absolutely nothing left to do except sleep, eat gingerbread, and worry about the continuation of world history—even then, out of pure ingratitude, sheer perversity, he'll commit some repulsive act. He'll even risk losing his gingerbread, and will intentionally desire the most wicked rubbish, the most uneconomical absurdity, simply in order to inject his own pernicious fantastic element into all this positive rationality. He wants to hold onto those most fantastic dreams, his own indecent stupidity solely for the purpose of assuring himself (as if it were necessary) that men are still men and not piano keys, and that even if the laws of nature play upon them with their own hands, they're still threatened by being overplayed until they won't possibly desire anything more than a schedule. But that's not all: even if man really turned out to be a piano key, even if this could be demonstrated to him by natural science and pure mathematics, even then he still won't become reasonable; he'll intentionally do something to the contrary, simply out of ingratitude, merely to have his own way. If he lacks the means, he'll cause destruction and chaos, he'll devise all kinds of suffering and have his own way! He'll leash a curse upon the world; and, since man alone can do so (it's his privilege and the thing that most distinguishes him from other animals), perhaps only through this curse will he achieve his goal, that is, become really convinced that he's a man and not a piano key! If you say that one can also calculate all this according to a table, this chaos and darkness, these curses, so that the mere possibility of calculating it all in advance would stop everything and that reason alone would prevail—in that case man would go insane deliberately in order not to have reason, but to have his own way! I believe this, I vouch for it, because, after all, the whole of man's work seems to consist only in proving to himself constantly that he's a man and not an organ stop! Even if he has to lose his own skin, he'll prove it; even if he has to become a troglodyte, he'll prove it. And after that, how can one not sin, how can one not praise the fact that all this hasn't yet come to pass and that desire still depends on the devil knows what . . . ?"

You'll shout at me (if you still choose to favor me with your shouts) that no one's really depriving me of my will; that they're merely attempting to arrange things so that my will, by its own free choice, will coincide with my normal interests, with the laws of nature, and with arithmetic.

"But gentlemen, what sort of free choice will there be when it comes down to tables and arithmetic, when all that's left is two times two makes four? Two times two makes four even without my will. Is that what you call free choice?" . . .

Let's suppose that the only thing man does is search for this two times two makes four; he sails across oceans, sacrifices his own life in the quest; but to seek it out and find it—really and truly, he's very frightened. After all, he feels that as soon as he finds it, there'll be nothing left to search for. Workers, after finishing work, at least receive their wages, go off to a tavern, and then wind up at a police station—now that's a full week's occupation. But where will man go? At any rate a certain awkwardness can be observed each time he approaches the achievement of similar goals. He loves the process, but he's not so fond of the achievement, and that, of course is terribly amusing. In short, man is made in a comical way; obviously there's some sort of catch in all this. But two times two makes four is an insufferable thing, nevertheless. Two times two makes four—why, in my opinion, it's mere insolence. Two times two makes four stands there brazenly with its hands on its hips, blocking your path and spitting at you. I agree that two times two makes four is a splendid thing; but if we're going to lavish praise, then two times two makes five is sometimes also a very charming little thing.

And why are you so firmly, so triumphantly convinced that only the normal and positive—in short, only well-being is advantageous to man? Doesn't reason ever make mistakes about advantage? After all, perhaps man likes something other than well-being? Perhaps he loves suffering just as much? Perhaps suffering is just as advantageous to him as well-being? Man sometimes loves suffering terribly, to the point of passion, and that's a fact. There's no reason to study world history on this point; if indeed you're a man and have lived at all, just ask yourself. As far as my own personal opinion is concerned, to love only well-being is somehow even indecent. Whether good or bad, it's sometimes also very pleasant to demolish something. After all, I'm not standing up for suffering here, nor for well-being, either. I'm standing up for . . . my own whim and for its being guaranteed to me whenever necessary. For instance, suffering is not permitted in vaudevilles, that I know. It's also inconceivable in the crystal palace; suffering is doubt and negation. What sort of crystal palace would it be if any doubt were allowed? Yet, I'm convinced that man will never renounce real suffering, that is, destruction and chaos. After all, suffering is the sole cause of consciousness. Although I stated earlier that in my opinion consciousness is man's greatest misfortune, still I know that man loves it and would not exchange it for any other sort of satisfaction. Consciousness, for example, is infinitely higher than two times two. Of course, after two times two, there's nothing left, not merely nothing to do, but nothing to learn. Then the only thing possible will be to plug up your five senses and plunge into contemplation. Well, even if you reach the same result with consciousness, that is, having nothing left to do, at least you'll be able to flog yourself from time to time, and that will liven things up a bit. Although it may be reactionary, it's still better than nothing.

You believe in the crystal palace, eternally indestructible, that is, one at which you can never stick out your tongue furtively nor make a rude gesture, even with your fist hidden away. Well, perhaps I'm so afraid of this building precisely because it's made of crystal and it's eternally indestructible, and because it won't be possible to stick one's tongue out even furtively.

Don't you see: if it were a chicken coop instead of a palace, and if it should rain, then perhaps I could crawl into it so as not to get drenched; but I would still not mistake a chicken coop for a palace out of gratitude, just because it sheltered me from the rain. You're laughing, you're even saying that in this case there's no difference between a chicken coop and a mansion. Yes, I reply, if the only reason for living is to keep from getting drenched.

But what if I've taken it into my head that this is not the only reason for living, and, that if one is to live at all, one might as well live in a mansion? Such is my wish, my desire. You'll expunge it from me only when you've changed my desires. Well, then, change them, tempt me with something else, give me some other ideal. In the meantime, I still won't mistake a chicken coop for a palace. But let's say that the crystal palace is a hoax, that according to the laws of nature it shouldn't exist, and that I've invented it only out of my own stupidity, as a result of certain antiquated, irrational habits of my generation. But what do I care if it doesn't exist? What difference does it make if it exists only in my own desires, or, to be more precise, if it exists as long as my desires exist? Perhaps you're laughing again? Laugh, if you wish;

I'll resist all your laughter and I still won't say I'm satiated if I'm really hungry; I know all the same that I won't accept a compromise, an infinitely recurring zero, just because it exists according to the laws of nature and it *really* does exist. I won't accept as the crown of my desires a large building with tenements for poor tenants to be rented for a thousand years and, just in case, with the name of the dentist Wagenheim on the sign. Destroy my desires, eradicate my ideals, show me something better and I'll follow you. You may say, perhaps, that it's not worth getting involved; but, in that case, I'll say the same thing in reply. We're having a serious discussion; if you don't grant me your attention, I won't grovel for it. I still have my underground.

And, as long as I'm still alive and feel desire—may my arm wither away before it contributes even one little brick to that building! Never mind that I myself have just rejected the crystal palace for the sole reason that it won't be possible to tease it by sticking out one's tongue at it. I didn't say that because I'm so fond of sticking out my tongue. Perhaps the only reason I got angry is that among all your buildings there's still not a single one where you don't feel compelled to stick out your tongue. On the contrary, I'd let my tongue be cut off out of sheer gratitude, if only things could be so arranged that I'd no longer want to stick it out. What do I care if things can't be so arranged and if I must settle for some tenements? Why was I made with such desires? Can it be that I was made this way only in order to reach the conclusion that my entire way of being is merely a fraud? Can this be the whole purpose? I don't believe it. . . .

Even now, after so many years, all this comes back to me *as very unpleasant*. A great deal that comes back to me now is very unpleasant, but . . . perhaps I should end these *Notes* here? I think that I made a mistake in beginning to write them. At least, I was ashamed all the time I was writing this *tale:* consequently, it's not really literature, but corrective punishment. After all, to tell you long stories about how, for example, I ruined my life through moral decay in my corner, by the lack of appropriate surroundings, by isolation from any living beings, and by futile malice in the underground—so help me God, that's not very interesting. A novel needs a hero, whereas here all the traits of an anti-hero have been assembled *deliberately;* but the most important thing is that all this produces an extremely unpleasant impression because we've all become estranged from life, we're all cripples, every one of us, more or less. We've become so estranged that at times we feel some kind of revulsion for genuine "real life," and therefore we can't bear to be reminded of it. Why, we've reached a point where we almost regard "real life" as hard work, as a job, and we've all agreed in private that it's really better in books. And why do we sometimes fuss, indulge in whims, and make demands? We don't know ourselves. It'd be even worse if all our whimsical desires were fulfilled. Go on, try it. Give us, for example, a little more independence; untie the hands of any one of us, broaden our sphere of activity, relax the controls, and . . . I can assure you, we'll immediately ask to have the controls reinstated. I know that you may get angry at me for saying this, you may shout and stamp your feet: "Speak for yourself," you'll say, "and for your own miseries in the underground, but don't you dare say *'all of us.'* " If you'll allow me, gentlemen; after all, I'm not trying to justify myself by saying *all of us*. What concerns me in particular, is that in my life I've only taken to an extreme that which you haven't even dared to take halfway; what's more, you've mistaken your cowardice for good sense; and, in so deceiving yourself, you've consoled yourself. So, in fact, I may even be "more alive" than you are. Just take a closer look! Why, we don't even know where this "real life" lives nowadays, what it really is, and what it's called. Leave us alone without books and we'll get confused and lose our way at once—we won't know what to join, what to hold on to, what to love or what to hate, what to respect or what to despise. We're even oppressed by being men—men with real bodies and blood of *our very own*. We're ashamed of it; we consider it a disgrace and we strive to become some kind of impossible "general-human-beings." We're still-born; for some time now we haven't been conceived by living fathers; we like it more and more. We're developing a taste for it. Soon we'll conceive of a way to be born from ideas. But enough; I don't want to write any more "from Underground. . . ."*

CRANE

Stephen Crane (1871–1900) is probably the most unusual selection in this volume. (Among the joys of editing a collection such as this is the opportunity of sharing representative classics, widely acknowledged to be important. Another delight, however, is to introduce readers to one's personal favorites.) Although best known for his Civil War coming-of-age novel, *The Red Badge of Courage,* Crane wrote other novels, short stories, and some notable, haunting poems. The following poems pretty much speak for themselves.

III

> In the desert
> I saw a creature, naked, bestial,
> Who, squatting upon the ground,
> Held his heart in his hands,
> And ate of it.
> I said, "Is it good, friend?"
> "It is bitter—bitter," he answered;
> "But I like it
> Because it is bitter,
> And because it is my heart."

XXIV

> I saw a man pursuing the horizon;
> Round and round they sped.
> I was disturbed at this;
> I accosted the man.
> "It is futile," I said,
> "You can never—"
>
> "You lie," he cried,
> And ran on.

XLIV

> I was in the darkness;
> I could not see my words
> Nor the wishes of my heart.
> Then suddenly there was a great light—
>
> "Let me into the darkness again."

*From *Notes from Underground* (1989). (M. R. Katz, Trans.). New York: Norton.

XLVI

Many red devils ran from my heart
And out upon the page.
They were so tiny
The pen could mash them.
And many struggled in the ink.
It was strange
To write in this red muck
Of things from my heart.*

STUDY QUESTIONS

1. Does the Underground Man use reason to defeat reason? (This question has two parts: (1) does he use reason? and (2) does he defeat reason?)

2. In Mozart's opera *The Marriage of Figaro* we are advised: "Drink when you are not thirsty, make love when you don't want to—this is what distinguishes us from the beasts" (Act II, scene 21). Would the Underground Man agree? Do you?

3. The quote "Untie our hands, give us independence and we would beg to be back under discipline" is from the famous Grand Inquisitor section of Dostoyevsky's *The Brother's Karamazov.* What does this say about the role of reason?

4. It is sometimes said that human beings are distinguished from other creatures by their capacity for suffering, a view with which Dostoyevsky and certain other Russian writers are very sympathetic. Why do some people value "lofty suffering" over "cheap happiness," and what relation does this bear to the question of tragedy, as opposed to mere pathos, and to the issue of reason?

SOME ADDITIONAL READINGS

Crawshay-Williams, Rupert (1947). *The Comforts of Unreason: A Study of the Motives Behind Irrational Thought.* London: K. Paul, Trench, Trubner & Co., Ltd.

Gardner, Sebastian (1993). *Irrationality and the Philosophy of Psychoanalysis.* New York: Cambridge University Press.

Harrison, Paul R. (1994). *The Disenchantment of Reason: The Problem of Socrates in Modernity.* Albany, N.Y.: SUNY Press.

Saul, John Ralston (1992). *Voltaire's Bastards: The Dictatorship of Reason in the West.* New York: Free Press.

Wheeler, Robert E. (1993). *Dragons for Sale: Studies in Unreason.* Buffalo, N.Y.: Prometheus Books.

*From *The Black Riders and Other Lines* (1895). New York: Alfred A. Knopf.

CHAPTER SIX

The Mind/Brain Problem

The "mind/brain problem" is very old. It may or may not be soluble. In any event, it speaks to the idea of human nature as follows: insofar as the "specialness" of human beings resides in their minds, then the question arises whether mind derives from anything more than physical properties, specifically, the anatomy, chemistry, electrophysiology, and so forth of brains. If not, then human nature can still be a meaningful concept, describing something that may be unique to human beings, but perhaps not qualitatively different from, say, the relationship of grasshoppers to grasshopper nature.

Older treatments often refer to "soul" (see Chapter 2); more recently, to "mind." Often, however, the two are virtually interchangeable, since the focus is on whether human beings partake of something that differs not just quantitatively, but also qualitatively, from other forms of matter. (Also, whether people might possess something potentially immortal, and that links them to the divine.) The nineteenth-century physician Karl Vogt expressed an extreme materialistic perspective when he claimed that the brain secretes thought just like the liver secretes bile. On the other hand, idealist philosophers such as George Berkeley argued that matter does not exist, and that the only thing that is "real" is immaterial mind! So-called dualists take an intermediate position, claiming that matter and mind both exist, but (somehow) independently. Plato was a dualist. So is the Nobel Prize–winning neurophysiologist John Eccles. Descartes, however, remains the preeminent spokesperson for this approach.

Advances in science have relentlessly forced Cartesian dualism to give ground. Milestones include the synthesis of urea, the first organic compound produced in the laboratory, which punctured the notion that life processes are inherently beyond material replication and, hence, explanation. Also Darwin's elaboration of evolution by natural selection, which bypassed special creation, thus further connecting human beings to the rest of the material world. The unraveling of the genetic code, the structure and functioning of DNA, also emphasized the material basis for living things. Nonetheless, the mind/brain problem seems likely to persist, and is as lively as ever.

DESCARTES

René Descartes (1596–1650) developed tuberculosis as an infant and was not expected to survive. It is tempting to conclude that his major contribution to the idea of human nature—the dualistic separation of mind from matter—derives from the situation of his own childhood: a powerful mind encased in a dangerously weak body. In any event, the young Descartes survived to enlist as an infantryman, and also to invent analytic geometry as well as to pioneer in physics, astronomy, anatomy, physiology, theology, and ethics. His dictum *cogito, ergo sum*—"I think, therefore I am"—is probably the most famous phrase in Western thought. (Actually, it had been prefigured by Augustine, who asked whether anyone really "doubts that he lives and thinks . . . for if he doubts, he lives." Ambrose Bierce suggested the following noteworthy "improvement": *"Cogito cogito, ergo cogito sum"*—"I think that I think, therefore I think that I am"—adding that this was "as close an approach to certainty as any philosopher has yet made"!)

Descartes repeatedly emphasizes the importance of rationality to human beings (see Chapter 4) and is in many ways the first modern philosopher. He adopts a rigorously mechanistic view of living things, paving the way for the application of anatomy and physiology to the human body. "Give me matter and motion," he wrote, "and I will make a world." Such an approach, often dubbed "materialism," continues a tradition from Democritus and Epicurus (including Lucretius, see Chapter 2) through Thomas Hobbes.

At the same time, Descartes radically distinguishes between the human mind (which, in his view is incorporeal—lacking length, breadth, weight, etc.,—and is also immortal) and matter, which occupies space and is subject to the recently discovered laws of physics and physiology, as well as to death and dissolution. Only human beings, in Descartes's view, possess mind; indeed, only they experience sensations. By contrast, bodies, whether animal or human, are mere automatons. He maintains that eventually, all the operations of human life will be reducible to mechanical principles, including sensation, but with the exception of reason itself.

Descartes was left with an insoluble dilemma, however: How can the material body influence the immaterial mind, and, vice versa, how could mind, which is not a "thing," act on the body (e.g., to produce movement)? His suggested answer, the pineal gland, is today only a historical curiosity, but Descartes's dilemma remains cogent even now. The following selections are from Descartes's *Discourse on the Method of Rightly Conducting the Reason and Seeking for Truth in the Sciences, Meditations on First Philosophy in which the Existence of God and the Distinction between Mind and Body Are Demonstrated,* and the *Treatise on Man.*

Because in this case I wished to give myself entirely to the search after Truth, I thought that it was necessary for me to take an apparently opposite course, and to reject as absolutely false everything as to which I could imagine the least ground of doubt, in order to see if afterwards there remained anything in my belief that was entirely certain. Thus, because our senses sometimes deceive us, I wished to suppose that nothing is just as they cause us to imagine it to be; and because there are men who deceive themselves in their reasoning and fall into paralogisms, even concerning the simplest matters of geometry, and judging that I was as subject to error as was any other, I rejected as false all the reasons formerly accepted by me as demonstrations. And since all the same thoughts and conceptions which we have while awake may also come to us in sleep, without any of them being at that time true, I resolved to assume that everything that ever entered into my mind was no more true than the illusions of my dreams. But immediately afterwards I noticed that whilst I thus wished to think all things false, it was absolutely essential that the 'I' who thought this should be somewhat, and remarking that this truth *'I think, therefore I am'* was so certain and so assured that all the most extravagant suppositions brought forward by the sceptics were incapable of shaking it, I came to the conclusion that I could receive it without scruple as the first principle of the Philosophy for which I was seeking.

And then, examining attentively that which I was, I saw that I could conceive that I had no body, and that there was no world nor place where I might be; but yet that I could not for all that conceive that I was not. On the contrary, I saw from the very fact that I thought of doubting the truth of other things, it very evidently and certainly followed that I was; on the other hand if I had only ceased from thinking, even if all the rest of what I had ever imagined had really existed, I should have no reason for thinking that I had existed. From that I knew that I was a substance the whole essence or nature of which is to think, and that for its existence there is no need of any place, nor does it depend on any material thing; so that this 'me,' that is to say, the soul by which I am what I am, is entirely distinct from body, and is even more easy to know than is the latter; and even if body were not, the soul would not cease to be what it is. . . .

But what then am I? A thing which thinks. What is a thing which thinks? It is a thing which doubts, understands, [conceives], affirms, denies, wills, refuses, which also imagines and feels.

But there is nothing which this nature teaches me more expressly [nor more sensibly] than that I have a body which is adversely affected when I feel pain, which has need of food or drink when I experience the feelings of hunger and thirst, and so on; nor can I doubt there being some truth in all this.

Nature also teaches me by these sensations of pain, hunger, thirst, etc., that I am not only lodged in my body as a pilot in a vessel, but that I am very closely united to it, and so to speak so intermingled with it that I seem to compose with it one whole. For if that were not the case, when my body is hurt, I, who am merely a thinking thing, should not feel pain, for I should perceive this wound by the understanding only, just as the sailor perceives by sight when something is damaged in his vessel; and when my body has need of drink or food, I should clearly understand the fact without being warned of it by confused feelings of hunger and thirst. For all these sensations of hunger, thirst, pain, etc., are in truth none other than certain confused modes of thought which are produced by the union and apparent intermingling of mind and body. . . .

I consider the body of a man as being a sort of machine so built up and composed of nerves, muscles, veins, blood and skin, that though there were no mind in it at all, it would not cease to have the same motions as at present, exception being made of those movements which are due to the direction of the will, and in consequence depend upon the mind [as opposed to those which operate by the disposition of its organs], . . .

I here say, in the first place, that there is a great difference between mind and body, inasmuch as body is by nature always divisible, and the mind is entirely indivisible. For, as a matter of fact, when I consider the mind, that is to say, myself inasmuch as I am only a thinking thing, I cannot distinguish in myself any parts, but apprehend myself to be clearly one and entire; and although the whole mind seems to be united to the whole body, yet if a foot, or an arm, or some other part, is separated from my body, I am aware that nothing has been taken away from my mind. And the faculties of willing, feeling, conceiving, etc., cannot be properly speaking said to be its parts, for it is one and the same mind which employs itself in willing and in feeling and understanding. But it is quite otherwise with corporeal or extended objects, for there is not one of these imaginable by me which my mind cannot easily divide into parts, and which consequently I do not recognise as being divisible; this would be sufficient to teach me that the mind or soul of man is entirely different from the body, if I have not already learned it from other sources. . . .

I assume that the body is nothing else than a statue or machine of clay which God forms expressly to make it as nearly like as possible to ourselves, so that not only does he give it externally the colour and the form of all our members, but also he puts within it all the parts necessary to make it walk, eat, breathe and, in fine, imitate all those of our functions which may be supposed to proceed from matter and to depend merely on the arrangement of organs.

We see clocks, artificial fountains, mills, and other similar machines, which, although made by men, are not without the power of moving of themselves in many different ways; and it seems to me that I should not be able to imagine so many kinds of movements in this one, which I am supposing to be made by the hand of God, nor attribute to it so much of artifice that you would not have reason to think there might still be more. . . .

I desire you to consider next that all the functions which I have attributed to this machine, such as the digestion of food, the beating of the heart and arteries, the nourishment and growth of the members, respiration, waking, and sleeping; the impressions of light, sounds, odours, tastes, heat and other such qualities on the organs of the external senses; the impression of their ideas on the common sense and the imagination; the retention of imprinting of these ideas upon the memory; the interior motions of the appetites and passions; and, finally, the external movements of all the members, which follow so suitably as well as the actions of objects which present themselves to sense, as the passions and impressions which are found in the memory, that they imitate in the most perfect manner possible those of a real man; I desire, I say, that you consider that all these functions follow naturally in this machine simply from the arrangement of its parts, no more nor less than do the movements of a clock, or other *automata*, from that of its weights and its wheels; so that it is not at all necessary for their explanation to conceive it in any other soul, vegetative or sensitive, nor any other principle of motion and life, than its blood and its spirits, set in a motion by the heat of the fire which burns continually in its heart, and which is of a nature no different from all fires in inanimate bodies.*

LA METTRIE

The eighteenth century in France saw the era of the philosophes, rationalist philosophers led by Voltaire, Diderot, and d'Alembert. Preceding them somewhat, and exceeding them in his materialism and atheism, was Julien de la Mettrie (1709–1751), a physician who scandalized (and fascinated) Europe with his books *The Natural History of the Soul,* and *Man a Machine.* These works conclude boldly "that man is a machine," and that "we can attribute the admirable property of thinking to matter, even without being able to see the connection between the two."

Descartes, in his dualism, had conceived the body as a mechanical contrivance while reserving immaterial status for the mind. La Mettrie carries Descartes's views a step further, concluding that human beings are machines, not only in their bodies but in their minds, which are neither more nor less than the result of material processes. La Mettrie was immensely impressed by findings in anatomy and physiology: for example, Harvey's discovery that blood circulates via a mechanical pump, the heart. La Mettrie also made much of the observation that

*From *Descartes Selections* (1927). (R. Eaton, Trans.). New York: Scribner's.

fresh-water hydras, previously thought to be plants, were actually animals—thereby suggesting continuity between the kingdoms, and also indicating that human beings might be continuous with other living things. Especially noteworthy for la Mettrie was the finding that after a hydra has been split up into many pieces, each piece is capable of regenerating whole bodies. This argues against life consisting of a mysterious "vital principle"; instead, it is a physical property of matter.

In *Man a Machine,* la Mettrie points to the connection between brain and mind, as in the influence of nutrition, drugs, sleep, the impact of a stroke, and so on. Also note that contrary to the widespread assumption that materialism is necessarily dark and pessimistic, la Mettrie maintains a gleeful sensualism and a zest worthy of Rabelais. The following selections are from *Man a Machine.*

The excellence of reason does not depend on its *immateriality,* a big word empty of meaning, but from its power, extent, and clear-sightedness. Thus, a *soul of mud* that could discern at a glance the relations and consequences of an infinity of ideas that are difficult to understand, would obviously be preferable to a foolish and stupid soul made of the most precious elements. To be a philosopher, it is not enough merely to be ashamed like Pliny of the wretchedness of our origin. Our seemingly base beginning is in fact the most precious thing in the world, for which nature seems to have used the most art and ceremony. . . .

Man is a machine so complicated that it is impossible at first to form a clear idea of it, and, consequently, to describe it. This is why all the investigations the greatest philosophers have made *a priori,* that is, by wanting to take flight with the wings of the mind, have been in vain. Only *a posteriori,* by unravelling the soul as one pulls out the guts of the body, can one, I do not say discover with clarity what the nature of man is, but rather attain the highest degree of probability possible on the subject. . . .

The human body is a self-winding machine, a living representation of perpetual motion. Food sustains what fever excites. Without food, the soul languishes, goes into a frenzy, and, exhausted, dies. The soul is a candle whose flame is relighted the moment it is put out. But feed the body, pour powerful juices and strong liquors into its pipes, and then the soul arms itself with proud courage, and the soldier, whom water would have made run away, becomes ferocious and runs gaily to his death to the beat of the drum. It is thus that hot water agitates the same blood that cold water calms.

What power a meal has! It rekindles joy in a sad heart, and joy flows into the souls of guests who sing glad songs in which the French excel. Only the melancholic is overcome, and the scholar is no longer good for anything.

Raw meat makes animals ferocious. Men would be the same if they ate the same meat. . . .

The various states of the soul always correlate to those of the body. To better demonstrate this dependence and its cause, I appeal to comparative anatomy. Slit open the guts of man and animals. How can you grasp human nature if you never see how the innards of the one exactly parallel the innards of the other?

The general form and arrangement of the quadruped brain is nearly the same as man's. Same shape, same structure everywhere, with this essential difference: Man has the largest and most convoluted brain of all the animals in proportion to the size of his body. . . .

Now look, all the faculties of the soul depend so much on the proper organization of the brain and of the entire body, since these faculties are obviously just this organized brain itself, there is a well-enlightened machine! Because really, why would man's having a share of the natural law make him any less a machine? A few more cog wheels and springs than in the most perfect animals, the brain proportionately nearer the heart so it receives more blood. The same reasons given, what, finally, am I saying? Unknown causes could produce both this delicate conscience so easy to offend, and this remorse, that are no more foreign to matter than thought is, and, in a word, any other faculty supposed here. Is organization therefore sufficient for everything? Yes, once again. Since thought obviously develops with the organs, why would the matter of which they are made not be susceptible to remorse once it has acquired in time the faculty of feeling?

Soul is, therefore, only an empty word to which no idea corresponds. An intelligent person ought to use it only to name the part in us that thinks. Given the least principle of movement, animated bodies have all they need to move, feel, think, repent, and in a word, to act in the physical world and also in the moral, which depends on the physical. . . .

The human body is an immense clock, constructed with so much artifice and skill that if the wheel that marks the seconds stops because of rust or derailment, the minutes wheel continues turning, as does the quarter hour wheel, and all the rest. Because is not the narrowing of a few veins enough to destroy or suspend the force of movement of the heart, as in the mainspring of a machine, since on the contrary, fluids whose volume is diminished, having less distance to cover, cover it that much faster, as by a new current that the force of the heart augments because of the resistance it finds in the extremities of the veins? When a compressed optic nerve prevents the passage of images of objects, this deprivation of sight no more impedes hearing than, when the functions of the *auditory nerve* are curtailed, deprivation of hearing impedes sight. So is it not because of such blockage that one sometimes hears without being able to say that he hears (unless this is caused by disease), and that someone who can hear nothing but whose lingual nerves are freely active in the brain automatically says out loud everything that passes through his head? These phenomena do not surprise well-informed physicians. They know what to expect of the nature of man. And, to remark in passing, of two physicians, the one who merits the most confidence is, in my opinion, always the one most versed in the physics or mechanics of the human body, the one who occupies himself seriously with pure naturalism alone and ignores the soul and all the anxieties this chimera raises in fools and ignoramuses. . . .

To be a machine, to feel, think, know good from evil like blue from yellow, in a word, to be born with intelligence and a sure instinct for morality, and yet to be only an animal, are things no more contradictory than to be an ape or parrot and know how to find sexual pleasure. And since the occasion presents itself for saying so, who would have ever divined *a priori* that shooting off a gob of sperm during copulation would make one feel such divine pleasure, and that from it would be born a tiny creature who one day, following certain laws, could enjoy the same delights? Thought is so far from being incompatible with organized matter that it seems to me to be just another of its properties, such as electricity, the motive faculty, impenetrability, extension, etc.*

CRICK

There has recently been a remarkable outpouring of interest in the mind/brain problem, from the perspective of neuroscience. The problem has been tackled not only by philosophers (such as John Searle, Paul and Patricia Churchland, and Daniel Dennett), but also by neuroscientists (such as Gerald Edelman, Nicholas Humphrey, and Antonio Damasio) who have begun to consider what had previously been unthinkable: that their discipline might eventually bridge the mind/brain gap.

*From *Man a Machine* (1994). (R. A. Watson and M. Rybalka, Trans.). Indianapolis: Hackett Publishing.

A vast amount has been learned about nerve cells, neuroanatomy, neurophysiology, and neurochemistry, and although the field of neuroscience is very exciting and promising, the fact remains that the details of anatomy, physiology, chemistry, and micro-electric circuitry have yet to be joined in a satisfying manner to the subjective mental experiences that human beings undergo. It does not seem appropriate to reproduce a primer of neuroscience in the present book. Instead, we excerpt a sample from one of the most prominent exponents of neuroscience as a bridge (he would say, "the" bridge) between brain and mind.

British-born biochemist Francis Crick was codiscoverer of the molecular structure of DNA, for which he was awarded the Nobel Prize in 1962. He has subsequently turned his attention to neurobiology. Crick's book, *The Astonishing Hypothesis,* excerpted below, is an authoritative layperson's guide to the field.

The Astonishing Hypothesis is that "You," your joys and your sorrows, your memories and your ambitions, your sense of personal identity and free will, are in fact no more than the behavior of a vast assembly of nerve cells and their associated molecules. As Lewis Carroll's Alice might have phrased it: "You're nothing but a pack of neurons." This hypothesis is so alien to the ideas of most people alive today that it can truly be called astonishing. . . .

A modern neurobiologist sees no need for the religious concept of a soul to explain the behavior of humans and other animals. One is reminded of the question Napoleon asked after Pierre-Simon Laplace had explained to him the workings of the solar system: Where does God come into all this? To which Laplace replied, "Sire, I have no need of that hypothesis." Not all neuroscientists believe that the idea of the soul is a myth—Sir John Eccles is the most notable exception—but certainly the majority do. It is not that they can yet prove the idea to be false. Rather, as things stand at the moment, they see no need for that hypothesis. Looked at in the perspective of human history, the main object of scientific research on the brain is not merely to understand and cure various medical conditions, important though this task may be, but to grasp the true nature of the human soul. Whether this term is metaphorical or literal is exactly what we are trying to discover.

Many educated people, especially in the Western world, also share the belief that the soul is a metaphor and that there is no personal life either before conception or after death. They may call themselves atheists, agnostics, humanists, or just lapsed believers, but they all deny the major claims of the traditional religions. Yet this does not mean that they normally think of themselves in a radically different way. The old habits of thought die hard. A man may, in religious terms, be an unbeliever but psychologically he may continue to think of himself in much the same way as a believer does, at least for everyday matters.

We need, therefore, to state the idea in stronger terms. The scientific belief is that our minds—the behavior of our brains—can be explained by the interactions of nerve cells (and other cells) and the molecules associated with them. This is to most people a really surprising concept. It does not come easily to believe that I am the detailed behavior of a set of nerve cells, however many there may be and however intricate their interactions. Try for a moment to imagine this point of view. ("Whatever he may say, Mabel, I know I'm in there somewhere, looking out on the world.")

Why does the Astonishing Hypothesis seem so surprising? I think there are three main reasons. The first is that many people are reluctant to accept what is often called the "reductionist approach"—that a complex system can be explained by the behavior of its parts and their interactions with each other. For a system with many levels of activity, this process may have to be repeated more than once—that is, the behavior of a particular part may have to be explained by the properties of *its* parts and their interactions. For example, to understand the brain we may need to know the many interactions of nerve cells with each other; in addition, the behavior of each nerve cell may need explanation in terms of the ions and molecules of which it is composed.

Where does this process end? Fortunately there is a natural stopping point. This is at the level of the chemical atoms. Each atom consists of a heavy atomic nucleus, carrying a positive charge, surrounded by an organized cloud of light, negatively charged nimble electrons. The chemical properties of each atom are determined almost entirely by its nuclear charge. The other properties of the nucleus—its mass, its secondary electrical properties such as the strengths of its dipole, and its quadripole—make in most cases only small differences to its chemical properties.

Now, to a first approximation, the mass and charge of the nucleus of an atom never change, at least in the mild environment in which life flourishes on earth. Thus the knowledge of the substructure of the nucleus is not needed for chemistry. It makes no difference that an atomic nucleus is composed of various combinations of protons and neutrons, and that they, in turn, are made up of quarks. All the chemist needs to know about each atom is its nuclear charge in order to explain most of the facts of chemistry. To do this he needs to understand the rather unexpected type of mechanics (called "quantum mechanics") that controls the behavior of very small particles and of electrons in particular. In practice, since the calculations soon become impossibly intricate, he mainly uses various rules-of-thumb that we now can see have a reasonable explanation in terms of quantum mechanics. Below this level he need not venture.

There have been a number of attempts to show that reductionism cannot work. They usually take the form of a rather formal definition, followed by an argument that reductionism of this type cannot be true. What is ignored is that reductionism is not the rigid process of explaining one fixed set of ideas in terms of another fixed set of ideas at a lower level, but a dynamic interactive process that modifies the concepts at both levels as knowledge develops. After all, "reductionism" is the main theoretical method that has driven the development of physics, chemistry, and molecular biology. It is largely responsible for the spectacular developments of modern science. It is the only sensible way to proceed until and unless we are confronted with strong experimental evidence that demands we modify our attitude. General philosophical arguments against reductionism will not do.

Another favorite philosophical argument is that reductionism involves a "category mistake." For example, in the 1920s this could have taken the form that to consider a gene to be a molecule (or as we should say now, part of a matched pair of molecules) would be a category mistake. A gene is one category and a molecule is a quite different category. One can see now how hollow such objections have turned out to be.* Categories are not given to us as absolutes. They are human inventions. History has shown that although a category may sound very plausible, it can, on occasion, turn out to be both misconceived and misleading. Recall the four Humors in ancient and medieval medicine: blood, phlegm, choler, and black bile.

The second reason why the Astonishing Hypothesis seems so strange is the nature of consciousness. We have, for example, a vivid internal picture of the external world. It might seem a category mistake to believe this is merely another way of talking about the behavior of neurons, but we have just seen that arguments of this type are not always to be trusted.

Philosophers have been especially concerned with the problem of qualia—for example, how to explain the redness of red or the painfulness of pain. This is a very thorny issue. The problem springs from the fact that the redness of red that I perceive so vividly cannot be precisely communicated to another human being, at least in the ordinary course of events. If you cannot describe the properties of a thing unambiguously, you are likely to have some difficulty trying to explain those properties in reductionist terms. This does not mean that, in the fullness of time, it may not be possible to explain to you the *neural correlate* of your seeing red. In other words, we may be able to say that you perceive red if and only if certain neurons (and/or molecules) in your head behave in a certain way. This may, or may not, suggest *why* you experience the vivid sensation of color and why one sort of neural behavior necessarily makes you see red while another makes you see blue, rather than vice versa.

Even if it turns out that the redness of red cannot be explained (because you cannot communicate that redness to me), it does not follow that we cannot be reasonably sure that you see red in the same way as I see red. If it turns out that the neural correlate of red is exactly the same in your brain as in mine, it would be scientifically plausible to infer that you see red as I do. The problem lies in the word "exactly." How precise we have to be will depend on a detailed knowledge of the processes involved. If the neural correlate of red depends, in an important way, on my past experience, and if my past experience is significantly different from yours, then we may not be able to deduce that we both see red in exactly the same way.

One may conclude, then, that to understand the various forms of consciousness we first need to know their neural correlates.

The third reason why the Astonishing Hypothesis seems strange springs from our undeniable feeling that our Will is free. Two problems immediately arise: Can we find a neural correlate of events we consider to show the free exercise of our Will? And could it not be that our Will only appears to be free? I believe that if we first solve the problem of awareness (or consciousness), the explanation of Free Will is likely to be easier to solve. . . .

How did this extraordinary neuronal machine arise? To understand the brain, it is important to grasp that it is the end product of a long process of evolution by natural selection. It has not been designed by an engineer, even though, as we shall see, it does a fantastic job in a small space and uses relatively little energy to do it. The genes we received from our parents have, over many millions of years, been influenced by the experience of our distant ancestors. These genes, and the processes directed by them before birth, lay down much of the structure of the parts of our brain. The brain at birth, we now know, is not a tabula rasa but an elaborate structure with many of its parts already in place. Experience then tunes this rough-and-ready apparatus until it can do a precision job.

Evolution is not a clean designer. Indeed, as François Jacob, the French molecular biologist, has written. "Evolution is a tinkerer." It builds, mainly in a series of smallish steps, on what was there before. It is opportunistic. If a new device works, in however odd a manner, evolution will try to promote it. This means that changes and improvements that can be added to the existing structures with relative ease are more likely to be selected, so the final design may not be a clean one but rather a messy accumulation of interacting gadgets. Surprisingly, such a system often works better than a more straightforward mechanism that is designed to do the job in a more direct manner.

Thus the mature brain is the product of both Nature and Nurture. We can see this easily in the case of language. The ability to handle a complex language fluently appears to be unique to human beings. Our nearest relatives, the apes, perform very poorly at language use even after extensive training. Yet the actual language we learn is obviously heavily dependent on where and how we were brought up.

Two more philosophical points need to be made. The first is that much of the behavior of the brain is "emergent"—that is, behavior does not exist in its separate parts, such as the individual neurons. An individual neuron is in fact rather dumb. It is the intricate interaction of many of them together that can do such marvelous things.

There are two meanings of the term *emergent*. The first has mystical overtones. It implies that the emergent behavior cannot in any way, even in principle, be understood as the combined behavior of its separate parts. I find it difficult to relate to this type of thinking. The scientific meaning of emergent, or at least the one I use, assumes that, while the whole may not be the simple sum of the separate parts, its behavior can, at least in principle, be *understood* from the nature and behavior of its parts *plus* the knowledge of how all these parts interact.

A simple example, from elementary chemistry, would be any organic compound, such as benzene. A benzene molecule is made of six carbon atoms arranged symmetrically in a ring with a hydrogen atom attached, on the outside of the ring, to each carbon atom. Apart from its mass, the properties of a benzene molecule are not in any sense the simple arithmetical sum of the properties of its twelve constituent atoms. Nevertheless, the behavior of benzene, such as its chemical reactivity and its absorption of light, can be calculated if we know how these parts interact, although we need quantum mechanics to tell us how to do this. It is curious that nobody derives some kind of mystical satisfaction by saying "the benzene molecule is more than the sum of its parts," whereas too many people are happy to make such statements about the brain and nod their heads wisely as they do so. The brain is so complicated, and each brain is so individual, that we may never be able to obtain second-to-second detailed knowledge of how a particular brain works but we may hope at least to understand the general principles of how complex sensations and behaviors arise in the brain from the interactions of its many parts.

Of course there may be important processes going on that have not yet been discovered. I suspect that even if we were told the exact behavior of one part of the brain we might in some cases not immediately understand the explanation, since it might involve new concepts and new ideas that have yet to be articulated. However, I do not share the pessimism of some who think that our brains are inherently incapable of grasping such ideas. I prefer to confront such difficulties, if indeed they exist, when we come to them. Our brains have evolved and developed so that we can deal fluently with many concepts related to our everyday world. Nevertheless, well-trained brains can grasp ideas about phenomena that are not part of our normal experience, such as those of relativity and quantum mechanics. Such ideas are very counterintuitive, but constant practice with them enables the trained brain to grasp them and manipulate them easily. Ideas *about* our brains are likely to have the same general character. They may appear very strange at first but with practice we may hope to handle them with confidence.

There is no obvious reason why we should not be able to obtain this knowledge—both of the components of the brain and also how they interact together. It is the sheer variety and complexity of the processes involved that makes our progress so slow.

The second philosophical conundrum that needs clarification concerns the reality of the outside world. Our brains have evolved mainly to deal with our body and its interactions with the world it senses to be around us. Is this world real? This is a venerable philosophical issue and I do not wish to be embroiled in the finely honed squabbles to which it has led. I merely state my own working hypotheses: that there is indeed an outside world, and that it is largely independent of our observing it. We can never fully know this outside world, but we can obtain approximate information about some aspects of its properties by using our senses and the operations of our brain. Nor, as we shall see, are we aware of everything that goes on in our brains, but only of some aspects of that activity. Moreover, both these processes—our interpretations of the nature of the outside world and of our own introspections—are open to error. We may think we know our motives for a particular action, but it is easy to show that, in some cases at least, we are in fact deceiving ourselves. . . .

Many philosophers and psychologists believe it is premature to think about neurons now. But just the contrary is the case. It is premature to try to describe how the brain really works using just a black-box approach, especially when it is couched in the language of common words or the language of a digital programmable computer. *The language of the brain is based on neurons.* To understand the brain you must understand neurons and especially how vast numbers of them act together in parallel. . . .

It is important to emphasize that the Astonishing Hypothesis is a hypothesis. What we already know is certainly enough to make it plausible, but it is not enough to make it as certain as science has done for many new ideas about the nature of the world, and about physics and chemistry in particular. Other hypotheses about man's nature, especially those based on religious beliefs, are based on evidence that is even more flimsy but this is not in itself a decisive argument against them. Only scientific certainty (with all its limitations) can in the long run rid us of the superstitions of our ancestors.

A critic could argue that, whatever scientists may say, they really do believe in the Astonishing Hypothesis. There is a restricted sense in which this is true. You cannot successfully pursue a difficult program of scientific research without some preconceived ideas to guide you. Thus, loosely speaking, you "believe" in such ideas. But to a scientist these are only provisional beliefs. He does not have a blind faith in them. On the contrary, he knows that he may, on occasion, make real progress by disproving one of his cherished ideas. That scientists have a preconceived bias toward scientific explanations I would not deny. This is justified, not just because it bolsters their morale but mainly because science in the past few centuries has been so spectacularly successful.

The next thing to stress is that the study of consciousness is a scientific problem. Science is not separated from it by some insurmountable barrier. If there is any lesson to be learned from this book it is that we can now see ways of approaching the problem experimentally. There is no justification for the view that only philosophers can deal with it. Philosophers have had such a poor record over the last two thousand years that they would do better to show a certain modesty rather than the lofty superiority that they usually display. Our tentative ideas about the workings of the brain will almost certainly need clarification and extension. I hope that more philosophers will learn enough about the brain to suggest ideas about how it works, but they must also learn how to abandon their pet theories when the scientific evidence goes against them or they will only expose themselves to ridicule.

The record of religious beliefs in explaining scientific phenomena has been so poor in the past that there is little reason to believe that the conventional religions will do much better in the future. It is certainly possible that there may be aspects of consciousness, such as qualia, that science will not be able to explain. We have learned to live with such limitations in the past (e.g., limitations of quantum mechanics) and we may have to live with them again. This does not necessarily mean that we shall be driven to embrace traditional religious beliefs. Not only do the beliefs of most popular religions contradict each other but, by scientific standards, they are based on evidence so flimsy that only an act of blind faith can make them acceptable. If the members of a church really believe in a life after death, why do they not conduct sound experiments to establish it? They may not succeed but at least they could try. History has shown that mysteries which the churches thought only they could explain (e.g., the age of the earth) have yielded to a concerted scientific attack. Moreover, the true answers are usually far from those of conventional religions. If revealed religions have revealed anything it is that they are usually wrong. The case for a scientific attack on the problem of consciousness is extremely strong. The only doubts are how to go about it, and when. What I am urging is that we should pursue it now.

There are, of course, educated people who believe that the Astonishing Hypothesis is so plausible that it should not be called astonishing. I have touched on this briefly in the first chapter. I suspect that such people have often not seen the full implications of the hypothesis. I myself find it difficult at times to avoid the idea of a homunculus. One slips into it so easily. The Astonishing Hypothesis states that *all* aspects of the brain's behavior are due to the activities of neurons. It will not do to explain all the various complex stages of visual processing in terms of neurons and then carelessly assume that some aspect of the act of seeing does not need an explanation because it is what "I" do naturally. For example, you cannot be aware of a defect in your brain unless there are neurons whose firing symbolizes that defect. There is no separate "I" who can recognize the defect independent of neural firing. In the same way, you do not normally know where something is happening in your brain because there are no neurons in your brain whose firing symbolizes where they or any other neurons in your brain are situated. . . .

Of course, there are people who say that they do not wish to know how their minds work. They believe that to understand Nature is to diminish her, since it removes the mystery and thus the natural awe that we feel when we are confronted with things that impress us but about which we know very little. They prefer the myths of the past even when they are in clear contradiction to the science of the present. I do not share this view. It seems to me that the modern picture of the universe—far, far older and bigger than our ancestors imagined, and full of marvelous and unexpected objects, such as rapidly rotating neutron stars—makes our earlier picture of an earth-centered world seem far too cozy and provincial. This new knowledge has not diminished our sense of awe but increased it immeasurably. The same is true of our detailed biological knowledge of the structure of plants and animals, and of our own bodies in particular. The psalmist said, "I am fearfully and wonderfully made," but he had only a very indirect glimpse of the delicate and sophisticated nature of our molecular construction. The processes of evolution have produced wonders of which our civilized ancestors had no knowledge at all. The mechanism of DNA replication, while basically unbelievably simple and elegant, has been elaborated by evolution to one of great complexity and precision. One must be dull of soul indeed to read about it and not feel how marvelous it is. To say that our behavior is based on a vast, interacting assembly of neurons should not diminish our view of ourselves but enlarge it tremendously.

It has been reported that a religious leader, shown a large drawing of a single neuron, exclaimed, "So that is what the brain is like!" But it is not the single neuron, wonderful though it is as an elaborate and well-organized piece of molecular machinery, that is built in our image. The true description of us is the complex, ever-changing pattern of interactions of billions of them, connected together in ways that, in their details, are unique to each one of us. The abbreviated and approximate shorthand that we employ every day to describe human behavior is a smudged caricature of our true selves. "What a piece of work is a man!" said Shakespeare. Had he been living today he might have given us the poetry we so sorely need to celebrate all these remarkable discoveries. . . .

It should always be remembered that our brains largely developed during the period when humans were hunter-gatherers. There was strong selective pressure for cooperation within small groups of people and also for hostility to neighboring, competing tribes. Even in this century, in the forests of the Amazon, the major cause of death among the competing tribes in the remote parts of Ecuador is from spear wounds inflicted by members of rival tribes. Under such circumstances a shared set of overall beliefs strengthens the bond between tribal members. It is more than likely that the need for them was built into our brains by evolution. Our highly developed brains, after all, were not evolved under the pressure of discovering scientific truths but only to enable us to be clever enough to survive and leave descendants.

From this point of view there is no need for these shared beliefs to be completely correct, provided people can believe in them. The single most characteristic human ability is that we can handle a complex language fluently. We can use words to denote not only objects and events in the outside world but also more abstract concepts. This ability leads to another strikingly human characteristic, one that is seldom mentioned: our almost limitless capacity for self-deception. The very nature of our brains—evolved to guess the most plausible interpretations of the limited evidence available—makes it almost inevitable that, without the discipline of scientific research, we shall often jump to wrong conclusions, especially about rather abstract matters.

How it will all turn out remains to be seen. The Astonishing Hypothesis may be proved correct. Alternatively, some view closer to the religious one may become more plausible. There is always a third possibility: that the facts support a new, alternative way of looking at the mind-brain problem that is significantly different from the rather crude materialistic view many neuroscientists hold today and also from the religious point of view. Only time, and much further scientific work, will enable us to decide. Whatever the answer, the only sensible way to arrive at it is through detailed scientific research. All other approaches are little more than whistling to keep our courage up. Man is endowed with a relentless curiosity about the world. We cannot be satisfied forever by the guesses of yesterday, however much the charms of tradition and ritual may, for a time, lull our doubts about their validity. We must hammer away until we have forged a clear and valid picture not only of this vast universe in which we live but also of our very selves.*

STUDY QUESTIONS

1. Are there some aspects of the human mind that seem less likely than others to be explained in material terms?

2. If the mind is ultimately found to be nothing but the sum total of physical processes, what basis is there for assuming that other living things are radically discontinuous? Does this have any implications for the likely truth or falsehood of materialism itself?

3. If you insist that material explanations do not as of yet encompass subjective experience such as consciousness, is there any kind of finding that might eventually satisfy you on this score?

4. What characteristics would a computer have to possess in order to be called "conscious"? What implications, if any, would such a computer have for the mind/brain problem? For the question of human nature?

SOME ADDITIONAL READINGS

Dennett, Daniel C. (1991). *Consciousness Explained.* Boston: Little, Brown.

Dimascio, Antonio (1994). *Descartes' Error: Emotion, Reason, and the Human Brain.* New York: G. P. Putnam.

Edelman, Gerald (1992). *Bright Air, Brilliant Fire.* New York: Basic Books.

Gazzaniga, Michael (1988). *Mind Matters: How the Mind and Brain Interact to Create our Conscious Lives.* Boston: Houghton Mifflin.

Searle, John (1992). *The Rediscovery of the Mind.* Boston: MIT Press.

*From *The Astonishing Hypothesis* (1994). New York: Scribner's.

CHAPTER SEVEN

Behaviorism

Psychology is a relatively new discipline; it has only existed for about a century. Its roots lie in philosophy, as evidenced by the fact that the first American professor of psychology, Harvard's William James (1842–1910), was also an eminent philosopher, one of the founders of pragmatism. Although some aspects of psychology, such as psychoanalysis and humanistic psychology, have largely remained comfortably within the humanistic tradition, most of the field has struggled to establish itself as a bona fide science.

For many psychologists in the first half of the twentieth century, this meant separating psychology from the introspective approach that smacked of "unscientific" philosophy. The discipline of behaviorism, a distinctively American branch of psychology, concerns itself entirely with observable, measurable forms of *behavior,* denying the usefulness (even the possibility) of studying feelings, thoughts, ideas, and other "inner" experiences.

Behaviorism also developed, secondarily, as a reaction to another early trend in psychology, namely, a proliferation of theories that emphasized the importance of instincts in human beings as well as in animals. Particularly under the influence of William McDougall (who was, in turn, influenced by evolution and Darwinism, see Chapter 16), "instinct psychologists" had by the early twentieth century identified a parental instinct, gregarious instinct, instincts of acquisition and construction, dominance, companionship, climbing trees, mating and "purposive striving."

Behaviorists, by contrast, concern themselves with behavior and only behavior. Moreover, they are inclined to identify every behavior as being a response, which, in turn, implies the existence of a stimulus that evoked the response in question. Hence, behaviorism is sometimes called *S-R psychology,* (for "stimulus-response"). In this approach, the nature of human beings resides somewhere, somehow, between the stimulus and the response, but is not knowable, and thus, not worth studying.

WATSON

John B. Watson (1878–1958) was the founder of behaviorism and, for many years, its foremost advocate. His initial work concerned animals, and he argued forcefully for the importance of carefully controlled laboratory research in which the outcome is quantified or somehow objectively measured. He soon thereafter pioneered studies of human infants, continuing to emphasize observable behavior over presumed instincts or internal states of consciousness. In his textbook, *Behavior: An Introduction to Comparative Psychology,* Watson wrote that "psychology, as the behaviorist views it, is a purely objective, experimental branch of natural science which needs introspection as little as do the sciences of chemistry and physics."

For Watson, the goal of behaviorism was not to understand behavior or the psyche (he considered the latter to be either nonexistent or a *deus ex machina,* invoked to hide our ignorance), but rather, "the prediction and control of behavior," such that its techniques would be useful to "the educator, the physician, the jurist, and the businessman." After he left Johns Hopkins University in the aftermath of a notorious marital scandal, Watson devoted his final decades to a successful career in advertising. The following selections are from *Behaviorism.*

Behaviorism, . . . holds that the subject matter of human psychology *is the behavior of the human being.* Behaviorism claims that consciousness is neither a definite nor a usable concept. The behaviorist, who has been trained always as an experimentalist, holds, further, that belief in the existence of consciousness goes back to the ancient days of superstition and magic.

The great mass of the people even today has not yet progressed very far away from savagery—it wants to believe in magic. The savage believes that incantations can bring rain, good crops, good hunting, that an unfriendly voodoo doctor can bring disaster to a person or to a whole tribe; that an enemy who has obtained a nail paring or a lock of your hair can cast a harmful spell over you and control your actions. There is always interest and news in magic. Almost every era has its new magic, black or white, and its new magician. Moses had his magic: he smote the rock and water gushed out. Christ had his magic: he turned water into wine and raised the dead to life. Coué had his magic word formula. Mrs. Eddy had a similar one.

Magic lives forever. As time goes on, all of these critically undigested, innumerably told tales get woven into the folk lore of the people. Folk lore in turn gets organized into religions. Religions get caught up into the political and economic network of the country. Then they are used as tools. The public is forced to accept all of the old wives' tales, and it passes them on as gospel to its children's children.

The extent to which most of us are shot through with a savage background is almost unbelievable. Few of us escape it. Not even a college education seems to correct it. If anything, it seems to strengthen it, since the colleges themselves are filled with instructors who have the same background. Some of our greatest biologists, physicists, and chemists, when outside of their laboratories, fall back upon folk lore which has become crystallized into religious concepts. These concepts—these heritages of a timid savage past—have made the emergence and growth of scientific psychology extremely difficult. . . . One example of such a religious concept is that every individual has a *soul* which is separate and distinct from the *body.* This soul is really a part of a supreme being. This ancient view led to the philosophical platform called "dualism." This dogma has been present in human psychology from earliest antiquity. No one has ever touched a soul, or seen one in a test tube, or has in any way come into relationship with it as he has with the other objects of his daily experience. Nevertheless, to doubt its existence is to become a heretic and once might possibly even have led to the loss of one's head. Even today the man holding a public position dare not question it.

With the development of the physical sciences which came with the renaissance, a certain release from this stifling soul cloud was obtained. A man could think of astronomy, of the celestial bodies and their motions, of gravitation and the like, without involving soul. Although the early scientists were as a rule devout Christians, nevertheless they began to leave soul out of their test tubes.

Psychology and philosophy, however, in dealing as they thought with non-material objects, found it difficult to escape the language of the church, and hence the concept of mind or soul as distinct from the body came down almost unchanged in essence to the latter part of the nineteenth century. . . .

Literally hundreds of thousands of printed pages have been published on the minute analysis of this intangible something called "consciousness." And how do we begin work upon it? Not by analyzing it as we would a chemical compound, or the way a plant grows. No, those things are material things. This thing we call consciousness can be analyzed only by *introspection*—a looking in on what takes place inside of us.

As a result of this major assumption that there is such a thing as consciousness and that we can analyze it by introspection, we find as many analyses as there are individual psychologists. There is no way of experimentally attacking and solving psychological problems and standardizing methods.) . . .

In his first efforts to get uniformity in subject matter and in methods the behaviorist began his own formulation of the problem of psychology by sweeping aside all mediaeval conceptions. He dropped from his scientific vocabulary all subjective terms such as sensation, perception, image, desire, purpose, and even thinking and emotion as they were subjectively defined.

The behaviorist asks: Why don't we make what we can *observe* the real field of psychology? Let us limit ourselves to things that can be observed, and formulate laws concerning only those things. Now what can we observe? We can observe *behavior*—*what the organism does or says.* And let us point out at once: that *saying* is doing—that is, *behaving.* Speaking overtly or to ourselves (thinking) is just as objective a type of behavior as baseball.

The rule, or measuring rod, which the behaviorist puts in front of him always is: Can I describe this bit of behavior I see in terms of "stimulus and response"? By stimulus we mean any object in the general environment or any change in the tissues themselves due to the physiological condition of the animal, such as the change we get when we keep an animal from sex activity, when we keep it from feeding, when we keep it from building a nest. By response we mean anything the animal does—such as turning toward or away from a light, jumping at a sound, and more highly organized activities such as building a skyscraper, drawing plans, having babies, writing books, and the like.

You will find, then, the behaviorist working like any other scientist. His sole object is to gather facts about behavior—verify his data—subject them both to logic and to mathematics (the tools of every scientist). He brings the new-born individual *into his experimental nursery* and begins to set problems: What is the baby doing now? What is the stimulus that makes him behave this way? He finds that the stimulus of tickling the cheek brings the response of turning the mouth to the side stimulated. The stimulus of the nipple brings out the sucking response. The stimulus of a rod placed on the palm of the hand brings closure of the hand and the suspension of the whole body by that hand and arm if the rod is raised. Stimulating the infant with a rapidly moving shadow across the eye will not produce blinking until the individual is sixty-five days of age. Stimulating the infant with an apple or stick of candy or any other object will not call out attempts at reaching until the baby is around 120 days of age. Stimulating a properly brought up infant at any age with snakes, fish, darkness, burning paper, birds, cats, dogs, monkeys, will not bring out that type of response which we call "fear" (which to be objective we might call reaction "X") which is a catching of the breath, a stiffening of the whole body, a turning away of the body from the source of stimulation, a running or crawling away from it. . . .

Behaviorism, as you have already grasped from our preliminary discussion, is, then, a natural science that takes the whole field of human adjustments as its own. Its closest scientific companion is physiology. Indeed you may wonder, as we proceed, whether behaviorism can be differentiated from that science. It is different from physiology only in the grouping of its problems, not in fundamentals or in central viewpoint. Physiology is particularly interested in the functioning of parts of the animal—for example, its digestive system, the circulatory system, the nervous system, the excretory systems, the mechanics of neural and muscular response. Behaviorism, on the other hand, while it is intensely interested in all of the functioning of these parts, is intrinsically interested in what the whole animal will do from morning to night and from night to morning.

The interest of the behaviorist in man's doings is more than the interest of the spectator—he wants to control man's reactions as physical scientists want to control and manipulate other natural phenomena. It is the business of behavioristic psychology to be able to predict and to control human activity. To do this it must gather scientific data by experimental methods. Only then can the trained behaviorist predict, given the stimulus, what reaction will take place; or, given the reaction, state what the situation or stimulus is that has caused the reaction. . . .

On the inside of us we have an equally large realm in which stimuli can exert their effect. For example, just before dinner the muscles of your stomach begin to contract and expand rhythmically because of the absence of food. As soon as food is eaten those contractions cease. By swallowing a small balloon and attaching it to a recording instrument we can easily register the response of the stomach to lack of food and note the lack of response when food is present. In the male, at any rate, the pressure of certain fluids (semen) may lead to sex activity. In the case of the female possibly the presence of certain chemical bodies can lead in a similar way to overt sex behavior. The muscles of our arms and legs and trunk are not only subject to stimuli coming from the blood; they are also stimulated by their own responses—that is, the muscle is under constant tension; any increase in that tension, as when a movement is made, gives rise to a stimulus which leads to another response in that same muscle or in one in some distant part of the body; any decrease in that tension, as when the muscle is relaxed, similarly gives rise to a stimulus.

So we see that the organism is constantly assailed by stimuli—which come through the eye, the ear, the nose and the mouth—the so-called objects of our environment; at the same time the inside of our body is likewise assailed at every movement by stimuli arising from changes in the tissues themselves. . . .

We have already brought out the fact that from birth to death the organism is being assailed by stimuli on the outside of the body and by stimuli arising in the body itself. Now the organism does something when it is assailed by stimuli. It responds. It moves. The response may be so slight that it can be observed only by the use of instruments. The response may confine itself merely to a change in respiration, or to an increase or decrease in blood pressure. It may call out merely a movement of the eye. The more commonly observed responses, however, are movements of the whole body, movements of the arm, leg, trunk, or combinations of all the moving parts.

Usually the response that the organism makes to a stimulus brings about an adjustment, though not always. By an adjustment we mean merely that the organism by moving so alters its physiological state that the stimulus no longer arouses reaction. This may sound a bit complicated, but examples will clear it up. If I am hungry, stomach contractions begin to drive me ceaselessly to and fro. If, in these restless seeking movements, I spy apples on a tree, I immediately climb the tree and pluck the apples and begin to eat. When surfeited, the stomach contractions cease. Although there are apples still hanging round about me, I no longer pluck and eat them. Again, the cold air stimulates me. I move around about until I am out of the wind. In the open I may even dig a hole. Having escaped the wind, it no longer stimulates me to further action. Under sex excitement the male may go to any length to capture a willing female. Once sex activity has been completed the restless seeking movements disappear. The female no longer stimulates the male to sex activity. . . .

We can throw all of our psychological problems and their solutions into terms of stimulus and response. Let us use the abbreviations S for *stimulus* (or the more complex *situation*) and R for *response*. We may schematise our psychological problems as follows:

$$S \ldots\ldots\ldots\ldots\ldots\ldots\ldots\ldots\ldots\ldots\ldots\ldots R$$

Given   ?(to be determined)

$$S \ldots\ldots\ldots\ldots\ldots\ldots\ldots\ldots\ldots\ldots\ldots\ldots R$$

?(to be determined)   given

Your problem reaches its explanation always when:

$$S \ldots\ldots\ldots\ldots\ldots\ldots\ldots\ldots\ldots\ldots\ldots\ldots R$$

has been determined   has been determined . . .

Man is an animal born with certain definite types of structure. Having that kind of structure, he is forced to respond to stimuli at birth in certain ways (for example: breathing, heart beat, sneezing, and the like. A fairly full list will be given later on). This repertoire of responses is in general the same for each of us. Yet there exists a certain amount of variation in each—the variation is probably merely proportional to the variation there is in structure (including in structure, of course, chemical constitution). It is probably the same repertoire now that it was when the *genus homo* first appeared many millions of years ago. Let us call this group of reactions man's *unlearned behavior.*

In this relatively simple list of human responses there is none corresponding to what is called an "instinct" by present-day psychologists and biologists. There are then for us no instincts—we no longer need the term in psychology. Everything we have been in the habit of calling an "instinct" today is a result largely of training—belongs to man's *learned behavior.*

As a corollary from this we draw the conclusion that there is no such thing as an inheritance of *capacity, talent, temperament, mental constitution* and *characteristics.* These things again depend on training that goes on mainly in the cradle. The behaviorist would *not* say: "He inherits his father's capacity or talent for being a fine swordsman." He would say: "This child certainly has his father's slender build of body, the same type of eyes. His build is wonderfully like his father's. He, too, has the build of a swordsman." And he would go on to say: "—and his father is very fond of him. He put a tiny sword into his hand when he was a year of age, and in all their walks he talks sword play, attack and defense, the code of duelling and the like." A certain type of structure, plus early training—*slanting*—accounts for adult performance. . . .

I should like to go one step further now and say, "Give me a dozen healthy infants, well-formed, and my own specified world to bring them up in and I'll guarantee to take any one at random and train him to become any type of specialist I might select—doctor, lawyer, artist, merchant-chief and, yes, even beggar-man and thief, regardless of his talents, penchants, tendencies, abilities, vocations, and race of his ancestors." I am going beyond my facts and I admit it, but so have the advocates of the contrary and they have been doing it for many thousands of years. Please note that when this experiment is made I am to be allowed to specify the way the children are to be brought up and the type of world they have to live in. . . .

This brings us now to our central thought. If the boomerang has no instinct (aptitude, capacity, tendency, trait) to return to the hand of the thrower; if we need no mysterious way of accounting for the motion of the boomerang, if the laws of physics will account for its motions—cannot psychology see in this a much needed lesson in simplicity? Can it not dispense with instincts? Can we not say that man is built of certain materials put together in certain complex ways, and *as a corollary of the way he is put together and of the material out of which he is made—he must act (until learning has reshaped him) as he does act?* . . .

Behaviorism ought to be a science that prepares men and women for understanding the principles of their own behavior. It ought to make men and women eager to rearrange their own lives, and especially eager to prepare themselves to bring up their own children in a healthy way. I wish I could picture for you what a rich and wonderful individual we should make of every healthy child if only we could let it shape itself properly and then provide for it a universe in which it could exercise that organization—a universe unshackled by legendary folk-lore of happenings thousands of years ago; unhampered by disgraceful political history; free of foolish customs and conventions which have no significance in themselves, yet which hem the individual in like taut steel bands. I am not asking here for revolution; I am not asking people to go out to some God-forsaken place, form a colony, go naked and live a communal life, nor am I asking for a change to a diet of roots and herbs. I am not asking for "free love." I am trying to dangle a stimulus in front of you, a verbal stimulus which, if acted upon, will gradually change this universe. For the universe will change if you bring up your children, not in the freedom of the libertine, but in behavioristic freedom—a freedom which we cannot even picture in words, so little do we know of it. Will not these children in turn, with their better ways of living and thinking, replace us as society and in turn bring up their children in a still more scientific way, until the world finally becomes a place fit for human habitation?*

SKINNER

If John Watson was the founding prophet and strategist of behaviorism, B. F. Skinner (1904–1990) became its leading apostle and tactician, in many ways exceeding his master's contribution. Skinner devised experimental equipment that standardized the use of so-called operant conditioning, whereby animals are trained to modify their responses as a result of carefully orchestrated patterns of stimuli. Best known is the Skinner box, an apparatus in which laboratory rats press a bar to receive food.

In Skinner's view, the crucial characteristic of behavior is that it is modifiable by its consequences; that is, it changes (or can *be changed*) as a result of what befalls the behaving individual. Like Watson, Skinner disapproved of speculation regarding internal mental states—of humans as well as of animals. He emphasized, for example, that we must think in terms of "reinforcement" (anything contributing to a behavior), rather than "reward" (which implies a subjective experience). He and his many students studied the influence upon behavior of differing "contingencies of reinforcement," leading to so-called teaching machines, as well as very effective techniques of animal training.

Skinner also was not shy about proposing to use behavioral techniques to modify, and, in his mind, improve, the behavior of human beings. Our first selection is from his *Science and Human Behavior.*

We are concerned, then, with the causes of human behavior. We want to know why men behave as they do. Any condition or event which can be shown to have an effect upon behavior must be taken into account. By discovering and analyzing these causes we can predict behavior; to the extent that we can manipulate them, we can control behavior.

There is a curious inconsistency in the zeal with which the doctrine of personal freedom has been defended, because men have always been fascinated by the search for causes. The spontaneity of human behavior is apparently no more challenging than its "why and wherefore." So strong is the urge to explain behavior that men have been led to anticipate legitimate scientific inquiry and to construct highly

*From *Behaviorism* (1924). Chicago: University of Chicago Press.

implausible theories of causation. This practice is not unusual in the history of science. The study of any subject begins in the realm of superstition. The fanciful explanation precedes the valid. Astronomy began as astrology; chemistry as alchemy. The field of behavior has had, and still has, its astrologers and alchemists. A long history of prescientific explanation furnishes us with a fantastic array of causes which have no function other than to supply spurious answers to questions which must otherwise go unanswered in the early stages of a science. . . .

Every science has at some time or other looked for causes of action inside the things it has studied. Sometimes the practice has proved useful, sometimes it has not. There is nothing wrong with an inner explanation as such, but events which are located inside a system are likely to be difficult to observe. For this reason we are encouraged to assign properties to them without justification. Worse still, we can invent causes of this sort without fear of contradiction. The motion of a rolling stone was once attributed to its *vis viva*. The chemical properties of bodies were thought to be derived from the *principles* or *essences* of which they were composed. Combustion was explained by the *phlogiston* inside the combustible object. Wounds healed and bodies grew well because of a *vis medicatrix*. It has been especially tempting to attribute the behavior of a living organism to the behavior of an inner agent, as the following examples may suggest.

Neural Causes. The layman uses the nervous system as a ready explanation of behavior. The English language contains hundreds of expressions which imply such a causal relationship. At the end of a long trial we read that the jury shows signs of *brain fag*, that the *nerves* of the accused are *on edge*, that the wife of the accused is on the verge of a *nervous breakdown*, and that his lawyer is generally thought to have lacked the *brains* needed to stand up to the prosecution. Obviously, no direct observations have been made of the nervous systems of any of these people. Their "brains" and "nerves" have been invented on the spur of the moment to lend substance to what might otherwise seem a superficial account of their behavior. . . .

An even more common practice is to explain behavior in terms of an inner agent which lacks physical dimensions and is called "mental" or "psychic." The purest form of the psychic explanation is seen in the animism of primitive peoples. From the immobility of the body after death it is inferred that a spirit responsible for movement has departed. The *enthusiastic* person is, as the etymology of the word implies, energized by a "god within." It is only a modest refinement to attribute every feature of the behavior of the physical organism to a corresponding feature of the "mind" or of some inner "personality." The inner man is regarded as driving the body very much as the man at the steering wheel drives a car. The inner man wills an action, the outer executes it. The inner loses his appetite, the outer stops eating. The inner man wants and the outer gets. The inner has the impulse which the outer obeys. . . .

In discussing human behavior, we often refer to "tendencies" or "predispositions" to behave in particular ways. Almost every theory of behavior uses some such term as "excitatory potential," "habit strength," or "determining tendency." But how do we observe a tendency? And how can we measure one?

If a given sample of behavior existed in only two states, in one of which it always occurred and in the other never, we should be almost helpless in following a program of functional analysis. An all-or-none subject matter lends itself only to primitive forms of description. It is a great advantage to suppose instead that the *probability* that a response will occur ranges continuously between these all-or-none extremes. We can then deal with variables which, unlike the eliciting stimulus, do not "cause a given bit of behavior to occur" but simply make the occurrence more probable. We may then proceed to deal, for example, with the combined effect of more than one such variable.

The everyday expressions which carry the notion of probability, tendency, or predisposition describe the frequencies with which bits of behavior occur. We never observe a probability as such. We say that someone is "enthusiastic" about bridge when we observe that he plays bridge often and talks about it often. To be "greatly interested" in music is to play, listen to, and talk about music a good deal.

The "inveterate" gambler is one who gambles frequently. The camera "fan" is to be found taking pictures, developing them, and looking at pictures made by himself and others. The "highly sexed" person frequently engages in sexual behavior. The "dipsomaniac" drinks frequently.

In characterizing a man's behavior in terms of frequency, we assume certain standard conditions: he must be able to execute and repeat a given act, and other behavior must not interfere appreciably. We cannot be sure of the extent of a man's interest in music, for example, if he is necessarily busy with other things. When we come to refine the notion of probability of response for scientific use, we find that here, too, our data are frequencies and that the conditions under which they are observed must be specified. The main technical problem in designing a controlled experiment is to provide for the observation and interpretation of frequencies. We eliminate, or at least hold constant, any condition which encourages behavior which competes with the behavior we are to study. An organism is placed in a quiet box where its behavior may be observed through a one-way screen or recorded mechanically. This is by no means an environmental vacuum, for the organism will react to the features of the box in many ways; but its behavior will eventually reach a fairly stable level, against which the frequency of a selected response may be investigated. . . .

Giving food to a hungry organism will do. We can feed our subject conveniently with a small food tray which is operated electrically. When the tray is first opened, the organism will probably react to it in ways which interfere with the process we plan to observe. Eventually, after being fed from the tray repeatedly, it eats readily, and we are then ready to make this consequence contingent upon behavior and to observe the result.

We select a relatively simple bit of behavior which may be freely and rapidly repeated, and which is easily observed and recorded. If our experimental subject is a pigeon, for example, the behavior of raising the head above a given height is convenient. This may be observed by sighting across the pigeon's head at a scale pinned on the far wall of the box. We first study the height at which the head is normally held and select some line on the scale which is reached only infrequently. Keeping our eye on the scale we then begin to open the food tray very quickly whenever the head rises above the line. If the experiment is conducted according to specifications, the result is invariable: we observe an immediate change in the frequency with which the head crosses the line. We also observe, and this is of some importance theoretically, that higher lines are now being crossed. We may advance almost immediately to a higher line in determining when food is to be presented. In a minute or two, the bird's posture has changed so that the top of the head seldom falls below the line which we first chose. . . .

A single instance in which a pigeon raises its head is a *response*. It is a bit of history which may be reported in any frame of reference we wish to use. The behavior called "raising the head," regardless of when specific instances occur, is an *operant*. It can be described, not as an accomplished act, but rather as a set of acts defined by the property of the height to which the head is raised. In this sense an operant is defined by an effect which may be specified in physical terms; the "cutoff" at a certain height is a property of behavior.

The term "learning" may profitably be saved in its traditional sense to describe the reassortment of responses in a complex situation. Terms for the process of stamping in may be borrowed from Pavlov's analysis of the conditioned reflex. Pavlov himself called all events which strengthened behavior "reinforcement" and all the resulting changes "conditioning." In the Pavlovian experiment, however, a reinforcer is paired with a *stimulus;* whereas in operant behavior it is contingent upon a *response*. Operant reinforcement is therefore a separate process and requires a separate analysis. In both cases, the strengthening of behavior which results from reinforcement is appropriately called "conditioning." In operant conditioning we "strengthen" an operant in the sense of making a response more probable or, in actual fact, more frequent. In Pavlovian or "respondent" conditioning we simply increase the magnitude of the response elicited by the conditioned stimulus and shorten the time which elapses between stimulus and response. (We note, incidentally, that these two cases exhaust the possibilities: an organism is conditioned when a reinforcer [1] accompanies another stimulus or [2] follows upon the organism's own behavior. Any event which does neither has no effect in changing a probability of response.) In the pigeon experiment, then, food is the *reinforcer* and presenting food when a response is emitted is the *reinforcement*. The *operant* is defined by the property upon which reinforcement is contingent—the height to which the head must be raised. The change in frequency with which the head is lifted to this height is the process of *operant conditioning.*

While we are awake, we act upon the environment constantly, and many of the consequences of our actions are reinforcing. Through operant conditioning the environment builds the basic repertoire with which we keep our balance, walk, play games, handle instruments and tools, talk, write, sail a boat, drive a car, or fly a plane. A change in the environment—a new car, a new friend, a new field of interest, a new job, a new location—may find us unprepared, but our behavior usually adjusts quickly as we acquire new responses and discard old. We shall see in the following chapter that operant reinforcement does more than build a behavioral repertoire. It improves the efficiency of behavior and maintains behavior in strength long after acquisition or efficiency has ceased to be of interest. . . .

The experimental procedure in operant conditioning is straightforward. We arrange a contingency of reinforcement and expose an organism to it for a given period. We then explain the frequent emission of the response by pointing to this history. . . .

When reinforcement is no longer forthcoming, a response becomes less and less frequent in what is called "operant extinction." If food is withheld, the pigeon will eventually stop lifting its head. In general when we engage in behavior which no longer "pays off," we find ourselves less inclined to behave in that way again. If we lose a fountain pen, we reach less and less often into the pocket which formerly held it. If we get no answer to telephone calls, we eventually stop telephoning. If our piano goes out of tune, we gradually play it less and less. If our radio becomes noisy or if programs become worse, we stop listening. . . .

Operant conditioning shapes behavior as a sculptor shapes a lump of clay. Although at some point the sculptor seems to have produced an entirely novel object, we can always follow the process back to the original undifferentiated lump, and we can make the successive stages by which we return to this condition as small as we wish. At no point does anything emerge which is very different from what preceded it. The final product seems to have a special unity or integrity of design, but we cannot find a point at which this suddenly appears. In the same sense, an operant is not something which appears full grown in the behavior of the organism. It is the result of a continuous shaping process. . . .

Social behavior may be defined as the behavior of two or more people with respect to one another or in concert with respect to a common environment. It is often argued that this is different from individual behavior and that there are "social situations" and "social forces" which cannot be described in the language of natural science. A special discipline called "social science" is said to be required because of this apparent break in the continuity of nature. There are, of course, many facts—concerning governments, wars, migrations, economic conditions, cultural practices, and so on—which would never present themselves for study if people did not gather together and behave in groups, but whether the basic data are fundamentally different is still a question. We are interested here in the methods of the natural sciences as we see them at work in physics, chemistry, and biology, and as we have so far applied them in the field of behavior. How far will they carry us in the study of the behavior of groups?

Many generalizations at the level of the group need not refer to behavior at all. There is an old law in economics, called Gresham's Law, which states that bad money drives good money out of circulation. If we can agree as to what money is, whether it is good or bad, and when it is in circulation, we can express this general principle without making specific reference to the use of money by individuals. Similar generalizations are found in sociology, cultural anthropology, linguistics, and history. But a "social law" must be generated by the behavior of individuals. It is always an individual who behaves, and he behaves with the same body and according to the same processes as in a nonsocial situation. If an individual possessing two pieces of money, one good and one bad, tends to spend the bad and save the good—a tendency which may be explained in terms of reinforcing contingencies—and if this is true of a large number of people, the phenomenon described by Gresham's Law arises. The individual behavior explains the group phenomenon. Many economists feel the need for some such explanation of all economic law, although there are others who would accept the higher level of description as valid in its own right.

We are concerned here simply with the extent to which an analysis of the behavior of the individual which has received substantial validation under the favorable conditions of a natural science may contribute to the understanding of social phenomena. To apply our analysis to the phenomena of the group is an excellent way to test its adequacy, and if we are able to account for the behavior of people in groups without using any new term or presupposing any new process or principle, we shall have revealed a promising simplicity in the data. This does not mean that the social sciences will then inevitably state their generalizations in terms of individual behavior, since another level of description may also be valid and may well be more convenient.

The Social Environment

Social behavior arises because one organism is important to another as part of its environment. A first step, therefore, is an analysis of the social environment and of any special features it may possess.

Social Reinforcement. Many reinforcements require the presence of other people. In some of these, as in certain forms of sexual and pugilistic behavior, the other person participates merely as an object. We cannot describe the reinforcement without referring to another organism. But social reinforcement is usually a matter of personal mediation. When a mother feeds her child, the food, as a primary reinforcer, is not social, but the mother's behavior in presenting it is. The difference is slight—as one may see by comparing breast-feeding with bottle-feeding. Verbal behavior always involves social reinforcement and derives its characteristic properties from this fact. The response, "A glass of water, please," has no effect upon the mechanical environment, but in an appropriate verbal environment it may lead to primary reinforcement. In the field of social behavior special emphasis is laid upon reinforcement with attention, approval, affection, and submission. These important generalized reinforcers are social because the process of generalization usually requires the mediation of another organism. Negative reinforcement—particularly as a form of punishment—is most often administered by others in the form of unconditioned aversive stimulation or of disapproval, contempt, ridicule, insult, and so on.

Behavior reinforced through the mediation of other people will differ in many ways from behavior reinforced by the mechanical environment. Social reinforcement varies from moment to moment, depending upon the condition of the reinforcing agent. Different responses may therefore achieve the same effect, and one response may achieve different effects, depending upon the occasion. As a result, social behavior is more extensive than comparable behavior in a nonsocial environment. It is also more flexible, in the sense that the organism may shift more readily from one response to another when its behavior is not effective. . . .

Another person is often an important source of stimulation. Since some properties of such stimuli appear to defy physical description, it has been tempting to assume that a special process of intuition or empathy is involved when we react to them. What, for example, are the physical dimensions of a smile? In everyday life we identify smiles with considerable accuracy and speed, but the scientist would find it a difficult task. He would have to select some identifying response in the individual under investigation—perhaps the verbal response, "That is a smile"—and then investigate all the facial expressions which evoked it. These expressions would be physical patterns and presumably susceptible to geometric analysis, but the number of different patterns to be tested would be very great. Moreover, there would be borderline instances where the stimulus control was defective or varied from moment to moment. . . .

The social stimulus which is least likely to vary from culture to culture is . . . imitative behavior . . . The ultimate consequences of imitative behavior may be peculiar to the culture, but the correspondence between the behavior of the imitator and that of the imitatee is relatively independent of it. Imitative behavior is not entirely free of style or convention, but the special features of the imitative repertoire characteristic of a group are slight. When a sizable repertoire has once been developed, imitation may be so skillful, so easy, so "instinctive," that we are likely to attribute it to some such special mode of interpersonal contact as empathy. It is easy to point to a history of reinforcement, however, which generates behavior of this sort. . . .

We turn now to the use of positive reinforcement in the practical control of behavior. This consists in general of the presentation of food, clothing, shelter, and other things which we call "goods." The etymology is significant. Like the behavior of the individual which is positively reinforcing to the group, goods are "good" in the sense of being positively reinforcing. We sometimes speak of them also as "wealth." This term has a similar etymological connection with positive reinforcement, but it also includes generalized conditioned reinforcers, such as money and credit, which are effective because they may be exchanged for goods.

Reinforcing Behavior with Money

As a simple example of economic control an individual is induced to perform labor through reinforcement with money or goods. The controller makes the payment of a wage contingent upon the performance of work. In actual practice, however, the process is seldom as simple as this. When we tip a man or pay him for performing a small service and thereby increase the probability of his performing a similar service in the future, we do not depart far from the laboratory study of operant reinforcement. Behavior has occurred and has been strengthened by its consequences. This is also roughly true when a man is steadily employed. His performance at a given time is mainly determined by the contingencies of reinforcement which have prevailed up to that time. When an explicit agreement is made, however, prior verbal stimuli must be analyzed in order to account for the effect of the economic contingency. Thus when we agree to pay a man a given amount for a given piece of work, our promise to pay is not far from the command analyzed in Chapter XXII, except that reinforcement is now positive rather than negative. Payment is contingent upon the verbal stimulus of the promise to pay and upon a correspondence between the topography of the behavior and certain verbal specifications. The offer, "I'll pay you two dollars if you mow the lawn" specifies (1) behavior ("mowing the lawn"), (2) a reinforcement ("two dollars"), and (3) a contingency ("if"). To the prospective employee the whole remark serves as an occasion which, if the offer is to be effective, must be similar to other occasions upon which similar contingencies have prevailed. . . .

In an American school if you ask for the salt in good French, you get an A. In France you get the salt. The difference reveals the nature of educational control. Education is the establishing of behavior which will be of advantage to the individual and to others at some future time. The behavior will eventually be reinforced in many of the ways we have already considered; meanwhile reinforcements are arranged by the educational agency for the purposes of conditioning. The reinforcers it uses are artificial, as such expressions as "drill," "exercise," and "practice" suggest. . . .

The prior importance of the environment has slowly come to be recognized by those who are concerned with changing the lot of mankind. It is more effective to change the culture than the individual because any effect upon the individual as such will be lost at his death. Since cultures survive for much longer periods, any effect upon them is more reinforcing. There is a similar distinction between clinical medicine, which is concerned with the health of the individual, and the science of medicine, which is concerned with improving medical practices which will eventually affect the health of billions of individuals. Presumably, the emphasis on culture will grow as the relevance of the social environment to the behavior of the individual becomes clearer. We may therefore find it necessary to change from a philosophy which emphasizes the individual to one which emphasizes the culture or the group. But cultures also change and perish, and we must not forget that they are created by individual action and survive only through the behavior of individuals.

Science does not set the group or the state above the individual or vice versa. All such interpretations derive from an unfortunate figure of speech, borrowed from certain prominent instances of control. In analyzing the determination of human conduct we choose as a starting point a conspicuous link in a longer causal chain. When an individual conspicuously manipulates the variables of which the behavior of another individual is a function, we say that the first individual controls the second, but we do not ask who or what controls the first. When a government conspicuously controls its citizens, we consider this fact without identifying the events which control the government. When the individual is strengthened as a measure of countercontrol, we may, as in democratic philosophies, think of him as a starting point. Actually, however, we are not justified in assigning to anyone or anything the role of prime mover. Although it is necessary that science confine itself to selected segments in a continuous series of events, it is to the whole series that any interpretation must eventually apply.

Even so, the conception of the individual which emerges from a scientific analysis is distasteful to most of those who have been strongly affected by democratic philosophies. As we saw in Chapter I, it has always been the unfortunate task of science to dispossess cherished beliefs regarding the place of man in the universe. It is easy to understand why men so frequently flatter themselves—why they characterize the world in ways which reinforce them by providing escape from the consequences of criticism or other forms of punishment. But although flattery temporarily strengthens behavior, it is questionable whether it has any ultimate survival value. If science does not confirm the assumptions of freedom, initiative, and responsibility in the behavior of the individual, these assumptions will not ultimately be effective either as motivating devices or as goals in the design of culture. We may not give them up easily, and we may, in fact, find it difficult to control ourselves or others until alternative principles have been developed. But the change will probably be made. It does not follow that newer concepts will necessarily be less acceptable. We may console ourselves with the reflection that science is, after all, a cumulative progress in knowledge which is due to man alone, and that the highest human dignity may be to accept the facts of human behavior regardless of their momentary implications.*

Skinner wrote a controversial, futuristic novel, *Walden Two,* in which his conditioning techniques were employed upon human beings on a large scale. He also boldly confronted resistance to behaviorism. (Incidentally, readers expecting to find in Skinner a real-life Dr. Strangelove confront, instead, a humanistically sophisticated scholar, as comfortable in dealing with Shakespeare, Thoreau, or Shaw as with the apparatus of his laboratory.) In these selections, from *Beyond Freedom and Dignity,* Skinner first takes on traditional views of human freedom, then dignity.

Almost all living things act to free themselves from harmful contacts. A kind of freedom is achieved by the relatively simple forms of behavior called reflexes. A person sneezes and frees his respiratory passages

*From *Science and Human Behavior* (1953). New York: Macmillan.

from irritating substances. He vomits and frees his stomach from indigestible or poisonous food. He pulls back his hand and frees it from a sharp or hot object. More elaborate forms of behavior have similar effects. When confined, people struggle ("in rage") and break free. When in danger they flee from or attack its source. Behavior of this kind presumably evolved because of its survival value; it is as much a part of what we call the human genetic endowment as breathing, sweating, or digesting food. And through conditioning similar behavior may be acquired with respect to novel objects which could have played no role in evolution. These are no doubt minor instances of the struggle to be free, but they are significant. We do not attribute them to any love of freedom; they are simply forms of behavior which have proved useful in reducing various threats to the individual and hence to the species in the course of evolution. . . .

The literature of freedom has encouraged escape from or attack upon all controllers. It has done so by making any indication of control aversive. Those who manipulate human behavior are said to be evil men, necessarily bent on exploitation. Control is clearly the opposite of freedom, and if freedom is good, control must be bad. What is overlooked is control which does not have aversive consequences at any time. Many social practices essential to the welfare of the species involve the control of one person by another, and no one can suppress them who has any concern for human achievements. We shall see later that in order to maintain the position that all control is wrong, it has been necessary to disguise or conceal the nature of useful practices, to prefer weak practices just because they can be disguised or concealed, and—a most extraordinary result indeed!—to perpetuate punitive measures.

The problem is to free men, not from control, but from certain kinds of control, and it can be solved only if our analysis takes all consequences into account. How people feel about control, before or after the literature of freedom has worked on their feelings, does not lead to useful distinctions.

Were it not for the unwarranted generalization that all control is wrong, we should deal with the social environment as simply as we deal with the nonsocial. Although technology has freed men from certain aversive features of the environment, it has not freed them from the environment. We accept the fact that we depend upon the world around us, and we simply change the nature of the dependency. In the same way, to make the social environment as free as possible of aversive stimuli we do not need to destroy that environment or escape from it; we need to redesign it.

Man's struggle for freedom is not due to a will to be free, but to certain behavioral processes characteristic of the human organism, the chief effect of which is the avoidance of or escape from so-called "aversive" features of the environment. Physical and biological technologies have been mainly concerned with natural aversive stimuli; the struggle for freedom is concerned with stimuli intentionally arranged by other people. The literature of freedom has identified the other people and has proposed ways of escaping from them or weakening or destroying their power. It has been successful in reducing the aversive stimuli used in intentional control, but it has made the mistake of defining freedom in terms of states of mind or feelings, and it has therefore not been able to deal effectively with techniques of control which do not breed escape or revolt but nevertheless have aversive consequences. It has been forced to brand all control as wrong and to misrepresent many of the advantages to be gained from a social environment. It is unprepared for the next step, which is not to free men from control but to analyze and change the kinds of control to which they are exposed. . . .

Any evidence that a person's behavior may be attributed to external circumstances seems to threaten his dignity or worth. We are not inclined to give a person credit for achievements which are in fact due to forces over which he has no control. We tolerate a certain amount of such evidence, as we accept without alarm some evidence that a man is not free. No one is greatly disturbed when important details of works of art and literature, political careers, and scientific discoveries are attributed to "influences" in the lives of artists, writers, statesmen, and scientists respectively. But as an analysis of behavior adds further evidence, the achievements for which a person himself is to be given credit seem to approach zero, and both the evidence and the science which produces it are then challenged.

Freedom is an issue raised by the aversive consequences of behavior, but dignity concerns positive reinforcement. When someone behaves in a way we find reinforcing, we make him more likely to do so again by praising or commending him. We applaud a performer precisely to induce him to repeat his performance, as the expressions "Again!" "Encore!" and *"Bis!"* indicate. We attest to the value of a person's behavior by patting him on the back, or saying "Good!" or "Right!" or giving him a "token of our esteem" such as a prize, honor, or award. Some of these things are reinforcing in their own right—a pat on the back may be a kind of caress, and prizes include established reinforcers—but others are conditioned—that is, they reinforce only because they have been accompanied by or exchanged for established reinforcers. Praise and approval are generally reinforcing because anyone who praises a person or approves what he has done is inclined to reinforce him in other ways. . . .

We recognize a person's dignity or worth when we give him credit for what he has done. The amount we give is inversely proportional to the conspicuousness of the causes of his behavior. If we do not know why a person acts as he does, we attribute his behavior to him. We try to gain additional credit for ourselves by concealing the reasons why we behave in given ways or by claiming to have acted for less powerful reasons. We avoid infringing on the credit due to others by controlling them inconspicuously. We admire people to the extent that we cannot explain what they do, and the word "admire" then means "marvel at." What we may call the literature of dignity is concerned with preserving due credit. It may oppose advances in technology, including a technology of behavior, because they destroy chances to be admired and a basic analysis because it offers an alternative explanation of behavior for which the individual himself has previously been given credit. The literature thus stands in the way of further human achievements. . . .

It is in the nature of an experimental analysis of human behavior that it should strip away the functions previously assigned to autonomous man and transfer them one by one to the controlling environment. The analysis leaves less and less for autonomous man to do. But what about man himself? Is there not something about a person which is more than a living body? Unless something called a self survives, how can we speak of self-knowledge or self-control? To whom is the injunction "Know thyself" addressed? . . .

A self is a repertoire of behavior appropriate to a given set of contingencies. A substantial part of the conditions to which a person is exposed may play a dominant role, and under other conditions a person may report, "I'm not myself today," or, "I couldn't have done what you said I did, because that's not like me." The identity conferred upon a self arises from the contingencies responsible for the behavior. Two or more repertoires generated by different sets of contingencies compose two or more selves. A person possesses one repertoire appropriate to his life with his friends and another appropriate to his life with his family, and a friend may find him a very different person if he sees him with his family or his family if they see him with his friends. The problem of identity arises when situations are intermingled, as when a person finds himself with both his family and his friends at the same time.

Self-knowledge and self-control imply two selves in this sense. The self-knower is almost always a product of social contingencies, but the self that is known may come from other sources. The controlling self (the conscience or superego) is of social origin, but the controlled self is more likely to be the product of genetic susceptibilities to reinforcement (the id, or the Old Adam). The controlling self generally represents the interests of others, the controlled self the interests of the individual.

The picture which emerges from a scientific analysis is not of a body with a person inside, but of a body which *is* a person in the sense that it displays a complex repertoire of behavior. . . .

What is being abolished is autonomous man—the inner man, the homunculus, the possessing demon, the man defended by the literatures of freedom and dignity.

His abolition has long been overdue. Autonomous man is a device used to explain what we cannot explain in any other way. He has been constructed from our ignorance, and as our understanding increases, the very stuff of which he is composed vanishes. Science does not dehumanize man, it dehomunculizes him, and it must do so if it is to prevent the abolition of the human species. To man *qua* man we readily say good riddance. Only by dispossessing him can we turn to the real causes of human behavior. Only then can we turn from the inferred to the observed, from the miraculous to the natural, from the inaccessible to the manipulable.

It is often said that in doing so we must treat the man who survives as a mere animal. "Animal" is a pejorative term, but only because "man" has been made spuriously honorific. Krutch has argued that whereas the traditional view supports Hamlet's exclamation, "How like a god!," Pavlov, the behavioral scientist, emphasized "How like a dog!" But that was a step forward. A god is the archetypal pattern of an explanatory fiction, of a miracle-working mind, of the metaphysical. Man is much more than a dog, but like a dog he is within range of a scientific analysis. . . .

No theory changes what it is a theory about. Nothing is changed because we look at it, talk about it, or analyze it in a new way. Keats drank confusion to Newton for analyzing the rainbow, but the rainbow remained as beautiful as ever and became for many even more beautiful. Man has not changed because we look at him, talk about him, and analyze him scientifically. His achievements in science, government, religion, art, and literature remain as they have always been, to be admired as one admires a storm at sea or autumn foliage or a mountain peak, quite apart from their origins and untouched by a scientific analysis. What does change is our chance of doing something about the subject of a theory. Newton's analysis of the light in a rainbow was a step in the direction of the laser.

The traditional conception of man is flattering; it confers reinforcing privileges. It is therefore easily defended and can be changed only with difficulty. It was designed to build up the individual as an instrument of countercontrol, and it did so effectively but in such a way as to limit progress. We have seen how the literatures of freedom and dignity, with their concern for autonomous man, have perpetuated the use of punishment and condoned the use of only weak nonpunitive techniques, and it is not difficult to demonstrate a connection between the unlimited right of the individual to pursue happiness and the catastrophes threatened by unchecked breeding, the unrestrained affluence which exhausts resources and pollutes the environment, and the imminence of nuclear war.

Physical and biological technologies have alleviated pestilence and famine and many painful, dangerous, and exhausting features of daily life, and behavioral technology can begin to alleviate other kinds of ills. In the analysis of human behavior it is just possible that we are slightly beyond Newton's position in the analysis of light, for we are beginning to make technological applications. There are wonderful possibilities—and all the more wonderful because traditional approaches have been so ineffective. It is hard to imagine a world in which people live together without quarreling, maintain themselves by producing the food, shelter, and clothing they need, enjoy themselves and contribute to the enjoyment of others in art, music, literature, and games, consume only a reasonable part of the resources of the world and add as little as possible to its pollution, bear no more children than can be raised decently, continue to explore the world around them and discover better ways of dealing with it, and come to know themselves accurately and, therefore, manage themselves effectively. Yet all this is possible, and even the slightest sign of progress should bring a kind of change which in traditional terms would be said to assuage wounded vanity, offset a sense of hopelessness or nostalgia, correct the impression that "we neither can nor need to do anything for ourselves," and promote a "sense of freedom and dignity" by building "a sense of confidence and worth." In other words, it should abundantly reinforce those who have been induced by their culture to work for its survival.

An experimental analysis shifts the determination of behavior from autonomous man to the environment—an environment responsible both for the evolution of the species and for the repertoire acquired by each member. Early versions of environmentalism were inadequate because they could not explain how the environment worked, and much seemed to be left for autonomous man to do. But environmental contingencies now take over functions once attributed to autonomous man, and certain questions arise. Is man then "abolished"? Certainly not as a species or as an individual achiever. It is the autonomous inner man who is abolished, and that is a step forward. But does man not then become merely a victim or passive observer of what is happening to him? He is indeed controlled by his environment, but we must remember that it is an environment largely of his own making. The evolution of a culture is a gigantic exercise in self-control. It is often said that a scientific view of man leads to wounded vanity, a sense of hopelessness, and nostalgia. But no theory changes what it is a theory about; man remains what he has always been. And a new theory may change what can be done with its subject matter. A scientific view of man offers exciting possibilities. We have not yet seen what man can make of man.*

STUDY QUESTIONS

1. The following postulates have been listed by The Association for Humanistic Psychology: "Man, as man, supersedes the sum of his parts; man has his being in a human context; man is aware; man has choice; and, man is intentional." Respond to the above as a behaviorist.

2. What are some particular strengths of behaviorism? What are some weaknesses?

3. Agree or disagree with Skinner's contention that a behaviorist approach is not necessarily incompatible with a humane or humanitarian one. Explain.

4. Where would behaviorists likely stand on the "mind/brain problem"? How would they line up relative to the ideas of Locke, Hume, and Kant, depicted in Chapter 3?

SOME ADDITIONAL READINGS

Bjork, Daniel W. (1993). *B. F. Skinner: A Life.* New York: Basic Books.

Buckley, Kerry W. (1989). *Mechanical Man: John Broadus Watson and the Beginnings of Behaviorism.* New York: Guilford Press.

Schwartz, Barry (1982). *Behaviorism, Science, and Human Nature.* New York: Norton.

Smith, Laurence D., and Woodward, William R., eds. (1996). *B. F. Skinner and Behaviorism in American Culture.* Bethlehem, Pa.: Lehigh University Press.

Todd, James T., and Morris, Edward K., eds. (1995). *Modern Perspectives on B. F. Skinner and Contemporary Behaviorism.* Westport, Conn.: Greenwood Press.

*From *Beyond Freedom and Dignity* (1971). New York: Knopf.

CHAPTER EIGHT

Psychoanalysis

Freud once suggested that human beings have suffered three major blows to their self-importance: (1) the demonstration by Copernicus, Kepler, and Galileo that the earth was not the center of the universe; (2) the demonstration by Darwin that human beings were not specially created by God; and (3) Freud's own revelation that our conscious minds represent only a small part of what goes on inside our heads. (Humility was not one of Freud's virtues!) It is also legitimate to point out, however, that much of psychoanalysis has become dogma, and some of its ideas, downright weird.

But despite the many criticisms, we are all Freudians in a sense, at least insofar as we use some of the language of psychoanalysis: ego, id, and superego, dreams as wish fulfillment, "Freudian slips" in everyday life, the pervasive importance of sexuality, narcissism, repression and other "defense mechanisms," including denial, phallic symbols, the Oedipus complex, differing childhood stages of psychological and emotional development, the importance of free associating, and—most important of all—the existence of the unconscious.

Philosopher Paul Ricoeur writes that there have been three "masters of suspicion"—he lists Marx, Nietzsche, and Freud—thinkers who have transformed our way of viewing human reality by skeptically questioning what others had taken for granted. Today, the triumph of Freud's "suspicion" is that virtually no one seriously believes that the human mind consists only of what is conscious and superficially apparent, that "what you see is what you get" (or that what we knowingly think is all that we are).

To be sure, there have been other significant contributors to psychoanalysis. Many of them were early colleagues and acolytes of Freud, who subsequently broke with him over questions of theory or practice. For example, Carl Jung emphasized the role of a specieswide "collective unconscious," reflected in the existence of what he called archetypes. Alfred Adler focused on the importance of inter-personal status, in the process coining the phrase *inferiority complex*. Helene Deutch and Melanie Klein explored questions of maternal attachment and infant development. But on balance, Freud's contribution is so formative and so immense that he deserves to have this chapter to himself.

FREUD

Sigmund Freud (1856–1939) was an Austrian physician who, after initially studying neurology, became intrigued with mental illness. He was especially concerned with certain neuroses, notably hysteria. It is useful, however, to divide Freud's contributions into three broad categories (admittedly, with considerable overlap): the psychological structure of the mind; clinical

accounts of mental illness and Freud's recommendations as to treatment (that is, psychoanalysis as a clinical therapy); and a variety of broader social and historical speculations. For
our purposes, we shall ignore psychoanalysis as therapy—so-called Freudian analysis, or dynamic psychotherapy—and concentrate on the first and third, since they speak most broadly
to the uniquely "analytic" view of human nature.

Although people have long been intrigued and/or troubled by their dreams, it was Freud
who made the first organized inquiry into dreams as a means of providing access to otherwise
hidden aspects of the human mind. Freud called the interpretation of dreams the "high road
to the unconscious." He distinguished importantly between a dream's manifest content and its
latent content, and emphasized the importance of dreamwork as a psychological mechanism,
notably wish fulfillment, as well as interpreting their frequent erotic content. The following selections are from *The Interpretation of Dreams*.

During the epoch which may be described as pre-scientific, men had no difficulty in finding an explanation of dreams. When they remembered a dream after waking up, they regarded it as either a
favourable or a hostile manifestation by higher powers, daemonic and divine. When modes of thought
belonging to natural science began to flourish, all this ingenious mythology was transformed into psychology, and to-day only a small minority of educated people doubt that dreams are a product of the
dreamer's own mind.

Since the rejection of the mythological hypothesis, however, dreams have stood in need of explanation. The conditions of their origin, their relation to waking mental life, their dependence upon stimuli
which force their way upon perception during the state of sleep, the many peculiarities of their content
which are repugnant to waking thought, the inconsistency between their ideational images and the affects attaching to them, and lastly their transitory character, the manner in which waking thought pushes
them on one side as something alien to it, and mutilates or extinguishes them in memory—all of these
and other problems besides have been awaiting clarification for many hundreds of years, and till now
no satisfactory solution of them has been advanced. But what stands in the foreground of our interest
is the question of the *significance* of dreams, a question which bears a double sense. It enquires in the first
place as to the psychical significance of dreaming, as to the relation of dreams to other mental processes,
and as to any biological function that they may have; in the second place it seeks to discover whether
dreams can be interpreted, whether the content of individual dreams has a 'meaning', such as we are
accustomed to find in other psychical structures. . . .

In order to contrast the dream as it is retained in my memory with the relevant material discovered
by analysing it, I shall speak of the former as the '*manifest* content of the dream' and the latter—without, in the first instance, making any further distinction—as the '*latent* content of the dream.' I am now
faced by two new problems which have not hitherto been formulated. (1) What is the psychical process
which has transformed the latent content of the dream into the manifest one which is known to me from
my memory? (2) What are the motive or motives which have necessitated this transformation? I shall describe the process which transforms the latent into the manifest content of dreams as the 'dreamwork'.
The counterpart to this activity—one which brings about a transformation in the opposite direction—
is already known to us as the work of analysis. . . . Since I attribute all the contradictory and incorrect
views upon dream-life which appear in the literature of the subject to ignorance of the latent content
of dreams as revealed by analysis, I shall be at the greatest pains henceforward to avoid confusing the
manifest dream with the *latent dream-thoughts*.

The transformation of the latent dream-thoughts into the manifest dream-content deserves all our attention, since it is the first instance known to us of psychical material being changed over from one mode of expression to another, from a mode of expression which is immediately intelligible to us to another which we can only come to understand with the help of guidance and effort, though it too must be recognized as a function of our mental activity. . . .

Even when the content of children's dreams becomes complicated and subtle, there is never any difficulty in recognizing them as wish-fulfilments. An eight-year-old boy had a dream that he was driving in a chariot with Achilles and that Diomede was the charioteer. It was shown that the day before he had been deep in a book of legends about the Greek heroes; and it was easy to see that he had taken the heroes as his models and was sorry not to be living in their days.

This small collection throws a direct light on a further characteristic of children's dreams: their connection with daytime life. The wishes which are fulfilled in them are carried over from daytime and as a rule from the day before, and in waking life they have been accompanied by intense emotion. Nothing unimportant or indifferent, or nothing which would strike a child as such, finds its way into the content of their dreams.

Numerous examples of dreams of this infantile type can be found occurring in adults as well, though, as I have said, they are usually brief in content. Thus a number of people regularly respond to a stimulus of thirst during the night with dreams of drinking, which thus endeavour to get rid of the stimulus and enable sleep to continue. . . . Under unusual or extreme conditions dreams of this infantile character are particularly common. Thus the leader of a polar expedition has recorded that the members of his expedition, while they were wintering in the ice-field and living on a monotonous diet and short rations, regularly dreamt like children of large meals, of mountains of tobacco, and of being back at home.

It by no means rarely happens that in the course of a comparatively long, complicated and on the whole confused dream one particularly clear portion stands out, which contains an unmistakable wish-fulfilment, but which is bound up with some other, unintelligible material. But in the case of adults, anyone with some experience in analysing their dreams will find to his surprise that even those dreams which have an appearance of being transparently clear are seldom as simple as those of children, and that behind the obvious wish-fulfilment some other meaning may lie concealed.

It would indeed be a simple and satisfactory solution of the riddle of dreams if the work of analysis were to enable us to trace even the meaningless and confused dreams of adults back to the infantile type of fulfilment of an intensely felt wish of the previous day. There can be no doubt, however, that appearances do not speak in favour of such an expectation. Dreams are usually full of the most indifferent and strangest material, and there is no sign in their content of the fulfilment of any wish. . . .

No one who accepts the view that the censorship is the chief reason for dream-distortion will be surprised to learn from the results of dream-interpretation that most of the dreams of adults are traced back by analysis to *erotic wishes*. This assertion is not aimed at dreams with an *undisguised* sexual content, which are no doubt familiar to all dreamers from their own experience and are as a rule the only ones to be described as 'sexual dreams'. Even dreams of this latter kind offer enough surprises in their choice of the people whom they make into sexual objects, in their disregard of all the limitations which the dreamer imposes in his waking life upon his sexual desires, and by their many strange details, hinting at what are commonly known as 'perversions'. A great many other dreams, however, which show no sign of being erotic in their manifest content, are revealed by the work of interpretation in analysis as sexual wish-fulfilments; and, on the other hand, analysis proves that a great many of the thoughts left over from the activity of waking life as 'residues of the previous day' only find their way to representation in dreams through the assistance of repressed erotic wishes.

There is no theoretical necessity why this should be so; but to explain the fact it may be pointed out that no other group of instincts has been submitted to such far-reaching suppression by the demands of cultural education, while at the same time the sexual instincts are also the ones which, in most people, find it easiest to escape from the control of the highest mental agencies. Since we have become acquainted with infantile sexuality, which is often so unobtrusive in its manifestations and is always overlooked and misunderstood, we are justified in saying that almost every civilized man retains the infantile forms of sexual life in some respect or other. We can thus understand how it is that repressed infantile sexual wishes provide the most frequent and strongest motive-forces for the construction of dreams.

There is only one method by which a dream which expresses erotic wishes can succeed in appearing innocently non-sexual in its manifest content. The material of the sexual ideas must not be represented as such, but must be replaced in the content of the dream by hints, allusions and similar forms of indirect representation. But, unlike other forms of indirect representation, that which is employed in dreams must not be immediately intelligible. The modes of representation which fulfil these conditions are usually described as 'symbols' of the things which they represent. Particular interest has been directed to them since it has been noticed that dreamers speaking the same language make use of the same symbols, and that in some cases, indeed, the use of the same symbols extends beyond the use of the same language. Since dreamers themselves are unaware of the meaning of the symbols they use, it is difficult at first sight to discover the source of the connection between the symbols and what they replace and represent. The fact itself, however, is beyond doubt, and it is important for the technique of dream-interpretation. For, with the help of a knowledge of dream-symbolism, it is possible to understand the meaning of separate elements of the content of a dream or separate pieces of a dream or in some cases even whole dreams, without having to ask the dreamer for his associations. Here we are approaching the popular ideal of translating dreams and on the other hand are returning to the technique of interpretation used by the ancients, to whom dream-interpretation was identical with interpretation by means of symbols.

Although the study of dream-symbols is far from being complete, we are in a position to lay down with certainty a number of general statements and a quantity of special information on the subject. There are some symbols which bear a single meaning almost universally: thus the Emperor and Empress (or the King and Queen) stand for the parents, rooms represent women and their entrances and exits the openings of the body. The majority of dream-symbols serve to represent persons, parts of the body and activities invested with erotic interest; in particular, the genitals are represented by a number of often very surprising symbols, and the greatest variety of objects are employed to denote them symbolically. Sharp weapons, long and stiff objects, such as tree-trunks and sticks, stand for the male genital; while cupboards, boxes, carriages or ovens may represent the uterus. In such cases as these the *tertium comparationis*, the common element in these substitutions, is immediately intelligible; but there are other symbols in which it is not so easy to grasp the connection. Symbols such as a staircase or going upstairs to represent sexual intercourse, a tie or cravat for the male organ, or wood for the female one, provoke our unbelief until we can arrive at an understanding of the symbolic relation underlying them by some other means. Moreover a whole number of dream-symbols are bisexual and can relate to the male or female genitals according to the context.

Some symbols are universally disseminated and can be met with in all dreamers belonging to a single linguistic or cultural group; there are others which occur only within the most restricted and individual limits, symbols constructed by an individual out of his own ideational material. Of the former class we can distinguish some whose claim to represent sexual ideas is immediately justified by linguistic usage (such, for instance, as those derived from agriculture, e.g. 'fertilization' or 'seed') and others whose relation to sexual ideas appears to reach back into the very earliest ages and to the most obscure depths of our conceptual functioning. The power of constructing symbols has not been exhausted in our own days in the case of either of the two sorts of symbols which I have distinguished at the beginning of this paragraph. Newly discovered objects (such as airships) are, as we may observe, at once adopted as universally available sexual symbols.

It would, incidentally, be a mistake to expect that if we had a still profounder knowledge of dream-symbolism (of the 'language of dreams') we could do without asking the dreamer for his associations to the dream and go back entirely to the technique of dream-interpretation of antiquity. Quite apart from individual symbols and oscillations in the use of universal ones, one can never tell whether any particular element in the content of a dream is to be interpreted symbolically or in its proper sense, and one can be certain that the *whole* content of a dream is not to be interpreted symbolically. A knowledge of dream-symbolism will never do more than enable us to translate certain constituents of the dream-content, and will not relieve us of the necessity for applying the technical rules which I gave earlier. It will, however, afford the most valuable assistance to interpretation precisely at points at which the dreamer's associations are insufficient or fail altogether.

Dream-symbolism is also indispensable to an understanding of what are known as 'typical' dreams, which are common to everyone, and of 'recurrent' dreams in individuals.*

Freud's initial theory of the mind distinguished between conscious (immediately available to our awareness), unconscious (inaccessible except via dreams, unintentional errors, etc.) and pre-conscious (normally hidden but nonetheless accessible if called for, e.g., your telephone number or your birthday). Later, he modified this conception into a more "topographic" theory, consisting of the id (representing biological instincts), the ego (which, unlike the id, distinguishes between the internal mind and external reality, and has the job of mediating between the two), and the super-ego (which represents society's, and the parents', moral code, and which rides herd on the id's demands). According to Freud, mental health requires harmony among these three components.

The following material is taken from *The Ego and the Id.*

The division of the psychical into what is conscious and what is unconscious is the fundamental premise of psycho-analysis; and it alone makes it possible for psycho-analysis to understand the pathological processes in mental life, which are as common as they are important, and to find a place for them in the framework of science. To put it once more, in a different way: psycho-analysis cannot situate the essence of the psychical in consciousness, but is obliged to regard consciousness as a quality of the psychical, which may be present in addition to other qualities or may be absent.

If I could suppose that everyone interested in psychology would read this book, I should also be prepared to find that at this point some of my readers would already stop short and would go no further; for here we have the first shibboleth of psycho-analysis. To most people who have been educated in philosophy the idea of anything psychical which is not also conscious is so inconceivable that it seems to them absurd and refutable simply by logic. I believe this is only because they have never studied the relevant phenomena of hypnosis and dreams, which—quite apart from pathological manifestations—necessitate this view. Their psychology of consciousness is incapable of solving the problems of dreams and hypnosis. . . .

*From *The Interpretation of Dreams* (1913). (A. A. Brill, Trans.). New York: Macmillan.

We have formed the idea that in each individual there is a coherent organization of mental processes; and we call this his *ego*. It is to this ego that consciousness is attached; the ego controls the approaches to motility—that is, to the discharge of excitations into the external world; it is the mental agency which supervises all its own constituent processes, and which goes to sleep at night, though even then it exercises the censorship on dreams. From this ego proceed the repressions, too, by means of which it is sought to exclude certain trends in the mind not merely from consciousness but also from other forms of effectiveness and activity. In analysis these trends which have been shut out stand in opposition to the ego, and the analysis is faced with the task of removing the resistances which the ego displays against concerning itself with the repressed. Now we find during analysis that, when we put certain tasks before the patient, he gets into difficulties; his associations fail when they should be coming near the repressed. We then tell him that he is dominated by a resistance; but he is quite unaware of the fact, and, even if he guesses from his unpleasurable feelings that a resistance is now at work in him, he does not know what it is or how to describe it. Since, however, there can be no question but that this resistance emanates from his ego and belongs to it, we find ourselves in an unforeseen situation. We have come upon something in the ego itself which is also unconscious, which behaves exactly like the repressed—that is, which produces powerful effects without itself being conscious and which requires special work before it can be made conscious. From the point of view of analytic practice, the consequence of this discovery is that we land in endless obscurities and difficulties if we keep to our habitual forms of expression and try, for instance, to derive neuroses from a conflict between the conscious and the unconscious. We shall have to substitute for this antithesis another, taken from our insight into the structural conditions of the mind—the antithesis between the coherent ego and the repressed which is split off from it.

For our conception of the unconscious, however, the consequences of our discovery are even more important. Dynamic considerations caused us to make our first correction; our insight into the structure of the mind leads to the second. We recognize that the *Ucs.* does not coincide with the repressed; it is still true that all that is repressed is *Ucs.*, but not all that is *Ucs.* is repressed. A part of the ego, too—and Heaven knows how important a part—may be *Ucs.*, undoubtedly is *Ucs.* And this *Ucs.* belonging to the ego is not latent like the *Pcs.;* for if it were, it could not be activated without becoming *Cs.*, and the process of making it conscious would not encounter such great difficulties. When we find ourselves thus confronted by the necessity of postulating a third *Ucs.*, which is not repressed, we must admit that the characteristic of being unconscious begins to lose significance for us. It becomes a quality which can have many meanings, a quality which we are unable to make, as we should have hoped to do, the basis of far-reaching and inevitable conclusions. Nevertheless we must beware of ignoring this characteristic, for the property of being conscious or not is in the last resort our one beacon-light in the darkness of depth-psychology. . . .

If the ego were merely the part of the id modified by the influence of the perceptual system, the representative in the mind of the real external world, we should have a simple state of things to deal with. But there is a further complication.

The considerations that led us to assume the existence of a grade in the ego, a differentiation within the ego, which may be called the 'ego ideal' or 'super-ego'. . . .

The broad general outcome of the sexual phase dominated by the Oedipus complex may, therefore, be taken to be the forming of a precipitate in the ego, consisting of these two identifications in some way united with each other. This modification of the ego retains its special position; it confronts the other contents of the ego as an ego ideal or super-ego.

The super-ego is, however, not simply a residue of the earliest object-choices of the id; it also represents an energetic reaction-formation against those choices. Its relation to the ego is not exhausted by the precept: 'You *ought* to *be* like this (like your father).' It also comprises the prohibition: 'You *may not be* like this (like your father)—that is, you may not do all that he does; some things are his prerogative.' This double aspect of the ego ideal derives from the fact that the ego ideal had the task of repressing the Oedipus complex; indeed, it is to that revolutionary event that it owes its existence. Clearly the repression of the Oedipus complex was no easy task. The child's parents, and especially his father, were perceived as the obstacle to a realization of his Oedipus wishes; so his infantile ego fortified itself for the carrying out of the repression by erecting this same obstacle within itself. It borrowed strength to do this, so to speak, from the father, and this loan was an extraordinarily momentous act. The super-ego retains the character of the father, while the more powerful the Oedipus complex was and the more rapidly it succumbed to repression (under the influence of authority, religious teaching, schooling and reading), the stricter will be the domination of the super-ego over the ego later on—in the form of conscience or perhaps of an unconscious sense of guilt. I shall presently bring forward a suggestion about the source of its power to dominate in this way—the source, that is, of its compulsive character which manifests itself in the form of a categorical imperative.

If we consider once more the origin of the super-ego as we have described it, we shall recognize that it is the outcome of two highly important factors, one of a biological and the other of a historical nature: namely, the lengthy duration in man of his childhood helplessness and dependence, and the fact of his Oedipus complex, the repression of which we have shown to be connected with the interruption of libidinal development by the latency period and so with the diphasic onset of man's sexual life. According to one psycho-analytic hypothesis {by Ferenczi}, the last-mentioned phenomenon, which seems to be peculiar to man, is a heritage of the cultural development necessitated by the glacial epoch. We see, then, that the differentiation of the super-ego from the ego is no matter of chance; it represents the most important characteristics of the development both of the individual and of the species; indeed, by giving permanent expression to the influence of the parents it perpetuates the existence of the factors to which it owes its origin.

Psycho-analysis has been reproached time after time with ignoring the higher, moral, supra-personal side of human nature. The reproach is doubly unjust, both historically and methodologically. For, in the first place, we have from the very beginning attributed the function of instigating repression to the moral and aesthetic trends in the ego, and secondly, there has been a general refusal to recognize that psycho-analytic research could not, like a philosophical system, produce a complete and ready-made theoretical structure, but had to find its way step by step along the path towards understanding the intricacies of the mind by making an analytic dissection of both normal and abnormal phenomena. So long as we had to concern ourselves with the study of what is repressed in mental life, there was no need for us to share in any agitated apprehensions as to the whereabouts of the higher side of man. But now that we have embarked upon the analysis of the ego we can give an answer to all those whose moral sense has been shocked and who have complained that there must surely be a higher nature in man: 'Very true,' we can say, 'and here we have that higher nature, in this ego ideal or super-ego, the representative of our relation to our parents. When we were little children we knew these higher natures, we admired them and feared them; and later we took them into ourselves.'

The ego ideal is therefore the heir of the Oedipus complex, and thus it is also the expression of the most powerful impulses and most important libidinal vicissitudes of the id. By setting up this ego ideal, the ego has mastered the Oedipus complex and at the same time placed itself in subjection to the id. Whereas the ego is essentially the representative of the external world, of reality, the super-ego stands in contrast to it as the representative of the internal world, of the id. Conflicts between the ego and the ideal will, as we are now prepared to find, ultimately reflect the contrast between what is real and what is psychical, between the external world and the internal world.*

*From *The Ego and the Id* (1923). New York: Norton.

One of Freud's most controversial (yet productive) theories involves childhood sexuality and development, specifically the notion that young children harbor erotic desire for their opposite-sex parent, combined with competitive, even homicidal, inclinations toward the same-sex parent. In Freud's view, this is particularly pronounced among boys, who experience what Freud calls an Oedipal attachment, named after the mythical and tragic Greek king who killed his father and married his mother. For Freud, normal sexual identity and personal maturation require that the Oedipal dilemma be resolved by strengthening the super-ego, and eventually identifying with the same-sex parent. Along the way, he introduced some of his most hotly disputed concepts, including penis envy and castration anxiety.

The following selections, from *Totem and Taboo*, illustrate Freud's inclination to extrapolate from individual psychoanalysis to theorize about group-processes and anthropology. In the process, he combines idiosyncratic, almost crackpot fantasy with startling profundity and originality.

Psycho-analysis has revealed that the totem animal is in reality a substitute for the father; and this tallies with the contradictory fact that, though the killing of the animal is as a rule forbidden, yet its killing is a festive occasion—with the fact that it is killed and yet mourned. The ambivalent emotional attitude, which to this day characterizes the father-complex in our children and which often persists into adult life, seems to extend to the totem animal in its capacity as substitute for the father.

If, now, we bring together the psycho-analytic translation of the totem with the fact of the totem meal and with Darwin's theories of the earliest state of human society, the possibility of a deeper understanding emerges—a glimpse of a hypothesis which may seem fantastic but which offers the advantage of establishing an unsuspected correlation between groups of phenomena that have hitherto been disconnected.

There is, of course, no place for the beginnings of totemism in Darwin's primal horde. All that we find there is a violent and jealous father who keeps all the females for himself and drives away his sons as they grow up. This earliest state of society has never been an object of observation. The most primitive kind of organization that we actually come across—and one that is in force to this day in certain tribes—consists of bands of males; these bands are composed of members with equal rights and are subject to the restrictions of the totemic system, including inheritance through the mother. Can this form of organization have developed out of the other one? and if so along what lines?

If we call the celebration of the totem meal to our help, we shall be able to find an answer. One day the brothers who had been driven out came together, killed and devoured their father and so made an end of the patriarchal horde. United, they had the courage to do and succeeded in doing what would have been impossible for them individually. (Some cultural advance, perhaps, command over some new weapon, had given them a sense of superior strength.) Cannibal savages as they were, it goes without saying that they devoured their victim as well as killing him. The violent primal father had doubtless been the feared and envied model of each one of the company of brothers: and in the act of devouring him they accomplished their identification with him, and each one of them acquired a portion of his strength. The totem meal, which is perhaps mankind's earliest festival, would thus be a repetition and a commemoration of this memorable and criminal deed, which was the beginning of so many things—of social organization, of moral restrictions and of religion.

In order that these latter consequences may seem plausible, leaving their premises on one side, we need only suppose that the tumultuous mob of brothers were filled with the same contradictory feelings which we can see at work in the ambivalent father-complexes of our children and of our neurotic patients. They hated their father, who presented such a formidable obstacle to their craving for power and their sexual desires; but they loved and admired him too. After they had got rid of him, had satisfied their hatred and had put into effect their wish to identify themselves with him, the affection which had all this time been pushed under was bound to make itself felt. It did so in the form of remorse. A sense of guilt made its appearance, which in this instance coincided with the remorse felt by the whole group. The dead father became stronger than the living one had been—for events took the course we so often see them follow in human affairs to this day. What had up to then been prevented by his actual existence was thenceforward prohibited by the sons themselves, in accordance with the psychological procedure so familiar to us in psycho-analyses under the name of 'deferred obedience'. They revoked their deed by forbidding the killing of the totem, the substitute for their father; and they renounced its fruits by resigning their claim to the women who had now been set free. They thus created out of their filial sense of guilt the two fundamental taboos of totemism, which for that very reason inevitably corresponded to the two repressed wishes of the Oedipus complex. Whoever contravened those taboos became guilt of the only two crimes with which primitive society concerned itself.

The two taboos of totemism with which human morality has its beginning are not on a par psychologically. The first of them, the law protecting the totem animal, is founded wholly on emotional motives: the father had actually been eliminated, and in no real sense could the deed be undone. But the second rule, the prohibition of incest, has a powerful practical basis as well. Sexual desires do not unite men but divide them. Though the brothers had banded together in order to overcome their father, they were all one another's rivals in regard to the women. Each of them would have wished, like his father, to have all the women to himself. The new organization would have collapsed in a struggle of all against all, for none of them was of such over-mastering strength as to be able to take on his father's part with success. Thus the brothers had no alternative, if they were to live together, but—not, perhaps, until they had passed through many dangerous crises—to institute the law against incest, by which they all alike renounced the women whom they desired and who had been their chief motive for despatching their father. In this way they rescued the organization which had made them strong—and which may have been based on homosexual feelings and acts, originating perhaps during the period of their expulsion from the horde. Here, too, may perhaps have been the germ of the institution of matriarchy, described by Bachofen, which was in turn replaced by the patriarchal organization of the family.

On the other hand, the claim of totemism to be regarded as a first attempt at a religion is based on the first of these two taboos—that upon taking the life of the totem animal. The animal struck the sons as a natural and obvious substitute for their father; but the treatment of it which they found imposed on themselves expressed more than the need to exhibit their remorse. They could attempt, in their relation to this surrogate father, to allay their burning sense of guilt, to bring about a kind of reconciliation with their father. The totemic system was, as it were, a covenant with their father, in which he promised them everything that a childish imagination may expect from a father—protection, care and indulgence— while on their side they undertook to respect his life, that is to say, not to repeat the deed which had brought destruction on their real father. Totemism, moreover, contained an attempt at self-justification: 'If our father had treated us in the way the totem does, we should never have felt tempted to kill him.' In this fashion totemism helped to smooth things over and to make it possible to forget the event to which it owed its origin.

Features were thus brought into existence which continued thenceforward to have a determining influence on the nature of religion. Totemic religion arose from the filial sense of guilt, in an attempt to allay that feeling and to appease the father by deferred obedience to him. All later religions are seen to be attempts at solving the same problem. They vary according to the stage of civilization at which they arise and according to the methods which they adopt; but all have the same end in view and are reactions to the same great event with which civilization began and which, since it occurred, has not allowed mankind a moment's rest.

There is another feature which was already present in totemism and which has been preserved unaltered in religion. The tension of ambivalence was evidently too great for any contrivance to be able to counteract it; or it is possible that psychological conditions in general are unfavourable to getting rid of these antithetical emotions. However that may be, we find that the ambivalence implicit in the father-complex persists in totemism and in religions generally. Totemic religion not only comprised expressions of remorse and attempts at atonement, it also served as a remembrance of the triumph over the father. Satisfaction over that triumph led to the institution of the memorial festival of the totem meal, in which the restrictions of deferred obedience no longer held. Thus it became a duty to repeat the crime of parricide again and again in the sacrifice of the totem animal, whenever, as a result of the changing conditions of life, the cherished fruit of the crime—appropriation of the paternal attributes—threatened to disappear. We shall not be surprised to find that the element of filial rebelliousness also emerges, in the *later* products of religion, often in the strangest disguises and transformations. . . .

At the conclusion, then, of this exceedingly condensed inquiry, I should like to insist that its outcome shows that the beginnings of religion, morals, society and art converge in the Oedipus complex. This is in complete agreement with the psycho-analytic finding that the same complex constitutes the nucleus of all neuroses, so far as our present knowledge goes. It seems to me a most surprising discovery that the problems of social psychology, too, should prove soluble on the basis of one single concrete point—man's relation to his father. It is even possible that yet another psychological problem belongs in this same connection. I have often had occasion to point out that emotional ambivalence in the proper sense of the term—that is, the simultaneous existence of love and hate towards the same object—lies at the root of many important cultural institutions. We know nothing of the origin of this ambivalence. One possible assumption is that it is a fundamental phenomenon of our emotional life. . . .

The analogy between primitive men and neurotics will be far more fully established if we suppose that in the former instance, too, psychical reality—as to the form taken by which we are in no doubt—coincided at the beginning with factual reality: the primitive men actually *did* what all the evidence shows that they intended to do.

Nor must we let ourselves be influenced too far in our judgement of primitive men by the analogy of neurotics. There are distinctions, too, which must be borne in mind. It is no doubt true that the sharp contrast that *we* make between thinking and doing is absent in both of them. But neurotics are above all *inhibited* in their actions: with them the thought is a complete substitute for the deed. Primitive men, on the other hand, are *uninhibited:* thought passes directly into action. With them it is rather the deed that is a substitute for the thought. And that is why, without laying claim to any finality of judgement, I think that in the case before us it may safely be assumed that 'in the beginning was the Deed'.*

Although Freud's clinical papers are difficult reading for the uninitiated, his numerous short books are surprisingly accessible. Probably the most widely read of these is *Civilization and Its Discontents,* one of Freud's last efforts. Others, not excerpted here, but which well repay attention to them, include *Beyond the Pleasure Principle,* which introduces the concept of the "death instinct," *Group Psychology and the Analysis of the Ego,* which develops the idea that the behavior of groups involves a "transference" whereby the relationship of child to parent is recapitulated in that of group-member to political leader, and *The Future of an Illusion,* in which Freud mercilessly attacks religion as an "organized neurosis," based on attempts to re-create an all-powerful father figure. *Civilization and Its Discontents,* written as Hitler's shadow

*From *Totem and Taboo* (1913). (A. A. Brill, Trans.). New York: Vintage.

began to fall across Europe, is perhaps the most pessimistic of Freud's books. In it, Freud suggests that human beings face a dilemma that is both immense and unavoidable: They rely utterly upon civilization for their happiness and even their survival, and yet, civilization itself is founded on the suppression of fundamental human traits.

We come upon a contention which is so astonishing that we must dwell upon it. This contention holds that what we call our civilization is largely responsible for our misery, and that we should be much happier if we gave it up and returned to primitive conditions. I call this contention astonishing because, in whatever way we may define the concept of civilization, it is a certain fact that all the things with which we seek to protect ourselves against the threats that emanate from the sources of suffering are part of that very civilization.

How has it happened that so many people have come to take up this strange attitude of hostility to civilization? I believe that the basis of it was a deep and long-standing dissatisfaction with the then existing state of civilization and that on that basis a condemnation of it was built up, occasioned by certain specific historical events. I think I know what the last and the last but one of those occasions were. I am not learned enough to trace the chain of them far back enough in the history of the human species; but a factor of this kind hostile to civilization must already have been at work in the victory of Christendom over the heathen religions. For it was very closely related to the low estimation put upon earthly life by the Christian doctrine. The last but one of these occasions was when the progress of voyages of discovery led to contact with primitive peoples and races. In consequence of insufficient observation and a mistaken view of their manners and customs, they appeared to Europeans to be leading a simple, happy life with few wants, a life such as was unattainable by their visitors with their superior civilization. Later experience has corrected some of those judgements. In many cases the observers had wrongly attributed to the absence of complicated cultural demands what was in fact due to the bounty of nature and the ease with which the major human needs were satisfied. The last occasion is especially familiar to us. It arose when people came to know about the mechanism of the neuroses, which threaten to undermine the modicum of happiness enjoyed by civilized men. It was discovered that a person becomes neurotic because he cannot tolerate the amount of frustration which society imposes on him in the service of its cultural ideals, and it was inferred from this that the abolition or reduction of those demands would result in a return to possibilities of happiness. . . .

Human life in common is only made possible when a majority comes together which is stronger than any separate individual and which remains united against all separate individuals. The power of this community is then set up as 'right' in opposition to the power of the individual, which is condemned as 'brute force'. This replacement of the power of the individual by the power of a community constitutes the decisive step of civilization. The essence of it lies in the fact that the members of the community restrict themselves in their possibilities of satisfaction, whereas the individual knew no such restrictions. The first requisite of civilization, therefore, is that of justice—that is, the assurance that a law once made will not be broken in favour of an individual. This implies nothing as to the ethical value of such a law. The further course of cultural development seems to tend towards making the law no longer an expression of the will of a small community—a caste or a stratum of the population or a racial group—which, in its turn, behaves like a violent individual towards other, and perhaps more numerous, collections of people. The final outcome should be a rule of law to which all—except those who are not capable of entering a community—have contributed by a sacrifice of their instincts, and which leaves no one—again with the same exception—at the mercy of brute force.

The liberty of the individual is no gift of civilization. It was greatest before there was any civilization, though then, it is true, it had for the most part no value, since the individual was scarcely in a position to defend it. The development of civilization imposes restrictions on it, and justice demands that no one shall escape those restrictions. What makes itself felt in a human community as a desire for freedom may be their revolt against some existing injustice, and so may prove favourable to a further development of civilization; it may remain compatible with civilization. But it may also spring from the remains of their original personality, which is still untamed by civilization and may thus become the basis in them of hostility to civilization. The urge for freedom, therefore, is directed against particular forms and demands of civilization or against civilization altogether. It does not seem as though any influence could induce a man to change his nature into a termite's. No doubt he will always defend his claim to individual liberty against the will of the group. A good part of the struggles of mankind centre round the single task of finding an expedient accommodation—one, that is, that will bring happiness—between this claim of the individual and the cultural claims of the group; and one of the problems that touches the fate of humanity is whether such an accommodation can be reached by means of some particular form of civilization or whether this conflict is irreconcilable.

By allowing common feeling to be our guide in deciding what features of human life are to be regarded as civilized, we have obtained a clear impression of the general picture of civilization; but it is true that so far we have discovered nothing that is not universally known. At the same time we have been careful not to fall in with the prejudice that civilization is synonymous with perfecting, that it is the road to perfection pre-ordained for men. But now a point of view presents itself which may lead in a different direction. The development of civilization appears to us as a peculiar process which mankind undergoes, and in which several things strike us as familiar. We may characterize this process with reference to the changes which it brings about in the familiar instinctual dispositions of human beings, to satisfy which is, after all, the economic task of our lives. A few of these instincts are used up in such a manner that something appears in their place which, in an individual, we describe as a character-trait. The most remarkable example of such a process is found in the anal erotism of young human beings. Their original interest in the excretory function, its organs and products, is changed in the course of their growth into a group of traits which are familiar to us as parsimony, a sense of order and cleanliness—qualities which, though valuable and welcome in themselves, may be intensified till they become markedly dominant and produce what is called the anal character. How this happens we do not know, but there is no doubt about the correctness of the finding. Now we have seen that order and cleanliness are important requirements of civilization, although their vital necessity is not very apparent, any more than their suitability as sources of enjoyment. At this point we cannot fail to be struck by the similarity between the process of civilization and the libidinal development of the individual. Other instincts [besides anal erotism] are induced to displace the conditions for their satisfaction, to lead them into other paths. In most cases this process coincides with that of the *sublimation* (of instinctual aims) with which we are familiar, but in some it can be differentiated from it. Sublimation of instinct is an especially conspicuous feature of cultural development; it is what makes it possible for higher psychical activities, scientific, artistic or ideological, to play such an important part in civilized life. If one were to yield to a first impression, one would say that sublimation is a vicissitude which has been forced upon the instincts entirely by civilization. But it would be wiser to reflect upon this a little longer. In the third place, finally, and this seems the most important of all, it is impossible to overlook the extent to which civilization is built up upon a renunciation of instinct, how much it presupposes precisely the non-satisfaction (by suppression, repression or some other means?) of powerful instincts. This 'cultural frustration' dominates the large field of social relationships between human beings. As we already know, it is the cause of the hostility against which all civilizations have to struggle. It will also make severe demands on our scientific work, and we shall have much to explain here. It is not easy to understand how it can become possible to deprive an instinct of satisfaction. Nor is doing so without danger. If the loss is not compensated for economically, one can be certain that serious disorders will ensue.

But if we want to know what value can be attributed to our view that the development of civilization is a special process, comparable to the normal maturation of the individual, we must clearly attack another problem. We must ask ourselves to what influences the development of civilization owes its origin, how it arose, and by what its course has been determined. . . .

Heterosexual genital love, which has remained exempt from outlawry, is itself restricted by further limitations, in the shape of insistence upon legitimacy and monogamy. Present-day civilization makes it plain that it will only permit sexual relationships on the basis of a solitary, indissoluble bond between one man and one woman, and that it does not like sexuality as a source of pleasure in its own right and is only prepared to tolerate it because there is so far no substitute for it as a means of propagating the human race.

This, of course, is an extreme picture. Everybody knows that it has proved impossible to put it into execution, even for quite short periods. Only the weaklings have submitted to such an extensive encroachment upon their sexual freedom, and stronger natures have only done so subject to a compensatory condition, which will be mentioned later. Civilized society has found itself obliged to pass over in silence many transgressions which, according to its own rescripts, it ought to have punished. But we must not err on the other side and assume that, because it does not achieve all its aims, such an attitude on the part of society is entirely innocuous. The sexual life of civilized man is notwithstanding severely impaired; it sometimes gives the impression of being in process of involution as a function, just as our teeth and hair seem to be as organs. One is probably justified in assuming that its importance as a source of feelings of happiness, and therefore in the fulfilment of our aim in life, has sensibly diminished. Sometimes one seems to perceive that it is not only the pressure of civilization but something in the nature of the function itself which denies us full satisfaction and urges us along other paths. This may be wrong; it is hard to decide. . . .

The element of truth behind all this, which people are so ready to disavow, is that men are not gentle creatures who want to be loved, and who at the most can defend themselves if they are attacked; they are, on the contrary, creatures among whose instinctual endowments is to be reckoned a powerful share of aggressiveness. As a result, their neighbour is for them not only a potential helper or sexual object, but also someone who tempts them to satisfy their aggressiveness on him, to exploit his capacity for work without compensation, to use him sexually without his consent, to seize his possessions, to humiliate him, to cause him pain, to torture and to kill him. *Homo homini lupus.* Who, in the face of all his experience of life and of history, will have the courage to dispute this assertion? As a rule this cruel aggressiveness waits for some provocation or puts itself at the service of some other purpose, whose goal might also have been reached by milder measures. In circumstances that are favourable to it, when the mental counter-forces which ordinarily inhibit it are out of action, it also manifests itself spontaneously and reveals man as a savage beast to whom consideration towards his own kind is something alien. Anyone who calls to mind the atrocities committed during the racial migrations or the invasions of the Huns, or by the people known as Mongols under Jenghiz Khan and Tamerlane, or at the capture of Jerusalem by the pious Crusaders, or even, indeed, the horrors of the recent World War—anyone who calls these things to mind will have to bow humbly before the truth of this view.

The existence of this inclination to aggression, which we can detect in ourselves and justly assume to be present in others, is the factor which disturbs our relations with our neighbour and which forces civilization into such a high expenditure [of energy]. In consequence of this primary mutual hostility of human beings, civilized society is perpetually threatened with disintegration. The interest of work in common would not hold it together; instinctual passions are stronger than reasonable interests. Civilization has to use its utmost efforts in order to set limits to man's aggressive instincts and to hold the manifestations of them in check by psychical reaction-formations. Hence, therefore, the use of methods intended to incite people into identifications and aim-inhibited relationships of love, hence the restriction upon sexual life, and hence too the ideal's commandment to love one's neighbour as oneself—a commandment which is really justified by the fact that nothing else runs so strongly counter to the original nature of man. In spite of every effort, these endeavours of civilization have not so far achieved very much. It hopes to prevent the crudest excesses of brutal violence by itself assuming the right to use violence against criminals, but the law is not able to lay hold of the more cautious and refined manifestations of human aggressiveness. The time comes when each one of us has to give up as illusions the expectations which, in his youth, he pinned upon his fellow-men, and when he may learn how much difficulty and pain has been added to his life by their ill-will. At the same time, it would be unfair to reproach civilization with trying to eliminate strife and competition from human activity. These things are undoubtedly indispensable. But opposition is not necessarily enmity; it is merely misused and made an *occasion* for enmity.

The communists believe that they have found the path to deliverance from our evils. According to them, man is wholly good and is well-disposed to his neighbour; but the institution of private property has corrupted his nature. The ownership of private wealth gives the individual power, and with it the temptation to ill-treat his neighbour; while the man who is excluded from possession is bound to rebel in hostility against his oppressor. If private property were abolished, all wealth held in common, and everyone allowed to share in the enjoyment of it, ill-will and hostility would disappear among men. Since everyone's needs would be satisfied, no one would have any reason to regard another as his enemy; all would willingly undertake the work that was necessary. I have no concern with any economic criticisms of the communist system; I cannot enquire into whether the abolition of private property is expedient or advantageous. But I am able to recognize that the psychological premises on which the system is based are an untenable illusion. In abolishing private property we deprive the human love of aggression of one of its instruments, certainly a strong one, though certainly not the strongest; but we have in no way altered the differences in power and influence which are misused by aggressiveness, nor have we altered anything in its nature. Aggressiveness was not created by property. It reigned almost without limit in primitive times, when property was still very scanty, and it already shows itself in the nursery almost before property has given up its primal, anal form; it forms the basis of every relation of affection and love among people (with the single exception, perhaps, of the mother's relation to her male child). If we do away with personal rights over material wealth, there still remains prerogative in the field of sexual relationships, which is bound to become the source of the strongest dislike and the most violent hostility among men who in other respects are on an equal footing. If we were to remove this factor, too, by allowing complete freedom of sexual life and thus abolishing the family, the germ-cell of civilization, we cannot, it is true, easily foresee what new paths the development of civilization could take; but one thing we can expect, and that is that this indestructible feature of human nature will follow it there. . . .

Starting from speculations on the beginning of life and from biological parallels, I drew the conclusion that, besides the instinct to preserve living substance and to join it into ever larger units, there must exist another, contrary instinct seeking to dissolve those units and to bring them back to their primaeval, inorganic state. That is to say, as well as Eros there was an instinct of death. The phenomena of life could be explained from the concurrent or mutually opposing action of these two instincts. It was not easy, however, to demonstrate the activities of this supposed death instinct. The manifestations of Eros were conspicuous and noisy enough. It might be assumed that the death instinct operated silently within the organism towards its dissolution, but that, of course, was no proof. A more fruitful idea was that a portion of the instinct is diverted towards the external world and comes to light as an instinct of aggressiveness and destructiveness. In this way the instinct itself could be pressed into the service of Eros, in that the organism was destroying some other thing, whether animate or inanimate, instead of destroying its own self. Conversely, any restriction of this aggressiveness directed outwards would be bound to increase the self-destruction, which is in any case proceeding. At the same time one can suspect from this example that the two kinds of instinct seldom—perhaps never—appear in isolation from each other, but are alloyed with each other in varying and very different proportions and so become unrecognizable to our judgement. In sadism, long since known to us as a component instinct of sexuality, we should have before us a particularly strong alloy of this kind between trends of love and the destructive instinct; while its counterpart, masochism, would be a union between destructiveness directed inwards and sexuality— a union which makes what is otherwise an imperceptible trend into a conspicuous and tangible one.

The assumption of the existence of an instinct of death or destruction has met with resistance even in analytic circles; I am aware that there is a frequent inclination rather to ascribe whatever is dangerous and hostile in love to an original bipolarity in its own nature. To begin with it was only tentatively that I put forward the views I have developed here, but in the course of time they have gained such a hold upon me that I can no longer think in any other way. To my mind, they are far more serviceable from a theoretical standpoint that any other possible ones; they provide that simplification, without either ignoring or doing violence to the facts, for which we strive in scientific work. I know that in sadism and masochism we have always seen before us manifestations of the destructive instinct (directed outwards and inwards), strongly alloyed with erotism; but I can no longer understand how we can have overlooked the ubiquity of non-erotic aggressivity and destructiveness and can have failed to give it its due place in our interpretation of life. (The desire for destruction when it is directed *inwards* mostly eludes our perception, of course, unless it is tinged with erotism.) I remember my own defensive attitude when the idea of an instinct of destruction first emerged in psychoanalytic literature, and how long it took before I became receptive to it. That others should have shown, and still show, the same attitude of rejection surprises me less. For 'little children do not like it' when there is talk of the inborn human inclination to 'badness', to aggressiveness and destructiveness, and so to cruelty as well. God has made them in the image of His own perfection; nobody wants to be reminded how hard it is to reconcile the undeniable existence of evil—despite the protestations of Christian Science—with His all-powerfulness or His all-goodness. The Devil would be the best way out as an excuse for God; in that way he would be playing the same part as an agent of economic discharge as the Jew does in the world of the Aryan ideal. But even so, one can hold God responsible for the existence of the Devil just as well as for the existence of the wickedness which the Devil embodies. In view of these difficulties, each of us will be well advised, on some suitable occasion, to make a low bow to the deeply moral nature of mankind; it will help us to be generally popular and much will be forgiven us for it.

The name 'libido' can once more be used to denote the manifestations of the power of Eros in order to distinguish them from the energy of the death instinct. It must be confessed that we have much greater difficulty in grasping that instinct; we can only suspect it, as it were, as something in the background behind Eros, and it escapes detection unless its presence is betrayed by its being alloyed with Eros. It is in sadism, where the death instinct twists the erotic aim in its own sense and yet at the same time fully satisfies the erotic urge, that we succeed in obtaining the clearest insight into its nature and its relation to Eros. But even where it emerges without any sexual purpose, in the blindest fury of destructiveness, we cannot fail to recognize that the satisfaction of the instinct is accompanied by an extraordinarily high degree of narcissistic enjoyment, owing to its presenting the ego with a fulfilment of the latter's old wishes for omnipotence. The instinct of destruction, moderated and tamed, and, as it were, inhibited in its aim, must, when it is directed towards objects, provide the ego with the satisfaction of its vital needs and with control over nature. Since the assumption of the existence of the instinct is mainly based on theoretical grounds, we must also admit that it is not entirely proof against theoretical objections. But this is how things appear to us now, in the present state of our knowledge; future research and reflection will no doubt bring further light which will decide the matter.

In all that follows I adopt the standpoint, therefore, that the inclination to aggression is an original, self-subsisting instinctual disposition in man, and I return to my view [p. 69] that it constitutes the greatest impediment to civilization. At one point in the course of this enquiry [p. 50] I was led to the idea that civilization was a special process which mankind undergoes, and I am still under the influence of that idea. I may now add that civilization is a process in the service of Eros, whose purpose is to combine single human individuals, and after that families, then races, peoples and nations, into one great unity, the unity of mankind. . . .

For a wide variety of reasons, it is very far from my intention to express an opinion upon the value of human civilization. I have endeavoured to guard myself against the enthusiastic prejudice which holds that our civilization is the most precious thing that we possess or could acquire and that its path will necessarily lead to heights of unimagined perfection. I can at least listen without indignation to the critic who is of the opinion that when one surveys the aims of cultural endeavour and the means it employs, one is bound to come to the conclusion that the whole effort is not worth the trouble, and that the outcome of it can only be a state of affairs which the individual will be unable to tolerate. My impartiality is made all the easier to me by my knowing very little about all these things. One thing only do I know for certain and that is that man's judgements of value follow directly his wishes for happiness—that, accordingly, they are an attempt to support his illusions with arguments. I should find it very understandable if someone were to point out the obligatory nature of the course of human civilization and were to say, for instance, that the tendencies to a restriction of sexual life or to the institution of a humanitarian ideal at the expense of natural selection were developmental trends which cannot be averted or turned aside and to which it is best for us to yield as though they were necessities of nature. I know, too, the objection that can be made against this, to the effect that in the history of mankind, trends such as these, which were considered unsurmountable, have often been thrown aside and replaced by other trends. Thus I have not the courage to rise up before my fellow-men as a prophet, and I bow to their reproach that I can offer them no consolation: for at bottom that is what they are all demanding—the wildest revolutionaries no less passionately than the most virtuous believers.

The fateful question for the human species seems to me to be whether and to what extent their cultural development will succeed in mastering the disturbance of their communal life by the human instinct of aggression and self-destruction. It may be that in this respect precisely the present time deserves a special interest. Men have gained control over the forces of nature to such an extent that with their help they would have no difficulty in exterminating one another to the last man. They know this, and hence comes a large part of their current unrest, their unhappiness and their mood of anxiety. And now it is to be expected that the other of the two 'Heavenly Powers' [p. 96f.], eternal Eros, will make an effort to assert himself in the struggle with his equally immortal adversary. But who can foresee with what success and with what result?*

STUDY QUESTIONS

1. Freud was very concerned that psychoanalysis be considered "scientific." How did he attempt to achieve this? Did he succeed?

2. Does psychoanalysis assume that people are basically not free in that their behavior is determined by forces beyond their control? Read about transference, and discuss its wider significance beyond clinical psychoanalysis.

*From *Civilization and Its Discontents* (1930). (J. Strachey, Trans.). New York: Norton.

3. This chapter consists entirely of selections from Freud. What were some contributions to psychoanalysis from other people?

4. Compare Freud's view of the relationship between human nature and civilization with that of Rousseau; Nietzsche; existentialists; behaviorists.

SOME ADDITIONAL READINGS

Fine, Reuben (1990). *The History of Psychoanalysis.* Northvale, N.J.: J. Aronson.

Gay, Peter (1988). *Freud: A Life for Our Time.* New York: Norton.

Hughes, Judith M. (1994). *From Freud's Consulting Room: The Unconscious in a Scientific Age.* Cambridge, Mass.: Harvard University Press.

Mitchell, Stephen A., and Black, Margaret J., eds. (1995). *Freud and Beyond: A History of Modern Psychoanalytic Thought.* New York: BasicBooks.

Webster, Richard (1995). *Why Freud Was Wrong: Sin, Science, and Psychoanalysis.* New York: BasicBooks.

PART THREE
THE SOCIAL SETTING

Even as debate continues over the precise nature of human nature, one thing seems beyond doubt: Human beings are social creatures. To be sure, there is the occasional hermit, but a solitary human being is about as rare, and as unnatural, as a solitary ant, or an object without mass. But even in the social dimension (and perhaps, especially so!) there are substantial unanswered questions and room for disagreement. What kind of social creature is *Homo sapiens?* What is our relationship to society more generally? Is there a private self, different from our public self? Are there ethical implications to be derived from our social or antisocial inclinations?

CHAPTER NINE

People Are Basically Bad

When people look at themselves, they are often less than delighted with what they find. In extreme cases, the result is outright loathing, often stimulated, at least in part, by a theological conviction that humanity is soiled by original sin. For example, according to the zealous Protestant theologian John Calvin,

> The mind of man has been so completely estranged from God's righteousness that it conceives, desires, and undertakes, only that which is impious, perverted, foul, impure and infamous. The human heart is so steeped in the poison of sin, that it can breathe out nothing but a loathesome stench.

Misanthropy can also be purely secular, as in this observation from Aldous Huxley:

> The leech's kiss, the squid's embrace,
> The prurient ape's defiling touch:
> And do you like the human race?
> No, not much.

Others focus on a particular aspect of human nastiness, notably a supposed "natural" tendency for selfishness. Many thinkers accept this premise, then attempt to show how even selfishness may have its redeeming virtues, when (if?) it generates cumulative social benefit. Probably the classic statement in this regard comes from Scottish economist Adam Smith, who argues in *The Wealth of Nations* that personal, capitalist greed leads to a society that is wealthy, and thus, happy:

> It is not from the benevolence of the butcher, the brewer or the baker, that we expect our dinner, but from their regard to their own interest. We address ourselves, not to their humanity, but to their self-love, and never talk to them of our own necessities, but of their advantages.

Criticism of human nature is especially intense, however, with respect to violence. Anthropologist Raymond Dart, for example, speaks for many when he laments that "the atrocities that have been committed . . . from the altars of antiquity to the abattoirs of every modern city proclaim the persistently bloodstained progress of man." An unruly, ingrained savagery, verging on bloodlust, is a favorite theme of fiction, including, for example, Joseph Conrad's *Heart of Darkness* and William Golding's *Lord of the Flies,* while Robert Louis Stevenson's *The Strange Case of Dr. Jeckyll and Mr. Hyde* develops the notion that a predisposition to violence and evil lurks within the most outwardly civilized and kindly person.

Human beings have also been accused (wrongly, we now know) of being the only species that kills its own kind. Nonetheless, considering just the horrors of the twentieth century, it remains difficult for any sensitive, fair-minded person to be wholly enthusiastic about the nature of human nature.

PLATO

Don't misunderstand: Plato did *not* believe that people are basically bad at heart. In his various *Dialogues,* Plato typically placed views with which he disagreed in the mouths of other speakers, to be later demolished by the arguments of Socrates. Fundamental to Platonism is the insistence that there exist certain "ideals" or "forms" that constitute ultimate truth; and for Plato (and, we presume, for Socrates, about whom Plato wrote), among the most important of these ideals are Justice and the Good. Early in Plato's most renowned dialogue, *The Republic,* Thrasymachus proposes that "justice is nothing but the advantage of the stronger," whereupon his brother, Glaucon, elaborates this argument with the famous story of the Ring of Gyges.

In a sense, the remainder of *The Republic* is Plato's answer to Glaucon's claim: The unjust person cannot be happy, Socrates explains, because true happiness requires harmony between the three parts of the human soul (see Chapter 2) with "reason" dominating "spirit" which, in turn, rides herd on "desire" (see also Chapter 8). Plato then proceeds to develop his proposals for the ideal political state modelled after this tripartite system, and governed by philosopher kings.

In this selection, from the beginning of Book II of *The Republic,* Glaucon speaks first, and "I" refers to Socrates.

Socrates, do you wish really to persuade us, or only to seem to have persuaded us, that to be just is always better than to be unjust?

I should wish really to persuade you, I replied, if I could.

Then you certainly have not succeeded. Let me ask you now:—How would you arrange goods—are there not some which we welcome for their own sakes, and independently of their consequences, as, for example, harmless pleasures and enjoyments, which delight us at the time, although nothing follows from them?

I agree in thinking that there is such a class, I replied.

Is there not also a second class of good, such as knowledge, sight, health, which are desirable not only in themselves, but also for their results?

Certainly, I said.

And would you not recognize a third class, such as gymnastic, and the care of the sick, and the physician's art; also the various ways of money-making—these do us good but we regard them as disagreeable; and no one would choose them for their own sakes, but only for the sake of some reward or result which flows from them?

There is, I said, this third class also. But why do you ask?

Because I want to know in which of the three classes you would place justice?

In the highest class, I replied,—among those goods which he who would be happy desires both for their own sake and for the sake of their results.

Then the many are of another mind; they think that justice is to be reckoned in the troublesome class, among goods which are to be pursued for the sake of rewards and of reputation, but in themselves are disagreeable and rather to be avoided.

I know, I said, that this is their manner of thinking, and that this was the thesis which Thrasymachus was maintaining just now, when he censured justice and praised injustice. But I am too stupid to be convinced by him.

I wish, he said, that you would hear me as well as him, and then I shall see whether you and I agree. For Thrasymachus seems to me, like a snake, to have been charmed by your voice sooner than he ought to have been; but to my mind the nature of justice and injustice have not yet been made clear. Setting aside their rewards and results, I want to know what they are in themselves, and how they inwardly work in the soul. If you please, then, I will revive the argument of Thrasymachus. And first I will speak of the nature and origin of justice according to the common view of them. Secondly, I will show that all men who practise justice do so against their will, of necessity, but not as a good. And thirdly, I will argue that there is reason in this view, for the life of the unjust is after all better far than the life of the just—if what they say is true, Socrates, since I myself am not of their opinion. But still I acknowledge that I am perplexed when I hear the voices of Thrasymachus and myriads of others dinning in my ears; and, on the other hand, I have never yet heard the superiority of justice to injustice maintained by any one in a satisfactory way. I want to hear justice praised in respect of itself; then I shall be satisfied, and you are the person from whom I think that I am most likely to hear this; and therefore I will praise the unjust life to the utmost of my power, and my manner of speaking will indicate the manner in which I desire to hear you too praising justice and censuring injustice. Will you say whether you approve of my proposal?

Indeed I do; nor can I imagine any theme about which a man of sense would oftener wish to converse.

I am delighted, he replied, to hear you say so, and shall begin by speaking, as I proposed, of the nature and origin of justice.

They say that to do injustice is, by nature, good; to suffer injustice, evil; but that the evil is greater than the good. And so when men have both done and suffered injustice and have had experience of both, not being able to avoid the one and obtain the other, they think that they had better agree among themselves to have neither; hence there arise laws and mutual covenants; and that which is ordained by law is termed by them lawful and just. This they affirm to be the origin and nature of justice;—it is a mean or compromise, between the best of all, which is to do injustice and not be punished, and the worst of all, which is to suffer injustice without the power of retaliation; and justice, being at a middle point between the two, is tolerated not as a good, but as the lesser evil, and honoured by reason of the inability of men to do injustice. For no man who is worthy to be called a man would ever submit to such an agreement if he were able to resist; he would be mad if he did. Such is the received account, Socrates, of the nature and origin of justice.

Now that those who practise justice do so involuntarily and because they have not the power to be unjust will best appear if we imagine something of this kind: having given both to the just and the unjust power to do what they will, let us watch and see whither desire will lead them; then we shall discover in the very act the just and unjust man to be proceeding along the same road, following their interest, which all natures deem to be their good, and are only diverted into the path of justice by the force of law. The liberty which we are supposing may be most completely given to them in the form of such a power as is said to have been possessed by Gyges, the ancestor of Croesus the Lydian. According to the tradition, Gyges was a shepherd in the service of the king of Lydia; there was a great storm, and an earthquake made an opening in the earth at the place where he was feeding his flock. Amazed at the sight, he descended into the opening, where, among other marvels, he beheld a hollow brazen horse, having doors, at which he stooping and looking in saw a dead body of stature, as appeared to him, more than human, and having nothing on but a gold ring; this he took from the finger of the dead and reascended. Now the shepherds met together, according to custom, that they might send their monthly report about the flocks to the king; into their assembly he came having the ring on his finger, and as he was sitting among them he chanced to turn the collet of the ring inside his hand, when instantly he became invisible to the rest of the company and they began to speak of him as if he were no longer present. He was astonished at this, and again touching the ring he turned the collet outwards and reappeared; he made several trials of the ring, and always with the same result—when he turned the collet inwards he became invisible, when outwards he reappeared. Whereupon he contrived to be chosen one of the messengers who were sent to the court; where as soon as he arrived he seduced the queen, and with her help conspired against the king and slew him, and took the kingdom. Suppose now that there were two such magic rings, and the just put on one of them and the unjust the other; no man can be imagined to be of such an iron nature that he would stand fast in justice. No man would keep his hands off what was not his own when he could safely take what he liked out of the market, or go into houses and lie with any one at his pleasure, or kill or release from prison whom he would, and in all respects be like a god among men. Then the actions of the just would be as the actions of the unjust; they would both come at last to the same point. And this we may truly affirm to be a great proof that a man is just, not willingly or because he thinks that justice is any good to him individually, but of necessity, for wherever any one thinks that he can safely be unjust, there he is unjust. For all men believe in their hearts that injustice is far more profitable to the individual than justice, and he who argues as I have been supposing, will say that they are right. If you could imagine any one obtaining this power of becoming invisible, and never doing any wrong or touching what was another's, he would be thought by the lookers-on to be a most wretched idiot, although they would praise him to one another's faces, and keep up appearances with one another from a fear that they too might suffer injustice. Enough of this.

Now, if we are to form a real judgement of the life of the just and unjust, we must isolate them; there is no other way; and how is the isolation to be effected? I answer: Let the unjust man be entirely unjust, and the just man entirely just; nothing is to be taken away from either of them, and both are to be perfectly furnished for the work of their respective lives. First, let the unjust be like other distinguished masters of craft; like the skilful pilot or physician, who knows intuitively his own powers and keeps within their limits, and who, if he fails at any point, is able to recover himself. So let the unjust make his unjust attempts in the right way, and lie hidden if he means to be great in his injustice: (he who is found out is nobody:) for the highest reach of injustice is, to be deemed just when you are not. Therefore I say that in the perfectly unjust man we must assume the most perfect injustice; there is to be no deduction, but we must allow him, while doing the most unjust acts, to have acquired the greatest reputation for justice. If he have taken a false step he must be able to recover himself; he must be one who can speak with effect, if any of his deeds come to light, and who can force his way where force is required by his courage and strength, and command of money and friends. And at his side let us place the just man in his nobleness and simplicity, wishing, as Aeschylus says, to be and not to seem good. There must be no seeming, for if he seem to be just he will be honoured and rewarded, and then we shall not know whether he is just for the sake of justice or for the sake of honours and rewards; therefore, let him be clothed in justice only, and have no other covering; and he must be imagined in a state of life the opposite to the former. Let him be the best of men, and let him be thought the worst; then he will have been put to the proof; and we shall see whether he will be affected by the fear of infamy and its consequences. And let him continue thus to the hour of death; being just and seeming to be unjust. When both have reached the uttermost extreme, the one of justice and the other of injustice, let judgement be given which of them is the happier of the two.

Heavens! my dear Glaucon, I said, how energetically you polish them up for the decision, first one and then the other, as if they were two statues.

I do my best, he said. And now that we know what they are like there is no difficulty in tracing out the sort of life which awaits either of them. This I will proceed to describe; but as you may think the description a little too coarse, I ask you to suppose, Socrates, that the words which follow are not mine.— Let me put them into the mouths of the eulogists of injustice: They will tell you that the just man who is thought unjust will be scourged, racked, bound—will have his eyes burnt out; and, at last, after suffering every kind of evil, he will be impaled: Then he will understand that he ought to seem only, and not to be, just; the words of Aeschylus may be more truly spoken of the unjust than of the just. For the unjust is pursuing a reality; he does not live with a view to appearances—he wants to be really unjust and not to seem only:—

His mind has a soil deep and fertile,
Out of which spring his prudent counsels.

In the first place, he is thought just, and therefore bears rule in the city; he can marry whom he will, and give in marriage to whom he will; also he can trade and deal where he likes, and always to his own advantage, because he has no misgivings about injustice; and at every contest, whether in public or private, he gets the better of his antagonists, and gains at their expense, and is rich, and out of his gains he can benefit his friends, and harm his enemies; moreover, he can offer sacrifices, and dedicate gifts to the gods abundantly and magnificently, and can honour the gods or any man whom he wants to honour in a far better style than the just, and therefore he is likely to be dearer than they are to the gods. And thus, Socrates, gods and men are said to unite in making the life of the unjust better than the life of the just.*

*From *The Republic* (1901). (B. Jowett, Trans.). London: Oxford University Press.

AUGUSTINE

For Saint Augustine, original human sin is primarily sexual. Others subsequently emphasized Adam and Eve's disobedience as the primal human sin; John Milton's *Paradise Lost* is a poetical elaboration of this theme. (In contrast to Augustine, the monk Pelagius argues his "heresy" that humans are not innately sinful but can save themselves by their own good works.) Augstine reserves the power of absolving sin and conferring immortal bliss to God. He maintains that human beings cannot by themselves derive genuine freedom or even morality: "Men will not do what is right, either because the right is hidden from them or because they find no delight in it. But that what was hidden may become clear, what delighted not may become sweet—this belongs to the grace of God."

The following is from Augustine's *City of God.*

Book 12

22. That God foreknew that the first man would sin, and that He at the same time foresaw how large a multitude of godly persons would by His grace be translated to the fellowship of the angels

And God was not ignorant that man would sin, and that, being himself made subject now to death, he would propagate men doomed to die, and that these mortals would run to such enormities in sin, that even the beasts devoid of rational will, and who were created in numbers from the waters and the earth, would live more securely and peaceably with their own kind than men, who had been propagated from one individual for the very purpose of commending concord. For not even lions or dragons have ever waged with their kind such wars as men have waged with one another.[42] But God foresaw also that by His grace a people would be called to adoption, and that they, being justified by the remission of their sins, would be united by the Holy Ghost to the holy angels in eternal peace, the last enemy, death, being destroyed; and He knew that this people would derive profit from the consideration that God had caused all men to be derived from one, for the sake of showing how highly He prizes unity in a multitude. . . .

Book 13

13. What was the first punishment of the transgression of our first parents?

For, as soon as our first parents had transgressed the commandment, divine grace forsook them, and they were confounded at their own wickedness; and therefore they took fig-leaves (which were possibly the first that came to hand in their troubled state of mind), and covered their shame; for though their members remained the same, they had shame now where they had none before. They experienced a new motion of their flesh, which had become disobedient to them, in strict retribution of their own disobedience to God. For the soul, revelling in its own liberty, and scorning to serve God, was itself deprived of the command it had formerly maintained over the body. And because it had wilfully deserted its superior Lord, it no longer held its own inferior servant; neither could it hold the flesh subject, as it would always have been able to do had it remained itself subject to God. Then began the flesh to lust against the Spirit,[17] in which strife we are born, deriving from the first transgression a seed of death, and bearing in our members, and in our vitiated nature, the contest or even victory of the flesh.

14. IN WHAT STATE MAN WAS MADE BY GOD, AND INTO WHAT ESTATE HE FELL BY THE CHOICE OF HIS OWN WILL

For God, the author of natures, not of vices, created man upright; but man, being of his own will corrupted, and justly condemned, begot corrupted and condemned children. For we all were in that one man, since we all were that one man who fell into sin by the woman who was made from him before the sin. For not yet was the particular form created and distributed to us, in which we as individuals were to live, but already the seminal nature was there from which we were to be propagated; and this being vitiated by sin, and bound by the chain of death, and justly condemned, man could not be born of man in any other state. And thus, from the bad use of free will, there originated the whole train of evil, which, with its concatenation of miseries, convoys the human race from its depraved origin, as from a corrupt root, on to the destruction of the second death, which has no end, those only being excepted who are freed by the grace of God. . . .

Book 14

1. THAT THE DISOBEDIENCE OF THE FIRST MAN WOULD HAVE PLUNGED ALL MEN INTO THE ENDLESS MISERY OF THE SECOND DEATH, HAD NOT THE GRACE OF GOD RESCUED MANY

We have already stated in the preceding books that God, desiring not only that the human race might be able by their similarity of nature to associate with one another, but also that they might be bound together in harmony and peace by the ties of relationship, was pleased to derive all men from one individual, and created man with such a nature that the members of the race should not have died, had not the two first (of whom the one was created out of nothing, and the other out of him) merited this by their disobedience; for by them so great a sin was committed, that by it the human nature was altered for the worse, and was transmitted also to their posterity, liable to sin and subject to death. And the kingdom of death so reigned over men, that the deserved penalty of sin would have hurled all headlong even into the second death, of which there is no end, had not the undeserved grace of God saved some therefrom. And thus it has come to pass, that though there are very many and great nations all over the earth, whose rites and customs, speech, arms, and dress, are distinguished by marked differences, yet there are no more than two kinds of human society, which we may justly call two cities, according to the language of our Scriptures. The one consists of those who wish to live after the flesh, the other of those who wish to live after the spirit; and when they severally achieve what they wish, they live in peace, each after their kind. . . .

Book 22

22. OF THE MISERIES AND ILLS TO WHICH THE HUMAN RACE IS JUSTLY EXPOSED THROUGH THE FIRST SIN, AND FROM WHICH NONE CAN BE DELIVERED SAVE BY CHRIST'S GRACE

That the whole human race has been condemned in its first origin, this life itself, if life it is to be called, bears witness by the host of cruel ills with which it is filled. Is not this proved by the profound and dreadful ignorance which produces all the errors that enfold the children of Adam, and from which no man can be delivered without toil, pain, and fear? Is it not proved by his love of so many vain and hurtful things, which produces gnawing cares, disquiet, griefs, fears, wild joys, quarrels, law-suits, wars, treasons, angers, hatreds, deceit, flattery, fraud, theft, robbery, perfidy, pride, ambition, envy, murders, parricides, cruelty, ferocity, wickedness, luxury, insolence, impudence, shamelessness, fornications, adulteries, incests, and the numberless uncleannesses and unnatural acts of both sexes, which it is shameful so much as to mention; sacrileges, heresies, blasphemies, perjuries, oppression of the innocent, calumnies, plots, false-hoods, false witnessings, unrighteous judgments, violent deeds, plunderings, and whatever similar wicked-ness has found its way into the lives of men, though it cannot find its way into the conception of pure minds? These are indeed the crimes of wicked men, yet they spring from that root of error and misplaced love which is born with every son of Adam. For who is there that has not observed with what profound ignorance, manifesting itself even in infancy, and with what superfluity of foolish desires, beginning to appear in boyhood, man comes into this life, so that, were he left to live as he pleased, and to do what-ever he pleased, he would plunge into all, or certainly into many of those crimes and iniquities which I mentioned, and could not mention?

But God does not wholly desert those whom He condemns nor shuts up in His anger His tender mercies. . . .*

HOBBES

It may be significant that Thomas Hobbes (1588–1679) was born just as the Spanish Armada was threatening England; he claims to have been permanently influenced by the fear that per-vaded his country at that time, not to mention the carnage of the English civil war through which he subsequently lived. In any event, Hobbes became one of the preeminent apostles of human nastiness; not that he was in favor of it, but rather, he maintained that human beings are so aggressive, self-aggrandizing, and obsessed with their own personal advantage that social controls are necessary to protect them from each other. Hobbes's most famous work, *The Leviathan,* is a political treatise, justifying a powerful ruling government: the whalelike "Leviathan," headed by a supreme monarch. However, it is directly informed by Hobbes's dark view of individual human nature.

In addition to propounding an early form of egoistic psychology, Hobbes was much taken with mathematics. He also weighed in on the mind/brain problem, as a hard-line materialist who interpreted life, sensation, and desire as the movement of appropriate body parts. Hobbes would not have agreed with Aristotle that man is a political animal, since he thought that the original state of nature was one of mutual hostility governed only by the balance between de-sires and fear.

By *manners,* I mean not here, decency of behavior; as how one should salute another, or how a man should wash his mouth, or pick his teeth before company, and such other points of the *small morals;* but those qualities of mankind, that concern their living together in peace, and unity. To which end we are to con-sider, that the felicity of this life, consisteth not in the repose of a mind satisfied. For there is no such *finis ultimus,* utmost aim, nor *summum bonum,* greatest good, as is spoken of in the books of the old moral philosophers. Nor can a man any more live, whose desires are at an end, than he, whose senses and imag-inations are at a stand. Felicity is a continual progress of the desire, from one object to another; the at-taining of the former, being still but the way to the latter. The cause whereof is, that the object of man's desire, is not to enjoy once only, and for one instant of time; but to assure for ever, the way of his future desire. And therefore the voluntary actions, and inclinations of all men, tend, not only to the procuring,

*From *The City of God* (1871). (M. Dods, Trans.). Edinburg: T and T Clark.

but also to the assuring of a contented life; and differ only in the way: which ariseth partly from the diversity of passions, in divers men; and partly from the difference of the knowledge, or opinion each one has of the causes, which produce the effect desired.

So that in the first place, I put for a general inclination of all mankind, a perpetual and restless desire of power after power, that ceaseth only in death. And the cause of this, is not always that a man hopes for a more intensive delight, than he has already attained to; or that he cannot be content with a moderate power: but because he cannot assure the power and means to live well, which he hath present, without the acquisition of more. And from hence it is, that kings, whose power is greatest, turn their endeavors to the assuring it at home by laws, or abroad by wars: and when that is done, there succeedeth a new desire; in some, of fame from new conquest; in others, of ease and sensual pleasure; in others, of admiration, or being flattered for excellence in some art, or other ability of the mind. . . .

Nature hath made men so equal, in the faculties of the body and mind; as that, though there be found one man sometimes manifestly stronger in body or of quicker mind than another, yet when all is reckoned together, the difference between man and man is not so considerable, as that one man can thereupon claim to himself any benefit, to which another may not pretend as well as he. For as to the strength of body, the weakest has strength enough to kill the strongest, either by secret machination, or by confederacy with others that are in the same danger with himself.

And as to the faculties of the mind—setting aside the arts grounded upon words, and especially that skill of proceeding upon general and infallible rules, called science; which very few have, and but in few things; as being not a native faculty, born with us; nor attained, as prudence, while we look after somewhat else— I find yet a greater equality amongst men, than that of strength. For prudence is but experience which equal time equally bestows on all men, in those things they equally apply themselves unto. That which may perhaps make such equality incredible, is but a vain conceit of one's own wisdom, which almost all men think they have in a greater degree than the vulgar; that is, than all men but themselves, and a few others, whom by fame, or for concurring with themselves, they approve. For such is the nature of men, that howsoever they may acknowledge many others to be more witty, or more eloquent, or more learned, yet they will hardly believe there be many so wise as themselves; for they see their own wit at hand, and other men's at a distance. But this proveth rather that men are in that point equal, than unequal. For there is not ordinarily a greater sign of the equal distribution of anything, than that every man is contented with his share.

From this equality of ability, ariseth equality of hope in the attaining of our ends. And therefore if any two men desire the same thing, which nevertheless they cannot both enjoy, they become enemies; and in the way to their end, which is principally their own conservation, and sometimes their delectation only, endeavor to destroy, or subdue one another. And from hence it comes to pass that where an invader hath no more to fear than another man's single power; if one plant, sow, build, or possess a convenient seat, others may probably be expected to come prepared with forces united, to dispossess and deprive him, not only of the fruit of his labor, but also of his life or liberty. And the invader again is in the like danger of another.

And from this diffidence of one another, there is no way for any man to secure himself so reasonable as anticipation; that is, by force or wiles to master the persons of all men he can, so long, till he see no other power great enough to endanger him: and this is no more than his own conservation requireth, and is generally allowed. Also because there be some, that taking pleasure in contemplating their own power in the acts of conquest, which they pursue farther than their security requires; if others, that otherwise would be glad to be at ease within modest bounds, should not by invasion increase their power, they would not be able long time, by standing only on their defense, to subsist. And by consequence, such augmentation of dominion over men being necessary to a man's conservation, it ought to be allowed him.

Again, men have no pleasure, but on the contrary a great deal of grief, in keeping company, where there is no power able to overawe them all. For every man looketh that his companion should value him at the same rate he sets upon himself; and upon all signs of contempt, or undervaluing, naturally endeavors, as far as he dares (which amongst them that have no common power to keep them in quiet, is far enough to make them destroy each other), to extort a greater value from his contemners by damage, and from others by the example.

So that in the nature of man, we find three principal causes of quarrel. First, competition; second, diffidence; thirdly, glory.

The first maketh men invade for gain; the second, for safety; and the third, for reputation. The first use violence to make themselves masters of other men's persons, wives, children, and cattle; the second, to defend them; the third, for trifles, as a word, a smile, a different opinion, and any other sign of undervalue, either direct in their persons, or by reflection in their kindred, their friends, their nation, their profession, or their name.

Hereby it is manifest that during the time men live without a common power to keep them all in awe, they are in that condition which is called war; and such a war as is of every man against every man. For *war* consisteth not in battle only, or the act of fighting, but in a tract of time wherein the will to contend by battle is sufficiently known, and therefore the notion of *time* is to be considered in the nature of war, as it is in the nature of weather. For as the nature of foul weather lieth not in a shower or two of rain, but in an inclination thereto of many days together; so the nature of war consisteth not in actual fighting, but in the known disposition thereto, during all the time there is no assurance to the contrary. All other time is *peace*.

Whatsoever therefore is consequent to a time of war, where every man is enemy to every man; the same is consequent to the time, wherein men live without other security than what their own strength and their own invention shall furnish them withal. In such condition there is no place for industry, because the fruit thereof is uncertain: and consequently no culture of the earth; no navigation, nor use of the commodities that may be imported by sea; no commodious building; no instruments of moving, and removing, such things as require much force; no knowledge of the face of the earth; no account of time; no arts; no letters; no society; and which is worst of all, continual fear, and danger of violent death; and the life of man, solitary, poor, nasty, brutish, and short.

It may seem strange to some man that has not well weighed these things, that nature should thus dissociate, and render men apt to invade and destroy one another; and he may therefore, not trusting to this inference, made from the passions, desire perhaps to have the same confirmed by experience. Let him therefore consider with himself, when taking a journey, he arms himself and seeks to go well accompanied; when going to sleep, he locks his doors; when even in his house he locks his chests; and this when he knows there be laws, and public officers, armed, to revenge all injuries shall be done him: what opinion he has of his fellow-subjects, when he rides armed; of his fellow-citizens, when he locks his doors; and of his children, and servants, when he locks his chests. Does he not there as much accuse mankind by his actions, as I do by my words? But neither of us accuse man's nature in it. The desires, and other passions of man, are in themselves no sin. No more are the actions that proceed from those passions, till they know a law that forbids them: which till laws be made they cannot know; nor can any law be made, till they have agreed upon the person that shall make it.

It may peradventure be thought, there was never such a time nor condition of war as this; and I believe it was never generally so, over all the world: but there are many places where they live so now. For the savage people in many places of America, except the government of small families, the concord whereof dependeth on natural lust, have no government at all; and live at this day in that brutish manner, as I said before. Howsoever, it may be perceived what manner of life there would be, where there were no common power to fear; by the manner of life which men that have formerly lived under a peaceful government, use to degenerate into in a civil war.

But though there had never been any time wherein particular men were in a condition of war one against another; yet in all times, kings, and persons of sovereign authority, because of their independency, are in continual jealousies, and in the state and posture of gladiators; having their weapons pointing, and their eyes fixed on one another; that is, their forts, garrisons, and guns upon the frontiers of their kingdoms; and continual spies upon their neighbors; which is a posture of war. But because they uphold thereby the industry of their subjects, there does not follow from it that misery which accompanies the liberty of particular men.

To this war of every man against every man, this also is consequent: *that nothing can be unjust.* The notions of right and wrong, justice and injustice, have there no place. Where there is no common power, there is no law; where no law, no injustice. Force and fraud are in war the two cardinal virtues. Justice and injustice are none of the faculties neither of the body nor mind. If they were, they might be in a man that were alone in the world, as well as his senses and passions. They are qualities that relate to men in society, not in solitude. It is consequent also to the same condition, that there be no propriety, no dominion, no *mine* and *thine* distinct; but only that to be every man's, that he can get; and for so long as he can keep it. And thus much for the ill condition which man by mere nature is actually placed in; though with a possibility to come out of it, consisting partly in the passions, partly in his reason.

The passions that incline men to peace are fear of death, desire of such things as are necessary to commodious living, and a hope by their industry to obtain them. And reason suggesteth convenient articles of peace, upon which men may be drawn to agreement. These articles are they which otherwise are called the Laws of Nature whereof I shall speak more particularly in the two following chapters. . . .

The right of nature, which writers commonly call *jus naturale,* is the liberty each man hath to use his own power, as he will himself, for the preservation of his own nature; that is to say, of his own life; and consequently, of doing anything, which in his own judgment and reason, he shall conceive to be the aptest means thereunto.

By *liberty,* is understood, according to the proper signification of the word, the absence of external impediments: which impediments, may oft take away part of a man's power to do what he would; but cannot hinder him from using the power left him, according as his judgment and reason shall dictate to him.

A *law of nature, lex naturalis,* is a precept or general rule, found out by reason, by which a man is forbidden to do that which is destructive of his life, or taketh away the means of preserving the same; and to omit that by which he thinketh it may be best preserved. For though they that speak of this subject, use to confound *jus* and *lex, right* and *law;* yet they ought to be distinguished: because *right* consisteth in liberty to do or to forbear, whereas *law* determineth and bindeth to one of them; so that law, and right differ as much as obligation and liberty; which in one and the same matter are inconsistent.

And because the condition of man, as hath been declared in the precedent chapter, is a condition of war of everyone against everyone; in which case everyone is governed by his own reason, and there is nothing he can make use of that may not be a help unto him in preserving his life against his enemies: it followeth, that in such a condition every man has a right to everything; even to one another's body. And therefore, as long as this natural right of every man to everything endureth, there can be no security to any man, how strong or wise soever he be, of living out the time which nature ordinarily alloweth men to live. And consequently it is a precept, or general rule of reason, *that every man ought to endeavor peace, as far as he has hope of obtaining it; and when he cannot obtain it, that he may seek and use all helps and advantages of war.* The first branch of which rule containeth the first and fundamental law of nature; which is, *to seek peace and follow it.* The second, the sum of the right of nature; which is, *by all means we can, to defend ourselves.*

From this fundamental law of nature, by which men are commanded to endeavor peace, is derived this second law: *that a man be willing, when others are so too, as far forth as for peace and defense of himself he shall think it necessary, to lay down this right to all things; and be contented with so much liberty against other men, as he would allow other men against himself.* For as long as every man holdeth this right, of doing anything he liketh, so long are all men in the condition of war. But if other men will not lay down their right, as well as he, then there is no reason for anyone to divest himself of his: for that were to expose himself to prey, which no man is bound to, rather than to dispose himself to peace. . . .

The final cause, end, or design of men who naturally love liberty and dominion over others, in the introduction of that restraint upon themselves in which we see them live in commonwealths, is the foresight of their own preservation, and of a more contented life thereby; that is to say, of getting themselves out from that miserable condition of war, which is necessarily consequent, as hath been shown in Chapter XIII, to the natural passions of men, when there is no visible power to keep them in awe, and tie them by fear of punishment to the performance of their covenants and observation of those laws of nature set down in the fourteenth and fifteenth chapters.

For the laws of nature, as justice, equity, modesty, mercy, and, in sum, *doing to others as we would be done to,* of themselves, without the terror of some power to cause them to be observed, are contrary to our natural passions, that carry us to partiality, pride, revenge, and the like. And covenants, without the sword, are but words, and of no strength to secure a man at all. Therefore notwithstanding the laws of nature, which everyone hath then kept, when he has the will to keep them when he can do it safely; if there be no power erected, or not great enough for our security, every man will, and may, lawfully rely on his own strength and art, for caution against all other men. And in all places where men have lived by small families, to rob and spoil one another has been a trade, and so far from being reputed against the law of nature, that the greater spoils they gained, the greater was their honor; and men observed no other laws therein but the laws of honor; that is, to abstain from cruelty, leaving to men their lives, and instruments of husbandry. And as small families did then; so now do cities and kingdoms, which are but greater families, for their own security enlarge their dominions, upon all pretenses of danger and fear of invasion, or assistance that may be given to invaders, and endeavor as much as they can to subdue or weaken their neighbors, by open force and secret arts, for want of other caution, justly; and are remembered for it in after ages with honor.

Nor is it the joining together of a small number of men, that gives them this security; because in small numbers, small additions on the one side or the other make the advantage of strength so great, as is sufficient to carry the victory, and therefore gives encouragement to an invasion. The multitude sufficient to confide in for our security, is not determined by any certain number, but by comparison with the enemy we fear; and is then sufficient, when the odds of the enemy is not of so visible and conspicuous moment, to determine the event of war, as to move him to attempt.

And be there never so great a multitude, yet if their actions be directed according to their particular judgments and particular appetites, they can expect thereby no defense nor protection, neither against a common enemy nor against the injuries of one another. For being distracted in opinions concerning the best use and application of their strength, they do not help but hinder one another; and reduce their strength by mutual opposition to nothing: whereby they are easily, not only subdued by a very few that agree together; but also when there is no common enemy, they make war upon each other, for their particular interests. For if we could suppose a great multitude of men to consent in the observation of justice, and other laws of nature, without a common power to keep them all in awe, we might as well suppose all mankind to do the same; and then there neither would be, nor need to be any civil government or commonwealth at all, because there would be peace without subjection.

Nor is it enough for the security, which men desire should last all the time of their life, that they be governed and directed by one judgment for a limited time, as in one battle or one war. For though they obtain a victory by their unanimous endeavor against a foreign enemy; yet afterwards, when either they have no common enemy, or he that by one part is held for an enemy, is by another part held for a friend, they must needs by the difference of their interests dissolve, and fall again into a war amongst themselves.

It is true that certain living creatures, as bees and ants, live sociably one with another, which are therefore by Aristotle numbered amongst political creatures; and yet have no other direction than their particular judgments and appetites; nor speech, whereby one of them can signify to another what he thinks expedient for the common benefit: and therefore some man may perhaps desire to know why mankind cannot do the same. To which I answer:

First, that men are continually in competition for honor and dignity, which these creatures are not; and consequently amongst men there ariseth on that ground, envy and hatred, and finally war; but amongst these not so.

Secondly, that amongst these creatures, the common good differeth not from the private; and being by nature inclined to their private, they procure thereby the common benefit. But man, whose joy consisteth in comparing himself with other men, can relish nothing but what is eminent.

Thirdly, that these creatures, having not, as man, the use of reason, do not see, nor think they see, any fault in the administration of their common business; whereas amongst men, there are very many that think themselves wiser, and able to govern the public better, than the rest; and these strive to reform and innovate, one this way, another that way; and thereby bring it into distraction and civil war.

Fourthly, that these creatures, though they have some use of voice in making known to one another their desires and other affections; yet they want that art of words by which some men can represent to others, that which is good in the likeness of evil, and evil in the likeness of good, and augment or diminish the apparent greatness of good and evil; discontenting men and troubling their peace at their pleasure.

Fifthly, irrational creatures cannot distinguish between *injury* and *damage;* and therefore as long as they be at ease, they are not offended with their fellows: whereas man is then most troublesome when he is most at ease; for then it is that he loves to shew his wisdom, and control the actions of them that govern the commonwealth.

Lastly, the agreement of these creatures is natural; that of men is by covenant only, which is artificial: and therefore it is no wonder if there be somewhat else required, besides covenant, to make their agreement constant and lasting; which is a common power, to keep them in awe, and to direct their actions to the common benefit.

The only way to erect such a common power, as may be able to defend them from the invasion of foreigners and the injuries of one another, and thereby to secure them in such sort as that, by their own industry, and by the fruits of the earth, they may nourish themselves and live contentedly; is, to confer all their power and strength upon one man, or upon one assembly of men, that may reduce all their wills, by plurality of voices, unto one will: which is as much as to say, to appoint one man, or assembly of men, to bear their person; and everyone to own and acknowledge himself to be author of whatsoever he that so beareth their person, shall act or cause to be acted in those things which concern the common peace and safety; and therein to submit their wills, everyone to his will, and their judgments, to his judgment. This is more than consent, or concord; it is a real unity of them all, in one and the same person, made by covenant of every man with every man, in such manner as if every man should say to every man, *"I authorize and give up my right of governing myself to this man, or to this assembly of men, on this condition, that thou give up thy right to him, and authorize all his actions in like manner."* This done, the multitude so united in one person, is called a *commonwealth,* in Latin *civitas.* This is the generation of that great LEVIATHAN, or rather, to speak more reverently, of that *mortal god,* to which we owe under the *immortal God,* our peace and defense. For by this authority, given him by every particular man in the commonwealth, he hath the use of so much power and strength conferred on him, that by terror thereof he is enabled to perform the wills of them all, to peace at home and mutual aid against their enemies abroad. And in him consisteth the essence of the commonwealth; which, to define it, is *one person, of whose acts a great multitude, by mutual covenants one with another, have made themselves every one the author, to the end he may use the strength and means of them all, as he shall think expedient, for their peace and common defense.*

And he that carrieth this person, is called *sovereign,* and said to have sovereign power; and everyone besides, his *subject.*

The attaining to this sovereign power is by two ways. One, by natural force; as when a man maketh his children to submit themselves and their children to his government, as being able to destroy them if they refuse; or by war subdueth his enemies to his will, giving them their lives on that condition. The other, is when men agree amongst themselves to submit to some man, or assembly of men, voluntarily, on confidence to be protected by him against all others. This latter, may be called a political commonwealth, or commonwealth by *institution;* and the former, a commonwealth by *acquisition.**

KAFKA

Franz Kafka (1883–1924) wrote some of the most bizarre, disturbing, and baffling fictional accounts of the human condition. Critics agree that Kafka's work describes the absurdity and alienation of modern life, although his allegorical tales have a timeless quality. His novels *The Trial* and *The Castle,* for example, depict (among other things!) the impossibility of achieving justice or personal validation, and his short stories challenge our very notion of what it means to be human. But Kafka does not simply rail against a meaningless universe. Underlying his work is a persistent criticism of people: However bad our human situation, he seems to be saying, it would not be quite so dire if we didn't treat each other as we do.

In "The Bucket Rider," one of his shortest stories, Kafka poignantly indicts human selfishness.

Coal all spent; the bucket empty; the shovel useless; the stove breathing out cold; the room freezing; the leaves outside the window rigid, covered with rime; the sky a silver shield against any one who looks for help from it. I must have coal; I cannot freeze to death; behind me is the pitiless stove, before me the pitiless sky, so I must ride out between them and on my journey seek aid from the coaldealer. But he has already grown deaf to ordinary appeals; I must prove irrefutably to him that I have not a single grain of coal left, and that he means to me the very sun in the firmament. I must approach like a beggar, who, with the death rattle already in his throat, insists on dying on the doorstep, and to whom the grand people's cook accordingly decides to give the dregs of the coffeepot; just so must the coaldealer, filled with rage, but acknowledging the command, "Thou shalt not kill," fling a shovelful of coal into my bucket.

My mode of arrival must decide the matter; so I ride off on the bucket. Seated on the bucket, my hands on the handle, the simplest kind of bridle, I propel myself with difficulty down the stairs; but once down below my bucket ascends, superbly, superbly; camels humbly squatting on the ground do not rise

*From *The Leviathan* (1651; 1939). New York: The Modern Library.

with more dignity, shaking themselves under the sticks of their drivers. Through the hard frozen streets we go at a regular canter; often I am upraised as high as the first story of a house; never do I sink as low as the house doors. And at last I float at an extraordinary height above the vaulted cellar of the dealer, whom I see far below crouching over his table, where he is writing; he has opened the door to let out the excessive heat.

"Coaldealer!" I cry in a voice burned hollow by the frost and muffled in the cloud made by my breath, "please, coaldealer, give me a little coal. My bucket is so light that I can ride on it. Be kind. When I can I'll pay you."

The dealer puts his hand to his ear. "Do I hear rightly?" he throws the question over his shoulder to his wife. "Do I hear rightly? A customer."

"I hear nothing," says his wife, breathing in and out peacefully while she knits on, her back pleasantly warmed by the heat.

"Oh, yes, you must hear," I cry. "It's me; an old customer; faithful and true; only without means at the moment."

"Wife," says the dealer, "it's someone, it must be; my ears can't have deceived me so much as that; it must be an old, a very old customer, that can move me so deeply."

"What ails you, man?" says his wife, ceasing from her work for a moment and pressing her knitting to her bosom. "It's nobody, the street is empty, all our customers are provided for; we could close down the shop for several days and take a rest."

"But I'm sitting up here on the bucket," I cry, and unfeeling frozen tears dim my eyes, "please look up here, just once; you'll see me directly; I beg you, just a shovelful; and if you give me more it'll make me so happy that I won't know what to do. All the other customers are provided for. Oh, if I could only hear the coal clattering into the bucket!"

"I'm coming," says the coaldealer, and on his short legs he makes to climb the steps of the cellar, but his wife is already beside him, holds him back by the arm and says: "You stay here; seeing you persist in your fancies I'll go myself. Think of the bad fit of coughing you had during the night. But for a piece of business, even if it's one you've only fancied in your head, you're prepared to forget your wife and child and sacrifice your lungs. I'll go."

"Then be sure to tell him all the kinds of coal we have in stock; I'll shout out the prices after you."

"Right," says his wife, climbing up to the street. Naturally she sees me at once. "Frau Coaldealer," I cry, "my humblest greetings; just one shovelful of coal; here in my bucket; I'll carry it home myself. One shovelful of the worst you have. I'll pay you in full for it, of course, but not just now, not just now." What a knell-like sound the words "not just now" have, and how bewilderingly they mingle with the evening chimes that fall from the church steeple near by!

"Well, what does he want?" shouts the dealer. "Nothing," his wife shouts back, "there's nothing here; I see nothing, I hear nothing; only six striking, and now we must shut up the shop. The cold is terrible; tomorrow we'll likely have lots to do again."

She sees nothing and hears nothing; but all the same she loosens her apron strings and waves her apron to waft me away. She succeeds, unluckily. My bucket has all the virtues of a good steed except powers of resistance, which it has not; it is too light; a woman's apron can make it fly through the air.

"You bad woman!" I shout back, while she, turning into the shop, half contemptuous, half reassured, flourishes her fist in the air. "You bad woman! I begged you for a shovelful of the worst coal and you would not give it me." And with that I ascend into the regions of the ice mountains and am lost for ever.*

*From *Franz Kafka: The Complete Stories* (1971). (W. and E. Muir, Trans.). New York: Schocken Books.

STUDY QUESTIONS

1. Is it fair to equate egoism, or even selfishness, with evil or nastiness?

2. There seems to be a tendency for materialists, such as Hobbes and presumably Glaucon, to argue that human beings are comparatively nasty and for idealists to believe otherwise (not many people make a case for "ideal evil")! Agree or disagree, and explain why.

3. To what extent is it misleading or oversimplifying to equate the different ideas presented in this chapter? Distinguish between them.

4. If people are basically bad, why do they often act so good?

SOME ADDITIONAL READINGS

Bloch, R. Howard, and Ferguson, Frances, eds. (1989). *Misogyny, Misandry, and Misanthropy.* Berkeley, Calif.: University of California Press.

Caws, Peter, ed. (1989). *The Causes of Quarrel: Essays on Peace, War, and Thomas Hobbes.* Boston: Beacon Press.

Ferguson, Everett, ed. (1993). *Doctrines of Human Nature, Sin, and Salvation in the Early Church.* New York: Garland.

Gorringe, Timothy (1996). *God's Just Vengeance: Crime, Violence, and the Rhetoric of Salvation.* New York: Cambridge University Press.

Green, Arnold W. (1993). *Hobbes and Human Nature.* New Brunswick, N.J.: Transaction Publishers.

CHAPTER TEN

People Are Basically Good

Countering the image of human beings as fallen, beastly, and evil, is another perspective, as optimistic as the other is pessimistic, and, perhaps, as naive as the other is cynical. This perspective sees people as basically good, possessing such admirable traits as kindness and generosity, capable of love and also worthy of being loved—not only as individuals but also as a species. Although, as we have seen, there is theological justification and precedence (especially in Christian doctrine) for taking a dim view of humankind, there is also room for a more positive view, if only because according to Genesis, human beings were made in God's image.

Thus, Joseph Butler (1692–1752) Bishop of the Church of England, argued influentially that

> vice is contrary to the nature and reason of things . . . it is a violation or breaking in upon our own nature, . . . [which is] adopted to virtue, as a watch to measuring time. . . . [I]t is not a true representation of mankind to affirm, that they are wholly governed by self-love, the love of power and sensual appetites . . . since . . . the same persons, the generality, are frequently influenced by friendship, compassion, gratitude; and even a general abhorrence of what is base, and a liking of what is fair and just.

This perspective has also appealed to a number of secular thinkers. David Hume, for example, claimed that human beings are equipped not only with self-love, but also with love for others, and that compassion and benevolence (what he called "sympathy") are natural aspects of the human endowment, although his enthusiasm for human fellow-feeling was tinged with acknowledgment that people often act in their own self-interest.

John Locke argued that civil government is formed when free, well-meaning individuals gather together for mutual benefit, based on a shared respect for each other's fundamental rights. But whereas Locke saw human society as based on the good qualities of human nature, a widespread view posited that human nature was good but that society was fundamentally bad.

ROUSSEAU

The most noteworthy advocate of primal human goodness was Jean-Jacques Rousseau (1712–1778), a seminal figure in Western thought. Rousseau experienced physical and emotional difficulties throughout his life, remaining in many ways a social outcast, even as he made brilliant contributions in music, political theory, philosophy, and literature. More than anyone else, he is also responsible for the "back to nature" movement, as well as the reverencing of spontaneity and emotion over artifice and reason.

Rousseau's most famous phrase is probably "Man is born free, but is everywhere in chains," the opening line of *The Social Contract.* That book explored the basis of political organization and is less important for our purposes than Rousseau's approach to human nature itself. In 1749, The Academy of Dijon announced a competition for the best essay on the topic "Has the restoration of the sciences and the arts contributed to corrupt or to purify morals?" Rousseau wanted to enter, and one day, while walking, he received his inspiration:

> All at once I felt myself dazzled by a thousand sparkling lights . . . I sank down under one of the trees by the road . . . and . . . when I rose I saw that the front of my waistcoat was all wet with tears. . . . Ah, if ever I could have written a quarter of what I saw and felt under that tree, with what clarity I should have brought out all the contradictions of our social system! With what simplicity I should have demonstrated that man is by nature good, and that only our institutions have made him bad!

Historian Will Durant writes "that last sentence was to be the theme song of his life, and those tears that streaked his vest were among the headwaters of the Romantic movement." Rousseau's essay, which won first prize, was followed by fame and many other contributions, including his book *Emile,* an immensely popular and (to this day) influential guide to child-rearing, which argued that nature, including natural human inclinations, is the best guide:

> Let us lay it down as an incontrovertible rule that the first impulses of nature are always right. There is no original sin in the human heart. . . . Never punish your pupil, for he does not know what it means to do wrong. . . . First leave the germ of his character free to show itself; do not constrain him in anything; so you will better see him as he really is.

Rousseau's most effective development of the "noble savage" theme was stimulated by another question posed by the Dijon Academy: "What is the origin of the inequality among men and is it justified by natural law?" His essay, "Discourse on the Origin of Inequality" or the so-called Second Discourse, can be criticized as "arm-chair anthropology," with essentially no relationship to actual facts; our interest, however, is not so much in the scientific validity of Rousseau's thesis as in understanding it, because it embodies such an influential view of human nature. Note that although Rousseau was doubtless naive in his idealization of human life in a "state of nature," he took a very dim view of human life in society; in his view, the fault lay with *society,* not with human nature itself.

I conceive two species of inequality among men; one which I call natural, or physical inequality, because it is established by nature, and consists in the difference of age, health, bodily strength, and the qualities of the mind, or of the soul; the other which may be termed moral, or political inequality, because it depends on a kind of convention, and is established, or at least authorized, by the common consent of mankind. This species of inequality consists in the different privileges, which some men enjoy, to the prejudice of others, such as that of being richer, more honoured, more powerful, and even that of exacting obedience from them.

It were absurd to ask, what is the cause of natural inequality, seeing the bare definition of natural inequality answers the question: it would be more absurd still to enquire, if there might not be some essential connection between the two species of inequality, as it would be asking, in other words, if those who command are necessarily better men than those who obey; and if strength of body or of mind, wisdom or virtue are always to be found in individuals, in the same proportion with power, or riches: a question, fit perhaps to be discussed by slaves in the hearing of their masters, but unbecoming free and reasonable beings in quest of truth.

What therefore is precisely the subject of this discourse? It is to point out, in the progress of things, that moment, when, right taking place of violence, nature became subject to law; to display that chain of surprising events, in consequence of which the strong submitted to serve the weak, and the people to purchase imaginary ease, at the expense of real happiness.

The philosophers, who have examined the foundations of society, have, every one of them, perceived the necessity of tracing it back to a state of nature, but not one of them has ever arrived there. Some of them have not scrupled to attribute to man in that state the ideas of justice and injustice, without troubling their heads to prove, that he really must have had such ideas, or even that such ideas were useful to him: others have spoken of the natural right of every man to keep what belongs to him, without letting us know what they meant by the word belong; others, without further ceremony ascribing to the strongest an authority over the weakest, have immediately struck out government, without thinking of the time requisite for men to form any notion of the things signified by the words authority and government. All of them, in fine, constantly harping on wants, avidity, oppression, desires and pride, have transferred to the state of nature ideas picked up in the bosom of society. In speaking of savages they described citizens. Nay, few of our own writers seem to have so much as doubted, that a state of nature did once actually exist; though it plainly appears by Sacred History, that even the first man, immediately furnished as he was by God himself with both instructions and precepts, never lived in that state, and that, if we give to the books of Moses that credit which every Christian philosopher ought to give to them, we must deny that, even before the deluge, such a state ever existed among men, unless they fell into it by some extraordinary event: a paradox very difficult to maintain, and altogether impossible to prove.

Let us begin therefore, by laying aside facts, for they do not affect the question. The researches, in which we may engage on this occasion, are not to be taken for historical truths, but merely as hypothetical and conditional reasonings, fitter to illustrate the nature of things, than to show their true origin, . . .

However important it may be, in order to form a proper judgment of the natural state of man, to consider him from his origin, and to examine him, as it were, in the first embryo of the species; I shall not attempt to trace his organization through its successive approaches to perfection: I shall not stop to examine in the animal system what he might have been in the beginning, to become at last what he actually is; I shall not inquire whether, as Aristotle thinks, his neglected nails were no better at first than crooked talons; whether his whole body was not, bear-like, thick covered with rough hair; and whether, walking upon all-fours, his eyes, directed to the earth, and confined to a horizon of a few paces extent, did not at once point out the nature and limits of his ideas. I could only form vague, and almost imaginary, conjectures on this subject. Comparative anatomy has not as yet been sufficiently improved; neither have the observations of natural philosophy been sufficiently ascertained, to establish upon such foundations the basis of a solid system. For this reason, without having recourse to the supernatural informations with which we have been favoured on this head, or paying any attention to the changes, that must have happened in the conformation of the interior and exterior parts of man's body, in proportion as he applied his members to new purposes, and took to new aliments, I shall suppose his conformation to have always been, what we now behold it; that he always walked on two feet, made the same use of his hands that we do of ours, extended his looks over the whole face of nature, and measured with his eyes the vast extent of the heavens.

If I strip this being, thus constituted, of all the supernatural gifts which he may have received, and of all the artificial faculties, which we could not have acquired but by slow degrees; if I consider him, in a word, such as he must have issued from the hands of nature; I see an animal less strong than some, and less active than others, but, upon the whole, the most advantageously organized of any; I see him satisfying the calls of hunger under the first oak, and those of thirst at the first rivulet; I see him laying himself down to sleep at the foot of the same tree that afforded him his meal; and behold, this done, all his wants are completely supplied.

The earth left to its own natural fertility and covered with immense woods, that no hatchet ever disfigured, offers at every step food and shelter to every species of animals. Men, dispersed among them, observe and imitate their industry, and thus rise to the instinct of beasts; with this advantage, that, whereas every species of beasts is confined to one peculiar instinct, man, who perhaps has not any that particularly belongs to him, appropriates to himself those of all other animals, and lives equally upon most of the different aliments, which they only divide among themselves; a circumstance which qualifies him to find his subsistence, with more ease than any of them.

Men, accustomed from their infancy to the inclemency of the weather, and to the rigour of the different seasons; inured to fatigue, and obliged to defend, naked and without arms, their life and their prey against the other wild inhabitants of the forest, or at least to avoid their fury by flight, acquire a robust and almost unalterable habit of body; the children, bringing with them into the world the excellent constitution of their parents, and strengthening it by the same exercises that first produced it, attain by this means all the vigour that the human frame is capable of. Nature treats them exactly in the same manner that Sparta treated the children of her citizens; those who come well formed into the world she renders strong and robust, and destroys all the rest; differing in this respect from our societies, in which the state, by permitting children to become burdensome to their parents, murders them all without distinction, even in the wombs of their mothers.

The body being the only instrument that savage man is acquainted with, he employs it to different uses, of which ours, for want of practice, are incapable; and we may thank our industry for the loss of that strength and agility, which necessity obliges him to acquire. Had he a hatchet, would his hand so easily snap off from an oak so stout a branch? Had he a sling, would it dart a stone to so great a distance? Had he a ladder, would he run so nimbly up a tree? Had he a horse, would he with such swiftness shoot along the plain? Give civilized man but time to gather about him all his machines, and no doubt he will be an overmatch for the savage: but if you have a mind to see a contest still more unequal, place them naked and unarmed one opposite to the other; and you will soon discover the advantage there is in perpetually having all our forces at our disposal, in being constantly prepared against all events, and in always carrying ourselves, as it were, whole and entire about us. . . .

The extreme inequalities in the manner of living of the several classes of mankind, the excess of idleness in some, and of labour in others, the facility of irritating and satisfying our sensuality and our appetites, the too exquisite and out of the way aliments of the rich, which fill them with fiery juices, and bring on indigestions, the unwholesome food of the poor, of which even, bad as it is, they very often fall short, and the want of which tempts them, every opportunity that offers, to eat greedily and overload their stomachs; watchings, excesses of every kind, immoderate transports of all the passions, fatigues, waste of spirits, in a word, the numberless pains and anxieties annexed to every condition, and which the mind of man is constantly a prey to; these are the fatal proofs that most of our ills are of our own making, and that we might have avoided them all by adhering to the simple, uniform and solitary way of life prescribed to us by nature. Allowing that nature intended we should always enjoy good health, I dare almost affirm that a state of reflection is a state against nature, and that the man who meditates is a depraved animal. We need only call to mind the good constitution of savages, of those at least whom we have not destroyed by our strong liquors; we need only reflect, that they are strangers to almost every disease, except those occasioned by wounds and old age, to be in a manner convinced that the history of human diseases might be easily composed by pursuing that of civil societies. . . .

Let us therefore beware of confounding savage man with the men, whom we daily see and converse with. Nature behaves towards all animals left to her care with a predilection, that seems to prove how jealous she is of that prerogative. The horse, the cat, the bull, nay the ass itself, have generally a higher stature, and always a more robust constitution, more vigour, more strength and courage in their forests than in our houses; they lose half these advantages by becoming domestic animals; it looks as if all our attention to treat them kindly, and to feed them well, served only to bastardize them. It is thus with man himself. In proportion as he becomes sociable and a slave to others, he becomes weak, fearful, mean-spirited, and his soft and effeminate way of living at once completes the enervation of his strength and of his courage. We may add, that there must be still a wider difference between man and man in a savage and domestic condition, than between beast and beast; for as men and beasts have been treated alike by nature, all the conveniences with which men indulge themselves more than they do the beasts tamed by them, are so many particular causes which make them degenerate more sensibly.

Nakedness therefore, the want of houses, and of all these unnecessaries, which we consider as so very necessary, are not such mighty evils in respect to these primitive men, and much less still any obstacle to their preservation. Their skins, it is true, are destitute of hair; but then they have no occasion for any such covering in warm climates; and in cold climates they soon learn to apply to that use those of the animals they have conquered. . . .

But though the difficulties, in which all these questions are involved, should leave some room to dispute on this difference between man and beast, there is another very specific quality that distinguishes them, and a quality which will admit of no dispute; this is the faculty of improvement; a faculty which, as circumstances offer, successively unfolds all the other faculties, and resides among us not only in the species, but in the individuals that compose it; whereas a beast is, at the end of some months, all he ever will be during the rest of his life; and his species, at the end of a thousand years, precisely what it was the first year of that long period. Why is man alone subject to dotage? Is it not, because he thus returns to his primitive condition? And because, while the beast, which has acquired nothing and has likewise nothing to lose, continues always in possession of his instinct, man, losing by old age, or by accident, all the acquisitions he had made in consequence of his perfectibility, thus falls back even lower than beasts themselves? It would be a melancholy necessity for us to be obliged to allow, that this distinctive and almost unlimited faculty is the source of all man's misfortunes; that it is this faculty, which, though by slow degrees, draws them out of their original condition, in which his days would slide away insensibly in peace and innocence; that it is this faculty, which, in a succession of ages, produces his discoveries and mistakes, his virtues and his vices, and, at long run, renders him both his own and nature's tyrant. . . .

It appears at first sight that, as there was no kind of moral relations between men in this state, nor any known duties, they could not be either good or bad, and had neither vices nor virtues, unless we take these words in a physical sense, and call vices, in the individual, the qualities which may prove detrimental to his own preservation, and virtues those which may contribute to it; in which case we should be obliged to consider him as most virtuous, who made least resistance against the simple impulses of nature. But without deviating from the usual meaning of these terms, it is proper to suspend the judgment we might form of such a situation, and be upon our guard against prejudice, till, the balance in hand, we have examined whether there are more virtues or vices among civilized men; or whether the improvement of their understanding is sufficient to compensate the damage which they mutually do to each other, in proportion as they become better informed of the services which they ought to do; or whether, upon the whole, they would not be much happier in a condition, where they had nothing to fear or to hope from each other, than in that where they had submitted to an universal subserviency, and have obliged themselves to depend for everything upon the good will of those, who do not think themselves obliged to give anything in return.

But above all things let us beware concluding with Hobbes, that man, as having no idea of goodness, must be naturally bad; that he is vicious because he does not know what virtue is; that he always refuses to do any service to those of his own species, because he believes that none is due to them; that, in virtue of that right which he justly claims to everything he wants, he foolishly looks upon himself as proprietor of the whole universe. Hobbes very plainly saw the flaws in all the modern definitions of natural right: but the consequences, which he draws from his own definition, show that it is, in the sense he understands it, equally exceptionable. This author, to argue from his own principles, should say that the state of nature, being that where the care of our own preservation interferes least with the preservation of others, was of course the most favourable to peace, and most suitable to mankind; whereas he advances the very reverse in consequence of his having injudiciously admitted, as objects of that care which savage man should take of his preservation, the satisfaction of numberless passions which are the work of society, and have rendered laws necessary. A bad man, says he, is a robust child. But this is not proving that savage man is a robust child; and though we were to grant that he was, what could this philosopher infer from such a concession? That if this man, when robust, depended on others as much as when feeble, there is no excess that he would not be guilty of. He would make nothing of striking his mother when she delayed ever so little to give him the breast; he would claw, and bite, and strangle without remorse the first of his younger brothers, that ever so accidentally jostled or otherwise disturbed him. But these are two contradictory suppositions in the state of nature, to be robust and dependent. Man is weak when dependent, and his own master before he grows robust. Hobbes did not consider that the same cause, which hinders savages from making use of their reason, as our jurisconsults pretend, hinders them at the same time from making an ill use of their faculties, as he himself pretends; so that we may say that savages are not bad, precisely because they don't know what it is to be good; for it is neither the development of the understanding, nor the curb of the law, but the calmness of their passions and their ignorance of vice that hinders them from doing ill: *tantus plus in illis proficit vitiorum ignorantia, quam in his cognito virtutis.* There is besides another principle that has escaped Hobbes, and which, having been given to man to moderate, on certain occasions, the blind and impetuous sallies of self-love, or the desire of self-preservation previous to the appearance of that passion, allays the ardour, with which he naturally pursues his private welfare, by an innate abhorrence to see beings suffer that resemble him. I shall not surely be contradicted, in granting to man the only natural virtue, which the most passionate detractor of human virtues could not deny him, I mean that of pity, a disposition suitable to creatures weak as we are, and liable to so many evils; a virtue so much the more universal, and withal useful to man, as it takes place in him of all manner of reflection; and so natural, that the beasts themselves sometimes give evident signs of it. Not to speak of the tenderness of mothers for their young; and of the dangers they face to screen them from danger; with what reluctance are horses known to trample upon living bodies. . . .

It is reason that engenders self-love, and reflection that strengthens it; it is reason that makes man shrink into himself; it is reason that makes him keep aloof from everything that can trouble or afflict him: it is philosophy that destroys his connections with other men; it is in consequence of her dictates that he mutters to himself at the sight of another in distress, You may perish for aught I care, nothing can hurt me. Nothing less than those evils, which threaten the whole species, can disturb the calm sleep of the philosopher, and force him from his bed. One man may with impunity murder another under his windows; he has nothing to do but clap his hands to his ears, argue a little with himself to hinder nature, that startles within him, from identifying him with the unhappy sufferer. Savage man wants this admirable talent; and for want of wisdom and reason, is always ready foolishly to obey the first whispers of humanity. In riots and street-brawls the populace flock together, the prudent man sneaks off. They are the dregs of the people, the poor basket and barrow-women, that part the combatants, and hinder gentle folks from cutting one another's throats.

It is therefore certain that pity is a natural sentiment, which, by moderating in every individual the activity of self-love, contributes to the mutual preservation of the whole species. It is this pity which hurries us without reflection to the assistance of those we see in distress; it is this pity which, in a state of nature, stands for laws, for manners, for virtue, with this advantage, that no one is tempted to disobey her sweet and gentle voice: it is this pity which will always hinder a robust savage from plundering a feeble child, or infirm old man, of the subsistence they have acquired with pain and difficulty, if he has but the least prospect of providing for himself by any other means: it is this pity which, instead of that sublime maxim of argumentative justice, Do to others as you would have others do to you, inspires all men with that other maxim of natural goodness a great deal less perfect, but perhaps more useful, Consult your own happiness with as little prejudice as you can to that of others. It is in a word, in this natural sentiment, rather than in fine-spun arguments, that we must look for the cause of that reluctance which every man would experience to do evil, even independently of the maxims of education. Though it may be the peculiar happiness of Socrates and other geniuses of his stamp, to reason themselves into virtue, the human species would long ago have ceased to exist, had it depended entirely for its preservation on the reasonings of the individuals that compose it.

With passions so tame, and so salutary a curb, men, rather wild than wicked, and more attentive to guard against mischief than to do any to other animals, were not exposed to any dangerous dissensions: As they kept up no manner of correspondence with each other, and were of course strangers to vanity, to respect, to esteem, to contempt; as they had no notion of what we call Meum and Tuum, nor any true idea of justice; as they considered any violence they were liable to, as an evil that could be easily repaired, and not as an injury that deserved punishment; and as they never so much as dreamed of revenge, unless perhaps mechanically and unpremeditatedly, as a dog who bites the stone that has been thrown at him; their disputes could seldom be attended with bloodshed, were they never occasioned by a more considerable stake than that of subsistence: but there is a more dangerous subject of contention, which I must not leave unnoticed.

Among the passions which ruffle the heart of man, there is one of a hot and impetuous nature, which renders the sexes necessary to each other; a terrible passion which despises all dangers, bears down all obstacles, and to which in its transports it seems proper to destroy the human species which it is destined to preserve. What must become of men abandoned to this lawless and brutal rage, without modesty, without shame, and every day disputing the objects of their passion at the expense of their blood? . . .

Let us conclude that savage man, wandering about in the forests, without industry, without speech, without any fixed residence, an equal stranger to war and every social connection, without standing in any shape in need of his fellows, as well as without any desire of hurting them, and perhaps even without ever distinguishing them individually one from the other, subject to few passions, and finding in himself all he wants, let us, I say, conclude that savage man thus circumstanced had no knowledge or sentiment but such as are proper to that condition, that he was alone sensible of his real necessities, took notice of nothing but what it was his interest to see, and that his understanding made as little progress as his vanity. If he happened to make any discovery, he could the less communicate it as he did not even know his children. The art perished with the inventor; there was neither education nor improvement; generations succeeded generations to no purpose; and as all constantly set out from the same point, whole centuries rolled on in the rudeness and barbarity of the first age; the species was grown old, while the individual still remained in a state of childhood.

If I have enlarged so much upon the supposition of this primitive condition, it is because I thought it my duty, considering what ancient errors and inveterate prejudices I have to extirpate, to dig to the very roots, and show in a true picture of the state of nature, how much even natural inequality falls short in this state of that reality and influence which our writers ascribe to it.

In fact, we may easily perceive that among the differences, which distinguish men, several pass for natural, which are merely the work of habit and the different kinds of life adopted by men living in a social way. Thus a robust or delicate constitution, and the strength and weakness which depend on it, are oftener produced by the hardy or effeminate manner in which a man has been brought up, than by the primitive constitution of his body. It is the same thus in regard to the forces of the mind; and education not only produces a difference between those minds which are cultivated and those which are not, but even increases that which is found among the first in proportion to their culture; for let a giant and a dwarf set out in the same path, the giant at every step will acquire a new advantage over the dwarf. Now, if we compare the prodigious variety in the education and manner of living of the different orders of men in a civil state, with the simplicity and uniformity that prevails in the animal and savage life, where all the individuals make use of the same aliments, live in the same manner, and do exactly the same things, we shall easily conceive how much the difference between man and man in the state of nature must be less than in the state of society, and how much every inequality of institution must increase the natural inequalities of the human species.

But though nature in the distribution of her gifts should really affect all the preferences that are ascribed to her, what advantage could the most favoured derive from her partiality, to the prejudice of others, in a state of things, which scarce admitted any kind of relation between her pupils? Of what service can beauty be, where there is no love? What will wit avail people who don't speak, or craft those who have no affairs to transact? Authors are constantly crying out, that the strongest would oppress the weakest; but let them explain what they mean by the word oppression. One man will rule with violence, another will groan under a constant subjection to all his caprices: this is indeed precisely what I observe among us, but I don't see how it can be said of savage men, into whose heads it would be a harder matter to drive even the meaning of the words domination and servitude. One man might, indeed, seize on the fruits which another had gathered, on the game which another had killed, on the cavern which another had occupied for shelter; but how is it possible he should ever exact obedience from him, and what chains of dependence can there be among men who possess nothing? If I am driven from one tree, I have nothing to do but look out for another; if one place is made uneasy to me, what can hinder me from taking up my quarters elsewhere? But suppose I should meet a man so much superior to me in strength, and withal so wicked, so lazy and so barbarous as to oblige me to provide for his subsistence while he remains idle; he must resolve not to take his eyes from me a single moment, to bind me fast before he can take the least nap, lest I should kill him or give him the slip during his sleep: that is to say, he must expose himself voluntarily to much greater troubles than what he seeks to avoid, than any he gives me. And after all, let him abate ever so little of his vigilance; let him at some sudden noise but turn his head another way; I am already buried in the forest, my fetters are broke, and he never sees me again.

But without insisting any longer upon these details, every one must see that, as the bonds of servitude are formed merely by the mutual dependence of men one upon another and the reciprocal necessities which unite them, it is impossible for one man to enslave another, without having first reduced him to a condition in which he can not live without the enslaver's assistance; a condition which, as it does not exist in a state of nature, must leave every man his own master, and render the law of the strongest altogether vain and useless.

Having proved that the inequality, which may subsist between man and man in a state of nature, is almost imperceivable, and that it has very little influence, I must now proceed to show its origin, and trace its progress, in the successive developments of the human mind. After having showed, that perfectibility, the social virtues, and the other faculties, which natural man had received *in potentia*, could never be developed of themselves, that for that purpose there was a necessity for the fortuitous concurrence of several foreign causes, which might never happen, and without which he must have eternally remained in his primitive condition; I must proceed to consider and bring together the different accidents which may have perfected the human understanding by debasing the species, render a being wicked by rendering him sociable, and from so remote a term bring man at last and the world to the point in which we now see them. . . .

The first man, who, after enclosing a piece of ground, took it into his head to say, "This is mine," and found people simple enough to believe him, was the true founder of civil society. How many crimes, how many wars, how many murders, how many misfortunes and horrors, would that man have saved the human species, who pulling up the stakes or filling up the ditches should have cried to his fellows: Be sure not to listen to this imposter; you are lost, if you forget that the fruits of the earth belong equally to us all, and the earth itself to nobody! But it is highly probable that things were now come to such a pass, that they could not continue much longer in the same way; for as this idea of property depends on several prior ideas which could only spring up gradually one after another, it was not formed all at once in the human mind: men must have made great progress; they must have acquired a great stock of industry and knowledge, and transmitted and increased it from age to age before they could arrive at this last term of the state of nature. Let us therefore take up things a little higher, and collect into one point of view, and in their most natural order, this slow succession of events and mental improvements.

The first sentiment of man was that of his existence, his first care that of preserving it. The productions of the earth yielded him all the assistance he required; instinct prompted him to make use of them. Among the various appetites, which made him at different times experience different modes of existence, there was one that excited him to perpetuate his species; and this blind propensity, quite void of anything like pure love or affection, produced nothing but an act that was merely animal. The present heat once allayed, the sexes took no further notice of each other, and even the child ceased to have any tie in his mother, the moment he ceased to want her assistance.

Such was the condition of infant man; such was the life of an animal confined at first to pure sensations, and so far from harbouring any thought of forcing her gifts from nature, that he scarcely availed himself of those which she offered to him of her own accord. But difficulties soon arose, and there was a necessity for learning how to surmount them: the height of some trees, which prevented his reaching their fruits; the competition of other animals equally fond of the same fruits; the fierceness of many that even aimed at his life; these were so many circumstances, which obliged him to apply to bodily exercise. There was a necessity for becoming active, swift-footed, and sturdy in battle. The natural arms, which are stones and the branches of trees, soon offered themselves to his assistance. He learned to surmount the obstacles of nature, to contend in case of necessity with other animals, to dispute his subsistence even with other men, or indemnify himself for the loss of whatever he found himself obliged to part with to the strongest.

In proportion as the human species grew more numerous, and extended itself, its pains likewise multiplied and increased. The difference of soils, climates and seasons, might have forced men to observe some difference in their way of living. Bad harvests, long and severe winters, and scorching summers which parched up all the fruits of the earth, required extraordinary exertions of industry. On the sea shore, and the banks of rivers, they invented the line and the hook, and became fishermen and ichthyophagous. In the forests they made themselves bows and arrows, and became huntsmen and warriors. In the cold countries they covered themselves with the skins of the beasts they had killed; thunder, a volcano, or some happy accident made them acquainted with fire, a new resource against the rigours of winter: they discovered the method of preserving this element, then that of reproducing it, and lastly the way of preparing with it the flesh of animals, which heretofore they devoured raw from the carcass.

This reiterated application of various beings to himself, and to one another, must have naturally engendered in the mind of man the idea of certain relations. These relations, which we express by the words, great, little, strong, weak, swift, slow, fearful, bold, and the like, compared occasionally, and almost without thinking of it, produced in him some kind of reflection, or rather a mechanical prudence, which pointed out to him the precautions most essential to his preservation and safety. . . .

Everything now begins to wear a new aspect. Those who heretofore wandered through the woods, by taking to a more settled way of life, gradually flock together, coalesce into several separate bodies, and at length form in every country distinct nations, united in character and manners, not by any laws or regulations, but by an uniform manner of life, a sameness of provisions, and the common influence of the climate. A permanent neighborhood must at last infallibly create some connection between different families. The transitory commerce required by nature soon produced, among the youth of both sexes living in contiguous cabins, another kind of commerce, which besides being equally agreeable is rendered more durable by mutual intercourse. Men begin to consider different objects, and to make comparisons; they insensibly acquire ideas of merit and beauty, and these soon produce sentiments of preference. By seeing each other often they contract a habit, which makes it painful not to see each other always. Tender and agreeable sentiments steal into the soul, and are by the smallest opposition wound up into the most impetuous fury: Jealousy kindles with love; discord triumphs; and the gentlest of passions requires sacrifices of human blood to appease it.

In proportion as ideas and sentiments succeed each other, and the head and the heart exercise themselves, men continue to shake off their original wildness, and their connections become more intimate and extensive. They now begin to assemble round a great tree: singing and dancing, the genuine offspring of love and leisure, become the amusement or rather the occupation of the men and women, free from care, thus gathered together. Every one begins to survey the rest, and wishes to be surveyed himself; and public esteem acquires a value. He who sings or dances best; the handsomest, the strongest, the most dexterous, the most eloquent, comes to be the most respected: this was the first step towards inequality, and at the same time towards vice. From these first preferences there proceeded on one side vanity and contempt, on the other envy and shame; and the fermentation raised by these new leavens at length produced combinations fatal to happiness and innocence.

Men no sooner began to set a value upon each other, and know what esteem was, than each laid claim to it, and it was no longer safe for any man to refuse it to another. Hence the first duties of civility and politeness, even among savages; and hence every voluntary injury became an affront, as besides the mischief, which resulted from it as an injury, the party offended was sure to find in it a contempt for his person more intolerable than the mischief itself. It was thus that every man, punishing the contempt expressed for him by others in proportion to the value he set upon himself, the effects of revenge became terrible and men learned to be sanguinary and cruel. . . .

But we must take notice, that the society now formed and the relations now established among men required in them qualities different from those, which they derived from their primitive constitution; that as a sense of morality began to insinuate itself into human actions, and every man, before the enacting of laws, was the only judge and avenger of the injuries he had received, that goodness of heart suitable to the pure state of nature by no means suited infant society; that it was necessary punishments should become severer in the same proportion that the opportunities of offending became more frequent, and the dread of vengeance add strength to the too weak curb of the law. Thus, though men were become less patient, and natural compassion had already suffered some alteration, this period of the development of the human faculties, holding a just mean between the indolence of the primitive state, and the petulant activity of self-love, must have been the happiest and most durable epoch. The more we reflect on this state, the more convinced we shall be, that it was the least subject of any to revolutions, the best for man, and that nothing could have drawn him out of it but some fatal accident, which, for the public good, should never have happened. The example of the savages, most of whom have been found in this condition, seems to confirm that mankind was formed ever to remain in it, that this condition is the real youth of the world, and that all ulterior improvements have been so many steps, in appearance towards the perfection of individuals, but in fact towards the decrepitness of the species.

As long as men remained satisfied with their rustic cabins; as long as they confined themselves to the use of clothes made of the skins of other animals, and the use of thorns and fish-bones, in putting these skins together; as long as they continued to consider feathers and shells as sufficient ornaments, and to paint their bodies of different colours, to improve or ornament their bows and arrows, to form and scoop out with sharp-edged stones some little fishing boats, or clumsy instruments of music; in a word, as long as they undertook such works only as a single person would finish, and stuck to such arts as did not require the joint endeavours of several hands, they lived free, healthy, honest and happy, as much as their nature would admit, and continued to enjoy with each other all the pleasures of an independent intercourse; but from the moment one man began to stand in need of another's assistance; from the moment it appeared an advantage for one man to possess the quantity of provisions requisite for two, all equality vanished; property started up; labour became necessary; and boundless forests became smiling fields, which it was found necessary to water with human sweat, and in which slavery and misery were soon seen to sprout out and grow with the fruits of the earth. . . .

Such was, or must have been, had man been left to himself, the origin of society and of the laws, which increased the fetters of the weak, and the strength of the rich; irretrievably destroyed natural liberty, fixed for ever the laws of property and inequality; changed an artful usurpation into an irrevocable title; and for the benefit of a few ambitious individuals subjected the rest of mankind to perpetual labour, servitude, and misery. We may easily conceive how the establishment of a single society rendered that of all the rest absolutely necessary, and how, to make head against united forces, it became necessary for the rest of mankind to unite in their turn. Societies once formed in this manner, soon multiplied or spread to such a degree, as to cover the face of the earth; and not to leave a corner in the whole universe, where a man could throw off the yoke, and withdraw his head from under the often ill-conducted sword which he saw perpetually hanging over it.*

KROPOTKIN

Peter Kropotkin (1842–1921) is an oxymoron: an anarchist prince! A renowned geographer, zoologist, and historian, he achieved his greatest fame as the leading theorist of the anarchist movement, both in his native Russia and in Europe, to which he fled in the 1880s. A person's perspective on human nature is often influenced by his or her personal political leanings (and vice versa). In Kropotkin's case, opposition to governments and devotion to small-scale social networks as both more desirable and "more human" led him to dispute the role of competition and to emphasize the importance of cooperation. His masterpiece, *Mutual Aid*, presents many examples of sociability and cooperation among animals as well as human beings.

Ironically, a revised edition of *Mutual Aid* appeared in 1914, as the ravages of World War

*From *The Second Discourse* (1910). (Trans. P. Eckler). New York: Collier.

I were beginning. In a dramatic example of seeing a glass half-full instead of half-empty, Kropotkin wrote in his preface to that edition,

> The peasant women who, on seeing German and Austrian war prisoners wearily trudging through the streets of Kiev, thrust into their hands bread, apples, and occasionally a copper coin; the thousands of women and men who attend the wounded, without making any distinction between friend and foe . . . all these facts and many more similar ones are the seeds of new forms of life. They will lead to new institutions, just as mutual aid in the earlier ages of mankind gave origin later on to the best progressive institutions of civilized society.

The following selections are from the text of *Mutual Aid: A Factor of Evolution.*

The immense part played by mutual aid and mutual support in the evolution of the animal world has been briefly analysed in the preceding chapters. We have now to cast a glance upon the part played by the same agencies in the evolution of mankind. We saw how few are the animal species which live an isolated life, and how numberless are those which live in societies, either for mutual defence, or for hunting and storing up food, or for rearing their offspring, or simply for enjoying life in common. We also saw that, though a good deal of warfare goes on between different classes of animals, or different species, or even different tribes of the same species, peace and mutual support are the rule within the tribe or the species; and that those species which best know how to combine, and to avoid competition, have the best chances of survival and of a further progressive development. They prosper, while the unsociable species decay.

It is evident that it would be quite contrary to all that we know of nature if men were an exception to so general a rule: if a creature so defenceless as man was at his beginnings should have found his protection and his way to progress, not in mutual support, like other animals, but in a reckless competition for personal advantages, with no regard to the interests of the species. To a mind accustomed to the idea of unity in nature, such a proposition appears utterly indefensible. And yet, improbable and unphilosophical as it is, it has never found a lack of supporters. There always were writers who took a pessimistic view of mankind. They knew it, more or less superficially, through their own limited experience; they knew of history what the annalists, always watchful of wars, cruelty and oppression, told of it, and little more besides; and they concluded that mankind is nothing but a loose aggregation of beings, always ready to fight with each other, and only prevented from so doing by the intervention of some authority.

Hobbes took that position; and while some of his eighteenth-century followers endeavoured to prove that at no epoch of its existence—not even in its most primitive condition—mankind lived in a state of perpetual warfare; that men have been sociable even in 'the state of nature', and that want of knowledge, rather than the natural bad inclinations of man, brought humanity to all the horrors of its early historical life,—his idea was, on the contrary, that the so-called 'state of nature' was nothing but a permanent fight between individuals, accidentally huddled together by the mere caprice of their bestial existence. True, that science has made some progress since Hobbes's time, and that we have safer ground to stand upon than the speculations of Hobbes or Rousseau. But the Hobbesian philosophy has plenty of admirers still; and we have had of late quite a school of writers who, taking possession of Darwin's terminology rather than of his leading ideas, made of it an argument in favour of Hobbes's views upon primitive man, and even succeeded in giving them a scientific appearance. Huxley, as is known, took the lead of that school, and in a paper written in 1888 he represented primitive men as a sort of tigers or lions, deprived of all ethical conceptions, fighting out the struggle for existence to its bitter end, and living a life of 'continual free fight'; to quote his own words—'beyond the limited and temporary relations of the family, the Hobbesian war of each against all was the normal state of existence'. . . .

Far from being a primitive form of organization, the family is a very late product of human evolution. As far as we can go back in the palaeo-ethnology of mankind, we find men living in societies—in tribes similar to those of the highest mammals; and an extremely slow and long evolution was required to bring these societies to the gentile, or clan organization, which, in its turn, had to undergo another, also very long evolution, before the first germs of family, polygamous or monogamous, could appear. Societies, bands, or tribes—not families—were thus the primitive form of organization of mankind and its earliest ancestors. That is what ethnology has come to after its painstaking researches. And in so doing it simply came to what might have been foreseen by the zoologist. None of the higher mammals, save a few carnivores and a few undoubtedly decaying species of apes (orang-utans and gorillas), live in small families, isolatedly straggling in the woods. All others live in societies. And Darwin so well understood that isolately-living apes never could have developed into man-like beings, that he was inclined to consider man as descended from some comparatively weak *but social species*, like the chimpanzee, rather than from some stronger but unsociable species, like the gorilla. Zoology and palaeo-ethnology are thus agreed in considering that the band, not the family, was the earliest form of social life. The first human societies simply were a further development of those societies which constitute the very essence of life of the higher animals. . . .

It is not possible to study primitive mankind without being deeply impressed by the sociability it has displayed since its very first steps in life. Traces of human societies are found in the relics of both the oldest and the later stone age; and, when we come to observe the savages whose manners of life are still those of neolithic man, we find them closely bound together by an extremely ancient clan organization which enables them to combine their individually weak forces, to enjoy life in common, and to progress. Man is no exception in nature. He also is subject to the great principle of Mutual Aid which grants the best chances of survival to those who best support each other in the struggle for life. These were the conclusions arrived at in the previous chapters.

However, as soon as we come to a higher stage of civilization, and refer to history which already has something to say about that stage, we are bewildered by the struggles and conflicts which it reveals. The old bonds seem entirely to be broken. Stems are seen to fight against stems, tribes against tribes, individuals against individuals; and out of this chaotic contest of hostile forces, mankind issues divided into castes, enslaved to despots, separated into States always ready to wage war against each other. And, with this history of mankind in his hands, the pessimist philosopher triumphantly concludes that warfare and oppression are the very essence of human nature; that the warlike and predatory instincts of man can only be restrained within certain limits by a strong authority which enforces peace and thus gives an opportunity to the few and nobler ones to prepare a better life for humanity in times to come.

And yet, as soon as the everyday life of man during the historical period is submitted to a closer analysis—and so it has been, of late, by many patient students of very early institutions—it appears at once under quite a different aspect. Leaving aside the preconceived ideas of most historians and their pronounced predilection for the dramatic aspects of history, we see that the very documents they habitually peruse are such as to exaggerate the part of human life given to struggles and to underrate its peaceful moods. The bright and sunny days are lost sight of in the gales and storms. Even in our own time, the cumbersome records which we prepare for the future historian, in our Press, our law courts, our Government offices and even in our fiction and poetry, suffer from the same one-sidedness. They hand down to posterity the most minute descriptions of every war, every battle and skirmish, every contest and act of violence, every kind of individual suffering; but they hardly bear any trace of the countless acts of mutual support and devotion which every one of us knows from his own experience; they hardly take notice of what makes the very essence of our daily life—our social instincts and manners. No wonder, then, if the records of the past were so imperfect. The annalists of old never failed to chronicle the petty wars and calamities which harassed their contemporaries; but they paid no attention whatever to the life of the masses, although the masses chiefly used to toil peacefully while the few indulged in fighting. The epic poems, the inscriptions on monuments, the treaties of peace—nearly all historical documents bear the same character; they deal with breaches of peace, not with peace itself. So that the best-intentioned historian unconsciously draws a distorted picture of the times he endeavours to depict; and, to restore the real proportion between conflict and union, we are now bound to enter into a minute analysis of thousands of small facts and faint indications accidentally preserved in the relics of the past; to interpret them with the aid of comparative ethnology; and, after having heard so much about what used to divide men, to reconstruct stone by stone the institutions which used to unite them.

Ere long history will have to be rewritten on new lines, so as to take into account these two currents of human life and to appreciate the part played by each of them in evolution. But in the meantime we may avail ourselves of the immense preparatory work recently done towards restoring the leading features of the second current, so much neglected. From the better-known periods of history we may take some illustrations of the life of the masses, in order to indicate the part played by mutual support during those periods; and, in so doing, we may dispense (for the sake of brevity) from going as far back as the Egyptian, or even the Greek and Roman antiquity. For, in fact, the evolution of mankind has not had the character of one unbroken series. Several times civilization came to an end in one given region, with one given race, and began anew elsewhere, among other races. But at each fresh start it began again with the same clan institutions which we have seen among the savages. So that if we take the last start of our own civilization, when it began afresh in the first centuries of our era, among those whom the Romans called the 'barbarians', we shall have the whole scale of evolution, beginning with the gentes and ending in the institutions of our own time. To these illustrations the following pages will be devoted. . . .

Sociability and need of mutual aid and support are such inherent parts of human nature that at no time of history can we discover men living in small isolated families, fighting each other for the means of subsistence. On the contrary, modern research, as we saw it in the two preceding chapters, proves that since the very beginning of their prehistoric life men used to agglomerate into *gentes*, clans, or tribes, maintained by an idea of common descent and by worship of common ancestors. For thousands and thousands of years this organization has kept men together, even though there was no authority whatever to impose it. It has deeply impressed all subsequent development of mankind; and when the bonds of common descent had been loosened by migrations on a grand scale, while the development of the separated family within the clan itself had destroyed the old unity of the clan, a new form of union, territorial in its principle—the village community—was called into existence by the social genius of man. This institution, again, kept men together for a number of centuries, permitting them to further develop their social institutions and to pass through some of the darkest periods of history, without being dissolved into loose aggregations of families and individuals, to make a further step in their evolution, and to work out a number of secondary social institutions, several of which have survived down to the present time. We have now to follow the further developments of the same ever-living tendency for mutual aid. Taking the village communities of the so-called barbarians at a time when they were making a new start of civilization after the fall of the Roman Empire, we have to study the new aspects taken by the sociable wants of the masses in the middle ages, and especially in the medieval guilds and the medieval city.

Far from being the fighting animals they have often been compared to, the barbarians of the first centuries of our era (like so many Mongolians, Africans, Arabs, and so on, who still continue in the same barbarian stage) invariably preferred peace to war. With the exception of a few tribes which had been driven during the great migrations into unproductive deserts or highlands, and were thus compelled periodically to prey upon their better-favoured neighbours—apart from these, the great bulk of the Teutons, the Saxons, the Celts, the Slavonians, and so on, very soon after they had settled in their newly conquered abodes, reverted to the spade or to their herds. . . .

The fact is, that the slave-hunters, the ivory robbers, the fighting kings, the Matabele and the Madagascar 'heroes' pass away, leaving their traces marked with blood and fire; but the nucleus of mutual-aid institutions, habits and customs, grown up in the tribe and the village community, remains; and it keeps men united in societies, open to the progress of civilization, and ready to receive it when the day comes that they shall receive civilization instead of bullets.

The same applies to our civilized world. The natural and social calamities pass away. Whole populations are periodically reduced to misery or starvation; the very springs of life are crushed out of millions of men, reduced to city pauperism; the understanding and the feelings of the millions are vitiated by teachings worked out in the interest of the few. All this is certainly a part of our existence. But the nucleus of mutual-support institutions, habits and customs remains alive with the millions; it keeps them together; and they prefer to cling to their customs, beliefs and traditions rather than to accept the teachings of a war of each against all, which are offered to them under the title of science, but are no science at all. . . .

If we take now the teachings which can be borrowed from the analysis of modern society, in connection with the body of evidence relative to the importance of mutual aid in the evolution of the animal world and of mankind, we may sum up our inquiry as follows.

In the animal world we have seen that the vast majority of species live in societies, and that they find in association the best arms for the struggle for life: understood, of course, in its wide Darwinian sense—not as a struggle for the sheer means of existence, but as a struggle against all natural conditions unfavourable to the species. The animal species in which individual struggle has been reduced to its narrowest limits, and the practice of mutual aid has attained the greatest development are invariably the most numerous, the most prosperous and the most open to further progress. The mutual protection which is obtained in this case, the possibility of attaining old age and of accumulating experience, the higher intellectual development, and the further growth of sociable habits, secure the maintenance of the species, its extension, and its further progressive evolution. The unsociable species, on the contrary, are doomed to decay.

Going next over to man, we found him living in clans and tribes at the very dawn of the stone age; we saw a wide series of social institutions developed already in the lower savage stage, in the clan and the tribe; and we found that the earliest tribal customs and habits gave to mankind the embryo of all the institutions which made later on the leading aspects of further progress. Out of the savage tribe grew up the barbarian village community; and a new, still wider, circle of social customs, habits and institutions, numbers of which are still alive among ourselves, was developed under the principles of common possession of a given territory and common defence of it, under the jurisdiction of the village folkmote, and in the federation of villages belonging, or supposed to belong, to one stem. And when new requirements induced men to make a new start, they made it in the city, which represented a double network of territorial units (village communities), connected with guilds—these latter arising out of the common prosecution of a given art or craft, or for mutual support and defence. . . .

It will probably be remarked that mutual aid, even though it may represent one of the factors of evolution, covers nevertheless one aspect only of human relations; that by the side of this current, powerful though it may be, there is, and always has been, the other current—the self-assertion of the individual, not only in its efforts to attain personal or caste superiority, economical, political and spiritual, but also in its much more important although less evident function of breaking through the bonds, always prone to become crystallized, which the tribe, the village community, the city, and the State impose upon the individual. In other words, there is the self-assertion of the individual taken as a progressive element.

It is evident that no review of evolution can be complete, unless these two dominant currents are analysed. However, the self-assertion of the individual or of groups of individuals, their struggles for superiority, and the conflicts which resulted therefrom, have already been analysed, described, and glorified from time immemorial. In fact, up to the present time, this current alone has received attention from the epical poet, the annalist, the historian and the sociologist. History, such as it has hitherto been written, is almost entirely a description of the ways and means by which theocracy, military power, autocracy and, later on, the richer classes' rule have been promoted, established and maintained. The struggles between these forces make, in fact, the substance of history. We may thus take the knowledge of the individual factor in human history as granted—even though there is full room for a new study of the subject on the lines just alluded to; while, on the other side, the mutual-aid factor has been hitherto totally lost sight of; it was simply denied, or even scoffed at, by the writers of the present and past generation. It was therefore necessary to show, first of all, the immense part which this factor plays in the evolution of both the animal world and human societies. Only after this has been fully recognized will it be possible to proceed to a comparison between the two factors.

To make even a rough estimate of their relative importance by any method more or less statistical, is evidently impossible. One single war—we all know—may be productive of more evil, immediate and subsequent, than hundreds of years of the unchecked action of the mutual-aid principle may be productive of good. But when we see that in the animal world, progressive development and mutual aid go hand in hand, while the inner struggle within the species is concomitant with retrogressive development; when we notice that with man, even success in struggle and war is proportionate to the development of mutual aid in each of the two conflicting nations, cities, parties, or tribes, and that in the process of evolution war itself (so far as it can go this way) has been made subservient to the ends of progress in mutual aid within the nation, the city or the clan—we already obtain a perception of the dominating influence of the mutual-aid factor as an element of progress. But we see also that the practice of mutual aid and its successive developments have created the very conditions of society life in which man was enabled to develop his arts, knowledge and intelligence; and that the periods when institutions based on the mutual-aid tendency took their greatest development were also the periods of the greatest progress in arts, industry, and science. . . .

To attribute, therefore, the industrial progress of our century to the war of each against all which it has proclaimed, is to reason like the man who, knowing not the causes of rain, attributes it to the victim he has immolated before his clay idol. For industrial progress, as for each other conquest over nature, mutual aid and close intercourse certainly are, as they have been, much more advantageous than mutual struggle.

However, it is especially in the domain of ethics that the dominating importance of the mutual-aid principle appears in full. That mutual aid is the real foundation of our ethical conceptions seems evident enough. But whatever the opinions as to the first origin of the mutual-aid feeling or instinct may be—whether a biological or a supernatural cause is ascribed to it—we must trace its existence as far back as to the lowest stages of the animal world; and from these stages we can follow its uninterrupted evolution, in opposition to a number of contrary agencies, through all degrees of human development, up to the present times. Even the new religions which were born from time to time—always at epochs when the mutual-aid principle was falling into decay in the theocracies and despotic States of the East, or at the decline of the Roman Empire—even the new religions have only reaffirmed that same principle. They found their first supporters among the humble, in the lowest, downtrodden layers of society, where the mutual-aid principle is the necessary foundation of everyday life; and the new forms of union which were introduced in the earliest Buddhist and Christian communities, in the Moravian brotherhoods and so on, took the character of a return to the best aspects of mutual aid in early tribal life.

Each time, however, that an attempt to return to this old principle was made, its fundamental idea itself was widened. From the clan it was extended to the stem, to the federation of stems, to the nation, and finally—in ideal, at least—to the whole of mankind. It was also refined at the same time. In primitive Buddhism, in primitive Christianity, in the writings of some of the Mussulman teachers, in the early movements of the Reform, and especially in the ethical and philosophical movements of the last century and of our own times, the total abandonment of the idea of revenge, or of 'due reward'—of good for good and evil for evil—is affirmed more and more vigorously. The higher conception of 'no revenge for wrongs', and of freely giving more than one expects to receive from his neighbours, is proclaimed as being the real principle of morality—a principle superior to mere equivalence, equity, or justice, and more conducive to happiness. And man is appealed to to be guided in his acts, not merely by love, which is always personal, or at the best tribal, but by the perception of his oneness with each human being. In the practice of mutual aid, which we can retrace to the earliest beginnings of evolution, we thus find the positive and undoubted origin of our ethical conceptions; and we can affirm that in the ethical progress of man, mutual support—not mutual struggle—has had the leading part. In its wide extension, even at the present time, we also see the best guarantee of a still loftier evolution of our race.*

STUDY QUESTIONS

1. Rousseau sent a copy of the *Second Discourse* to Voltaire, who wrote back: "I have received, Monsieur, your new book against the human race. . . . You paint in very true colors the horrors of human society; . . . no one has ever employed so much intellect to persuade men to be beasts. In reading your work one is seized with a desire to walk on four paws. However, as it is more than sixty years since I lost that habit, I feel, unfortunately, that it is impossible for me to resume it. . . ." Did Voltaire misunderstand Rousseau?

2. "In spite of everything," wrote Anne Frank, in her *Diary of a Young Girl,* "I still believe that people are really good at heart. I simply can't build up my hope on a foundation consisting of confusion, misery and death." Such sentiments are especially poignant, given that Anne Frank and her family (along with millions of others) were subsequently killed by the Nazis. How would Rousseau have responded?

3. Compare views of human society and culture from this chapter with those presented in Chapter 9.

4. If people are naturally good, why do they often act so bad?

SOME ADDITIONAL READINGS

Hunt, Morton (1990). *The Compassionate Beast: What Science Is Discovering about the Humane Side of Humankind.* New York: Morrow.

Kohn, Alfie (1990). *The Brighter Side of Human Nature: Altruism and Empathy in Everyday Life.* New York: Basic Books.

*From *Mutual Aid: A Factor of Evolution* (1914; 1972). New York: New York University Press.

McFarland, Thomas (1995). *Romanticism and the Heritage of Rousseau.* New York: Oxford University Press.

Melzer, Arthur M. (1990). *The Natural Goodness of Man: On the System of Rousseau's Thought.* Chicago: University of Chicago Press.

Woodcock, George, and Avakumovic, Ivan (1990). *Peter Kropotkin: From Prince to Rebel.* Montreal: Black Rose Books.

CHAPTER ELEVEN

People Are Basically a Product of Their Cultures

The Greek historian Herodotus (485?–430? B.C.E.) tells the following story. Darius, king of Persia, was intrigued to learn that east of his empire, in India, the Callatians ostensibly cannibalized their dead. At the same time, he was told that to the west, the Greeks cremated theirs. Darius sent emissaries to each, asking what it would take to get them to switch practices. The Callatians responded indignantly that nothing would ever induce them to be so barbaric as to burn their deceased friends and relatives; at the same time, the Greeks were equally adamant that they would never eat theirs! Darius concluded that not he, but *custom* was king.

What we might call "Darius's Dictum" has persisted to this day in much of the social sciences, notably sociology and anthropology. Callatians and Greeks are both human, yet they behave very differently. The idea, then, is that to get to the root of human differences you must get to the root of custom, tradition, social learning, cultural expectations, social mores—all of the accumulated details of what people in society are induced to do and/or to refrain from doing, the elaborate trappings of rules, regulations, symbolic meaning, received wisdom, and complex teachings that make people Callatians or Greeks, Croatians or Greenlanders.

DURKHEIM

Some consider human behavior to be like those famous Russian dolls, or the layers of an onion: Different levels are contained each within the other. Thus, individual nerve cells would be among the innermost, whole civilizations would be outermost, with individual people and societies residing somewhere in between. For the French researcher and social theoretician Emile Durkheim (1858–1917), however, it is not possible to understand human social life by looking reductionistically at the next smaller level, that of the individual. Durkheim was among the first to emphasize the validity of studying what he called "social facts" as freestanding phenomena in their own right. He was also concerned that these facts must be understood at their own level of analysis. He emphasized that they cannot be derived, for example, from the study of human psychology: "a social fact can be explained only by another social fact."

Just as a half-century earlier, John Stuart Mill had argued that basic principles of human psychology could not be derived from the study of physiology or anatomy (even neurophysiology and neuroanatomy), Durkheim made the case that students of human social life must work at the level of social facts themselves rather than the details of individual psychology. At the same time, he acknowledged how difficult it is to look objectively at these facts, especially when the researcher is personally embedded in the society being studied.

In addition to his theoretical contributions—Durkheim was one of the founders of sociol-ogy—he conducted path-breaking research on religion and suicide. The following excerpt is from Durkheim's *Rules of Sociological Method.*

We assert not that social facts are material things but that they are things by the same right as material things, although they differ from them in type.

What, precisely, is a "thing"? A thing differs from an idea in the same way as that which we know from without differs from that which we know from within. Things include all objects of knowledge that can-not be conceived by purely mental activity, those that require for their conception data from outside the mind, from observations and experiments, those which are built up from the more external and imme-diately accessible characteristics to the less visible and more profound. To treat the facts of a certain order as things is not, then, to place them in a certain category of reality but to assume a certain mental atti-tude toward them on the principle that when approaching their study we are absolutely ignorant of their nature, and that their characteristic properties, like the unknown causes on which they depend, cannot be discovered by even the most careful introspection.

With the terms thus defined, our proposition, far from being a paradox, could almost pass for a tru-ism if it were not too often misinterpreted in the human sciences and especially in sociology. One might even say in this sense that, with the possible exception of mathematical units, every object of science is a thing. In mathematics, to proceed from the simplest to the most complex concepts we need only our own mental processes and analyses; but in the case of "facts" properly so called, these are, at the mo-ment when we undertake to study them scientifically, necessarily unknown things of which we are ig-norant; and any "representations" which we have been able to make of them in the course of our life, having been made without method and criticism, are devoid of scientific value, and must be distinguished from the scientific mentality. The facts of individual psychology are excellent examples of this distinc-tion, for although they are by definition purely mental, yet the consciousness we have of them reveals to us neither their nature nor their genesis. It permits us to know them up to a certain point, just as our sensations give us a certain familiarity with heat or light, sound or electricity; it gives us confused, fleet-ing, subjective impressions of them but no clear and scientific notions or explanatory concepts. It is pre-cisely for this reason that there has been founded in the course of this century an objective psychology whose fundamental purpose is to study mental facts from the outside, that is, as things.

Such a procedure is all the more necessary with social facts, for consciousness is even more helpless in knowing them than in knowing its own life. The objection will be raised that, since social facts are our own personal constructs, we have only to resort to introspection in order to determine what we put into them and how we formed them. But we must remember that the greater part of our social institutions was bequeathed to us by former generations. We ourselves took no part in their formation, and conse-quently we cannot by introspection discover the causes which brought them about. Furthermore, even when we have collaborated in their genesis, we can only with difficulty obtain even a confused and in-exact insight into the true nature of our action and the causes which determined it. When it is simply a matter of our private acts, we know very imperfectly the relatively simple motives that guide us. We be-lieve ourselves disinterested when we act egoistically; we think we are motivated by hate when we are yielding to love, and obeying reason when we are the slaves of unreasoned prejudices, etc. How, then, should we have the faculty of discerning with greater clarity the causes, otherwise complex, from which collective acts proceed? For, at the very least, each one of us participates in them only as an infinitesimal unit; we have a multitude of collaborators, and what takes place in other consciousnesses escapes us.

Our principle, then, implies no metaphysical conception, no speculation about the fundamental nature of beings. What it demands is that the sociologist put himself in the same state of mind as the physicist, chemist, or physiologist when he probes into a still unexplored region of the scientific domain. When he penetrates the social world, he must be aware that he is penetrating the unknown; he must feel himself in the presence of facts whose laws are as unsuspected as were those of life before the era of biology; he must be prepared for discoveries which will surprise and disturb him. Sociology is far from having arrived at this degree of intellectual maturity. While the scientist who studies physical nature is very keenly aware of the resistance it offers him, and which he has so much difficulty in overcoming, the sociologist seems to move in a sphere perfectly transparent to his view, so great is the ease with which the most obscure questions are resolved. In the present state of the science we really do not even know what are the principal social institutions, such as the state, or the family; what is the right of property or contract, of punishment and responsibility. We are almost completely ignorant of the factors on which they depend, the functions they fulfil, the laws of their development; we are scarcely beginning to shed even a glimmer of light on some of these points. Yet one has only to glance through the works on sociology to see how rare is the appreciation of this ignorance and these difficulties. Not only do social theorists consider themselves at once obliged to dogmatize on all problems, but they find themselves able to set forth in a few pages or phrases the very essence of the most complex phenomena. Theorizing of this sort cannot have its source in facts, for facts could not be so quickly disposed of; it springs from the prejudices which the author held prior to his research. To be sure, each man's individual conception of what our social customs are, or what they ought to be, is itself a factor in their development. But these conceptions in turn are additional facts which must be properly identified and studied objectively. The important thing to know is not the way in which a certain thinker individually conceives a certain institution but the group's conception of it; this conception alone is socially significant. Nor can this conception be arrived at by simple introspection, since it does not exist in its entirety in any one individual; we must find external objective signs that will make it perceptible. Further, even a product of spontaneous generation is in itself an effect of external causes which must also be determined in order to estimate its role in the future. Ultimately, we must always return to the same method.

Another proposition has been argued no less vehemently than the preceding one, namely, that social phenomena are external to individuals. Today our critics grant, willingly enough, that the facts of individual and of collective life are not altogether coterminous; one can even say that a quite general, if not unanimous, understanding on this point is in process of being achieved. Practically all sociologists now demand a separate existence for their science; but because society is composed only of individuals, the common-sense view still holds that sociology is a superstructure built upon the substratum of the individual consciousness and that otherwise it would be suspended in a social vacuum.

   What is so readily judged inadmissible in the matter of social facts is freely admitted in the other realms of nature. Whenever certain elements combine and thereby produce, by the fact of their combination, new phenomena, it is plain that these new phenomena reside not in the original elements but in the totality formed by their union. The living cell contains nothing but mineral particles, as society contains nothing but individuals. Yet it is patently impossible for the phenomena characteristic of life to reside in the atoms of hydrogen, oxygen, carbon, and nitrogen. How could the properties of life exist in inanimate elements? How would the biological properties be divided among these elements? These properties could not exist equally in all the elements because the latter are dissimilar by nature; carbon is not nitrogen and consequently cannot have the same properties as nitrogen or function in the same way. It is equally inadmissible that each of the principal characteristics of life be resident in a certain group of atoms. Life could not be thus separated into discrete parts; it is a unit, and consequently its substratum can be only the living substance in its totality and not the element parts of which it is composed. The inanimate particles of the cell do not assimilate food, reproduce, and, in a word, live; only the cell itself as a unit can achieve these functions.

What we say of life could be repeated for all possible compounds. The hardness of bronze is not in the copper, the tin, or the lead, which are its ingredients and which are soft and malleable bodies; it is in their mixture. The fluidity of water and its nutritional and other properties are not to be found in the two gases of which it is composed but in the complex substance which they form by their association.

Let us apply this principle to sociology. If, as we may say, this synthesis constituting every society yields new phenomena, differing from those which take place in individual consciousnesses, we must, indeed, admit that these facts reside exclusively in the very society itself which produces them, and not in its parts, i.e., its members. They are, then, in this sense external to individual consciousnesses, considered as such, just as the distinctive characteristics of life are external to the mineral substances composing the living being. These new phenomena cannot be reduced to their elements without contradiction in terms, since, by definition, they presuppose something different from the properties of these elements. Thus we have a new justification for the separation which we have established between psychology, which is properly the science of the mind of the individual, and sociology.

Social facts do not differ from psychological facts in quality only: *they have a different substratum;* they evolve in a different milieu; and they depend on different conditions. This does not mean that they are not also mental after a fashion, since they all consist of ways of thinking or behaving. But the states of the collective consciousness are different in nature from the states of the individual consciousness; they are "representations" of another type. The mentality of groups is not the same as that of individuals; it has its own laws. The two sciences are thus as clearly distinct as two sciences can be, whatever relationships there may otherwise be between them.*

BOAS

For a time—especially under the influence of evolutionary theory, which was just unfolding in the mid- to late-nineteenth-century—anthropology labored under a racist bias. It was widely thought that the different human races could be arrayed along a continuum from "primitive" to "advanced," along with their cultural accomplishments. The German-born American anthropologist Franz Boas (1858–1942) caused, almost single-handedly, a sea change in this intellectual environment. He championed the idea of "cultural relativism," pointing out that

> it is somewhat difficult for us to recognize that the value which we attribute to our own civilization is due to the fact that we participate in this civilization, and that it has been controlling all our actions since the time of our birth; but it is certainly conceivable that there may be other civilizations . . . which are of no less value than ours, although it may be impossible for us to appreciate their values without having grown up under their influence. [Anthropology] . . . teaches us a higher tolerance than the one we now profess. *(The Mind of Primitive Man)*

Boas is also responsible for popularizing what has become known as the "psychic unity of mankind," the idea that "there is no fundamental difference in the ways of thinking of primitive and

*From *Rules of Sociological Method* (2nd ed., 1938). (Trans. Sarah A. Solovay and John H. Mueller). Chicago: University of Chicago Press.

civilized man." In his landmark book *The Mind of Primitive Man,* which is excerpted below, Boas powerfully disputes the presumption that the different human races differ in important biological ways, and that these differences, in turn, are reflected in cultural distinctions. His work is the major step along the road whereby modern anthropology came to consider that human cultures must be considered in their own terms, and not a result of particular traits characteristic of a particular human group.

Considerations show that, at least at the present time, anatomical type, language and culture have not necessarily the same fates; that a people may remain constant in type and language, and change in culture; that it may remain constant in type, but change in language; or that it may remain constant in language, and change in type and culture. It is obvious, therefore, that attempts to classify mankind, based on the present distribution of type, language and culture, must lead to different results, according to the point of view taken; that a classification based primarily on type alone will lead to a system which represents more or less accurately the blood-relationships of the people; but these do not need to coincide with their cultural relationships. In the same way classifications based on language and culture do not need to coincide with a biological classification.

If this be true, then a problem like the Aryan problem does not exist, because it relates to the history of the Aryan languages; and the assumption that a certain definite people whose members have always been related by blood must have been the carriers of this language throughout history; and the other assumption, that a certain cultural type must have always belonged to peoples speaking Aryan languages—are purely arbitrary ones, and not in accord with the observed facts.

Nevertheless it must be granted that in a theoretical consideration of the history of the types of mankind, of languages and of cultures, we are led back to the assumption of early conditions, during which each type was much more isolated from the rest of mankind than it is at the present time. For this reason the culture and the language belonging to a single type must have been much more sharply separated from those of other types than we find them to be at the present period. Such a condition has nowhere been observed; but the knowledge of historical developments almost compels us to assume its existence at a very early period in the development of mankind. If this be true, the question would arise, whether an isolated group at an early period was necessarily characterized by a single type, a single language and a single culture, or whether in such a group different types, different languages and different cultures may have been represented.

The historical development of mankind would afford a simpler and clearer picture if we were justified in the belief that in primitive communities the three phenomena had been intimately associated. No proof, however, of such an assumption can be given. On the contrary, the present distribution of languages, as compared with the distribution of types, makes it plausible that even at the earliest times within the biological units more than one language and more than one culture were represented. I believe it may safely be said that all over the world the biological unit—disregarding minute local differences—is much larger than the linguistic one; in other words, that groups of men who are so closely related in bodily appearance that we must consider them as representatives of the same variety of mankind, embrace a much larger number of individuals than the number of men speaking languages which we know to be genetically related. . . .

It may be asked whether the cultural achievements of races may be arranged in a progressive series, some races having produced inferior values while others have created nobler ones. If a progression of culture could be established and if, at the same time, it could be shown that the simpler forms always occur in some races, higher ones in others, it might be possible to conclude that there are differences in racial ability. It is easily shown that the most varied cultural forms appear in most races. In America the high civilizations of Peru and Mexico may be compared with the primitive tribes of Tierra del Fuego or with those of northern Canada. In Asia Chinese, Japanese and the primitive Yukaghir; in Africa the Negroes of the Sudan and the hunters of the primeval forests are found side by side. Only in Australia no higher forms of culture are found, and our own modern civilization had nothing alike to it among other races until the most recent time when Japan and China participate in many of our most valued activities, as in earlier times we have taken on many of their achievements.

The errors underlying all conclusions based on the achievements of various races have been dwelt on before. . . . It should be emphasized again that we can never be sure whether the mental character of a primitive tribe is the cause of its low culture so that under favorable conditions it could not attain a more advanced cultural life, or whether its mental character is the effect of its low culture and would change with advancing culture. It is all but impossible to find material for answering this question, except for the peoples of eastern Asia, because nowadays no large populations of alien races are placed in a position in which they are socially and politically equal to Whites and enjoy the same opportunities for intellectual, economic and social development. The chasm between our society and theirs is the wider the greater the contrast in outer appearance. For this reason we may not expect the same kind of mental development in these groups.

The considerations which in the beginning of our discussion led us to the conclusion that in modern times primitive tribes have no opportunity to develop their innate abilities, prevents us from forming any opinion in regard to their racial hereditary faculty. . . .

Culture may be defined as the totality of the mental and physical reactions and activities that characterize the behavior of the individuals composing a social group collectively and individually in relation to their natural environment, to other groups, to members of the group itself and of each individual to himself. It also includes the products of these activities and their role in the life of the groups. The mere enumeration of these various aspects of life, however, does not constitute culture. It is more, for its elements are not independent, they have a structure.

The activities enumerated here are not by any means the sole property of man, for the life of animals is also regulated by their relations to nature, to other animals and by the interrelation of the individuals composing the same species or social group.

It has been customary to describe culture in order as material culture, social relations, art and religion. Ethical attitudes and rational activities have generally been treated slightly, and language has seldom been included in the description of culture. Under the first of these headings the gathering, preserving and preparation of food, shelter and clothing, processes and products of manufacture, methods of locomotion are described. Rational knowledge is generally included as part of this subject. Under social relations the general economic conditions, property rights, relation to foreign tribes in war and peace, the position of the individual in the tribe, the organization of the tribe, forms of communication, sexual and other individual relations are discussed. Decorative, pictorial and plastic art, song, narrative and dance are the subject matter of art; the attitudes and activities centering around everything that is considered as sacred or outside of the sphere of ordinary human acts, that of religion. Here are generally also included customary behavior, referring to what is considered as good, bad, proper or improper and other fundamental ethical concepts. . . .

Our previous considerations enable us also to evaluate the claim that the biological character of a race determines its culture. Let us admit for the moment that the genetic make-up of an individual determines his behavior. The actions of his glands, his basal metabolism and so on are elements that find expression in his personality. Personality in this sense means the biologically determined emotional, volitional and intellectual characteristics which determine the way in which an individual reacts to the culture in which he lives. The biological constitution does not make the culture. It influences the reactions of the individual to the culture. As little as geographical environment or economic conditions create a culture, just as little does the biological character of a race create a culture of a definite type. Experience has shown that members of most races placed in a certain culture can participate in it. In America men like Juárez, President of Mexico, or the highly educated Indians in North and South America are examples. In Asia the modern history of Japan and China; in America the successes of educated Negroes as scientists, physicians, lawyers, economists are ample proof showing that the racial position of an individual does not hinder his participation in modern civilization. Culture is rather the result of innumerable interacting factors and there is no evidence that the differences between human races, particularly not between the members of the White race have any directive influence upon the course of development of culture. Individual types, ever since the glacial period, have always found an existing culture to which they reacted.

The range of individual differences that occur within a race has never been investigated in a satisfactory manner. We have shown that the variability of bodily form of individuals composing each race is great. We cannot yet give exact data regarding the variability of fundamental physiological traits, much less of more intangible features such as physiologically determined personality, but even qualitative observation shows that the variability in each racial unit is great. The almost insurmountable difficulty lies in the fact that physiological and psychological processes and particularly personality cannot be reduced to an absolute standard that is free of environmental elements. It is, therefore, gratuitous to claim that a race has a definite personality. We have seen that on account of the variability of individuals composing a race, differences between larger groups of slightly varying human types are much smaller than the differences between the individuals composing each group, so that any considerable influence of the biologically determined distribution of personalities upon the form of culture seems very unlikely. No proof has ever been given that a sufficiently large series of normal individuals of an identical social environment but representing different European types, perhaps the one group, blond, tall, longheaded, with large nose; the other darker, shorter, roundheaded, with smaller noses will behave differently. The opposite, that people of the same type—like the Germans in Bohemia and the Czechs—behave quite differently is much more easily given.*

KROEBER

The tradition of Franz Boas was continued and extended by his many distinguished students, including Ruth Benedict, Margaret Mead, and Alfred Kroeber. Of these, it was Kroeber (1876–1960) who initially took the Boasian approach the furthest, proclaiming the virtual independence of culture from biology, in other words, from human nature, narrowly defined. In Kroeber's celebrated formulation, human culture is a "superorganism," which must be considered on its own terms. He draws a hard line between the cultural and the biological, maintaining that human nature is unique in producing culture, which then exists independently of biology (or as he calls it, the "organic"). Note that culture, in this context, does not refer simply to "high culture," namely opera, poetry, painting, and so forth. Rather it refers to what Edward B. Tylor, one of the founders of anthropology, defined in 1871 as "that complex whole which includes knowledge, belief, art, morals, law, custom, and any other capabilities and habits acquired by man as a member of society."

The anthropologist Robert Lowie, building on this approach, argues that *omnia cultura ex cultura* ("all culture comes from culture"), by which he meant that the anthropologist should "account for a given cultural fact by merging it in a group of cultural facts or by demonstrating some other cultural fact out of which it has developed." Another influential anthropologist, Leslie White, maintains that "The culture process . . . is to be explained in terms of culture it-

*From *The Mind of Primitive Man* (1911). New York: Macmillan.

self . . . in short, culturalogically rather than biologically or psychologically." White even argues that "what one takes for 'human nature' is not natural at all but cultural."

This excerpt is from Kroeber's important article, "The Superorganic," published in the journal *American Anthropologist* in 1917. (In a subsequent revision, Kroeber urged that the word "social" should be replaced with "cultural.")

A way of thought characteristic of our western civilization has been the formulation of complementary antitheses, a balancing of exclusive opposites. One of these pairs of ideas with which our world has been laboring for some two thousand years is expressed in the words *body* and *soul*. Another couplet that has served its useful purpose, but which science is now often endeavoring to rid itself of, at least in certain aspects, is the distinction of the *physical* from the *mental*. A third discrimination is that of the *vital* from the *social*, or in other phraseology, of the *organic* from the *cultural*. The implicit recognition of the difference between organic qualities and processes and social qualities and processes is of long standing. The formal distinction is however recent. In fact the full import of the significance of the antithesis may be said to be only dawning upon the world. For every occasion on which some human mind sharply separates organic and social forces, there are dozens of other times when the distinction between them is not thought of, or an actual confusion of the two ideas takes place.

One reason for this current confusion of the organic and the social is the predominance, in the present phase of the history of thought, of the idea of evolution. This idea, one of the earliest, simplest, and also vaguest ever attained by the human mind, has received its strongest ground and fortification in the domain of the organic; in other words, through biological science. At the same time, there is an evolution, or growth, or gradual development, apparent also in other realms than that of plant and animal life. We have theories of stellar or cosmic evolution; and there is obvious, even to the least learned, a growth or evolution of civilization. In the nature of things there is little danger of the carrying over of the Darwinian or post-Darwinian principles of the evolution of life into the realm of burning suns and lifeless nebulae. Human civilization or progress, on the other hand, which exists only in and through living members of the species, is outwardly so similar to the evolution of plants and animals, that it has been inevitable that there should have been sweeping applications of the principles of organic development to the facts of cultural growth. This of course is reasoning by analogy, or arguing that because two things resemble each other in one point they will also be similar in others. In the absence of knowledge, such assumptions are justifiable as assumptions. Too often, however, their effect is to predetermine mental attitude, with the result that when the evidence begins to accumulate which could prove or disprove the assumption based on analogy, this evidence is no longer viewed impartially and judiciously, but is merely distributed and disposed of in such a way as not to interfere with the established conviction into which the original tentative guess has long since turned.

This is what has happened in the field of organic and social evolution. This distinction between them, which is so obvious that to former ages it seemed too commonplace to remark upon, except incidentally and indirectly, has been largely obscured in the last fifty years through the hold which thoughts connected with the idea of organic evolution have had on minds of the time. It even seems fair to say that this confusion has been greater and more general among those to whom study and scholarship are a daily pursuit than to the remainder of the world. . . .

It has long been the custom to say that the difference is that between body and mind; that animals have their physiques adapted to their circumstances, but that man's superior intelligence enables him to rise superior to such lowly needs. But this is not the most significant point of the difference. It is true that without the much greater mental faculties of man, he could not achieve the attainments the lack of which keeps the brute chained to the limitations of his anatomy. But the greater human intelligence in itself does not cause the differences that exist. This psychic superiority is only the indispensable condition of what is peculiarly human; civilization. Directly, it is the civilization in which every Eskimo, every Alaskan miner or arctic discoverer is reared, and not any greater inborn faculty, that leads him to build houses, ignite fire, and wear clothing. The distinction between animal and man which counts is not that of the physical and mental, which is one of relative degree, but that of the organic and social which is one of kind. The beast has mentality, and we have bodies; but in civilization man has something that no animal has. . . .

There have been many attempts to make precise the distinction between instinct and civilization, between the organic and the social, between animal and man. Man as the clothing animal, the fire-using animal, the tool-using or tool-making animal, the speaking animal, are all summations that contain some approximation. But for the conception of the discrimination that is at once most complete and most compact, we must go back, as for the first precise expression of so many of the ideas with which we operate, to the unique mind that impelled Aristotle: "Man is a political animal." The word political has changed in import. We use instead the Latin term social. This, both philosopher and philologist tell us, is what the great Greek would have said were he speaking in English today. Man is a social animal, then; a social organism. He has organic constitution; but he has also civilization. To ignore one element is as short-sighted as to overlook the other; to convert one into the other, if each has its reality, is negation. With this basic formulation more than two thousand years old, and known to all the generations, there is something puny, as well as obtinately destructive, in the endeavor to abrogate the distinction, or to hinder its completest fruition. The attempt today to treat the social as organic, to understand civilization as hereditary, is as essentially narrow as the alleged mediaeval inclination to withdraw man from the realm of nature and from the ken of the scientist because he was believed to possess an immaterial soul.

But unfortunately the denials, and for every denial a dozen confusions, still persist. They pervade the popular mind; and thence they rise, again and again, into the thoughts of avowed and recognized science. It seems, even, that in a hundred years we have retrograded. A century and two centuries ago, with a generous impulse, the leaders of thought devoted their energies, and the leaders of men their lives, to the cause that all men are equal. With all that this idea involves, and with its correctness, we need not here concern ourselves; but it certainly implied the proposition of equality of racial capacity. Possibly our ancestors were able to maintain this liberal stand because its full practical imports did not yet face them. But, whatever the reason, we have certainly gone back, in America and in Europe and in their colonies, in our application of the assumption; and we have receded too in our theoretic analysis of the evidence. Hereditary racial differences of ability pass as approved doctrine, in many quarters. There are men of eminent learning who would be surprised to know that serious doubts were held in the matter. . . .

The reason why mental heredity has so little if anything to do with civilization, is that civilization is not mental action but a body or stream of products of mental exercise. Mental activity, as biologists have dealt with it, being organic, any demonstration concerning it consequently proves nothing whatever as to social events. Mentality relates to the individual. The social or cultural, on the other hand, is in its essence nonindividual. Civilization, as such, begins only where the individual ends; and whoever does not in some measure perceive this fact, even though only as a brute and rootless one, can find no meaning in civilization, and history for him must be only a wearying jumble, or an opportunity for the exercise of art.

All biology necessarily has this direct reference to the individual. A social mind is as meaningless a nonentity as a social body. There can be only one kind of organicness: the organic on another plane would no longer be organic. The Darwinian doctrine relates, it is true, to the race; but the race, except as an abstraction, is only a collection of individuals; and the bases of this doctrine, heredity, variation, and competition, deal with the relation of individual to individual, from individual, and against individual. The whole key of the success of the Mendelian methods of studying heredity lies in isolating traits and isolating individuals.

But a thousand individuals do not make a society. They are the potential basis of a society; but they do not themselves cause it; and they are also the basis of a thousand other potential societies.

The findings of biology as to heredity, mental and physical alike, may then, in fact must be, accepted without reservation. But that therefore civilization can be understood by psychological analysis, or explained by observations or experiments in heredity, or, to revert to a concrete example, that the destiny of nations can be predicted from an analysis of the organic constitution of their members, assumes that society is merely a collection of individuals; that civilization is only an aggregate of psychic activities and not also an entity beyond them; in short, that the social can be wholly resolved into the mental as it is thought this resolves into the physical.

It is accordingly in this point of the tempting leap from the individually mental to the culturally social which presupposes but does not contain mentality, that the source of the distracting transferences of the organic into the social is to be sought. . . .

All civilization in a sense exists only in the mind. Gunpowder, textile arts, machinery, laws, telephones are not themselves transmitted from man to man or from generation to generation, at least not permanently. It is the perception, the knowledge and understanding of them, their *ideas* in the Platonic sense, that are passed along. Everything social can have existence only through mentality. Of course, civilization is not mental action itself; it is carried by men, without being in them. But its relation to mind, its absolute rooting in human faculty, is obvious.

What, then, has occurred is that biology, which correlates and often identifies the "physical" and the mental, has gone one natural but as yet unjustified step further, and assumed the social as mental; whence the explanation of civilization in physiological and mechanical terms was an unavoidable consequence.

Now, the correlation by modern science of the physical and mental is certainly correct. That is, it is justifiable as a method which can be consistently employed toward a coherent explanation of phenomena, and which leads to intellectually satisfactory and practically useful results. The correlation of the two sets of phenomena is made, or admitted, by all psychologists; it clearly holds for all faculties and instincts; and it has some definite physiological and chemical corroboration, though of a more crude and less completely established kind than is sometimes imagined. At any rate, this correlation is an unchallenged axiom of those who concern themselves with science: all mental equipment and all mental activity have an organic basis. And that is sufficient for present purposes. . . .

[T]wo wholly disparate evolutions must be recognized: that of the substance which we call organic and that of the phenomena called social. . . .

[W]ith the unknown bearers of the primeval and gradually manifesting beginnings of civilization, there took place a profound alteration rather than an improved passing of the existing. A new factor has arisen which was to work out its own independent consequences, slowly and of little apparent import at first, but gathering weight, and dignity, and influence; a factor that had passed beyond natural selection, that was no longer wholly dependent on any agency of organic evolution, and that, however rocked and swayed by the oscillations of the heredity that underlay it, nevertheless floated unimmersibly upon it.

The dawn of the social thus is not a link in a chain, not a step in a path, but a leap to another plane. It may be likened to the first occurrence of life in the hitherto lifeless universe, the hour when that one of infinite chemical combinations took place which put the organic into existence, and made it that from this moment on there should be two worlds in place of one. Atomic qualities and movements were not interfered with when that seemingly slight event took place; the majesty of the mechanical laws of the cosmos was not diminished; but something new was inextinguishably added to the history of this planet.

One might compare the inception of civilization to the end of the process of slowly heating water. The expansion of the liquid goes on a long time. Its alteration can be observed by the thermometer as well as in bulk, in its solvent power as well as in its internal agitation. But it remains water. Finally, however, the boiling point is attained. Steam is produced: the rate of enlargement of volume is increased a thousand fold; and in place of a glistening, percolating fluid, a volatile gas diffuses invisibly. Neither the laws of physics nor those of chemistry are violated; nature is not set aside; but yet a saltation has taken place: the slow transitions that accumulated from zero to one hundred have been transcended in an instant, and a condition of substance with new properties and new possibilities of effect is in existence.

Such, in some manner, must have been the result of the appearance of this new thing, civilization. . . .

Here, then, we have to come to our conclusion; and here we rest. The mind and the body are but facets of the same organic material or activity; the social substance—or unsubstantial fabric, if one prefers the phrase—the thing that we call civilization, transcends them for all its being rooted in life. The processes of civilization activity are almost unknown to us. The factors that govern their workings are unresolved. The forces and principles of mechanistic science can indeed analyze our civilization; but in so doing they destroy its essence, and leave us without understanding of the very thing which we seek. The historian as yet can do little but picture. He traces and he connects what seems far removed; he balances; he integrates; but he does not really explain, nor does he transmute phenomena into something else. His method is not mechanistic; but neither can the physicist or physiologist deal with historical material and leave it civilization nor convert it into concepts of life and leave nothing else to be done. What we all are able to do is to realize this gap, to be impressed by it with humility, and to go our paths on its respective sides without self-deluding boasts that the chasm has been bridged.*

STUDY QUESTIONS

1. What sort of evidence would confirm the idea that culture is independent of human nature? What would refute it?

2. Anthropologist Leslie White claimed that "culture may be regarded as a thing *sui generis,* with a life of its own and its own laws." Assume for the sake of argument that this is true; what are the implications?

3. Suggest one or more definitions of "culture." Do any animals have culture? Can any people lack it?

4. What is wrong with investigating "social facts" as the outgrowth of individual behavior? What is right about it? Even when the whole is greater than the sum of its parts, does this mean that the whole is qualitatively different from its parts?

SOME ADDITIONAL READINGS

Benedict, Ruth (1946). *Patterns of Culture.* New York: Penguin Books.

Degler, Carl N. (1991). *In Search of Human Nature: The Rise and Fall of Darwinism in American Social Thought.* New York: Oxford University Press.

Geertz, Clifford (1973). *The Interpretation of Cultures: Selected Essays.* New York: Basic Books.

Harris, Marvin (1968). *The Rise of Anthropological Theory: A History of Theories of Culture.* New York: Crowell.

White, Leslie A. (1969). *The Science of Culture.* New York: Farrar, Straus and Giroux.

*From "The Superorganic" (1917). *American Anthropologist* 19: 23–51.

CHAPTER TWELVE

Marxist "Man" and Alienation

To some degree, every social, political, or economic system is based on an idea of human nature, even though that idea is not always made explicit. Democracy, for example, assumes that human beings are essentially reasonable (see Chapter 4) and well-meaning (see Chapter 10); hence, they can be trusted with self-government. Despotisms, on the other hand, generally assume a darker view of human inclinations (see Chapters 5 and 9), such that people require a strong hand in order to be "kept in line." Capitalism, to some degree, presupposes a penchant for competition (see Chapter 16), and Marxism? Well, that is the topic of this chapter.

MARX

The ideas of Karl Marx (1818–1883) are generally thought to be social, historical, economic, and revolutionary—all of which is true. However, Marx developed his ideas from several sources, one of which was a conviction that human beings, because of their nature as human beings, were ill-served by capitalism. He maintained that systems of labor, production, and capital do genuine violence to the human-ness of humanity, leading to profound psychological isolation and dissatisfaction; in other words, alienation.

Marx developed this line of thinking in some of his earlier writings, most of which were not available to English-speaking scholars until the 1930s and later. Although the exact logical and historical connections are still debated, it is increasingly agreed that Marx's later, and better known works, notably *The Communist Manifesto* (coauthored with Friedrich Engels) and *Das Kapital,* developed as a logical outgrowth of his concept of worker alienation.

The following selections are, in order, from Marx's *Comments on James Mill, The Economic and Philosophical Manuscripts of 1844, The Grundrisse,* and *Das Kapital.*

Man *produces* only in order to *have*—this is the basic presupposition of private property. The aim of production is *having.* And not only does production have this kind of *useful* aim; it has also a *selfish* aim; man produces only in order to *possess* for himself; the object he produces is the objectification of his *immediate,* selfish *need.* For man himself—in a savage, barbaric condition—therefore, the amount of his production is determined by the *extent* of his immediate need, the content of which is *directly* the object produced.

Under these conditions, therefore, man produces *no more* than he immediately requires. The *limit of his need* forms the *limit of his production.* Thus demand and supply exactly coincide. The extent of his production is *measured* by his need. In this case no exchange takes place, or exchange is reduced to the exchange of his labour for the product of his labour, and this exchange is the latent form, the germ, of real exchange.

As soon as exchange takes place, a surplus is produced beyond the immediate limit of possession. But this surplus production does not mean rising above selfish need. On the contrary, it is only an *indirect* way of satisfying a need which finds its objectification not in *this* production but in the production of someone else. Production has become a *means of gaining a living*, labour to gain a living. Whereas under the first state of affairs, therefore, need is the measure of production, under the second state of affairs production, or rather *ownership of the product*, is the measure of how far needs can be satisfied.

I have produced for myself and not for you, just as you have produced for yourself and not for me. In itself, the result of my production has as little connection with you as the result of your production has directly with me. That is to say, our production is not man's production for man as a man, i.e., it is not *social* production. Neither of us, therefore, as a man stands in a relation of enjoyment to the other's product. As men, we do not exist as far as our respective products are concerned. Hence our exchange, too, cannot be the mediating process by which it is confirmed that my product is [for] you, because it is an *objectification* of your own nature, your need. For it is not *man's nature* that forms the link between the products we make for one another. Exchange can only set in *motion*, only confirm, the *character* of the relation which each of us has in regard to his own product, and therefore to the product of the other. Each of us sees in his product only the objectification of his *own* selfish need, and therefore in the product of the other the objectification of a *different* selfish need, independent of him and alien to him.

As a man you have, of course, a human relation to my product: you have *need* of my product. Hence it exists for you as an object of your desire and your will. But your need, your desire, your will, are powerless as regards my product. That means, therefore, that your *human* nature, which accordingly is bound to stand in intimate relation to my human production, is not your *power* over this production, your possession of it, for it is not the *specific character*, not the *power*, of man's nature that is recognised in my production. They [your need, your desire, etc.] constitute rather the *tie* which makes you dependent on me, because they put you in a position of dependence on my product. Far from being the *means* which would give you *power* over my production, they are instead the *means* for giving me power over you.

When I produce *more of* an object than I myself can directly use, my *surplus* production is cunningly *calculated* for your need. It is only in *appearance* that I produce a surplus of this object. In reality I produce a *different* object, the object of your production, which I intend to exchange against this surplus, an exchange which in my mind I have already completed. The *social* relation in which I stand to you, my labour for your need, is therefore also a mere *semblance*, and our complementing each other is likewise a mere *semblance*, the basis of which is mutual plundering. The intention of *plundering*, of *deception*, is necessarily present in the background, for since our exchange is a selfish one, on your side as on mine, and since the selfishness of each seeks to get the better of that of the other, we necessarily seek to deceive each other. It is true though, that the power which I attribute to my object over yours requires your *recognition* in order to become a real power. Our mutual recognition of the respective powers of our objects, however, is a struggle, and in a struggle the victor is the one who has more energy, force, insight, or adroitness. If I have sufficient physical force, I plunder you directly. If physical force cannot be used, we try to impose on each other by bluff, and the more adroit overreaches the other. For the *totality* of the relationship, it is a matter of chance who overreaches whom. The *ideal, intended* overreaching takes place on both sides, i.e., each in his own judgment has overreached the other.

On both sides, therefore, exchange is necessarily mediated by the *object* which each side produces and possesses. The ideal relationship to the respective objects of our production is, of course, our mutual need. But the *real, true* relationship, which *actually* occurs and takes effect, is only the mutually *exclusive pos-*

session of our respective products. What gives your need of my article its *value, worth* and *effect* for me is solely your *object*, the *equivalent* of my object. Our respective products, therefore, are the *means*, the *mediator*, the *instrument*, the *acknowledged power* of our mutual needs. Your *demand* and the *equivalent of your possession*, therefore, are for me terms that are *equal in significance* and validity, and your demand only acquires a *meaning*, owing to having an effect, when it has meaning and effect in relation to me. As a mere human being without this instrument your demand is an unsatisfied aspiration on your part and an idea that does not exist for me. As a human being, therefore, you stand in no relationship to my object, because *I myself* have no human relationship to it. But the *means* is the *true power* over an object and therefore we mutually regard our products as the *power* of each of us over the other and over himself. That is to say, our own product has risen up against us; it seemed to be our property, but in fact we are its property. We ourselves are excluded from *true* property because our *property* excludes other men.

The only intelligible language in which we converse with one another consists of our objects in their relation to each other. We would not understand a human language and it would remain without effect. By one side it would be recognised and felt as being a request, an entreaty, and therefore a *humiliation*, and consequently uttered with a feeling of shame, of degradation. By the other side it would be regarded as *impudence* or *lunacy* and rejected as such. We are to such an extent estranged from man's essential nature that the direct language of this essential nature seems to us a *violation of human dignity*, whereas the estranged language of material values seems to be the well-justified assertion of human dignity that is self-confident and conscious of itself. . . .*

We have proceeded from the premises of political economy. We have accepted its language and its laws. We presupposed private property, the separation of labour, capital and land, and of wages, profit of capital and rent of land—likewise division of labour, competition, the concept of exchange-value, etc. On the basis of political economy itself, in its own words, we have shown that the worker sinks to the level of a commodity and becomes indeed the most wretched of commodities; that the wretchedness of the worker is in inverse proportion to the power and magnitude of his production; that the necessary result of competition is the accumulation of capital in a few hands, and thus the restoration of monopoly in a more terrible form; and that finally the distinction between capitalist and land rentier, like that between the tiller of the soil and the factory workers, disappears and that the whole of society must fall apart into the two classes—the *property owners* and the propertyless *workers*.

Political economy starts with the fact of private property; it does not explain it to us. It expresses in general, abstract formulas the *material* process through which private property actually passes, and these formulas it then takes for *laws*. It does not *comprehend* these laws, i.e., it does not demonstrate how they arise from the very nature of private property. Political economy throws no light on the cause of the division between labour and capital, and between capital and land. When, for example, it defines the relationship of wages to profit, it takes the interest of the capitalists to be the ultimate cause, i.e., it takes for granted what it is supposed to explain. Similarly, competition comes in everywhere. It is explained from external circumstances. As to how far these external and apparently accidental circumstances are but the expression of a necessary course of development, political economy teaches us nothing. We have seen how exchange itself appears to it as an accidental fact. The only wheels which political economy sets in motion are *greed* and the *war amongst the greedy—competition*.

*From *Comments on James Mill* (1986) (J. Elster, Trans.) New York: Cambridge University Press.

Precisely because political economy does not grasp the way the movement is connected, it was possible to oppose, for instance, the doctrine of competition to the doctrine of monopoly, the doctrine of the freedom of the crafts to the doctrine of the guild, the doctrine of the division of landed property to the doctrine of the big estate—for competition, freedom of the crafts and the division of landed property were explained and comprehended only as accidental, premeditated and violent consequences of monopoly, of the guild system, and of feudal property, not as their necessary, inevitable and natural consequences.

Now, therefore, we have to grasp the intrinsic connection between private property, avarice, the separation of labour, capital and landed property; the connection of exchange and competition, of value and the devaluation of men, of monopoly and competition, etc.—we have to grasp this whole estrangement connected with the *money* system.

Do not let us go back to a fictitious primordial condition as the political economist does, when he tries to explain. Such a primordial condition explains nothing; it merely pushes the question away into a grey nebulous distance. The economist assumes in the form of a fact, of an event, what he is supposed to deduce—namely, the necessary relationship between two things—between, for example, division of labour and exchange. Thus the theologian explains the origin of evil by the fall of man; that is, he assumes as a fact, in historical form, what has to be explained.

We proceed from an *actual* economic fact.

The worker becomes all the poorer the more wealth he produces, the more his production increases in power and size. The worker becomes an ever cheaper commodity the more commodities he creates. The *devaluation* of the world of men is in direct proportion to the *increasing value* of the world of things. Labour produces not only commodities: it produces itself and the worker as a *commodity*—and this at the same rate at which it produces commodities in general.

This fact expresses merely that the object which labour produces—labour's product—confronts it as *something alien*, as a *power independent* of the producer. The product of labour is labour which has been embodied in an object, which has become material: it is the *objectification* of labour. Labour's realisation is its objectification. Under these economic conditions this realisation of labour appears as *loss of realisation* for the workers; objectification as *loss of the object and bondage to it*, appropriation as *estrangement, as alienation*.

So much does labour's realisation appear as loss of realisation that the worker loses realisation to the point of starving to death. So much does objectification appear as loss of the object that the worker is robbed of the objects most necessary not only for his life but for his work. Indeed, labour itself becomes an object which he can obtain only with the greatest effort and with the most irregular interruptions. So much does the appropriation of the object appear as estrangement that the more objects the worker produces the less he can possess and the more he falls under the sway of his product capital.

All these consequences are implied in the statement that the worker is related to the *product of his labour* as to an *alien* object. For on this premise it is clear that the more the worker spends himself, the more powerful becomes the alien world of objects which he creates over and against himself, the poorer he himself—his inner world—becomes, the less belongs to him as his own. It is the same in religion. The more man puts into God, the less he retains in himself. The worker puts his life into the object; but now his life no longer belongs to him but to the object. Hence, the greater the activity, the more the worker lacks objects. Whatever the product of his labour is, he is not. Therefore the greater this product, the less is he himself. The *alienation* of the worker in his product means not only that his labour becomes an object, an *external* existence, but that it exists *outside* him, independently, as something alien to him, and that it becomes a power on its own confronting him. It means that the life which he has conferred on the object confronts him as something hostile and alien.

Let us now look more closely at the *objectification*, at the production of the worker; and in it at the *estrangement*, the *loss* of the object, of his product.

The worker can create nothing without *nature*, without the *sensuous external world*. It is the material on which his labour is realised, in which it is active, from which and by means of which it produces.

But just as nature provides labour with [the] *means of life* in the sense that labour cannot *live* without objects on which to operate, on the other hand, it also provides the *means of life* in the more restricted sense, i.e., the means for the physical subsistence of the *worker* himself.

Thus the more the worker by his labour *appropriates* the external world, sensuous nature, the more he deprives himself of *means of life* in two respects: first, in that the sensuous external world more and more ceases to be an object belonging to his labour—to be his labour's *means of life;* and secondly, in that it more and more ceases to be *means of life* in the immediate sense, means for the physical subsistence of the worker.

In both respects, therefore, the worker becomes a servant of his object, first, in that he receives an *object of labour,* i.e., in that he receives *work;* and secondly, in that he receives *means of subsistence.* This enables him to exist, first, as a *worker;* and, second, as a *physical subject.* The height of this servitude is that it is only as a *worker* that he can maintain himself as a *physical subject,* and that it is only as a *physical subject* that he is a worker.

(According to the economic laws the estrangement of the worker in his object is expressed thus: the more the worker produces, the less he has to consume; the more values he creates, the more valueless, the more unworthy he becomes; the better formed his product, the more deformed becomes the worker; the more civilised his object, the more barbarous becomes the worker; the more powerful labour becomes, the more powerless becomes the worker; the more ingenious labour becomes, the less ingenious becomes the worker and the more he becomes nature's servant.)

Political economy conceals the estrangement inherent in the nature of labour by not considering the **direct** *relationship between the* **worker** (labour) *and production.* It is true that labour produces wonderful things for the rich—but for the worker it produces privation. It produces palaces—but for the worker, hovels. It produces beauty—but for the worker, deformity. It replaces labour by machines, but it throws one section of the workers back to a barbarous type of labour, and it turns the other section into a machine. It produces intelligence—but for the worker, stupidity, cretinism.

The direct relationship of labour to its products is the relationship of the worker to the objects of his production. The relationship of the man of means to the objects of production and to production itself is only a *consequence* of this first relationship—and confirms it. We shall consider this other aspect later. When we ask, then, what is the essential relationship of labour we are asking about the relationship of the *worker* to production.

Till now we have been considering the estrangement; the alienation of the worker only in one of its aspects, i.e., the worker's *relationship to the products of his labour.* But the estrangement is manifested not only in the result but in the *act of production,* within the *producing activity* itself. How could the worker come to face the product of his activity as a stranger, were it not that in the very act of production he was estranging himself from himself? The product is after all but the summary of the activity, of production. If then the product of labour is alienation, production itself must be active alienation, the alienation of activity, the activity of alienation. In the estrangement of the object of labour is merely summarised the estrangement, the alienation, in the activity of labour itself.

What, then, constitutes the alienation of labour?

First, the fact that labour is *external* to the worker, i.e., it does not belong to his intrinsic nature; that in his work, therefore, he does not affirm himself but denies himself, does not feel content but unhappy, does not develop freely his physical and mental energy but mortifies his body and ruins his mind. The worker therefore only feels himself outside his work, and in his work feels outside himself. He feels at home when he is not working, and when he is working he does not feel at home. His labour is therefore not voluntary, but coerced; it is *forced labour.* It is therefore not the satisfaction of a need; it is merely a *means* to satisfy needs external to it. Its alien character emerges clearly in the fact that as soon as no physical or other compulsion exists, labour is shunned like the plague. External labour, labour in which man alienates himself, is a labour of self-sacrifice, of mortification. Lastly, the external character of labour for the worker appears in the fact that it is not his own, but someone else's, that it does not belong to him, that in it he belongs, not to himself, but to another. Just as in religion the spontaneous activity of the human imagination, of the human brain and the human heart, operates on the individual independently of him—that is, operates as an alien, divine or diabolical activity—so is the worker's activity not his spontaneous activity. It belongs to another; it is the loss of his self.

As a result, therefore, man (the worker) only feels himself freely active in his animal functions—eating, drinking, procreating, or at most in his dwelling and in dressing-up, etc.; and in his human functions he no longer feels himself to be anything but an animal. What is animal becomes human and what is human becomes animal.

Certainly eating, drinking, procreating, etc., are also genuinely human functions. But taken abstractly, separated from the sphere of all other human activity and turned into sole and ultimate ends, they are animal functions.

We have considered the act of estranging practical human activity, labour, in two of its aspects. (1) The relation of the worker to the *product of labour* as an alien object exercising power over him. This relation is at the same time the relation to the sensuous external world, to the objects of nature, as an alien world inimically opposed to him. (2) The relation of labour to the *act of production* within the *labour* process. This relation is the relation of the worker to his own activity as an alien activity not belonging to him; it is activity as suffering, strength as weakness, begetting as emasculating, the worker's *own* physical and mental energy, his personal life—for what is life but activity?—as an activity which is turned against him, independent of him and not belonging to him. Here we have *self-estrangement,* as previously we had the estrangement of the *thing.*

We have still a third aspect of *estranged labour* to deduce from the two already considered.

Man is a species-being, not only because in practice and in theory he adopts the species (his own as well as those of other things) as his object, but—and this is only another way of expressing it—also because he treats himself as the actual, living species; because he treats himself as a *universal* and therefore a free being.

The life of the species, both in man and in animals, consists physically in the fact that man (like the animal) lives on inorganic nature; and the more universal man (or the animal) is, the more universal is the sphere of inorganic nature on which he lives. Just as plants, animals, stones, air, light, etc., constitute theoretically a part of human consciousness, partly as objects of natural science, partly as objects of art — his spiritual inorganic nature, spiritual nourishment which he must first prepare to make palatable and digestible—so also in the realm of practice they constitute a part of human life and human activity. Physically man lives only on these products of nature, whether they appear in the form of food, heating, clothes, a dwelling, etc. The universality of man appears in practice precisely in the universality which makes all nature his *inorganic* body—both inasmuch as nature is (1) his direct means of life, and (2) the material, the object, and the instrument of his life activity. Nature is man's *inorganic body*—nature, that is, insofar as it is not itself human body. Man *lives* on nature—means that nature is his *body,* with which he must remain in continuous interchange if he is not to die. That man's physical and spiritual life is linked to nature means simply that nature is linked to itself, for man is a part of nature.

In estranging from man (1) nature, and (2) himself, his own active functions, his life activity, estranged labour estranges the *species* from man. It changes for him the *life of the species* into a means of individual life. First it estranges the life of the species and individual life, and secondly it makes individual life in its abstract form the purpose of the life of the species, likewise in its abstract and estranged form.

For labour, *life activity, productive life* itself, appears to man in the first place merely as a *means* of satisfying a need—the need to maintain physical existence. Yet the productive life is the life of the species. It is life-engendering life. The whole character of a species—its species-character—is contained in the character of its life activity; and free, conscious activity is man's species-character. Life itself appears only as a *means to life.*

The animal is immediately one with its life activity. It does not distinguish itself from it. It is *its life activity.* Man makes his life activity itself the object of his will and of his consciousness. He has conscious life activity. It is not a determination with which he directly merges. Conscious life activity distinguishes man immediately from animal life activity. It is just because of this that he is a species-being. Or it is only because he is a species-being that he is a conscious being, i.e., that his own life is an object for him. Only because of that is his activity free activity. Estranged labour reverses this relationship, so that it is just because man is a conscious being that he makes his life activity, his *essential being*, a mere means to his *existence.*

In creating a *world of objects* by his practical activity, in his *work upon* inorganic nature, man proves himself a conscious species-being, i.e., as a being that treats the species as its own essential being, or that treats itself as a species-being. Admittedly animals also produce. They build themselves nests, dwellings, like the bees, beavers, ants, etc. But an animal only produces what it immediately needs for itself or its young. It produces one-sidedly, whilst man produces universally. It produces only under the dominion of immediate physical need, whilst man produces even when he is free from physical need and only truly produces in freedom therefrom. An animal produces only itself, whilst man reproduces the whole of nature. An animal's product belongs immediately to its physical body, whilst man freely confronts his product. An animal forms objects only in accordance with the standard and the need of the species to which it belongs, whilst man knows how to produce in accordance with the standard of every species, and knows how to apply everywhere the inherent standard to the object. Man therefore also forms objects in accordance with the laws of beauty.

It is just in his work upon the objective world, therefore, that man really proves himself to be a *species-being.* This production is his active species-life. Through this production, nature appears as *his* work and his reality. The object of labour is, therefore, the *objectification of man's species-life:* for he duplicates himself not only, as in consciousness, intellectually, but also actively, in reality, and therefore he sees himself in a world that he has created. In tearing away from man the object of his production, therefore, estranged labour tears from him his *species-life*, his real objectivity as a member of the species, and transforms his advantage over animals into the disadvantage that his inorganic body, nature, is taken away from him.

Similarly, in degrading spontaneous, free activity to a means, estranged labour makes man's species-life a means to his physical existence.

The consciousness which man has of his species is thus transformed by estrangement in such a way that species[-life] becomes for him a means.

Estranged labour turns thus:

(3)   *Man's species-being*, both nature and his spiritual species-property, into a being *alien* to him, into a *means* for his *individual existence*. It estranges from man his own body, as well as external nature and his spiritual aspect, his *human* aspect.

(4)   An immediate consequence of the fact that man is estranged from the product of his labour, from his life activity, from his species-being is the *estrangement of man* from *man*. When man confronts himself, he confronts the *other* man. What applies to a man's relation to his work, to the product of his labour and to himself, also holds of a man's relation to the other man, and to the other man's labour and object of labour.

In fact, the proposition that man's species-nature is estranged from him means that one man is estranged from the other, as each of them is from man's essential nature.

The estrangement of man, and in fact every relationship in which man [stands] to himself, is realised and expressed only in the relationship in which a man stands to other men.

Hence within the relationship of estranged labour each man views the other in accordance with the standard and the relationship in which he finds himself as a worker.

We took our departure from a fact of political economy—the estrangement of the life and his product. We have formulated this fact in conceptual terms as *estranged, alienated* labour. We have analysed this concept—hence analysing merely a fact of political economy.

Let us now see, further, how the concept of estranged, alienated labour must express and present itself in real life.

If the product of labour is alien to me, if it confronts me as an alien power, to whom, then, does it belong?

If my own activity does not belong to me, if it is an alien, a coerced activity, to whom, then, does it belong?

To a being *other* than myself.

Who is this being?

The *gods?* To be sure, in the earliest times the principle production (for example, the building of temples, etc., in Egypt, India and Mexico) appears to be in the service of the gods, and the product belongs to the gods. However, the gods on their own were never the lords of labour. No more was *nature*. And what a contradiction it would be if, the more man subjugated nature by his labour and the more the miracles of the gods were rendered superfluous by the miracles of industry, the more man were to renounce the joy of production and the enjoyment of the product to please these powers.

The *alien* being, to whom labour and the product of labour belongs, in whose service labour is done and for whose benefit the product of labour is provided, can only be *man* himself.

If the product of labour does not belong to the worker, if it confronts him as an alien power, then this can only be because it belongs to some *other man than the worker.* If the worker's activity is a torment to him, to another it must give *satisfaction* and pleasure. Not the gods, not nature, but only man himself can be this alien power over man.

We must bear in mind the previous proposition that man's relation to himself only becomes for him *objective* and *actual* through his relation to the other man. Thus, if the product of his labour, his labour objectified, is for him an *alien, hostile,* powerful object independent of him, then his position towards it is such that someone else is master of this object, someone who is alien, hostile, powerful, and independent of him. If he treats his own activity as an unfree activity, then he treats it as an activity performed in the service, under the dominion, the coercion, and the yoke of another man.

Every self-estrangement of man, from himself and from nature, appears in the relation in which he places himself and nature to men other than and differentiated from himself. For this reason religious self-estrangement necessarily appears in the relationship of the layman to the priest, or again to a mediator, etc., since we are here dealing with the intellectual world. In the real practical world self-estrangement can only become manifest through the real practical relationship to other men. The medium through which estrangement takes place is itself *practical.* Thus through estranged labour man not only creates his relationship to the object and to the act of production as to powers that are alien and hostile to him; he also creates the relationship in which other men stand to his production and to his product, and the relationship in which he stands to these other men. Just as he creates his own production as the loss of his reality, as his punishment; his own product as a loss, as a product not belonging to him; so he creates the domination of the person who does not produce over production and over the product. Just as he estranges his own activity from himself, so he confers upon the stranger an activity which is not his own.

We have until now considered this relationship only from the standpoint of the worker and later we shall be considering it also from the standpoint of the non-worker.

Through *estranged, alienated labour,* then, the worker produces the relationship to this labour of a man alien to labour and standing outside it. The relationship of the worker to labour creates the relation to it of the capitalist (or whatever one chooses to call the master of labour). *Private property* is thus the product, the result, the necessary consequence, of *alienated labour,* of the external relation of the worker to nature and to himself.

Private property thus results by analysis from the concept of *alienated labour,* i.e., of *alienated man,* of estranged labour, of estranged life, of *estranged* man.

True, it is as a result of the *movement of private property* that we have obtained the concept of *alienated labour (of alienated life)* in political economy. But analysis of this concept shows that though private property appears to be the reason, the cause of alienated labour, it is rather its consequence, just as the gods are *originally* not the cause but the effect of man's intellectual confusion. Later this relationship becomes reciprocal.

Only at the culmination of the development of private property does this, its secret, appear again, namely, that on the one hand it is the *product* of alienated labour, and that on the other it is the *means* by which labour alienates itself, the *realisation of this alienation.* . . .*

[It has been said and may be said that this is precisely the beauty and the greatness of it: this spontaneous interconnection, this material and mental metabolism which is independent of the knowing and willing of individuals, and which presupposes their reciprocal independence and indifference. And, certainly, this objective connection is preferable to the lack of any connection, or to a merely local connection resting on blood ties, or on primeval, natural or master-servant relations. Equally certain is it that individuals cannot gain mastery over their own social interconnections before they have created them. But it is an insipid notion to conceive of this merely *objective bond* as a spontaneous, natural attribute inherent in individuals and inseparable from their nature (in antithesis to their conscious knowing and willing). This bond is their product. It is a historic product. It belongs to a specific phase of their development. The alien and independent character in which it presently exists *vis-à-vis* individuals proves only that the latter are still engaged in the creation of the conditions of their social life, and that they have not yet begun, on the basis of these conditions, to live it. It is the bond natural to individuals within specific and limited relations of production. Universally developed individuals, whose social relations, as their own communal relations, are hence also subordinated to their own communal control, are no product of nature, but of history. The degree and the universality of the development of wealth where *this* individuality becomes possible supposes production on the basis of exchange values as a prior condition, whose universality produces not only the alienation of the individual from himself and from others, but also the universality and the comprehensiveness of his relations and capacities. In earlier stages of development the single individual seems to be developed more fully, because he has not yet worked out his relationships in their fullness, or erected them as independent social powers and relations opposite himself. It is as ridiculous to yearn for a return to that original fullness as it is to believe that with this complete emptiness history has come to a standstill. The bourgeois viewpoint has never advanced beyond this antithesis between itself and this

*From *The Economic and Philosophical Manuscripts of 1844* (1986). (J. Elster, Trans.) New York: Cambridge University Press.

romantic viewpoint, and therefore the latter will accompany it as legitimate antithesis up to its blessed end.] . . .*

A commodity appears, at first sight, a very trivial thing, and easily understood. Its analysis shows that it is, in reality, a very queer thing, abounding in metaphysical subtleties and theological niceties. So far as it is a value in use, there is nothing mysterious about it, whether we consider it from the point of view that by its properties it is capable of satisfying human wants, or from the point that those properties are the product of human labour. It is as clear as noon-day, that man, by his industry, changes the forms of the materials furnished by Nature, in such a way as to make them useful to him. The form of wood, for instance, is altered, by making a table out of it. Yet, for all that, the table continues to be that common, every-day thing, wood. But, so soon as it steps forth as a commodity, it is changed into something transcendent. It not only stands with its feet on the ground, but, in relation to all other commodities, it stands on its head, and evolves out of its wooden brain grotesque ideas, far more wonderful than "table-turning" ever was.

The mystical character of commodities does not originate, therefore, in their use-value. Just as little does it proceed from the nature of the determining factors of value. For, in the first place, however varied the useful kinds of labour, or productive activities, may be, it is a physiological fact, that they are functions of the human organism, and that each such function, whatever may be its nature or form, is essentially the expenditure of human brain, nerves, muscles, &c. Secondly, with regard to that which forms the ground-work for the quantitative determination of value, namely, the duration of that expenditure, or the quantity of labour, it is quite clear that there is a palpable difference between its quantity and quality. In all states of society, the labour-time that it costs to produce the means of subsistence, must necessarily be an object of interest to mankind, though not of equal interest in different stages of development. And lastly, from the moment that men in any way work for one another, their labour assumes a social form.

Whence, then, arises the enigmatical character of the product of labour, so soon as it assumes the form of commodities? Clearly from this form itself. The equality of all sorts of human labour is expressed objectively by their products all being equally values; the measure of the expenditure of labour-power by the duration of that expenditure, takes the form of the quantity of value of the products of labour; and finally, the mutual relations of the producers, within which the social character of their labour affirms itself, take the form of a social relation between the products.

A commodity is therefore a mysterious thing, simply because in it the social character of men's labour appears to them as an objective character stamped upon the product of that labour: because the relation of the producers to the sum total of their own labour is presented to them as a social relation, existing not between themselves, but between the products of their labour. This is the reason why the products of labour become commodities, social things whose qualities are at the same time perceptible and imperceptible by the senses. In the same way the light from an object is perceived by us not as the subjective excitation of our optic nerve, but as the objective form of something outside the eye itself. But, in the act of seeing, there is at all events, an actual passage of light from one thing to another, from the external object to the eye. There is a physical relation between physical things. But it is different with commodities. There, the existence of the things *quâ* commodities, and the value-relation between the

---

*From *The Grundrisse* (1973). (M. Nicolaus, Trans.). London: Pelican Marx Library.

products of labour which stamps them as commodities, have absolutely no connexion with their physical properties and with the material relations arising therefrom. There it is a definite social relation between men, that assumes, in their eyes, the fantastic form of a relation between things. In order, therefore, to find an analogy, we must have recourse to the mist-enveloped regions of the religious world. In that world the productions of the human brain appear as independent beings endowed with life, and entering into relation both with one another and the human race. So it is in the world of commodities with the products of men's hands. This I call the Fetishism which attaches itself to the products of labour, so soon as they are produced as commodities, and which is therefore inseparable from the production of commodities.

This Fetishism of commodities has its origin, as the foregoing analysis has already shown, in the peculiar social character of the labour that produces them.[*]

MARKHAM

Edwin Markham (1852–1940) was an American lecturer and poet who acquired fame in 1899 when the *San Francisco Examiner* published his work of social protest, "The Man with the Hoe." This poem was inspired by Jean-Francois Millet's painting, and for a time it made French peasantry the worldwide symbol of exploited and alientated labor.

The Man with the Hoe

> Bowed by the weight of centuries he leans
> Upon his hoe and gazes on the ground,
> The emptiness of ages in his face,
> And on his back the burden of the world.
> Who made him dead to rapture and despair,
> A thing that grieves not and that never hopes,
> Stolid and stunned, a brother to the ox?
> Who loosened and let down this brutal jaw?
> Whose was the hand that slanted back this brow?
> Whose breath blew out the light within this brain?
>
> Is this the Thing the Lord God made and gave
> To have dominion over sea and land?
> To trace the stars and search the heavens for power;
> To feel the passion of Eternity?
> Is this the dream He dreamed who shaped the suns
> And markt their ways upon the ancient deep?
> Down all the caverns of Hell to their last gulf
> There is no shape more terrible than this—
> More tongued with censure of the world's blind greed—
> More filled with signs and portents for the soul—
> More packt with danger to the universe.

[*]From *Das Kapital* (1906). (S. Moore and E. Aveling, Trans.). New York: Modern Library.

What gulfs between him and the seraphim!
Slave of the wheel of labor, what to him
Are Plato and the swing of Pleiades?
What the long reaches of the peaks of song,
The rift of dawn, the reddening of the rose?
Through this dread shape the suffering ages look;
Time's tragedy is in that aching stoop;
Through this dread shape humanity betrayed,
Plundered, profaned and disinherited,
Cries protest to the Powers that made the world,
A protest that is also prophecy.

O masters, lords and rulers in all lands,
Is this the handiwork you give to God,
This monstrous thing distorted and soul-quencht?
How will you ever straighten up this shape;
Touch it again with immortality;
Give back the upward looking and the light;
Rebuild in it the music and the dream;
Make right the immemorial infamies,
Perfidious wrongs, immedicable woes?

O masters, lords and rulers in all lands,
How will the future reckon with this Man?
How answer his brute question in that hour
When whirlwinds of rebellion shake all shores?
How will it be with kingdoms and with kings—
With those who shaped him to the thing he is—
When this dumb Terror shall rise to judge the world,
After the silence of the centuries?*

STUDY QUESTIONS

1. For people to be "alienated," it is necessary not only that they be alienated *from* something, but also that they consist of something within themselves; that is, there must be a human nature which is alienated. In Marx's view, what is that human nature which is alienated by capitalism?

2. Compare the sources of alienation as seen by Marx with the other major view of human alienation, existentialism (see Chapter 14). Compare with Rousseau, Nietzsche, and Augustine.

3. The collapse of the Soviet Union has been seen as indicating the failure of Marxism. Alternatively, some have interpreted this collapse as analogous to C. K. Chesterton's observation about Christianity, that "it has not been tried and found wanting; rather, it has been found

*From *The Man with the Hoe and Other Poems* (1899). New York: Doubleday & McClure.

difficult and left untried." Assuming either interpretation, what might there be about human nature that makes communism so difficult?

4. Is "alienated labor" a special case of a deeper, more fundamental aspect of the human condition, in which people are unavoidably alienated from each other, as well as from nature, and even from themselves, regardless of economic system?

SOME ADDITIONAL READINGS

Bien, Joseph (1984). *History, Revolution and Human Nature: Marx's Philosophical Anthropology.* Amsterdam: B. R. Gruner.

Fromm, Erich (1961). *Marx's Concept of Man.* New York: F. Ungar Publishing Co.

Heyer, Paul (1982). *Nature, Human Nature, and Society: Marx, Darwin, Biology and the Human Sciences.* Westport, Conn.: Greenwood Press.

Plamenatz, J. (1975). *Karl Marx's Theory of Man.* New York: Oxford University Press.

Wallimann, Isidor (1981). *Estrangement: Marx's Conception of Human Nature and the Division of Labor.* Westport, Conn.: Greenwood Press.

CHAPTER THIRTEEN

The Pursuit of Power

When someone says "It's just human nature," the likelihood is that the speaker is about to excuse some unpleasant act. Leaving aside for now the question of whether human nature can ever provide such a defense, let's look at the behavior in question. Most of the time, the "it" that is supposedly just human nature is aggressive, deceitful, or otherwise selfish, related to what we might call the pursuit of personal power. Such a perspective often implies a pessimistic assessment of human beings generally; hence it could have been included in our earlier consideration that people are basically nasty (Chapter 9). Thus, Niccolo Machiavelli wrote that from the perspective of practical politics,

> all men are bad and ever ready to display their vicious nature, whenever they may find occasion for it. If their evil disposition remains concealed for a time, it must be attributed to some unknown reason, and we must assume that it lacked occasion to show itself; but time, which has been said to be the father of all truth, does not fail to bring it to light. (*The Discourses,* I, ch. 3)

Such views, in turn, introduce fundamental questions of ethics, as well as the interesting issue of whether *theorists* of a particular aspect of human nature become its *advocates* as well. On the other hand, there is something ennobling about human striving. Goethe apparently thought so, since in his version of Faust, this yearning for transcendence sufficed to save a soul that would otherwise have been damned. And when striving for power is seen as "self-actualization" instead of the domination of others, the result can be inspiring. Consider, for example, the following words, put into the mouth of the warrior Tamburlaine by Elizabethan playwright Christopher Marlowe. (You might also consider improving upon the last line!)

Nature, that fram'd us of four elements
Warring within our breasts for regiment,
Doth teach us all to have aspiring minds:
Our souls, whose faculties can comprehend
The wondrous architecture of the world,
And measure every wandering planet's course,
Still climbing after knowledge infinite,
And always moving as the restless spheres,
Wills us to wear ourselves and never rest,
Until we reach the ripest fruit of all,
That perfect bliss and sole felicity,
The sweet fruition of an earthly crown.

MACHIAVELLI

Niccolò Machiavelli (1469–1527) is one of those remarkable people whose name has become an adjective (a distinction achieved, incidentally, by more than a few of the thinkers encountered in this book!). *Machiavellian* has come to be associated with ruthlessness, treachery, and an insistence that when it comes to politics, the end—power—justifies virtually any means. In Elizabethan England, in fact, Machiavelli was synonymous with the devil. While ethicists have consistently denounced his work, politicians have assiduously practiced his precepts.

Born in Florence, Machiavelli was actively engaged in political intrigue among the Italian city-states, and was especially fascinated by the notorious Cesare Borgia, who served in many ways as the model for Machiavelli's best-known work, *The Prince.* This relatively brief and readable treatise was intended as a practical handbook for the aspiring politician. It remains a classic document in political theory, one that has been consulted not only by scholars but by politicians and military leaders (such as Lenin, Mussolini, and Hitler), many of whose reputations are none too savory. However, *The Prince* is not simply a primer for the politically ambitious and unprincipled; it is of particular interest for our purposes as history's clearest, most influential, and thoroughly unabashed document extolling the role of power in human affairs.

Machiavelli was not simply an apostle of immorality. He was the founder of the realist tradition in political theory and the father of power politics. He had the clear-eyed daring to distinguish between what people ought to be and what, in his opinion at least, they actually are. Machiavelli penetrated the gap between outward appearance and inner reality, in some ways unmasking aspects of human nature that many of us would rather keep unacknowledged. He insisted on pursuing human motives with an unswerving, unsentimental determination that makes us shiver today—not so much because he is so cynical but because, in many ways, he was so perceptive.

Machiavelli's other major work is *The Discourses,* ostensibly a commentary on Livy's *History of Rome,* but actually a longer, more detailed account of Machiavelli's thought. *The Prince,* however, is by far the most renowned (and accessible) of Machiavelli's works. It consists of 26 short chapters; here are two of them.

Passing to the other qualities above referred to, I say that every Prince should desire to be accounted merciful and not cruel. Nevertheless, he should be on his guard against the abuse of this quality of mercy. Cesare Borgia was reputed cruel, yet his cruelty restored Romagna, united it, and brought it to order and obedience; so that if we look at things in their true light, it will be seen that he was in reality far more merciful than the people of Florence, who, to avoid the imputation of cruelty, suffered Pistoja to be torn to pieces by factions.

A Prince should therefore disregard the reproach of being thought cruel where it enables him to keep his subjects united and obedient. For he who quells disorder by a very few signal examples will in the end be more merciful than he who from too great leniency permits things to take their course and so to result in rapine and bloodshed; for these hurt the whole State, whereas the severities of the Prince injure individuals only.

And for a new Prince, of all others, it is impossible to escape a name for cruelty, since new States are full of dangers. . . .

And here comes in the question whether it is better to be loved rather than feared, or feared rather than loved. It might perhaps be answered that we should wish to be both; but since love and fear can hardly exist together; if we must choose between them, it is far safer to be feared than loved. For of men it may generally be affirmed that they are thankless, fickle, false, studious to avoid danger, greedy of gain, devoted to you while you are able to confer benefits upon them, and ready, as I said before, while danger is distant, to shed their blood, and sacrifice their property, their lives, and their children for you; but in the hour of need they turn against you. The Prince, therefore, who without otherwise securing himself builds wholly on their professions is undone. For the friendships which we buy with a price, and do not gain by greatness and nobility of character, though they be fairly earned are not made good, but fail us when we have occasion to use them.

Moreover, men are less careful how they offend him who makes himself loved than him who makes himself feared. For love is held by the tie of obligation, which, because men are a sorry breed, is broken on every whisper of private interest; but fear is bound by the apprehension of punishment which never relaxes its grasp.

Nevertheless a Prince should inspire fear in such a fashion that if he do not win love he may escape hate. For a man may very well be feared and yet not hated, and this will be the case so long as he does not meddle with the property or with the women of his citizens and subjects. And if constrained to put any to death, he should do so only when there is manifest cause or reasonable justification. But, above all, he must abstain from the property of others. For men will sooner forget the death of their father than the loss of their patrimony. Moreover, pretexts for confiscation are never to seek, and he who has once begun to live by rapine always finds reasons for taking what is not his; whereas reasons for shedding blood are fewer, and sooner exhausted.

But when a Prince is with his army, and has many soldiers under his command, he must needs disregard the reproach of cruelty, for without such a reputation in its Captain, no army can be held together or kept under any kind of control. Among other things remarkable in Hannibal this has been noted, that having a very great army, made up of men of many different nations and brought to fight in a foreign country, no dissension ever arose among the soldiers themselves, nor any mutiny against their leader, either in his good or in his evil fortunes. This we can only ascribe to the transcendent cruelty, which, joined with numberless great qualities, rendered him at once venerable and terrible in the eyes of his soldiers; for without this reputation for cruelty these other virtues would not have produced the like results.

Unreflecting writers, indeed, while they praise his achievements, have condemned the chief cause of them; but that his other merits would not by themselves have been so efficacious we may see from the case of Scipio, one of the greatest Captains, not of his own time only but of all times of which we have record, whose armies rose against him in Spain from no other cause than his too great leniency in allowing them a freedom inconsistent with military strictness. With which weakness Fabius Maximus taxed him in the Senate House, calling him the corrupter of the Roman soldiery. Again, when the Locrians were shamefully outraged by one of his lieutenants, he neither avenged them, nor punished the insolence of his officer; and this from the natural easiness of his disposition. So that it was said in the Senate by one who sought to excuse him, that there were many who knew better how to refrain from doing wrong themselves than how to correct the wrong-doing of others. This temper, however, must in time have marred the name and fame even of Scipio, had he continued in it, and retained his command. But living as he did under the control of the Senate, this hurtful quality was not merely disguised, but came to be regarded as a glory.

Returning to the question of being loved or feared, I sum up by saying, that since his being loved depends upon his subjects, while his being feared depends upon himself, a wise Prince should build on what is his own, and not on what rests with others. Only, as I have said, he must do his utmost to escape hatred. . . .

Every one understands how praiseworthy it is in a Prince to keep faith, and to live uprightly and not craftily. Nevertheless, we see from what has taken place in our own days that Princes who have set little store by their word, but have known how to overreach men by their cunning, have accomplished great things, and in the end got the better of those who trusted to honest dealing.

Be it known, then, that there are two ways of contending, one in accordance with the laws, the other by force; the first of which is proper to men, the second to beasts. But since the first method is often ineffectual, it becomes necessary to resort to the second. A Prince should, therefore, understand how to use well both the man and the beast. And this lesson has been covertly taught by the ancient writers, who relate how Achilles and many others of these old Princes were given over to be brought up and trained by Chiron the Centaur; since the only meaning of their having for instructor one who was half man and half beast is, that it is necessary for a Prince to know how to use both natures, and that the one without the other has no stability.

But since a Prince should know how to use the beast's nature wisely, he ought of beasts to choose both the lion and the fox; for the lion cannot guard himself from the toils, nor the fox from wolves. He must therefore be a fox to discern toils, and a lion to drive off wolves.

To rely wholly on the lion is unwise; and for this reason a prudent Prince neither can nor ought to keep his word when to keep it is hurtful to him and the causes which led him to pledge it are removed. If all men were good, this would not be good advice, but since they are dishonest and do not keep faith with you, you, in return, need not keep faith with them; and no prince was ever at a loss for plausible reasons to cloak a breach of faith. Of this numberless recent instances could be given, and it might be shown how many solemn treaties and engagements have been rendered inoperative and idle through want of faith in Princes, and that he who was best known to play the fox has had the best success.

It is necessary, indeed, to put a good colour on this nature, and to be skilful in simulating and dissembling. But men are so simple, and governed so absolutely by their present needs, that he who wishes to deceive will never fail in finding willing dupes. One recent example I will not omit. Pope Alexander VI had no care or thought but how to deceive, and always found material to work on. No man ever had a more effective manner of asseverating, or made promises with more solemn protestations, or observed them less. And yet, because he understood this side of human nature, his frauds always succeeded.

It is not essential, then, that a Prince should have all the good qualities which I have enumerated above, but it is most essential that he should seem to have them; I will even venture to affirm that if he has and invariably practises them all, they are hurtful, whereas the appearance of having them is useful. Thus, it is well to seem merciful, faithful, humane, religious, and upright, and also to be so; but the mind should remain so balanced that were it needful not to be so, you should be able and know how to change to the contrary.

And you are to understand that a Prince, and most of all a new Prince, cannot observe all those rules of conduct in respect whereof men are accounted good, being often forced, in order to preserve his Princedom, to act in opposition to good faith, charity, humanity, and religion. He must therefore keep his mind ready to shift as the winds and tides of Fortune turn, and, as I have already said, he ought not to quit good courses if he can help it, but should know how to follow evil courses if he must.

A Prince should therefore be very careful that nothing ever escapes his lips which is not replete with the five qualities above named, so that to see and hear him, one would think him the embodiment of mercy, good faith, integrity, humanity, and religion. And there is no virtue which it is more necessary for him to seem to possess than this last; because men in general judge rather by the eye than by the hand, for every one can see but few can touch. Every one sees what you seem, but few know what you are, and these few dare not oppose themselves to the opinion of the many who have the majesty of the State to back them up.

Moreover, in the actions of all men, and most of all of Princes, where there is no tribunal to which we can appeal, we look to results. Wherefore if a Prince succeeds in establishing and maintaining his authority, the means will always be judged honourable and be approved by every one. For the vulgar are always taken by appearances and by results, and the world is made up of the vulgar, the few only finding room when the many have no longer ground to stand on.

A certain Prince of our own days, whose name it is as well not to mention, is always preaching peace and good faith, although the mortal enemy of both; and both, had he practised them as he preaches them, would, oftener than once, have lost him his kingdom and authority.*

NIETZSCHE

Friedrich Nietzsche (1844–1900) was one of the most influential theorists of human nature; he is also, at times, maddeningly difficult and widely misunderstood. His best writing is a kind of poetry, consisting of brief aphorisms, striking metaphors, and powerful yet puzzling allegories. In his first work, *The Birth of Tragedy,* Nietzsche suggested that Greek civilization (and humanity generally) could be understood as expressing a conflict between two tendencies, the Apollonian, which strives for order and clarity, and its unbridled and orgiastic opposite, the Dionysian.

Nietzsche is also famous for proclaiming in *Thus Spake Zarathustra* that "God is dead" (to which someone responded years later by writing: "Nietzsche is dead—God"). But Nietzsche was not so much blatantly atheistic as he was convinced that religion had lost meaning for modern society, which, in turn, required that people establish their own meaning and values. Nietzsche sought to achieve this with extraordinary intensity and passion, as well as iconoclasm. As part of this overall reevaluation, Nietzsche argued, especially in *Beyond Good and Evil* and *The Genoology of Morals,* that Christianity fostered a "slave morality" that elevated the good of underlings, in opposition to the true good, reflected in the power of rulers, warriors, and innovators.

Nietzsche believed that immortality was a flattering but misleading doctrine, appealing to the conceit that one's death has cosmic significance, whereas in fact it is only the quality of one's life that matters. Whereas Machiavelli described the uses of power in the political sphere, Nietzsche was the preeminent theorist of the personal "will to power," which included not only physical and social power, but also power over one's own emotions and the freedom to define one's own destiny.

Despite his faults, and occasional incoherence, there is something terrifying and exhilarating, yet sobering in Nietzsche's lonely, passionate, defiant struggle over what it means to be human. It is tempting—but misleading—to dismiss Nietzsche because he died insane, and because his ideas (particularly the *Ubermensch* or Overman) were subsequently misappropriated by the Nazis. Nietzsche himself was not crazy during his productive period; moreover, he was an ardent foe of anti-Semitism, nationalism, and power politics. It is ironic that posthumously, his name was invoked to support what in life he had thoroughly loathed. The following selections are from *The Portable Nietzsche.* First, a bit of *The Antichrist.*

*From *The Prince* (1910). (N. H. Thomson, Trans.). London: Collier.

What is good? Everything that heightens the feeling of power in man, the will to power, power itself.

What is bad? Everything that is born of weakness.

What is happiness? The feeling that power is *growing*, that resistance is overcome.

Not contentedness but more power; not peace but war; not virtue but fitness (Renaissance virtue, *virtù*, virtue that is moraline-free).

The weak and the failures shall perish: first principle of *our* love of man. And they shall even be given every possible assistance.

What is more harmful than any vice? Active pity for all the failures and all the weak: Christianity.

The problem I thus pose is not what shall succeed mankind in the sequence of living beings (man is an *end*), but what type of man shall be *bred*, shall be *willed*, for being higher in value, worthier of life, more certain of a future.

Even in the past this higher type has appeared often—but as a fortunate accident, as an exception, never as something *willed*. In fact, this has been the type most dreaded—almost *the* dreadful—and from dread the opposite type was willed, bred, and *attained:* the domestic animal, the herd animal, the sick human animal—the Christian.

Mankind does *not* represent a development toward something better or stronger or higher in the sense accepted today. "Progress" is merely a modern idea, that is, a false idea. The European of today is vastly inferior in value to the European of the Renaissance: further development is altogether *not* according to any necessity in the direction of elevation, enhancement, or strength.

In another sense, success in individual cases is constantly encountered in the most widely different places and cultures: here we really do find a *higher type*, which is, in relation to mankind as a whole, a kind of overman. Such fortunate accidents of great success have always been possible and *will* perhaps always be possible. And even whole families, tribes, or peoples may occasionally represent such a *bull's-eye*.

Christianity should not be beautified and embellished: it has waged deadly war against this higher type of man; it has placed all the basic instincts of this type under the ban; and out of these instincts it has distilled evil and the Evil One: the strong man as the typically reprehensible man, the "reprobate." Christianity has sided with all that is weak and base, with all failures; it has made an ideal of whatever *contradicts* the instinct of the strong life to preserve itself; it has corrupted the reason even of those strongest in spirit by teaching men to consider the supreme values of the spirit as something sinful, as something that leads into error—as temptations. The most pitiful example: the corruption of Pascal, who believed in the corruption of his reason through original sin when it had in fact been corrupted only by his Christianity.

It is a painful, horrible spectacle that has dawned on me: I have drawn back the curtain from the *corruption* of man. In my mouth, this word is at least free from one suspicion: that it might involve a moral accusation of man. It is meant—let me emphasize this once more—*moraline-free*. So much so that I experience this corruption most strongly precisely where men have so far aspired most deliberately to "virtue" and "godliness." I understand corruption, as you will guess, in the sense of decadence: it is my contention that all the values in which mankind now sums up its supreme desiderata are *decadence-values*.

I call an animal, a species, or an individual corrupt when it loses its instincts, when it chooses, when it prefers, what is disadvantageous for it. A history of "lofty sentiments," of the "ideals of mankind"—and it is possible that I shall have to write it—would almost explain too *why* man is so corrupt. Life itself is to my mind the instinct for growth, for durability, for an accumulation of forces, for *power:* where the will to power is lacking there is decline. It is my contention that all the supreme values of mankind *lack* this will—that the values which are symptomatic of decline, *nihilistic* values, are lording it under the holiest names.

Christianity is called the religion of *pity*. Pity stands opposed to the tonic emotions which heighten our vitality: it has a depressing effect. We are deprived of strength when we feel pity. That loss of strength which suffering as such inflicts on life is still further increased and multiplied by pity. Pity makes suffering contagious. Under certain circumstances, it may engender a total loss of life and vitality out of all proportion to the magnitude of the cause (as in the case of the death of the Nazarene). That is the first consideration, but there is a more important one.

Suppose we measure pity by the value of the reactions it usually produces; then its perilous nature appears in an even brighter light. Quite in general, pity crosses the law of development, which is the law of *selection*. It preserves what is ripe for destruction; it defends those who have been disinherited and condemned by life; and by the abundance of the failures of all kinds which it keeps alive, it gives life itself a gloomy and questionable aspect.

Some have dared to call pity a virtue (in every *noble* ethic it is considered a weakness); and as if this were not enough, it has been made *the* virtue, the basis and source of all virtues. To be sure—and one should always keep this in mind—this was done by a philosophy that was nihilistic and had inscribed the *negation of life* upon its shield. Schopenhauer was consistent enough: pity negates life and renders it *more deserving of negation*.

Pity is the *practice* of nihilism. To repeat: this depressive and contagious instinct crosses those instincts which aim at the preservation of life and at the enhancement of its value. It multiplies misery and conserves all that is miserable, and is thus a prime instrument of the advancement of decadence: pity persuades men to *nothingness!* Of course, one does not say "nothingness" but "beyond" or "God," or "*true* life," or Nirvana, salvation, blessedness.

This innocent rhetoric from the realm of the religious-moral idiosyncrasy appears much less innocent as soon as we realize which tendency it is that here shrouds itself in sublime words: *hostility against life*. Schopenhauer was hostile to life, therefore pity became a virtue for him.

Aristotle, as is well known, considered pity a pathological and dangerous condition, which one would be well advised to attack now and then with a purge: he understood tragedy as a purge. From the standpoint of the instinct of life, a remedy certainly seems necessary for such a pathological and dangerous accumulation of pity as is represented by the case of Schopenhauer (and unfortunately by our entire literary and artistic decadence from St. Petersburg to Paris, from Tolstoi to Wagner)—to puncture it and make it *burst*.

In our whole unhealthy modernity there is nothing more unhealthy than Christian pity. To be physicians *here*, to be inexorable *here*, to wield the scalpel *here*—that is *our* part, that is *our* love of man, that is how *we* are philosophers, we *Hyperboreans*.

It is necessary to say whom we consider our antithesis: it is the theologians and whatever has theologians' blood in its veins—and that includes our whole philosophy.

Whoever has seen this catastrophe at close range or, better yet, been subjected to it and almost perished of it, will no longer consider it a joking matter (the free-thinking of our honorable natural scientists and physiologists is, to my mind, a joke: they lack passion in these matters, they do not suffer them as their passion and martyrdom). This poisoning is much more extensive than is generally supposed: I have found the theologians' instinctive arrogance wherever anyone today considers himself an "idealist"—wherever a right is assumed, on the basis of some higher origin, to look at reality from a superior and foreign vantage point.

The idealist, exactly like the priest, holds all the great concepts in his hand (and not only in his hand!); he plays them out with a benevolent contempt for the "understanding," the "senses," "honors," "good living," and "science"; he considers all that *beneath* him, as so many harmful and seductive forces over which "the spirit" hovers in a state of pure for-itselfness—as if humility, chastity, poverty, or, in one word, *holiness,* had not harmed life immeasurably more than any horrors or vices. The pure spirit is the pure lie.

As long as the priest is considered a *higher* type of man—this *professional* negator, slanderer, and poisoner of life—there is no answer to the question: what *is* truth? For truth has been stood on its head when the conscious advocate of nothingness and negation is accepted as the representative of "truth."*

Nietzsche's best-known work is a difficult, novel-length parable, *Thus Spoke Zarathustra,* which tells of a prophet who seeks to inform human beings of their true nature and of their possibilities:

When Zarathustra came into the next town, which lies on the edge of the forest, he found many people gathered together in the market place; for it had been promised that there would be a tightrope walker. And Zarathustra spoke thus to the people:

"*I teach you the overman.* Man is something that shall be overcome. What have you done to overcome him?

"All beings so far have created something beyond themselves; and do you want to be the ebb of this great flood and even go back to the beasts rather than overcome man? What is the ape to man? A laughingstock or a painful embarrassment. And man shall be just that for the overman: a laughingstock or a painful embarrassment. You have made your way from worm to man, and much in you is still worm. Once you were apes, and even now, too, man is more ape than any ape.

"Whoever is the wisest among you is also a mere conflict and cross between plant and ghost. But do I bid you become ghosts or plants?

"Behold, I teach you the overman. The overman is the meaning of the earth. Let your will say: the overman *shall be* the meaning of the earth! I beseech you, my brothers, *remain faithful to the earth,* and do not believe those who speak to you of otherworldly hopes! Poison-mixers are they, whether they know it or not. Despisers of life are they, decaying and poisoned themselves, of whom the earth is weary: so let them go.

"Once the sin against God was the greatest sin; but God died, and these sinners died with him. To sin against the earth is now the most dreadful thing, and to esteem the entrails of the unknowable higher than the meaning of the earth.

"Once the soul looked contemptuously upon the body, and then this contempt was the highest: she wanted the body meager, ghastly, and starved. Thus she hoped to escape it and the earth. Oh, this soul herself was still meager, ghastly, and starved: and cruelty was the lust of this soul. But you, too, my brothers, tell me: what does your body proclaim of your soul? Is not your soul poverty and filth and wretched contentment?

"Verily, a polluted stream is man. One must be a sea to be able to receive a polluted stream without becoming unclean. Behold, I teach you the overman: he is this sea; in him your great contempt can go under.

"What is the greatest experience you can have? It is the hour of the great contempt. The hour in which your happiness, too, arouses your disgust, and even your reason and your virtue.

"The hour when you say, 'What matters my happiness? It is poverty and filth and wretched contentment. But my happiness ought to justify existence itself.'

"The hour when you say, 'What matters my reason? Does it crave knowledge as the lion his food? It is poverty and filth and wretched contentment.'

*From *The Portable Nietzsche* (1954). (Walter Kaufmann, Trans.). New York: Viking Press.

"The hour when you say, 'What matters my virtue? As yet it has not made me rage. How weary I am of my good and my evil! All that is poverty and filth and wretched contentment.'

"The hour when you say, 'What matters my justice? I do not see that I am flames and fuel. But the just are flames and fuel.'

"The hour when you say, 'What matters my pity? Is not pity the cross on which he is nailed who loves man? But my pity is no crucifixion.'

"Have you yet spoken thus? Have you yet cried thus? Oh, that I might have heard you cry thus!

"Not your sin but your thrift cries to heaven; your meanness even in your sin cries to heaven.

"Where is the lightning to lick you with its tongue? Where is the frenzy with which you should be inoculated?

"Behold, I teach you the overman: he is this lightning, he is this frenzy."

When Zarathustra had spoken thus, one of the people cried: "Now we have heard enough about the tightrope walker; now let us see him too!" And all the people laughed at Zarathustra. But the tightrope walker, believing that the word concerned him, began his performance.

Zarathustra, however, beheld the people and was amazed. Then he spoke thus:

"Man is a rope, tied between beast and overman—a rope over an abyss. A dangerous across, a dangerous on-the-way, a dangerous looking-back, a dangerous shuddering and stopping.

"What is great in man is that he is a bridge and not an end: what can be loved in man is that he is an *overture* and a *going under.*

"I love those who do not know how to live, except by going under, for they are those who cross over.

"I love the great despisers because they are the great reverers and arrows of longing for the other shore.

"I love those who do not first seek behind the stars for a reason to go under and be a sacrifice, but who sacrifice themselves for the earth, that the earth may some day become the overman's.

"I love him who lives to know, and who wants to know so that the overman may live some day. And thus he wants to go under.

"I love him who works and invents to build a house for the overman and to prepare earth, animal, and plant for him: for thus he wants to go under.

"I love him who loves his virtue, for virtue is the will to go under and an arrow of longing.

"I love him who does not hold back one drop of spirit for himself, but wants to be entirely the spirit of his virtue: thus he strides over the bridge as spirit.

"I love him who makes his virtue his addiction and his catastrophe: for his virtue's sake he wants to live on and to live no longer.

"I love him who does not want to have too many virtues. One virtue is more virtue than two, because it is more of a noose on which his catastrophe may hang.

"I love him whose soul squanders itself, who wants no thanks and returns none: for he always gives away and does not want to preserve himself.

"I love him who is abashed when the dice fall to make his fortune, and asks, 'Am I then a crooked gambler?' For he wants to perish.

"I love him who casts golden words before his deeds and always does even more than he promises: for he wants to go under.

"I love him who justifies future and redeems past generations: for he wants to perish of the present.

"I love him who chastens his god because he loves his god: for he must perish of the wrath of his god.

"I love him whose soul is deep, even in being wounded, and who can perish of a small experience: thus he goes gladly over the bridge.

"I love him whose soul is overfull so that he forgets himself, and all things are in him: thus all things spell his going under.

"I love him who has a free spirit and a free heart: thus his head is only the entrails of his heart, but his heart drives him to go under.

"I love all those who are as heavy drops, falling one by one out of the dark cloud that hangs over men: they herald the advent of lightning, and, as heralds, they perish.

"Behold, I am a herald of the lightning and a heavy drop from the cloud; but this lightning is called *overman*." . . .

Then something happened that made every mouth dumb and every eye rigid. For meanwhile the tightrope walker had begun his performance: he had stepped out of a small door and was walking over the rope, stretched between two towers and suspended over the market place and the people. When he had reached the exact middle of his course the small door opened once more and a fellow in motley clothes, looking like a jester, jumped out and followed the first one with quick steps.

"Forward, lamefoot!" he shouted in an awe-inspiring voice. "Forward, lazybones, smuggler, pale-face, or I shall tickle you with my heel! What are you doing here between towers? The tower is where you belong. You ought to be locked up; you block the way for one better than yourself." And with every word he came closer and closer; but when he was but one step behind, the dreadful thing happened which made every mouth dumb and every eye rigid: he uttered a devilish cry and jumped over the man who stood in his way. This man, however, seeing his rival win, lost his head and the rope, tossed away his pole, and plunged into the depth even faster, a whirlpool of arms and legs. The market place became as the sea when a tempest pierces it: the people rushed apart and over one another, especially at the place where the body must hit the ground.

Zarathustra, however, did not move; and it was right next to him that the body fell, badly maimed and disfigured, but not yet dead. After a while the shattered man recovered consciousness and saw Zarathustra kneeling beside him. "What are you doing here?" he asked at last. "I have long known that the devil would trip me. Now he will drag me to hell. Would you prevent him?"

"By my honor, friend," answered Zarathustra, "all that of which you speak does not exist: there is no devil and no hell. Your soul will be dead even before your body: fear nothing further."

The man looked up suspiciously. "If you speak the truth," he said, "I lose nothing when I lose my life. I am not much more than a beast that has been taught to dance by blows and a few meager morsels."

"By no means," said Zarathustra. "You have made danger your vocation; there is nothing contemptible in that. Now you perish of your vocation: for that I will bury you with my own hands."

When Zarathustra had said this, the dying man answered no more; but he moved his hand as if he sought Zarathustra's hand in thanks. . . .

I want to speak to the despisers of the body. It is their respect that begets their contempt. What is it that created respect and contempt and worth and will? The creative self created respect and contempt; it created pleasure and pain. The creative body created the spirit as a hand for its will.

Even in your folly and contempt, you despisers of the body, you serve your self. I say unto you: your self itself wants to die and turns away from life. It is no longer capable of what it would do above all else: to create beyond itself. That is what it would do above all else, that is its fervent wish.

But now it is too late for it to do this: so your self wants to go under, O despisers of the body. Your self wants to go under, and that is why you have become despisers of the body! For you are no longer able to create beyond yourselves.

And that is why you are angry with life and the earth. An unconscious envy speaks out of the squint-eyed glance of your contempt.

I shall not go your way, O despisers of the body! You are no bridge to the overman!

Thus spoke Zarathustra. . . .

For this is *our* height and our home: we live here too high and steep for all the unclean and their thirst. Cast your pure eyes into the well of my pleasure, friends! How should that make it muddy? It shall laugh back at you in its own purity.

On the tree, Future, we build our nest; and in our solitude eagles shall bring us nourishment in their beaks. Verily, no nourishment which the unclean might share: they would think they were devouring fire and they would burn their mouths. Verily, we keep no homes here for the unclean: our pleasure would be an ice cave to their bodies and their spirits.

And we want to live over them like strong winds, neighbors of the eagles, neighbors of the snow, neighbors of the sun: thus live strong winds. And like a wind I yet want to blow among them one day, and with my spirit take the breath of their spirit: thus my future wills it.

Verily, a strong wind is Zarathustra for all who are low; and this counsel he gives to all his enemies and all who spit and spew: "Beware of spitting *against* the wind!"

Thus spoke Zarathustra. . . .

Where I found the living, there I found will to power; and even in the will of those who serve I found the will to be master.

That the weaker should serve the stronger, to that it is persuaded by its own will, which would be master over what is weaker still: this is the one pleasure it does not want to renounce. And as the smaller yields to the greater that it may have pleasure and power over the smallest, thus even the greatest still yields, and for the sake of power risks life. That is the yielding of the greatest: it is hazard and danger and casting dice for death.

And where men make sacrifices and serve and cast amorous glances, there too is the will to be master. Along stealthy paths the weaker steals into the castle and into the very heart of the more powerful—and there steals power.

And life itself confided this secret to me: "Behold," it said, "I am *that which must always overcome itself.* Indeed, you call it a will to procreate or a drive to an end, to something higher, farther, more manifold: but all this is one, and one secret.

"Rather would I perish than forswear this; and verily, where there is perishing and a falling of leaves, behold, there life sacrifices itself—for power. That I must be struggle and a becoming and an end and an opposition to ends—alas, whoever guesses what is my will should also guess on what *crooked* paths it must proceed.

"Whatever I create and however much I love it—soon I must oppose it and my love; thus my will wills it. And you too, lover of knowledge, are only a path and footprint of my will; verily, my will to power walks also on the heels of your will to truth.

"Indeed, the truth was not hit by him who shot at it with the word of the 'will to existence': that will does not exist. For, what does not exist cannot will; but what is in existence, how could that still want existence? Only where there is life is there also will: not will to life but—thus I teach you—will to power.

"There is much that life esteems more highly than life itself; but out of the esteeming itself speaks the will to power." . . .

Not long ago I walked gloomily through the deadly pallor of dusk—gloomy and hard, with lips pressed together. Not only one sun had set for me. A path that ascended defiantly through stones, malicious, lonely, not cheered by herb or shrub—a mountain path crunched under the defiance of my foot.

Striding silently over the mocking clatter of pebbles, crushing the rock that made it slip, my foot forced its way upward. Upward—defying the spirit that drew it downward toward the abyss, the spirit of gravity, my devil and archenemy. Upward—although he sat on me, half dwarf, half mole, lame, making lame, dripping lead into my ear, leaden thoughts into my brain.

"O Zarathustra," he whispered mockingly, syllable by syllable; "you philosopher's stone! You threw yourself up high, but every stone that is thrown must fall. O Zarathustra, you philosopher's stone, you slingstone, you star-crusher! You threw yourself up so high; but every stone that is thrown must fall. Sentenced to yourself and to your own stoning—O Zarathustra, far indeed have you thrown the stone, but it will fall back on yourself."

Then the dwarf fell silent, and that lasted a long time. His silence, however, oppressed me; and such twosomeness is surely more lonesome than being alone. I climbed, I climbed, I dreamed, I thought; but everything oppressed me. I was like one sick whom his wicked torture makes weary, and who as he falls asleep is awakened by a still more wicked dream. But there is something in me that I call courage; that has so far slain my every discouragement. This courage finally bade me stand still and speak: "Dwarf! It is you or I!"

For courage is the best slayer, courage which *attacks;* for in every attack there is playing and brass.

Man, however, is the most courageous animal: hence he overcame every animal. With playing and brass he has so far overcome every pain; but human pain is the deepest pain.

Courage also slays dizziness at the edge of abysses: and where does man not stand at the edge of abysses? Is not seeing always—seeing abysses?

Courage is the best slayer: courage slays even pity. But pity is the deepest abyss: as deeply as man sees into life, he also sees into suffering.

Courage, however, is the best slayer—courage which attacks: which slays even death itself, for it says, "Was *that* life? Well then! Once more!"

In such words, however, there is much playing and brass. He that has ears to hear, let him hear!

"Stop, dwarf!" I said. "It is I or you! But I am the stronger of us two: you do not know my abysmal thought. *That* you could not bear!"

Then something happened that made me lighter, for the dwarf jumped from my shoulder, being curious; and he crouched on a stone before me. But there was a gateway just where we had stopped.

"Behold this gateway, dwarf!" I continued. "It has two faces. Two paths meet here; no one has yet followed either to its end. This long lane stretches back for an eternity. And the long lane out there, that is another eternity. They contradict each other, these paths; they offend each other face to face; and it is here at this gateway that they come together. The name of the gateway is inscribed above: 'Moment.' But whoever would follow one of them, on and on, farther and farther—do you believe, dwarf, that these paths contradict each other eternally?"

"All that is straight lies," the dwarf murmured contemptuously. "All truth is crooked; time itself is a circle."

"You spirit of gravity," I said angrily, "do not make things too easy for yourself! Or I shall let you crouch where you are crouching, lamefoot; and it was I that carried you to this *height.*

"Behold," I continued, "this moment! From this gateway, Moment, a long, eternal lane leads *backward:* behind us lies an eternity. Must not whatever *can* walk have walked on this lane before? Must not whatever *can* happen have happened, have been done, have passed by before? And if everything has been there before—what do you think, dwarf, of this moment? Must not this gateway too have been there before? And are not all things knotted together so firmly that this moment draws after it *all* that is to come? Therefore—itself too? For whatever *can* walk—in this long lane out *there* too, it *must* walk once more.

"And this slow spider, which crawls in the moonlight, and this moonlight itself, and I and you in the gateway, whispering together, whispering of eternal things—must not all of us have been there before? And return and walk in that other lane, out there, before us, in this long dreadful lane—must we not eternally return?"

Thus I spoke, more and more softly; for I was afraid of my own thoughts and the thoughts behind my thoughts. Then suddenly I heard a dog howl nearby. Had I ever heard a dog howl like this? My thoughts raced back. Yes, when I was a child, in the most distant childhood: then I heard a dog howl like this. And I saw him too, bristling, his head up, trembling, in the stillest midnight when even dogs believe in ghosts—and I took pity: for just then the full moon, silent as death, passed over the house; just then it stood still, a round glow—still on the flat roof, as if on another's property—that was why the dog was terrified, for dogs believe in thieves and ghosts. And when I heard such howling again I took pity again.

Where was the dwarf gone now? And the gateway? And the spider? And all the whispering? Was I dreaming, then? Was I waking up?

Among wild cliffs I stood suddenly alone, bleak, in the bleakest moonlight. *But there lay a man.* And there—the dog, jumping, bristling, whining—now he saw me coming; then he howled again, he *cried.* Had I ever heard a dog cry like this for help? And verily, what I saw—I had never seen the like. A young shepherd I saw, writhing, gagging, in spasms, his face distorted, and a heavy black snake hung out of his mouth. Had I ever seen so much nausea and pale dread on one face? He seemed to have been asleep when the snake crawled into his throat, and there bit itself fast. My hand tore at the snake and tore in vain; it did not tear the snake out of his throat. Then it cried out of me: "Bite! Bite its head off! Bite!" Thus it cried out of me—my dread, my hatred, my nausea, my pity, all that is good and wicked in me cried out of me with a single cry.

You bold ones who surround me! You searchers, researchers, and whoever among you has embarked with cunning sails on unexplored seas. You who are glad of riddles! Guess me this riddle that I saw then, interpret me the vision of the loneliest. For it was a vision and a foreseeing. *What* did I see then in a parable? And *who* is it who must yet come one day? *Who* is the shepherd into whose throat the snake crawled thus? *Who* is the man into whose throat all that is heaviest and blackest will crawl thus?

The shepherd, however, bit as my cry counseled him; he bit with a good bite. Far away he spewed the head of the snake—and he jumped up. No longer shepherd, no longer human—one changed, radiant, *laughing!* Never yet on earth has a human being laughed as he laughed! O my brothers, I heard a laughter that was no human laughter; and now a thirst gnaws at me, a longing that never grows still. My longing for this laughter gnaws at me; oh, how do I bear to go on living! And how could I bear to die now!

Thus spoke Zarathustra.*

LONDON

Jack London (1876–1916) was a best-selling author of stories and adventure novels, and neither a scientist nor a philosopher. Why, then, is his work included in this volume? Because it demonstrates how a perspective on human nature can underlie works of art—and also because it is so refreshingly readable!

Before becoming one of the most popular writers in American history, London was an oyster pirate, a hobo, and an unsuccessful participant in the Klondike gold rush. Jack London became a militant socialist, and yet, his writing celebrated unbridled individualism. To some ex-

*From *The Portable Nietzsche* (1954). (Walter Kaufman, Trans.). New York: Viking Press.

tent, he wrote about people as though they were animals and animals as though they were people, the heroes triumphing (via their own power) in the face of difficult circumstances. Consider this account from London's novel *White Fang:*

> Hated by his kind and by mankind, indomitable, perpetually warred upon and himself waging perpetual war, his development was rapid and one-sided. . . . The code he learned was to obey the strong and to oppress the weak. . . . He became quicker of movement than the other dogs, swifter of foot, craftier, deadlier, more lithe, more lean with iron-like muscle and sinew, more enduring, more cruel, more ferocious, and more intelligent. He had to become all these things, else he would not have held his own nor survived the hostile environment in which he found himself.

And here is Jack London's triumphant description of the dog hero, Buck, which concludes his best-known novel, *The Call of the Wild:*

> When the long winter nights come on and the wolves follow their meat into the lower valleys, he may be seen running at the head of the pack through the pale moonlight or glimmering borealis, leaping gigantic above his fellows, his great throat a-bellow as he sings a song of the younger world, which is the song of the pack.

Jack London also wrote two semiautobiographical novels, *Martin Eden* (about a brawling sailor who becomes a writer before committing suicide) and *John Barleycorn* (about his struggle with alcoholism). Our selection is from *The Sea-Wolf* (1904), the tale of an effete intellectual who finds himself in the clutches of a supremely powerful and utterly amoral captain, Wolf Larsen. Ironically, London intended this novel as an attack on Nietzscheanism, and yet, Larsen emerges as the book's most memorable character. Here is the narrator's first impression of Wolf Larsen, followed by their discussion of "the meaning of life."

Pacing back and forth the length of the hatchway, and savagely chewing the end of cigar, was the man whose casual glance had rescued me from the sea. His height was probably five feet ten inches, or ten and a half; but my first impression, or feel of the man, was not of this, but of his strength. And yet, while he was of massive build, with broad shoulders and deep chest, I could not characterize his strength as massive. It was what might be termed a sinewy, knotty strength, of the kind we ascribe to lean and wiry men, but which, in him, because of his heavy build, partook more of the enlarged gorilla order. Not that in appearance he seemed in the least gorilla-like. What I am striving to express is this strength itself, more as a thing apart from his physical semblance. It was a strength we are wont to associate with things primitive, with wild animals, and the creatures we imagine our tree-dwelling prototypes to have been—a strength savage, ferocious, alive in itself, the essence of life in that it is the potency of motion, the elemental stuff itself out of which the many forms of life have been molded; in short, that which writhes in the body of a snake when the head is cut off, and the snake, as a snake, is dead, or which lingers in a shapeless lump of turtle-meat and recoils and quivers from the prod of a finger.

Such was the impression of strength I gathered from this man who paced up and down. He was firmly planted on his legs; his feet struck the deck squarely and with surety; every movement of a muscle, from the heave of the shoulders to the tightening of the lips about the cigar, was decisive, and seemed to come out of a strength that was excessive and overwhelming. In fact, though this strength pervaded every action of his, it seemed but the advertisement of a greater strength that lurked within, that lay dormant and no more than stirred from time to time, but which might arouse, at any moment, terrible and compelling, like the rage of a lion or the wrath of a storm. . . .

"What do you believe, then?" I countered.

"I believe that life is a mess," he answered promptly. "It is like yeast, a ferment, a thing that moves and may move for a minute, an hour, a year, or a hundred years, but that in the end will cease to move. The big eat the little that they may continue to move, the strong eat the weak that they may retain their strength. The lucky eat the most and move the longest, that is all. What do you make of those things?"

He swept his arm in an impatient gesture toward a number of the sailors who were working on some kind of rope stuff amidships.

"They move; so does the jellyfish move. They move in order to eat in order that they may keep moving. There you have it. They live for their belly's sake, and the belly is for their sake. It's a circle; you get nowhere. Neither do they. In the end they come to a standstill. They move no more. They are dead."

"They have dreams," I interrupted, "radiant, flashing dreams—"

"Of grub," he concluded sententiously.

"And of more—"

"Grub. Of a larger appetite and more luck in satisfying it." His voice sounded harsh. There was no levity in it. "For look you, they dream of making lucky voyages which will bring them more money, of becoming the mates of ships, of finding fortunes—in short, of being in a better position for preying on their fellows, of having all night in, good grub, and somebody else to do the dirty work. You and I are just like them. There is no difference, except that we have eaten more and better. I am eating them now, and you, too. But in the past you have eaten more than I have. You have slept in soft beds, and worn fine clothes, and eaten good meals. Who made those beds? and those clothes? and those meals? Not you. You never made anything in your own sweat. You live on an income which your father earned. You are like a frigate bird swooping down upon the boobies and robbing them of the fish they have caught. You are one with a crowd of men who have made what they call a government, who are masters of all the other men, and who eat the food the other men get and would like to eat themselves. You wear the warm clothes. They made the clothes, but they shiver in rags and ask you, the lawyer, or business agent who handles your money, for a job."

"But that is beside the matter," I cried.

"Not at all." He was speaking rapidly, now, and his eyes were flashing. "It is piggishness, and it is life. Of what use or sense is an immortality of piggishness? What is the end? What is it all about? You have made no food. Yet the food you have eaten or wasted might have saved the lives of a score of wretches who made the food but did not eat it. What immortal end did you serve? Or did they? Consider yourself and me. What does your boasted immortality amount to when your life runs foul of mine? You would like to go back to the land, which is a favorable place for your kind of piggishness. It is a whim of mine to keep you aboard this ship, where my piggishness flourishes. And keep you I will. I can make or break you. You may die today, this week, or next month. I could kill you now, with a blow of my fist, for you are a miserable weakling. But if we are immortal, what is the reason for this? To be piggish as you and I have been all our lives does not seem to be just the thing for immortals to be doing. Again, what's it all about? Why have I kept you here?—"

"Because you are stronger," I managed to blurt out.

"But why stronger?" he went on at once with his perpetual queries. "Because I am a bigger bit of the ferment than you? Don't you see? Don't you see?"

"But the hopelessness of it," I protested.

"I agree with you," he answered. "Then why move at all, since moving is living? Without moving and being part of the yeast there would be no hopelessness. But,—and there it is,—we want to live and move, though we have no reason to, because it happens that it is the nature of life to live and move, to want to live and move. If it were not for this, life would be dead. It is because of this life that is in you that you dream of your immortality. The life that is in you is alive and wants to go on being alive forever. Bah! An eternity of piggishness!" . . .

"Just so," he went on. "The earth is as full of brutality as the sea is full of motion. And some men are made sick by the one, and some by the other. That's the only reason."

"But you, who make a mock of human life, don't you place any value upon it whatever?" I demanded.

"Value? What value?" He looked at me, and though his eyes were steady and motionless, there seemed a cynical smile in them. "What kind of value? How do you measure it? Who values it?"

"I do," I made answer.

"Then what is it worth to you? Another man's life, I mean. Come, now, what is it worth?"

The value of life? How could I put a tangible value upon it? Somehow, I, who have always had expression, lacked expression when with Wolf Larsen. I have since determined that a part of it was due to the man's personality, but that the greater part was due to his totally different outlook. Unlike other materialists I had met and with whom I had something in common to start on, I had nothing in common with him. Perhaps, also, it was the elemental simplicity of his mind that baffled me. He drove so directly to the core of the mater, divesting a question always of all superfluous details, and with such an air of finality, that I seemed to find myself struggling in deep water with no footing under me. Value of life? How could I answer the question on the spur of the moment? The sacredness of life I had accepted as axiomatic. That it was intrinsically valuable was a truism I had never questioned. But when he challenged the truism I was speechless.

"We were talking about this yesterday," he said. "I held that life was a ferment, a yeasty something which devoured life that it might live, and that living was merely successful piggishness. Why, if there is anything in supply and demand, life is the cheapest thing in the world. There is only so much water, so much earth, so much air; but the life that is demanding to be born is limitless. Nature is a spendthrift. Look at the fish and their millions of eggs. For that matter, look at you and me. In our loins are the possibilities of millions of lives. Could we but find time and opportunity and utilize the last bit and every bit of the unborn life that is in us, we could become the fathers of nations and populate continents. Life? Bah! It has no value. Of cheap things it is the cheapest. Everywhere it goes begging. Nature spills it out with a lavish hand. Where there is room for one life, she sows a thousand lives, and it's life eat life till the strongest and most piggish life is left."

"You have read Darwin," I said. "But you read him misunderstandingly when you conclude that the struggle for existence sanctions your wanton destruction of life."

He shrugged his shoulders. "You know you only mean that in relation to human life, for of the flesh and the fowl and the fish you destroy as much as I or any other man. And human life is in no wise different, though you feel it is and think that you reason why it is. Why should I be parsimonious with this life which is cheap and without value? There are more sailors than there are ships on the sea for them, more workers than there are factories or machines for them. Why, you who live on the land know that you house your poor people in the slums of cities and loose famine and pestilence upon them, and that there still remain more poor people, dying for want of a crust of bread and a bit of meat, (which is life destroyed), than you know what to do with. Have you ever seen the London dockers fighting like wild beasts for a chance to work?"

He started for the companion stairs, but turned his head for a final word. "Do you know the only value life has is what life puts upon itself? And it is of course overestimated, since it is of necessity prejudiced in its own favor. Take that man I had aloft. He held on as if he were a precious thing, a treasure beyond diamonds or rubies. To you? No. To me? Not at all. To himself? Yes. But I do not accept his estimate. He sadly overrates himself. There is plenty more life demanding to be born. Had he fallen and dripped his brains upon the deck like honey from the comb, there would have been no loss to the world. He was worth nothing to the world. The supply is too large. To himself only was he of value, and to show how fictitious even this value was, being dead he is unconscious that he has lost himself. He alone rated himself beyond diamonds and rubies. Diamonds and rubies are gone, spread out on the deck to be washed away by a bucket of sea-water, and he does not even know that the diamonds and rubies are gone. He does not lose anything, for with the loss of himself he loses the knowledge of loss. Don't you see? And what have you to say?"

"That you are at least consistent," was all I could say, and I went on washing the dishes.*

STUDY QUESTIONS

1. Immanuel Kant argued that as a basic ethical precept, human beings must always be treated as ends, never as means. Compare this with the attitudes of Machiavelli and Nietzsche, paying special attention to the practical consequences of each approach.

2. Nietzsche and Machiavelli would probably argue that they did not invent power or cause it to be important, any more than Copernicus, say, invented the fact that the earth revolves around the sun. To what extent, however, does "acknowledging a reality" help create that reality, and also legitimize a course of action?

3. Make arguments for and/or against the proposition that the "will to power" is natural, ethical, original, or useful.

4. Discuss the meaning of Nietzsche's dwarf for Nietzsche himself, for Christianity, for Rousseau, for Marx, for yourself. Also, take a stab at the young shepherd and his snake!

SOME ADDITIONAL READINGS

Masters, Roger D. (1996). *Machiavelli, Leonardo, and the Science of Power.* Notre Dame, Ind.: University of Notre Dame Press.

Parkes, Graham (1994). *Composing the Soul: Reaches of Nietzsche's Psychology.* Chicago: University of Chicago Press.

Rosen, Stanley (1995). *The Mask of Enlightenment: Nietzsche's Zarathustra.* New York: Cambridge University Press.

Stack, George J. (1994). *Nietzsche: Man, Knowledge, and Will to Power.* Durango, Colo.: Hollowbrook Publishing.

Strauss, Leo (1959). *Thoughts on Machiavelli.* Glencoe, Ill.: Free Press.

*From *The Sea-Wolf* (1904). London: Macmillan.

CHAPTER FOURTEEN

The Existential Imagination

Of all schools of thought, existentialism has probably concerned itself more than any other with the problem of human existence. Its emphasis is not on human beings as knowers, but rather, as personal, subjective creatures struggling with some of the most intense and problematic aspects of what it means to be alive: with fear, death, absurdity, isolation, alienation, the condition of human beings in the here and now—and what, if anything, they can do about it.

Existentialism has both religious and atheistic roots, the former notably in the Danish philosopher Søren Kierkegaard, whose overwhelming concern was that each individual must make personal choices, often wrenchingly painful ones, about his or her relationship to God. Twentieth-century manifestations of religious existentialism can be found especially in the work of Gabriel Marcel and Karl Barth. Atheistic existentialism originated largely in the writings of Friedrich Nietzsche (see Chapter 13), with twentieth-century development especially by Martin Heidegger, Jean-Paul Sartre, and Albert Camus. It deals with the question of how human life can be meaningful in an uncaring universe bereft of God. Either way, the existential quest is to understand the role of subjective personhood, and in doing so, existentialism has developed distinctive notions of human nature.

Existential approaches are also reflected in the work of theologians such as Paul Tillich, psychiatrists such as Karl Jaspers, and in literary works ranging from Shakespeare's *King Lear* to Dostoyevsky's *The Brothers Karamazov*, to the work of Franz Kafka as well as recent treatments of the alienated individual, including Samuel Beckett and the so-called "theater of the absurd."

KIERKEGAARD

Anyone whose books include *Fear and Trembling* and *The Sickness Unto Death* is unlikely to have been especially lighthearted. Indeed, the Danish philosopher and religious thinker Søren Kierkegaard (1813–1855) appears to have led a tormented life, especially after he learned that his father had once cursed God, and later, when he broke off his engagement to a young woman, the great and only romantic love of his life. Kierkegaard was deeply religious, although he fought bitterly with the state (Lutheran) Church of Denmark, claiming that it lacked the absolute, unconditional devotion that, in his opinion, Christianity demanded. For Kierkegaard, faith required acceptance of the "absurd," as well as unquestioning obedience to religious commands (such as God's demand that Abraham sacrifice his son, Isaac) that are not only irrational, but even unethical.

Kierkegaard was also passionately devoted to the idea of subjectivity and the over-whelming importance of the individual, whose highest calling was to become a "Knight of Faith." He insisted that the most important issues in life require painful, honest choices, which he formulated in the stark contrast: either/or—as opposed to wishy-washy attempted compromises such as both/and. Only in this way, he felt, can the individual become a self, that is, he or she must go beyond "not willing to be himself" or "willing despairingly to be himself," or re-maining "despairingly unconscious of having a Self and an eternal Self."

Sometimes, Kierkegaard is downright infuriating, as in this notorious opening passage of *The Sickness Unto Death:*

> Man is spirit. But what is spirit? Spirit is the self. But what is the self? The self is a rela-tion which relates itself to its own self, or it is that in the relation which accounts for it that the relation relates itself to its own self; the self is not the relation but consists in the fact that the relation relates itself to its own self. . . . So regarded, man is not yet a self.

(Your earnest, hard-working editor would be deeply grateful if anyone would care to send him a clarification of the above!)

At other times, however, Kierkegaard is clear, even funny, but he is consistently de-manding and always intense.

The selections that follow, concerned with the necessity of human choice, are from *Either/Or,* followed by a brief selection on the "knight of faith" from *Fear and Trembling,* and then some material on subjectivity and truth, from *Concluding Unscientific Postscript to the "Philo-sophical Fragments."*

That which has to be chosen stands in the deepest relationship to the chooser and, when it is a question of a choice involving a life problem, the individual must naturally be living in the meantime; hence it comes about that the longer he postpones the choice the easier it is for him to alter its character, notwith-standing that he is constantly deliberating and deliberating and believes that thereby he is holding the alternatives distinctly apart. When life's either/or is regarded in this way, one is not easily tempted to jest with it. One sees, then, that the inner drift of the personality leaves no time for thought-experiments, that it constantly hastens onward and in one way or another posits this alternative or that, making the choice more difficult the next instant, because what has thus been posited must be revoked. Think of the captain on his ship at the instant when it has to come about. He will perhaps be able to say, "I can ei-ther do this or that"; but in case he is not a pretty poor navigator, he will be aware at the same time that the ship is all the while making its usual headway, and that therefore it is only an instant when it is in-different whether he does this or that. So it is with a man. If he forgets to take account of the headway, there comes at last an instant when there no longer is any question of an either/or, not because he has chosen but because he has neglected to choose, which is equivalent to saying, because others have cho-sen for him, because he has lost his self. . . .

If you will understand me aright, I should like to say that in making a choice it is not so much a ques-tion of choosing the right as of the energy, the earnestness, the pathos with which one chooses. Thereby the personality announces its inner infinity, and thereby, in turn, the personality is consolidated. There-fore, even if a man were to choose the wrong, he will nevertheless discover, precisely by reason of the energy with which he chose, that he has chosen the wrong. For, the choice being made with the whole inwardness of his personality, his nature is purified and he himself brought into immediate relation to the eternal Power whose omnipresence interpenetrates the whole of existence. This transfiguration, this higher consecration, is never attained by that man who chooses merely aesthetically. The rhythm in that man's soul, in spite of all its passion, is a *spiritus levis.*

So, like a Cato, I shout at you my either/or, and yet not like a Cato, for my soul has not yet acquired the resigned coldness which he possessed. But I know that only this incantation, if I have the strength for it, will be capable of rousing you, not to an activity of thought, for of that you have no lack, but to earnestness of spirit. Perhaps you will succeed without that in accomplishing much, perhaps even in astonishing the world (for I am not niggardly), and yet you will miss the highest thing, the only thing which truly has significance—perhaps you will gain the whole world and lose your own self.

What is it, then, that I distinguish in my either/or? Is it good and evil? No, I would only bring you up to the point where the choice between the evil and the good acquires significance for you. Everything hinges upon this. As soon as one can get a man to stand at the crossways in such a position that there is no recourse but to choose, he will choose the right. Hence if it should chance that, while you are in the course of reading this somewhat lengthy dissertation, you were to feel that the instant for choice had come, then throw the rest of this away, never concern yourself about it, you have lost nothing—but choose, and you shall see what validity there is in this act, yea, no young girl can be so happy in the choice of her heart as is a man who knows how to choose. . . .

And this is the pitiful thing to one who contemplates human life, that so many live on in a quiet state of perdition; they outlive themselves, not in the sense that the content of life is successively unfolding and now is possessed in this expanded state, but they live their lives, as it were, outside of themselves, they vanish like shadows, their immortal soul is blown away, and they are not alarmed by the problem of its immortality, for they are already in a state of dissolution before they die. They do not live aesthetically, but neither has the ethical manifested itself in its entirety, so they have not exactly rejected it either; they therefore are not sinning, except insofar as it is sin not to be either one thing or the other; neither are they ever in doubt about their immortality, for he who deeply and sincerely is in doubt of it on his own behalf will surely find the right, and surely it is high time to utter a warning against the great-hearted, heroic objectivity with which many thinkers think on behalf of others and not on their own behalf. If one would call this which I here require selfishness, I would reply that this comes from the fact that people have no conception of what this "self" is, and that it would be of very little use to a man if he were to gain the whole world and lose himself, and that it must necessarily be a poor proof which does not first of all convince the man who presents it.

My either/or does not in the first instance denote the choice between good and evil, it denotes the choice whereby one chooses good *and* evil/or excludes them. Here the question is under what determinants one would contemplate the whole of existence and would himself live. That the man who chooses good and evil chooses the good is indeed true, but this becomes evident only afterwards; for the aesthetical is not the evil but neutrality, and that is the reason why I affirmed that it is the ethical which constitutes the choice. It is, therefore, not so much a question of choosing between willing the good *or* the evil, as of choosing to *will*, but by this in turn the good and the evil are posited. He who chooses the ethical chooses the good, but here the good is entirely abstract, only its being is posited, and hence it does not follow by any means that the chooser cannot in turn choose the evil, in spite of the fact that he chose the good. Here you see again how important it is that a choice be made, and that the crucial thing is not deliberation, but the baptism of the will which lifts up the choice into the ethical. The longer the time that elapses, the more difficult it is to choose, for the soul is constantly attached to one side of the dilemma, and it becomes more and more difficult, therefore, to tear oneself loose. And yet this is necessary if one is truly to choose. . . .*

[For my part I can well describe the movements of faith, but I cannot make them. When one would learn to make the motions of swimming one can let oneself be hung by a swimming-belt from the ceiling and go through the motions (describe them, so to speak, as we speak of describing a circle), but one is not swimming. In that way I can describe the movements of faith, but when I am thrown into the water, I swim, it is true (for I don't belong to the beach-waders), but I make other movements, I make the movements of infinity, whereas faith does the opposite: after having made the movements of infinity, it makes those of finiteness. Hail to him who can make those movements, he performs the marvelous and I shall never grow tired of admiring him, whether he be Abraham or a slave in Abraham's house; whether he be a professor of philosophy or a servant-girl, I look only at the movements. But at them I *do* look and do not let myself be fooled, either by myself or by any other man. The knights of the infinite resignation are easily recognized: their gait is gliding and assured. Those on the other hand who carry the jewel of faith are likely to be delusive, because their outward appearance bears a striking resemblance to that which both the infinite resignation and faith profoundly despise—to Philistinism.

I candidly admit that in my practice I have not found any reliable example of the knight of faith, though I would not therefore deny that every second man may be such an example. I have been trying, however, for several years to get on the track of this, and all in vain. People commonly travel around the world to see rivers and mountains, new stars, birds of rare plumage, queerly deformed fishes, ridiculous breeds of men—they abandon themselves to the bestial stupor which gapes at existence, and they think they have seen something. This does not interest me. But if I knew where there was such a knight of faith, I would make a pilgrimage to him on foot, for this prodigy interests me absolutely. I would not let go of him for an instant, every moment I would watch to see how he managed to make the movements, I would regard myself as secured for life and would divide my time between looking at him and practicing the exercises myself, and thus would spend all my time admiring him.

As was said, I have not found any such person, but I can well think him. Here he is. Acquaintance made, I am introduced to him. The moment I set eyes on him I instantly push him from me, I myself leap backwards, I clasp my hands and say half aloud, "Good Lord, is this the man? Is it really he? Why, he looks like a tax-collector!" However, it is the man after all. I draw closer to him, watching his least movements to see whether there might not be visible a little heterogeneous fractional telegraphic message from the infinite, a glance, a look, a gesture, a note of sadness, a smile, which betrayed the infinite in its heterogeneity with the finite. No! I examine his figure from tip to toe to see if there might not be a cranny through which the infinite was peeping. No! He is solid through and through. His tread? It is vigorous, belonging entirely to finiteness.] . . .†

Christianity proposes to endow the individual with an eternal happiness, a good which is not distributed wholesale, but only to one individual at a time. Though Christianity assumes that there inheres in the sub-

---

*From *Either/Or* (1944). (D. F. Swenson and L. M. Swenson, Trans.). Princeton, N.J.: Princeton University Press.

†From *Fear and Trembling* (1941). (W. Lowrie, Trans.). Princeton, N.J.: Princeton University Press.

jectivity of the individual, as being the potentiality of the appropriation of this good, the possibility for its acceptance, it does not assume that the subjectivity is immediately ready for such acceptance or even that it has, without further ado, a real conception of the significance of such a good. The development or transformation of the individual's subjectivity, its infinite concentration in itself over against the conception of an eternal happiness, that highest good of the infinite—this constitutes the developed potentiality of the primary potentiality which subjectivity as such presents. In this way Christianity protests every form of objectivity; it desires that the subject should be infinitely concerned about himself. It is subjectivity that Christianity is concerned with, and it is only in subjectivity that its truth exists, if it exists at all; objectively, Christianity has absolutely no existence. If its truth happens to be in only a single subject, it exists in him alone; and there is greater Christian joy in heaven over this one individual than over universal history and the System, which as objective entities are incommensurable with that which is Christian.

It is commonly assumed that no art or skill is required in order to be subjective. To be sure, every human being is a bit of a subject, in a sense. But now to strive to become what one already is: who would take the pains to waste his time on such a task, involving the greatest imaginable degree of resignation? Quite so. But for this very reason alone it is a very difficult task, the most difficult of all tasks in fact, precisely because every human being has a strong natural bent and passion to become something more and different. And so it is with all such apparently insignificant tasks: precisely their seeming insignificance makes them infinitely difficult. In such cases the task itself is not directly alluring, so as to support the aspiring individual; instead it works against him, and it needs an infinite effort on his part merely to discover that his task lies here, that this is his task—an effort from which he is otherwise relieved. To think about the simple things of life, about what the plain man also knows after a fashion, is extremely forbidding; for the differential distinction attainable even through the utmost possible exertion is by no means obvious to the sensual man. No indeed, thinking about the high-falutin is very much more attractive and glorious. . . .

When *the question of truth is raised in an objective manner, reflection is directed objectively to the truth, as an object to which the knower is related. Reflection is not focused upon the relationship, however, but upon the question of whether it is the truth to which the knower is related. If only the object to which he is related is the truth, the subject is accounted to be in the truth. When the question of the truth is raised subjectively, reflection is directed subjectively to the nature of the individual's relationship: if only the mode of this relationship is in the truth, the individual is in the truth, even if he should happen to be thus related to what is not true.* Let us take as an example the knowledge of God. Objectively, reflection is directed to the problem of whether this object is the true God; subjectively, reflection is directed to the question whether the individual is related to a something *in such a manner* that his relationship is in truth a God-relationship. . . .

There is only one kind of ethical contemplation, namely, self-contemplation. Ethics closes immediately about the individual, and demands that he exist ethically; it does not make a parade of millions or of generations of men; it does not take humanity in the lump any more than the police arrest humanity at large. The ethical is concerned with particular human beings, and with each and every one of them by himself. If God knows how many hairs there are on a man's head, the ethical knows how many human beings there are; and its enumeration is not in the interest of a total sum, but for the sake of each individual. The ethical requirement is imposed upon each individual, and when it judges, it judges each individual by himself; only a tyrant or an impotent man is content to decimate. The ethical lays hold of each individual and demands that he refrain from all contemplation, especially of humanity and the world; for the ethical, as being the internal, cannot be observed by an outsider. It can be realized only by the individual subject, who alone can know what it is that moves within him.*

*From *Concluding Unscientific Postscript to the "Philosophical Fragments"* (1941). (D. F. Swenson, Trans.). Princeton, N.J.: Princeton University Press.

SARTRE

Jean-Paul Sartre (1905–1980) is, for many, *the* existentialist. Sartre's voluminous works (plays and novels as well as nonfiction) established his brand of existentialism as undoubtedly the most influential, despite the fact that his writing is often terribly dense. Although Sartre did not believe in the existence of an immaterial soul, he distinguished between material objects ("beings in themselves") and conscious human beings ("beings for themselves"). His idea of human nature can best be approached through his own account of his experiences in the anti-Nazi French resistance, during World War II:

> We were never more free than during the German occupation. We had lost all our rights, beginning with the right to talk. Every day we were insulted to our faces and had to take it in silence. Under one pretext or another, as workers, Jews, or political prisoners, we were deported en masse. Everywhere, on billboards, in the newspapers, on the screen, we encountered the revolting and insipid picture of ourselves that our suppressors wanted us to accept. And because of all this we were free. Because the Nazi venom seeped into our thoughts, every accurate thought was a conquest. Because an all-powerful police tried to force us to hold our tongues, every word took on the value of a declaration of principles. Because we were hunted down, every one of our gestures had the weight of a solemn commitment. . . .
>
> Exile, captivity, and especially death (which we usually shrink from facing at all in happier days) became for us the habitual objects of our concern. We learned that they were neither inevitable accidents, nor even constant and inevitable dangers, but they must be considered as our lot itself, our testing, the profound source of our reality as men. At every instant we lived up to the full sense of this commonplace little phrase: 'Man is mortal!' And the choice that each of us made of his life was an authentic choice because it was made face to face with death, because it could always have been expressed in these terms: 'Rather death than . . .' And here I am not speaking of the elite among us who were real Resistants, but of all Frenchmen who, at every hour of the night and day throughout four years, answered NO. *(The Republic of Silence)*

Among the cardinal points of existentialism—and of particular importance for the question of human nature as perceived by existentialists—is the dictum that "existence precedes essence." In his most accessible work, *Existentialism and Humanism,* Sartre states that all existentialists (religious or atheistic) have in common "the fact that they believe that existence comes before essence—or, if you will, that we must begin from the subjective." The following is from *Existentialism and Humanism.*

There are two kinds of existentialists. There are, on the one hand, the Christians, amongst whom I shall name Jaspers and Gabriel Marcel, both professed Catholics; and on the other the existential atheists, amongst whom we must place Heidegger as well as the French existentialists and myself. What they have in common is simply the fact that they believe that *existence* comes before *essence*—or, if you will, that we must begin from the subjective. What exactly do we mean by that?

If one considers an article of manufacture—as, for example, a book or a paper-knife—one sees that it has been made by an artisan who had a conception of it; and he has paid attention, equally, to the conception of a paper-knife and to the pre-existent technique of production which is a part of that conception and is, at bottom, a formula. Thus the paper-knife is at the same time an article producible in a certain manner and one which, on the other hand, serves a definite purpose, for one cannot suppose that a man would produce a paper-knife without knowing what it was for. Let us say, then, of the paper-knife that its essence—that is to say the sum of the formulae and the qualities which made its production and its definition possible—precedes its existence. The presence of such-and-such a paper-knife or book is thus determined before my eyes. Here, then, we are viewing the world from a technical standpoint, and we can say that production precedes existence.

When we think of God as the creator, we are thinking of him, most of the time, as a supernal artisan. Whatever doctrine we may be considering, whether it be a doctrine like that of Descartes, or of Leibnitz himself, we always imply that the will follows, more or less, from the understanding or at least accompanies it, so that when God creates he knows precisely what he is creating. Thus, the conception of man in the mind of God is comparable to that of the paper-knife in the mind of the artisan: God makes man according to a procedure and a conception, exactly as the artisan manufactures a paper-knife, following a definition and a formula. Thus each individual man is the realisation of a certain conception which dwells in the divine understanding. In the philosophic atheism of the eighteenth century, the notion of God is suppressed, but not, for all that, the idea that essence is prior to existence; something of that idea we still find everywhere, in Diderot, in Voltaire and even in Kant. Man possesses a human nature; that "human nature," which is the conception of human being, is found in every man; which means that each man is a particular example of an universal conception, the conception of Man. In Kant, this universality goes so far that the wild man of the woods, man in the state of nature and the bourgeois are all contained in the same definition and have the same fundamental qualities. Here again, the essence of man precedes that historic existence which we confront in experience.

Atheistic existentialism, of which I am a representative, declares with greater consistency that if God does not exist there is at least one being whose existence comes before its essence, a being which exists before it can be defined by any conception of it. That being is man or, as Heidegger has it, the human reality. What do we mean by saying that existence precedes essence? We mean that man first of all exists, encounters himself, surges up in the world—and defines himself afterwards. If man as the existentialist sees him is not definable, it is because to begin with he is nothing. He will not be anything until later, and then he will be what he makes of himself. Thus, there is no human nature, because there is no God to have a conception of it. Man simply is. Not that he is simply what he conceives himself to be, but he is what he wills, and as he conceives himself after already existing—as he wills to be after that leap towards existence. Man is nothing else but that which he makes of himself. That is the first principle of existentialism. And this is what people call its "subjectivity," using the word as a reproach against us. But what do we mean to say by this, but that man is of a greater dignity than a stone or a table? For we mean to say that man primarily exists—that man is, before all else, something which propels itself towards a future and is aware that it is doing so. Man is, indeed, a project which possesses a subjective life, instead of being a kind of moss, or a fungus or a cauliflower. Before that projection of the self nothing exists; not even in the heaven of intelligence: man will only attain existence when he is what he purposes to be.*

For Sartre, as for other existentialists, human freedom is crucially important, and, in a sense, unavoidable. Recall B. F. Skinner's contention that we are not really free but like to pretend that we are (Chapter 7); Sartre insists that we really *are* free, but like to pretend that we aren't! In a famous phrase, we are "condemned to be free." There are no excuses.

*From *Existentialism and Humanism* (1948). (P. Mairet, Trans.). London: Methuen.

Dostoievsky once wrote "If God did not exist, everything would be permitted"; and that, for existentialism, is the starting point. Everything is indeed permitted if God does not exist, and man is in consequence forlorn, for he cannot find anything to depend upon either within or outside himself. He discovers forthwith, that he is without excuse. For if indeed existence precedes essence, one will never be able to explain one's action by reference to a given and specific human nature; in other words, there is no determinism—man is free, man *is* freedom. Nor, on the other hand, if God does not exist, are we provided with any values or commands that could legitimise our behaviour. Thus we have neither behind us, nor before us in a luminous realm of values, any means of justification or excuse. We are left alone, without excuse. That is what I mean when I say that man is condemned to be free. Condemned, because he did not create himself, yet is nevertheless at liberty, and from the moment that he is thrown into this world he is responsible for everything he does. The existentialist does not believe in the power of passion. He will never regard a grand passion as a destructive torrent upon which a man is swept into certain actions as by fate, and which, therefore, is an excuse for them. He thinks that man is responsible for his passion. Neither will an existentialist think that a man can find help through some sign being vouchsafed upon earth for his orientation: for he thinks that the man himself interprets the sign as he chooses. He thinks that every man, without any support or help whatever, is condemned at every instant to invent man. As Ponge has written in a very fine article, "Man is the future of man." That is exactly true. Only, if one took this to mean that the future is laid up in Heaven, that God knows what it is, it would be false, for then it would no longer even be a future. If, however, it means that, whatever man may now appear to be, there is a future to be fashioned, a virgin future that awaits him—then it is a true saying. But in the present one is forsaken.

As an example by which you may the better understand this state of abandonment, I will refer to the case of a pupil of mine, who sought me out in the following circumstances. His father was quarrelling with his mother and was also inclined to be a "collaborator"; his elder brother had been killed in the German offensive of 1940 and this young man, with a sentiment somewhat primitive but generous, burned to avenge him. His mother was living alone with him, deeply afflicted by the semi-treason of his father and by the death of her eldest son, and her one consolation was in this young man. But he, at this moment, had the choice between going to England to join the Free French Forces or of staying near his mother and helping her to live. He fully realised that this woman lived only for him and that his disappearance—or perhaps his death—would plunge her into despair. He also realised that, concretely and in fact, every action he performed on his mother's behalf would be sure of effect in the sense of aiding her to live, whereas anything he did in order to go and fight would be an ambiguous action which might vanish like water into sand and serve no purpose. For instance, to set out for England he would have to wait indefinitely in a Spanish camp on the way through Spain; or, on arriving in England or in Algiers he might be put into an office to fill up forms. Consequently, he found himself confronted by two very different modes of action; the one concrete, immediate, but directed towards only one individual; and the other an action addressed to an end infinitely greater, a national collectivity, but for that very reason ambiguous—and it might be frustrated on the way. At the same time, he was hesitating between two kinds of morality; on the one side the morality of sympathy, of personal devotion and, on the other side, a morality of wider scope but of more debatable validity. He had to choose between those two. What could help him to choose? Could the Christian doctrine? No. Christian doctrine says: Act with charity, love your neighbour, deny yourself for others, choose the way which is hardest, and so forth. But which is the harder road? To whom does one owe the more brotherly love, the patriot or the mother? Which is the more useful aim, the general one of fighting in and for the whole community, or the precise aim of helping one particular person to live? Who can give an answer to that *à priori?* No one. Nor is it given in any ethical scripture. The Kantian ethic says, Never regard another as a means, but always as an end. Very well; if I remain with my mother, I shall be regarding her as the end and not as a means: but by the same token I am in danger of treating as means those who are fighting on my behalf; and the converse is also true, that if I go to the aid of the combatants I shall be treating them as the end at the risk of treating my mother as a means. . . .

Quietism is the attitude of people who say, "let others do what I cannot do." The doctrine I am presenting before you is precisely the opposite of this, since it declares that there is no reality except in action. It goes further, indeed, and adds, "Man is nothing else but what he purposes, he exists only in so far as he realises himself, he is therefore nothing else but the sum of his actions, nothing else but what his life is." Hence we can well understand why some people are horrified by our teaching. For many have but one resource to sustain them in their misery, and that is to think, "Circumstances have been against me, I was worthy to be something much better than I have been. I admit I have never had a great love or a great friendship; but that is because I never met a man or a woman who were worthy of it; if I have not written any very good books, it is because I had not the leisure to do so; or, if I have had no children to whom I could devote myself it is because I did not find the man I could have lived with. So there remains within me a wide range of abilities, inclinations and potentialities, unused but perfectly viable, which endow me with a worthiness that could never be inferred from the mere history of my actions." But in reality and for the existentialist, there is no love apart from the deeds of love; no potentiality of love other than that which is manifested in loving; there is no genius other than that which is expressed in works of art. The genius of Proust is the totality of the works of Proust; the genius of Racine is the series of his tragedies, outside of which there is nothing. Why should we attribute to Racine the capacity to write yet another tragedy when that is precisely what he did not write? In life, a man commits himself, draws his own portrait and there is nothing but that portrait. No doubt this thought may seem comfortless to one who has not made a success of his life. On the other hand, it puts everyone in a position to understand that reality alone is reliable; that dreams, expectations and hopes serve to define a man only as deceptive dreams, abortive hopes, expectations unfulfilled; that is to say, they define him negatively, not positively. Nevertheless, when one says, "You are nothing else but what you live," it does not imply that an artist is to be judged solely by his works of art, for a thousand other things contribute no less to his definition as a man. What we mean to say is that a man is no other than a series of undertakings, that he is the sum, the organisation, the set of relations that constitute these undertakings.

In the light of all this, what people reproach us with is not, after all, our pessimism, but the sternness of our optimism. . . .

Existentialism is nothing else but an attempt to draw the full conclusions from a consistently atheistic position. Its intention is not in the least that of plunging men into despair. And if by despair one means—as the Christians do—any attitude of unbelief, the despair of the existentialists is something different. Existentialism is not atheist in the sense that it would exhaust itself in demonstrations of the non-existence of God. It declares, rather, that even if God existed that would make no difference from its point of view. Not that we believe God does exist, but we think that the real problem is not that of His existence; what man needs is to find himself again and to understand that nothing can save him from himself, not even a valid proof of the existence of God. In this sense existentialism is optimistic, it is a doctrine of action, and it is only by self-deception, by confusing their own despair with ours that Christians can describe us as without hope.*

One consequence of all this freedom is what Sartre calls "anguish," as developed in this excerpt from his *Being and Nothingness.*

If freedom is the being of consciousness, consciousness ought to exist as a consciousness of freedom. What form does this consciousness of freedom assume? In freedom the human being is his own past (as

*From *Existentialism and Humanism* (1948). (P. Mairet, Trans.). London: Methuen.

also his own future) in the form of nihilation. If our analysis has not led us astray, there ought to exist for the human being, in so far as he is conscious of being, a certain mode of standing opposite his past and his future, as being both this past and this future and as not being them. We shall be able to furnish an immediate reply to this question; it is in anguish that man gets the consciousness of his freedom, or if you prefer, anguish is the mode of being of freedom as consciousness of being; it is in anguish that freedom is, in its being, in question for itself.

Kierkegaard describing anguish in the face of what one lacks characterizes it as anguish in the face of freedom. But Heidegger, whom we know to have been greatly influenced by Kierkegaard, considers anguish instead as the apprehension of nothingness. These two descriptions of anguish do not appear to us contradictory; on the contrary the one implies the other.

First we must acknowledge that Kierkegaard is right; anguish is distinguished from fear in that fear is fear of beings in the world whereas anguish is anguish before myself. Vertigo is anguish to the extent that I am afraid not of falling over the precipice, but of throwing myself over. A situation provokes fear if there is a possibility of my life being changed from without; my being provokes anguish to the extent that I distrust myself and my own reactions in that situation. The artillery preparation which precedes the attack can provoke fear in the soldier who undergoes the bombardment, but anguish is born in him when he tries to foresee the conduct with which he will face the bombardment, when he asks himself if he is going to be able to "hold up."*

Another consequence is what Sartre calls "bad faith," recounted in this excerpt from *Being and Nothingness.*

To be sure, the one who practices bad faith is hiding a displeasing truth or presenting as truth a pleasing untruth. Bad faith then has in appearance the structure of falsehood. Only what changes everything is the fact that in bad faith it is from myself that I am hiding the truth. Thus the duality of the deceiver and the deceived does not exist here. Bad faith on the contrary implies in essence the unity of a single consciousness. . . .

Take the example of a woman who has consented to go out with a particular man for the first time. She knows very well the intentions which the man who is speaking to her cherishes regarding her. She knows also that it will be necessary sooner or later for her to make a decision. But she does not want to realize the urgency; she concerns herself only with what is respectful and discreet in the attitude of her companion. She does not apprehend this conduct as an attempt to achieve what we call "the first approach"; that is, she does not want to see possibilities of temporal development which his conduct presents. She restricts this behavior to what is in the present; she does not wish to read in the phrases which he addresses to her anything other than their explicit meaning. If he says to her, "I find you so attractive!" she disarms this phrase of its sexual background; she attaches to the conversation and to the behavior of the speaker, the immediate meanings, which she imagines as objective qualities. The man who is speaking to her appears to her sincere and respectful as the table is round or square, as the wall coloring is blue or gray. The qualities thus attached to the person she is listening to are in this way fixed in a permanence like that of things, which is no other than the projection of the strict present of the qualities into the temporal flux. This is because she does not quite know what she wants. She is profoundly aware of the desire which she inspires, but the desire cruel and naked would humiliate and horrify her. Yet she would find no charm in a respect which would be only respect. In order to satisfy her, there must be a feeling which is addressed wholly to her *personality*—that is, to her full freedom—and which would

*From *Being and Nothingness* (1957). (Hazel Barnes, Trans.). New York: Washington Square Press.

be a recognition of her freedom. But at the same time this feeling must be wholly desire; that is, it must address itself to her body as object. This time then she refuses to apprehend the desire for what it is; she does not even give it a name; she recognizes it only to the extent that it transcends itself toward admiration, esteem, respect and that it is wholly absorbed in the more refined forms which it produces, to the extent of no longer figuring anymore as a sort of warmth and density. But then suppose he takes her hand. This act of her companion risks changing the situation by calling for an immediate decision. To leave the hand there is to consent in herself to flirt, to engage herself. To withdraw it is to break the troubled and unstable harmony which gives the hour its charm. The aim is to postpone the moment of decision as long as possible. We know what happens next; the young woman leaves her hand there, but she *does not notice* that she is leaving it. She does not notice because it happens by chance that she is at this moment all intellect. She draws her companion up to the most lofty regions of sentimental speculation; she speaks of Life, of her life, she shows herself in her essential aspect—a personality, a consciousness. And during this time the divorce of the body from the soul is accomplished; the hand rests inert between the warm hands of her companion—neither consenting nor resisting—a thing.

We shall say that this woman is in bad faith.*

CAMUS

Albert Camus (1913–1960), along with Sartre, was the major representative of atheistic existentialism. He, too, was French, and he, too, participated in the Resistance to Nazi occupation, running a Resistance news sheet. Camus wrote essays, novels, and plays and, again, like Sartre, he was awarded a Nobel Prize for literature. His novel *The Stranger* is a popular depiction of the alienated Outsider; Camus's work regularly turns to the problems of human isolation (from others and even from one's self), the existence of evil, and the pressing finality of death. In his essay "The Myth of Sisyphus," reprinted below, Camus encapsulates a surprising, yet powerful view of the human predicament.

The gods had condemned Sisyphus to ceaselessly rolling a rock to the top of a mountain, whence the stone would fall back of its own weight. They had thought with some reason that there is no more dreadful punishment than futile and hopeless labor.

If one believes Homer, Sisyphus was the wisest and most prudent of mortals. According to another tradition, however, he was disposed to practice the profession of highwayman. I see no contradiction in this. Opinions differ as to the reasons why he became the futile laborer of the underworld. To begin with, he is accused of a certain levity in regard to the gods. He stole their secrets. Ægina, the daughter of Æsopus, was carried off by Jupiter. The father was shocked by that disappearance and complained to Sisyphus. He, who knew of the abduction, offered to tell about it on condition that Æsopus would give water to the citadel of Corinth. To the celestial thunderbolts he preferred the benediction of water. He was punished for this in the underworld. Homer tells us also that Sisyphus had put Death in chains. Pluto could not endure the sight of his deserted, silent empire. He dispatched the god of war, who liberated Death from the hands of her conqueror.

It is said also that Sisyphus, being near to death, rashly wanted to test his wife's love. He ordered her to cast his unburied body into the middle of the public square. Sisyphus woke up in the underworld. And there, annoyed by an obedience so contrary to human love, he obtained from Pluto permission to return to earth in order to chastise his wife. But when he had seen again the face of this world, enjoyed water

*From *Being and Nothingness* (1957). (Hazel Barnes, Trans.). New York: Washington Square Press.

and sun, warm stones and the sea, he no longer wanted to go back to the infernal darkness. Recalls, signs of anger, warnings were of no avail. Many years more he lived facing the curve of the gulf, the sparkling sea, and the smiles of earth. A decree of the gods was necessary. Mercury came and seized the impudent man by the collar and, snatching him from his joys, led him forcibly back to the underworld, where his rock was ready for him.

You have already grasped that Sisyphus is the absurd hero. He *is*, as much through his passions as through his torture. His scorn of the gods, his hatred of death, and his passion for life won him that unspeakable penalty in which the whole being is exerted toward accomplishing nothing. This is the price that must be paid for the passions of this earth. Nothing is told us about Sisyphus in the underworld. Myths are made for the imagination to breathe life into them. As for this myth, one sees merely the whole effort of a body straining to raise the huge stone, to roll it and push it up a slope a hundred times over; one sees the face screwed up, the cheek tight against the stone, the shoulder bracing the clay-covered mass, the foot wedging it, the fresh start with arms outstretched, the wholly human security of two earth-clotted hands. At the very end of his long effort measured by skyless space and time without depth, the purpose is achieved. Then Sisyphus watches the stone rush down in a few moments toward that lower world whence he will have to push it up again toward the summit. He goes back down to the plain.

It is during that return, that pause, that Sisyphus interests me. A face that toils so close to stones is already stone itself! I see that man going back down with a heavy yet measured step toward the torment of which he will never know the end. That hour like a breathing-space which returns as surely as his suffering, that is the hour of consciousness. At each of those moments when he leaves the heights and gradually sinks toward the lairs of the gods, he is superior to his fate. He is stronger than his rock.

If this myth is tragic, that is because its hero is conscious. Where would his torture be, indeed, if at every step the hope of succeeding upheld him? The workman of today works every day in his life at the same tasks, and this fate is no less absurd. But it is tragic only at the rare moments when it becomes conscious. Sisyphus, proletarian of the gods, powerless and rebellious, knows the whole extent of his wretched condition: it is what he thinks of during his descent. The lucidity that was to constitute his torture at the same time crowns his victory. There is no fate that cannot be surmounted by scorn.

If the descent is thus sometimes performed in sorrow, it can also take place in joy. This word is not too much. Again I fancy Sisyphus returning toward his rock, and the sorrow was in the beginning. When the images of earth cling too tightly to memory, when the call of happiness becomes too insistent, it happens that melancholy rises in man's heart: this is the rock's victory, this is the rock itself. The boundless grief is too heavy to bear. These are our nights of Gethsemane. But crushing truths perish from being acknowledged. Thus, Œdipus at the outset obeys fate without knowing it. But from the moment he knows, his tragedy begins. Yet at the same moment, blind and desperate, he realizes that the only bond linking him to the world is the cool hand of a girl. Then a tremendous remark rings out: "Despite so many ordeals, my advanced age and the nobility of my soul make me conclude that all is well." Sophocles' Œdipus, like Dostoevsky's Kirilov, thus gives the recipe for the absurd victory. Ancient wisdom confirms modern heroism.

One does not discover the absurd without being tempted to write a manual of happiness. "What! by such narrow ways—?" There is but one world, however. Happiness and the absurd are two sons of the same earth. They are inseparable. It would be a mistake to say that happiness necessarily springs from the absurd discovery. It happens as well that the feeling of the absurd springs from happiness. "I conclude that all is well," says Œdipus, and that remark is sacred. It echoes in the wild and limited universe of man. It teaches that all is not, has not been, exhausted. It drives out of this world a god who had come into it with dissatisfaction and a preference for futile sufferings. It makes of fate a human matter, which must be settled among men.

All Sisyphus' silent joy is contained therein. His fate belongs to him. His rock is his thing. Likewise, the absurd man, when he contemplates his torment, silences all the idols. In the universe suddenly restored to its silence, the myriad wondering little voices of the earth rise up. Unconscious, secret calls, invitations from all the faces, they are the necessary reverse and price of victory. There is no sun without shadow, and it is essential to know the night. The absurd man says yes and his effort will henceforth be unceasing. If there is a personal fate, there is no higher destiny, or at least there is but one which he concludes is inevitable and despicable. For the rest, he knows himself to be the master of his days. At that subtle moment when man glances backward over his life, Sisyphus returning toward his rock, in that slight pivoting he contemplates that series of unrelated actions which becomes his fate, created by him, combined under his memory's eye and soon sealed by his death. Thus, convinced of the wholly human origin of all that is human, a blind man eager to see who knows that the night has no end, he is still on the go. The rock is still rolling.

I leave Sisyphus at the foot of the mountain! One always finds one's burden again. But Sisyphus teaches the higher fidelity that negates the gods and raises rocks. He too concludes that all is well. This universe henceforth without a master seems to him neither sterile nor futile. Each atom of that stone, each mineral flake of that night-filled mountain, in itself forms a world. The struggle itself toward the heights is enough to fill a man's heart. One must imagine Sisyphus happy.*

Camus's novel *The Plague* describes the struggle of several residents of the Algerian city of Oran to counter an outbreak of bubonic plague. (It is also a metaphor for the German occupation of France, for the inevitability of death, for the absurd impossibility of defeating an uncaring universe, etc.) On the final page, Camus explores the ruminations of its central character, the courageous Dr. Rieux, when the plague appears to have been defeated, and the survivors are celebrating their "victory."

And it was in the midst of shouts rolling against the terrace wall in massive waves that waxed in volume and duration, while cataracts of colored fire fell thicker through the darkness, that Dr. Rieux resolved to compile this chronicle, so that he should not be one of those who hold their peace but should bear witness in favor of those plague-stricken people; so that some memorial of the injustice and outrage done them might endure; and to state quite simply what we learn in a time of pestilence: that there are more things to admire in men than to despise.

None the less, he knew that the tale he had to tell could not be one of a final victory. It could be only the record of what had had to be done, and what assuredly would have to be done again in the never ending fight against terror and its relentless onslaughts, despite their personal afflictions, by all who, while unable to be saints but refusing to bow down to pestilences, strive their utmost to be healers.

And, indeed, as he listened to the cries of joy rising from the town, Rieux remembered that such joy is always imperiled. He knew what those jubilant crowds did not know but could have learned from books: that the plague bacillus never dies or disappears for good; that it can lie dormant for years and years in furniture and linen-chests; that it bides its time in bedrooms, cellars, trunks, and bookshelves; and that perhaps the day would come when, for the bane and the enlightening of men, it would rouse up its rats again and send them forth to die in a happy city.†

---

*"The Myth of Sisyphus" (1955). (J. O'Brien, Trans.). New York: Alfred A. Knopf.
†From *The Plague* (1948). (S. Gilbert, Trans.). New York: The Modern Library.

STUDY QUESTIONS

1. Kierkegaard once wrote about a man who was so abstract and absentminded that he didn't even realize he existed—until one day he woke up and found that he was dead! Relate this story to the material presented here.

2. Is existentialism necessarily pessimistic? Optimistic?

3. In his play *No Exit,* one of Sartre's characters says "One always dies too soon—or too late. And yet one's whole life is complete at that moment, with a line drawn neatly under it, ready for the summing up. You are—your life, and nothing else." Comment.

4. Blaise Pascal, not normally considered an existentialist, once wrote that "We burn with the desire to find solid ground and an ultimate sure foundation, whereupon to build a tower reaching to the Infinite. But our whole groundwork cracks, and the earth opens to abysses." Relate this to the ideas in the present chapter.

SOME ADDITIONAL READINGS

Barrett, William (1990). *Irrational Man.* New York: Doubleday.

Harper, Ralph (1948). *Existentialism, a Theory of Man.* Cambridge, Mass.: Harvard University Press.

Kaufmann, Walter Arnold (1975). *Existentialism from Dostoevsky to Sartre.* New York: New American Library.

Scott, Jr., Nathan A. (1978). *Mirrors of Man in Existentialism.* New York: Collins.

Solomon, Robert C. (1985). *From Rationalism to Existentialism: The Existentialists and Their Nineteenth-century Backgrounds.* Lanham, Md.: University Press of America.

CHAPTER FIFTEEN

Sex and Gender

There is nothing in any of the preceding chapters that is specific to either gender. And yet, this has not always been the prevailing opinion. Seemingly responsible and intelligent people have seriously debated, for example, whether women have souls, whether they are capable of reason (or are particularly prone to irrationality), whether they are especially "good," and so forth. Take Immanuel Kant, whose essay "On the Distinction of the Beautiful and Sublime in the Interrelations of the Two Sexes" included this bit of wisdom:

> Laborious learning or painful pondering, even if a woman should greatly succeed in it, destroy the merits that are proper to her sex, and because of their rarity they can make of her an object of cold admiration; but at the same time they will weaken the charms with which she exercises her great power over the other sex. A woman who has a head full of Greek . . . or carries on fundamental controversies about mechanics . . . might as well even have a beard.

Others have been even more avowedly misogynistic, as in these observations from Nietzsche's *Thus Spoke Zarathustra:*

> A real man wants two things: danger and play. Therefore he wants woman as the most dangerous plaything. Man should be educated for war, and woman for the recreation of the warrior; all else is folly. The warrior does not like all-too-sweet fruit; therefore he likes woman: even the sweetest woman is bitter. . . . You are going to women? Do not forget your whip!

On the other hand, Plato, in *The Republic,* argued that women, like men, should perform whatever functions they did best.

Most ideas about human nature, however, have either ignored male-female differences, or have implicitly assumed that "human" equals "male." Nonetheless, the question of gender differences remains an active area of research in at least one scientific approach to human nature (see Chapter 17).

It is useful to make a distinction between "sex," the biological qualities of male and female, and "gender," which refers to socially constructed roles and distinctions. The question arises whether the latter is derived from the former. Men and women, together, comprise the human species; the existence of any fundamental differences, beyond obvious anatomy and physiology, could have important implications for society as well as for what it means to be human.

215

WOLLSTONECRAFT

Mary Wollstonecraft (1759–1797) wrote the first sustained classic work of feminism, *A Vindication of the Rights of Woman,* at a time when English women lacked the right to vote, and, upon marriage, even gave up the right to own property. Socialism and feminism were closely linked, and the French Revolution, having claimed that all men were brothers, inspired some people at least to consider that there were also sisters. Wollstonecraft was especially concerned with the need to reform the educational system, so it would prepare women for gratifying, independent lives. Her own life was exciting, radical, and considered rather scandalous, associated with the likes of Thomas Paine, and the "Three Williams": Godwin, Blake, and Wordsworth. Mary Wollstonecraft died shortly after giving birth to her daughter, Mary (later Shelley), who was to write *Frankenstein.*

I have sighed when obliged to confess that either Nature has made a great difference between man and man, or that the civilisation which has hitherto taken place in the world has been very partial. I have turned over various books written on the subject of education, and patiently observed the conduct of parents and the management of schools; but what has been the result?—a profound conviction that the neglected education of my fellow-creatures is the grand source of the misery I deplore, and that women, in particular, are rendered weak and wretched by a variety of concurring causes, originating from one hasty conclusion. The conduct and manners of women, in fact, evidently prove that their minds are not in a healthy state; for, like the flowers which are planted in too rich a soil, strength and usefulness are sacrificed to beauty; and the flaunting leaves, after having pleased a fastidious eye, fade, disregarded on the stalk, long before the season when they ought to have arrived at maturity. One cause of this barren blooming I attribute to a false system of education, gathered from the books written on this subject by men who, considering females rather as women than human creatures, have been more anxious to make them alluring mistresses than affectionate wives and rational mothers; and the understanding of the sex has been so bubbled by this specious homage, that the civilised women of the present century, with a few exceptions, are only anxious to inspire love, when they ought to cherish a nobler ambition, and by their abilities and virtues exact respect. . . .

The education of women has of late been more attended to than formerly; yet they are still reckoned a frivolous sex, and ridiculed or pitied by the writers who endeavour by satire or instruction to improve them. It is acknowledged that they spend many of the first years of their lives in acquiring a smattering of accomplishments; meanwhile strength of body and mind are sacrificed to libertine notions of beauty, to the desire of establishing themselves—the only way women can rise in the world—by marriage. And this desire making mere animals of them, when they marry they act as such children may be expected to act,—they dress, they paint, and nickname God's creatures. Surely these weak beings are only fit for a scraglio! Can they be expected to govern a family with judgment, or take care of the poor babes whom they bring into the world?

If, then, it can be fairly deduced from the present conduct of the sex, from the prevalent fondness for pleasure which takes place of ambition and those nobler passions that open and enlarge the soul, that the instruction which women have hitherto received has only tended, with the constitution of civil society, to render them insignificant objects of desire—mere propagators of fools!—if it can be proved that in aiming to accomplish them, without cultivating their understandings, they are taken out of their sphere of duties, and made ridiculous and useless when the short-lived bloom of beauty is over, I presume that *rational* men will excuse me for endeavouring to persuade them to become more masculine and respectable. . . .

Contending for the rights of woman, my main argument is built on this simple principle, that if she be not prepared by education to become the companion of man, she will stop the progress of knowledge and virtue; for truth must be common to all, or it will be inefficacious with respect to its influence on general practice. And how can woman be expected to co-operate unless she knows why she ought to be virtuous? unless freedom strengthens her reason till she comprehends her duty, and see in what manner it is connected with her real good. If children are to be educated to understand the true principle of patriotism, their mother must be a patriot; and the love of mankind, from which an orderly train of virtues spring, can only be produced by considering the moral and civil interest of mankind; but the education and situation of woman at present shuts her out from such investigations. . . .

To account for, and excuse the tyranny of man, many ingenious arguments have been brought forward to prove, that the two sexes, in the acquirement of virtue, ought to aim at attaining a very different character; or, to speak explicitly, women are not allowed to have sufficient strength of mind to acquire what really deserves the name of virtue. Yet it should seem, allowing them to have souls, that there is but one way appointed by Providence to lead *mankind* to either virtue or happiness.

If then women are not a swarm of ephemeron triflers, why should they be kept in ignorance under the specious name of innocence? Men complain, and with reason, of the follies and caprices of our sex, when they do not keenly satirise our headstrong passions and grovelling vices. Behold, I should answer, the natural effect of ignorance! The mind will ever be unstable that has only prejudices to rest on, and the current will run with destructive fury when there are no barriers to break its force. Women are told from their infancy, and taught by the example of their mothers, that a little knowledge of human weakness, justly termed cunning, softness of temper, *outward* obedience, and a scrupulous attention to a puerile kind of propriety, will obtain for them the protection of man; and should they be beautiful, everything else is needless, for at least twenty years of their lives. . . .

[T]hough moralists have agreed that the tenor of life seems to prove that *man* is prepared by various circumstances for a future state, they constantly concur in advising *woman* only to provide for the present. Gentleness, docility, and a spaniellike affection are, on this ground, consistently recommended as the cardinal virtues of the sex; and, disregarding the arbitrary economy of nature, one writer has declared that it is masculine for a woman to be melancholy. She was created to be the toy of man, his rattle, and it must jingle in his ears whenever, dismissing reason, he chooses to be amused. . . .

But should it be proved that woman is naturally weaker than man, whence does it follow that it is natural for her to labour to become still weaker than nature intended her to be? Arguments of this cast are an insult to common sense, and savour of passion. The *divine right* of husbands, like the divine right of kings, may, it is to be hoped, in this enlightened age, be contested without danger; and though conviction may not silence many boisterous disputants, yet, when any prevailing prejudice is attacked, the wise will consider, and leave the narrow-minded to rail with thoughtless vehemence at innovation. . . .

It would be an endless task to trace the variety of meannesses, cares, and sorrows, into which women are plunged by the prevailing opinion, that they were created rather to feel than reason, and that all the power they obtain must be obtained by their charms and weakness:

Fine by defect, and amiably weak!

And, made by this amiable weakness entirely dependent, excepting what they gain by illicit sway, on man, not only for protection, but advice, is it surprising that, neglecting the duties that reason alone points out, and shrinking from trials calculated to strengthen their minds, they only exert themselves to give their defects a graceful covering, which may serve to heighten their charms in the eye of the voluptuary, though it sink them below the scale of moral excellence.

Fragile in every sense of the word, they are obliged to look up to man for every comfort. In the most trifling danger they cling to their support, with parasitical tenacity, piteously demanding succour; and their *natural* protector extends his arm, or lifts up his voice, to guard the lovely trembler—from what? Perhaps the frown of an old cow, or the jump of a mouse; a rat would be a serious danger. In the name of reason, and even common sense, what can save such beings from contempt; even though they be soft and fair.

These fears, when not affected, may produce some pretty attitudes; but they show a degree of imbecility which degrades a rational creature in a way women are not aware of—for love and esteem are very distinct things.

I am fully persuaded that we should hear of none of these infantine airs, if girls were allowed to take sufficient exercise, and not confined in close rooms till their muscles are relaxed, and their powers of digestion destroyed. To carry the remark still further, if fear in girls, instead of being cherished, perhaps, created, were treated in the same manner as cowardice in boys, we should quickly see women with more dignified aspects. It is true, they could not then with equal propriety be termed the sweet flowers that smile in the walk of man; but they would be more respectable members of society, and discharge the important duties of life by the light of their own reason. "Educate women like men," says Rousseau, "and the more they resemble our sex the less power will they have over us." This is the very point I aim at. I do not wish them to have power over men; but over themselves. . . .

But what have women to do in society? I may be asked, but to loiter with easy grace; surely you would not condemn them all to suckle fools and chronicle small beer! No. Women might certainly study the art of healing, and be physicians as well as nurses. . . .

Business of various kinds, they might likewise pursue, if they were educated in a more orderly manner, which might save many from common and legal prostitution. Women would not then marry for a support, as men accept of places under Government, and neglect the implied duties; nor would an attempt to earn their own subsistence, a most laudable one! sink them almost to the level of those poor abandoned creatures who live by prostitution. . . .

How much more respectable is the woman who earns her own bread by fulfilling any duty, than the most accomplished beauty!—beauty did I say!—so sensible am I of the beauty of moral loveliness, or the harmonious propriety that attunes the passions of a well-regulated mind, that I blush at making the comparison; yet I sigh to think how few women aim at attaining this respectability by withdrawing from the giddy whirl of pleasure, or the indolent calm that stupefies the good sort of women it sucks in. . . .

Would men but generously snap our chains, and be content with rational fellowship instead of slavish obedience, they would find us more observant daughters, more affectionate sisters, more faithful wives, more reasonable mothers—in a word, better citizens. We should then love them with true affection, because we should learn to respect ourselves. . . .*

MILL

The British philosopher, logician, ethicist, and pioneering social scientist John Stuart Mill (1806–1873) was associated with many of the progressive causes of his day, including profit sharing in business and agriculture, and utilitarianism ("the greatest good for the greatest number"). In this, he was strongly influenced by political economist Jeremy Bentham. Also in-

*From *A Vindication of the Rights of Woman* (1792; 1992). London: J.M. Dent.

fluential in Mill's life and thought was his wife, Harriet Taylor Mill. In the introduction to his important book, *On Liberty,* J. S. Mill wrote that Harriet was "the inspirer, and in part the author, of all that is best in my writing."

For many readers at the time, including the growing band of American women's rights advocates such as Lucretia Mott, Elizabeth Cady Stanton, and Susan B. Anthony, the best of Mill's writing was *The Subjection of Women,* from which we take the following selections.

The object of this Essay is to explain as clearly as I am able, the grounds of an opinion which I have held from the very earliest period when I had formed any opinions at all on social or political matters, and which, instead of being weakened or modified, has been constantly growing stronger by the progress of reflection and the experience of life: That the principle which regulates the existing social relations between the two sexes—the legal subordination of one sex to the other—is wrong in itself, and now one of the chief hindrances to human improvement; and that it ought to be replaced by a principle of perfect equality, admitting no power or privilege on the one side, nor disability on the other.

The generality of a practice is in some cases a strong presumption that it is, or at all events once was, conducive to laudable ends. This is the case, when the practice was first adopted, or afterwards kept up, as a means to such ends, and was grounded on experience of the mode in which they could be most effectually attained. If the authority of men over women, when first established, had been the result of a conscientious comparison between different modes of constituting the government of society; if, after trying various other modes of social organization—the government of women over men, equality between the two, and such mixed and divided modes of government as might be invented—it had been decided, on the testimony of experience, that the mode in which women are wholly under the rule of men, having no share at all in public concerns, and each in private being under the legal obligation of obedience to the man with whom she has associated her destiny, was the arrangement most conducive to the happiness and well being of both; its general adoption might then be fairly thought to be some evidence that, at the time when it was adopted, it was the best: though even then the considerations which recommended it may, like so many other primeval social facts of the greatest importance, have subsequently, in the course of ages, ceased to exist. But the state of the case is in every respect the reverse of this. In the first place, the opinion in favour of the present system, which entirely subordinates the weaker sex to the stronger, rests upon theory only; for there never has been trial made of any other: so that experience, in the sense in which it is vulgarly opposed to theory, cannot be pretended to have pronounced any verdict. And in the second place, the adoption of this system of inequality never was the result of deliberation, or forethought, or any social ideas, or any notion whatever of what conduced to the benefit of humanity or the good order of society. It arose simply from the fact that from the very earliest twilight of human society, every woman (owing to the value attached to her by men, combined with her inferiority in muscular strength) was found in a state of bondage to some man. Laws and systems of polity always begin by recognising the relations they find already existing between individuals. They convert what was a mere physical fact into a legal right, give it the sanction of society, and principally aim at the substitution of public and organized means of asserting and protecting these rights, instead of the irregular and lawless conflict of physical strength. . . .

We now live—that is to say, one or two of the most advanced nations of the world now live—in a state in which the law of the strongest seems to be entirely abandoned as the regulating principle of the world's affairs: nobody professes it, and, as regards most of the relations between human beings, nobody is permitted to practise it. When any one succeeds in doing so, it is under cover of some pretext which gives him the semblance of having some general social interest on his side. This being the ostensible state of things, people flatter themselves that the rule of mere force is ended; that the law of the strongest cannot be the reason of existence of anything which has remained in full operation down to the present time. However any of our present institutions may have begun, it can only, they think, have been preserved to this period of advanced civilization by a well-grounded feeling of its adaptation to human nature, and conduciveness to the general good. They do not understand the great vitality and durability of institutions which place right on the side of might; how intensely they are clung to; how the good as well as the bad propensities and sentiments of those who have power in their hands, become identified with retaining it; how slowly these bad institutions give way, one at a time, the weakest first, beginning with those which are least interwoven with the daily habits of life; and how very rarely those who have obtained legal power because they first had physical, have ever lost their hold of it until the physical power had passed over to the other side. Such shifting of the physical force not having taken place in the case of women; this fact, combined with all the peculiar and characteristic features of the particular case, made it certain from the first that this branch of the system of right founded on might, though softened in its most atrocious features at an earlier period than several of the others, would be the very last to disappear. It was inevitable that this one case of a social relation grounded on force, would survive through generations of institutions grounded on equal justice, an almost solitary exception to the general character of their laws and customs; but which, so long as it does not proclaim its own origin, and as discussion has not brought out its true character, is not felt to jar with modern civilization, any more than domestic slavery among the Greeks jarred with their notion of themselves as a free people. . . .

There was a time when the division of mankind into two classes, a small one of masters and a numerous one of slaves, appeared, even to the most cultivated minds, to be a natural, and the only natural, condition of the human race. . . .

Again, the theorists of absolute monarchy have always affirmed it to be the only natural form of government; issuing from the patriarchal, which was the primitive and spontaneous form of society, framed on the model of the paternal, which is anterior to society itself, and, as they contend, the most natural authority of all. . . .

So true is it that unnatural generally means only uncustomary, and that everything which is usual appears natural. The subjection of women to men being a universal custom, any departure from it quite naturally appears unnatural. But how entirely, even in this case, the feeling is dependent on custom, appears by ample experience. Nothing so much astonishes the people of distant parts of the world, when they first learn anything about England, as to be told that it is under a queen: the thing seems to them so unnatural as to be almost incredible. To Englishmen this does not seem in the least degree unnatural, because they are used to it; but they do feel it unnatural that women should be soldiers or members of parliament. In the feudal ages, on the contrary, war and politics were not thought unnatural to women, because not unusual; it seemed natural that women of the privileged classes should be of manly character, inferior in nothing but bodily strength to their husbands and fathers. . . .

But, it will be said, the rule of men over women differs from all these others in not being a rule of force: it is accepted voluntarily; women make no complaint, and are consenting parties to it. In the first place, a great number of women do not accept it. Ever since there have been women able to make their sentiments known by their writings (the only mode of publicity which society permits to them), an increasing number of them have recorded protests against their present social condition: and recently many thousands of them, headed by the most eminent women known to the public, have petitioned Parliament for their admission to the Parliamentary Suffrage. The claim of women to be educated as solidly, and in the same branches of knowledge, as men, is urged with growing intensity, and with a great prospect of success; while the demand for their admission into professions and occupations hitherto closed against them, becomes every year more urgent. Though there are not in this country, as there are in the United States, periodical Conventions and an organized party to agitate for the Rights of Women, there is a numerous and active Society organized and managed by women, for the more limited object of obtaining the political franchise. Nor is it only in our own country and in America that women are beginning to protest, more or less collectively, against the disabilities under which they labour. France, and Italy, and Switzerland, and Russia now afford examples of the same thing. How many more women there are who silently cherish similar aspirations, no one can possibly know; but there are abundant tokens how many *would* cherish them, were they not so strenuously taught to repress them as contrary to the proprieties of their sex. It must be remembered, also, that no enslaved class ever asked for complete liberty at once. . . .

It is a political law of nature that those who are under any power of ancient origin, never begin by complaining of the power itself, but only of its oppressive exercise. There is never any want of women who complain of ill usage by their husbands. There would be infinitely more, if complaint were not the greatest of all provocatives to a repetition and increase of the ill usage. It is this which frustrates all attempts to maintain the power but protect the woman against its abuses. In no other case (except that of a child) is the person who has been proved judicially to have suffered an injury, replaced under the physical power of the culprit who inflicted it. Accordingly wives, even in the most extreme and protracted cases of bodily ill usage, hardly ever dare avail themselves of the laws made for their protection: and if, in a moment of irrepressible indignation, or by the interference of neighbours, they are induced to do so, their whole effort afterwards is to disclose as little as they can, and to beg off their tyrant from his merited chastisement.

All causes, social and natural, combine to make it unlikely that women should be collectively rebellious to the power of men. They are so far in a position different from all other subject classes, that their masters require something more from them than actual service. Men do not want solely the obedience of women, they want their sentiments. All men, except the most brutish, desire to have, in the woman most nearly connected with them, not a forced slave but a willing one, not a slave merely, but a favourite. They have therefore put everything in practice to enslave their minds. The masters of all other slaves rely, for maintaining obedience, on fear; either fear of themselves, or religious fears. The masters of women wanted more than simple obedience, and they turned the whole force of education to effect their purpose. All women are brought up from the very earliest years in the belief that their ideal of character is the very opposite to that of men; not self-will, and government by self-control, but submission, and yielding to the control of others. All the moralities tell them that it is the duty of women, and all the current sentimentalities that it is their nature, to live for others; to make complete abnegation of themselves, and to have no life but in their affections. And by their affections are meant the only ones they are allowed to have—those to the men with whom they are connected, or to the children who constitute an additional and indefeasible tie between them and a man. When we put together three things—first, the natural attraction between opposite sexes; secondly, the wife's entire dependence on the husband, every privilege or pleasure she has being either his gift, or depending entirely on his will; and lastly, that the principal object of human pursuit, consideration, and all objects of social ambition, can in general be sought or obtained by her only through him, it would be a miracle if the object of being attractive to men had not become the polar star of feminine education and formation of character. And, this great means of influence over the minds of women having been acquired, an instinct of selfishness made men avail themselves of it to the utmost as a means of holding women in subjection, by representing to them meekness, submissiveness, and resignation of all individual will into the hands of a man, as an essential part of sexual attractiveness. Can it be doubted that any of the other yokes which mankind have succeeded in breaking, would have subsisted till now if the same means had existed, and had been as sedulously used, to bow down their minds to it? . . .

Neither does it avail anything to say that the *nature* of the two sexes adapts them to their present functions and position, and renders these appropriate to them. Standing on the ground of common sense and the constitution of the human mind, I deny that any one knows, or can know, the nature of the two sexes, as long as they have only been seen in their present relation to one another. If men had ever been found in society without women, or women without men, or if there had been a society of men and women in which the women were not under the control of the men, something might have been positively known about the mental and moral differences which may be inherent in the nature of each. What is now called the nature of women is an eminently artificial thing—the result of forced repression in some directions, unnatural stimulation in others. It may be asserted without scruple, that no other class of dependents have had their character so entirely distorted from its natural proportions by their relation with their masters; for, if conquered and slave races have been, in some respects, more forcibly repressed, whatever in them has not been crushed down by an iron heel has generally been let alone, and if left with any liberty of development, it has developed itself according to its own laws; but in the case of women, a hothouse and stove cultivation has always been carried on of some of the capabilities of their nature, for the benefit and pleasure of their masters. . . .

Even the preliminary knowledge, what the differences between the sexes now are, apart from all questions as to how they are made what they are, is still in the crudest and most incomplete state. Medical practitioners and physiologists have ascertained, to some extent, the differences in bodily constitution; and this is an important element to the psychologist: but hardly any medical practitioner is a psychologist. Respecting the mental characteristics of women; their observations are of no more worth than those of common men. It is a subject on which nothing final can be known, so long as those who alone can really know it, women themselves, have given but little testimony, and that little, mostly suborned. It is easy to know stupid women. Stupidity is much the same all the world over. A stupid person's notions and feelings may confidently be inferred from those which prevail in the circle by which the person is surrounded. Not so with those whose opinions and feelings are an emanation from their own nature and faculties. It is only a man here and there who has any tolerable knowledge of the character even of the women of his own family. I do not mean, of their capabilities; these nobody knows, not even themselves, because most of them have never been called out. I mean their actually existing thoughts and feelings. Many a man thinks he perfectly understands women, because he has had amatory relations with several, perhaps with many of them. If he is a good observer, and his experience extends to quality as well as quantity, he may have learnt something of one narrow department of their nature—an important department, no doubt. But of all the rest of it, few persons are generally more ignorant, because there are few from whom it is so carefully hidden. The most favourable case which a man can generally have for studying the character of a woman, is that of his own wife: for the opportunities are greater, and the cases of complete sympathy not so unspeakably rare. And in fact, this is the source from which any knowledge worth having on the subject has, I believe, generally come. But most men have not had the opportunity of studying in this way more than a single case: accordingly one can, to an almost laughable degree, infer what a man's wife is like, from his opinions about women in general. To make even this one case yield any result, the women must be worth knowing, and the man not only a competent judge, but of a character so sympathetic in itself, and so well adapted to hers, that he can either read her mind by sympathetic intuition, or has nothing in himself which makes her shy of disclosing it. Hardly anything, I believe, can be more rare than this conjunction. It often happens that there is the most complete unity of feeling and community of interests as to all external things, yet the one has as little admission into the internal life of the other as if they were common acquaintance. Even with true affection, authority on the one side and subordination on the other prevent perfect confidence. Though nothing may be intentionally withheld, much is not shown. . . .

When we further consider that to understand one woman is not necessarily to understand any other woman; that even if he could study many women of one rank, or of one country, he would not thereby understand women of other ranks or countries; and even if he did, they are still only the women of a single period of history; we may safely assert that the knowledge which men can acquire of women, even as they have been and are, without reference to what they might be, is wretchedly imperfect and superficial, and always will be so, until women themselves have told all that they have to tell. . . .

One thing we may be certain of—that what is contrary to women's nature to do, they never will be made to do by simply giving their nature free play. The anxiety of mankind to interfere in behalf of nature, for fear lest nature should not succeed in effecting its purpose, is an altogether unnecessary solicitude. What women by nature cannot do, it is quite superfluous to forbid them from doing. What they can do, but not so well as the men who are their competitors, competition suffices to exclude them from; since nobody asks for protective duties and bounties in favour of women; it is only asked that the present bounties and protective duties in favour of men should be recalled. If women have a greater natural inclination for some things than for others, there is no need of laws or social inculcation to make the majority of them do the former in preference to the latter. . . .

The general opinion of men is supposed to be, that the natural vocation of a woman is that of a wife and mother. I say, is supposed to be, because, judging from acts—from the whole of the present constitution of society—one might infer that their opinion was the direct contrary. They might be supposed to think that the alleged natural vocation of women was of all things the most repugnant to their nature; insomuch that if they are free to do anything else—if any other means of living, or occupation of their time and faculties, is open, which has any chance of appearing desirable to them—there will not be enough of them who will be willing to accept the condition said to be natural to them. If this is the real opinion of men in general, it would be well that it should be spoken out. I should like to hear somebody openly enunciating the doctrine (it is already implied in much that is written on the subject)—"It is necessary to society that women should marry and produce children. They will not do so unless they are compelled. Therefore it is necessary to compel them." . . .

With regard to the fitness of women, not only to participate in elections, but themselves to hold offices or practise professions involving important public responsibilities; I have already observed that this consideration is not essential to the practical question in dispute: since any woman, who succeeds in an open profession, proves by that very fact that she is qualified for it. And in the case of public offices, if the political system of the country is such as to exclude unfit men, it will equally exclude unfit women: while if it is not, there is no additional evil in the fact that the unfit persons whom it admits may be either women or men. As long therefore as it is acknowledged that even a few women may be fit for these duties, the laws which shut the door on those exceptions cannot be justified by any opinion which can be held respecting the capacities of women in general. . . .

It will be said, perhaps, that the greater nervous susceptibility of women is a disqualification for practice, in anything but domestic life, by rendering them mobile, changeable, too vehemently under the influence of the moment, incapable of dogged perseverance, unequal and uncertain in the power of using their faculties. I think that these phrases sum up the greater part of the objections commonly made to the fitness of women for the higher class of serious business. Much of all this is the mere overflow of nervous energy run to waste, and would cease when the energy was directed to a definite end. Much is also the result of conscious or unconscious cultivation; as we see by the almost total disappearance of "hysterics" and fainting fits, since they have gone out of fashion. Moreover, when people are brought up, like many women of the higher classes (though less so in our own country than in any other) a kind of hothouse plants, shielded from the wholesome vicissitudes of air and temperature, and untrained in any of the occupations and exercises which give stimulus and development to the circulatory and muscular system, while their nervous system, especially in its emotional department, is kept in unnaturally active play; it is no wonder if those of them who do not die of consumption, grow up with constitutions liable to derangement from slight causes, both internal and external, and without stamina to support any task, physical or mental, requiring continuity of effort. But women brought up to work for their livelihood show none of these morbid characteristics, unless indeed they are chained to an excess of sedentary work in confined and unhealthy rooms. Women who in their early years have shared in the healthful physical education and bodily freedom of their brothers, and who obtain a sufficiency of pure air and exercise in after-life, very rarely have any excessive susceptibility of nerves which can disqualify them for active pursuits. There is indeed a certain proportion of persons, in both sexes, in whom an unusual degree of nervous sensibility is constitutional, and of so marked a character as to be the feature of their organization which exercises the greatest influence over the whole character of the vital phenomena. . . . We will assume this as a fact: and let me then ask, are men of nervous temperament found to be unfit for the duties and pursuits usually followed by men? If not, why should women of the same temperament be unfit for them? The peculiarities of the temperament are, no doubt, within certain limits, an obstacle to success in some employments, though an aid to it in others. But when the occupation is suitable to the temperament, and sometimes even when it is unsuitable, the most brilliant examples of success are continually given by the men of high nervous sensibility. They are distinguished in their practical manifestations chiefly by this, that being susceptible of a higher degree of excitement than those of another physical constitution, their powers when excited differ more than in the case of other people, from those shown in their ordinary state: they are raised, as it were, above themselves, and do things with ease which they are wholly incapable of at other times. . . .

Supposing it, however, to be true that women's minds are by nature more mobile than those of men, less capable of persisting long in the same continuous effort, more fitted for dividing their faculties among many things than for travelling in any one path to the highest point which can be reached by it: this may be true of women as they now are (though not without great and numerous exceptions), and may account for their having remained behind the highest order of men in precisely the things in which this absorption of the whole mind in one set of ideas and occupations may seem to be most requisite. Still, this difference is one which can only affect the kind of excellence, not the excellence itself, or its practical worth: and it remains to be shown whether this exclusive working of a part of the mind, this absorption of the whole thinking faculty in a single subject, and concentration of it on a single work, is the normal and healthful condition of the human faculties, even for speculative uses. I believe that what is gained in special development by this concentration, is lost in the capacity of the mind for the other purposes of life; and even in abstract thought, it is my decided opinion that the mind does more by frequently returning to a difficult problem, than by sticking to it without interruption. For the purposes, at all events, of practice, from its highest to its humblest departments, the capacity of passing promptly from one subject of consideration to another, without letting the active spring of the intellect run down between the two, is a power far more valuable; and this power women pre-eminently possess, by virtue of the very mobility of which they are accused. . . .

To so ridiculous an extent are the notions formed of the nature of women, mere empirical generalizations, framed, without philosophy or analysis, upon the first instances which present themselves, that the popular idea of it is different in different countries, according as the opinions and social circumstances of the country have given to the women living in it any specialty of development or non-development. An Oriental thinks that women are by nature peculiarly voluptuous; see the violent abuse of them on this ground in Hindoo writings. An Englishman usually thinks that they are by nature cold. The sayings about women's fickleness are mostly of French origin; from the famous distich of Francis the First, upward and downward. In England it is a common remark, how much more constant women are than men. Inconstancy has been longer reckoned discreditable to a woman, in England than in France; and Englishwomen are besides, in their inmost nature, much more subdued to opinion. It may be remarked by the way, that Englishmen are in peculiarly unfavourable circumstances for attempting to judge what is or is not natural, not merely to women, but to men, or to human beings altogether, at least if they have only English experience to go upon: because there is no place where human nature shows so little of its original lineaments. Both in a good and a bad sense, the English are farther from a state of nature than any other modern people. They are, more than any other people, a product of civilization and discipline. England is the country in which social discipline has most succeeded, not so much in conquering, as in suppressing, whatever is liable to conflict with it. The English, more than any other people, not only act but feel according to rule. . . .

The association of men with women in daily life is much closer and more complete than it ever was before. Men's life is more domestic. Formerly, their pleasures and chosen occupations were among men, and in men's company: their wives had but a fragment of their lives. At the present time, the progress of civilization, and the turn of opinion against the rough amusements and convivial excesses which formerly occupied most men in their hours of relaxation—together with (it must be said) the improved tone of modern feeling as to the reciprocity of duty which binds the husband towards the wife—have thrown the man very much more upon home and its inmates, for his personal and social pleasures: while the kind and degree of improvement which has been made in women's education, has made them in some degree capable of being his companions in ideas and mental tastes, while leaving them, in most cases, still hopelessly inferior to him. His desire of mental communion is thus in general satisfied by a communion from which he learns nothing. An unimproving and unstimulating companionship is substituted for (what he might otherwise have been obliged to seek) the society of his equals in powers and his fellows in the higher pursuits. We see, accordingly, that young men of the greatest promise generally cease to improve as soon as they marry, and, not improving, inevitably degenerate. If the wife does not push the husband forward, she always holds him back. He ceases to care for what she does not care for; he no longer desires, and ends by disliking and shunning, society congenial to his former aspirations, and which would now shame his falling-off from them; his higher faculties both of mind and heart cease to be called into activity. And this change coinciding with the new and selfish interests which are created by the family, after a few years he differs in no material respect from those who have never had wishes for anything but the common vanities and the common pecuniary objects.

What marriage may be in the case of two persons of cultivated faculties, identical in opinions and purposes, between whom there exists that best kind of equality, similarity of powers and capacities with reciprocal superiority in them—so that each can enjoy the luxury of looking up to the other, and can have alternately the pleasure of leading and of being led in the path of development—I will not attempt to describe. To those who can conceive it, there is no need; to those who cannot, it would appear the dream of an enthusiast. But I maintain, with the profoundest conviction, that this, and this only, is the ideal of marriage; and that all opinions, customs, and institutions which favour any other notion of it, or turn the conceptions and aspirations connected with it into any other direction, by whatever pretences they may be coloured, are relics of primitive barbarism. The moral regeneration of mankind will only really commence, when the most fundamental of the social relations is placed under the rule of equal justice, and when human beings learn to cultivate their strongest sympathy with an equal in rights and in cultivation.

Thus far, the benefits which it has appeared that the world would gain by ceasing to make sex a disqualification for privileges and a badge of subjection, are social rather than individual; consisting in an increase of the general fund of thinking and acting power, and an improvement in the general conditions of the association of men with women. But it would be a grievous understatement of the case to omit the most direct benefit of all, the unspeakable gain in private happiness to the liberated half of the species; the difference to them between a life of subjection to the will of others, and a life of rational freedom. After the primary necessities of food and raiment, freedom is the first and strongest want of human nature.*

STANTON

Elizabeth Cady Stanton (1815–1902) was, along with Susan B. Anthony (1820–1906), especially connected with the rise of the women's rights movement in the United States during the nineteenth and early twentieth centuries. The two women were close friends and collaborators from their meeting in 1851. Initially, their focus included abolitionism (opposition to slavery) as well as women's rights. After the Civil War, however, many former abolitionists became less enthusiastic about women's issues. Anthony emerged as the master strategist of women's suffrage, although her concerns also included economic issues more generally; Stanton was if anything more radical and wide-ranging in her intellectual approach to women's liberation generally, extending beyond the right to vote to embrace more fundamental social problems: what she saw as the struggle against women's oppression more generally, including concern for a woman's status within the family and before God. The following selections are from Stanton's introduction to *The Woman's Bible,* a controversial attempt at reworking the Old and New Testaments that she edited in 1895.

From the inauguration of the movement for woman's emancipation the Bible has been used to hold her in the "divinely ordained sphere," prescribed in the Old and New Testaments.

The canon and civil law; church and state; priests and legislators; all political parties and religious denominations have alike taught that woman was made after man, of man, and for man, an inferior being, subject to man. Creeds, codes, Scriptures and statutes, are all based on this idea. The fashions, forms, ceremonies and customs of society, church ordinances and discipline all grow out of this idea.

Of the old English common law, responsible for woman's civil and political status, Lord Brougham said, "it is a disgrace to the civilization and Christianity of the Nineteenth Century." Of the canon law, which is responsible for woman's status in the church, Charles Kingsley said, "this will never be a good world for women until the last remnant of the canon law is swept from the face of the earth."

The Bible teaches that woman brought sin and death into the world, that she precipitated the fall of the race, that she was arraigned before the judgment seat of Heaven, tried, condemned and sentenced. Marriage for her was to be a condition of bondage, maternity a period of suffering and anguish, and in silence and subjection, she was to play the role of a dependent on man's bounty for all her material wants, and for all the information she might desire on the vital questions of the hour, she was commanded to ask her husband at home. Here is the Bible position of woman briefly summed up.

Those who have the divine insight to translate, transpose and transfigure this mournful object of pity into an exalted, dignified personage, worthy our worship as the mother of the race, are to be congratulated as having a share of the occult mystic power of the eastern Mahatmas.

The plain English to the ordinary mind admits of no such liberal interpretation. The unvarnished texts speak for themselves. The canon law, church ordinances and scriptures, are homogeneous, and all reflect the same spirit and sentiments.

*From *The Subjection of Women* (1869; 1992). London: J.M. Dent.

These familiar texts are quoted by clergymen in their pulpits, by statesmen in the halls of legislation, by lawyers in the courts, and are echoed by the press of all civilized nations, and accepted by woman herself as "The Word of God." So perverted is the religious element in her nature, that with faith and works she is the chief support of the church and clergy; the very powers that make her emancipation impossible. When, in the early part of the Nineteenth Century, women began to protest against their civil and political degradation, they were referred to the Bible for an answer. When they protested against their unequal position in the church, they were referred to the Bible for an answer.

This led to a general and critical study of the Scriptures. Some, having made a fetish of these books and believing them to be the veritable "Word of God," with liberal translations, interpretations, allegories and symbols, glossed over the most objectionable features of the various books and clung to them as divinely inspired. Others, seeing the family resemblance between the Mosaic code, the canon law, and the old English common law, came to the conclusion that all alike emanated from the same source; wholly human in their origin and inspired by the natural love of domination in the historians. Others, bewildered with their doubts and fears, came to no conclusion. While their clergymen told them on the one hand, that they owed all the blessings and freedom they enjoyed to the Bible, on the other, they said it clearly marked out their circumscribed sphere of action: that the demands for political and civil rights were irreligious, dangerous to the stability of the home, the state and the church. Clerical appeals were circulated from time to time conjuring members of their churches to take no part in the anti-slavery or woman suffrage movements, as they were infidel in their tendencies, undermining the very foundations of society. No wonder the majority of women stood still, and with bowed heads, accepted the situation. . . .

Bible historians claim special inspiration for the Old and New Testaments containing most contradictory records of the same events, of miracles opposed to all known laws, of customs that degrade the female sex of all human and animal life, stated in most questionable language that could not be read in a promiscuous assembly, and call all this "The Word of God."

The only points in which I differ from all ecclesiastical teaching is that I do not believe that any man ever saw or talked with God, I do not believe that God inspired the Mosaic code, or told the historians what they say he did about woman, for all the religions on the face of the earth degrade her, and so long as woman accepts the position that they assign her, her emancipation is impossible. Whatever the Bible may be made to do in Hebrew or Greek, in plain English it does not exalt and dignify woman. My standpoint for criticism is the revised edition of 1888. I will so far honor the revising committee of nine men who have given us the best exegesis they can according to their ability, although Disraeli said the last one before he died, contained 150,000 blunders in the Hebrew, and 7,000 in the Greek.

But the verbal criticism in regard to woman's position amounts to little. The spirit is the same in all periods and languages, hostile to her as an equal.

There are some general principles in the holy books of all religions that teach love, charity, liberty, justice and equality for all the human family, there are many grand and beautiful passages, the golden rule has been echoed and re-echoed around the world. There are lofty examples of good and true men and women, all worthy our acceptance and example whose lustre cannot be dimmed by the false sentiments and vicious characters bound up in the same volume. The Bible cannot be accepted or rejected as a whole, its teachings are varied and its lessons differ widely from each other. In criticising the peccadilloes of Sarah, Rebecca and Rachel, we would not shadow the virtues of Deborah, Huldah and Vashti. In criticising the Mosaic code we would not question the wisdom of the golden rule and the fifth Commandment. Again the church claims special consecration for its cathedrals and priesthood, parts of these aristocratic churches are too holy for women to enter, boys were early introduced into the choirs for this reason, women singing in an obscure corner closely veiled. A few of the more democratic denominations accord women some privileges, but invidious discriminations of sex are found in all religious organizations, and the most bitter outspoken enemies of woman are found among clergymen and bishops of the Protestant religion.

The canon law, the Scriptures, the creeds and codes and church discipline of the leading religions bear the impress of fallible man, and not of our ideal great first cause, "the Spirit of all Good," that set the universe of matter and mind in motion, and by immutable law holds the land, the sea, the planets, revolving round the great centre of light and heat, each in its own elliptic, with millions of stars in harmony all singing together, the glory of creation forever and ever.*

WOOLF

Virginia Woolf (1882–1941) was an important and highly original literary critic and novelist. Her notable works of fiction include *Jacob's Room, Mrs. Dalloway, Orlando, The Waves,* and *To The Lighthouse.* Woolf was one of the founding members of an informal gathering of rational-minded, free-thinking English intellectuals that became known as the "Bloomsbury Group," and included the economist John Maynard Keynes, art critic Clive Bell, literary critic Lytton Strachey, authors E. M. Forster and Leonard Woolf, and, on occasion, writer Aldous Huxley, poet T. S. Eliot, and philosopher Bertrand Russell.

Woolf delivered two lectures on "Women and Fiction" at Cambridge University, which were published in 1929 as *A Room of One's Own.* In it, Woolf examined the many difficulties faced by creative, literary women. She concluded, among other things, that because of these obstacles, women need "guineas and keys": a degree of economic independence as well as social insulation from family-generated pressures—i.e., a room of one's own. In part of that work—excerpted below—she speculated as follows:

Let me imagine, . . . what would have happened had Shakespeare had a wonderfully gifted sister, called Judith, let us say. Shakespeare himself went, very probably . . . to the grammar school, where he may have learnt Latin—Ovid, Virgil, and Horace—and the elements of grammar and logic. He . . . had, rather sooner than he should have done, to marry a woman in the neighbourhood, who bore him a child rather quicker than was right. That escapade sent him to seek his fortune in London. He had, it seemed, a taste for the theatre . . . Very soon he got work . . . became a successful actor, and lived at the hub of the universe, meeting everybody, knowing everybody, practising his art on the boards, exercising his wits in the streets, and even getting access to the palace of the queen. Meanwhile his extraordinarily gifted sister, let us suppose, remained at home. She was as adventurous, as imaginative, as agog to see the world as he was. But she was not sent to school. She had not a chance of learning grammar and logic, let alone of reading Horace and Virgil. She picked up a book now and then, one of her brother's perhaps, and read a few pages. But then her parents came in and told her to mend the stockings or mind the stew and not moon about with books and papers. . . .

Perhaps she scribbled some pages up in an apple loft on the sly, but was careful to hide them or set fire to them. Soon, however, before she was out of her teens, she was to be betrothed to the son of a neighbouring wool-stapler. . . . She made up a small parcel of her belongings, let herself down by a rope one summer's night and took the road to London. She was not seventeen. The birds that sang in the hedge were not more musical than she was. She had the quickest fancy, a gift like her brother's, for the

---

*From *The Woman's Bible* (1895). New York: European.

tune of words. Like him, she had a taste for the theatre. She stood at the stage door; she wanted to act, she said. Men laughed in her face. . . . She could get no training in her craft. Could she even seek her dinner in a tavern or roam the streets at midnight? Yet her genius was for fiction and lusted to feed abundantly upon the lives of men and women and the study of their ways. At last . . . she found herself with child and so—who shall measure the heat and violence of the poet's heart when caught and tangled in a woman's body?—killed herself one winter's night and lies buried at some cross-roads . . .

Now my belief is that this poet who never wrote a word and was buried at the cross-roads still lives. She lives in you and in me, and in many other women . . . but she lives; for great poets do not die; . . . they need only the opportunity to walk among us in the flesh.*

BEAUVOIR

The French philosopher and novelist Simone de Beauvoir (1908–1986) wrote eloquently on existential themes and also on aging. In her scholarly, two-volume work, *The Second Sex,* de Beauvoir argued forcefully for the abolition of what she considered the myth of the "eternal feminine." She vigorously decried the fact that women have long been defined as "the Other," existing only in relation to "real human beings," namely, men. She pointed out that men have typically considered themselves to be "subjects," who control their lives, whereas women have been the "objects" of men, largely restrained from developing and experiencing their own personal freedom and identity. (Given this commitment on de Beauvoir's part, it is especially ironic that when the life and work of Simone de Beauvoir is acknowledged, she is nearly always identified as: the long-time companion of Jean-Paul Sartre!) The following is from *The Second Sex.*

Just as for the ancients there was an absolute vertical with reference to which the oblique was defined, so there is an absolute human type, the masculine. Woman has ovaries, a uterus; these peculiarities imprison her in her subjectivity, circumscribe her within the limits of her own nature. It is often said that she thinks with her glands. Man superbly ignores the fact that his anatomy also includes glands, such as the testicles, and that they secrete hormones too. . . .

Along with the ethical urge of each individual to affirm his subjective existence, there is also the temptation to forgo liberty and become a thing. This is an inauspicious road, for he who takes it—passive, lost, ruined—becomes henceforth the creature of another's will, frustrated in his transcendence and deprived of every value. But it is an easy road, on it one avoids the strain involved in undertaking an authentic existence. When man makes of woman the *Other,* he may, then, expect her to manifest deep-seated tendencies toward complicity. Thus, woman may fail to lay claim to the status of subject because she lacks definite resources, because she feels the necessary bond that ties her to man regardless of reciprocity, and because she is often very well pleased with her role as the *Other.* . . .

Woman is defined and differentiated with reference to man and not he with reference to her; she is the incidental, the inessential as opposed to the essential. He is the Subject, he is the Absolute—she is the Other. . . .

Otherness is a fundamental category of human thought. Thus it is that no group ever sets itself up as the One without at once setting up the Other over against itself. . . .

Now what peculiarly signalizes the situation of woman is that she—a free and autonomous being like all human creatures—nevertheless finds herself living in a world where men compel her to assume the status of the Other. . . .

*From *A Room of One's Own* (1929). New York: Harcourt, Brace, Jovanovich.

It is as absurd to speak of the "eternal woman" in general as of the "eternal" man. And we understand why all comparisons are idle which purport to show that woman is superior, inferior, or equal to man, for their situations are profoundly different. . . .

To begin with, there will always be certain differences between man and woman. . . . To emancipate woman is to refuse to confine her to the relations she bears to man, not to deny them to her; let her have her independent existence and she will continue none the less to exist for him *also:* Mutually recognizing each other as subject, each will yet remain for the other an *other.* The reciprocity of their relations will not do away with the miracles—desire, possession, love, dream, adventure—worked by the division of human beings into two separate categories; and the words that move us—giving, conquering, uniting—will not lose their meaning. . . . To gain the supreme victory, it is necessary . . . that by and through their natural differentiation men and women unequivocally affirm their brotherhood.*

GILLIGAN

There is currently an immense feminist literature, covering innumerable aspects of this complex issue. For the next selection, we turn to a different approach from that taken by Wollstonecraft and de Beauvoir. Whereas most feminist scholarship has focused on making a case for male-female *comparability,* a contrasting tendency—sometimes called "difference feminism"—has developed. It seeks to identify, and to celebrate, certain presumed *differences* between women and men.

Much of this literature has involved new psychoanalytic perspectives. An especially influential approach argues for significant male-female differences in moral reasoning and in the expectation of what constitutes "success." A notable voice in this regard belongs to Carol Gilligan, professor of education at Harvard University. Her example of "Heinz's dilemma" has become a modern classic.

This book records different modes of thinking about relationships and the association of these modes with male and female voices in psychological and literary texts and in the data of my research. The disparity between women's experience and the representation of human development, noted throughout the psychological literature, has generally been seen to signify a problem in women's development. Instead, the failure of women to fit existing models of human growth may point to a problem in the representation, a limitation in the conception of human condition, an omission of certain truths about life. . . .

Relationships, and particularly issues of dependency, are experienced differently by women and men. For boys and men, separation and individuation are critically tied to gender identity since separation from the mother is essential for the development of masculinity. For girls and women, issues of femininity or feminine identity do not depend on the achievement of separation from the mother or on the progress of individuation. Since masculinity is defined through separation while femininity is defined through attachment, male gender identity is threatened by intimacy while female gender identity is threatened by separation. Thus males tend to have difficulty with relationships, while females tend to have problems with individuation. The quality of embeddedness in social interaction and personal relationships that characterizes women's lives in contrast to men's, however, becomes not only a descriptive difference but also a developmental liability when the milestones of childhood and adolescent development in the psychological literature are markers of increasing separation. Women's failure to separate then becomes by definition a failure to develop. . . .

*From *The Second Sex* (1952). (H. M. Parshley, Trans.). New York: Vintage Books.

Women's deference is rooted not only in their social subordination but also in the substance of their moral concern. Sensitivity to the needs of others and the assumption of responsibility for taking care lead women to attend to voices other than their own and to include in their judgment other points of view. Women's moral weakness, manifest in an apparent diffusion and confusion of judgment, is thus inseparable from women's moral strength, an overriding concern with relationships and responsibilities. The reluctance to judge may itself be indicative of the care and concern for others that infuse the psychology of women's development and are responsible for what is generally seen as problematic in its nature.

Thus women not only define themselves in a context of human relationship but also judge themselves in terms of their ability to care. Women's place in man's life cycle has been that of nurturer, caretaker, and helpmate, the weaver of those networks of relationships on which she in turn relies. But while women have thus taken care of men, men have, in their theories of psychological development, as in their economic arrangements, tended to assume or devalue that care. When the focus on individuation and individual achievement extends into adulthood and maturity is equated with personal autonomy, concern with relationships appears as a weakness of women rather than as a human strength. . . .

The discovery now being celebrated by men in mid-life of the importance of intimacy, relationships, and care is something that women have known from the beginning. However, because that knowledge in women has been considered "intuitive" or "instinctive," a function of anatomy coupled with destiny, psychologists have neglected to describe its development. . . .

The shift in imagery that creates the problem in interpreting women's development is elucidated by the moral judgments of two eleven-year-old children, a boy and a girl, who see, in the same dilemma, two very different moral problems. While current theory brightly illuminates the line and the logic of the boy's thought, it casts scant light on that of the girl. The choice of a girl whose moral judgments elude existing categories of developmental assessment is meant to highlight the issue of interpretation rather than to exemplify sex differences per se. Adding a new line of interpretation, based on the imagery of the girl's thought, makes it possible not only to see development where previously development was not discerned but also to consider differences in the understanding of relationships without scaling these differences from better to worse.

The two children were in the same sixth-grade class at school and were participants in the rights and responsibilities study, designed to explore different conceptions of morality and self. The sample selected for this study was chosen to focus the variables of gender and age while maximizing developmental potential by holding constant, at a high level, the factors of intelligence, education, and social class that have been associated with moral development, at least as measured by existing scales. The two children in question, Amy and Jake, were both bright and articulate and, at least in their eleven-year-old aspirations, resisted easy categories of sex-role stereotyping, since Amy aspired to become a scientist while Jake preferred English to math. Yet their moral judgments seem initially to confirm familiar notions about differences between the sexes, suggesting that the edge girls have on moral development during the early school years gives way at puberty with the ascendance of formal logical thought in boys.

The dilemma that these eleven-year-olds were asked to resolve was one in the series devised by Kohlberg to measure moral development in adolescence by presenting a conflict between moral norms and exploring the logic of its resolution. In this particular dilemma, a man named Heinz considers whether or not to steal a drug which he cannot afford to buy in order to save the life of his wife. In the standard format of Kohlberg's interviewing procedure, the description of the dilemma itself—Heinz's predicament, the wife's disease, the druggist's refusal to lower his price—is followed by the question, "Should Heinz steal the drug?" The reasons for and against stealing are then explored through a series of questions that vary and extend the parameters of the dilemma in a way designed to reveal the underlying structure of moral thought.

Jake, at eleven, is clear from the outset that Heinz should steal the drug. Constructing the dilemma, as Kohlberg did, as a conflict between the values of property and life, he discerns the logical priority of life and uses that logic to justify his choice:

> For one thing, a human life is worth more than money, and if the druggist only makes $1,000, he is still going to live, but if Heinz doesn't steal the drug, his wife is going to die. *(Why is life worth more than money?)* Because the druggist can get a thousand dollars later from rich people with cancer, but Heinz can't get his wife again. *(Why not?)* Because people are all different and so you couldn't get Heinz's wife again.

Asked whether Heinz should steal the drug if he does not love his wife, Jake replies that he should, saying that not only is there "a difference between hating and killing," but also, if Heinz were caught, "the judge would probably think it was the right thing to do." Asked about the fact that, in stealing, Heinz would be breaking the law, he says that "the laws have mistakes, and you can't go writing up a law for everything that you can imagine."

Thus, while taking the law into account and recognizing its function in maintaining social order (the judge, Jake says, "should give Heinz the lightest possible sentence"), he also sees the law as man-made and therefore subject to error and change. Yet his judgment that Heinz should steal the drug, like his view of the law as having mistakes, rests on the assumption of agreement, a societal consensus around moral values that allows one to know and expect others to recognize what is "the right thing to do."

Fascinated by the power of logic, this eleven-year-old boy locates truth in math, which, he says, is "the only thing that is totally logical." Considering the moral dilemma to be "sort of like a math problem with humans," he sets it up as an equation and proceeds to work out the solution. Since his solution is rationally derived, he assumes that anyone following reason would arrive at the same conclusion and thus that a judge would also consider stealing to be the right thing for Heinz to do. Yet he is also aware of the limits of logic. Asked whether there is a right answer to moral problems, Jake replies that "there can only be right and wrong in judgment," since the parameters of action are variable and complex. Illustrating how actions undertaken with the best of intentions can eventuate in the most disastrous of consequences, he says, "like if you give an old lady your seat on the trolley, if you are in a trolley crash and that seat goes through the window, it might be that reason that the old lady dies."

Theories of developmental psychology illuminate well the position of this child, standing at the juncture of childhood and adolescence, at what Piaget describes as the pinnacle of childhood intelligence, and beginning through thought to discover a wider universe of possibility. The moment of preadolescence is caught by the conjunction of formal operational thought with a description of self still anchored in the factual parameters of his childhood world—his age, his town, his father's occupation, the substance of his likes, dislikes, and beliefs. Yet as his self-description radiates the self-confidence of a child who has arrived, in Erikson's terms, at a favorable balance of industry over inferiority—competent, sure of himself, and knowing well the rules of the game—so his emergent capacity for formal thought, his ability to think about thinking and to reason things out in a logical way, frees him from dependence on authority and allows him to find solutions to problems by himself.

This emergent autonomy follows the trajectory that Kohlberg's six stages of moral development trace, a three-level progression from an egocentric understanding of fairness based on individual need (stages one and two), to a conception of fairness anchored in the shared conventions of societal agreement (stages three and four), and finally to a principled understanding of fairness that rests on the freestanding logic of equality and reciprocity (stages five and six). While this boy's judgments at eleven are scored as conventional on Kohlberg's scale, a mixture of stages three and four, his ability to bring deductive logic to bear on the solution of moral dilemmas, to differentiate morality from law, and to see how laws can be considered to have mistakes points toward the principled conception of justice that Kohlberg equates with moral maturity.

In contrast, Amy's response to the dilemma conveys a very different impression, an image of development stunted by a failure of logic, an inability to think for herself. Asked if Heinz should steal the drug, she replies in a way that seems evasive and unsure:

> Well, I don't think so. I think there might be other ways besides stealing it, like if he could borrow the money or make a loan or something, but he really shouldn't steal the drug—but his wife shouldn't die either.

Asked why he should not steal the drug, she considers neither property nor law but rather the effect that theft could have on the relationship between Heinz and his wife:

> If he stole the drug, he might save his wife then, but if he did, he might have to go to jail, and then his wife might get sicker again, and he couldn't get more of the drug, and it might not be good. So, they should really just talk it out and find some other way to make the money.

Seeing in the dilemma not a math problem with humans but a narrative of relationships that extends over time, Amy envisions the wife's continuing need for her husband and the husband's continuing concern for his wife and seeks to respond to the druggist's need in a way that would sustain rather than sever connection. Just as she ties the wife's survival to the preservation of relationships, so she considers the value of the wife's life in a context of relationships, saying that it would be wrong to let her die because, "if she died, it hurts a lot of people and it hurts her." Since Amy's moral judgment is grounded in the belief that, "if somebody has something that would keep somebody alive, then it's not right not to give it to them," she considers the problem in the dilemma to arise not from the druggist's assertion of rights but from his failure of response.

As the interviewer proceeds with the series of questions that follow from Kohlberg's construction of the dilemma, Amy's answers remain essentially unchanged, the various probes serving neither to elucidate nor to modify her initial response. Whether or not Heinz loves his wife, he still shouldn't steal or let her die; if it were a stranger dying instead, Amy says that "if the stranger didn't have anybody near or anyone she knew," then Heinz should try to save her life, but he should not steal the drug. But as the interviewer conveys through the repetition of questions that the answers she gave were not heard or not right, Amy's confidence begins to diminish, and her replies become more constrained and unsure. Asked again why Heinz should not steal the drug, she simply repeats, "Because it's not right." Asked again to explain why, she states again that theft would not be a good solution, adding lamely, "if he took it, he might not know how to give it to his wife, and so his wife might still die." Failing to see the dilemma as a self-contained problem in moral logic, she does not discern the internal structure of its resolution; as she constructs the problem differently herself, Kohlberg's conception completely evades her.

Instead, seeing a world comprised of relationships rather than of people standing alone, a world that coheres through human connection rather than through systems of rules, she finds the puzzle in the dilemma to lie in the failure of the druggist to respond to the wife. Saying that "it is not right for someone to die when their life could be saved," she assumes that if the druggist were to see the consequences of his refusal to lower his price, he would realize that "he should just give it to the wife and then have the husband pay back the money later." Thus she considers the solution to the dilemma to lie in making the wife's condition more salient to the druggist or, that failing, in appealing to others who are in a position to help.

Just as Jake is confident the judge would agree that stealing is the right thing for Heinz to do, so Amy is confident that, "if Heinz and the druggest had talked it out long enough, they could reach something besides stealing." As he considers the law to "have mistakes," so she sees this drama as a mistake, believing that "the world should just share things more and then people wouldn't have to steal." Both children thus recognize the need for agreement but see it as mediated in different ways—he impersonally through systems of logic and law, she personally through communication in relationship. Just as he relies on the conventions of logic to deduce the solution to this dilemma, assuming these conventions to be shared, so she relies on a process of communication, assuming connection and believing that her voice will be heard. Yet while his assumptions about agreement are confirmed by the convergence in logic between his answers and the questions posed, her assumptions are belied by the failure of communication, the interviewer's inability to understand her response.

Although the frustration of the interview with Amy is apparent in the repetition of questions and its ultimate circularity, the problem of interpretation is focused by the assessment of her response. When considered in the light of Kohlberg's definition of the stages and sequence of moral development, her moral judgments appear to be a full stage lower in maturity than those of the boy. Scored as a mixture of stages two and three, her responses seem to reveal a feeling of powerlessness in the world, an inability to think systematically about the concepts of morality or law, a reluctance to challenge authority or to examine the logic of received moral truths, a failure even to conceive of acting directly to save a life or to consider that such action, if taken, could possibly have an effect. As her reliance on relationships seems to reveal a continuing dependence and vulnerability, so her belief in communication as the mode through which to resolve moral dilemmas appears naive and cognitively immature.

Yet Amy's description of herself conveys a markedly different impression. Once again, the hallmarks of the preadolescent child depict a child secure in her sense of herself, confident in the substance of her beliefs, and sure of her ability to do something of value in the world. Describing herself at eleven as "growing and changing," she says that she "sees some things differently now, just because I know myself really well now, and I know a lot more about the world." Yet the world she knows is a different world from that refracted by Kohlberg's construction of Heinz's dilemma. Her world is a world of relationships and psychological truths where an awareness of the connection between people gives rise to a recognition of responsibility for one another, a perception of the need for response. Seen in this light, her understanding of morality as arising from the recognition of relationship, her belief in communication as the mode of conflict resolution, and her conviction that the solution to the dilemma will follow from its compelling representation seem far from naive or cognitively immature. Instead, Amy's judgments contain the insights central to an ethic of care, just as Jake's judgments reflect the logic of the justice approach. Her incipient awareness of the "method of truth," the central tenet of nonviolent conflict resolution, and her belief in the restorative activity of care, lead her to see the actors in the dilemma arrayed not as opponents in a contest of rights but as members of a network of relationships on whose continuation they all depend. Consequently her solution to the dilemma lies in activating the network by communication, securing the inclusion of the wife by strengthening rather than severing connections.

But the different logic of Amy's response calls attention to the interpretation of the interview itself. Conceived as an interrogation, it appears instead as a dialogue, which takes on moral dimensions of its own, pertaining to the interviewer's uses of power and to the manifestations of respect. With this shift in the conception of the interview, it immediately becomes clear that the interviewer's problem in understanding Amy's response stems from the fact that Amy is answering a different question from the one the interviewer thought had been posed. Amy is considering not *whether* Heinz should act in this situation ("*should* Heinz steal the drug?") but rather *how* Heinz should act in response to his awareness of his wife's need ("Should Heinz *steal* the drug?"). The interviewer takes the mode of action for granted, presuming it to be a matter of fact; Amy assumes the necessity for action and considers what form it should take. In the interviewer's failure to imagine a response not dreamt of in Kohlberg's moral philosophy lies the failure to hear Amy's question and to see the logic in her response, to discern that what appears, from one perspective, to be an evasion of the dilemma signifies in other terms a recognition of the problem and a search for a more adequate solution.

Thus in Heinz's dilemma these two children see two very different moral problems—Jake a conflict between life and property that can be resolved by logical deduction, Amy a fracture of human relationship that must be mended with its own thread. Asking different questions that arise from different conceptions of the moral domain, the children arrive at answers that fundamentally diverge, and the arrangement of these answers as successive stages on a scale of increasing moral maturity calibrated by the logic of the boy's response misses the different truth revealed in the judgment of the girl. To the question, "What does he see that she does not?" Kohlberg's theory provides a ready response, manifest in the scoring of Jake's judgments a full stage higher than Amy's in moral maturity; to the question, "What does she see that he does not?" Kohlberg's theory has nothing to say. Since most of her responses fall through the sieve of Kohlberg's scoring system, her responses appear from his perspective to lie outside the moral domain. . . .

In this way, these two eleven-year-old children, both highly intelligent and perceptive about life, though in different ways, display different modes of moral understanding, different ways of thinking about conflict and choice. In resolving Heinz's dilemma, Jake relies on theft to avoid confrontation and turns to the law to mediate the dispute. Transposing a hierarchy of power into a hierarchy of values, he defuses a potentially explosive conflict between people by casting it as an impersonal conflict of claims. In this way, he abstracts the moral problem from the interpersonal situation, finding in the logic of fairness an objective way to decide who will win the dispute. But this hierarchical ordering, with its imagery of winning and losing and the potential for violence which it contains, gives way in Amy's construction of the dilemma to a network of connection, a web of relationships that is sustained by a process of communication. With this shift, the moral problem changes from one of unfair domination, the imposition of property over life, to one of unnecessary exclusion, the failure of the druggist to respond to the wife.*

STUDY QUESTIONS

1. With the exception of John Stuart Mill, the writers chosen for this chapter are all women; this is not accidental, although it is also possible to find men such as Mill who have written sympathetically, cogently, and influentially about sex and gender. Does the gender of the writer matter to the writer? To you? Should it matter?

2. When it comes to male-female differences, are there any ways to separate the effects of culture and social tradition from possible additional effects of biology?

3. Make a case for or against including current "radical feminists" in a chapter of this sort. Be specific.

4. Assume, for the sake of argument, that there are in fact differences in the "human nature" of men and women, boys and girls. In what way(s), if at all, would it matter? In what way(s), if at all, should it matter?

*From *In a Different Voice* (1982). Cambridge, MA: Harvard University Press.

SOME ADDITIONAL READINGS

Barash, David P. and Lipton, Judith Eve (1997). *Making Sense of Sex: How Genes and Gender Influence Our Relationships.* Washington, D.C.: Island Press.

Freeman, Jo, ed. (1995). *Women: A Feminist Perspective.* Mountain View, Calif.: Mayfield Publishing Co.

Goldberger, Nancy Rule et al., eds. (1996). *Knowledge, Difference, and Power: Essays Inspired by Women's Ways of Knowing.* New York: Basic Books.

Jaggar, Alison M. (1983). *Feminist Politics and Human Nature.* Totowa, N.J.: Rowman and Allanheld.

Pollitt, Katha (1994). *Reasonable Creatures: Essays on Women and Feminism.* NY: Alfred A. Knopf.

PART FOUR
THE HUMAN ANIMAL?

It does not require an immense imagination to see the similarity between human beings and other living things. Accordingly, any effort to identify the nature of human nature must come to grips with the question of *Homo sapiens'* relationship with animals. At the risk of oversimplifying, the basic question is typically: Are human beings unique among animals, or is there an essential continuity in their "natures," just as there undoubtedly is in physiology and structure?

When observing animals, people are strongly tempted to indulge in anthropomorphism ("human shape"), the assumption that animals essentially think and act like human beings. At the other extreme, anthropologist Margaret Mead warned against "zoomorphism," the assumption that human beings essentially think and act like animals. Biologist Julian Huxley urged, similarly, that we beware of "nothing-butism," the mistaken notion that because people are animals, they are nothing but animals. Some argue, nonetheless, that we have much to learn by likening human beings to apes, wolves, or geese, and vice versa. Others caution that this runs the risk of denigrating human dignity by focusing precisely on those traits that do *not* distinguish human beings.

In his poem, "The White-tailed Hornet," Robert Frost catches some of the outrage that results from comparing human beings with animals:

> . . . As long on earth
> As our comparisons were stoutly upward
> With gods and angels, we were men at least,
> But little lower than the gods and angels.
> But once comparisons were yielded downward,
> Once we began to see our images
> Reflected in the mud and even dust,
> 'Twas disillusion upon disillusion.
> We were lost piecemeal to the animals,
> Like people thrown out to delay the wolves.
> Nothing but fallibility was left us,
> And this day's work made even that seem doubtful.

For others, including Charles Darwin, the connection is exalting (as well as true!). Here is the final paragraph of *The Origin of Species:*

> It is interesting to contemplate a tangled bank, clothed with many plants of many kinds, with birds singing on the bushes, with various insects flitting about, and with worms crawling through the damp earth, and to reflect that these elaborately constructed forms, so different from each other, and dependent upon each other in so complex a manner, have all been produced by laws acting around us. . . . Thus, from the war of nature, from famine and death, the most exalted object which we are capable of conceiving, namely, the production of the higher animals, directly follows. There is grandeur in this view of life, with its several powers, having been originally breathed by the Creator into a few forms or into one; and that, whilst this planet has gone cycling on according to the fixed law of gravity, from so simple a beginning endless forms most beautiful and most wonderful have been, and are being evolved.

CHAPTER SIXTEEN

Humans as Animals, and Vice Versa

From Aesop's *Fables* to the Bible, to George Orwell's *Animal Farm* and the cartoons of Walt Disney, people have pictured animals as human, and the other way around. Sometimes the purpose has been allegory, to instruct the young. Sometimes it has been in the service of satire that might otherwise be unacceptable. Sometimes attempts to break down the human-animal barrier have reflected an honest belief in a fundamental, qualitative continuity between people and (other) animals. Such efforts span the gap from fiction to science, as we shall now see.

SWIFT

Jonathan Swift (1667–1745) was no sentimental lover of the human species. He served as Dean of St. Patrick's Cathedral in Dublin, was politically active on behalf of the Irish, and wrote bitterly about human foibles. His novel, *Gulliver's Travels,* often mistakenly considered a children's story, is in fact a biting social criticism, if not a downright misanthropic work. Thus, during one of Gulliver's encounters, the giant king of Brobdingnag describes human beings as "the most pernicious race of little odious vermin that nature ever suffered to crawl upon the surface of the earth." It is Gulliver's final voyage, however, to the land of the admirable, rational, horse creatures known as Houynhnms (pronounced "whin-ums," developed from "whinny"), that constitutes what is probably the most sardonic human-animal comparison ever written. Sir Walter Scott even wrote that this work "holds mankind forth in a light too degrading for contemplation, and which, if admitted, would justify or palliate the worst vices, by exhibiting them as natural attributes, and rendering reformation from a state of such depravity a task too desperate to be attempted."

An English physician, Edward Tyson had published his anatomical investigations of chimpanzees in 1698; the effect was potent, emphasizing the similarities in structure between man and animal. But the mind, especially the power of reason, still remained as a bastion of human specialness. In his satire, Swift was taking issue with the prevailing view of his day, that human beings were *the* rational animal (see Chapter 4). That view had been clearly depicted by the neo-Platonist Porphyry more than a thousand years earlier, as follows:

> Man is a Substance; but because an Angel is also a Substance, That it may appear how Man differs from an Angel, Substance ought to be divided into Corporeal and Incorporeal. A Man is a Body, an Angel without a Body: But a Stone also is a Body: That therefore a Man may be distinguished from a Stone, divide Bodily or Corporeal Substance into Ani-

mate and Inanimate, that is, with or without a Soul. Man is a Corporeal Substance Animate, Stone Inanimate. But Plants are also Animate:* Let us divide therefore again Corporeal Substance Animate into Feeling and void of Feeling. Man feels, a Plant not: But a Horse also feels, and likewise other Beasts. Divide we therefore Animate Corporeal Feeling Substance into Rational and Irrational. Here therefore are we to stand, since it appears that every, and only Man is Rational.

Swift's Yahoos most assuredly are *not* rational. The Houynhnms are, however, and it is at least possible to read Gulliver's adventures among them as the author's yearning for greater rationality on the part of human beings; that is, a devout wish that people were *more* human. Swift himself wrote "I hate and detest that animal called Man, yet I heartily love John, Peter, Thomas and so forth." He also announced that he writes "to vex the world rather than divert it." The following vexatious selections are from *Gulliver's Travels,* Part IV, a voyage to the country of the Houynhnms.

At last I beheld several Animals in a Field, and one or two of the same Kind sitting in Trees. Their Shape was very singular, and deformed, which a little discomposed me, so that I lay down behind a Thicket to observe them better. Some of them coming forward near the Place where I lay, gave me an Opportunity of distinctly marking their Form. Their Heads and Breasts were covered with a thick Hair, some frizzled and others lank; they had Beards like Goats, and a long Ridge of Hair down their Backs, and the fore Parts of their Legs and Feet; but the rest of their Bodies were bare, so that I might see their Skins, which were of a brown Buff Colour. They had no Tails, nor any Hair at all on their Buttocks, except about the *Anus;* which, I presume Nature had placed there to defend them as they sat on the Ground; for this Posture they used, as well as lying down, and often stood on their hind Feet. They climbed high Trees, as nimbly as a Squirrel, for they had strong extended Claws before and behind, terminating in sharp Points, and hooked. They would often spring, and bound, and leap with prodigious Agility. The Females were not so large as the Males; they had long lank Hair on their Heads, and only a Sort of Down on the rest of their Bodies, except about the *Anus*, and *Pudenda*. Their Dugs hung between their fore Feet, and often reached almost to the Ground as they walked. The Hair of both Sexes was of several Colours, brown, red, black and yellow. Upon the whole, I never beheld in all my Travels so disagreeable an Animal, or one against which I naturally conceived so strong an Antipathy. So that thinking I had seen enough, full of Contempt and Aversion, I got up and pursued the beaten Road, hoping it might direct me to the Cabbin of some *Indian.* I had not gone far when I met one of these Creatures full in my Way, and coming up directly to me. The ugly Monster, when he saw me, distorted several Ways every Feature of his Visage, and stared as at an Object he had never seen before; then approaching nearer, lifted up his fore Paw, whether out of Curiosity or Mischief, I could not tell: But I drew my Hanger, and gave him a good Blow with the flat Side of it; for I durst not strike him with the Edge, fearing the Inhabitants might be provoked against me, if they should come to know, that I had killed or maimed any of their Cattle. When the Beast felt the Smart, he drew back, and roared so loud, that a Herd of at least forty came flocking about me from the next Field, howling and making odious Faces; but I ran to the Body of a Tree, and leaning my Back against it, kept them off, by waving my Hanger. Several of this cursed Brood getting hold of the Branches behind, leaped up into the Tree, from whence they began to discharge their Excrements on my Head: However, I escaped pretty well, by sticking close to the Stem of the Tree, but was almost stifled with the Filth, which fell about me on every Side.

In the Midst of this Distress, I observed them all to run away on a sudden as fast as they could; at which

*Editor's note: that is, alive.

I ventured to leave the Tree, and pursue the Road, wondering what it was that could put them into this Fright. But looking on my Left-Hand, I saw a Horse walking softly in the Field; which my Persecutors having sooner discovered, was the Cause of their Flight. The Horse started a little when he came near me, but soon recovering himself, looked full in my Face with manifest Tokens of Wonder: He viewed my Hands and Feet, walking round me several times. I would have pursued my Journey, but he placed himself directly in the Way, yet looking with a very mild Aspect, never offering the least Violence. We stood gazing at each other for some time; at last I took the Boldness, to reach my Hand towards his Neck, with a Design to stroak it; using the common Style and Whistle of Jockies when they are going to handle a strange Horse. But, this Animal seeming to receive my Civilities with Disdain, shook his Head, and bent his Brows, softly raising up his Left Fore-Foot to remove my Hand. Then he neighed three or four times, but in so different a Cadence, that I almost began to think he was speaking to himself in some Language of his own.

While He and I were thus employed, another Horse came up; who applying himself to the first in a very formal Manner, they gently struck each others Right Hoof before, neighing several times by Turns, and varying the Sound, which seemed to be almost articulate. They went some Paces off, as if it were to confer together, walking Side by Side, backward and forward, like Persons deliberating upon some Affair of Weight; but often turning their Eyes towards me, as it were to watch that I might not escape. I was amazed to see such Actions and Behaviour in Brute Beasts; and concluded with myself, that if the Inhabitants of this Country were endued with a proportionable Degree of Reason, they must needs be the wisest People upon Earth. This Thought gave me so much Comfort, that I resolved to go forward untill I could discover some House or Village, or meet with any of the Natives; leaving the two Horses to discourse together as they pleased. But the first, who was a Dapple-Grey, observing me to steal off, neighed after me in so expressive a Tone, that I fancied myself to understand what he meant; whereupon I turned back, and came near him, to expect his farther Commands; but concealing my Fear as much as I could; for I began to be in some Pain, how this Adventure might terminate; and the Reader will easily believe I did not much like my present Situation.

The two Horses came up close to me, looking with great Earnestness upon my Face and Hands. The grey Steed rubbed my Hat all round with his Right Fore-hoof, and discomposed it so much, that I was forced to adjust it better, by taking it off, and settling it again; whereat both he and his Companion (who was a brown Bay) appeared to be much surprized; the latter felt the Lappet of my Coat, and finding it to hang loose about me, they both looked with new Signs of Wonder. He stroked my Right Hand, seeming to admire the Softness, and Colour; but he squeezed it so hard between his Hoof and his Pastern, that I was forced to roar; after which they both touched me with all possible Tenderness. They were under great Perplexity about my Shoes and Stockings, which they felt very often, neighing to each other, and using various Gestures, not unlike those of a Philosopher, when he would attempt to solve some new and difficult Phænomenon.

Upon the whole, the Behaviour of these Animals was so orderly and rational, so acute and judicious, that I at last concluded, they must needs be Magicians, who had thus metamorphosed themselves upon some Design; and seeing a Stranger in the Way, were resolved to divert themselves with him; or perhaps were really amazed at the Sight of a Man so very different in Habit, Feature and Complexion from those who might probably live in so remote a Climate. Upon the Strength of this Reasoning, I ventured to address them in the following Manner: Gentlemen, if you be Conjurers, as I have good Cause to believe, you can understand any Language; therefore I make bold to let your Worships know, that I am a poor distressed *Englishman*, driven by his Misfortunes upon your Coast; and I entreat one of you, to let me ride upon his Back, as if he were a real Horse, to some House or Village, where I can be relieved. In return of which Favour, I will make you a Present of this Knife and Bracelet, (taking them out of my Pocket.) The two Creatures stood silent while I spoke, seeming to listen with great Attention; and when I had ended, they neighed frequently towards each other, as if they were engaged in serious Conversation. I plainly observed, that their Language expressed the Passions very well, and the Words might with little Pains be resolved into an Alphabet more easily than the *Chinese.*

I could frequently distinguish the Word *Yahoo,* which was repeated by each of them several times; and although it were impossible for me to conjecture what it meant, yet while the two Horses were busy in Conversation, I endeavoured to practice this word upon my Tongue; and as soon as they were silent, I boldly pronounced *Yahoo* in a loud Voice, imitating, at the same time, as near as I could, the Neighing of a Horse; at which they were both visibly surprized, and the Grey repeated the same Word twice, as if he meant to teach me the right Accent, wherein I spoke after him as well as I could, and found myself perceivably to improve every time, although very far from any Degree of Perfection. Then the Bay tried me with a second Word, much harder to be pronounced; but reducing it to the *English Orthography,* may be spelt thus, *Houyhnhnm.* I did not succeed in this so well as the former, but after two or three farther Trials, I had better Fortune; and they both appeared amazed at my Capacity.

After some farther Discourse, which I then conjectured might relate to me, the two Friends took their Leaves, with the same Compliment of striking each other's Hoof; and the Grey made me Signs that I should walk before him; wherein I thought it prudent to comply, till I could find a better Director. When I offered to slacken my Pace, he would cry *Hhuun, Hhuun;* I guessed his Meaning, and gave him to understand, as well as I could, that I was weary, and not able to walk faster; upon which, he would stand a while to let me rest. . . .

[W]hen I asserted that the *Yahoos* were the only governing Animals in my Country, which my Master said was altogether past his Conception, he desired to know, whether we had *Houyhnhnms* among us, and what was their Employment: I told him, we had great Numbers; that in Summer they grazed in the Fields, and in Winter were kept in Houses, with Hay and Oats, where *Yahoo* Servants were employed to rub their Skins smooth, comb their Manes, pick their Feet, serve them with Food, and make their Beds. I understand you well, said my Master; it is now very plain from all you have spoken, that whatever Share of Reason the *Yahoos* pretend to, the *Houyhnhnms* are your Masters; I heartily wish our *Yahoos* would be so tractable. I begged his Honour would please to excuse me from proceeding any farther, because I was very certain that the Account he expected from me would be highly displeasing. But he insisted in commanding me to let him know the best and the worst: I told him he should be obeyed. I owned, that the *Houyhnhnms* among us, whom we called *Horses,* were the most generous and comely Animal we had; that they excelled in Strength and Swiftness; and when they belonged to Persons of Quality, employed in Travelling, Racing, and drawing Chariots, they were treated with much Kindness and Care, till they fell into Diseases, or became foundered in the Feet; but then they were sold, and used to all kind of Drudgery till they died; after which their Skins were stripped and sold for what they were worth, and their Bodies left to be devoured by Dogs and Birds of Prey. But the common Race of Horses had not so good Fortune, being kept by Farmers and Carriers, and other mean People, who put them to greater Labour, and feed them worse. I described as well as I could, our Way of Riding; the Shape and Use of a Bridle, a Saddle, a Spur, and a Whip; of Harness and Wheels. I added, that we fastened Plates of a certain hard Substance called *Iron* at the Bottom of their Feet, to preserve their Hoofs from being broken by the Stony Ways on which we often travelled.

My Master, after some Expressions of great Indignation, wondered how we dared to venture upon a *Houyhnhnm*'s Back; for he was sure, that the weakest Servant in his House would be able to shake off the strongest *Yahoo;* or by lying down, and rouling upon his Back, squeeze the Brute to Death. I answered,

That our Horses were trained up from three or four Years old to the several Uses we intended them for; That if any of them proved intolerably vicious, they were employed for Carriages; that they were severely beaten while they were young for any mischievous Tricks: That the Males, designed for the common Use of Riding or Draught, were generally *castrated* about two Years after their Birth, to take down their Spirits, and make them more tame and gentle: That they were indeed sensible of Rewards and Punishments; but his Honour would please to consider, that they had not the least Tincture of Reason any more than the *Yahoos* in this Country.

It put me to the Pains of many Circumlocutions to give my Master a right Idea of what I spoke; for their Language doth not abound in Variety of Words, because their Wants and Passions are fewer than among us. But it is impossible to express his noble Resentment at our savage Treatment of the *Houyhnhnm* Race; particularly after I had explained the Manner and Use of *Castrating* Horses among us, to hinder them from propagating their Kind, and to render them more servile. He said, if it were possible there could be any Country where *Yahoos* alone were endued with Reason, they certainly must be the governing Animal, because Reason will in Time always prevail against Brutal Strength. But, considering the Frame of our Bodies, and especially of mine, he thought no Creature of equal Bulk was so ill-contrived, for employing that Reason in the common Offices of Life. . . .

What you have told me, (said my Master) upon the Subject of War, doth indeed discover most admirably the Effects of that Reason you pretend to: However, it is happy that the *Shame* is greater than the *Danger;* and that Nature hath left you utterly uncapable of doing much Mischief: For your Mouths lying flat with your Faces, you can hardly bite each other to any Purpose, unless by Consent. Then, as to the Claws upon your Feet before and behind, they are so short and tender, that one of our *Yahoos* would drive a Dozen of yours before him. And therefore in recounting the Numbers of those who have been killed in Battle, I cannot but think that you have *said the Thing which is not.*

I could not forbear shaking my Head and smiling a little at his Ignorance. And, being no Stranger to the Art of War, I gave him a Description of Cannons, Culverins, Muskets, Carabines, Pistols, Bullets, Powder, Swords, Bayonets, Battles, Sieges, Retreats, Attacks, Undermines, Countermines, Bombardments, Seafights; Ships sunk with a Thousand Men; twenty Thousand killed on each Side; dying Groans, Limbs flying in the Air: Smoak, Noise, Confusion, trampling to Death under Horses Feet: Flight, Pursuit, Victory; Fields strewed with Carcases left for Food to Dogs, and Wolves, and Birds of Prey; Plundering, Stripping, Ravishing, Burning and Destroying. And, to set forth the Valour of my own dear Countrymen, I assured him, that I had seen them blow up a Hundred Enemies at once in a Siege, and as many in a Ship; and beheld the dead Bodies drop down in Pieces from the Clouds, to the great Diversion of all the Spectators.

I was going on to more Particulars, when my Master commanded me Silence. He said, whoever understood the Nature of *Yahoos* might easily believe it possible for so vile an Animal, to be capable of every Action I had named, if their Strength and Cunning equalled their Malice. But, as my Discourse had increased his Abhorrence of the whole Species, so he found it gave him a Disturbance in his Mind, to which he was wholly a Stranger before. He thought his Ears being used to such abominable Words, might by Degrees admit them with less Detestation. That, although he hated the *Yahoos* of this Country, yet he no more blamed them for their odious Qualities, than he did a *Gnnayh* (a Bird of Prey) for its Cruelty, or a sharp Stone for cutting his Hoof. But, when a Creature pretending to Reason, could be capable of such Enormities, he dreaded lest the Corruption of that Faculty might be worse than Brutality itself. . . .

As these noble *Houyhnhnms* are endowed by Nature with a general Disposition to all Virtues, and have no Conceptions or Ideas of what is evil in a rational Creature; so their grand Maxim is, to cultivate *Reason,* and to be wholly governed by it. Neither is *Reason* among them a Point problematical as with us, where Men can argue with Plausibility on both Sides of a Question; but strikes you with immediate

Conviction; as it must needs do where it is not mingled, obscured, or discoloured by Passion and Interest. I remember it was with extreme Difficulty that I could bring my Master to understand the Meaning of the Word *Opinion,* or how a Point could be disputable; because *Reason* taught us to affirm or deny only where we are certain; and beyond our Knowledge we cannot do either. So that Controversies, Wranglings, Disputes, and Positiveness in false or dubious Propositions, are Evils unknown among the *Houyhnhnms.* . . .

There take a final Leave of my Courteous Readers, and return to enjoy my own Speculations in my little Garden at *Redriff;* to apply those excellent Lessons of Virtue which I learned among the *Houyhnhnms;* to instruct the *Yahoos* of my own Family as far as I shall find them docible Animals; to behold my Figure often in a Glass, and thus if possible habituate my self by Time to tolerate the Sight of a human Creature: To lament the Brutality of *Houyhnhnms* in my own Country, but always treat their Persons with Respect, for the Sake of my noble Master, his Family, his Friends, and the whole *Houyhnhnm* Race, whom these of ours have the Honour to resemble in all their Lineaments, however their Intellectuals came to degenerate.

I began last Week to permit my Wife to sit at Dinner with me, at the farthest End of a long Table; and to answer (but with the utmost Brevity) the few Questions I ask her. Yet the Smell of a *Yahoo* continuing very offensive, I always keep my Nose well stopt with Rue, Lavender, or Tobacco-Leaves. And although it be hard for a Man late in Life to remove old Habits; I am not altogether out of Hopes in some Time to suffer a Neighbour *Yahoo* in my Company, without the Apprehensions I am yet under of his Teeth or his Claws.

My Reconcilement to the *Yahoo*-kind in general might not be so difficult, if they would be content with those Vices and Follies only which Nature hath entitled them to. I am not in the least provoked at the Sight of a Lawyer, a Pick-pocket, a Colonel, a Fool, a Lord, a Gamster, a Politician, a Whoremunger, a Physician, an Evidence, a Suborner, an Attorney, a Traytor, or the like: This is all according to the due Course of Things: But, when I behold a Lump of Deformity, and Diseases both in Body and Mind, smitten with *Pride,* it immediately breaks all the Measures of my Patience; neither shall I be ever able to comprehend how such an Animal and such a Vice could tally together. The wise and virtuous *Houyhnhnms,* who abound in all Excellencies that can adorn a rational Creature, have no Name for this Vice in their Language, which hath no Terms to express any thing that is evil, except those whereby they describe the detestable Qualities of their *Yahoos;* among which they were not able to distinguish this of Pride, for want of thoroughly understanding Human Nature, as it sheweth it self in other Countries, where that Animal presides. But I, who had more Experience, could plainly observe some Rudiments of it among the wild *Yahoos.*

But the *Houyhnhnms,* who live under the Government of Reason, are no more proud of the good Qualities they possess, than I should be for not wanting a Leg or an Arm, which no Man in his Wits would boast of, although he must be miserable without them. I dwell the longer upon this Subject from the Desire I have to make the Society of an *English Yahoo* by any Means not insupportable; and therefore I here intreat those who have any Tincture of this absurd Vice, that they will not presume to appear in my Sight.*

LORENZ

Konrad Lorenz (1903–1989) made very different use of human-animal comparisons. Trained originally as a physician, the Austrian-born Lorenz was one of the founders of ethology, the biological study of animal behavior (for which he shared the Nobel Prize in 1973). His work emphasized the stereotyped, genetically based aspects of animal life, with especially detailed

*From *Gulliver's Travels* (1735; 1961). New York: Norton.

studies of social behavior and species-typical learning, especially the phenomenon known as imprinting. Lorenz was not shy, however, about occasional anthropomorphism, especially in his more popular writings, such as *King Solomon's Ring, Man Meets Dog,* and *On Aggression.* He also did not hesitate to suggest parallels between human and animal behavior, as in the following selection from *On Aggression.*

It is on principle impossible to make any scientifically legitimate assertion about the subjective experiences of animals. The central nervous system of animals is constructed differently from ours, and the physiological processes in it are also different from what happens in our brain. These qualitative differences are sufficient to make us conclude that whatever subjective phenomena may correspond to neural processes in animals must be considerably different from what we, ourselves, experience. However, similarities and analogies in the nervous processes of animals and men are sufficiently great to justify the conclusion that higher animals do indeed have subjective experiences which are qualitatively different from but in essence akin to our own. We are convinced that animals do have emotions, though we shall never be able to say exactly what these emotions are. My teacher Heinroth, who was most careful to describe animal behavior as objectively as possible, was often accused by animal lovers of misrepresenting living creatures as being machines, because of his mechanistic interpretations of behavior. To such aspersions he used to answer: "Quite the contrary, I regard animals as very emotional people with very little intelligence!" We cannot know what a gander is feeling when he stands about displaying all the symptoms of human grief on the loss of his mate, or when he rushes at her in an ecstasy of triumph calling on finding her again. But we cannot help feeling that whatever he may experience is closely akin to our own emotions in an analogous situation.

Considered objectively, the whole behavior of a wild goose deprived of its triumph bond is highly similar to that of a highly territorial animal if it is uprooted from its home environment and put in a strange one. We see the same desperate searching and the same ebbing of courage all the time the animal is looking for its old surroundings. The greylag goose behaves toward her triumph partner just as a resident animal does toward the center of its territory, being the more tied to it the longer she has known it. Near the center of the territory, not only intra-specific aggression but many other autonomous activities of the species reach their highest intensity. Monika Meyr-Holzapfel called the partner that is a personal friend "the animal with the home valency," and with this term, avoiding all anthropomorphic subjectivity, she has apprehended the fullness of the emotional values pertaining to the true friend.

Poet and psychoanalyst alike have long known how close love and hate are, and we know that in human beings also the object of love is nearly always, in an ambivalent way, an object of aggression too. The triumph ceremony of geese—and this cannot be stressed too often—is at most an extremely simplified model of human friendship, but it shows significantly how such an ambivalence can arise. Though in the greylag the second act of the ceremony, the friendly turning toward the partner, normally contains almost no more aggression, the ceremony as a whole, particularly the first part with its accompaniment of "rolling," contains a certain measure of autochthonous aggression directed, if only latently, toward the well-loved friend and partner. We know that this is so, not only from the phylogenetic considerations discussed in this chapter, but also from observations of exceptional cases throwing light on the interaction of the original aggression and the now autonomous triumph-ceremony activation.

Our oldest snow gander, Paulchen, paired in his second year with a snow goose of the same age but kept at the same time a triumph bond with a second snow gander, Schneerot, with whom he lived in brotherly affection. Now snow geese have a habit, common in perching and diving ducks but uncommon in geese, of raping strange females, particularly when they are incubating. The following year, when Paulchen's wife built her nest, laid her eggs, and was sitting on them, an interesting but nasty situation arose: Schneerot raped her persistently and brutally and Paulchen made not the slightest attempt to do anything about it. When Schneerot came to the nest and set upon the female, Paulchen rushed at him furiously but at the last moment swerved past him and attacked any harmless nearby object, for instance our photographer who was filming the scene. Never before was the power of redirection, fixed by ritualization, brought home to me so forcibly: Paulchen wanted to attack Schneerot but could not, because the fixed path of the ritualized movement pattern directed him as firmly past the object of his anger as the points of a railway line direct a locomotive into a siding.

As the behavior of this gander conclusively shows aggression-eliciting stimuli, if proceeding from the partner, release only the triumph cry and not attack. In the Snow Goose the two acts of this ceremony—the first more aggressive and directed outward, the second an almost entirely socially motivated turning toward the partner—are not so markedly divided as they are in the Greylag. A snow goose, particularly in its triumph ceremony, seems to be more imbued with aggression than the friendly greylag, and its triumph cry is more primitive than that of its gray relative. So in the abnormal case just described we may find a behavior corresponding in the mechanisms of its impulses with the primal redirected attack glancing past the partner, such as we have already learned about in cichlid fishes. The Freudian concept of regression is applicable here.

A rather different kind of regression may cause certain changes in the second, less aggressive phase of the triumph cry of the Greylag which show the original participation of the aggression drive. The highly dramatic scene is enacted only when two strong ganders have formed a triumph bond. Since even the most belligerent goose is inferior in strength to the smallest gander, no normal goose pair can ever win a fight against two such friends. Therefore such ganders regularly stand high in the ranking order of the colony. Now with age and with long tenure of high rank "self-assurance," that is assurance of victory, increases, and with it intensity of aggression.

Since at the same time the intensity of the triumph ceremony increases, as we have seen on page 185, with the degree of acquaintance of the partners, that is with the duration of their association, it is understandable that the ceremony of alliance in such a gander couple reaches grades of intensity never attained by pairs of unlike sex. The ganders Max and Kopfschlitz, "married" for the last nine years, are recognizable from afar by the wild enthusiasm of their triumph ceremony.

Now the triumph ceremony of such ganders sometimes increases beyond all measure, to the pitch of ecstasy, and then something very remarkable and sinister happens: the sounds become increasingly stronger, quicker, and more concentrated, the necks more and more horizontal till the upright attitude typical of the ceremony is lost and the angle between the line of the redirected movement and the line pointing directly toward the partner becomes smaller and smaller. In other words, with extreme increase of intensity the ritualized ceremony loses more and more those characteristics which differentiate it from its unritualized prototype. Thus it regresses, in the Freudian sense, to a phylogenetically earlier primitive condition. J. Nicolai was the first to discover this "deritualization" in bullfinches. In these birds the greeting ceremony of the female has arisen, like the triumph ceremony of geese, from ritualization of primally threatening gestures. If we increase the sexual drives of a female bullfinch by submitting her to a long period of solitary confinement, and afterwards put her with a male, she will pursue him with greeting gestures whose character is the more aggressive the more the sexual drives have been dammed. The tumult of such ecstatic love-hate can, in the gander couple, halt at any stage and subside; then follows a triumph ceremony still very excited but normally ending in quiet, tender cackling even if the gestures still have the expression of furious aggression. When one sees such an exhibition of fervent love for the first time, without yet knowing anything about the phenomena above described, one experiences a certain feeling of uneasiness: involuntarily one remembers such expressions as "I love you so much I could eat you" and one recalls what Freud so often stressed, that colloquialisms often reflect deepest psychological associations.

However, in our goose records of the last ten years we have only three cases in which the deritualization of the triumph ceremony, rising to highest ecstasy, did not subside. In these cases there occurs something irrevocable and of great consequence for the future life of the individuals: the threatening and fighting attitudes of the two ganders assume purer and purer forms, excitement rises to boiling point, and suddenly the two friends seize each other by the neck and beat each other with resounding blows of their wings, which are armed with hard little horns at the shoulder. Their grim fight can be heard from afar. While an ordinary fight between two ganders, induced by rivalry for status, for a female, or for a nesting place, seldom lasts more than a few seconds and never more than a minute, we registered in one of three fights between triumph-cry partners a full quarter of an hour after we had rushed to the scene, alarmed from afar by the sound of battle.

The embittered fury of these fights is only partly explained by the fact that the opponents know each other so well that they are less afraid of each other than of strangers. In human beings, too, the particular horror of marital quarrels springs only partly from this source. I am much more inclined to believe that in every case of genuine love there is such a high measure of latent aggression, normally obscured by the bond, that on the rupturing of this bond the horrible phenomenon known as hate makes its appearance. There is no love without aggression, but there is no hate without love!

The victor never pursues the vanquished, and we have never known a second fight to take place between the two ganders. On the contrary, they avoid each other meticulously from thenceforth, and when our big flock of geese is grazing on the marsh, the former friends that have fallen out with each other are always to be found at opposite sides of the periphery. If by chance, not having noticed each other in time, or owing to our experiments, they do come near each other, they show the most remarkable behavior that I have ever seen in animals, and I hesitate to describe it for fear of being accused of anthropomorphizing. The ganders are embarrassed! They cannot look at each other. Their glances dart hither and thither, magnetically attracted to the object of their love and hate, then they jerk away from it, as a finger jerks back from hot metal; in addition, both ganders constantly perform displacement activities, preening their feathers, shaking imaginary objects from their beaks, and so on. They cannot simply walk away, for any action suggestive of flight is forbidden by the age-old commandment to "save face" at any cost. One cannot help pitying them in their awkward situation.

The investigator of the problems of intra-specific aggression would give much to be able to determine, by an exact quantitative motivation analysis, the proportions of original aggression and autonomous triumph-cry drive contained in individual cases of this ceremony. We believe that we are gradually nearing the solution to this problem, but a description of the researches involved would take us too far here.

Let us recapitulate what has been said in the previous chapters about aggression and those special inhibiting mechanisms which, in certain permanently united individuals, not only exclude the possibility of their fighting each other but also create between them a bond such as the triumph ceremony of geese. Let us examine the relations between this bond and those of other mechanisms of community life described in the preceding chapters. As I read through these chapters for the purpose of making this summary, I realize how little I have succeeded in doing justice to the greatness and importance of the phylogenetic phenomena whose workings I think I really understand myself, but which are so difficult to explain, and I am overcome by the discouraging feeling of helplessness. One might think that a scholar with a certain gift for expressing himself, having dedicated his whole life to a specific subject, would be able to describe and communicate the results of his labors in such a way that his reader would understand not only what he knows but also what he feels about them. I can only hope that the following summary of my facts will convey to the reader at least a pale reflection of what I cannot put into words.

... [T]here are animals totally devoid of aggression which keep together for life in firmly united flocks. One would think that such animals would be predestined to develop permanent friendships and brotherly unions of individuals, and yet these characteristics are never found among such peaceable herd creatures; their association is always entirely anonymous. A personal bond, an individual friendship, is found only in animals with highly developed intra-specific aggression; in fact, this bond is the firmer, the more aggressive the particular animal and species is. There are few more aggressive fish than cichlids, few more aggressive birds than geese. Proverbially the most aggressive of all mammals, Dante's *bestia senza pace*, the wolf, is the most faithful of friends. Some animals are alternately territorial and aggressive, and nonaggressive and social, according to season, and in these species every personal bond is limited to the period of aggressiveness. Undoubtedly the personal bond developed at that phase of evolution when, in aggressive animals, the co-operation of two or more individuals was necessary for a species-preserving purpose, usually brood tending. Doubtless the personal bond, love, arose in many cases from intra-specific aggression, by way of ritualization of a redirected attack or threatening. Since these rites are tied up with the person of the partner, and since they later become a need as independent instinct actions, they make the presence of a partner an absolute necessity and make the partner itself the "animal with home valency"—having the same emotional value as the home.

Intra-specific aggression is millions of years older than personal friendship and love. During long epochs of the earth's history, there have been animals that were certainly extraordinarily fierce and aggressive. Nearly all reptiles of the present day are aggressive and it is unlikely that those of antiquity were less so. But the personal bond is known only in certain teleost fishes, birds, and mammals, that is in groups that did not appear before the Tertiary period. Thus intra-specific aggression can certainly exist without its counterpart, love, but conversely there is no love without aggression.

A behavior mechanism that must be sharply differentiated from intra-specific aggression is hate, the ugly little brother of love. As opposed to ordinary aggression, it is directed toward one individual, just as love is, and probably hate presupposes the presence of love: one can really hate only where one has loved and, even if one denies it, still does.

It is superfluous to point out the analogies between the social behavior patterns of many animals, particularly wild geese, and those of man. All the truisms in our proverbs seem to apply equally to geese. As good evolutionists and Darwinians, we can and must draw important conclusions from this fact. We know that the youngest common ancestors of birds and mammals were very low reptiles of the Upper Devonian and Lower Carboniferous strata, which certainly had no highly developed social life and were scarcely more intelligent than frogs. Thus the similarities in the social behavior patterns of the Greylag Goose and of man are not derived from a common ancestor but have arisen by so-called convergent adaptation. They do not owe their existence to chance; this would be an improbability which could be calculated, but could only be expressed in astronomical figures.

If, in the Greylag Goose and in man, highly complex norms of behavior, such as falling in love, strife for ranking order, jealousy, grieving, etc., are not only similar but down to the most absurd details the same, we can be sure that every one of these instincts has a very special survival value, in each case almost or quite the same in the Greylag and in man. Only in this way can the conformity of behavior have developed.

As natural scientists who do not believe in "infallible instincts" or other miracles, we of course assume that every one of these behavior patterns is the function of a corresponding special physical organization of the nervous system, sense organs, etc., in other words of a structure evolved in the organism by selection pressure. If we imagine how complicated a physiological apparatus such as an electronic brain would have to be to produce a social behavior pattern like the triumph ceremony, we realize with astonishment that a wonderful organ such as the eye or the ear seems simple in comparison. The more complex and differentiated two analogously constructed and similarly functioning organs are, the more right we have to group them in the same functional conception and to call them by the same name, however different their phylogenetic origin may be. When Cephalopods, like the Octopus, Squid, and Cuttlefish, on the one hand and vertebrates on the other have invented, independently of one another, eyes built on the same principle as the lens camera, and when in both cases these organs have similar constructional units such as lens, iris, vitreous humor and retina, no reasonable person will object to calling both the organ of the Cephalopods and that of the vertebrate an eye—without any quotation marks. We are equally justified in omitting the quotation marks when speaking of the social behavior patterns of higher animals which are analogous with those of man.

All that I have said in this chapter should be a warning to the spiritual pride of many people. In an animal not even belonging to the favored class of mammals we find a behavior mechanism that keeps certain individuals together for life, and this behavior pattern has become the strongest motive governing all action; it can overcome all "animal" drives, such as hunger, sexuality, aggression, and fear, and it determines social order in its species-characteristic form. In all these points this bond is analogous with those human functions that go hand in hand with the emotions of love and friendship in their purest and noblest form.*

GRIFFIN

Thus far in this chapter, we have looked at two very different approaches to "humans as animals." Now we turn to the inverse, "animals as humans," or, more precisely, animals as conscious creatures. The issue is important, not only for its scientific and ethical implications, but also because concern with human nature must confront whether that deeply prized and personal characteristic, our consciousness, is uniquely human.

Highly respected scientists do not generally venture into the murky and controversial realm of animal consciousness. The most notable exception has been Donald R. Griffin (1915–) a renowned biophysicist and animal behaviorist, whose research credits include detailed study of bird migration, as well as the demonstration that bats orient themselves via echolocation. Griffin's books include *Listening in the Dark, Echoes of Bats and Men, The Question of Animal Awareness,* and *Animal Thinking.* The following selection is from *Animal Minds.*

Mental experiences are real and important to us, and insofar as they occur in nonhuman animals they must be important to them as well. They are certainly important to our appreciation of animals, for we can only understand other species fully when we know what, if anything, they think and feel. It is therefore important for those interested in animals to learn as much as possible about whatever thoughts and feelings they experience. Unfortunately, almost all of the scientists who study animal behavior avoid this subject; and many deny the existence or the significance of animal consciousness. Because it is so difficult to prove rigorously whether any given animal is conscious, no matter how ingenious its behavior, scientists have tended to cling to the conservative assumption that all animal behavior is *un*conscious. But recent discoveries about animal behavior have rendered this tendency to minimize the implications of animal versatility more and more difficult to maintain. The dilemma faced by the conservative "nothing but" position preferred by many scientists is illustrated by two examples.

A hungry chimpanzee walking through his native rain forest in the Ivory Coast, comes upon a large *Panda oleosa* nut lying on the ground under one of the widely scattered Panda trees. He knows that these nuts are much too hard to open with his hands or teeth, and that although he can use pieces of wood

*From *On Aggression* (1966). New York: Harcourt Brace & World.

or relatively soft rocks to batter open the more abundant *Coula edulis* nuts, these tough Panda nuts can only be cracked by pounding them with a very hard piece of rock. Very few stones are available in the rain forest, but he walks for about 80 meters straight to another tree where several days ago he had cracked open a Panda nut with a large chunk of granite. He carries this rock back to the nut he has just found, places it in a crotch between two buttress roots, and cracks it open with a few well-aimed blows. (The loud noises of chimpanzees cracking nuts with rocks had led early European explorers to suspect that some unknown native tribe was forging metal tools in the depths of the rain forest.)

In a city park in Japan, a hungry green-backed heron picks up a twig, breaks it into small pieces, and carries one of these to the edge of a pond, where she drops it into the water. At first it drifts away, but she picks it up and brings it back. She watches the floating twig intently until small minnows swim up to it, and she then seizes one by a rapid thrusting grab with her long sharp bill. Another green-backed heron from the same colony carries bits of material to a branch extending out over the pond and tosses the bait into the water below. When minnows approach this bait, he flies down and seizes one on the wing.

Must we reject, or repress, any suggestion that the chimpanzee or the heron thinks consciously about the tasty food it manages to obtain by these coordinated actions? Many animals adapt their behavior to the challenges they face either under natural conditions or in laboratory experiments. This has persuaded many scientists that some sort of cognition must be required to orchestrate such versatile behavior. For example, in other parts of Africa chimpanzees select suitable branches from which they break off twigs to produce a slender probe, which they carry some distance to poke it into a termite nest and eat the termites clinging to it as it is withdrawn. Apes have also learned to use artificial communication systems to ask for objects and activities they want and to answer simple questions about pictures of familiar things. Vervet monkeys employ different alarm calls to inform their companions about particular types of predator.

Such ingenuity is not limited to primates. Lionesses sometimes cooperate in surrounding prey or drive prey toward a companion waiting in a concealed position. Captive beaver have modified their customary patterns of lodge and dam building behavior by piling material around a vertical pole at the top of which was located food that they could not otherwise reach. They are also very ingenious at plugging water leaks, sometimes cutting pieces of wood to fit a particular hole through which water is escaping. Under natural conditions, in late winter some beaver cut holes in the dams they have previously constructed, causing the water level to drop, which allows them to swim about under the ice without holding their breath.

Nor is appropriate adaptation of complex behavior to changing circumstances a mammalian monopoly. Bowerbirds construct and decorate bowers that help them attract females for mating. Plovers carry out injury-simulating distraction displays that lead predators away from their eggs or young, and they adjust these displays according to the intruder's behavior. A parrot uses imitations of spoken English words to ask for things he wants to play with and to answer simple questions such as whether two objects are the same or different, or whether they differ in shape or color. Even certain insects, specifically the honeybees, employ symbolic gestures to communicate the direction and distance their sisters must fly to reach food or other things that are important to the colony.

These are only a few of the more striking examples of versatile behavior on the part of animals. . . .

But does it really matter whether any animals are ever conscious, and, if any are, which ones and under what conditions? Strict behaviorists tend to argue that it doesn't matter, thereby impaling themselves on the horns of a dilemma. Either they must deny the importance of human consciousness, or they must accept its importance but hold that no other species can be conscious to a significant degree. A conscious organism is clearly different in an important way from one that lacks any subjective mental experiences. The former thinks and feels to a greater or lesser degree, while the latter is limited to existing and reacting. One important difference between unconscious and conscious thought is that the latter includes paying attention to internal images or representations, that is, thinking about them to oneself. Such representations may involve any sensory modalities; they may be directly elicited by contemporary external stimulation, they may be based on memories, or they may be anticipations of future events. They can also be literal imagination of objects and events that do not actually exist.

Many behaviorists claim that the distinction between conscious and unconscious mental states is an empty and meaningless one, at least when applied to nonhuman animals, because, they say, anything an animal does might equally well be done without any accompanying consciousness. In one sense this is simply a denial of concern, a confession of limited interests. But it is often combined with an appeal to scientific parsimony and an insistence that consciousness is a needless complication, and furthermore that it does not matter whether animals, or even people, are conscious of anything at all. This attitude often leads to such sweeping and dogmatically negative pronouncements as: "The idea that people are autonomous and possess within them the power and the reasons for making decisions has no place in behavior theory" (Schwartz and Lacey, 1982, 16).

Inclusive behaviorists see no way to determine what thoughts or feelings, if any, are experienced by a member of another species. Philosophical purists of the school known as skeptics make essentially the same argument about our conspecifics. Perhaps the most appropriate response to both these claims is to point out that total perfection of argument and proof is seldom available in science any more than in general affairs. We can only make stronger or weaker claims with a higher or lower probability of correctness. Even when vital practical decisions are at stake, we have no choice but to act on whatever interpretation appears most likely to be correct, based on the most balanced assessment of available evidence of which we are capable. We do not know whether conscious mental experiences are correlated with any specific and identifiable states or activities of central nervous systems, although of course certain parts of the human brain such as Wernicke's area are clearly of great importance. But this ignorance of ours does not mean that conscious experience is nonexistent. . . .

Many philosophers have wrestled with the question of how we can know anything about the minds of others, whether they be other people, animals, extraterrestrial creatures, or artifacts such as computer systems. Some are convinced that other minds are found only in our species, while others consider it possible, or even likely, that they can also be found in animals or computers. Philosophers struggle to devise logical and reasonable criteria for the presence of minds and consciousness, criteria that can be applied to animals or to computer systems as well as to borderline human cases such as newborn infants or persons with severe brain damage. When many of these criteria were first proposed they seemed to be impossible for any nonhuman animal to satisfy. But, as emphasized in previous chapters, increasing understanding of animals and their behavior has often disclosed cases where the criterion in question is satisfied after all. . . .

The whole kingdom of nonhuman animals, comprising millions of species and literally countless numbers of individuals, is clearly an important component of our planet, for the universe would be a very different one if they did not exist. For that reason alone it is important to understand animals as fully as possible; for without such understanding we will remain blind to an important aspect of reality. We cannot understand animals fully without knowing what their subjective lives are like. Until this is possible, and at present it is possible only to a very limited degree, we will remain unable to appreciate adequately either the nature of nonhuman animals, or how we differ from them. This zoological significance of the question of animal consciousness may lack the practical urgency of the ethical questions, and it may not appeal to philosophers as an intellectual challenge comparable in significance to the general problem of other minds. But it not only bears directly on the philosophical and ethical issues outlined above; it is also, in its own right, an important reason to inquire as deeply and critically as we can into the subjects discussed in this book.

Much of twentieth-century science has gradually slipped into an attitude that belittles nonhuman animals. Subtle but effective nonverbal signals to this effect emanate from much of the scientific literature. Physical and chemical science is assumed to be more fundamental, more rigorous, and more significant than zoology. Modern biology revels in being largely molecular, and this inevitably diverts attention away from the investigation of animals for their own sakes. Part of this trend may be due to an unrecognized reaction against the deflation of human vanity by the Darwinian revolution. The acceptance of biological evolution and the genetic relationship of our species to others was a shattering blow to the human ego, from which we may not have fully recovered, for it is not easy to give up a deep seated faith that our kind is unique and qualitatively superior. A psychological palliative that may be subconsciously attractive, even to many scientists, is to shift attention away from the embarrassing fact of our animal ancestry by accentuating those aspects of science that are more akin to physics. . . .

Evolutionary biology has been so concerned with identifying how the structure, function, and behavior of animals contribute to their fitness that it has tended to underemphasize those attributes that render animals importantly different from nonliving systems, plants, or protozoa. Independent mobility and a heterotrophic metabolism dependent on food materials synthesized by plants are the most obvious distinguishing features of multicellular animals. But animals are also clearly more than mobile metabolisms. They appear to *act*, that is, to do things spontaneously, on their own. What they do is determined in large part by outside influences; yet the complexity and the remoteness of animal actions from whatever external causes may be at work distinguishes them in an important fashion from microorganisms, plants, or physical systems. Most of these spontaneous activities are regulated by central nervous systems, and such systems, together with the adaptable behavior they make possible, are a special feature of living animals not found elsewhere in the known universe. In addition, members of at least one species also experience subjective feelings and conscious thoughts. We cannot be certain how common this additional feature actually is; but suggestive evidence such as that reviewed in this book makes it at least plausible that simple forms of conscious thinking may be quite widespread.

CONSCIOUS INSTINCTS

There is a strong tendency among contemporary behavioral scientists to assume that conscious mental states, on the one hand, and learning or evolutionary selection, on the other, are mutually exclusive alternatives. But this is by no means self-evident. An animal may or may not be conscious, and its behavior may be influenced to varying degrees by genetic programming. These are actually quite independent considerations, and any combination is possible. Learned behavior is not always consciously acquired or executed, even in our own species, and it may be even less closely linked to conscious awareness in nonhuman animals. Likewise, a genetically programmed behavior pattern may or may not be accompanied or guided by conscious thinking. There is no reason why genetic influences should not lead to a central nervous system that develops conscious thoughts, especially when such thinking is adaptive and has been selected in the course of the animal's evolutionary history. In short, the customary assumption that if some behavior has been genetically programmed, it cannot be guided by conscious thinking, is not supported by any solid evidence. . . .

Perhaps we should pull back for a moment and ask ourselves just what evidence supports this deep-rooted assumption that only learned behavior can be accompanied by conscious thinking. This belief arises, I suspect, from analogies to our own situation. Human lives clearly require an enormous amount of learning, so much so that many have denied the existence of instinctive, genetically programmed human behavior. It is widely believed that only the simplest human reactions such as eye blinks, knee jerks, sneezing, cries of pain, exclamations one makes when startled, or a newborn baby's suckling are under predominantly genetic control. Many of these reactions happen automatically, unintentionally, and without any learning, although we may be aware of them as they occur. We do not plan to sneeze although we certainly know we are sneezing. But we may not even realize that we have blinked in response to a flash of light or the sight of something moving rapidly toward us. From these experiences we reason that when animal behavior requires no learning it cannot be accompanied by conscious thought.

Consciousness of one's bodily activities falls into two general categories: we may consciously anticipate, plan, and intend to perform some action, or our bodies may simply do something without any conscious expectation and perhaps without our being able to affect the action. Yet even in the second case we may be completely conscious of what our body is doing. A typical case of the first type is reaching out to grasp something; this usually entails consciously deciding to pick up the object, although it may also occur unconsciously or even involuntarily. The second category might be exemplified by the withdrawal response to a painful stimulus. Such simple human reflexes have tended to serve as "type specimens" of instinctive behavior and to color our view of unlearned behavior as a whole. But perhaps it is unwisely anthropocentric to assume that this view accurately describes instinctive behavior in all other animals. The large genetic component underlying many sorts of animal behavior may not justify the conclusion that all instinctive behavior is a homogeneous category. In particular, the analogy to our own situation does not establish how tightly consciousness is linked to learned behavior as contrasted with behavior strongly influenced by hereditary constitution.

When animals behave instinctively, they might be fully aware of what they are doing, without necessarily having experienced a prior intention, still less understanding the causes of their behavior or its ultimate consequences. Our own conscious thoughts need not be tightly linked to any overt behavior at all. We can think about objects and events, including past or future activities, without doing anything. It can be argued that our previous learning has led indirectly to such unexpressed thoughts, yet we certainly experience conscious thoughts that are unrelated to any current behavior or sensory input. Recognizing this obvious fact, it is appropriate to inquire whether conscious thoughts might sometimes arise as a result of the brain's genetically guided development and functioning. . . .

The subject of animal thinking is usually discussed by Western intellectuals who try hard to be objective and realistic. But the content of much human consciousness does not conform to objective reality. Fear of ghosts and monsters is very basic and widespread in our species. Demons, spirits, miracles, and voices of departed ancestors are real and important to many people, as are religious beliefs that entail faith in the overriding significance of entities that lie far outside of the physical universe studied by objective science. Yet when we speculate about animal thoughts, we tend to assume that they must necessarily be confined to practical down-to-earth matters, such as how to get food or escape predators. We usually suppose that animal thinking must be a simpler version of our own thinking about the animal's situation.

But there is really no reason to assume that animal thoughts are rigorously realistic. Apes and porpoises often seem playful, mischievous, and fickle, and anything but businesslike, practical, and objective. Insofar as animals think and feel, they may fear imaginary predators, imagine unrealistically delicious foods, or think about objects and events that do not actually exist in the real world around them. The young vervet monkey that gives the eagle alarm call for a harmless songbird may really fear that this flying creature will attack. As we try to imagine the content of animal thoughts, we should consider the possibility that their thoughts, like some of ours, may be less than perfect replicas of reality. Animals may experience fantasies as well as realistic representations of their environments. . . .

The emergent property of consciousness confers an enormous advantage by allowing animals to select those actions that are most likely to get them what they want or to ward off what they fear, as suggested in chapter 1. To paraphrase Karl Popper, animals that think consciously can try out possible actions in their heads without the risk of actually performing them solely on a trial-and-error basis. Considering and then rejecting a possible action because one decides it is less promising than some alternative is far less risky than trying it out in the real world, where a mistake can easily be fatal. We carry out such trial-and-error behavior in our minds, and it is difficult to avoid the conclusion that animals often do something similar at a simple level. This activity, attribute, or capability is a truly marvelous phenomenon. Although almost all discoveries about animal behavior throw some light on animal mentality, scientists have devoted relatively little attention to it, at least in direct and explicit form. Once its significance is appreciated more fully, there is good reason to hope that we can learn much more about it.

I am confident that with patience and critical investigation we can begin to discern what life is like, subjectively, to particular animals under specific conditions, beginning with the sorts of evidence reviewed in previous chapters. Cognitive ethologists can certainly improve greatly on these preliminary inferences, once the creative ingenuity of scientists is directed constructively toward the important goal of answering Nagel's basic question: What is it like to be a bat, or any other animal? Contrary to the widespread pessimistic opinion that the content of animal thinking is hopelessly inaccessible to scientific inquiry, the communicative signals used by many animals provide empirical data on the basis of which much can reasonably be inferred about their subjective mental experiences. Because mentality is one of the most important capabilities that distinguishes living animals from the rest of the known universe, seeking to understand animal minds is even more exciting and significant than elaborating our picture of inclusive fitness or discovering new molecular mechanisms. Cognitive ethology presents us with one of the supreme scientific challenges of our times, and it calls for our best efforts of critical and imaginative investigation.*

STUDY QUESTIONS

1. Would you feel debased or ennobled (or neither) if you considered that human beings are animals? Why?

2. Would it be significant if it were shown that severely retarded human beings are less intelligent than, say, chimpanzees?

3. Discuss circumstances in which people have sought to raise and/or lower their opinion of other people by likening them to animals. Similarly, consider the effect on people's perceptions of animals when animals are likened to people.

4. In the movie *African Queen,* Katherine Hepburn's character announces rather stiffly to Humphrey Bogart's character "Nature . . . is something we were put on earth to rise above." What is your response?

SOME ADDITIONAL READINGS

Candland, Douglas Keith (1993). *Feral Children and Clever Animals: Reflections on Human Nature.* New York: Oxford University Press.

Gould, James L. and Gould, Carol Grant (1994). *The Animal Mind.* New York: W.H. Freeman.

*From *Animal Minds* (1992). Chicago: University of Chicago Press.

Savage-Rumbaugh, Sue and Lewin, Roger (1994). *Kanzi: The Ape at the Brink of the Human Mind.* New York: Wiley.

Shepard, Paul (1996). *The Others: How Animals Made Us Human.* Washington, D.C.: Island Press.

de Waal, Frans (1996). *Good Natured: The Origins of Right and Wrong in Humans and Other Animals.* Cambridge, Mass.: Harvard University Press.

CHAPTER SEVENTEEN

Evolution and Sociobiology

It can be argued that there is one and only one *scientific* theory of human nature. Not surprisingly, it is the one and only scientific theory of living things generally: namely, evolution. Evolution has emerged as the fundamental paradigm of the biological sciences, the organizing principle that makes sense out of the diversity of hypotheses and observations that comprise the study of life. Although it is sometimes protested that evolution is "only a theory," it should be emphasized that "theory" applies here in the same sense as in atomic theory or number theory. That is, it appears to be as close to fact as one can get in the natural sciences.

On the other hand, although there is "the theory" of evolution, there are also numerous "theories of evolution," that is, contending ideas as to its details. Evolution is often mistakenly thought to provide only an explanation of past events, such as fossils, anatomical structures, embryologic affinities, and so on. As such, it has been controversial enough, especially among religious fundamentalists who hold that it contradicts (or, rather, is contradicted by) biblical and other accounts of human creation. The important thing for our purposes, however, is that evolution also promises to explain and interpret behavior, including that of human beings. Whether it delivers on this promise is for the reader to judge.

DARWIN

Charles Darwin (1809–1882) did not discover evolution. Numerous workers before him had speculated that living things were somehow derived from each other, over a long time span, rather than having been specially created by a deity. Darwin's contribution was to identify a precise mechanism—natural selection—by which evolution took place, and then to document his thesis with an extraordinary array of evidence. Darwin's idea apparently developed gradually, stimulated in large part by the observations he made as official naturalist on an around-the-world voyage. He was impressed, for example, that the animal species inhabiting the various Galapagos Islands appeared to be closely related to each other, yet were distinct; this suggested to him that they all shared a common ancestor.

Darwin's insight was especially stimulated by Thomas Malthus's observation that populations tend to exceed available resources. Considering, then, that competition would necessarily result, and that individuals differ in heritable ways from each other, Darwin concluded that certain forms would leave a disproportionate representation in future generations. In short, they would have been naturally selected. (He was also impressed by the success of animal and plant breeders in producing evolutionary change by "artificial selection.")

Darwin's massive yet surprisingly readable book, *The Origin of Species by Means of Natural Selection or the Preservation of Favored Races in the Struggle for Life* (1859), was a milestone in scientific thought. It was also controversial, although its only direct reference to human beings is the prophetic comment, "Much light will be thrown on the origin of man and his history." Darwin researched and wrote widely on such topics as coral reefs, insectivorous plants, pollination, the movements of plants, animal and plant domestication, barnacles, earthworms, and the expression of human and animal emotions. In 1871 he published *The Descent of Man and Selection in Relation to Sex,* which directly treated human beings. It is difficult to overestimate the impact that Darwinism (that is, evolution by natural selection) has had on biology, and on humanity's idea of itself. The first paragraph of the reading below is from *The Origin of Species,* followed by a longer selection from *The Descent of Man.*

In the survival of favoured individuals and races, during the constantly-recurrent Struggle for Existence, we see a powerful and ever-acting form of Selection. The struggle for existence inevitably follows from the high geometrical ratio of increase which is common to all organic beings. This high rate of increase is proved by calculation,—by the rapid increase of many animals and plants during a succession of peculiar seasons, and when naturalised in new countries. More individuals are born than can possibly survive. A grain in the balance may determine which individuals shall live and which shall die,—which variety or species shall increase in number, and which shall decrease, or finally become extinct. As the individuals of the same species come in all respects into the closest competition with each other, the struggle will generally be most severe between them; it will be almost equally severe between the varieties of the same species, and next in severity between the species of the same genus. On the other hand the struggle will often be severe between beings remote in the scale of nature. The slightest advantage in certain individuals, at any age or during any season, over those with which they come into competition, or better adaptation in however slight a degree to the surrounding physical conditions, will, in the long run, turn the balance.*

The main conclusion here arrived at, and now held by many naturalists who are well competent to form a sound judgment is that man is descended from some less highly organised form. The grounds upon which this conclusion rests will never be shaken, for the close similarity between man and the lower animals in embryonic development, as well as in innumerable points of structure and constitution, both of high and of the most trifling importance,—the rudiments which he retains, and the abnormal reversions to which he is occasionally liable,—are facts which cannot be disputed. They have long been known, but until recently they told us nothing with respect to the origin of man. Now when viewed by the light of our knowledge of the whole organic world, their meaning is unmistakable. The great principle of evolution stands up clear and firm, when these groups or facts are considered in connection with others, such as the mutual affinities of the members of the same group, their geographical distribution in past and present times, and their geological succession. It is incredible that all these facts should speak falsely. He who is not content to look, like a savage, at the phenomena of nature as disconnected, cannot any longer believe that man is the work of a separate act of creation. He will be forced to admit that the close resemblance of the embryo of man to that, for instance, of a dog—the construction of his

*From *The Origin of Species by Means of Natural Selection.* (1859). London: Murray.

skull, limbs and whole frame on the same plan with that of other mammals, independently of the uses to which the parts may be put—the occasional re-appearance of various structures, for instance of several muscles, which man does not normally possess, but which are common to the Quadrumana—and a crowd of analogous facts—all point in the plainest manner to the conclusion that man is the co-descendant with other mammals of a common progenitor.

We have seen that man incessantly presents individual differences in all parts of his body and in his mental faculties. These differences or variations seem to be induced by the same general causes, and to obey the same laws as with the lower animals. In both cases similar laws of inheritance prevail. Man tends to increase at a greater rate than his means of subsistence; consequently he is occasionally subjected to a severe struggle for existence, and natural selection will have effected whatever lies within its scope. A succession of strongly-marked variations of a similar nature is by no means requisite; slight fluctuating differences in the individual suffice for the work of natural selection; not that we have any reason to suppose that in the same species, all parts of the organisation tend to vary to the same degree. We may feel assured that the inherited effects of the long-continued use or disuse of parts will have done much in the same direction with natural selection. Modifications formerly of importance, though no longer of any special use, are long-inherited. When one part is modified, other parts change through the principle of correlation, of which we have instances in many curious cases of correlated monstrosities. Something may be attributed to the direct and definite action of the surrounding conditions of life, such as abundant food, heat or moisture; and lastly, many characters of slight physiological importance, some indeed of considerable importance, have been gained through sexual selection.

No doubt man, as well as every other animal, presents structures, which seem to our limited knowledge, not to be now of any service to him, nor to have been so formerly, either for the general conditions of life, or in the relations of one sex to the other. Such structures cannot be accounted for by any form of selection, or by the inherited effects of the use and disuse of parts. We know, however, that many strange and strongly-marked peculiarities of structure occasionally appear in our domesticated productions, and if their unknown causes were to act more uniformly, they would probably become common to all the individuals of the species. We may hope hereafter to understand something about the causes of such occasional modifications, especially through the study of monstrosities: hence the labours of experimentalists such as those of M. Camille Dareste, are full of promise for the future. In general we can only say that the cause of each slight variation and of each monstrosity lies much more in the constitution of the organism, than in the nature of the surrounding conditions; though new and changed conditions certainly play an important part in exciting organic changes of many kinds.

Through the means just specified, aided perhaps by others as yet undiscovered, man has been raised to his present state. But since he attained to the rank of manhood, he has diverged into distinct races, or as they may be more fitly called, sub-species. Some of these, such as the Negro and European, are so distinct that, if specimens had been brought to a naturalist without any further information, they would undoubtedly have been considered by him as good and true species. Nevertheless all the races agree in so many unimportant details of structure and in so many mental peculiarities that these can be accounted for only by inheritance from a common progenitor; and a progenitor thus characterised would probably deserve to rank as man.

It must not be supposed that the divergence of each race from the other races, and of all from a common stock, can be traced back to any one pair of progenitors. On the contrary, at every stage in the process of modification, all the individuals which were in any way better fitted for their conditions of life, though in different degrees, would have survived in greater numbers than the less well-fitted. The process would have been like that followed by man, when he does not intentionally select particular individuals, but breeds from all the superior individuals, and neglects the inferior. He thus slowly but surely modifies his stock, and unconciously forms a new strain. So with respect to modifications acquired independently of selection, and due to variations arising from the nature of the organism and the action of the surrounding conditions, or from changed habits of life, no single pair will have been modified much more than the other pairs inhabiting the same country, for all will have been continually blended through free intercrossing.

By considering the embryological structure of man,—the homologies which he presents with the lower animals,—the rudiments which he retains,—and the reversions to which he is liable, we can partly recall in imagination the former condition of our early progenitors; and can approximately place them in their proper place in the zoological series. We thus learn that man is descended from a hairy, tailed quadruped, probably arboreal in its habits, and an inhabitant of the Old World. This creature, if its whole structure had been examined by a naturalist, would have been classed amongst the Quadrumana, as surely as the still more ancient progenitor of the Old and New World monkeys. The Quadrumana and all the higher mammals are probably derived from an ancient marsupial animal, and this through a long series of diversified forms, from some amphibian-like creature, and this again from some fish-like animal. In the dim obscurity of the past we can see that the early progenitor of all the Vertebrata must have been an aquatic animal provided with branchiæ, with the two sexes united in the same individual, and with the most important organs of the body (such as the brain and heart) imperfectly or not at all developed. This animal seems to have been more like the larvæ of the existing marine Ascidians than any other known form.

The high standard of our intellectual powers and moral disposition is the greatest difficulty which presents itself, after we have been driven to this conclusion on the origin of man. But every one who admits the principle of evolution, must see that the mental powers of the higher animals, which are the same in kind with those of man, though so different in degree, are capable of advancement. Thus the interval between the mental powers of one of the higher apes and of a fish, or between those of an ant and scale-insect, is immense; yet their development does not offer any special difficulty; for with our domesticated animals, the mental faculties are certainly variable, and the variations are inherited. No one doubts that they are of the utmost importance to animals in a state of nature. Therefore the conditions are favourable for their development through natural selection. The same conclusion may be extended to man; the intellect must have been all-important to him, even at a very remote period, as enabling him to invent and use language, to make weapons, tools, traps, &c., whereby with the aid of his social habits, he long ago became the most dominant of all living creatures.

A great stride in the development of the intellect will have followed, as soon as the half-art and half-instinct of language came into use; for the continued use of language will have reacted on the brain and produced an inherited effect; and this again will have reacted on the improvement of language. As Mr. Chauncey Wright has well remarked, the largeness of the brain in man relatively to his body, compared with the lower animals, may be attributed in chief part to the early use of some simple form of language,—that wonderful engine which affixes signs to all sorts of objects and qualities, and excites trains of thought which would never arise from the mere impression of the senses, or if they did arise could not be followed out. The higher intellectual powers of man, such as those of ratiocination, abstraction, self-consciousness, &c., probably follow from the continued improvement and exercise of the other mental faculties.

The development of the moral qualities is a more interesting problem. The foundation lies in the social instincts, including under this term the family ties. These instincts are highly complex, and in the case of the lower animals give special tendencies towards certain definite actions; but the more important elements are love, and the distinct emotion of sympathy. Animals endowed with the social instincts take pleasure in one another's company, warn one another of danger, defend and aid one another in many ways. These instincts do not extend to all the individuals of the species, but only to those of the same community. As they are highly beneficial to the species, they have in all probability been acquired through natural selection.

A moral being is one who is capable of reflecting on his past actions and their motives—of approving of some and disapproving of others; and the fact that man is the one being who certainly deserves this designation, is the greatest of all distinctions between him and the lower animals. But in the fourth chapter I have endeavoured to shew that the moral sense follows, firstly, from the enduring and ever-present nature of the social instincts; secondly, from man's appreciation of the approbation and disapprobation of his fellows; and thirdly, from the high activity of his mental faculties, with past impressions extremely vivid; and in these latter respects he differs from the lower animals. Owing to this condition of mind, man cannot avoid looking both backwards and forwards, and comparing past impressions. Hence after some temporary desire or passion has mastered his social instincts, he reflects and compares the now weakened impression of such past impulses with the ever-present social instincts; and he then feels that sense of dissatisfaction which all unsatisfied instincts leave behind them, he therefore resolves to act differently for the future,—and this is conscience. Any instinct, permanently stronger or more enduring than another, gives rise to a feeling which we express by saying that it ought to be obeyed. A pointer dog, if able to reflect on his past conduct, would say to himself, I ought (as indeed we say of him) to have pointed at that hare and not have yielded to the passing temptation of hunting it.

Social animals are impelled partly by a wish to aid the members of their community in a general manner, but more commonly to perform certain definite actions. Man is impelled by the same general wish to aid his fellows; but has few or no special instincts. He differs also from the lower animals in the power of expressing his desires by words, which thus become a guide to the aid required and bestowed. The motive to give aid is likewise much modified in man: it no longer consists solely of a blind instinctive impulse, but is much influenced by the praise or blame of his fellows. The appreciation and the bestowal of praise and blame both rest on sympathy; and this emotion, as we have seen, is one of the most important elements of the social instincts. Sympathy, though gained as an instinct, is also much strengthened by exercise or habit. As all men desire their own happiness, praise or blame is bestowed on actions and motives, according as they lead to this end; and as happiness is an essential part of the general good, the greatest-happiness principle indirectly serves as a nearly safe standard of right and wrong. As the reasoning powers advance and experience is gained, the remoter effects of certain lines of conduct on the character of the individual, and on the general good, are perceived; and then the self-regarding virtues come within the scope of public opinion, and receive praise, and their opposites blame. But with the less civilised nations reason often errs, and many bad customs and base superstitions come within the same scope, and are then esteemed as high virtues, and their breach as heavy crimes.

The moral faculties are generally and justly esteemed as of higher value than the intellectual powers. But we should bear in mind that the activity of the mind in vividly recalling past impressions is one of the fundamental though secondary bases of conscience. This affords the strongest argument for educating and stimulating in all possible ways the intellectual faculties of every human being. No doubt a man with a torpid mind, if his social affections and sympathies are well developed, will be led to good actions, and may have a fairly sensitive conscience. But whatever renders the imagination more vivid and strengthens the habit of recalling and comparing past impressions, will make the conscience more sensitive, and may even somewhat compensate for weak social affections and sympathies.

The moral nature of man has reached its present standard, partly through the advancement of his reasoning powers and consequently of a just public opinion, but especially from his sympathies having been rendered more tender and widely diffused through the effects of habit, example, instruction, and reflection. It is not improbable that after long practice virtuous tendencies may be inherited. With the more civilised races, the conviction of the existence of an all-seeing Deity has had a potent influence on the advance of morality. Ultimately man does not accept the praise or blame of his fellows as his sole guide, though few escape this influence, but his habitual convictions, controlled by reason, afford him the safest rule. His conscience then becomes the supreme judge and monitor. Nevertheless the first foundation or origin of the moral sense lies in the social instincts, including sympathy; and these instincts no doubt were primarily gained, as in the case of the lower animals, through natural selection.

The belief in God has often been advanced as not only the greatest, but the most complete of all the distinctions between man and the lower animals. It is however impossible, as we have seen, to maintain that this belief is innate or instinctive in man. On the other hand a belief in all-pervading spiritual agencies seems to be universal; and apparently follows from a considerable advance in man's reason, and from a still greater advance in his faculties of imagination, curiosity and wonder. I am aware that the assumed instinctive belief in God has been used by many persons as an argument for His existence. But this is a rash argument, as we should thus be compelled to believe in the existence of many cruel and malignant spirits, only a little more powerful than man; for the belief in them is far more general than in a beneficent Deity. The idea of a universal and beneficent Creator does not seem to arise in the mind of man, until he has been elevated by long-continued culture.

He who believes in the advancement of man from some low organised form, will naturally ask how does this bear on the belief in the immortality of the soul. The barbarous races of man, as Sir J. Lubbock has shewn, possess no clear belief of this kind; but arguments derived from the primeval beliefs of savages are, as we have just seen, of little or no avail. Few persons feel any anxiety from the impossibility of determining at what precise period in the development of the individual, from the first trace of a minute germinal vesicle, man becomes an immortal being; and there is no greater cause for anxiety because the period cannot possibly be determined in the gradually ascending organic scale.

I am aware that the conclusions arrived at in this work will be denounced by some as highly irreligious; but he who denounces them is bound to shew why it is more irreligious to explain the origin of man as a distinct species by descent from some lower form, through the laws of variation and natural selection, than to explain the birth of the individual through the laws of ordinary reproduction. The birth both of the species and of the individual are equally parts of that grand sequence of events, which our minds refuse to accept as the result of blind chance. The understanding revolts at such a conclusion, whether or not we are able to believe that every slight variation of structure,—the union of each pair in marriage,—the dissemination of each seed,—and other such events, have all been ordained for some special purpose.

Sexual selection has been treated at great length in this work; for, as I have attempted to shew, it has played an important part in the history of the organic world. I am aware that much remains doubtful, but I have endeavoured to give a fair view of the whole case. In the lower divisions of the animal kingdom, sexual selection seems to have done nothing: such animals are often affixed for life to the same spot, or have the sexes combined in the same individual, or what is still more important, their perceptive and intellectual faculties are not sufficiently advanced to allow of the feelings of love and jealousy, or of the exertion of choice. When, however, we come to the Arthropoda and Vertebrata, even to the lowest classes in these two great Sub-Kingdoms, sexual selection has effected much.

In the several great classes of the animal kingdom,—in mammals, birds, reptiles, fishes, insects, and even crustaceans,—the differences between the sexes follow nearly the same rules. The males are almost always the wooers; and they alone are armed with special weapons for fighting with their rivals. They are generally stronger and larger than the females, and are endowed with the requisite qualities of courage and pugnacity. They are provided, either exclusively or in a much higher degree than the females, with organs for vocal or instrumental music, and with odoriferous glands. They are ornamental with infinitely diversified appendages, and with the most brilliant or conspicuous colours, often arranged in elegant patterns, whilst the females are unadorned. When the sexes differ in more important structures, it is the male which is provided with special sense-organs for discovering the female, with locomotive organs for reaching her, and often with prehensile organs for holding her. These various structures for charming or securing the female are often developed in the male during only part of the year, namely the breeding-season. They have in many cases been more or less transferred to the females; and in the latter case they often appear in her as mere rudiments. They are lost or never gained by the males after emasculation. Generally they are not developed in the male during early youth, but appear a short time before the age for reproduction. Hence in most cases the young of both sexes resemble each other; and the female somewhat resembles her young offspring throughout life. In almost every great class a few anomalous cases occur, where there has been an almost complete transposition of the characters proper to the two sexes; the females assuming characters which properly belong to the males. This surprising uniformity in the laws regulating the differences between the sexes in so many and such widely separated classes, is intelligible if we admit the action of one common cause, namely sexual selection.

Sexual selection depends on the success of certain individuals over others of the same sex, in relation to the propagation of the species; whilst natural selection depends on the success of both sexes, at all ages, in relation to the general conditions of life. The sexual struggle is of two kinds; in the one it is between individuals of the same sex, generally the males, in order to drive away or kill their rivals, the females remaining passive; whilst in the other, the struggle is likewise between the individuals of the same sex, in order to excite or charm those of the opposite sex, generally the females, which no longer remain passive, but select the more agreeable partners. This latter kind of selection is closely analogous to that which man unintentionally, yet effectually, brings to bear on his domesticated productions, when he preserves during a long period the most pleasing or useful individuals, without any wish to modify the breed.

The laws of inheritance determine whether characters gained through sexual selection by either sex shall be transmitted to the same sex, or to both; as well as the age at which they shall be developed. It appears that variations arising late in life are commonly transmitted to one and the same sex. Variability is the necessary basis for the action of selection, and is wholly independent of it. It follows from this, that variations of the same general nature have often been taken advantage of and accumulated through sexual selection in relation to the propagation of the species, as well as through natural selection in relation to the general purposes of life. Hence secondary sexual characters, when equally transmitted to both sexes can be distinguished from ordinary specific characters only by the light of analogy. The modifications acquired through sexual selection are often so strongly pronounced that the two sexes have frequently been ranked as distinct species, or even as distinct genera. Such strongly-marked differences must be in some manner highly important; and we know that they have been acquired in some instances at the cost not only of inconvenience, but of exposure to actual danger.

The belief in the power of sexual selection rests chiefly on the following considerations. Certain characters are confined to one sex; and this alone renders it probable that in most cases they are connected with the act of reproduction. In innumerable instances these characters are fully developed only at maturity, and often during only a part of the year, which is always the breeding-season. The males (passing over a few exceptional cases) are the more active in courtship; they are the better armed, and are rendered the more attractive in various ways. It is to be especially observed that the males display their attractions with elaborate care in the presence of the females; and that they rarely or never display them excepting during the season of love. It is incredible that all this should be purposeless. Lastly we have distinct evidence with some quadrupeds and birds, that the individuals of one sex are capable of feeling a strong antipathy or preference for certain individuals of the other sex.

Bearing in mind these facts, and the marked results of man's unconscious selection, when applied to domesticated animals and cultivated plants, it seems to me almost certain that if the individuals of one sex were during a long series of generations to prefer pairing with certain individuals of the other sex, characterised in some peculiar manner, the offspring would slowly but surely become modified in this same manner. I have not attempted to conceal that, excepting when the males are more numerous than the females, or when polygamy prevails, it is doubtful how the more attractive males succeed in leaving a large number of offspring to inherit their superiority in ornaments or other charms than the less attractive males; but I have shewn that this would probably follow from the females,—especially the more vigorous ones, which would be the first to breed,—preferring not only the more attractive but at the same time the more vigorous and victorious males.

Although we have some positive evidence that birds appreciate bright and beautiful objects, as with the bower-birds of Australia, and although they certainly appreciate the power of song, yet I fully admit that it is astonishing that the females of many birds and some mammals should be endowed with sufficient taste to appreciate ornaments, which we have reason to attribute to sexual selection; and this is even more astonishing in the case of reptiles, fish, and insects. But we really know little about the minds of the lower animals. It cannot be supposed, for instance, that male birds of paradise or peacocks should take such pains in erecting, spreading, and vibrating their beautiful plumes before the females for no purpose. We should remember the fact given on excellent authority in a former chapter, that several peahens, when debarred from an admired male, remained widows during a whole season rather than pair with another bird.

Nevertheless I know of no fact in natural history more wonderful than that of the female Argus pheasant should appreciate the exquisite shading of the ball-and-socket ornaments and the elegant patterns on the wing-feathers of the male. He who thinks that the male was created as he now exists must admit that the great plumes, which prevent the wings from being used for flight, and which are displayed during courtship and at no other time in a manner quite peculiar to this one species, were given to him as an ornament. If so, he must likewise admit that the female was created and endowed with the capacity of appreciating such ornaments. I differ only in the conviction that the male Argus pheasant acquired his beauty gradually, through the preference of the females during many generations for the more highly ornamented males; the æsthetic capacity of the females having been advanced through exercise or habit, just as our own taste is gradually improved. In the male through the fortunate chance of a few feathers, being left unchanged, we can distinctly trace how simple spots with a little fulvous shading on one side may have been developed by small steps into the wonderful ball-and-socket ornaments; and it is probable that they were actually thus developed.

Everyone who admits the principle of evolution, and yet feels great difficulty in admitting that female mammals, birds, reptiles, and fish, could have acquired the high taste implied by the beauty of the males, and which generally coincides with our own standard, should reflect that the nerve-cells of the brain in the highest as well as in the lowest members of the Vertebrate series, are derived from those of the common progenitor of this great Kingdom. For we can thus see how it has come to pass that certain mental faculties, in various and widely distinct groups of animals, have been developed in nearly the same manner and to nearly the same degree.

The reader who has taken the trouble to go through the several chapters devoted to sexual selection, will be able to judge how far the conclusions at which I have arrived are supported by sufficient evidence. If he accepts these conclusions he may, I think, safely extend them to mankind; but it would be superfluous here to repeat what I have so lately said on the manner in which sexual selection apparently has acted on man, both on the male and female side, causing the two sexes to differ in body and mind, and the several races to differ from each other in various characters, as well as from their ancient and lowly-organised progenitors.

He who admits the principle of sexual selection will be led to the remarkable conclusion that the nervous system not only regulates most of the existing functions of the body, but has indirectly influenced the progressive development of various bodily structures and of certain mental qualities. Courage, pugnacity, perseverance, strength and size of body, weapons of all kinds, musical organs, both vocal and instrumental, bright colours and ornamental appendages, have all been indirectly gained by the one sex or the other, through the exertion of choice, the influence of love and jealousy, and the appreciation of the beautiful in sound, colour or form; and these powers of the mind manifestly depend on the development of the brain.

Man scans with scrupulous care the character and pedigree of his horses, cattle, and dogs before he matches them; but when he comes to his own marriage he rarely, or never, takes any such care. He is impelled by nearly the same motives as the lower animals, when they are left to their own free choice, though he is in so far superior to them that he highly values mental charms and virtues. On the other hand he is strongly attracted by mere wealth or rank. Yet he might by selection do something not only for the bodily constitution and frame of his offspring, but for their intellectual and moral qualities. Both sexes ought to refrain from marriage if they are in any marked degree inferior in body or mind; but such hopes are Utopian and will never be even partially realised until the laws of inheritance are thoroughly known. Everyone does good service, who aids towards this end. When the principles of breeding and inheritance are better understood, we shall not hear ignorant members of our legislature rejecting with scorn a plan for ascertaining whether or not consanguineous marriages are injurious to man.

The advancement of the welfare of mankind is a most intricate problem: all ought to refrain from marriage who cannot avoid abject poverty for their children; for poverty is not only a great evil, but tends to its own increase by leading to recklessness in marriage. On the other hand, as Mr. Galton has remarked, if the prudent avoid marriage, whilst the reckless marry, the inferior members tend to supplant the better members of society. Man, like every other animal, has no doubt advanced to his present high condition through a struggle for existence consequent on his rapid multiplication; and if he is to advance still higher, it is to be feared that he must remain subject to a severe struggle. Otherwise he would sink into indolence, and the more gifted men would not be more successful in the battle of life than the less gifted. Hence our natural rate of increase, though leading to many and obvious evils, must not be greatly diminished by any means. There should be open competition for all men; and the most able should not be prevented by laws or customs from succeeding best and rearing the largest number of offspring. Important as the struggle for existence has been and even still is, yet as far as the highest part of man's nature is concerned there are other agencies more important. For the moral qualities are advanced, either directly or indirectly, much more through the effects of habit, the reasoning powers, instruction, religion, &c., than through natural selection; though to this latter agency may be safely attributed the social instincts, which afforded the basis for the development of the moral sense.

The main conclusion arrived at in this work, namely, that man is descended from some lowly organised form, will, I regret to think, be highly distasteful to many. But there can hardly be a doubt that we are descended from barbarians. The astonishment which I felt on first seeing a party of Fuegians on a wild and broken shore will never be forgotten by me, for the reflection at once rushed into my mind—such were our ancestors. These men were absolutely naked and bedaubed with paint, their long hair was tangled, their mouths frothed with excitement, and their expression was wild, startled, and distrustful. They possessed hardly any arts, and like wild animals lived on what they could catch; they had no government, and were merciless to every one not of their own small tribe. He who has seen a savage in his native land will not feel much shame, if forced to acknowledge that the blood of some more humble creature flows in his veins. For my own part I would as soon be descended from that heroic little monkey, who braved his dreaded enemy in order to save the life of his keeper, or from that old baboon, who descending from the mountains, carried away in triumph his young comrade from a crowd of astonished dogs—as from a savage who delights to torture his enemies, offers up bloody sacrifices, practices infanticide without remorse, treats his wives like slaves, knows no decency, and is haunted by the grossest superstitions.

Man may be excused for feeling some pride at having risen, though not through his own exertions, to the very summit of the organic scale; and the fact of his having thus risen, instead of having been aboriginally placed there, may give him hope for a still higher destiny in the distant future. But we are not here concerned with hopes or fears, only with the truth as far as our reason permits us to discover it; and I have given the evidence to the best of my ability. We must, however, acknowledge, as it seems to me, that man with all his noble qualities, with sympathy which feels for the most debased, with benevolence which extends not only to other men but to the humblest living creature, with his god-like intellect which has penetrated into the movements and constitution of the solar system—with all these exalted powers—Man still bears in his bodily frame the indelible stamp of his lowly origin.*

WILSON

Evolution has influenced virtually every aspect of biology, ranging from the molecular biology of the gene to anatomy, physiology, biogeography, ecology, taxonomy, and behavior. With respect to ideas of human nature, one of the most portentous is sociobiology, a term especially associated with the work of Harvard zoologist Edward O. Wilson (1929–). Wilson is an authority on ants and has also made major contributions to population biology and the protection of biodiversity. His 1975 book *Sociobiology the New Synthesis* pulled together an immense literature in ecology, evolution, and ethology, defining *sociobiology* as "the study of the biological basis of social behavior."

Although sociobiology is generally noncontroversial when applied to animals, some have objected to the overt implication that similar biological insights can (or should) be applied to human beings. Others, particularly from the social sciences, were incensed by what they saw as an exercise in academic imperialism, with evolutionary biology threatening to take over their disciplines.

The underlying assumption of sociobiology is that living things, including human beings, have been selected to behave in a manner that maximizes their fitness, that is, their success in projecting copies of their genes into the future. The sociobiological approach employs a number of subordinate concepts, such as analyzing evolution at the level of the individual or gene rather than the group or species, interpreting so-called altruistic behavior as resulting from selection for the success of genes present within the beneficiaries (and hence, promoting nepotism as a means of achieving genetic success), evaluating male-female differences as a consequence of differing sexual patterns of "parental investment," and the use of mathematical

---

*From *The Descent of Man and Selection in Relation to Sex* (1871). London: Murray.

game theory to understand conflicting behavioral tendencies. The first selection is from E. O. Wilson's *Sociobiology* and the other is from *On Human Nature*.

In the process of natural selection, . . . any device that can insert a higher proportion of certain genes into subsequent generations will come to characterize the species. One class of such devices promotes prolonged individual survival. Another promotes superior mating performance and care of the resulting offspring. As more complex social behavior by the organism is added to the genes' techniques for replicating themselves, altruism becomes increasingly prevalent and eventually appears in exaggerated forms. This brings us to the central theoretical problem of sociobiology: how can altruism, which by definition reduces personal fitness, possibly evolve by natural selection? The answer is kinship: if the genes causing the altruism are shared by two organisms because of common descent, and if the altruistic act by one organism increases the joint contribution of these genes to the next generation, the propensity to altruism will spread through the gene pool. This occurs even though the altruist makes less of a solitary contribution to the gene pool as the price of its altruistic act.

To his own question, "Does the Absurd dictate death?" Camus replied that the struggle toward the heights is itself enough to fill a man's heart. This arid judgment is probably correct, but it makes little sense except when closely examined in the light of evolutionary theory. The hypothalamic-limbic complex of a highly social species, such as man, "knows," or more precisely it has been programmed to perform as if it knows, that its underlying genes will be proliferated maximally only if it orchestrates behavioral responses that bring into play an efficient mixture of personal survival, reproduction, and altruism. Consequently, the centers of the complex tax the conscious mind with ambivalences whenever the organisms encounter stressful situations. Love joins hate; aggression, fear; expansiveness, withdrawal; and so on; in blends designed not to promote the happiness and survival of the individual, but to favor the maximum transmission of the controlling genes.

The ambivalences stem from counteracting pressures on the units of natural selection. Their genetic consequences will be explored formally later in this book. For the moment suffice it to note that what is good for the individual can be destructive to the family; what preserves the family can be harsh on both the individual and the tribe to which its family belongs; what promotes the tribe can weaken the family and destroy the individual; and so on upward through the permutations of levels of organization. Counteracting selection on these different units will result in certain genes being multiplied and fixed, others lost, and combinations of still others held in static proportions. According to the present theory, some of the genes will produce emotional states that reflect the balance of counteracting selection forces at the different levels.

I have raised a problem in ethical philosophy in order to characterize the essence of sociobiology. Sociobiology is defined as the systematic study of the biological basis of all social behavior. For the present it focuses on animal societies, their population structure, castes, and communication, together with all of the physiology underlying the social adaptations. But the discipline is also concerned with the social behavior of early man and the adaptive features of organization in the more primitive contemporary human societies. Sociology *sensu stricto*, the study of human societies at all levels of complexity, still stands apart from sociobiology because of its largely structuralist and nongenetic approach. It attempts to explain human behavior primarily by empirical description of the outermost phenotypes and by unaided intuition, without reference to evolutionary explanations in the true genetic sense. It is most successful, in the way descriptive taxonomy and ecology have been most successful when it provides a detailed description of particular phenomena and demonstrates first-order correlations with features of the environment. Taxonomy and ecology, however, have been reshaped entirely during the past forty years by integration into neo-Darwinist evolutionary theory—the "Modern Synthesis," as it is often called—in which each phenomenon is weighed for its adaptive significance and then related to the basic principles of population genetics. It may not be too much to say that sociology and the other social sciences, as well as the humanities, are the last branches of biology waiting to be included in the Modern Synthesis. One of the functions of sociobiology, then, is to reformulate the foundations of the social sciences in a way that draws these subjects into the Modern Synthesis. Whether the social sciences can be truly biologicized in this fashion remains to be seen. . . .

The principal goal of a general theory of sociobiology should be an ability to predict features of social organization from a knowledge of these population parameters combined with information on the behavioral constraints imposed by the genetic constitution of the species. It will be a chief task of evolutionary ecology, in turn, to derive the population parameters from a knowledge of the evolutionary history of the species and of the environment in which the most recent segment of that history unfolded. The most important feature . . . then, is the sequential relation between evolutionary studies, ecology, population biology, and sociobiology.

In stressing the tightness of this sequence, however, I do not wish to underrate the filial relationship that sociobiology has had in the past with the remainder of behavioral biology. Although behavioral biology is traditionally spoken of as if it were a unified subject, it is now emerging as two distinct disciplines centered on neurophysiology and on sociobiology, respectively. The conventional wisdom also speaks of ethology, which is the naturalistic study of whole patterns of animal behavior, and its companion enterprise, comparative psychology, as the central, unifying fields of behavioral biology. They are not; both are destined to be cannibalized by neurophysiology and sensory physiology from one end and sociobiology and behavioral ecology from the other.

I hope not too many scholars in ethology and psychology will be offended by this vision of the future of behavioral biology. It seems to be indicated both by the extrapolation of current events and by consideration of the logical relationship behavioral biology holds with the remainder of science. The future, it seems clear, cannot be with the ad hoc terminology, crude models, and curve fitting that characterize most of contemporary ethology and comparative psychology. Whole patterns of animal behavior will inevitably be explained within the framework, first, of integrative neurophysiology, which classifies neurons and reconstructs their circuitry, and, second, of sensory physiology, which seeks to characterize the cellular transducers at the molecular level. Endocrinology will continue to play a peripheral role, since it is concerned with the cruder tuning devices of nervous activity. To pass from this level and reach the next really distinct discipline, we must travel all the way up to the society and the population. Not only are the phenomena best described by families of models different from those of cellular and molecular biology, but the explanations become largely evolutionary. There should be nothing surprising in this distinction. It is only a reflection of the larger division that separates the two greater domains of evolutionary biology and functional biology. . . .

Let us now consider man in the free spirit of natural history, as though we were zoologists from another planet completing a catalog of social species on Earth. In this macroscopic view the humanities and social sciences shrink to specialized branches of biology; history, biography, and fiction are the research protocols of human ethology; and anthropology and sociology together constitute the sociobiology of a single primate species.

Homo sapiens is ecologically a very peculiar species. It occupies the widest geographical range and maintains the highest local densities of any of the primates. An astute ecologist from another planet would not be surprised to find that only one species of *Homo* exists. Modern man has preempted all the conceivable hominid niches. Two or more species of hominid did coexist in the past, when the *Australopithecus* man-apes and possibly an early *Homo* lived in Africa. But only one evolving line survived into late Pleistocene times to participate in the emergence of the most advanced human social traits.

Modern man is anatomically unique. His erect posture and wholly bipedal locomotion are not even approached in other primates that occasionally walk on their hind legs, including the gorilla and chimpanzee. The skeleton has been profoundly modified to accommodate the change: the spine is curved to distribute the weight of the trunk more evenly down its length; the chest is flattened to move the center of gravity back toward the spine; the pelvis is broadened to serve as an attachment for the powerful striding muscles of the upper legs and reshaped into a basin to hold the viscera; the tail is eliminated, its vertebrae (now called the coccyx) curved inward to form part of the floor of the pelvic basin; the occipital condyles have rotated far beneath the skull so that the weight of the head is balanced on them; the face is shortened to assist this shift in gravity; the thumb is enlarged to give power to the hand; the leg is lengthened; and the foot is drastically narrowed and lengthened to facilitate striding. Other changes have taken place. Hair has been lost from most of the body. It is still not known why modern man is a "naked ape." One plausible explanation is that nakedness served as a device to cool the body during the strenuous pursuit of prey in the heat of the African plains. It is associated with man's exceptional reliance on sweating to reduce body heat; the human body contains from two to five million sweat glands, far more than in any other primate species.

The reproductive physiology and behavior of *Homo sapiens* have also undergone extraordinary evolution. In particular, the estrous cycle of the female has changed in two ways that affect sexual and social behavior. Menstruation has been intensified. The females of some other primate species experience slight bleeding, but only in women is there a heavy sloughing of the wall of the "disappointed womb" with consequent heavy bleeding. The estrus, or period of female "heat," has been replaced by virtually continuous sexual activity. Copulation is initiated not by response to the conventional primate signals of estrus, such as changes in color of the skin around the female sexual organs and the release of pheromones, but by extended foreplay entailing mutual stimulation by the partners. The traits of physical attraction are, moreover, fixed in nature. They include the pubic hair of both sexes and the protuberant breasts and buttocks of women. The flattened sexual cycle and continuous female attractiveness cement the close marriage bonds that are basic to human social life.

At a distance a perceptive Martian zoologist would regard the globular head as a most significant clue to human biology. The cerebrum of *Homo* was expanded enormously during a relatively short span of evolutionary time . . . Three million years ago *Australopithecus* had an adult cranial capacity of 400–500 cubic centimeters, comparable to that of the chimpanzee and gorilla. Two million years later its presumptive descendant *Homo erectus* had a capacity of about 1000 cubic centimeters. The next million years saw an increase to 1400–1700 cubic centimeters in Neanderthal man and 900–2000 cubic centimeters in modern *Homo sapiens*. The growth in intelligence that accompanied this enlargement was so great that it cannot yet be measured in any meaningful way. Human beings can be compared among themselves in terms of a few of the basic components of intelligence and creativity. But no scale has been invented that can objectively compare man with chimpanzees and other living primates.

We have leaped forward in mental evolution in a way that continues to defy self-analysis. The mental hypertrophy has distorted even the most basic primate social qualities into nearly unrecognizable forms. Individual species of Old World monkeys and apes have notably plastic social organizations; man has extended the trend into a protean ethnicity. Monkeys and apes utilize behavioral scaling to adjust aggressive and sexual interactions; in man the scales have become multidimensional, culturally adjustable, and almost endlessly subtle. Bonding and the practices of reciprocal altruism are rudimentary in other primates; man has expanded them into great networks where individuals consciously alter roles from hour to hour as if changing masks.

It is the task of comparative sociobiology to trace these and other human qualities as closely as possible back through time. Besides adding perspective and perhaps offering some sense of philosophical ease, the exercise will help to identify the behaviors and rules by which individual human beings increase their

Darwinian fitness through the manipulation of society. In a phrase, we are searching for the human biogram. . . . One of the key questions, never far from the thinking of anthropologists and biologists who pursue real theory, is to what extent the biogram represents an adaptation to modern cultural life and to what extent it is a phylogenetic vestige. Our civilizations were jerrybuilt around the biogram. How have they been influenced by it? Conversely, how much flexibility is there in the biogram, and in which parameters particularly? Experience with other animals indicates that when organs are hypertrophied, phylogeny is hard to reconstruct. This is the crux of the problem of the evolutionary analysis of human behavior. . . .

It was shown earlier that behavioral traits tend to be selected out by the principle of metabolic conservation when they are suppressed or when their original function becomes neutral in adaptive value. Such traits can largely disappear from populations in as few as ten generations, only two or three centuries in the case of human beings. With our present inadequate understanding of the human brain, we do not know how many of the most valued qualities are linked genetically to more obsolete, destructive ones. Cooperativeness toward groupmates might be coupled with aggressivity toward strangers, creativeness with a desire to own and dominate, athletic zeal with a tendency to violent response, and so on. In extreme cases such pairings could stem from pleiotropism, the control of more than one phenotypic character by the same set of genes. If the planned society—the creation of which seems inevitable in the coming century—were to deliberately steer its members past those stresses and conflicts that once gave the destructive phenotypes their Darwinian edge, the other phenotypes might dwindle with them. In this, the ultimate genetic sense, social control would rob man of his humanity.

It seems that our autocatalytic social evolution has locked us onto a particular course which the early hominids still within us may not welcome. To maintain the species indefinitely we are compelled to drive toward total knowledge, right down to the levels of the neuron and gene. When we have progressed enough to explain ourselves in these mechanistic terms, and the social sciences come to full flower, the result might be hard to accept. It seems appropriate therefore to close this book as it began, with the foreboding insight of Albert Camus:

> A world that can be explained even with bad reasons is a familiar world. But, on the other hand, in a universe divested of illusions and lights, man feels an alien, a stranger. His exile is without remedy since he is deprived of the memory of a lost home or the hope of a promised land.

This, unfortunately, is true. But we still have another hundred years.*

These are the central questions that the great philosopher David Hume said are of unspeakable importance: How does the mind work, and beyond that why does it work in such a way and not another, and from these two considerations together, what is man's ultimate nature?

We keep returning to the subject with a sense of hesitancy and even dread. For if the brain is a machine of ten billion nerve cells and the mind can somehow be explained as the summed activity of a finite number of chemical and electrical reactions, boundaries limit the human prospect—we are biological and our souls cannot fly free. If humankind evolved by Darwinian natural selection, genetic chance and environmental necessity, not God, made the species. Deity can still be sought in the origin of the ultimate units of matter, in quarks and electron shells (Hans Küng was right to ask atheists why there is something instead of nothing) but not in the origin of species. However much we embellish that

*From *Sociobiology* (1975). Cambridge, MA: Harvard University Press.

stark conclusion with metaphor and imagery, it remains the philosophical legacy of the last century of scientific research.

No way appears around this admittedly unappealing proposition. It is the essential first hypothesis for any serious consideration of the human condition. Without it the humanities and social sciences are the limited descriptors of surface phenomena, like astronomy without physics, biology without chemistry, and mathematics without algebra. With it, human nature can be laid open as an object of fully empirical research, biology can be put to the service of liberal education, and our self-conception can be enormously and truthfully enriched.

But to the extent that the new naturalism is true, its pursuit seems certain to generate two great spiritual dilemmas. The first is that no species, ours included, possesses a purpose beyond the imperatives created by its genetic history. Species may have vast potential for material and mental progress but they lack any immanent purpose or guidance from agents beyond their immediate environment or even an evolutionary goal toward which their molecular architecture automatically steers them. I believe that the human mind is constructed in a way that locks it inside this fundamental constraint and forces it to make choices with a purely biological instrument. If the brain evolved by natural selection, even the capacities to select particular esthetic judgments and religious beliefs must have arisen by the same mechanistic process. They are either direct adaptations to past environments in which the ancestral human populations evolved or at most constructions thrown up secondarily by deeper, less visible activities that were once adaptive in this stricter, biological sense.

The essence of the argument, then, is that the brain exists because it promotes the survival and multiplication of the genes that direct its assembly. The human mind is a device for survival and reproduction, and reason is just one of its various techniques. Steven Weinberg has pointed out that physical reality remains so mysterious even to physicists because of the extreme improbability that it was constructed to be understood by the human mind. We can reverse that insight to note with still greater force that the intellect was not constructed to understand atoms or even to understand itself but to promote the survival of human genes. The reflective person knows that his life is in some incomprehensible manner guided through a biological ontogeny, a more or less fixed order of life stages. He senses that with all the drive, wit, love, pride, anger, hope, and anxiety that characterize the species he will in the end be sure only of helping to perpetuate the same cycle. . . .

Reduction is the traditional instrument of scientific analysis, but it is feared and resented. If human behavior can be reduced and determined to any considerable degree by the laws of biology, then mankind might appear to be less than unique and to that extent dehumanized. Few social scientists and scholars in the humanities are prepared to enter such a conspiracy, let alone surrender any of their territory. But this perception, which equates the method of reduction with the philosophy of diminution, is entirely in error. The laws of a subject are necessary to the discipline above it, they challenge and force a mentally more efficient restructuring, but they are not sufficient for the purposes of the discipline. Biology is the key to human nature, and social scientists cannot afford to ignore its rapidly tightening principles. But the social sciences are potentially far richer in content. Eventually they will absorb the relevant ideas of biology and go on to beggar them. The proper study of man is, for reasons that now transcend anthropocentrism, man. . . .

Are human beings innately aggressive? This is a favorite question of college seminars and cocktail party conversations, and one that raises emotion in political ideologues of all stripes. The answer to it is yes. Throughout history, warfare, representing only the most organized technique of aggression, has been endemic to every form of society, from hunter-gatherer bands to industrial states. During the past three centuries a majority of the countries of Europe have been engaged in war during approximately half of all the years; few have ever seen a century of continuous peace. Virtually all societies have invented elaborate sanctions against rape, extortion, and murder, while regulating their daily commerce through complex customs and laws designed to minimize the subtler but inevitable forms of conflict. Most significantly of all, the human forms of aggressive behavior are species-specific: although basically primate in form, they contain features that distinguish them from aggression in all other species. Only by redefining the words "innateness" and "aggression" to the point of uselessness might we correctly say that human aggressiveness is not innate.

Theoreticians who wish to exonerate the genes and blame human aggressiveness wholly on perversities of the environment point to the tiny minority of societies that appear to be nearly or entirely pacific. They forget that innateness refers to the measurable probability that a trait will develop in a specified set of environments, not to the certainty that the trait will develop in all environments. By this criterion human beings have a marked hereditary predisposition to aggressive behavior. . . .

Like so many other forms of behavior and "instinct," aggression in any given species is actually an ill-defined array of different responses with separate controls in the nervous system. No fewer than seven categories can be distinguished: the defense and conquest of territory, the assertion of dominance within well-organized groups, sexual aggression, acts of hostility by which weaning is terminated, aggression against prey, defensive counterattacks against predators, and moralistic and disciplinary aggression used to enforce the rules of society. Rattlesnakes provide an instructive example of the distinctions between these basic categories. When two males compete for access to females, they intertwine their necks and wrestle as though testing each other's strength, but they do not bite, even though their venom is as lethal to other rattlesnakes as it is to rabbits and mice. When a rattlesnake stalks its prey it strikes from any number of positions without advance warning. But when the tables are turned and the snake is confronted by an animal large enough to threaten its safety, it coils, pulls its head forward to the center of the coil in striking position, and raises and shakes its rattle. Finally, if the intruder is a king snake, a species specialized for feeding on other snakes, the rattlesnake employs a wholly different maneuver: it coils, hides its head under its body, and slaps at the king snake with one of the raised coils. So to understand the aggression of rattlesnakes or human beings it is necessary to specify which of the particular forms of aggressive behavior is of interest. . . .

The quintessential female is an individual specialized for making eggs. The large size of the egg enables it to resist drying, to survive adverse periods by consuming stored yolk, to be moved to safety by the parent, and to divide at least a few times after fertilization before needing to ingest nutrients from the outside. The male is defined as the manufacturer of the sperm, the little gamete. A sperm is a minimum cellular unit, stripped down to a head packed with DNA and powered by a tail containing just enough stored energy to carry the vehicle to the egg.

When the two gametes unite in fertilization they create an instant mixture of genes surrounded by the durable housing of the egg. By cooperating to create zygotes, the female and male make it more likely that at least some of their offspring will survive in the event of a changing environment. A fertilized egg differs from an asexually reproducing cell in one fundamental respect: it contains a newly assembled mixture of genes.

The anatomical difference between the two kinds of sex cell is often extreme. In particular, the human egg is eighty-five thousand times larger than the human sperm. The consequences of this gametic dimorphism ramify throughout the biology and psychology of human sex. The most important immediate result is that the female places a greater investment in each of her sex cells. A woman can expect to produce only about four hundred eggs in her lifetime. Of these a maximum of about twenty can be converted into healthy infants. The costs of bringing an infant to term and caring for it afterward are relatively enormous. In contrast, a man releases 100 million sperm with each ejaculation. Once he has achieved fertilization his purely physical commitment has ended. His genes will benefit equally with those of the female, but his investment will be far less than hers unless she can induce him to contribute to the care of the offspring. If a man were given total freedom to act, he could theoretically inseminate thousands of women in his lifetime.

The resulting conflict of interest between the sexes is a property of not only human beings but also the majority of animal species. Males are characteristically aggressive, especially toward one another and most intensely during the breeding season. In most species, assertiveness is the most profitable male strategy. During the full period of time it takes to bring a fetus to term, from the fertilization of the egg to the birth of the infant, one male can fertilize many females but a female can be fertilized by only one male. Thus if males are able to court one female after another, some will be big winners and others will be absolute losers, while virtually all healthy females will succeed in being fertilized. It pays males to be aggressive, hasty, fickle, and undiscriminating. In theory it is more profitable for females to be coy, to hold back until they can identify males with the best genes. In species that rear young, it is also important for the females to select males who are more likely to stay with them after insemination.

Human beings obey this biological principle faithfully. It is true that the thousands of existing societies are enormously variable in the details of their sexual mores and the division of labor between the sexes. This variation is based on culture. Societies mold their customs to the requirements of the environment and in so doing duplicate in totality a large fraction of the arrangements encountered throughout the remainder of the animal kingdom: from strict monogamy to extreme forms of polygamy, and from a close approach to unisex to extreme differences between men and women in behavior and dress. People change their attitudes consciously and at will; the reigning fashion of a society can shift within a generation. Nevertheless, this flexibility is not endless, and beneath it all lie general features that conform closely to the expectations from evolutionary theory. So let us concentrate initially on the biologically significant generalities and defer, for the moment, consideration of the undeniably important plasticity controlled by culture.

We are, first of all, moderately polygynous, with males initiating most of the changes in sexual partnership. About three-fourths of all human societies permit the taking of multiple wives, and most of them encourage the practice by law and custom. In contrast, marriage to multiple husbands is sanctioned in less than one percent of societies. The remaining monogamous societies usually fit that category in a legal sense only, with concubinage and other extramarital strategems being added to allow de facto polygyny.

Because women are commonly treated by men as a limiting resource and hence as valued property, they are the beneficiaries of hypergamy, the practice of marrying upward in social position. Polygyny and hypergamy are essentially complementary strategies. In diverse cultures men pursue and acquire, while women are protected and bartered. Sons sow wild oats and daughters risk being ruined. When sex is sold, men are usually the buyers. . . .

Perhaps, to put the best possible construction on the matter, conscious altruism is a transcendental quality that distinguishes human beings from animals. But scientists are not accustomed to declaring any phenomenon off limits, and it is precisely through the deeper analysis of altruism that sociobiology seems best prepared at this time to make a novel contribution. . . .

Sharing the capacity for extreme sacrifice does not mean that the human mind and the "mind" of an insect (if such exists) work alike. But it does mean that the impulse need not be ruled divine or otherwise transcendental, and we are justified in seeking a more conventional biological explanation. A basic problem immediately arises in connection with such an explanation: fallen heroes do not have children. If self-sacrifice results in fewer descendants, the genes that allow heroes to be created can be expected to disappear gradually from the population. A narrow interpretation of Darwinian natural selection would predict this outcome: because people governed by selfish genes must prevail over those with altruistic genes, there should also be a tendency over many generations for selfish genes to increase in prevalence and for a population to become ever less capable of responding altruistically.

How then does altruism persist? In the case of social insects, there is no doubt at all. Natural selection has been broadened to include kin selection. The self-sacrificing termite soldier protects the rest of its colony, including the queen and king, its parents. As a result, the soldier's more fertile brothers and sisters flourish, and through them the altruistic genes are multiplied by a greater production of nephews and nieces.

It is natural, then, to ask whether through kin selection the capacity for altruism has also evolved in human beings. In other words, do the emotions we feel, which in exceptional individuals may climax in total self-sacrifice, stem ultimately from hereditary units that were implanted by the favoring of relatives during a period of hundreds or thousands of generations? This explanation gains some strength from the circumstance that during most of mankind's history the predominant social unit was the immediate family and a tight network of other close relatives. Such exceptional cohesion, combined with detailed kin classifications made possible by high intelligence, might explain why kin selection has been more forceful in human beings than in monkeys and other mammals.

To anticipate a common objection raised by many social scientists and others, let me grant at once that the form and intensity of altruistic acts are to a large extent culturally determined. Human social evolution is obviously more cultural than genetic. The point is that the underlying emotion, powerfully manifested in virtually all human societies, is what is considered to evolve through genes. The sociobiological hypothesis does not therefore account for differences among societies, but it can explain why human beings differ from other mammals and why, in one narrow aspect, they more closely resemble social insects. . . .

Can the cultural evolution of higher ethical values gain a direction and momentum of its own and completely replace genetic evolution? I think not. The genes hold culture on a leash. The leash is very long, but inevitably values will be constrained in accordance with their effects on the human gene pool. The brain is a product of evolution. Human behavior—like the deepest capacities for emotional response which drive and guide it—is the circuitous technique by which human genetic material has been and will be kept intact. Morality has no other demonstrable ultimate function.*

DAWKINS

Sociobiologists often analyze behavior from the perspective of individual genes. Living things, including human beings, can thus be considered temporary aggregates, created by genes for the sake of their own (the genes') propogation. The most effective exponent of this approach has been Oxford zoologist Richard Dawkins (1941–), who has become perhaps the most influential advocate of modern Darwinism generally, via such books as *The Extended Phenotype, The Blind Watchmaker,* and *River Out of Eden.* Dawkins's most noteworthy popularization and explication of sociobiology's gene-centered approach was his book *The Selfish Gene,* from which the following selections are taken.

Intelligent life on a planet comes of age when it first works out the reason for its own existence. If superior creatures from space ever visit earth, the first question they will ask, in order to assess the level of our civilization, is: 'Have they discovered evolution yet?' Living organisms had existed on earth, without ever knowing why, for over three thousand million years before the truth finally dawned on one of them. His name was Charles Darwin. To be fair, others had had inklings of the truth, but it was Darwin who first put together a coherent and tenable account of why we exist. Darwin made it possible for

*From *On Human Nature* (1978). Cambridge, MA: Harvard University Press.

us to give a sensible answer to the curious child whose question heads this chapter. We no longer have to resort to superstition when faced with the deep problems: Is there a meaning to life? What are we for? What is man? After posing the last of these questions, the eminent zoologist G. G. Simpson put it thus: 'The point I want to make now is that all attempts to answer that question before 1859 are worthless and that we will be better off if we ignore them completely.'

Today the theory of evolution is about as much open to doubt as the theory that the earth goes round the sun, but the full implications of Darwin's revolution have yet to be widely realized. Zoology is still a minority subject in universities, and even those who choose to study it often make their decision without appreciating its profound philosophical significance. Philosophy and the subjects known as 'humanities' are still taught almost as if Darwin had never lived. No doubt this will change in time. In any case, this book is not intended as a general advocacy of Darwinism. Instead, it will explore the consequences of the evolution theory for a particular issue. My purpose is to examine the biology of selfishness and altruism. . . .

Apart from its academic interest, the human importance of this subject is obvious. It touches every aspect of our social lives, our loving and hating, fighting and cooperating, giving and stealing, our greed and our generosity. . . .

Before beginning on my argument itself, I want to explain briefly what sort of an argument it is, and what sort of an argument it is not. If we were told that a man had lived a long and prosperous life in the world of Chicago gangsters, we would be entitled to make some guesses as to the sort of man he was. We might expect that he would have qualities such as toughness, a quick trigger finger, and the ability to attract loyal friends. These would not be infallible deductions, but you can make some inferences about a man's character if you know something about the conditions in which he has survived and prospered. The argument of this book is that we, and all other animals, are machines created by our genes. Like successful Chicago gangsters, our genes have survived, in some cases for millions of years, in a highly competitive world. This entitles us to expect certain qualities in our genes. I shall argue that a predominant quality to be expected in a successful gene is ruthless selfishness. This gene selfishness will usually give rise to selfishness in individual behaviour. However, as we shall see, there are special circumstances in which a gene can achieve its own selfish goals best by fostering a limited form of altruism at the level of individual animals. 'Special' and 'limited' are important words in the last sentence. Much as we might wish to believe otherwise, universal love and the welfare of the species as a whole are concepts that simply do not make evolutionary sense.

This brings me to the first point I want to make about what this book is *not*. I am not advocating a morality based on evolution. I am saying how things have evolved. I am not saying how we humans morally ought to behave. I stress this, because I know I am in danger of being misunderstood by those people, all too numerous, who cannot distinguish a statement of belief in what is the case from an advocacy of what ought to be the case. My own feeling is that a human society based simply on the gene's law of universal ruthless selfishness would be a very nasty society in which to live. But unfortunately, however much we may deplore something, it does not stop it being true. This book is mainly intended to be interesting, but if you would extract a moral from it, read it as a warning. Be warned that if you wish, as I do, to build a society in which individuals cooperate generously and unselfishly towards a common good, you can expect little help from biological nature. Let us try to *teach* generosity and altruism, because we are born selfish. Let us understand what our own selfish genes are up to, because we may then at least have the chance to upset their designs, something that no other species has ever aspired to.

As a corollary to these remarks about teaching, it is a fallacy—incidentally a very common one—to suppose that genetically inherited traits are by definition fixed and unmodifiable. Our genes may instruct us to be selfish, but we are not necessarily compelled to obey them all our lives. It may just be more difficult to learn altruism than it would be if we were genetically programmed to be altruistic.

Among animals, man is uniquely dominated by culture, by influences learned and handed down. Some would say that culture is so important that genes, whether selfish or not, are virtually irrelevant to the understanding of human nature. Others would disagree. It all depends where you stand in the debate over 'nature versus nurture' as determinants of human attributes. . . .

We do not know what chemical raw materials were abundant on earth before the coming of life, but among the plausible possibilities are water, carbon dioxide, methane, and ammonia: all simple compounds known to be present on at least some of the other planets in our solar system. Chemists have tried to imitate the chemical conditions of the young earth. They have put these simple substances in a flask and supplied a source of energy such as ultraviolet light or electric sparks—artificial simulation of primordial lightning. After a few weeks of this, something interesting is usually found inside the flask: a weak brown soup containing a large number of molecules more complex than the ones originally put in. In particular, amino acids have been found—the building blocks of proteins, one of the two great classes of biological molecules. Before these experiments were done, naturally-occurring amino acids would have been thought of as diagnostic of the presence of life. If they had been detected on, say Mars, life on that planet would have seemed a near certainty. Now, however, their existence need imply only the presence of a few simple gases in the atmosphere and some volcanoes, sunlight, or thundery weather. More recently, laboratory simulations of the chemical conditions of earth before the coming of life have yielded organic substances called purines and pyrimidines. These are building blocks of the genetic molecule, DNA itself. . . .

At some point a particularly remarkable molecule was formed by accident. We will call it the *Replicator*. It may not necessarily have been the biggest or the most complex molecule around, but it had the extraordinary property of being able to create copies of itself. This may seem a very unlikely sort of accident to happen. So it was. It was exceedingly improbable. In the lifetime of a man, things that are that improbable can be treated for practical purposes as impossible. That is why you will never win a big prize on the football pools. But in our human estimates of what is probable and what is not, we are not used to dealing in hundreds of millions of years. If you filled in pools coupons every week for a hundred million years you would very likely win several jackpots.

Actually a molecule that makes copies of itself is not as difficult to imagine as it seems at first, and it only had to arise once. Think of the replicator as a mould or template. Imagine it as a large molecule consisting of a complex chain of various sorts of building block molecules. The small building blocks were abundantly available in the soup surrounding the replicator. Now suppose that each building block has an affinity for its own kind. Then whenever a building block from out in the soup lands up next to a part of the replicator for which it has an affinity, it will tend to stick there. The building blocks that attach themselves in this way will automatically be arranged in a sequence that mimics that of the replicator itself. It is easy then to think of them joining up to form a stable chain just as in the formation of the original replicator. This process could continue as a progressive stacking up, layer upon layer. This is how crystals are formed. On the other hand, the two chains might split apart, in which case we have two replicators, each of which can go on to make further copies.

A more complex possibility is that each building block has affinity not for its own kind, but reciprocally for one particular other kind. Then the replicator would act as a template not for an identical copy, but for a kind of 'negative', which would in its turn re-make an exact copy of the original positive. For our purposes it does not matter whether the original replication process was positive-negative or positive-positive, though it is worth remarking that the modern equivalents of the first replicator, the DNA molecules, use positive-negative replication. What does matter is that suddenly a new kind of 'stability' came into the world. Previously it is probable that no particular kind of complex molecule was very abundant in the soup, because each was dependent on building blocks happening to fall by luck into a particular stable configuration. As soon as the replicator was born it must have spread its copies rapidly throughout the seas, until the smaller building block molecules became a scarce resource, and other larger molecules were formed more and more rarely.

So we seem to arrive at a large population of identical replicas. But now we must mention an important property of any copying process: it is not perfect. Mistakes will happen. I hope there are no misprints in this book, but if you look carefully you may find one or two. They will probably not seriously distort the meaning of the sentences, because they will be 'first generation' errors. But imagine the days before printing, when books such as the Gospels were copied by hand. All scribes, however careful, are bound to make a few errors, and some are not above a little wilful 'improvement'. If they all copied from a single master original, meaning would not be greatly perverted. But let copies be made from other copies, which in their turn were made from other copies, and errors will start to become cumulative and serious. We tend to regard erratic copying as a bad thing, and in the case of human documents it is hard to think of examples where errors can be described as improvements. I suppose the scholars of the Septuagint could at least be said to have started something big when they mistranslated the Hebrew word for 'young woman' into the Greek word for 'virgin', coming up with the prophecy: 'Behold a virgin shall conceive and bear a son . . .' Anyway, as we shall see, erratic copying in biological replicators can in a real sense give rise to improvement, and it was essential for the progressive evolution of life that some errors were made. We do not know how accurately the original replicator molecules made their copies. Their modern descendants, the DNA molecules, are astonishingly faithful compared with the most high-fidelity human copying process, but even they occasionally make mistakes, and it is ultimately these mistakes that make evolution possible. Probably the original replicators were far more erratic, but in any case we may be sure that mistakes were made, and these mistakes were cumulative.

As mis-copyings were made and propagated, the primeval soup became filled by a population not of identical replicas, but of several varieties of replicating molecules, all 'descended' from the same ancestor. Would some varieties have been more numerous than others? Almost certainly yes. Some varieties would have been inherently more stable than others. Certain molecules, once formed, would be less likely than others to break up again. These types would become relatively numerous in the soup, not only as a direct logical consequence of their 'longevity', but also because they would have a long time available for making copies of themselves. Replicators of high longevity would therefore tend to become more numerous and, other things being equal, there would have been an 'evolutionary trend' towards greater longevity in the population of molecules.

But other things were probably not equal, and another property of a replicator variety that must have had even more importance in spreading it through the population was speed of replication or 'fecundity'. If replicator molecules of type A make copies of themselves on average once a week while those of type B make copies of themselves once an hour, it is not difficult to see that pretty soon type A molecules are going to be far outnumbered, even if they 'live' much longer than B molecules. There would therefore probably have been an 'evolutionary trend' towards higher 'fecundity' of molecules in the soup. A third characteristic of replicator molecules which would have been positively selected is accuracy of replication. If molecules of type X and type Y last the same length of time and replicate at the same rate, but X makes a mistake on average every tenth replication while Y makes a mistake only every hundredth replication, Y will obviously become more numerous. The X contingent in the population loses not only the errant 'children' themselves, but also all their descendants, actual or potential.

If you already know something about evolution, you may find something slightly paradoxical about the last point. Can we reconcile the idea that copying errors are an essential prerequisite for evolution to occur, with the statement that natural selection favours high copying-fidelity? The answer is that although evolution may seem, in some vague sense, a 'good thing', especially since we are the product of it, nothing actually 'wants' to evolve. Evolution is something that happens, willy-nilly, in spite of all the efforts of the replicators (and nowadays of the genes) to prevent it happening. Jacques Monod made this point very well in his Herbert Spencer lecture, after wryly remarking: 'Another curious aspect of the theory of evolution is that everybody thinks he understands it!'

To return to the primeval soup, it must have become populated by stable varieties of molecule; stable in that either the individual molecules lasted a long time, or they replicated rapidly, or they replicated accurately. Evolutionary trends toward these three kinds of stability took place in the following sense: if you had sampled the soup at two different times, the later sample would have contained a higher proportion of varieties with high longevity/fecundity/copying-fidelity. This is essentially what a biologist means by evolution when he is speaking of living creatures, and the mechanism is the same—natural selection.

Should we then call the original replicator molecules 'living'? Who cares? I might say to you 'Darwin was the greatest man who ever lived', and you might say 'No, Newton was', but I hope we would not prolong the argument. The point is that no conclusion of substance would be affected whichever way our argument was resolved. The facts of the lives and achievements of Newton and Darwin remain totally unchanged whether we label them 'great' or not. Similarly, the story of the replicator molecules probably happened something like the way I am telling it, regardless of whether we choose to call them 'living'. Human suffering has been caused because too many of us cannot grasp that words are only tools for our use, and that the mere presence in the dictionary of a word like 'living' does not mean it necessarily has to refer to something definite in the real world. Whether we call the early replicators living or not, they were the ancestors of life; they were our founding fathers.

The next important link in the argument, one that Darwin himself laid stress on (although he was talking about animals and plants, not molecules) is *competition*. The primeval soup was not capable of supporting an infinite number of replicator molecules. For one thing, the earth's size is finite, but other limiting factors must also have been important. In our picture of the replicator acting as a template or mould, we supposed it to be bathed in a soup rich in the small building block molecules necessary to make copies. But when the replicators became numerous, building blocks must have been used up at such a rate that they became a scarce and precious resource. Different varieties or strains of replicator must have competed for them. We have considered the factors that would have increased the numbers of favoured kinds of replicator. We can now see that less-favoured varieties must actually have become *less* numerous because of competition, and ultimately many of their lines must have gone extinct. There was a struggle for existence among replicator varieties. They did not know they were struggling, or worry about it; the struggle was conducted without any hard feelings, indeed without feelings of any kind. But they were struggling, in the sense that any mis-copying that resulted in a new higher level of stability, or a new way of reducing the stability of rivals, was automatically preserved and multiplied. The process of improvement was cumulative. Ways of increasing stability and of decreasing rivals' stability became more elaborate and more efficient. Some of them may even have 'discovered' how to break up molecules of rival varieties chemically, and to use the building blocks so released for making their own copies. These proto-carnivores simultaneously obtained food and removed competing rivals. Other replicators perhaps discovered how to protect themselves, either chemically, or by building a physical wall of protein around themselves. This may have been how the first living cells appeared. Replicators began not merely to exist, but to construct for themselves containers, vehicles for their continued existence. The replicators that survived were the ones that built *survival machines* for themselves to live in. The first survival machines probably consisted of nothing more than a protective coat. But making a living got steadily harder as new rivals arose with better and more effective survival machines. Survival machines got bigger and more elaborate, and the process was cumulative and progressive.

Was there to be any end to the gradual improvement in the techniques and artifices used by the replicators to ensure their own continuation in the world? There would be plenty of time for improvement. What weird engines of self-preservation would the millennia bring forth? Four thousand million years on, what was to be the fate of the ancient replicators? They did not die out, for they are past masters of the survival arts. But do not look for them floating loose in the sea; they gave up that cavalier freedom long ago. Now they swarm in huge colonies, safe inside gigantic lumbering robots, sealed off from the outside world, communicating with it by tortuous indirect routes, manipulating it by remote control. They are in you and in me; they created us, body and mind; and their preservation is the ultimate rationale for our existence. They have come a long way, those replicators. Now they go by the name of genes, and we are their survival machines. . . .

We are survival machines, but 'we' does not mean just people. It embraces all animals, plants, bacteria, and viruses. The total number of survival machines on earth is very difficult to count and even the total number of species is unknown. Taking just insects alone, the number of living species has been estimated at around three million, and the number of individual insects may be a million million million.

Different sorts of survival machine appear very varied on the outside and in their internal organs. An octopus is nothing like a mouse, and both are quite different from an oak tree. Yet in their fundamental chemistry they are rather uniform, and, in particular, the replicators that they bear, the genes, are basically the same kind of molecule in all of us—from bacteria to elephants. We are all survival machines for the same kind of replicator—molecules called DNA—but there are many different ways of making a living in the world, and the replicators have built a vast range of machines to exploit them. A monkey is a machine that preserves genes up trees, a fish is a machine that preserves genes in the water; there is even a small worm that preserves genes in German beer mats. DNA works in mysterious ways. . . .

The point I am making now is that, even if we look on the dark side and assume that individual man is fundamentally selfish, our conscious foresight—our capacity to simulate the future in imagination—could save us from the worst selfish excesses of the blind replicators. We have at least the mental equipment to foster our long-term selfish interests rather than merely our short-term selfish interests. We can see the long-term benefits of participating in a 'conspiracy of doves', and we can sit down together to discuss ways of making the conspiracy work. We have the power to defy the selfish genes of our birth and, if necessary, the selfish memes of our indoctrination. We can even discuss ways of deliberately cultivating and nurturing pure, disinterested altruism—something that has no place in nature, something that has never existed before in the whole history of the world. We are built as gene machines and cultured as meme machines, but we have the power to turn against our creators. We, alone on earth, can rebel against the tyranny of the selfish replicators.*

STUDY QUESTIONS

1. What are some consequences of considering that evolution operates at the level of the gene rather than the individual?

2. Identify and discuss some examples of human behavior that appear to run counter to evolutionary (or sociobiological) expectation.

*From *The Selfish Gene* (2nd ed.) (1989). New York: Oxford University Press.

3. What ethical consequences, if any, derive from the demonstration that a given behavior has substantial biological (i.e., evolutionary or genetic) underpinnings?

4. Compare and contrast the implications of an evolutionary view of human nature with the view(s) presented in one or more of the previous chapters.

SOME ADDITIONAL READINGS

Alexander, Richard D. (1987). *The Biology of Moral Systems.* New York: Aldine De Gruyter.

Barash, David P., and Lipton, Judith Eve (1998). *Making Sense of Families: Altruism, Selfishness, and the Surprising Importance of Shared Genes.* Washington, D.C.: Island Press.

Barkow, Jerome H., Cosmides, Leda, and Tooby, John, eds. (1992). *The Adapted Mind: Evolutionary Psychology and the Generation of Culture.* New York: Oxford University Press.

Betzig, Laura, ed. (1997). *Human Nature.* New York: Oxford University Press.

Wright, Robert (1994). *The Moral Animal: Evolutionary Psychology and Everyday Life.* New York: Pantheon Books.

CHAPTER EIGHTEEN

Uniquely Human?

So, is there something that we might usefully identify as human nature? "Man has no nature," wrote Jose Ortega y Gassett in 1940. "What he has is history." Many social scientists would agree, adding that what human beings have is culture and social traditions (see Chapter 11). On the other hand, some anthropologists and biologists emphasize a specieswide heritage shared by all *Homo sapiens* (see Chapter 17). Accordingly, they look for what are sometimes called "cross-cultural universals," traits that are characteristic of all (or nearly all) human beings, regardless of cultural background or social tradition. In his *Enquiry Concerning the Human,* David Hume argued for the existence of such a common, universal human nature:

> Would you know the sentiments, inclinations, and core of life of the French and English; you cannot be much mistaken in transferring to the former most of the observations which you have made with regard to the latter. Mankind are so much the same in all times and places that history informs us of nothing new or strange in this particular. Its *[history's]* chief use is only to discover the constant and universal principles of human nature, by showing men in all varieties of circumstances and situations, and furnishing us with materials from which we may . . . become acquainted with the regular springs of human action and behavior.

A somewhat different approach is to search for characteristics of human beings that are uniquely human, that is, not shared by other living things. This has long been a popular enterprise, attempting to identify what is special about our own species. Many candidates have arisen, such as, tool-making, self-awareness, religious sentiments, language-using, only to be seriously questioned (language) or disproved outright (tools), when animals have been found to partake of one trait or another—although admittedly in limited form. Nonetheless, people generally retain belief in their specialness. Most human beings do not agree with the bleak conclusion of Shakespeare's King Lear, upon seeing the naked and shivering Edgar: "Thou art the thing itself; unaccommodated man is no more but such a poor, bare, forked animal as thou art."

In our final selections, we consider three notable explorations of possible human uniqueness.

BECKER

Only human beings, it has been said, are aware of their own inevitable death. "Man is a thinking reed, the weakest to be found in nature," wrote the French mathematical genius and religious mystic Blaise Pascal.

But he is a thinking reed. It is not necessary for the whole of nature to take up arms to crush him: a puff of smoke, a drop of water, is enough to kill him. But, even if the universe should crush him, man would still be more noble than that which destroys him, because he knows that he dies and he realises the advantage which the universe possesses over him. The universe knows nothing of this.

In recent times, the most effective exponent of the significance of "death awareness" has been Ernest Becker (1924–1974), an anthropologist by formal training and a psychoanalyst by inclination. His books include *The Birth and Death of Meaning, Revolution in Psychiatry,* and *Escape from Evil.* The following selections are from Becker's *The Denial of Death.*

One way of looking at the whole development of social science since Marx and of psychology since Freud is that it represents a massive detailing and clarification of the problem of human heroism. This perspective sets the tone for the seriousness of our discussion: we now have the scientific underpinning for a true understanding of the nature of heroism and its place in human life. If "mankind's common instinct for reality" is right, we have achieved the remarkable feat of exposing that reality in a scientific way.

One of the key concepts for understanding man's urge to heroism is the idea of "narcissism." As Erich Fromm has so well reminded us, this idea is one of Freud's great and lasting contributions. Freud discovered that each of us repeats the tragedy of the mythical Greek Narcissus: we are hopelessly absorbed with ourselves. If we care about anyone it is usually ourselves first of all. As Aristotle somewhere put it: luck is when the guy next to you gets hit with the arrow. Twenty-five hundred years of history have not changed man's basic narcissism; most of the time, for most of us, this is still a workable definition of luck. It is one of the meaner aspects of narcissism that we feel that practically everyone is expendable except ourselves. We should feel prepared, as Emerson once put it, to recreate the whole world out of ourselves even if no one else existed. The thought frightens us; we don't know how we could do it without others—yet at bottom the basic resource is there: we could suffice alone if need be, if we could trust ourselves as Emerson wanted. And if we don't feel this trust emotionally, still most of us would struggle to survive with all our powers, no matter how many around us died. Our organism is ready to fill the world all alone, even if our mind shrinks at the thought. This narcissism is what keeps men marching into point-blank fire in wars: at heart one doesn't feel that *he* will die, he only feels sorry for the man next to him. Freud's explanation for this was that the unconscious does not know death or time: in man's physiochemical, inner organic recesses he feels immortal. . . .

It doesn't matter whether the cultural hero-system is frankly magical, religious, and primitive or secular, scientific, and civilized. It is still a mythical hero-system in which people serve in order to earn a feeling of primary value, of cosmic specialness, of ultimate usefulness to creation, of unshakable meaning. They earn this feeling by carving out a place in nature, by building an edifice that reflects human value: a temple, a cathedral, a totem pole, a skyscraper, a family that spans three generations. The hope and belief is that the things that man creates in society are of lasting worth and meaning, that they outlive or outshine death and decay, that man and his products count. When Norman O. Brown said that Western society since Newton, no matter how scientific or secular it claims to be, is still as "religious" as any other, this is what he meant: "civilized" society is a hopeful belief and protest that science, money and goods *make man count* for more than any other animal. In this sense everything that man does is religious and heroic, and yet in danger of being fictitious and fallible. . . .

The first thing we have to do with heroism is to lay bare its underside, show what gives human heroics its specific nature and impetus. Here we introduce directly one of the great rediscoveries of modern thought: that of all things that move man, one of the principal ones is his terror of death. After Darwin the problem of death as an evolutionary one came to the fore, and many thinkers immediately saw that it was a major psychological problem for man. They also very quickly saw what real heroism was about, as Shaler wrote just at the turn of the century: heroism is first and foremost a reflex of the terror of death. We admire most the courage to face death; we give such valor our highest and most constant adoration; it moves us deeply in our hearts because we have doubts about how brave we ourselves would be. When we see a man bravely facing his own extinction we rehearse the greatest victory we can imagine. And so the hero has been the center of human honor and acclaim since probably the beginning of specifically human evolution. But even before that our primate ancestors deferred to others who were extrapowerful and courageous and ignored those who were cowardly. Man has elevated animal courage into a cult.

Anthropological and historical research also began, in the nineteenth century, to put together a picture of the heroic since primitive and ancient times. The hero was the man who could go into the spirit world, the world of the dead, and return alive. He had his descendants in the mystery cults of the Eastern Mediterranean, which were cults of death and resurrection. The divine hero of each of these cults was one who had come back from the dead. And as we know today from the research into ancient myths and rituals, Christianity itself was a competitor with the mystery cults and won out—among other reasons—because it, too, featured a healer with supernatural powers who had risen from the dead. The great triumph of Easter is the joyful shout "Christ has risen!", an echo of the same joy that the devotees of the mystery cults enacted at their ceremonies of the victory over death. These cults, as G. Stanley Hall so aptly put it, were an attempt to attain "an immunity bath" from the greatest evil: death and the dread of it. All historical religions addressed themselves to this same problem of how to bear the end of life. Religions like Hinduism and Buddhism performed the ingenious trick of pretending not to want to be reborn, which is a sort of negative magic: claiming not to want what you really want most. When philosophy took over from religion it also took over religion's central problem, and death became the real "muse of philosophy" from its beginnings in Greece right through Heidegger and modern existentialism.

We already have volumes of work and thought on the subject, from religion and philosophy and—since Darwin—from science itself. The problem is how to make sense out of it; the accumulation of research and opinion on the fear of death is already too large to be dealt with and summarized in any simple way. The revival of interest in death, in the last few decades, has alone already piled up a formidable literature, and this literature does not point in any single direction. . . .

We always knew that there was something peculiar about man, something deep down that characterized him and set him apart from the other animals. It was something that had to go right to his core, something that made him suffer his peculiar fate, that made it impossible to escape. For ages, when philosophers talked about the core of man they referred to it as his "essence," something fixed in his nature, deep down, some special quality or substance. But nothing like it was ever found; man's peculiarity still remained a dilemma. The reason it was never found, as Erich Fromm put it in an excellent discussion, was that there was no essence, that the essence of man is really his *paradoxical* nature, the fact that he is half animal and half symbolic. . . .

Man has a symbolic identity that brings him sharply out of nature. He is a symbolic self, a creature with a name, a life history. He is a creator with a mind that soars out to speculate about atoms and infinity, who can place himself imaginatively at a point in space and contemplate bemusedly his own planet. This immense expansion, this dexterity, this ethereality, this self-consciousness gives to man literally the status of a small god in nature, as the Renaissance thinkers knew.

Yet, at the same time, as the Eastern sages also knew man is a worm and food for worms. This is the paradox: he is out of nature and hopelessly in it; he is dual, up in the stars and yet housed in a heart-pumping, breath-gasping body that once belonged to a fish and still carries the gill-marks to prove it. His body is a material fleshy casing that is alien to him in many ways—the strangest and most repugnant way being that it aches and bleeds and will decay and die. Man is literally split in two: he has an awareness of his own splendid uniqueness in that he sticks out of nature with a towering majesty, and yet he goes back into the ground a few feet in order blindly and dumbly to rot and disappear forever. It is a terrifying dilemma to be in and to have to live with. The lower animals are, of course, spared this painful contradiction, as they lack a symbolic identity and the self-consciousness that goes with it. They merely act and move reflexively as they are driven by their instincts. If they pause at all, it is only a physical pause; inside they are anonymous, and even their faces have no name. They live in a world without time, pulsating, as it were, in a state of dumb being. This is what has made it so simple to shoot down whole herds of buffalo or elephants. The animals don't know that death is happening and continue grazing placidly while others drop alongside them. The knowledge of death is reflective and conceptual, and animals are spared it. They live and they disappear with the same thoughtlessness: a few minutes of fear, a few seconds of anguish, and it is over. But to live a whole lifetime with the fate of death haunting one's dreams and even the most sun-filled days—that's something else.

It is only if you let the full weight of this paradox sink down on your mind and feelings that you can realize what an impossible situation it is for an animal to be in. I believe that those who speculate that a full apprehension of man's condition would drive him insane are right, quite literally right. Babies are occasionally born with gills and tails, but this is not publicized—instead it is hushed up. Who wants to face up fully to the creatures we are, clawing and gasping for breath in a universe beyond our ken? I think such events illustrate the meaning of Pascal's chilling reflection: "Men are so necessarily mad that not to be mad would amount to another form of madness." *Necessarily* because the existential dualism makes an impossible situation, an excruciating dilemma. *Mad* because, as we shall see, everything that man does in his symbolic world is an attempt to deny and overcome his grotesque fate. He literally drives himself into a blind obliviousness with social games, psychological tricks, personal preoccupations so far removed from the reality of his situation that they are forms of madness—agreed madness, shared madness, disguised and dignified madness, but madness all the same. "Character-traits," said Sandor Ferenczi, one of the most brilliant minds of Freud's intimate circle of early psychoanalysts, "are secret psychoses." This is not a smug witticism offered in passing by a young science drunk with its own explanatory power and success; it is a mature scientific judgment of the most devastating self-revelatory kind ever fashioned by man trying to understand himself. Ferenczi had already seen behind the tight-lipped masks, the smiling masks, the earnest masks, the satisfied masks that people use to bluff the world and themselves about their secret psychoses. More recently Erich Fromm wondered why most people did not become insane in the face of the existential contradiction between a symbolic self, that seems to give man infinite worth in a timeless scheme of things, and a body that is worth about 98¢. How to reconcile the two?*

PINKER

Honeybees possess a language, or at least the ability to communicate complex information (the direction and desirability of a food source) using a system of seemingly arbitrary symbols. Different populations of white-crowned sparrows sing in different dialects. Chimpanzees and gorillas may or may not be able to organize and reorganize symbols for words into meaningful sentences. People, however, use language in ways that are far more complicated, varied,

*From *The Denial of Death* (1973). New York: The Free Press.

and creative; perhaps the difference between human and nonhuman languages is so great as to be qualitatively distinct.

In any event, human language has typically been considered entirely under the control of personal experience and cultural tradition: All people employ language, but the language in which people speak (and think) depends on what they have been exposed to. More recently, human language has been thought to derive directly from certain uniquely human mental predispositions. Linguist Noam Chomsky can be seen as the originator of this approach. Steven Pinker (1954–), director of the Center for Cognitive Neuroscience at MIT, is one of his intellectual descendents. These selections are from Pinker's book *The Language Instinct.*

As you are reading these words, you are taking part in one of the wonders of the natural world. For you and I belong to a species with a remarkable ability: we can shape events in each other's brains with exquisite precision. I am not referring to telepathy or mind control or the other obsessions of fringe science; even in the depictions of believers these are blunt instruments compared to an ability that is uncontroversially present in every one of us. That ability is language. Simply by making noises with our mouths, we can reliably cause precise new combinations of ideas to arise in each other's minds. The ability comes so naturally that we are apt to forget what a miracle it is. So let me remind you with some simple demonstrations. Asking you only to surrender your imagination to my words for a few moments, I can cause you to think some very specific thoughts:

> When a male octopus spots a female, his normally grayish body suddenly becomes striped. He swims above the female and begins caressing her with seven of his arms. If she allows this, he will quickly reach toward her and slip his eighth arm into her breathing tube. A series of sperm packets moves slowly through a groove in his arm, finally to slip into the mantle cavity of the female.

> Cherries jubilee on a white suit? Wine on an altar cloth? Apply club soda immediately. It works beautifully to remove the stains from fabrics.

> When Dixie opens the door to Tad, she is stunned, because she thought he was dead. She slams it in his face and then tries to escape. However, when Tad says, "I love you," she lets him in. Tad comforts her, and they become passionate. When Brian interrupts, Dixie tells a stunned Tad that she and Brian were married earlier that day. With much difficulty, Dixie informs Brian that things are nowhere near finished between her and Tad. Then she spills the news that Jamie is Tad's son. "My what?" says a shocked Tad.

Think about what these words have done. I did not simply remind you of octopuses; in the unlikely event that you ever see one develop stripes, you now know what will happen next. Perhaps the next time you are in a supermarket you will look for club soda, one out of the tens of thousands of items available, and then not touch it until months later when a particular substance and a particular object accidentally come together. You now share with millions of other people the secrets of protagonists in a world that is the product of some stranger's imagination, the daytime drama *All My Children.* True, my demonstrations depended on our ability to read and write, and this makes our communication even more impressive by bridging gaps of time, space, and acquaintanceship. But writing is clearly an optional accessory; the real engine of verbal communication is the spoken language we acquired as children.

In any natural history of the human species, language would stand out as the preeminent trait. To be sure, a solitary human is an impressive problem-solver and engineer. But a race of Robinson Crusoes would not give an extraterrestrial observer all that much to remark on. What is truly arresting about our kind is better captured in the story of the Tower of Babel, in which humanity, speaking a single language, came so close to reaching heaven that God himself felt threatened. A common language connects the members of a community into an information-sharing network with formidable collective powers. Anyone can benefit from the strokes of genius, lucky accidents, and trial-and-error wisdom accumulated by anyone else, present or past. And people can work in teams, their efforts coordinated by negotiated agreements. As a result, *Homo sapiens* is a species, like blue-green algae and earthworms, that has wrought far-reaching changes on the planet. Archeologists have discovered the bones of ten thousand wild horses at the bottom of a cliff in France, the remains of herds stampeded over the clifftop by groups of paleolithic hunters seventeen thousand years ago. These fossils of ancient cooperation and shared ingenuity may shed light on why saber-tooth tigers, mastodons, giant woolly rhinoceroses, and dozens of other large mammals went extinct around the time that modern humans arrived in their habitats. Our ancestors, apparently, killed them off.

Language is so tightly woven into human experience that it is scarcely possible to imagine life without it. Chances are that if you find two or more people together anywhere on earth, they will soon be exchanging words. When there is no one to talk with, people talk to themselves, to their dogs, even to their plants. In our social relations, the race is not to the swift but to the verbal—the spellbinding orator, the silver-tongued seducer, the persuasive child who wins the battle of wills against a brawnier parent. Aphasia, the loss of language following brain injury, is devastating, and in severe cases family members may feel that the whole person is lost forever. . . .

Some thirty-five years ago a new science was born. Now called "cognitive science," it combines tools from psychology, computer science, linguistics, philosophy, and neurobiology to explain the workings of human intelligence. The science of language, in particular, has seen spectacular advances in the years since. There are many phenomena of language that we are coming to understand nearly as well as we understand how a camera works or what the spleen is for. I hope to communicate these exciting discoveries, some of them as elegant as anything in modern science, but I have another agenda as well.

The recent illumination of linguistic abilities has revolutionary implications for our understanding of language and its role in human affairs, and for our view of humanity itself. Most educated people already have opinions about language. They know that it is man's most important cultural invention, the quintessential example of his capacity to use symbols, and a biologically unprecedented event irrevocably separating him from other animals. They know that language pervades thought, with different languages causing their speakers to construe reality in different ways. They know that children learn to talk from role models and caregivers. They know that grammatical sophistication used to be nurtured in the schools, but sagging educational standards and the debasements of popular culture have led to a frightening decline in the ability of the average person to construct a grammatical sentence. They also know that English is a zany, logic-defying tongue, in which one drives on a parkway and parks in a driveway, plays at a recital and recites at a play. They know that English spelling takes such wackiness to even greater heights—George Bernard Shaw complained that *fish* could just as sensibly be spelled *ghoti* (*gh* as in *tough, o* as in *women, ti* as in *nation*)—and that only institutional inertia prevents the adoption of a more rational, spell-it-like-it-sounds system.

In the pages that follow, I will try to convince you that every one of these common opinions is wrong! And they are all wrong for a single reason. Language is not a cultural artifact that we learn the way we learn to tell time or how the federal government works. Instead, it is a distinct piece of the biological makeup of our brains. Language is a complex, specialized skill, which develops in the child spontaneously, without conscious effort or formal instruction, is deployed without awareness of its underlying logic, is qualitatively the same in every individual, and is distinct from more general abilities to process information or behave intelligently. For these reasons some cognitive scientists have described language as a psychological faculty, a mental organ, a neural system, and a computational module. But I prefer the admittedly quaint term "instinct." It conveys the idea that people know how to talk in more or less the sense that spiders know how to spin webs. Web-spinning was not invented by some unsung spider genius and does not depend on having had the right education or on having an aptitude for architecture or the construction trades. Rather, spiders spin spider webs because they have spider brains, which give them the urge to spin and the competence to succeed. Although there are differences between webs and words, I will encourage you to see language in this way, for it helps to make sense of the phenomena we will explore.

Thinking of language as an instinct inverts the popular wisdom, especially as it has been passed down in the canon of the humanities and social sciences. Language is no more a cultural invention than is upright posture. It is not a manifestation of a general capacity to use symbols: a three-year-old, we shall see, is a grammatical genius, but is quite incompetent at the visual arts, religious iconography, traffic signs, and the other staples of the semiotics curriculum. Though language is a magnificent ability unique to *Homo sapiens* among living species, it does not call for sequestering the study of humans from the domain of biology, for a magnificent ability unique to a particular living species is far from unique in the animal kingdom. Some kinds of bats home in on flying insects using Doppler sonar. Some kinds of migratory birds navigate thousands of miles by calibrating the positions of the constellations against the time of day and year. In nature's talent show we are simply a species of primate with our own act, a knack for communicating information about who did what to whom by modulating the sounds we make when we exhale.

Once you begin to look at language not as the ineffable essence of human uniqueness but as a biological adaptation to communicate information, it is no longer as tempting to see language as an insidious shaper of thought, and, we shall see, it is not. Moreover, seeing language as one of nature's engineering marvels—an organ with "that perfection of structure and co-adaptation which justly excites our admiration," in Darwin's words—gives us a new respect for your ordinary Joe and the much-maligned English language (or any language). The complexity of language, from the scientist's point of view, is part of our biological birthright; it is not something that parents teach their children or something that must be elaborated in school—as Oscar Wilde said, "Education is an admirable thing, but it is well to remember from time to time that nothing that is worth knowing can be taught." A preschooler's tacit knowledge of grammar is more sophisticated than the thickest style manual or the most state-of-the-art computer language system, and the same applies to all healthy human beings, even the notorious syntax-fracturing professional athlete and the, you know, like, inarticulate teenage skateboarder. Finally, since language is the product of a well-engineered biological instinct, we shall see that it is not the nutty barrel of monkeys that entertainer-columnists make it out to be. I will try to restore some dignity to the English vernacular, and will even have some nice things to say about its spelling system.

The conception of language as a kind of instinct was first articulated in 1871 by Darwin himself. In *The Descent of Man* he had to contend with language because its confinement to humans seemed to present a challenge to his theory. As in all matters, his observations are uncannily modern:

> As . . . one of the founders of the noble science of philology observes, language is an art, like brewing or baking; but writing would have been a better simile. It certainly is not a true instinct, for every language has to be learned. It differs, however, widely from all ordinary arts, for man has an instinctive tendency to speak, as we see in the babble of our young children; while no child has an instinctive tendency to brew, bake, or write. Moreover, no philologist now supposes that any language has been deliberately invented; it has been slowly and unconsciously developed by many steps.

Darwin concluded that language ability is "an instinctive tendency to acquire an art," a design that is not peculiar to humans but seen in other species such as song-learning birds.

A language instinct may seem jarring to those who think of language as the zenith of the human intellect and who think of instincts as brute impulses that compel furry or feathered zombies to build a dam or up and fly south. But one of Darwin's followers, William James, noted that an instinct possessor need not act as a "fatal automaton." He argued that we have all the instincts that animals do, and many more besides; our flexible intelligence comes from the interplay of many instincts competing. Indeed, the instinctive nature of human thought is just what makes it so hard for us to see that it is an instinct:

> It takes . . . a mind debauched by learning to carry the process of making the natural seem strange, so far as to ask for the *why* of any instinctive human act. To the metaphysician alone can such questions occur as: Why do we smile, when pleased, and not scowl? Why are we unable to talk to a crowd as we talk to a single friend? Why does a particular maiden turn our wits so upside-down? The common man can only say, "*Of course* we smile, *of course* our heart palpitates at the sight of the crowd, *of course* we love the maiden, that beautiful soul clad in that perfect form, so palpably and flagrantly made for all eternity to be loved!"
>
> And so, probably, does each animal feel about the particular things it tends to do in presence of particular objects. . . . To the lion it is the lioness which is made to be loved; to the bear, the she-bear. To the broody hen the notion would probably seem monstrous that there should be a creature in the world to whom a nestful of eggs was not the utterly fascinating and precious and never-to-be-too-much-sat-upon object which it is to her.

Thus we may be sure that, however mysterious some animals' instincts may appear to us, our instincts will appear no less mysterious to them. And we may conclude that, to the animal which obeys it, every impulse and every step of every instinct shines with its own sufficient light, and seems at the moment the only eternally right and proper thing to do. What voluptuous thrill may not shake a fly, when she at last discovers the one particular leaf, or carrion, or bit of dung, that out of all the world can stimulate her ovipositor to its discharge? Does not the discharge then seem to her the only fitting thing? And need she care or know anything about the future maggot and its food? . . .

In this century, the most famous argument that language is like an instinct comes from Noam Chomsky, the linguist who first unmasked the intricacy of the system and perhaps the person most responsible for the modern revolution in language and cognitive science. In the 1950s the social sciences were dominated by behaviorism, the school of thought popularized by John Watson and B. F. Skinner. Mental terms like "know" and "think" were branded as unscientific; "mind" and "innate" were dirty words. Behavior was explained by a few laws of stimulus-response learning that could be studied with rats pressing bars and dogs salivating to tones. But Chomsky called attention to two fundamental facts about language. First, virtually every sentence that a person utters or understands is a brand-new combination of words, appearing for the first time in the history of the universe. Therefore a language cannot be a repertoire of responses; the brain must contain a recipe or program that can build an unlimited set of sentences out of a finite list of words. That program may be called a mental grammar (not to be confused with pedagogical or stylistic "grammars," which are just guides to the etiquette of written prose). The second fundamental fact is that children develop these complex grammars rapidly and without formal instruction and grow up to give consistent interpretations to novel sentence constructions that they have never before encountered. Therefore, he argued, children must innately be equipped with a plan common to the grammars of all languages, a Universal Grammar, that tells them how to distill the syntactic patterns out of the speech of their parents. . . .

So the language instinct suggests a mind of adapted computational modules rather than the blank slate, lump of wax, or general-purpose computer of the Standard Social Science Model. But what does

this view say about the secular ideology of equality and opportunity that the model has provided us? If we abandon the SSSM, are we forced to repugnant doctrines like "biological determinism"?

Let me begin with what I hope are obvious points. First, the human brain works however it works. Wishing for it to work in some way as a shortcut to justifying some ethical principle undermines both the science and the ethics (for what happens to the principle if the scientific facts turn out to go the other way?). Second, there is no foreseeable discovery in psychology that could bear on the self-evident truth that ethically and politically, all people are created equal, that they are endowed with certain inalienable rights, and that among these are life, liberty, and the pursuit of happiness. Finally, radical empiricism is not necessarily a progressive, humanitarian doctrine. A blank slate is a dictator's dream. Some psychology textbooks mention the "fact" that Spartan and samurai mothers smiled upon hearing that their sons fell in battle. Since history is written by generals, not mothers, we can dismiss this incredible claim, but it is clear what purposes it must have served.

With those points out of the way, I do want to point out some implications of the theory of cognitive instincts for heredity and humankind, for they are the opposite of what many people expect. It is a shame that the following two claims are so often confused:

Differences between people are innate.
Commonalities among all people are innate.

The two claims could not be more different. Take number of legs. The reason that some people have fewer legs than others is 100% due to the environment. The reason that all uninjured people have exactly two legs (rather than eight, or six, or none) is 100% due to heredity. But claims that a universal human nature is innate are often run together with claims that differences between individuals, sexes, or races are innate. One can see the misguided motive for running them together: if *nothing* in the mind is innate, then differences between people's minds cannot be innate; thus it would be good if the mind had no structure because then decent egalitarians would have nothing to worry about. But the logical inverse is false. Everyone could be born with identical, richly structured minds, and all differences among them could be bits of acquired knowledge and minor perturbations that accumulate through people's history of life experiences. So even for people who, inadvisably in my view, like to conflate science and ethics, there is no need for alarm at the search for innate mental structure, whatever the truth turns out to be.

One reason innate commonalities and innate differences are so easy to confuse is that behavior geneticists (the scientists who study inherited deficits, identical and fraternal twins, adopted and biological children, and so on) have usurped the word "heritable" as a technical term referring to the proportion of *variation* in some trait that correlates with genetic differences within a species. This sense is different from the everyday term "inherited" (or genetic), which refers to traits whose inherent structure or organization comes from information in the genes. Something can be ordinarily inherited but show zero heritability, like number of legs at birth or the basic structure of the mind. Conversely, something can be not inherited but have 100% heritability. Imagine a society where all and only the red-haired people were made priests. Priesthood would be highly "heritable," though of course not inherited in any biologically meaningful sense. For this reason, people are bound to be confused by claims like "Intelligence is 70% heritable," especially when the newsmagazines report them in the same breath (as they inevitably do, alas) with research in cognitive science on the basic workings of the mind.

All claims about a language instinct and other mental modules are claims about the commonalities among all normal people. They have virtually nothing to do with possible genetic differences between people. One reason is that, to a scientist interested in how complex biological systems work, differences between individuals are so *boring!* Imagine what a dreary science of language we would have if instead

of trying to figure out how people put words together to express their thoughts, researchers had begun by developing a Language Quotient (LQ) scale, and busied themselves by measuring thousands of people's relative language skills. It would be like asking how lungs work and being told that some people have better lungs than others, or asking how compact disks reproduce sound and being given a consumer magazine that ranked them instead of an explanation of digital sampling and lasers.

But emphasizing commonalities is not just a matter of scientific taste. The design of any adaptive biological system—the explanation of how it works—is almost certain to be uniform across individuals in a sexually reproducing species, because sexual recombination would fatally scramble the blueprints for qualitatively different designs. There is, to be sure, a great deal of genetic diversity among individuals; each person is biochemically unique. But natural selection is a process that feeds on that variation, and (aside from functionally equivalent varieties of molecules) when natural selection creates adaptive designs, it does so by using the variation up: the variant genes that specify more poorly designed organs disappear when their owners starve, get eaten, or die mateless. To the extent that mental modules are complex products of natural selection, genetic variation will be limited to quantitative variations, not differences in basic design. Genetic differences among people, no matter how fascinating they are to us in love, biography, personnel, gossip, and politics, are of minor interest to us when we appreciate what makes minds intelligent at all.

Similarly, an interest in mind design puts possible innate differences between sexes (as a psycholinguist I refuse to call them "genders") and races in a new light. With the exception of the maleness-determining gene on the Y-chromosome, every functioning gene in a man's body is also found in a woman's and vice versa. The maleness gene is a developmental switch that can activate some suites of genes and deactivate others, but the same blueprints are in both kinds of bodies, and the default condition is identity of design. There is some evidence that the sexes depart from this default in the case of the psychology of reproduction and the adaptive problems directly and indirectly related to it, which is not surprising; it seems unlikely that peripherals as different as the male and female reproductive systems would come with the same software. But the sexes face essentially similar demands for most of the rest of cognition, including language, and I would be surprised if there were differences in design between them.

Race and ethnicity are the most minor differences of all. The human geneticists Walter Bodmer and Luca Cavalli-Sforza have noted a paradox about race. Among laypeople, race is lamentably salient, but for biologists it is virtually invisible. Eighty-five percent of human genetic variation consists of the differences between one person and another within the same ethnic group, tribe, or nation. Another eight percent is between ethnic groups, and a mere seven percent is between "races." In other words, the genetic difference between, say, two randomly picked Swedes is about twelve times as large as the genetic difference between the average of Swedes and the average of Apaches or Warlpiris. Bodmer and Cavalli-Sforza suggests that the illusion is the result of an unfortunate coincidence. Many of the systematic differences among races are adaptations to climate: melanin protects skin against the tropical sun, eyelid folds insulate eyes from dry cold and snow. But the skin, the part of the body seen by the weather, is also the part of the body seen by other people. Race is, quite literally, skin-deep, but to the extent that perceivers generalize from external to internal differences, nature has duped them into thinking that race is important. The X-ray vision of the molecular geneticist reveals the unity of our species.

And so does the X-ray vision of the cognitive scientist. "Not speaking the same language" is a virtual synonym for incommensurability, but to a psycholinguist, it is a superficial difference. Knowing about the ubiquity of complex language across individuals and cultures and the single mental design underlying them all, no speech seems foreign to me, even when I cannot understand a word. The banter among New Guinean highlanders in the film of their first contact with the rest of the world, the motions of a

sign language interpreter, the prattle of little girls in a Tokyo playground—I imagine seeing through the rhythms to the structures underneath, and sense that we all have the same minds.*

WESTERMARCK

Incest avoidance (sometimes called the *incest taboo*) refers to the near-universal human tendency to avoid sexual relations with close relatives. It has received considerable attention from scholars eager to conceptualize human nature. Incest avoidance was long thought to be unique to human beings, even a defining human characteristic. Thus, the Freudian Oedipus complex assumed that children "naturally" desired sexual relations with their opposite-sex parents, and that full humanity and civilization was only achieved when that desire was effectively overcome. The anthropologist Claude Levi-Strauss theorized that exogamy (marrying outside the family) served to establish crucial social bonds and relationships, while others have stressed its role in preventing disruption to family dynamics.

Since the 1960s, however, it has become clear that most animals in fact avoid mating with close relatives, while the genetically deleterious disadvantages of inbreeding have also been clarified. Moreover, it has been demonstrated that human beings, and many animals as well, refrain from mating with individuals with whom they were closely associated as juveniles. This idea was first suggested by the Finnish anthropologist, philosopher, and sociologist Edward Westermarck (1862–1939) in his massive compilation, *The History of Human Marriage,* from which the following excerpt is taken. The "Westermarck hypothesis" currently enjoys strong support.

I cannot but believe that consanguineous marriages, in some way or other, are more or less detrimental to the species. And here, I think, we may find a quite sufficient explanation of the horror of incest; not because man at an early stage recognized the injurious influence of close intermarriage, but because the law of natural selection must inevitably have operated. Among the ancestors of man, as among other animals, there was no doubt a time when blood-relationship was no bar to sexual intercourse. But variations, here as elsewhere, would naturally present themselves; and those of our ancestors who avoided in-and-in breeding would survive, while the others would gradually decay and ultimately perish. Thus an instinct would be developed which would be powerful enough, as a rule, to prevent injurious unions. Of course it would display itself simply as an aversion on the part of individuals to union with others with whom they lived; but these, as a matter of fact, would be blood-relations, so that the result would be the survival of the fittest.

Whether man inherited the feeling from the predecessors from whom he sprang, or whether it was developed after the evolution of distinctly human qualities, we do not know. It must necessarily have arisen at a stage when family ties became comparatively strong, and children remained with their parents until the age of puberty, or even longer. Exogamy, as a natural extension of this instinct, would arise when single families united in small hordes. It could not but grow up if the idea of union between persons intimately associated with one another was an object of innate repugnance. There is no real reason why we should assume, as so many anthropologists have done, that primitive men lived in small endogamous communities, practising incest in every degree. The theory does not accord with what is known of the customs of existing savages; and it accounts for no facts which may not be otherwise far more satisfactorily explained.

*From *The Language Instinct* (1994). New York: Morrow.

The objection will perhaps be made that the aversion to sexual intercourse between persons living very closely together from early youth is too complicated a mental phenomenon to be a true instinct, acquired through spontaneous variations intensified by natural selection. But there are instincts just as complicated as this feeling, which, in fact, only implies that disgust is associated with the idea of sexual intercourse between persons who have lived in a long-continued, intimate relationship from a period of life at which the action of desire is naturally out of the question. This association is no matter of course, and certainly cannot be explained by the mere liking for novelty. *It* has all the characteristics of a real, powerful instinct and bears evidently a close resemblance to the aversion to sexual intercourse with individuals belonging to another species. . . .

Closely akin to the horror of bestiality is the horror of incest, which, almost without exception, is a characteristic of the races of men, though the degrees within which intercourse is forbidden vary in an extraordinary degree. It is nearly universally abominated between parents and children, generally between brothers and sisters, often between cousins, and, among a great many peoples uninfluenced by modern civilization, between all the members of the tribe or clan. We criticized the theories set forth by various writers as to the origin of such prohibitions. To each of these theories there are special objections; and all of them presuppose that men avoid incestuous marriages only because they are taught to do so. As a matter of fact, the home is kept pure from incestuous intercourse neither by laws, nor by customs, nor by education, but by an instinct which under normal circumstances makes sexual love between the nearest kin a psychical impossibility. Of course there is no innate aversion to marriage with near relations; but there is an innate aversion to marriage between persons living very closely together from early youth, and, as such persons are in most cases related, this feeling displays itself chiefly as a horror of intercourse between near kin. The existence of an innate aversion of this kind is proved, not only by common experience, but by an abundance of ethnographical facts which show that it is not in the first place by degrees of consanguinity, but by close living together, that prohibitory laws against intermarriage are determined. Thus many peoples have a rule of local exogamy, which is quite independent of kinship. The extent to which, among various nations, relatives are not allowed to intermarry, is obviously nearly connected with their close living together. There is so strong a coincidence (as statistical data prove) between exogamy and the "classificatory system of relationship"—which system springs, to a great extent, from the close living together of considerable numbers of kinsfolk—that they must, in fact, be regarded as two sides of one institution. Prohibitions of incest are very often more or less one-sided, applying more extensively either to the kinsfolk on the father's side or to those on the mother's, according as descent is reckoned through men or women; and we have seen that the line of descent is intimately connected with local relationships. In a large number of cases, however, prohibitions of intermarriage are only indirectly influenced by the close living together. Aversion to the intermarriage of persons who live in intimate connection with each other has provoked prohibitions of the intermarriage of relations; and, as kinship is traced by means of a system of names, the name comes to be considered identical with relationship. Generally speaking, the feeling that two persons are intimately connected in some way or other may, through an association of ideas, give rise to the notion that intercourse between them is incestuous. There are exceptions to the rule that close living together inspires an aversion to intermarriage. But most of the recorded instances of intermarriage of brother and sister refer to royal families, and are brought about simply by pride of birth. Incestuous unions may also take place on account of extreme isolation, and certain instances of such connection are evidently the results of vitiated instincts. Marriage between a half-brother and a half-sister, however, is not necessarily contrary to the principle here laid down, as polygyny breaks up each family into as many sub-families as there are wives who have children. The question arose:—Why is a feeling of disgust associated with the idea of marriage between persons who have lived in a long-continued, intimate relationship from a period of life at which the action of desire is naturally out of the question? We found an answer in the evil effects resulting from consanguineous marriages. It seems to be necessary for the welfare of the species that the sexual elements which unite shall be somewhat different from, as it is necessary that they shall be in some way similar to, one another. The injurious results of self-fertilization among plants and of close interbreeding among animals appear to prove the existence of such a law, and it is impossible to believe that it does not apply to man also. We stated several facts pointing in this direction, and found reason to believe that consanguineous marriages are much more injurious in savage regions, where the struggle for existence is often very severe, than they have proved to be in civilized society. We also observed that no evidence which can stand the test of scientific investigation has hitherto been adduced against the view that consanguineous marriages in some way or other, are more or less detrimental to the species. Through natural selection an instinct must have been developed, powerful enough, as a rule, to prevent injurious unions. This instinct displays itself simply as an aversion on the part of individuals to union with others with whom they have lived, but as these are for the most part blood-relations, the result is the survival of the fittest.*

STUDY QUESTIONS

1. Identify some other human characteristics that are possible candidates for human uniqueness (e.g., striving for technological transcendence, for better or worse, as in the case of Faust, Dr. Frankenstein, nuclear weapons, or genetic cloning).

2. Does it matter whether certain traits are uniquely human?

3. Mark Twain once wrote that "only human beings blush . . . or need to." Comment on this.

4. To what extent is an individual's "humanness" a consequence of whether he or she partakes of certain traits we might identify as *uniquely* human?

SOME ADDITIONAL READINGS

Brown, Norman O. (1985; 1959). *Life Against Death.* Middletown, Conn.: Wesleyan University Press.

Chomsky, Noam (1975). *Reflections on Language.* New York: Pantheon Books.

Count, Earl W. (1973). *Being and Becoming: Human Essays on the Biogram.* New York: Van Nostrand Reinhold.

Jackendoff, Ray (1994). *Patterns in the Mind: Language and Human Nature.* New York: Basic Books.

Shepher, Joseph (1983). *Incest, a Biosocial View.* New York: Academic Press.

*From *The History of Human Marriage* (3rd ed., 1903). London: Macmillan.

Credits

"At the very heart of the ecumenical movement is the reality of prayer. Jesus prayed that we may all be one, united in God in the mystery of the Trinity. That is the basis and the goal of our search for unity.

"Intercessory prayer is of the essence of the church's vocation. Through the daily discipline of intercession we affirm our solidarity with Christians all over the world, brothers and sisters living in diverse situations and experiencing diverse problems.

"*A World at Prayer: The New Ecumenical Prayer Cycle* includes prayers from the countries of the world. It enables us to journey in prayer through every region of the world and through every week of the year. It enables us to pray together, with all God's people and for all God's people, from within our concrete contexts."

Gregory Baum
McGill University

A WORLD AT PRAYER

The New Ecumenical Prayer Cycle

Compiled by John Carden
and the World Council of Churches
Foreword by Emilio Castro

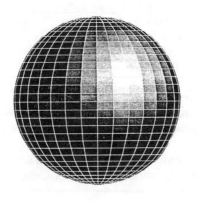

XXIII
TWENTY-THIRD PUBLICATIONS
Mystic, Connecticut

Orders of Service, a companion volume for *With All God's People: The New Ecumenical Prayer Cycle*, contains hymns, litanies, and other liturgical forms from around the world for use in different seasons of the church year and on special ecumenical occasions. Available from Forward Movement Publications, 412 Sycamore Street, Cincinati, Ohio 45202, 134 pages, $7.95, postpaid.

North American Edition 1990

Published by   Twenty-Third Publications
                 185 Willow Street
                 P.O. Box 180
                 Mystic, CT 06355
                 (203) 536-2611

Originally published as *With All God's People: The New Ecumenical Prayer Cycle* by World Council of Churches, Geneva, Switzerland.

ISBN 0-89622-427-9

Foreword

At the very heart of the ecumenical movement is the reality of prayer. Jesus prayed that we may all be one, united in God in the mystery of the Trinity. That is the basis and the goal of our search for unity.

Prayer is our pathway to unity. What we seek in and through the ecumenical movement is a communion that we cannot articulate in words because it belongs to our life in God. It is through prayer that we both seek and celebrate that communion.

Intercessory prayer is of the essence of the church's vocation. Like Abraham interceding for Sodom and Gomorrah, and following the example of Jesus' priestly prayer in the gospel of John, we raise our hearts and minds to God in worship and adoration, and we intercede on behalf of all with whom we share the world and all its joys and sorrows. Through the daily discipline of intercession we affirm our solidarity with Christians all over the world, brothers and sisters living in diverse situations and experiencing diverse problems.

The Vancouver Assembly of the World Council of Churches in 1983 reaffirmed the centrality of worship. Participants experienced there the power of prayer. They interceded for churches everywhere and for the nations and peoples of the world. A larger number than ever before at such gatherings were able to be part of one eucharistic community, sharing as they did in the memorable celebration of the Lima Liturgy, which tries to embody in liturgical form some of the ecumenical theological convergence achieved through the years.

It is out of such ecumenical worship experience that this edition of the Ecumenical Prayer Cycle has been prepared. It represents an attempt to identify with God's people in every place and to present before God their specific needs and aspirations.

A World at Prayer: The New Ecumenical Prayer Cycle includes prayers from many countries. It enables us to journey in prayer through every region of the world and through every week of the year. It enables us to pray together, *with* all God's people and *for* all God's people, from within our concrete contexts.

Many member churches and Christian groups have their own prayer cycles which follow their liturgical tradition and calendar. They have litanies and liturgies around denominational and congregational concerns. These serve an important purpose. But there is also the need to grow in an ecumenical spirituality of prayer. As churches and Christians we are committed together to the search for full visible unity.

During and within that search we must celebrate the unity that God has granted us; and we must hold up before God all the partners in the ecumenical pilgrimage in their disparate situations. Committing one another to God, we draw closer to one another and we grow in unity together.

For many people the first edition of the Ecumenical Prayer Cycle, *For All God's People,* published in 1978 and later translated into some twenty languages, was their first introduction to ecumenical prayer. *A World at Prayer* continues that tradition; it seeks to inform our public worship and private prayer with ecumenical concern and content. It demonstrates the old ecumenical conviction: *lex orandi, lex credendi.* Churches and Christians, men and women, live by a faith embodied in a variety of credal and doxological affirmations, but they enter the presence of God together, for and with one another.

In the process of preparing this volume, we have received a great variety of worship material from many sources. Available now at the worship resource center of the World Council of Churches at its Geneva headquarters, it indicates the richness of the liturgical traditions among our member churches and of the themes and styles of prayer that Christian people resort to in our time.

This book is offered to all churches and Christian groups in the conviction that it is responding to a demand for a spirituality that is contextual, local, and ecumenical.

Where there is no prayer for unity there can be no vision of unity. Let the Spirit so guide us that our human voices praying to God for the salvation of the world and the unity of the people of God may be heard and answered.

Emilio Castro

Preface

About This Book

Published in 1978 and subsequently translated into a number of languages, the first Ecumenical Prayer Cycle, *For All God's People*, has been widely used by many different churches, groups, and individuals all over the world. The present volume is a successor to it. The revised book, *A World at Prayer: The New Ecumenical Prayer Cycle*, carries with it an idea very familiar in WCC circles, that of staying together, struggling together, growing together, and praying together; and which, applied to the EPC, implies an effort not just to pray *for* all God's people, but also to understand, to stand alongside and to pray in solidarity *with* our fellow Christians around the world.

A World at Prayer takes its shape and content from the interaction of many different people, and from formal and informal dialogue with churches and councils of churches and with individual friends in the ecumenical movement in different parts of the world. We are grateful to those many people who provided inspiration, who have allowed us to use their prayers and words, who have made corrections, or in any other way participated in the process of preparing this new book.

The Cycle

It is obviously an aid to our sense of Christian solidarity and to the growing sense of interdependence on the part of all human beings if we can find some way of praying together on a regular and agreed basis. Solidarity is one of the recurring themes of this book, as of the ecumenical movement as a whole, and is articulated most forcefully by churches that are under pressure of one kind or another, and most appreciatively by individual Christians in situations of isolation and privation.

This Ecumenical Prayer Cycle is offered by the member churches of the WCC as one method of enabling Christians to broaden and also to focus their prayer and concern, and to familiarize themselves with, and bring into the local family, people of different parts of the world. Intended for the use of individuals and local congregations as well as for places of daily corporate prayer and ecumenical formation such as religious communities, ashrams, theological colleges, and lay training institutes, the weekly material can be used over the course of the week as it is in the Ecumenical Center in Geneva. Alternatively—especially in the case of congregations who use the EPC as the basis for their Sunday

intercessions, and find it difficult to assimilate more than one country on any given Sunday—the region can be prayed for as a whole, or, as is done in the German Democratic Republic, one country of the week each year, over what adds up to a three- or four-year cycle.

Some use the book as a resource, as the hub of the wheel rather than its perimeter, and when for whatever reason a particular country comes to their attention, perhaps in connection with their own confessional cycle, they turn to *A World at Prayer* for material for prayer. It is hoped that the index, which lists countries and regions and also themes of prayers, will be helpful. The aim of the cycle is to provide a system and discipline for those who would value it, and a resource book for all who are concerned in whatever way to pray with all God's people.

Format

In the interest of freshness and variety, and in order to do some justice to regional differences, the compilers were encouraged to approach different weeks in different ways. This means that the layout for each week is not standard. What is standard is that all the prayers are in larger type and the background of each country is in smaller type. Also, background pertaining to more than one country is presented in a wide column of type; that pertaining to one country, in a narrower column.

For various reasons some weeks seem to call for more explanatory or factual material than others, and the amount of prayer material made available varies greatly.

Language

As its title suggests, *A World at Prayer* is designed to include all people, and inclusive language is therefore used throughout. Since we are praying alongside those, both young and old, of every race and language, and using the prayers which they themselves use, there is a rich and varied way of addressing God, using such names as Father, Mother, Grandfather, Parent, Elder Brother, Weaverwoman. Certainly many prayers acknowledge that God has feminine attributes. For some, the word "Lord" may present problems. In one of his books Kosuke Koyama instances Philippians 2, in which Christ is shown as affirming his lordship by giving it up. He goes on: "Christians live in such a Lord and their lives must point to such a strange lordship." In praying the prayers and making them their own, it is hoped that users will feel free to appropriate these varied ways of addressing God or to transpose them into forms with which they feel more at ease.

Information

Prayers emerge out of and are related to given situations, and it is the blending of information, facts, and history with prayer that provides

one of the most satisfactory elements in ecumenical spirituality and makes this a book of living prayer rather than a bookish anthology. Within the limits of time available, care has been taken to check the accuracy of the information, and the compilers apologize for any mistakes. However, it must be remembered that situations can change quickly, and in the case of some countries, very significant changes have indeed already taken place. In some instances these are matters for thanksgiving. Users of the prayer cycle will wish to take these changes into their prayers.

Population figures throughout the book are all taken from one standard source, taking the latest official figure available and rounding it up to the next decimal point. This means that for most countries the figure given is too low, as populations are mostly rising and often rapidly. Religious statistics are more difficult. In most cases use has been made of Barrett's forecast figures,* but wherever statistics have been made available by the local Christian council these have been used.

The Prayers

While an effort has been made to achieve a degree of typicality in the prayers that have been chosen, and thus enable users to identify with the words and ways of different countries, the compilers have also had in mind the totality of the cycle and have sought to choose prayers not only for the sake of their local flavor but also because of what they contribute to the whole. So it is that Finland's prayer of blessing of a computer, or Canada's meditation on a crucified woman, are to be regarded as the gifts of those countries to the spirituality of the whole church rather than as being necessarily typical of the country concerned. Likewise prayers for those affected with AIDS are included under USA and Uganda because both of these countries have experience with AIDS, are open about it, are relating it to their Christian faith, and therefore share this pain and this problem with the rest of the world.

While in an increasingly interdependent world an ever-increasing number of prayers reflect common themes—peace, unity, cities, young people—some very striking differences of need and of emphasis are emerging. Elements of questioning, anger, anguish, penitence, silence, solidarity, affirmation, and rejoicing are all to be found, some more typical of certain areas of the world than others.

Every effort has been made to trace and acknowledge the origin of the prayers, and where these have not knowingly been adapted, to reproduce them in the form received. However, like birds released from captivity, prayers once published take on a life of their own and enjoy

---

*World Christian Encyclopedia, ed. David B. Barrett, Nairobi, OUP, 1982. Also used for general information: The Europa Year Book: a World Survey, 1987, London, Europa Publications Ltd.

the freedom of the universe. Flying in different environments, they sometimes acquire new meanings. This has surely happened in the case of a number of the prayers in the book, and as they continue to be used in many different situations and settings that process will undoubtedly continue and add to their richness.

Symbols

"Am I to believe that God's concern for the people of Taiwan, for instance, or Korea, began only 60, 80, or 90 years ago when we western missionaries arrived with the gospel of Jesus Christ?" asks Emilio Castro. To which, of course, the answer is "No." As far as this book is concerned, a number of things follow from that. The compilers have tried, first, to acknowledge the earlier history of each country and to affirm the dignity and rights of original inhabitants, and second, to affirm their belief that God also speaks in and through those of other faiths and all cultures. A third thing, which follows from the recognition of God's presence and activity in those who belong to largely non-literary cultures, is that God also speaks through visual images and symbols. It was at our very first meeting in Taizé that a Ghanaian member of the group challenged us to look at the possibility of introducing some non-literary elements into this new edition. To a West African the symbol on page 188 communicates immediately the need for unity and harmony in a way words can never do. Some of the symbols in this book, like the cross of St. Thomas and the one from Taxila, speak of a very early Christian presence in those lands. Others relate to more contemporary concerns. All stand as tokens for a great deal of sharing which could be enriching.

In response to the need for the world church to become fully ecumenical Walter Hollenweger, professor of Mission at Birmingham University in England, posed the question as to whether a proverb, a song, a snatch of poetry, a dance, a story, a parable was ever taken as seriously as a committee resolution. And if not, why not? His inference was that it is just those things that move human beings most deeply, that stir the imagination, that evoke the teaching of Jesus and inspire the spirit of prayer more unerringly and deeply than many more formal utterances.

Maps

The very many small "maps" used in this book are meant to serve as "locations," that is, to inform the reader where a particular country is located, say, Tunisia, Brunei, or Turkey. Used for this purpose, the maps show no topographical or other detail and are not all drawn to the same scale.

A number of well-known medieval pilgrim maps view the world as

centered on Jerusalem, and show the continents of Africa, Asia, and Europe as radiating from that center. This insight has been adopted to the extent of singling out Jerusalem as the only city to be shown, the place of our Lord's passion, resurrection, ascension, and the promise of his continued intercession, as the point of departure for users of this ecumenical cycle of prayer.

Updating

One of the staff at the Ecumenical Center said recently, "With things moving so quickly, every day away from Africa is one more day out of date." (To this add Eastern Europe.) Applied to the EPC, this suggests the need for constant updating on the part of the user. Users are invited to share in updating and renewal by submitting corrections, up-to-date information, prayers, and liturgical material to the Worship Resource Center of the Sub-unit on Renewal and Congregational Life.

This prayer cycle has been compiled under the guidance of a task force specially constituted for the purpose, made up of members of staff of the World Council of Churches. The work was carried out under the general direction of the WCC Sub-units on Faith and Order, and Renewal and Congregational Life. In the earlier stages, the Rev. Dr. Hans-Georg Link played a major role.

John Carden
Consultant for the EPC
Renewal and Congregational Life

Contents

Schedule

Ecumenical Prayer Cycle

Applicable to any calendar year, this schedule may be used for the ecumenical prayer cycle in this book. The weeks of the year are grouped according to geographical areas of the world. In each week are the country or countries that are the subject of prayer and concern for that week. For precise dates for the years 1990–1996, see pages 345–348.

Week 1   Egypt, Israel and the Occupied Territories, Jordan, Lebanon, Syria

Week 2   Countries of the Arabian Peninsula, Iran, Iraq

Week 3   Cyprus, Greece, Turkey

Week 4   Algeria, Libya, Morocco, Tunisia

Week 5   Hong Kong, Macao, People's Republic of China, Taiwan

Week 6   Democratic People's Republic of Korea, Japan, Republic of Korea

Week 7   The Philippines

Week 8   Brunei, Malaysia, Singapore

Week 9   Denmark, Finland, Iceland, Norway, Sweden

Week 10   Republic of Ireland, United Kingdom

Week 11   Belgium, Luxembourg, The Netherlands

Week 12   France, Portugal, Spain

Week 13   Djibouti, Ethiopia, Somalia

Week 14   Sudan, Uganda

Week 15   Kenya, Tanzania

Week 16   Madagascar, Malawi, Zambia

Week 17   Brazil

Week 18   Argentina, Paraguay, Uruguay

Week 19   Bolivia, Chile, Peru

Week 20   Czechoslovakia, Poland

Week 21   Albania, Bulgaria, Yugoslavia

Week 22   Hungary, Romania

Week 23   Mongolia, Union of Soviet Socialist Republics

Week 24   Liberia, Sierra Leone

Week 25   Cape Verde, Guinea, Guinea Bissau, Senegal, The Gambia

Week 26   Benin, Ghana, Ivory Coast, Togo

Week 27   Nigeria

Week 28	Kampuchea, Laos, Vietnam
Week 29	Burma, Thailand
Week 30	Indonesia
Week 31	United States of America
Week 32	Canada
Week 33	Australia, New Zealand
Week 34	The Pacific Islands
Week 35	The Islands of the Indian Ocean
Week 36	The Caribbean Islands, French Guiana, Guyana, Suriname
Week 37	Belize, Guatemala, Honduras, Mexico
Week 38	Costa Rica, El Salvador, Nicaragua, Panama
Week 39	Colombia, Ecuador, Venezuela
Week 40	Burkina Faso, Chad, Mali, Mauritania, Niger
Week 41	Cameroon, Central African Republic
Week 42	Congo, Equatorial Guinea, Gabon, São Tomé and Príncipe
Week 43	Burundi, Rwanda, Zaïre
Week 44	Federal Republic of Germany, German Democratic Republic
Week 45	Austria, Liechtenstein, Switzerland
Week 46	Italy, Malta
Week 47	Bangladesh, Bhutan, Nepal
Week 48	Afghanistan, Pakistan
Week 49	India, Sri Lanka
Week 50	Angola, Mozambique
Week 51	Botswana, Zimbabwe
Week 52	Lesotho, Namibia, South Africa, Swaziland

Jerusalem

Lord, dear Lord,
I long for Jerusalem;
The city built high in heaven
but also the one built on the rocks
over there in Israel.

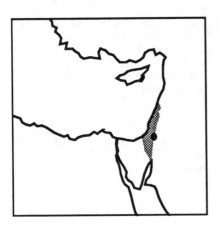

In all the countries and churches included in this cycle of prayer, there
can hardly be a single believer who
cannot identify with the prayer of
this Ghanaian Christian; and few of
us indeed who, in times of privation
and difficulty, have not taken comfort in the thought of the heavenly
city; or, at some time or another,
have not walked in imagination the
streets of Jerusalem, re-living those
events in the life of Jesus so central to
our faith.

Lord God,
then I would see, in my mind,
how he was pushed and lashed
through city streets to Golgotha
and see there how he died for us.
I'd mourn and weep
and mourn—but I would know!
I'd see how the temple curtain was torn,
and feel the earthquake under my feet.
Then Easter when he rose from the dead.
Rejoicing, dancing, and clapping
I would shout:
He is risen!
He is risen!

Since that first resurrection morning it is to Jerusalem that pilgrims have come; and it is from Jerusalem that our cycle of prayer begins, following the ever-increasing spread of the church since Pentecost to the present time. Over the centuries, the church's growth has been aided by countless preachers and evangelists, as well as by other social and political forces which have scattered Christians across the world.

Jerusalem remains also the meeting place of the three great monotheistic faiths: Judaism, Christianity, and Islam, each with its centers of devotion, hospitality, and scholarship and its own institutions of service. Due to the uncertainties of the future and the present political reality, many Christians and Muslims have left Jerusalem. In terms of the local Arab Christian community, for example, numbers have diminished since 1967, when there were an estimated 27,000, to something like 7,500. They belong to a number of different confessions, but are mostly Eastern Orthodox, Roman Catholics, Melkites, Lutherans, and Anglicans. There is a small community of Christian converts from Judaism.

Pray for this living presence in Jerusalem.

As in all greatly revered pilgrimage places, special sensitivities are involved, and relationships between the different Christian confessions in Jerusalem, as well as between the different faiths and peoples are often marked by conflict. Now, as ever, there is need to pray for the peace of Jerusalem, the city which gave rise to that great expression of the mother love of God.

O Jerusalem, Jerusalem...how often would I have gathered your children together as a hen gathers her brood under her wings, and you would not!

The figure of a pelican feeding her young with her own life-blood is to be seen in the "Upper Room" in Jerusalem, and is an ancient reminder of the self-giving love of God in Christ. To him we pray:

Blessed Jesus,
lifting up holy hands perpetually for all humankind;
breathe by thy Spirit such love into the prayers that we offer,
that they may be taken into thine, and prevail with thine. Amen.

Pray
for the city of Jerusalem distracted and divided until this day, yet still pregnant with promise for the children and for

all who seek the common good of its diverse people
  Gather them together, O Lord.

for men and women of peace and reconciliation in every
community
  Gather them together, O Lord.

for the custodians of holy places; for priests and pastors
and for the continuing life of local congregations
  Gather them together, O Lord.

for the Christians of many backgrounds and traditions,
who take part in the Palm Sunday walk, but find other
steps towards unity less easy to take
  Gather them together, O Lord.

Lord Jesus, we pray for the church which is one in the
greatness of your love, but divided in the littleness of our
own. May we be less occupied with the things which divide us, and more with the things we hold in common.
Amen.

Jesus comes to Benares
As he does to Mecca
and to Jerusalem and to Rome
In each place
he raises his hand in peace
And in each place
he is crucified again.
                    The Christian Conference of Asia

Jesus, ride again into our cities, temples,
Upper Rooms and Gethsemanes.
  Give us sight so that this time we might recognize you.
Amen.
                    Prayer for peace

Week 1

Egypt • Israel and the Occupied Territories• Jordan • Lebanon• Syria

O God of the ever-present crosses,
help us, your servants.

4th-century Egyptian

O Master, Lord God, Almighty, the Father of our Lord, our God and our Savior Jesus Christ, we thank you in every condition, for any condition and in whatever condition. For that you have covered us, preserved us, accepted us, had compassion on us, sustained us, and brought us to this hour.

Coptic Orthodox prayer of thanksgiving
which precedes all acts of worship

Accept, our Lord, from us—at this hour and all hours—our supplications; make our life easy; direct us to behave in accordance with your commandments. Sanctify our spirits; purify our bodies, straighten our thoughts; cleanse our desires; heal our sicknesses; forgive our sins; and save us from all evil, sorrow, and heartache. Surround us by your holy angels that we may be kept in their camp, and guided so as to arrive at the unity of faith and the knowledge of your glory, imperceptible and boundless.

Seven times, each Egyptian day is punctuated by the Horlogion commemorating the resurrection, the sentencing of Jesus, and the coming of the Spirit, the crucifixion, death, deposition, and burial of Jesus, each recollection concluding with the prayer above.

God of grace and providence, Lord of our going out and of our coming in, we pray for Egypt, shelter of the Holy Family from the old tyranny of Herod, and first resting place be-

4

yond the manger of the eternal glory. Bless her land and people, once entertaining unawares the earth's redeemer. Make the church in Egypt the patient means of thy purpose and ready custodian of the peace of Christ, ever left with his servants and ever passing through and from them to the saving of the world. We pray in his name. Amen.

Kenneth Cragg, sometime assistant bishop in Jerusalem

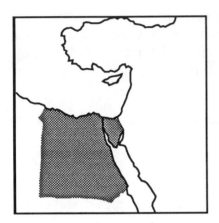

Egypt

Population: 48.6 million, and increasing by at least one million annually.
Language: Arabic.
Government: Multi-party republic.
Religion: Muslims 85%; Christians 15%, mostly members of the Coptic Orthodox Church who number some 7 million. The ancient Greek Orthodox Patriarchate of Alexandria also has its roots here. There are considerably smaller Evangelical Coptic, Armenian, Catholic, Anglican, and Protestant communities.

If the unforgettable words in St. John's Gospel "And the word was made flesh" were written originally to meet the needs of Hellenic Jews in Alexandria, and if—as is firmly believed in Egypt—St. Mark himself visited Alexandria and preached the gospel throughout the country, then there must have been a Christian presence in Egypt from a very early date. Unquestionably, Egyptian Christians died in thousands in the bitter persecution of the 3rd and 4th centuries, and formed the nucleus of the great desert communities, an experience which fortified the Coptic Church for the years to come. The rise of Islam brought problems and opportunities which continue to this day.

Today, give thanks

for the ordinary people of Egypt who remain cheerful in the face of adversity, aspiring only to live a decent and reasonable life

for the lives of all the saints, known and unknown, from apostolic times until now (for Copts, the Book of the Acts of the Apostles does not conclude with Amen, but continues in the lives of today's saints)

for the movement of renewal in the church; for classes and Sunday schools; for the hospitality of monasteries and an expanding diakonia

for the provision of Christian literature and cassettes and for the spiritual enrichment they provide in the lives of the people.

Today, share
with the church in Egypt its concern for work among up-rooted people come to the cities, for a ministry to a quarter of a million university students, and for the work among the Zabbaleen living on and by means of the rubbish dumps of Cairo.

In my faith is comprised the love of the city and its inhabitants.

Sufi saying

Lord, give us such a faith as will encompass cities the like of Cairo, and loving prayers that will uphold and serve its 10 million people.

Today, pray
for the bulk of Egypt's population cultivating the land of the Nile delta, often for little reward

for the Fellaheen and countless others who have left the countryside to seek for laboring jobs in the cities and in surrounding countries; separated from their families, doing hard work and often underpaid, the Christians among them are sustained by the presence of the Coptic church or other Christian fellowship.

We pray, Lord, for the rising of the water of the Nile this year. May Christ, our Savior, bless it and raise it, cheering the earth and sustaining us, his creatures. And may the rising water remind us of the Living Water freely given to all who repent and believe.

From the Coptic Orthodox liturgy

Wherever there are two, they are not without God.
And where there is only one, I say I am with him.
Raise the stone and you will find me, cleave the wood,
and there am I.

> *Recovered from the rubbish heap at Oxyrhynchus in Upper Egypt, these words—claimed to be one of the promises of Jesus—seem particularly applicable to Egypt's scattered manual workers*

Israel and the Occupied Territories

Pray not for Arab or Jew,
for Palestinian or Israeli,
but pray rather for yourselves
that you may not divide them in your prayers,
but keep them both together in your hearts.

> *A Palestinian Christian*

As Christians especially do we pray for that land sanctified by Our Lord's footsteps, that it may become the crossroads of peace and fraternity.

> *Christian prayer for peace*
> *Pope John Paul II, Assisi, 1986*

Lord,
after all the talking; questioning; agonizing over your land,
grant that some compassionate breakthrough may occur.
Amen.

O Lord Jesus,
stretch forth your wounded hands in blessing over your people,
to heal and to restore,
and to draw them to yourself and to one another in love.
Amen.

> *Prayer from the Middle East*

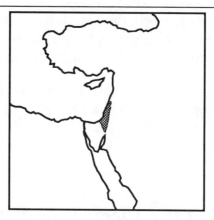

Israel

West Bank and Gaza

Population: 4.3 million, including E. Jerusalem, Israeli residents in certain other areas under Israeli military occupation, and non-Jews in the Golan.
Languages: Hebrew, immigrant languages from all over the world.
Government: Parliamentary state.
Religion: Jews 85%; Muslims 12%; Christians 3%.

Population: 1.4 million.
Language: Arabic.
Government: Under Israeli military administration.
Religion: Muslims 90%; Jews 5%; Christians 5%.

Something of the reality of this complex situation is apparent from these figures, but sensitivity and understanding are needed to appreciate the strength of feeling for this land, and the pain which is endured by many who live there. Each with an intense longing for the same particular land, Israeli and Palestinian struggle for a secure national autonomy.

Since the 19th century the Zionist movement has been dedicated to the creation of a Jewish state and the physical return of Jews to Palestine. Given added impetus by the holocaust in Europe, and increasing immigration, both legal and illegal, of Jews into Palestine, the state of Israel came into being in 1948. The early years were marked by idealism; and in the task of developing the land and building a nation the lifestyle of the kubbutzim made a significant contribution. For some, the current situation represents God's promises fulfilled through faith and hard work. Today, however, there are many in Israel who question the incursion into neighboring territory, Jewish settlement on the West Bank, and the subhuman treatment of Arabs living under military administration.

Initially, in 1948, some 750,000 Palestinian Arabs, by far the majority population, fled or were expelled, and the annexation by Israel of East Jerusalem, the West Bank, and Gaza in 1967 produced a further wave of refugees. There are now about 2.5 million Palestinians scattered through the Middle East—many of them living in refugee camps—and rather fewer living in Israeli-occupied territory and Israel proper. Dispossessed, or suffering severe discrimination and harassment, these are the victims of the Jewish return. For them, the situation represents a betrayal by the world community.

Of local Christians, concentrated in Galilee and the Occupied Territories, most are Arab; and fellowship between them and Hebrew converts is not easy. Palestinian Christians belong to a wide variety of religious communities, worshiping together Sunday by Sunday, running clinics and schools, and involving themselves in social service and reconciliation projects of one kind or another. Sometimes they are puzzled by the preoccupation of visiting tourists with holy places, and their seeming lack of interest in the living church. Always they are in need of encouragement and the assurance of understanding on the part of their fellow Christians. It is they who, at no small cost, maintain a Christian presence in the land in which Jesus lived.

We pray

that God will heal the pain of those who have suffered the loss of family or of land; that bitter hurt may be transformed into healing and love

for all those, Jew and Arab, who have the courage to meet together in the quest for understanding, reconciliation, and peace

for Palestinian Christians who more easily than most can reproduce a pattern of life close to that of Jesus, and yet who find that today, it is his experience of rejection and homelessness, and of living in a land ruled by aliens, that is the hardest to bear

for all Jews in Israel, that sensitivity and good will may prevail in the affairs of their country; and for those in diaspora

for Muslims and Druze, with their belief in one God, and devotion to the land of their forebears.

For all peoples, that thy light may shine upon them, that the spirit of justice and mutual forbearance may be established among them, the spirit of love and peace.

To Thee we cry, O Lord; hear and have mercy.

Melkite petition

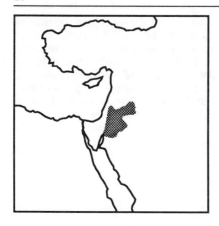

Jordan

Population: 2.7 million (including Palestinians).
Languages: Arabic, English.
Government: Constitutional monarchy.
Religion: Muslims 93%, Christians 5%.

Embracing the region traversed by our Lord in his journeys through Decapolis, the river bank where Jacob wrestled with the angel, the mountain from which Moses saw the Promised Land, the country of Ruth, and the range of hills which gave rise to the question "Is there no balm in Gilead?", the present-day nation of Jordan, being largely a Muslim nation, puts a rather different emphasis on its history. With a large influx of Palestinian refugees, very few economic resources of its own, and a geographical position which makes it both vulnerable and strategic, its preoccupation is the quest for peace in the Middle East. It is a quest shared by Muslims and Christians alike.

Amman has largely replaced Beirut as the business center of the area, and much political initiative arises here. Christians enjoy freedom of worship, and the church has made a major contribution in education and other forms of service. The majority of local Christians are Greek Orthodox, but there are also sizeable Armenian, Latin, Greek Catholic, and Anglican communities, as well as some small but thriving Protestant groups and churches. The Coptic Orthodox Church ministers to a large community of Egyptian laborers. Filipino, Sri Lankan, and Indian workers, mainly engaged in domestic work or in hospitals, are connected with various churches.

In response to the question "Is there no balm in Gilead?" a number of signs can be instanced: parish priests quietly and humbly working among their people; a new campsite for young people being constructed in those same Gilead hills; a vocational training school for the deaf, and a Mother Teresa home for the very deprived. In addition, other agencies run schools, clinics, and centers of various kinds, both inside and outside the refugee camps.

We pray
for political and church leaders, and all others who, often tired and discouraged, continue to work toward a solution to the Palestinian problem and peace in the region

for the people of Jordan—Bedouin herders, farmers, city-dwellers—outnumbered by their Palestinian neighbors

for Palestinians who continue to mourn the loss of home and land, that their sadness and unassuaged longing may find comfort and resolution.

"The problem in so many parts of the world," says one who worked with Palestinian refugees, "is still threefold; first to comfort and relieve, then to inspire patience founded on hope, and thirdly to provide a happy issue out of affliction." A traditional prayer, much used locally, sums it all up in one sentence:

We commend to thy fatherly goodness all those who are in any ways afflicted or distressed in mind, body, or estate; that it may please thee to comfort and relieve them, according to their several necessities, giving them patience under their sufferings, and happy issue out of all their afflictions...

Prayer Book of the Arab Evangelical Episcopal Church

We remember with gratitude
the many signs of balm in Gilead, and

pray
that they may continue to bring healing and wholeness to those who are deeply wounded by the vicissitudes of life.

O God, send into the hearts of the people of Jordan and its neighboring lands the spirit of Jesus; and upon us all be peace. Amen.

Lebanon

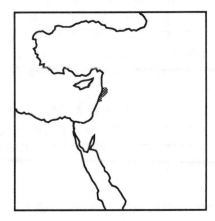

Population: Approximately 2.7 million (excluding Palestinian refugees in camps).
Languages: Arabic, Armenian, French, Kurdish, and others.
Government: Parliamentary republic.
Religion: Muslims (Shiah and Sunni) and Druze; Christians (Catholic, Orthodox, Protestant); the present ratio widely held to be 60-40, the majority being Muslim.

Linked in the Bible with images of glory, wealth and the sheltering cedar tree, later regarded as the commercial, financial, and tourist center of the Middle East, Lebanon today has a different kind of notoriety. Beirut, once the country's pride and joy, has been described as "one of the most violent capitals in the world"; and with 44 warring groups, about one out of every twenty people has been injured or wounded.

Lebanon became independent in 1944. It is characterized by great religious and cultural diversity, and probably contains the closest juxtaposition of different communities within a small area of any country in the Middle East. When the republic was established in 1943, the various communities agreed on a system of power sharing based on their relative proportions in the population at that time. This system worked for many years. However, the influx of Palestinians, and the higher rate of population increase in Muslim communities, upset the ratio. Israeli reprisals for Palestinian resistance activity added to the tension, and civil war broke out in 1975.

The majority of Christians in Lebanon are Maronite Catholics. This church, tracing its roots to the early undivided church at Antioch, claims unbroken communion with Rome. Seeking refuge in the 9th century, Maronites settled in the mountains of Lebanon. There are many other Christian communities of whom the Greek Orthodox, Greek Catholic, and Armenian Apostolic are the largest. Lebanon has become an important center for the Armenian community.

Life today in war-torn Lebanon reflects the extraordinary capacity of the Lebanese to carry on living more or less normally in the midst of such a situation. "It is as though we live in a huge coal mine," says Frieda Haddad of the Greek Orthodox Diocese of Mount Lebanon, "which nevertheless hides in its depths a shining diamond." Some cannot see it like that, and have become disillusioned and despairing. On the other hand, one priest from Beirut observed that Christians in the city were asking as never before: "What is God saying to us in all this?"

Let us join our prayers and presences to those of that company of witnesses called upon in this invocation:

Come in peace, prophets of the Spirit, who have prophesied concerning our Redeemer.

Come in peace, chosen apostles, who have preached the good news of the Only-begotten.

Come in peace, martyrs, friends of the heavenly Bridegroom.

Come in peace, all you Saints, friends of the Son.

Offer to him your prayers for us, that he for whose sake you travailed may be compassionate to us at your intercession, O holy ones.

Maronite liturgy

Pray

for peace; and for a change of heart in all those who seem intent on keeping the conflict alive

that Lebanon may be spared unwelcome intervention from outside, and may be given peaceful initiatives from within

for all of whatever nationality who are held hostage, and for their desperately anxious families

for all families in Lebanon who have lost loved ones.

Lord Christ, give me some of your Spirit to comfort the places in my heart where I hurt...Then give me some more of your Spirit, so that I can comfort other people.

Terry Waite

Pray also

for the life and work of the Middle East Council of Churches still going on in Beirut

for the Near East School of Theology, continuing to train men and women for Christian ministry

for the young people of Lebanon "suffering most from despair, needing most to have grounds for hope"

for renewal in worship and family life; and that in this time of testing, the different communities may grow closer to each other.

"At mid-day at the sixth hour, the hour of crucifixion, the praying church in the East lives each day anew this ultimate hour in which God's love for us was made fully manifest in the cross of Calvary." It is a rather special hour in Lebanon where every day involves a living out of the cross and resurrection.

Lord God, lover of peace and concord, look down with mercy upon Lebanon, that tormented country. Preserve its people and guide its rulers. Bless the peacemakers and those who love justice. May Lebanon become again in your loving purpose a place of unity in diversity, where men and women may learn to reverence life and humankind as your creation. Amen.

Syria

O glorious apostle Paul, who can describe your bondage and your tribulations in the cities? Who can tell the hardships and efforts you went through while preaching Christ in order to win all men and women and offer the church to Christ? O apostle Paul, founder of churches, pray that the church may be strengthened by you until the end of time.

From the Melkite liturgy

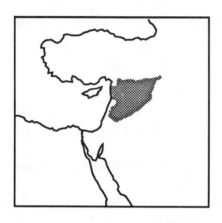

Population: 10.3 million.
Languages: Arabic; Kurdish, French, Armenian, Turkoman, Circassian, Aramaic, and others are also spoken.
Government: Socialist republic.
Religion: Muslims 90%, Christians approximately 8%; Druze approximately 3%.

Modern Syria became independent in 1946 and the socialist republic was proclaimed in 1973. Syria is unique among Arab countries in that, despite the large majority of Muslims, it is a secular state. Historically Syria has links with Lebanon and has played an active part in attempting to secure some kind of cease-fire in that country. Internally, although the administration keeps a tight rein, medical and educational facilities, never before widely available, are now enjoyed by the whole population.

Ancient Syria covered a wider area and included Antioch where "the disciples were first called Christians" (Acts 11:26) and which became one of the great centers of the early church associated with St. Peter and St. Paul. Division occurred in 451 when the family of Oriental Orthodox churches (Armenian, Coptic, and Syrian) separated. There are Armenian and Syrian Orthodox communities in Syria today and the Syrian Orthodox Church (see also week 49) has its See in Damascus. This church, which has suffered greatly through the centuries, has remained very close to the Jerusalem tradition of the ancient church. The ongoing (Greek) Orthodox Church of Antioch, whose membership is Arab and liturgical language Arabic, is now the largest Christian body. Catholics belong to six different rites. Most Protestants are members of either the National Evangelical Synod of Syria and Lebanon, or the Union of Armenian Evangelical Churches of the Near East. The churches are doing lively work in the field of Christian education.

Foreign missionaries were expelled in 1963, and Syrian nationals are not permitted to change their legal registration from Muslim to Christian. Syrian Christians, after the manner of St. Paul, faithfully playing their part in the life of the local church, have been joined in recent years by others of diverse nationality and background, whose informal and joyful worship must surely delight the heart of the apostle.

Christians in Syria, give thanks
for a long and rich history

and pray
that it may be constantly maintained and passed on to
their children, and that they may be ready, like their coun-
tryman Ananias, to welcome and embrace others.

Today there are signs of new vitality in the Syrian
church.

Thanks be to God.

To me who am but black cold charcoal
grant, O Lord,
that by the fire of Pentecost,
I may be set ablaze.

A prayer after St. John of Damascus

In peace let us make our supplication to the Lord—Lord,
have mercy.

For the peace that is from above, and the love of God,
and the salvation of our souls, let us make our supplication
to the Lord—Lord, have mercy.

For the peace of the whole world, and the unity of all the
holy churches of God—Lord, have mercy.

For them that bear fruit and do good deeds in the holy
churches of God, that remember the poor, the widows and
the orphans, the strangers, and them that are in need; and
for them that have desired of us to make mention of them
in our prayers—Lord, have mercy.

For them that are in old age and infirmity, the sick and
distressed, and them that are vexed in spirit, their speedy
healing from God and salvation—Lord, have mercy.

For them that lead their lives in celibacy and asceticism,
and in venerable marriage, and them that carry on their
struggle in the caves and dens and holes of the earth, our
holy fathers and brothers and sisters—Lord, have mercy.

For Christians that sail, that journey, that are strangers,
and for our brothers and sisters that are in bonds and ex-

iles, and imprisonment and bitter slavery, their peaceful return—Lord, have mercy.

For good temperature of the atmosphere, peaceful showers, pleasant dews, abundance of fruits, fullness of a good season, and for the crown of the year—Lord, have mercy.

And for every Christian soul in affliction and distress, and needing the mercy and succor of God, and for the conversion of the erring, the health of the sick, the rescue of the prisoners, the rest of them that have departed afore, our brothers and sisters—Lord, have mercy.

That our prayer may be heard and acceptable before God, and that his rich mercies and pities may be sent down upon us, let us make our supplications to the Lord—Lord, have mercy.

The divine liturgy of St. James

Week 2

Countries of the Arab Peninsula
Iran • Iraq

O God, I haven't recognized thee as thou ought to be recognized.

Prayer of Muhammad

O Lord, we beseech you, grant your blessing and guidance to all who are seeking to bring peace to the Middle East, stir the conscience of the nations, and break the bonds of covetousness and pride; make plain your way of deliverance, through Jesus Christ our Lord. Amen.

The Arabian Peninsula

Tradition holds that the apostle Bartholomew first brought the gospel to Arabia; and Scripture tells us (Acts 2:11) that Arabians were present at Pentecost. By whatever voice and means, Christianity certainly came to this area very early. A bishopric existed in Bahrain in the 3rd century, and by the 4th and 5th there were well-established Christian communities along the mainland coast. The spread of Islam in the 7th century virtually extinguished Christianity in the peninsula, although a legend exists of a small group of Christians, who had survived a thousand years without a priest, greeting the chaplain of a 15th-century Portuguese ship which called into Muscat. More recent evangelistic effort, both Roman Catholic and Protestant, began in the latter half of the 19th century, first in Aden (then under British rule) and shortly afterwards in the Gulf, with an emphasis on medical and educational work. Evangelism has never been permitted in Saudi Arabia. The presence of large numbers of immigrant workers, many of them Christians, means that there are probably more Christians in the Arabian Peninsula today than there have ever been.

Saudi Arabia (population 10.9 million) is the focal center of Islam. The Prophet (570–632 C.E.) was born and died here. Each year over a million Muslims come from all over the world on the hajj, which every devout Muslim hopes to make at least once in his or her lifetime. The strictly orthodox Wahhabi movement, dedicated to the reform of Islam, originated here, and indeed was the center of the first Sa'udi kingdom. The present-day monarch is the religious

head of the country, and custodian of the holy shrines. Islam is the only permitted religion. However, from 1970 onward, hundreds of thousands of immigrant workers from many lands have entered the country, men and women, separated from their families; they work long hours and face an insecure future. Meetings for worship are not officially permitted, and clergy are not allowed into the country, but groups meet informally for Bible study and prayer. The groups are constituted largely on a language basis, confessional differences becoming insignificant in this situation. "I'm Catholic really," said a recent resident, "but that was a long time ago. We've been to Saudi Arabia since then. Now we're just Christians."

Since the discovery of oil, *the Gulf States* (Kuwait, Bahrain, Qatar, United Arab Emirates, and Oman) have developed rapidly. Employment possibilities have brought large numbers of workers, especially Middle Eastern Arabs, Indians, and Pakistanis, as well as Europeans and Americans. In Qatar and UAE the immigrant work force far outnumbers the local population. It is the Christians among these expatriates who largely constitute the church in the Gulf, although there are a few local Christians in some areas. A wide range of confessional churches is represented: Orthodox, Catholic, Mar Thoma, Anglican, and various Protestant bodies; but in many instances congregations are ecumenical. Here, where local people observe Indian and Pakistani congregations meeting regularly and faithfully, Christianity is seen as an Asian religion. The freedom, or otherwise, of the church to worship openly varies in the different states. In some there are church buildings, in some not; and everywhere house groups are important. In general, open evangelism is not permitted, although in some areas the church is allowed to run schools, clinics, and hospitals. Throughout the Gulf a ministry is exercised through Family Bookshops.

In the southwest corner of the peninsula is the *Yemen Arab Republic* (North Yemen), the ancient biblical kingdom of Sheba. A relatively high rainfall and fertile soil mean good agricultural potential, but a large part of the work force is in oil-rich countries and sending home much needed money. The country has suffered civil war and intermittent warfare with neighboring South Yemen. Since the country's Jewish residents emigrated to Israel, the local population (9.3 million) has been 100% Muslim. At the invitation of the government, a number of Roman Catholic and Protestant bodies are assisting in clinics and hospitals, and Mother Teresa's Sisters of Charity have opened homes for the aged and helpless. Proselytization is not allowed.

The *Peoples' Democratic Republic of Yemen* (South Yemen) is a single-party Marxist state in which 99.5% of the population (2.3 million) are Muslim. There are tiny Hindu and Christian minorities. In 1973 all missionaries were expelled except one Catholic priest who remained to minister to the foreign community. Since then "he has presided over the church in Aden, maintaining a place for Christian worship, and a large heart to welcome Christians of any background."

The YAR/PDRY Yemen council, established in 1981 and scheduled to meet every six months, is working toward the reunification of Yemen.

Give thanks to God
for a Christian presence on the soil of this Peninsula; and
for all acts of mercy undertaken in the spirit of Jesus
that just as myrrh (traditionally believed to have come

from Salalah in Oman) was offered at Christ's epiphany, so the gifts and devotions of contemporary dwellers in the region are being offered to Christ.

O God, who by a star guided the wise men to the worship of your Son; we pray you to lead to yourself the wise and the great of every land, that unto you every knee may bow, and every thought be brought into captivity; through Jesus Christ our Lord.

Epiphany collect from the Church of South India, adapted

Call upon God
for all migrant workers in the Gulf and other parts of the Middle East
for Christian house groups, composed of many nationalities and allegiances, seeking to "sing the Lord's song in a strange land"
that Christians of the land may be encouraged and renewed
for today's "apostles" to the Arabian Peninsula—visiting bishops, itinerant pastors, and other enablers—who provide much-needed links with otherwise isolated congregations.

How often it happens that special destiny is given not to the great and complacent majorities, but to the little bands of people who never succeed so well as to be able to forget the Source of their strength and life.

Robert Brendon Betts
Christians in the Arab East

For all such we pray

We pray, O Father, for the land that nurtured the prophet Mohammed and for the people who follow his path. Guard them from the temptations of affluence; lead them into the ways of peace; and help them to see the fullness of your revelation in Jesus the Lord.

Iran

God protect this country from foe, famine, and falsehood.

2,000-year-old Persian prayer

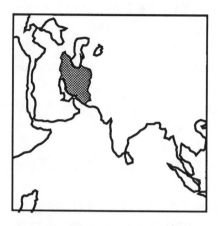

Population: 48.2 million

The Christian witness in Iran has been unbroken since the 3rd century, carried on mainly through the Assyrian Church of the East. At the turn of the 16th–17th centuries, Shah Abbas the Great invited Armenian craftsmen to beautify his capital city (Isfahan), thus introducing an Armenian community together with the Armenian church. Two-thirds of the Christians of contemporary Iran belong to these two ancient churches. Roman Catholic missionary orders came in the time of Shah Abbas, and again in the 19th century—along with Protestants and Anglicans.

Zoroastrianism was born in Iran in approximately the 6th century B.C.E., later becoming the state religion and a symbol of national and cultural identity. There is still a Zoroastrian minority. The Bahai faith also originated here. Bahais have been persecuted almost since the faith began, particularly so under the present regime.

Iran, formerly Persia, and with a long history of civilization, has experienced tragic turmoil in recent years. Since the Islamic fundamentalist revolution of 1979, many Iranians have left. "There is hardly a major city in the West in which there are not a great number of Iranian wanderers in search of a second home." In addition, the recent costly war with Iraq means that most families have lost a male relative. News of the church trickles out. Traditional missionary work is no longer possible, Christians are allowed to worship but sometimes meet with difficulties, and clergy cannot travel freely. "Priests these days are a very rare commodity. If one is found anywhere, even of a different denomination, demand on his time is enormous—very much like a medical doctor appearing in a place where they have had no doctor for a long time—patients won't leave him alone—like our Lord himself who sometimes could not get away from the crowds...."

Give thanks

that in the long history of Iran to the present time, there have always been men and women of faith, integrity, and courage ready to withstand both foe and falsehood even at the cost of their own lives

for the faithful life and worship of the ancient churches of Iran.

Thou who didst spread thy creating arms to the stars, strengthen our arms with power to intercede when we lift up our hands unto thee.

Armenian liturgy

O God, thou hast not endowed conscience with material force to compel from human beings a reluctant obedience. So grant them inwardly a spiritual compulsion, in which they will follow it out of choice and delight...O God, guide thy servants who have gone almost irretrievably astray. Thou art the Hearer and the Answerer.

City of Wrong, Kamil Hussein

We intercede
for the leaders of Iran and Iraq, that in the name of One who is most compassionate they may take steps to end the bitter conflict between them
for all who are victims of repression
for the church in Iran: "Our condition is very much like the condition of Peter," writes a group of Irani Christians, "when, with his eyes on Christ, he was able to walk on the water, but at other times would sink to the depths crying 'Lord, save me.'"

The cross of our Lord protect those who belong to Jesus and strengthen your hearts in faith to Christ in hardship and in ease, in life and in death, now and forever.

Blessing given by Simon, a Bishop of Iran
at the time of his martyrdom in 339 C.E.

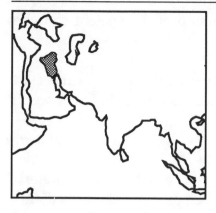

Iraq

Traditionally thought to contain the Garden of Eden, and certainly one of the oldest civilizations in the world, Iraq was laid waste by the Mongols in 1256 and was thereafter under some kind of foreign domination until achieving independence in 1932. Since the recent bitter conflict with Iran has drained the nation and drastically reduced oil exports, a potential source of wealth. Predominantly Arab, but with Kurdish and other minorities, this socialist republic allows religious freedom. Islam is the state religion and about 95% of the population of 14.2 million are Muslims.

Jewish communities in Mesopotamia were evangelized in the 1st century, traditionally by St. Thomas; and the church was later strengthened by the work of Assyrian missions. Islam increased in importance in the 7th century, but the church continued. In 1552, in consequence of an internal split, a large segment of the Assyrian Church became linked with Rome, and this Chaldean Catholic Church is today by far the largest Christian community in Iraq. There are other ancient churches of Mesopotamian origin. Roman Catholic missions date from the Crusades, and sustained Protestant work from this century.

Today's Christians number about half a million. Their participation as Iraqi nationals in the war effort has brought them greater acceptability, and they contribute in all areas of society.

Litany for Iraq

For lasting peace in this war-torn land—From you, O Lord.

For wisdom and compassion for all in authority—From you, O Lord.

For comfort for families separated or bereaved—From you, O Lord.

For the release of captives—From you, O Lord.

For refreshment for the weary and healing for the sick—From you, O Lord.

For continuing faithfulness of the ancient churches of this land—From you, O Lord.

For tenacity of spirit for small Christian groups—From you, O Lord.

For the mutual enrichment and support of those of different Christian traditions—From you, O Lord.

You, Lord of all, we confess;
You, Lord Jesus, we glorify;
For you are the life of our bodies
And you are the Savior of our souls.

The response in the litany and this hymn both come from the Chaldean liturgy. The ancient hymn celebrates Christ the source of resurrection in all situations of death and deprivation.

Week 3

Cyprus • Greece • Turkey

Lord, who through a vision to your servant John on Patmos revealed yourself amid the seven churches of Asia, encouraging, reproving, and challenging those first Christian communities; continue to walk, we beseech you, to this same end, amid today's churches in Cyprus, Greece, and Turkey; and grant that we all may be heedful of your presence and obedient to your commands. Amen.

To God be glory;
To the angels, honor;
To Satan, confusion;
To the cross, reverence;
To the church, exaltation;
To the departed, quickening;
To the penitent, acceptance;
To the sick and infirm, recovery and healing;
And to the four quarters of the world, great peace and tranquility;
And on us who are weak and sinful may the compassion and mercies of our God come, and may they overshadow us continually. Amen.

A prayer from the old Syriac,
used by Christians in Turkey, Iran, and South India

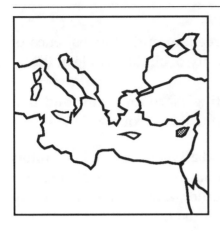

Cyprus

Population: Approximately 666,000, of whom 80% are Greek Cypriots and 19% Turkish Cypriots. Britons, Armenians, and others account for the rest.
Languages: Greek, Turkish, English, Armenian, Arabic, and others.
Government: Republic.
Religion: Christians 80%; Muslims 18.5%

The island is currently divided into Greek and Turkish sectors, with a United Nations peacekeeping force present. The British continue to maintain military bases on the island.

Greek colonies were established in Cyprus in the 2nd millennium B.C.E. Since then the island has had a troubled history, being occupied and ruled in turn by Romans, Byzantines, Arabs, Franks, Venetians, Ottomans, and the British. The people won their independence in 1960 after a five-year guerrilla war conducted by Greek Cypriots. Since independence there has been tension between the two Cypriot communities, and in 1963 the Turkish Cypriots ceased to participate in government. Following a coup inspired by the Greek military junta, the armed forces of Turkey occupied the northern sector in 1974; 200,000 Greek Cypriots and 55,000 Turkish Cypriots were displaced from their homes and the economy was devastated. A de facto partition has existed since then. In a unilateral declaration of independence, the Turkish Republic of Northern Cyprus was declared in 1983. Only Turkey has recognized this government.

Founded by the apostles Paul and Barnabas, the Eastern Orthodox Church of Cyprus, to which 96% of Christians on the island belong, has been officially recognized as autocephalous since the 5th century. Since Ottoman rule the archbishop has had considerable political significance as head of the nation. For ordinary people religion centers on home and family as well as liturgical and sacramental life, and local priests are close to their people. Family life here, as throughout the region, is a source of great stability. The fate of the refugees from the north constitutes a major concern of the church. The Armenian Apostolic Church has been represented here since the 11th century, and the Maronite Church since the Crusades. There are a number of small Protestant groups. Roman Catholics and Anglicans are mostly expatriate.

Cyprus today has become something of a meeting place for the Middle East. Numerous Christian organizations have opened headquarters here, and it provides a venue for regional meetings, as well as a haven for rest and refreshment. The tourist industry is considerable, bringing prosperity but also social problems. Arabic Christian literature is printed and stored here for distribution in neighboring countries.

We pray

for the restoration of the freedom and independence of Cyprus and for the peaceful unity of all the people of the island

that Cyprus will be a meeting place for many, and that the peace of God may flow out to other troubled lands.

O God of peace, good beyond all that is good, in whom is calmness and concord: Do thou make up the dissensions which divide us from one another, and bring us into unity of love in thee; through Jesus Christ our Lord.

Liturgy of St. Dionysius

In spite of the impression that the Middle East gives to the West of great instability, of being just about to break out into some great conflagration, underneath there is a great deal of stability, and many forces that pull together.

A bishop in Cyprus

We give thanks

for religion; for home and family life; for traditional values and all else that unites and stabilizes in the life of the people of Cyprus

for the haven this island provides for those of many nationalities.

We identify

with Orthodox Christians of Cyprus in giving thanks for St. Barnabas:

O Barnabas, who art equal unto the angels,[1] thy godly and blameless soul[2] dwelleth in the Jerusalem which is above[3] and thy body that bore much torment hath Cyprus for its earthly resting place, the which thou didst bring unto the faith. Thy spirit joyeth on high with the angels before the throne of the invisible God[4], delighting in the sweet

vision of his unassailable glory, thyself made godlike[5] in a union with the consubstantial Trinity: and below thy precious relics[6] spring forth health and cure;[7] and thy shrine is called "the place of healing," for as such hath it long endured through the often working of thy power. Wherefore, being united with us invisibly at this present time, watch over us in God from the heavenly height; and forasmuch as thou art tenderhearted, keep from us all wrath that is laid upon us for our sins; shield us from the crafts of the devil, and entreat that peace be upon us and great mercy.[8]

From the service to St. Barnabas the Apostle, founder of the Church of Cyprus; the work of Hilarion, Archbishop of Cyprus 1624–1682

1. Lk 20:36; 2. 1 Th 5:23; 3. Ga 4:26; 4. Rv 14:5; Col 1:15; 5. 2 P 1:4; Ps 82:6; Jn 10:34; 6. cf. 2 K 13:21; 7. Jr 33:6; 8. cf Ga 6:16

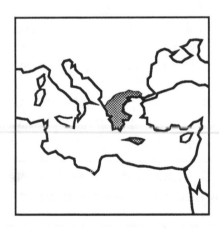

Greece

Population: 10 million, of whom 95% are ethnic Greeks; Turks are the largest indigenous minority.
Language: Greek.
Government: Parliamentary republic.
Religion: Christians 98%, of whom the vast majority are Greek Orthodox; Muslims 1.5%, a very small Jewish community.

St. Paul's obedience to his vision of the Macedonian urging him to "Come over...and help us" (Acts 16:9,10) marks the beginning of Christianity in this land. Then part of the Roman Empire, later under Ottoman rule for nearly 400 years, Greece fought in the 19th century for independence. The church took an active part in the struggle, and after liberation declared independence from the Ecumenical Patriarchate of Constantinople which was still under Ottoman rule. Autocephaly was officially recognized in 1850. In recent years, following German occupation, the country has suffered civil war and a period of rule by military juntas before the present parliamentary democracy became established in 1974.

The Greek Orthodox Church is the established religion of Greece, and has a profound influence in the nation. Monastic communities have played an important part in the spiritual life of the people, particularly the communities of Mount Athos which, in Byzantine times, was a great center of theological learning. The twenty monasteries, which re-

main under the jurisdiction of the Ecumenical Patriarchate, form a self-governing unit within the country.

The Catholic Church is represented by three different rites, of whom the Latins (the most numerous) have been here since the Crusades. The main Protestant body is the Greek Evangelical Church. Jehovah's Witnesses entered the country in 1900 and now have a relatively large following. There are strict rules about proselytization.

Apostolic Service, the church's organization for home missions, together with other movements, is active in evangelistic and educational work, and there are important theological faculties in Athens and Thessaloniki.

Kyrie eleison—Lord, have mercy.

In the English language "mercy" has a rather limited and constricting meaning. In Orthodox use, however, and according to its meaning in modern Greek, it has none of this narrowness, but conveys the sense of every good thing that God wills for creation.

For the land and people of Greece—Kyrie eleison.

For the authorities in church and state—Kyrie eleison.

For monastic communities, and especially those for women, which are growing today—Kyrie eleison.

For theologians and priests of the future, studying in theological schools and faculties—Kyrie eleison.

For all Orthodox parishes, priests, and people—Kyrie eleison.

For the activities of organizations and groups devoted to strengthening and deepening the spiritual life of the church—Kyrie eleison.

For the bond established by Greek Orthodox young people with their counterparts in North America, Western Europe and the Middle East—Kyrie eleison.

For the small Helleniké Evangeliké Ekklesia, its lay participation, and its Sunday School and youth movement—Kyrie eleison.

Lord Jesus Christ,
Son of the living God,
have mercy on me,
a sinner.

The constant rhythmic use of this prayer to Jesus originated in Sinai, but from the 10th century onward it has been practiced mainly at Mount Athos

Grant, O God, that the Christians of the Orthodox Church who preserved for the world the Jesus Prayer, may themselves live by that mercy and enjoy its fruits.

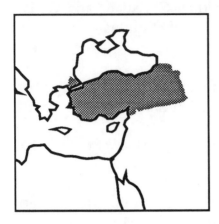

Turkey

Population: 50.7 million, of whom 80% are ethnic Turks. There are a number of other groups and some 600,000 Iranian refugees.
Language: Turkish.
Government: Republic.
Religion. Muslims 99%, Christians less than 0.5%.

Present-day Turkey incorporates the territory of much of Paul's missionary journeys and the Seven Churches of Revelation. The early ecumenical councils and the first serious divisions of the church took place in this region. Constantinople (Istanbul), capital of the Byzantine empire, was for many centuries one of the greatest centers of Christianity. From here missionary work extended in many directions. Muslim invasions and the establishment of the Ot-toman empire greatly reduced the number of Christians, but at the beginning of the first world war the population was still 20% Christian. The massacres and deportations of Armenians and Chaldeans, a massive exodus of survivors, and the forced exchange of Greek Orthodox Christians from Anatolia for Turkish Muslims from Greece have drastically reduced the Christian presence.

The Republic of Turkey was established in 1923, and a program of modernization begun. In spite of the large Muslim majority it became a secular state. Incidents of social disorder resulted in much loss of life, and periods of military rule have been repressive. Democratic government was reestablished in 1983, but the military still holds considerable power.

The principal centers of Christianity today are Istanbul and the southeastern part of the country, although there are scattered and isolated Christians in other areas, often without church or priest. Numerically the largest church family is the Oriental Orthodox—Armenian in Istanbul, and Syrian in the southeast. Of great significance is the Ecumenical Patriarchate of Constantinople which holds the highest honor for Eastern Orthodox Christians and was one of the first participants in the ecumenical movement. There are Catholic communities of five different rites, and the United Church Board for World Ministries (USA) is involved in educational and medical work.

We give thanks
for the continued presence of the Christian church in
Turkey, small as it now is
for the ways in which individual Christians and Christian-inspired organizations can be of stimulus and service
to the community.

Our thoughts rest for a few moments with them and we
pray that your love and compassion may sustain them always.

Week of Prayer for World Peace

We pray
for all depleted and fearful Christian communities, and
for courage and integrity for individual Christians.

for relationships between Christians and Muslims in Turkey

for our Muslim brethren who repeat your name of grace,
in their fasting, their praying, and their almsgiving with
faith and piety. Receive their worship and cause the light of
your Holy Spirit to shine upon them and illumine in their
hearts the way of love and redemption and peace,
To you we cry, O Lord.
Hear and have mercy.

Petition: Melkite rite

Week 4

Algeria • Libya • Morocco • Tunisia

Lord of the lovers of humankind,
who for your sake broke the alabaster box of life:
quicken your church today with the ardor of the saints,
so that by prayer and scholarship
by discipline and sacrifice,
your name may be made truly known.

Collect for Raymond Lull of Tunis:
Calendar of Middle East Saints

Lord, let me offer you in sacrifice the service of my thoughts
and my tongue, but first give me what I may offer you.

St. Augustine of Hippo, born 354 at Tagaste
in North Africa, died 430 in Hippo

Another day of sand and prayer. I tried to remember
some of the 99 names of God handed down to us by the tradition of Islam. And I wondered whether the 99 names revealed God or hid him. Perhaps they do both.

I recall some names I particularly like. God the Merciful,
the Compassionate, the Peaceful, the Faithful, the Tolerant.
But the one I like best is God the Patient.

Nevertheless, none of these names struck me as apposite
in my situation in the desert. I felt that yet another name
had to be added to the list: God the Difficult. In the desert I
was always wrestling with a difficult God.

Abu Hurayra affirms that whoever knows these 99 beautiful names of God will enter heaven. But I am inclined to
believe that the one who knows the hundredth name of
God is more likely to get there first. After all, the road that
leads to heaven is narrow and difficult.

Meditations on the Sand, Alessandro Pronzato

Give, O God, peace and harmony to the Islamic nations of North Africa. Strengthen in faith and witness the Christian minorities that live and work among them. And hasten the time when your Son may again be known in these ancient lands as Lord and Savior.

Once one of the most significant centers of Christianity in the Roman Empire, North Africa was the home of such early saints and scholars as Cyprian, Tertullian, and Augustine. The Mediterranean coastal plain of the region has been invaded and settled by Phoenicians, Romans, Vandals, Byzantines, Arabs, and Europeans successively, some of whom integrated the local population into their way of life. Many of the indigenous Berbers, however, remained nomadic pastoralists, carrying out frequent raids from the mountains and the desert beyond.

Christianity persisted on into the 6th century, but had begun to decline well before the Muslim invasion. Later Christian work, from the 13th century onward, has produced a number of martyrs, notably Raymond Lull (a lay Franciscan) and some of the early Missionaries of Africa. They were organized in Algeria in the 19th century to carry on missionary work throughout the rest of Africa.

Charles de Foucauld, whose dramatic conversion was prompted by his experience of observing Muslims at prayer, lived a hermit life among the Tuaregs. Protestant work dates from the 19th century. Radio programs and Bible correspondence courses operated from outside the area are features of contemporary evangelistic effort.

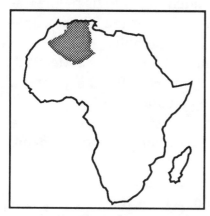

Algeria

Population: 20.5 million, of whom about 1.7 million are migrants in Europe.
Languages: Arabic, French, Berber.

Government: Single-party socialist republic.
Religion: Muslims 99.5%; Christians 0.3%.

Attached to France for just over a century, Algeria gained independence in 1962 after an 8-year war which left the country drained. However, in recent years it has experienced rapid industrialization and economic expansion. With few exceptions the Algerian people are Muslims.

The church is mainly composed of former French colonialists who stayed on, and Europeans and other expatriates working or living in the country, some of whom have taken Algerian nationality. The majority are Roman Catholics. Three Protestant bodies—the North Africa Mission (interdenominational), the

Methodist Church of the USA, and the Reformed Church—joined together in 1973 to form the Protestant Church in Algeria. There is also an Orthodox community. Although the Christian churches have no legal status and proselytization is forbidden, Muslim-Christian relationships are good and there is freedom to worship. Service to the community is a major emphasis of all the churches.

Following the death in 1916 of Charles de Foucauld in Tamantasset deep in the Algerian desert, others have continued to go to the Sahara to be a Christian presence similar to his. A more organized attempt to follow in his footsteps led to the founding in 1933 of the Little Sisters and Brothers of Jesus, who retain a link with Algeria and the Sahara but now locate their "desert" wherever the poorest, most helpless, and underprivileged of this earth are to be found.

Formerly an Italian colony, Libya was the scene of bitter fighting in the second world war, and was subsequently administered by France and Britain until 1951, when it became independent. Islam, the state religion, is regarded also as an ideological alternative to capitalism or communism, and thus has added significance for Libyan nationals.

The Christian church is almost entirely expatriate. A major confessional body is the Coptic Orthodox Church of Egypt. There are also Catholics (Eastern rite) and Orthodox from Greece and the Middle East, Presbyterians from Korea, and Roman Catholics, Anglicans, and other Protestants from various countries. Missionaries were not permitted entry after the 1969 revolution but in more recent years some Roman Catholic nursing sisters have been invited in. The very few local Christians are nurtured by informal means. Communication between expatriates and local people on matters of religion is difficult.

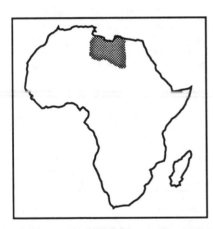

Libya

Population: 3.7 million.
Languages: Arabic; English and Italian are also spoken.
Government: Single-party socialist republic.
Religion: Muslims 98%, Christians 2%.

Morocco

Population: 20.5 million, including 164,000 inhabitants of Western Sahara.
Languages: Arabic, Berber, French, Spanish.

Government: Modified constitutional monarchy.
Religion: Muslims 99%. There are about 60,000 Christians and half that number of Jews.

After being divided into French and Spanish protectorates for nearly half a century, Morocco became independent in 1956. Islamization, among the Berbers also, has been profound in this area. Islam is the state religion. The exercise of monotheistic religions is guaranteed by the constitution. The fact that Christian leaders supported the move toward independence has created considerable good will toward the churches. All over the country Christian churches enjoy hospitality and respect which are traditional values in Morocco. A number of church-related and other Christian humanitarian organizations are working in areas of social service, health care, and development, and thus contribute in solidarity and mutual respect to the country's most urgent needs. The Moroccan Council of Christian Churches incorporates the Roman Catholic, Greek and Russian Orthodox, and Anglican churches, and the Evangelical (Reformed) Church of Morocco.

The disputed territory of *Western Sahara* (formerly Spanish Sahara) was ceded to Morocco (and Mauritania) in 1976. The claim of the *Sahrawi Arab Democratic Republic* for the territory is recognized by a number of countries. The proposal has been made for a referendum, and has to be worked out with the assistance of the United Nations.

Tunisia

Population: 7.3 million.
Languages: Arabic, Berber, French.
Government: Republic.
Religion: Muslims 99.5%. There are small Christian and Jewish minorities.

Formerly a French protectorate, Tunisia became independent in 1956. In spite of relative political stability, unemployment and a high rate of population increase have led to hardship, and there have been times of civil unrest. The people are renowned for their hospitality and the government for moderation in foreign relations.

The church today is small and almost entirely expatriate. Most Christians are Roman Catholics, but there are also Greek and Russian Orthodox churches, and a number of very small Protestant congregations. Missionaries are not allowed in the country, but the government shows tolerance to foreign religious minorities.

We give thanks

for the North African saints and scholars and hermits of the early centuries—Augustine and Monica, Tertullian and Cyprian—whose experience was also of a difficult and demanding God

for missionaries such as Raymond Lull, Archbishop La-
vigerie, and the Missionaries of Africa, Charles de Foucauld and all who have followed them; some in martyrdom, and others by patient presence in the deserts and
towns of North Africa

for all small Christian congregations in North Africa today who continue to bear these countries on their hearts
and in their intercessions.

My brother, bridge the Christian centuries
and touch us now.
Least calm of all the saints,
your white-hot African blood
not stilled by your conversion to the faith.

Ranging among Algerian hills you tasted all
our depth of self-despair
before you reached in middle-life
the calm of sin forgiven

We need your strength in our slow decadence
to understand
re-birth through pain and hope
and on this Gadarene hillside
the sovereignty of God.

A prayer in honor of St. Augustine of Hippo

We pray

for wisdom, integrity and compassion for the rulers of
these lands

for local Christians, often isolated, some able to meet in
small groups; that they may be faithful in the circumstances
in which they are set

for Christian expatriates of all nationalities in these different countries, and for the churches to which they belong

for a Christian-inspired consortium in Tunisia offering personnel for community service and development projects for the church's ministry through orphanages and homes for people with disabilities, the poor and the destitute

that the churches may mirror the proverbial hospitality of these lands, and may reach out to those who are lost and lonely

for the dialogue between Christians and Muslims being promoted in Tunis, and for all informal contact and conversation between Muslims and Christians.

Almighty God, whose Son our Savior Jesus taught us that to serve the least of his brethren is to serve him; we give you thanks that Simon from Africa was there to help Jesus our Lord to carry his cross, and we beseech you to grant us compassion like his and a ready willingness to serve the weak and helpless as though we were serving Jesus.

Collect for Simon of Cyrene; Calendar for Middle East Saints

"Islam...takes God with awful seriousness," writes Dr. Hendrik Kraemer. "Whoever has listened with his inmost being to the passionate call that vibrates through those well-known sentences: Allahu Akhbar (God is Great) and La Sharika Lahu (He has no associates), knows that Islam has religious tones of elemental power and quality. The apprehension of the naked majesty of God in Islam is simply unsurpassed...."

Almighty God, grant that we may listen with deep attention to those awesome words from the minarets of the Muslim world, and listening, hopefully gain a hearing for those other resonances of your divine nature embodied in the life and death and resurrection of Jesus Christ. Amen.

As the needle naturally turns to the north when it is touched by the magnet, so it is fitting, O Lord, that your servant should turn to love and praise and serve you; seeing that out of love for him you were willing to endure such grievous pangs and sufferings.

Prayer to Jesus by Raymond Lull,
stoned, Bugi, Algeria, 30 June 1315

Middle East Council of Churches

"The 12 million or so Christians in the region are today the heirs of rich Christian traditions, which by remaining indigenous to the areas where Christianity began, link the world church historically with its origins," wrote David Kerr.

A further link with this rich Christian tradition was established in 1974 when, on the inception of the Middle East Council of Churches, member churches of an earlier ecumenical body were joined by Oriental and Byzantine churches. Thus, with the inclusion also of the Church of Cyprus, and churches from Iran, the council ceased to be a forum only for the Arab churches, and began to reflect some of the richness and diversity of the whole Middle East. Its geographical area now stretches from Iran to Morocco and from Turkey to the Gulf. With its main office still in Beirut, but with regional offices in Egypt, Cyprus, and Bahrain, the MECC represents about 75% of the Christians of the region.

Over the years the principal concern of the MECC has been the continuity of Christian presence in this area, with renewal, the quest for Christian unity, and the pursuit of justice and peace as integral parts of that concern. Its program units and its related organizations concerned with theological education, with the study and observation of Middle East Christianity, and with the production and sale of literature, all stem from this same concern. A more wide-ranging brief is to facilitate the link between the world church and its origins through visits and prayer. "The solidarity we are seeking between our churches and churches everywhere," declares Gabriel Habib, MECC general secretary, "must mainly be manifested through prayer, with full awareness of the suffering and joy of the members of Christ's body, the church, to which we all belong..."

God bless the countries of the Middle East
Guard their children
Guide their leaders
Grant them peace with justice
for Jesus Christ's sake. Amen.

Week 5

Hong Kong • Macau • People's Republic of China • Taiwan

(The listing and description of the People's Republic of China and Taiwan in this way are done for the sake of convenience, acknowledging the present reality. This in no way reflects any policy of the WCC on issues related to China.)

Christ,
look upon us in this city
and keep our sympathy and pity fresh
and our faces heavenward
lest we grow hard.

These words of Thomas Ashe provide the inspiration
for St. Thomas' Clinic, Hong Kong

Heavenly Parent, as the miry bottom of the pond helps the lotus flower to grow, so may our often unlovely environment encourage growth in us. And as the lotus blossom in all its radiance rises above the mire, so help us to transcend our earthly environment to become heavenly personalities worthy to be called your children. Amen.

Prayer of a Chinese Christian

O God our Father,
we thank you for our daily bread. We thank you for the providence which has sustained this restless city where millions have found their home. The restlessness has sapped our strength, and oftentimes tempted our eyes toward the vulgarity of life. But we thank you for the hard-earned daily bread which sustains our bodies and our pride.

On the verge of rejoining China's mainstream destiny, we come to you with trembling hope and fearful joy.

Lord of the churches, make us one. Help us love one an-

other as you have loved us, so that all may come to know we are yours.

Lord of history, make us strong. Help us to live this day as if it is tomorrow, so that the past no longer binds the future.

May your will be done in this city. May you be pleased with this land and this people on which to build a concrete token of your kingdom.

In Jesus' name. Amen.

Raymond Fung, Hong Kong

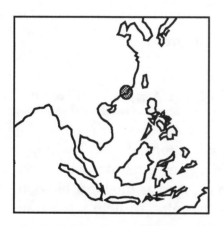

Hong Kong

With a population of 5.5 million, the British Crown Colony of Hong Kong has one of the highest population densities in the world, swollen even more by waves of refugees. It comprises Hong Kong island, Kowloon Peninsula, and the New Territories on the mainland. Chinese and English are the official languages, but Cantonese is widely spoken. The majority of people are Buddhists. Christians number about 8%, of whom just over half are Roman Catholics. There are many Protestant denominations. Christianity came to Hong Kong mainly from China, and acted as the social conscience, promoting educational and social services of every kind. Such work continues today on a scale unique in Asia.

In recent years Hong Kong has gone through a period of uncertainty and anxiety during which China and Britain negotiated the future of the territory. An agreement providing for the reversion of Hong Kong's sovereignty to China and turning it into a highly autonomous Special Administrative Region of the Peoples' Republic in 1997, was officially signed in December 1984 by the Chinese and British governments. The church fully supports this and is playing an active part in the drafting of the Basic Law and encouraging a new political awareness among the people. A source of comfort and encouragement, it looks for a spirituality to match its involvement in society. Searching for an authentic Chinese Christian identity some recall the earlier use of Chinese thought-forms, symbols, and practices. Others define their identity in much more contemporary Western terms and are actively committed to the use of the media as a stimulus to faith and a means of sharing it with others. Hong Kong has been described as "a place of baffling contradictions—anxiety and hope, insecurity and indomitable courage."

Give thanks

for the Sino-British Agreement about the future of Hong Kong

for the church's obedience to God's calling to be a servant people, especially during recent uncertainties

for the gifts of the Spirit constantly at work in the lives and affairs of Chinese people.

Pray

for the many refugees whose future continues to be uncertain

for those who work toward a new and suitable government structure in Hong Kong, and for the emerging political leadership

for those who work among the mass of the population especially in the field of civic education.

Pray for us, brothers and sisters in Christ,
that we may not fail in the oil of comfort,
the wine of justice, the involvement of the patient mule,
and the generosity which, having given, promises more,
until recovery is complete.

A plea from Hong Kong

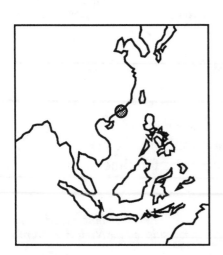

Macau

Population: Approximately 0.5 million (of whom 2–3,000 are Portuguese).
Languages: Portuguese, Cantonese, English, Burmese.
Government: Special territory under Portuguese jurisdiction.
Religion: Buddhists 66%; Christians 15% (mostly Roman Catholics, but with a small Protestant, mainly Baptist, community).

Lying opposite Hong Kong, and comprising a small hilly peninsula on the mainland and three nearby is-

lands, Macau was established by the Portuguese as a trading post with China in 1557. It was used as a stepping stone for missionaries entering China, notably the Jesuits, and later (1807) the Presbyterian Robert Morrison, who here had his vision of "millions who shall believe."

In 1976 Macau's status as an overseas province of Portugal was redefined, and in 1999 the territory is due to be transferred to the People's Republic of China. In recent years the population has been greatly swollen by refugees. Gambling, dog-racing, and the Macau Grand Prix are tourist attractions, facing the church with all the opportunities and problems innate to such a situation. From an early date the Roman Catholic church has played a major role in education. The churches remain active in education and social work, but numbers—certainly in the Protestant community—are steadily diminishing. Commenting on the return of the territory to China in 1999, and the consequent loss of government subsidies, the Roman Catholic bishop has declared that the church must become "more a church of the poor."

Give thanks to God
for Macau's long association with the Christian faith.

Pray
for the encouragement and renewal of the church.

God the Father,
the voice of John the Baptist challenges us to repentance
and points the way to Christ the Lord.
Open our ears to his message, and free our hearts
to turn from our sins and receive the life of the gospel.
We ask this through Christ our Lord.

Mass, Feast of St. John the Baptist,
Patron Saint of Macau, Roman Missal

People's Republic of China

We reverently worship
the mysterious Person, God the Father;
the responding Person, God the Son;
the witnessing Person, the Spirit of Holiness.
We worship the Holy Trinity
Three persons in one.

Ancient Chinese ascription,
used in worship by the Nestorian church

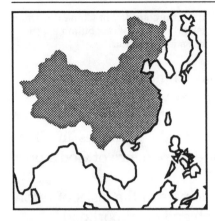

Population: 1 billion.
Languages: Putonghua, various local dialects, and languages of minority groups.
Government: Socialist republic.
Religion: Traditional religions and philosophies of China are Buddhism, Confucianism, and Taoism. Today many are atheists. There are significant Muslim and Christian communities.

Chinese civilization and culture has a continuous history of over 5,000 years. The last of the dynasties was overthrown and a republic established in 1911. Following a traumatic period of international and civil wars Communist forces took over in 1949 and the People's Republic was proclaimed.

Christianity entered China with the Nestorians in the 7th century, but disappeared after about 200 years. At the time of the Mongol occupation it appeared again temporarily, but it was not until sea routes were discovered in the 16th century that the Roman Catholic Church began to take root in China. The first Protestants arrived early in the 19th century when a considerable missionary impact followed the expansion of Western commercial and political interest.

With the establishment of the People's Republic, churches and institutions receiving foreign funds were registered at a government bureau, all foreign missionaries left or were expelled, and the Three-Self Movement (self-government, self-support, self-propagation) began to take root. The Cultural Revolution (1966–1976) led to the closure of all churches and theological colleges, and Christians as well as others suffered greatly. The church—like the grain of wheat—went underground.

Now new fruits are appearing. The government has adopted a policy of religious liberalization. The emerging church has developed an independence and discovered a sense of selfhood hitherto unknown. The Catholic Church continues to function apart from Rome. Among Protestants, united in the China Christian Council, denominational labels have ceased to be relevant. Local churches, while using a variety of liturgies, regard themselves as post-denominational churches. Structure and form, and pattern of ministry have yet to emerge, but the churches rejoice in using a new common hymnal. Church buildings are reopening. Many have been closed or used for other purposes for as long as thirty years; and the task of restoration, compensation, and negotiating their re-use demands much patience. The rebuilding of relationships, and more particularly the working out of the church's relationship within the world Christian community requires much sensitivity.

The Three-Self Movement provides a framework for Christians to participate with the government in the task of nation-building. "Christians need to care for the welfare of the people of the whole world..." says Bishop K.H. Ting, "it means for us caring for China, not exclusively but as our point of departure, the first stage in our love for humankind." In this period of rebuilding after the trauma of the Cultural Revolution, reconciliation and forgiveness, and selfless service to others are

dominant themes. "Although dynamic and growing," says Emilio Castro, following a visit, "the Christian church today in China is a small island in a sea of one billion people—but a joyful island."

Let us rejoice with present-day Chinese Christians

in their recovery of freedom to worship and to speak openly of their faith

that the historical experience of the churches in China has brought to Christians a wider experience of God's presence and activity

in their opportunities to participate in the tasks of reconciliation and rebuilding in nation and neighborhood.

Reconciliation is a theme that can speak to the mind and heart of the Chinese people. And reconciliation, we think, is *the* permanent theme of Christian theology.

Bishop K.H. Ting, Chairman of the China Christian Council and the Three-Self National Committee

Help each one of us, gracious God,
to live in such magnanimity and restraint
that the Head of the church
may never have cause to say of us:
This is my body, broken by you.

Prayer from China

Let us pray with Chinese Christians
at the local level

meeting for worship; some in church buildings, and many in homes and other meeting places

for all believers bearing witness to Christ in the places where they live and work

for the pastoral care and Christian nurture of growing congregations, and the faithful work of a largely elderly ministry

and more widely

for the work of the China Christian Council and the Chinese Protestant Three-Self Movement

for the theological training programs in Nanjing, Shanghai, Beijing, Hangzhou, and Fuzhou; for men and women in training, and for the establishment of an appropriate form of ministry

for efforts to relate theology to life and to make the Christian gospel understandable and acceptable in the New China

for the Amity Foundation for the promotion of education, health, and social work.

O God, teach us to be understanding friends
to our fellow Christians in China,
that endeavoring to sit where they sit
and to kneel where they kneel
we may share their vision and their hope.

God, creator of heaven and earth and giver of human life, we thank you for the witness to your truth, your goodness and your beauty which the long history of China has borne. We thank you for the church in China which is bearing witness to Christ in ways beyond our hopes. Strengthen ties that bind Christians together beyond national boundaries. Help us to accept the idea that all local churches are part of your church universal and are witnessing on its behalf and with its blessing. To the glory of Jesus Christ in whom all riches abide. Amen.

A contemporary prayer from China

Following the foundation of the People's Republic, and in response to what they describe as "secular revolutionary goodness," Chinese lay Christians have been challenged to re-examine their understanding of Christ and their expression of the Christian faith in China. Turning to St. John and the epistles to the Ephesians, Colossians, and Hebrews, they affirm the pre-existent, risen, ascended, upholding, and sustaining Christ "who liberates and enables us":

Now may the God of peace who brought again from the dead our Lord Jesus, the great shepherd of the sheep, by the blood of the eternal covenant; equip you with every-

thing good that you may do his will, working in you that which is pleasing in his sight, through Jesus Christ; to whom be glory forever and ever. Amen.

Hebrews 13:20-21

Taiwan

If the Lord is in prison with me,
what do I fear?
Lonely and solitary though I am,
  I believe
  I praise
  I give thanks.
If the Lord is in prison with me,
why do I grieve?
The Lord knows my trouble and pain,
to him I entrust my heart and my all,
  I believe
  I rejoice
  I sing.

Hsu T'ien Hsien

The biblical prayer most frequently used by leaders of the Presbyterian church in Taiwan on behalf of their president, his government and the whole people of Taiwan is that found in Micah 6:8:

You have shown us, O God, what is good.
Enable us, we pray,
  to act justly,
  to love mercy,
  and to walk humbly with you. Amen.

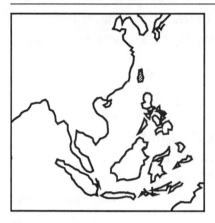

Population: 19.3 million.
Languages: Mandarin, Hoklo, Hakka, various tribal languages.
Government: Republic.
Religion: Chinese religions and philosophies are widely practiced. Christians 5% (Protestants—of whom the majority are Presbyterians—3.6%, Roman Catholic 1.4%); Muslims 0.5%.

Comprising one large and several smaller islands off the coast of the Chinese mainland, Taiwan is the second most densely populated country in the world. The original inhabitants—less than half a million—are considerably outnumbered by Hoklo and Hakka-speaking people who arrived from southeast China over the last four centuries. In 1949 Taiwan became the refuge of the Nationalist Chinese government, bringing in over 2 million Mandarin-speaking mainlanders. This Kuomintang regime has continued to dominate the local population ever since.

Roman Catholic priests arrived in Taiwan from South China in 1859. The Presbyterian church, established in the 1860s, is mainly a church of the original inhabitants and therefore of the rural areas and small towns. The years 1945–1960 saw the arrival of other Protestant churches, and considerable growth in the Chinese church in the cities. More recently there has been both a resurgence of Chinese religions, and a growing secularism, but the work of the Protestant churches has continued to grow in the rural and mountain areas in spite of an acute shortage of pastors. The Presbyterian church in particular has come into conflict with the government on major issues concerning human rights. Long prison sentences have been imposed on pastors and laypeople, whose courage and faithfulness must rank among the most challenging and inspiring of this century (see *Testimonies of Faith: Letters and Poems from Prison in Taiwan*).

Praise God
for the witness of the Presbyterian church in Taiwan in the struggle for freedom and justice for the people.

Pray
that the peoples' desire for their integrity, and for democracy in their state may be recognized
for the many who work under bad labor conditions
for aboriginal children lured into prostitution, and for all who strive for its prevention

that in the midst of much materialism the church may continue to speak to the deep needs of the people of Taiwan.

Gracious God,
let your will for Taiwan be known,
Hakka, Mainlander, Taiwanese, Tribal...
Let all be partners in shaping the future
with a faith that quarrels with the present
for the sake of what yet might be.

Prayer from Taiwan

Week 6

Democratic People's Republic of Korea • Japan • Republic of Korea

If I had not suffered,
I would not have known the love of God.

If many people had not suffered,
God's love would not have been passed on.

If Jesus had not suffered,
God's love would not have been made visible.

Mizuno Genzo, Japan

Japan

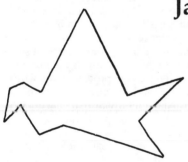

"I will write *peace* on your wings, and you will fly all over the world." Praying for peace for all victims of war as she folded paper cranes, these words were composed by Sadako Sasaki, child victim of atomic radiation in Hiroshima. They serve as a continuing stimulus to prayer for peace.

Lord, make us one as You are One.

Population: 120.3 million.
Language: Japanese.
Government: Parliamentary democracy, with constitutionally limited monarchy.
Religion: Buddhism, Shintoism, and Confucianism are the traditional religions and philosophies, and are often practiced together. Many syncretistic "new religions" have sprung up in recent years. Less than 1% of the population is Christian.

In history books Japan is an an-

cient country whose traditions reach back into the mists of mythology. Yet few countries belong so actively to the here-and-now of the modern world. In this hyperactive, industrialized, technological country 90% of the population regard themselves as middle class, a situation unique in Asia. Since mountains account for about 85% of the total land area, of which only 17% is arable, most people live in the cities.

Christianity was first brought to Japan in 1549 by Francis Xavier. At first the church grew rapidly, but later was outlawed, and hundreds of Christians were martyred. In spite of persecution the church survived in secret through more than two centuries of isolation (see Shusaku Endo's historical novel *Silence*) until Japan became open to foreign trade in the mid-19th century, and a process of modernization began. Many Catholic and Protestant missionaries entered the country. In 1861 Nicholas Kassathin, later canonized, established the Orthodox Church in Japan. In 1887 the Nippon Sei Ko Kai (Anglican Church) was formed by the uniting of three separate Episcopalian missions. The church again suffered during the second world war and was required to conform to the militaristic regime. In order to fulfill the requirements for recognition many Protestant groups joined together in 1941 to form the Nippon Kirisuto Kyodan (United Church of Christ in Japan).

At the end of the second world war the religious laws were abolished, and a number of bodies withdrew from the Kyodan which, however, remains the largest of the Protestant churches and seeks to work out its life and witness in the ecumenical context. Nearly half of Japan's Christians are Roman Catholic. Significant, albeit small in numbers (5,000), the Korean Christian Church in Japan ministers to the descendants of Koreans forcibly brought to Japan during the annexation of Korea between 1910–1945.

In addition to many social issues the Christian churches as well as other groups are concerned about the discriminatory practice of fingerprinting foreign residents, including the 800,000 Koreans who were born in Japan. The NCC of Japan has led a campaign against it. "As a Catholic I feel that fingerprints are given by God," says Kim Myong Shik. "They are beautiful. It is to defy the will of God to use them for purposes which are violent...This is the message and the prayer addressed by Jesus to me: this is why I personally refuse to be fingerprinted."

Confession of responsibility during the second world war is deeply felt by Japanese Christians and is embodied in a resolution, seeking the forgiveness of God and of all people, adopted by the Kyodan. "Indeed, even as our country committed sin, so we too as a church fell into the same sin. We neglected to perform our mission as a 'watchman.'" The importance given to the Yasukuni Shrine—a Shinto war memorial symbolic of Japan's pre-war militarism—has long been protested by Christians. Seen by many as a sign of increasing militaristic patriotism, it is interpreted as a threat to peace. Peace and the need for international cooperation are deeply felt concerns.

Starting the new day with a Japanese Christian

Try to read into this prayer some of the circumstances you know to apply to members of the Japanese Christian community who may use it. Nearly all of them start their new day and do their work in artificial light in the midst of city smog. Ask, therefore, what kind of renewal and freshness they seek from God; what kind of work they do (there is a high level of employment in Japan); what form of captivity it is that holds them, and what kind of justice and freedom they seek.

Eternal God,
we say good morning to you;
hallowed be your name.
Early in the morning, before we begin our work
we praise your glory.
Renew our bodies as fresh as the morning flowers.
Open our inner eyes, as the sun casts new light upon the
darkness
which prevailed over the night.
Deliver us from all captivity.
Give us wings of freedom like the birds in the sky,
to begin a new journey.
Restore justice and freedom, as a mighty stream
running continuously as day follows day.
We thank you for the gift of this morning,
and a new day to work with you.

Masao Takenaka, Japan

We remember
the witness for peace of Christians in Japan and the anxiety felt at signs of official endorsement of all that Yasukuni
Shrine symbolizes
the struggle against the practice of fingerprinting aliens

Lord, touch with your fingers those who are so de-
meaned,
and restore to them their proper dignity.

the work of Christian education in Japan
those with disability, and especially the hibakusha who
continue to survive and to suffer from atomic bomb exposure
the continuing presence of the cross of Christ in the lives
of Japanese people.

O God, we do not protest even if our life is destined to

lead to the cross, or if the way leads to our losing our lives. Teach us how to dispense with unnecessary things.

Toyohiko Kagawa

"Those who would pray for the Christian church in Japan might do worse than start with the yellow pages in the telephone directory," writes a recent visitor. "Some towns list as many as 150 different churches and religious groups. Just where would a potential inquirer make a start?"

Lord, bless the work of the national Christian Council of Churches in Japan, the Bible Society, all uniting and community churches, the Japanese Overseas Christian Medical Service, and all who in their work for unity seek to make sense of the prayer of Jesus that they all may be one. Amen.

Korea

O God,
you have made us glad
by those Koreans who,
by dying for you,
received a crown of glory.
Grant that through their example
our resolve may be strengthened
and our faith in you deepened.

Thanksgiving for Korean martyrs,
observed in Korea on September 20 or 26

The people of the Korean peninsula have a distinctive history and culture extending over 4,000 years. Formerly an independent kingdom, Korea was annexed by Japan early in this century, and remained under Japanese colonial rule until the end of the second world war when it was divided at the 38th parallel into military occupation zones with Soviet forces in the North and US forces in the South. North Koreans entered the South in 1950; and the ensuing 3-year war hardened attitudes and generated fear and suspicion. Today the Dem-

ocratic People's Republic of Korea (North) and the Republic of Korea (South) are divided by an impenetrable barrier of reinforced concrete across which, until recently, there has been virtually no communication.

Even though there had been several contacts with Christianity, the first missionary work was done in the 18th century by Koreans themselves, who in the course of official visits to China came into contact with Roman Catholic priests and Christian literature. In the 19th century Christians were persecuted by the government and many gave their lives. The country was closed to foreigners. Following a treaty with the USA the first Protestant missionary arrived in 1884. Others followed and the church grew. During the Japanese occupation the church again came under pressure. Imbued with the love of God Christians continued to witness to Jesus Christ and many joined the great company of Korean martyrs.

Democratic People's Republic of Korea

Population: 20.4 million.
Language: Korean.
Government: Unitary single-party republic.

Religion: Buddhism, Confucianism, Taoism, Shamanism, and Chundo Kyo (a syncretistic religion peculiar to Korea) are the traditional religions and philosophies. The number of Christians in unknown, but is estimated at about 10,000.

The constitution speaks of "religious liberty" but also of "liberty of anti-religious propaganda," and it seems likely that all religion is discouraged in this communist country. Many Christians fled to the South during the 1950–1953 war, and there has been little contact with those in the North since. The indications are that they are continuing to meet in house churches. "Christians in North Korea have been worshiping in the privacy of homes for over 30 years," writes Erich Weingärtner. "It has become a way of Christian life and witness. To forsake the intimacy of this experience in favor of a showcase edifice would be to forsake what links them to the early church of New Testament times."

What, then, shall we pray for them—unless we pray that prayer which has always stood Christians in good stead?

Our Father
Hallowed be your name, in Korea;
your kingdom come, in Korea;

your will be done, in Korea;

Give them today their daily bread, in Korea.

Deliver them from evil, in Korea.

For the kingdom, the power and the glory are yours, in Korea, now and forever. Amen.

Republic
of Korea

Population: 41.1 million.
Language: Korean.
Government: Republic, with power centered in the executive.
Religion: Buddhists 20%; Christians 21%, of whom 80% are Protestants. Confucianism and Chundo Kyo are also prevalent.

Since the bitter war of 1950–1953, South Korea has developed a flourishing capitalist economy, but a wide gap remains between rich and poor. In the face of what is felt to be a constant threat of invasion from the North, the government has been strongly autocratic, and a sizable American military presence remains. Christians opposing the government's oppressive policies have been dealt with harshly, but changes have occurred and greater moderation has been shown recently. There continues to be considerable political ferment and student unrest. On the other hand, the church in the cities continues to flourish and grow, with congregations numbering thousands. A number of Christians belonging to these congregations serve in parliament and in the armed forces, and also take an active part in evangelism. In recent years alongside a phenomenal growth of the Protestant community with a strong emphasis on Korean initiative, there have also been major splits in most of the large denominations and a proliferation of Christian groups.

"On Sunday morning in Seoul the number of Christians going in cars to their different churches is liable to cause a traffic jam."

We give thanks, O God, for the rapid growth of the church in Korea. We pray that zeal may be tempered with sensitivity and that numerical growth may be accompanied by spiritual deepening. May the divided Christian communities in Korea become one in faith and purpose, that they

may grow into a credible sign of that unity in love promised by Jesus to his followers.

We must not forget that today there are many people who
cannot come to the big evangelistic meetings. I mean those
workers who are laboring hard with beads of sweat; those
young boys and girls who are continually running, like rats;
those sick people who are living in the wood-and-tarpaper
shacks and wondering how to get their next meal; those who
are struggling to live with polluted air and water in rural and
fishing villages; and those who are poor, enviously watching
the luxurious life of the cats and dogs of the rich, despite
the fact that they themselves were born as human beings.

Rev. Park Hyung Kyu,
written shortly before one of his arrests.

O Christ, whose loving eyes see those we so often fail to
see, bless these your needy children in Korea.

North and South Korea are both interested in reunification, albeit each on its
own terms. Contact at government level has been sporadic and fraught with
difficulties. Significantly, a meeting was negotiated recently between Christians
from both sides who, in spite of ideological differences, were able to celebrate
the Lord's supper together, and to reaffirm the role Christians in their two
countries should play in breaking down barriers.

"The story is told of an aging South Korean pastor, who,
on his death, donated his eyes to a young person needing
sight. He wished his eyes to be able to see the reunification
of his homeland."

Lord, with Korean Christians, we pray for the unification
of their land, and the creation of a new, just, and peaceful
future. Amen.

Lord, thanks to you
the dividing wall of the temple is no longer a problem for
us,

but the separating walls which we continue to build
most certainly are.
So Lord,
whether we are in Berlin, Soweto,
Belfast, or on the 38th parallel,
or a member of an ordinary Christian congregation
somewhere,
putting up all the barriers common to human communities
the world over,
show us how we may begin instead to take them down.
Amen.

Lord, break down the walls that separate us
and unite us in a single body.

Chorus of the theme song;
Fifth Assembly of the WCC, Nairobi

Week 7

The Philippines

United through grace with all the members of your universal church, we offer you, Lord, our being, our working, our thinking, our feeling, our desiring; so that by these we may serve your greater glory.

Offering of the day: a prayer used in the Philippines

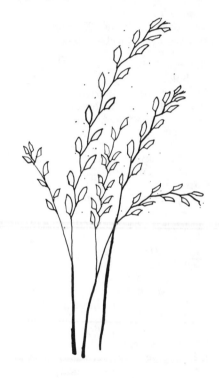

Often heavily laden with grains, sometimes bent over and broken, and so common a sight as to go almost unnoticed, the stalk of rice in the Philippines stands as a symbol for burden and struggle, and for all that satisfies and sustains. It symbolizes the potential richness of the land, which, because of maldistribution and the profitability of international trade, fails to reach the hands of the very poor who continue to struggle.

In every country in the world local Christians take what are often very well-known words and, praying them in their own particular situation, invest those words with new meaning for themselves and others. Such is the familiar affirmation used at every eucharist throughout the Philipines, said with special intention for their country and its people, and in which we are invited to join.

Your death, O Lord, we commemorate—Amen.
Your glory as our Risen Lord, we now celebrate—Amen.
Your return, as Lord in glory, together we await—Amen.

Acclamation as used by Filipino members
of Cursillos in Christianity

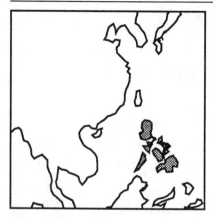

Population: 55 million.
Languages: Filipino, English, Spanish, and many local languages.
Government: Presidential republic.
Religion: Christians 95% (Roman Catholics 80.6%, Protestants 14%; there are 140 different denominations and sects); Muslims 4.3%, mostly in the south, and dating from the 14th century.

Made up of over 7,000 islands, many of them uninhabitable, the Philippine Republic is the only predominantly Christian country in Asia. Two-thirds of the population live on the islands of Luzon and Mindanao. The economy is mixed agricultural and industrial. There are extensive US military bases.

The Philippine Republic is "a young nation made up of old peoples" who lived in a large number of independent groups in the islands for something like 25,000 years before the advent of the Spanish in 1565. Some then retreated to the mountains and remain today as minority tribes. Revolution in 1896 resulted in freedom from Spain, but the country then found itself under United States rule. It was occupied by the Japanese from 1942–1945. Independence was gained in 1946.

Under the Spaniards, political and ecclesiastical domination went together, and within a hundred years the Spanish missionary orders had established the only Christian nation in Asia. Protestant missions became active around the turn of this century, and several of them formed the Evangelical Union to avoid duplication of work. Meanwhile, a desire for reform and nationalization within the Roman Catholic Church led to the formation of the Iglesia Filipina Independiente (Philippine Independent Church). A number of Protestant indigenous groups grew up, of which the Iglesia Ni Cristo is the fastest growing. In this century, the history of the church has been one of schism, union, and proliferation. The Council of Churches in the Philippines (NCCP) was formed in 1963, offering new possibilities for unity and cooperation.

Since independence the Filipino people have continued to experience exploitation, with large areas of peasant land appropriated by the government for "development" by large multinational companies, from which the poor do not benefit. In the mountains tribal minorities, both Christian and Muslim, have suffered steady encroachment of their lands. Resistance to domination of various kinds has been a continuing thread of Philippine history, and the churches are much involved in the struggle for justice and peace. Under the Marcos regime many people, including church leaders, were harassed and imprisoned. There are now a variety of people's organizations working for social change; and many facets of the women's movement, coordinated by GABRIELA, are strong.

In 1986, what began as an electoral exercise designed to shore up the sagging credibility of the martial law regime quickly became a democratic movement which resulted in a change of government, thus giving the people a new hope and a greater sense of unity. Much, however, remains to be done if a genuine democracy is to be realized. Land reform re-

mains a crucial issue. In the words of Dr. Edicio de la Torre: "The first half of the Magnificat has been fulfilled, and the mighty put down from their seats; but the lowly are not yet exalted." In this situation the church has an important role to fulfill. Dr. Feli-

ciano Cariño, general secretary of the NCCP, writes of a new political incarnation "requiring a renewed church that will be a companion in the making of a new society...living a spirituality of justice and freedom, rooted among the poor..."

In company with the church in the Philippines

we offer thanks for
all those who proclaim and work for the betterment of the whole person
signs of awakening in the church
the hope in Jesus Christ which sustains Filipino Christians.

We pray
that God's presence may continue to be felt in this changing period of Philippine history
that in days of economic stringency those who live in plenty may share with those who are without
for the struggle of women in the Philippines against sex tourism
for courage as Christians continue to involve themselves in the struggle for justice, peace, truth, and freedom.

As you anointed kings and called prophets of old, lead us to recognize our true representatives and authentic leaders: men and women
who love your people and can walk with them
who feel their pain and share their joys,
who dream their dreams
and strive to accompany them to their common goal.

In your fire—with your spirit—
embolden and commission us
to transform our political system,

to serve your people
and to bring real glory to your name. Amen.

Prayer from the Philippines

We pray that we may be truly sensitive to the poverty and oppression around us, of the marginalized of our society—the poor peasants, the poor estate and city workers, shanty-dwellers, unemployed youth, exploited women and children, depressed classes, ethnic minorities; of those repressed, imprisoned and put to death in the struggle for democratic and human rights—Lord, hear us.

We call on you to succor them and to show us how we may participate in their struggle for justice, as co-workers together with Jesus, the servant Lord—Lord, hear us.

We pray for true spiritual resources necessary for these tasks. We pray for a true awareness of the corruptible forces and influences in our society and in ourselves, and for trust in your grace and strength in building a new spirituality for our times—Lord, hear us. Amen.

Prayers for Asia Sunday; the Christian Conference of Asia,
of which many Philippine churches are members

Week 8

Brunei • Malaysia • Singapore

May the peaceful nature of multi-racialism in our lands grow into a Christ-like family; we ask in the name of Jesus, the Elder Brother.

Prayer of a Malaysian Christian

O God of many names
Lover of all nations
We pray for peace
   in our hearts
   in our homes
   in our nations
   in our world
the peace of your will
the peace of our need.

Week of Prayer for World Peace

In the brightness of your Son
we spend each day;
in the darkness of the night
you light our way;
always you protect us
with the umbrella of your love.
To you, God, be all praise
and glory forever and forever.

Opening recollection and benediction,
from Christian Conference of Asia resource
for Delhi 1984 Asia Youth Assembly

The population of these nations is multi-racial and multi-faith. Muslims form the largest religious group overall, but are outnumbered by Buddhists and Taoists in Singapore. There are appreciable Christian and Hindu communities. The indigenous people are Malays, who are almost all Muslim, and other tribal races in Sarawak and Sabah (formerly North Borneo). Chinese from

southeast China have migrated to the area over the centuries, and are usually Buddhists or adherents of Chinese folk religion (syncretistic), although a considerable number are Christian. There are significant Indian (mostly Hindu) and Pakistani (Muslim) communities—also Eurasian and European groups. The latter, as well as some Indians and Pakistanis, are Christians.

Christianity was brought to the region by colonialists: the Portuguese in the 16th century and the Dutch in the 17th. Areas were later annexed piecemeal by the British, and the East India Company appointed chaplains in Malaya and Singapore. Other Protestant churches were introduced, initially ministering to European congregations, but later working also among the Chinese. Methodism came from the United States and Britain, and is now the largest Protestant church in Malaysia and Singapore.

Europeans. Malay and English are official languages. The Christian church is small and confined to the Chinese and expatriate population. Evangelism is not permitted, but existing churches are allowed freedom of worship.

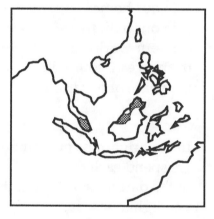

Brunei

The Sultanate of Brunei is a traditional Islamic monarchy. Formerly it consisted of most of the coastal region of the island of North Borneo, but in the 19th century its rulers ceded large areas to the United Kingdom. In 1888 it became a British protected state, and was invaded by the Japanese during the second world war. The Sultan decided not to join the Malaysian Federation in 1963, and Brunei attained internal self-government in 1971 and full independence in 1984.

The majority of the population of 200,000 are Muslim Malays, and Islam is the official religion. Other indigenous races are mostly animist. The second largest group are the Chinese and there are some Indians and

Malaysia

The Federation of Malaysia consists of 13 states, 11 on the Malayan peninsula (West Malaysia) and two, Sarawak and Sabah (East Malaysia), on the north coast of Borneo. All have a colonial history. The 11 peninsular states united under British protection, becoming the Federation of Malaya in 1948, and achieving independence in 1957. The Federation of Malaysia came into being in 1963.

The population of 14.5 million is

multi-racial, and proportions vary in different areas. In West Malaysia approximately 55% are Malays who are all Muslims, and about 34% are Chinese. The remainder are Indians (9%), Pakistanis, Eurasians, and Europeans. In Sarawak and Sabah, other indigenous races and Chinese predominate over the Malays. The country received many refugees from Indochina, especially Vietnam, some of whom have been resettled elsewhere. The official language is Malay, but others are widely spoken.

With such a racial and religious mix, it is not surprising that there have been tensions and even riots in the past; nor that today, although tolerance and accommodation prevail, life is influenced by political and communal decisions made along racial lines. Terrorist activity by communist insurgents was a problem in the later 1970s, and is still perceived as a potential threat.

As in some other parts of the world, a revival of Islamic fundamentalism has challenged the government to be more overtly Islamic in its policies. As a result, an interfaith organization representing Buddhists, Christians, Hindus, and Sikhs, and the Christian Federation of Malaysia (made up of Roman Catholic and evangelical churches as well as the Council of Churches of Malaysia) have emerged as watchdogs to protect the rights of minority religions. Islam is the state religion, and evangelism among Muslims is not permitted. In West Malaysia, Christians number about 7%, with three and four times that in Sabah and Sarawak where there has been considerable outreach among the tribal peoples. The church is increasingly aware of its moral responsibility to address issues like racial polarization and the disparity between rich and poor. Individual churches are steadily growing, but ecumenical activity is hampered by the use of so many different languages.

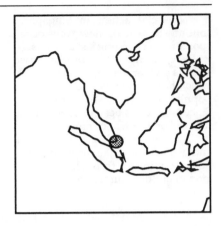

Singapore

The Republic of Singapore, with its mixed population of 2.5 million, has one of the highest per capita incomes in Asia. Natural resources are limited and the country relies on imports, but it is a thriving center of international trade. In the colonial era it was linked with Malaya, and became part of the Federation of Malaysia in 1963, but separated two years later to become a fully independent country. It has enjoyed considerable political stability. Chinese (Mandarin), English, Malay, and Tamil are official languages.

About one quarter of the population is Buddhist, and another quarter practices Chinese folk religions. There are appreciable Muslim, Christian, and Hindu minorities, and some who profess no religion at all. Christians number about 12%, of whom nearly half are Roman Catholics.

In this highly entrepreneurial society the pressure to succeed pushes some to the breaking point. With every third person under 15, schools are overflowing and competition is keen. The social cost of high-rise, high-density living is making itself felt and there are many who live in poverty. The churches, which pio-

neered social action in Singapore, continue to develop new ways of responding to changing social needs.

Here, at the heart of Southeast Asia, is a vigorously growing church which has risen from 2 to 12% of the population in the last twenty years. Since 1972 it has been experiencing a renewal of its life and ministry. Trinity Theological College trains men and women of different denominations for ministry throughout the region in multi-cultural societies.

According to the Christian Conference of Asia, Christians of this region are being called to act upon their prayer and to speak courageous words and perform courageous deeds in all places where there is injustice and oppression, and the pressure of materialism. It is for doing precisely this that the CCA was asked to leave Singapore.

We identify with Christians in Malaysia in seeking to build a church in which all races may feel at home—Lord, turn our thought into a blessing.

We warm to the apostolic style of ministry exercised among tribal people in Sabah, and respond to their request to "give thanks to God for the Christian joy that is never exhausted, even when living through troubled times and dealing with difficult people"—Lord, turn our thought into a blessing.

We sit with Singaporean Christians to hear afresh the story of Jesus' synagogue sermon; to rejoice where charismatic gifts have been truly experienced; and to pray with them for a spirit of questioning, disquiet, and boldness at all that falls short of being good news for the poor, the needy, the prisoner, and the oppressed—Lord, turn our thought into a blessing.

We remember men and women being trained for the ministry in the region and visualize the different situations in which they will serve—Lord, turn our thought into a blessing.

We think of young people under such heavy pressure to succeed and, with many of them crowding into various Christian fellowships, offering enormous potential for Christian discipleship—Lord, turn our thought into a blessing.

Just call me by my name is the prayer of many young people in today's Singapore and Malaysia:

Thank you, Father, for your blessing upon this land: for peace, for freedom from natural calamities; for stability of government; for tolerance between races; for freedom of worship; for rich resources beneath the soil and in the sea. But Father, prevent your children from becoming fat and lazy, and content to meet needs that do not call for much sacrifice. Help your churches to bring the good news to the poor, and to be touched by those who sit in the darkness of sin.

Prayer of a leading Chinese Christian businessman in Malaysia

Week 9

Denmark • Finland • Iceland • Norway • Sweden

Destroy, O Lord, the spirit of self-seeking in individuals and nations. Give to the peoples and their leaders thoughts of peace and reconciliation. For you, O Lord, can find a way where human beings know not what to do.

Prayer from Sweden

Nine "prayer strokes," three times three on the largest bell, signify the beginning of Sunday service in Denmark, followed by this prayer said together:

O Lord, I have come into your house to hear what
You, God, my Creator,
You, Lord Jesus, my Savior,
You, Good Holy Spirit, my Comforter in life and death
will speak to me....

Father in heaven
in the evening when we prepare to go to sleep, we are consoled by the thought that you are the one who watches over us—and yet, what a desolation if you were not present and watching over us when we wake up in the morning and remain awake during the day. The distinction that we make between sleep and waking is an artificial one, as if we needed your wakefulness only as long as we are asleep, but not when we ourselves are awake.

The Prayers of Sören Kierkegaard, 1813–1855

O God, our Father and Mother,
we confess today that your own sons and daughters in
Christ have let you down.
Dominated by our fears, we have trampled and smothered one another.
We have smothered the tenderness of man and the creative thinking of woman.

Help women to discover honest and life-giving
sisterhood.
Help men to open their hearts to each other
in true brotherhood.
Help us to create a community of brothers and sisters
where we can live with each other in creative community
man with man, woman with woman,
man with woman....

Help us to share with each other our pain and joy,
our fears and hope.
Save us from chilliness and distance,
from teaching without life,
from seeking prestige and struggling for power.

We pray for those who hesitate to confess your name.
You know them and their secret longing.
Do not let your sinful church and its fearful followers
hinder them in their seeking for you.

Taken from a prayer by
Kerstin Lindqvist and Ulla Bardh, Sweden

Population, language, and government

Denmark: 5.1 million; Danish.

Finland: 4.9 million; Finnish, Swedish, Lappish.

Iceland: 242,000; Icelandic.

Norway: 4.2 million; Norwegian, Finnish, Lappish.

Sweden: 8.4 million; Swedish, Finnish, Lappish.

Denmark, Norway, and Sweden are constitutional monarchies; Finland and Iceland are parliamentary republics.

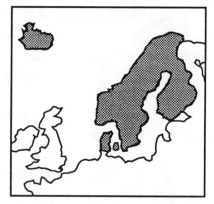

These five countries have close historical, cultural, and confessional ties and all are now joined in the Nordic Council founded in 1952. The Lutheran Church is the major religious body throughout the region.

The Christian message was brought to the Nordic countries from three directions. It was carried into Norway, Denmark, and Sweden from the British Isles and from Germany. Best known of the apostles to the Scandinavian countries are Ansgar, later Archbishop of Hamburg/Bremen, and the English Bishop Henrik. The latter, accompanying the Swedish king, also carried the gospel into Finland. At the same time, Orthodox Christianity was extending from Russia. Except in Karelia (the easternmost province of Finland) the Western tradition prevailed. Bishop Henrik, eventually martyred, became the patron saint of Finland. Women played an important part in spreading the faith, notably in Iceland in the 9th and 10th centuries. Christianity had spread throughout all these countries by the end of the 12th century.

The Reformation reached northern Europe by various means, and on the whole proceeded without violence, former Catholic dioceses quietly becoming Lutheran. During the 16th and 17th centuries devastating wars between Sweden and Russia brought severe persecution to the Orthodox in Karelia, many of whom fled to Russia. During the 20th century the Nordic churches have been influential in the development of ecumenism. Particularly important was the work of Archbishop Nathan Söderblom of Uppsala in the Life and Work movement.

In an area where East and West still meet, the need for disarmament and detente is felt acutely. Although their foreign policies diverge, these countries are concerted in their efforts to promote worldwide justice and international peace.

More than 90% of the people nominally belong to the Lutheran folk churches, although, with variations from place to place, relatively few attend church regularly or take part in church activities. Secularization is widespread, and in Denmark and Sweden the number of children baptized has fallen drastically, especially in the cities. The provision of Christian education for both adults and children has become an urgent necessity. In all these countries discussion is proceeding about the traditional relationship between the state and the (Lutheran) church. This could eventually lead to disestablishment. The Pentecostal movement has considerable influence, many people being active in this and the Lutheran church. In Finland and Sweden the Orthodox church, although numerically small (about 1.5%), is widespread; in Finland it is recognized as a national church.

In Denmark and Sweden especially, recent immigrations of foreign workers have brought members of other faiths; and there are considerable numbers of

Turkish Muslims in Finland. The problem of refugees is a burning issue in all these countries. Small Jewish communities have been established throughout the region for centuries. In Iceland the reintroduction of traditional Norse pre-Christian religion has gained a small following.

In *Denmark*, where the bond between church and culture is close, the Lutheran church embraces many different, sometimes opposing groups. Voluntary organization and missions within the church promote renewal and outreach. Sharing in the region's long tradition of humanitarian concern on peace themes and human rights, Denmark recently opened the world's first-ever treatment clinic for the victims of torture. In Greenland, Denmark's self-governing Arctic colony, 50% of the sparse population is Christian, nearly all Lutheran. Catechists primarily care for these scattered groups.

Although the church in *Finland* is not directly involved in political activity, parishes are independently active in a range of socioethical issues. Among a number of Christians there is a growing concern that the privileges and benefits of life in their country may be shared with the deprived and dispossessed of other lands. As a result of the cession of Karelia to the USSR, the entire population moved in 1944. Orthodox Christians (of whom 75% lived in Karelia) thus became spread throughout the country.

In *Iceland* the movement of people into the capital, and the inability of many diminished rural congregations to support a pastor, have called for new ways of working. With the whole island a single diocese and 97% of the people Lutheran, the church is looking anew at its role in society. This small church has, since the second world war, undertaken missionary work in Africa, and contributed generously to development projects overseas.

In *Norway* the church's involvement in sociopolitical issues stems from its wartime experience. Because the country is so mountainous and people scattered, habitual church attendance has never been widespread, and the church faces a shortage of pastors. However, membership and belief are strong and religious broadcasts provide a much-needed service. Voluntary organizations and lay movements have sprung up, and many Norwegian missionaries serve overseas.

In *Sweden* the Free churches account for 10% of the population, and as a result of the influx of refugees and foreign workers there is an appreciable Orthodox community. In this country, with its exceptionally high standard of living, many church people are expressing in positive action a new sense of responsibility for those in the third world, and the country's longstanding concern for peace is well known.

Ecumenical awareness and cooperation are growing, and the Roman Catholic Church is a member of the three national ecumenical councils of Denmark, Finland, and Sweden. In Iceland, an interdenominational committee including Roman Catholics and Pentecostals organizes the Week of Prayer for Christian Unity. The ecumenical climate in Norway is changing, and there is now a forum for dialogue on theological matters.

While for many Nordic Christians today the way of holiness lies through personal piety and devotion, for others a truly contemporary spirituality involves active involvement in the struggles and needs of the world. For some people the appeal of Orthodoxy lies in its facility for uniting these and other dimensions of the Christian faith in a single whole. This diverse spiritual quest is the key to the prayers that follow.

We thank God

for the Christian church in these lands, for the rich and varied Lutheran heritage, and for the saints, missionaries, and ascetics of the Orthodox church

for the invigorating contribution of minority churches

for the spiritual intensity and depth brought by movements of revival and renewal

for the work of missionaries from northern Europe in other lands

for all movements concerned to protect the environment.

We pray God

for these countries, that they may share not only their material goods but also spiritual gifts in solidarity with people inside and outside northern Europe

for Christian education in an increasingly secularized consumer society

for the strengthening and growth of trusting and sustaining relationships within families and between generations

that Christ's people may continue to fulfill their mission and service to the world, especially in their efforts for disarmament and detente

for a creative response on the part of the churches to changing conditions; and a willingness to enter into new relationships with state and society

for more ecumenical openness and cooperation locally, nationally, and internationally.

Pray

with and for the people of Iceland as they prepare to commemorate one thousand years of Christianity in the year 2000:

God, grant that in my mother tongue
Thy gospel may be sounded,

To rich and poor, to old and young,
Its blessings be expounded,
Over vale and glen
By lip and pen,
To each remotest dwelling,
While Thy strong hand
Safeguards our land,
Dangers and foes repelling.

Regarded as among the public treasures of the Icelandic people, the 200-year-old passion hymns of Hallgrimur Petersson are commonly read aloud in homes during Lent, and recited on state radio after the evening news.

Affirming that for Orthodox "knowledge and faith belong to the one wholeness of God," the Finnish Orthodox church offers this prayer, used in the blessing of their newly installed computer in the monastery of New Valamo, and which may be adapted for the blessing of computers anywhere:

Lord our God, who taught wisdom to Solomon, and who by sending your All-Holy Spirit made the fishermen your disciples and proclaimers of your Gospel, you who by your word, make light to shine in darkness; grant that the work done with this computer may be to your glory, and lead to the benefit of your church and to blessing for this holy monastery.

Lord, you who are the guide into wisdom, giver of understanding, teacher of the ignorant and refuge of the poor; sanctify and bless computers which you have inspired people to create. Grant that they may be used to promote truth. Grant that they may serve the unity of humankind, and the sanctification of life, peace, and justice. Amen.

In the towns of Finland an increasing number of families, having become disenchanted with apartment living, are getting together with friends and relatives to build their own houses, thus giving rise to occasions when the blessing of God is sought upon home and family life:

Heavenly Father, we thank you that in the building of this home many hopes and aspirations have been fulfilled.

We thank you for hard work and tiredness, for protection and rest, and for all the people who have helped in this work.

Come and be the Master of our homes so that family members may grow up as your children in mutual confidence and love. Grant that the homes of our land may be places of rest and relaxation for their members as well as those who visit.

The New Lutheran Manual, adapted

Lord, we bring you thanks for the care and attention you gave to women when you lived among us. We thank you for your solidarity with them, for returning human dignity to women and for inviting them to service.

Lord, we pray:

for women, who are victims of war, or refugees, or left behind alone with their children

for women living in poverty, not having food and other necessities for themselves and the ones they love

for women without education and employment, women who suffer from their economic dependency

for children and young girls exploited like slaves for their labor

for women despised and used for prostitution and pornography

for women who are victims of drugs and alcohol

for women living in oppressive cultures and systems

for women subject to violence and abuse in their own homes.

Lord, help them and give them strength and courage in their struggle for better lives.

Lord, help all of us to show the same solidarity and care as you, help us to persist in the struggle so that your kingdom may come to every person. Amen.

This prayer for solidarity with women
is taken from a prayer used on the Norwegian radio,
March 6, 1987.

God, our Creator,

as we join the large spectrum of Christians in different churches who are praying for refugees,

we realize that we are, in fact, asking for changes in our own society.

We pray for politicians,

that they may be willing to share the prosperity of our country with all people—not only with their own citizens.

Send to them someone who will give a name and a human face to the refugee problem, and thus show them the inhumanity of the legislation.

We pray for journalists and others who work in the media, and thus influence public opinion.

Send into their experience events which will safeguard them from cynicism and invite them to use their capacities to generate a friendlier atmosphere toward refugees.

We pray for the police and immigration officers at our airports, who exercise power over the lives of people— often without a real knowledge of their situation.

Send into their lives people who are able to help them understand the reality of the asylum seekers.

We pray for ordinary citizens in our country,

that we may not be naive or indifferent, but join those who are working to alleviate the lot of refugees.

God, our Creator, have mercy on us
we who are acting as if freedom, peace and the well-being of our country were meant for our benefit alone.

God, our Creator, help us to become changed people, and to change our attitudes, as well as our legislation. Amen.

Prayer from Finland

Week 10

Republic of Ireland • United Kingdom

O Holy Spirit, giver of light and life,
free us from all that is matter-of-fact, stale, bored, tired;
all that takes things for granted.
Open our eyes to see and excite our minds to marvel.

After a prayer by Monica Furlong

Lord Jesus Christ, you are the way of peace.
Come into the brokenness of our lives and our land with
your healing love.
Help us to be willing to bow before you in true repentance,
and to bow to one another in real forgiveness.
By the fire of your Holy Spirit, melt our hard hearts and
consume the pride and prejudice which separate us.
Fill us, O Lord, with your perfect love which casts out
fear and bind us together in that unity which you share
with the Father and the Holy Spirit.

Emerging out of the movement of charismatic renewal,
this prayer is used in both the Republic and Northern Ireland.
Unity, the newsletter of the Irish School of Ecumenics.

We are tired, Lord,
weary of the long night without rest.
We grow complaining and bitter.
We sorrow for ourselves
as we grow hardened to the pain of others.
Another death leaves us unmoved.
A widow's tears fall unnoticed.
Our children know only the bitterness
already possessing their parents.
Our violent words

explode into violent acts
by the hands of youth
bringing destruction without thought or reason.
Lord, have mercy upon us.
Lead us to repentance that we may forgive
and be forgiven. Amen.

Presbyterian minister, Northern Ireland

God our Mother and Father, we come to you as children. Be with us as we learn to see one another with new eyes, hear one another with new hearts, and treat one another in a new way. Amen.

Corrymeela community

Republic of Ireland

Population: 3.6 million.
Languages: Irish, English.
Government: Unitary multi-party republic.
Religion: Christians 99.5% (Roman Catholics 94%, Anglicans 3%, Presbyterians, Methodists, and others).

Although Christianity first appeared in these islands around 2000 C.E., during the Roman occupation, its spread was uneven over the next 500 years, and owes much to the missionary work of many saints of both the Celtic and Roman traditions. Both of these strands have continued to contribute to the spirituality of these lands to this day.

From the 12th century until the 20th, Anglo-Irish relations have fluctuated through varying degrees of discord, perceived by many as centuries of English oppression. During this period the Church of England was imposed as state religion upon Ireland; and Scottish and English "planters," mostly Presbyterians and Anglicans, were introduced into Ulster (Northern Ireland) in order to settle this area under English control. Ireland became part of the United Kingdom in 1801. The 26 southern counties obtained full independent sovereignty in 1937, the six northern counties remaining part of the United Kingdom. This partition of Ireland has resulted in much bitterness and bloodshed affecting both the Republic and the United Kingdom, the worst impact being felt in Northern Ireland.

The Irish Roman Catholic Church has great importance overseas, partly as a result of large-scale emigrations, and partly because of the country's

remarkable missionary contribution. Despite its strongly traditional character it is increasingly participating in ecumenical ventures. In the Irish Interchurch Meeting, Roman Catholics and Protestants are deeply committed in an ongoing initiative with permanent working departments on theological questions and social issues. The Irish School of Ecumenics is sponsored by the Anglican, Methodist, Presbyterian, and Catholic churches. The Irish Council of Churches, established in Belfast in 1922, serves both the Republic and Northern Ireland, and in the Republic includes the Anglican and six Protestant churches. In both North and South, matters of justice and peace, as well as social problems, are being increasingly handled on an ecumenical basis, and the charismatic movement is bringing some Catholics and Protestants together in a new way. Most of the recently formed Christian women's groups recruit members without reference to denomination, thus contributing to understanding and fellowship. Women play an increasingly active role in the life of all the churches, pastorally, liturgically, and administratively.

Of course, the traditional Catholicism of Ireland has its own immense strengths. With a long tradition of reverence for holy places and holy people, and a strong emphasis on the family and the Christian education of children, this church retains the loyalty and active participation of its members both at home and abroad. They have a reputation for homely and practical piety, and speak easily of their faith.

We pray

for all ecumenical initiatives and all occasions which bring together Christians of different traditions

for the people of Ireland, for Irish missionaries, and those many other Irish men and women living and working overseas.

Three things are of the Evil One:
　　an evil eye;
　　an evil tongue;
　　an evil mind.

Three things are of God,
and these three are what Mary told her Son,
for she heard them in heaven:
　　the merciful word,
　　the singing word,
　　and the good word.

May the power of these three holy things
be on all men and women of Erin for evermore. Amen.

15th-century Irish benediction

United Kingdom

Population: 56.7 million.
Languages: English, Welsh, Gaelic, and various languages of immigrant communities.
Government: Parliamentary constitutional monarchy.
Religion: The majority count themselves Christian, but there are significant numbers of Muslims, Jews, Hindus, Sikhs, Buddhists, and others.

Waves of invasion in times past have resulted in a considerable mixing of peoples in Great Britain, although the Celtic groups to the west have been better able to retain their original identity and languages. Britain's history as a colonial power has resulted in a more recent influx of immigrants from many parts of the world.

The figures, 7 million adult church members (of whom approximately 2.3 million are Roman Catholics, 2.1 million Anglicans, 1.5 million Presbyterians) and 2 million of other faiths, speak for themselves, and indicate something of the secular and spiritual dimensions of multi-racial, multi-cultural, and multi-faith Britain. Together with increasing contact with continental Europe, these contribute to the development of a new relationship with the wider international community. On the other hand, large-scale unemployment, urban decay, racial tension, and a wide disparity in standards of living all contribute to the adverse sociological climate in which the church carries out its mission in Britain today.

Many movements of reform and renewal have contributed to a complex pattern of church life in which the Roman Catholic church plays a significant part. The Church of England (Anglican) and Church of Scotland (Presbyterian) are the established churches in England and Scotland, respectively. In Wales, which has no established church, a strong sense of cultural identity, owing much to the Welsh Bible and Welsh hymnody, has molded the life of the chapels and churches. Of the other mainstream Protestant churches, Methodists and Baptists form the largest groups. There are 100,000 members of Orthodox churches, and Black Pentecostal churches are growing numerically. The Society of Friends and the Salvation Army have made distinctive contributions, not least in areas of social concern and missionary outreach. Many churches are currently struggling to understand better the role of women in mission and ministry, and there is a growing consciousness among women themselves of their call to serve.

In exploring new forms of prayer and worship, in contact with those of other faiths, and in responding to the problems of inner cities, the churches in Britain have been increasingly acting together. This has provided the momentum for the development of an interchurch process of prayer, reflection, and debate on the nature, purpose, and unity of the church involving upward of a million people in England, Scotland, and Wales. According to the general secretary of the British Council of Churches the ensuing conference was "the most representative gathering of churches

since the Reformation, including Orthodox, Catholic, Anglican, Reformed, Lutheran, and all the way across the spectrum to Black Pentecostals and Brethren." Under the banner "Not Strangers but Pilgrims," they are now committed to some very practical proposals for the church's ministry and unity in the years that lie ahead.

Northern Ireland has its own complex difficulties. Most Protestants wish to retain their British citizenship and are opposed to unification with the Republic, while a high percentage of Roman Catholics aspire to a united Ireland. Paramilitary organizations, particularly the IRA, have resorted to violence as a means of promoting their ends, with the result that thousands of people have been killed and injured and there has been widespread suffering. The reconciling role of the churches is vital in this situation, and both Protestants and Catholics have become involved in peacemaking in a host of community organizations operating at the "sharp end" of things.

"In contrast to the beauty and wealth of nature, in Northern Ireland especially, we are torn apart by hate and fear. Every attempt at peace comes under immediate attack and is never allowed to establish itself. Violence is always ready to erupt, bringing sorrow and shame."

Let us kneel alongside those in Britain who seek forgiveness for
false pride and complacency
unthinking consumerism
insularity, and reluctance to accept new ways
acquiescence in a society which is often ruthless in its pursuit of progress and profit; and heedless of the hurt and anger felt by its victims.

All-merciful tender God
you have given birth to our world,
conceiving and bearing all that lives and breathes.
We come to you as your daughters and sons,
aware of our aggression and anger,
our drive to dominate and manipulate others.
We ask you to forgive us,
and by the gentle touch of your Spirit
help us to find a renewed sense of compassion

that we may truly live as your people
in service to all humanity.

Janet Berry, South West Manchester Group of Churches

Let us pray

for a willingness to live lives with a bias toward the poor, the needy, the unemployed and the deprived

for the people of Wales, concerned to preserve their cultural identity and for their various churches exploring ways of recognizing each others' ministries

for the diverse ministry of the church in Scotland: in city areas, the Highlands and islands, and the Lowlands

for the church in Britain, diminished in size, beset with problems, but increasingly alert to its task

for Christians of different traditions on converging paths.

Lord God, we thank you
For calling us into the company
Of those who trust in Christ
And seek to obey his will.
May your Spirit guide and strengthen us
In mission and service to our world;
For we are strangers no longer
But pilgrims together on the way to your kingdom.
Amen.

Prayer for the interchurch process, Jamie Wallace

Week 11

Belgium • Luxembourg • The Netherlands

O Lord Jesus,
let not your word become a judgment upon us,
that we hear it and do not do it,
that we believe it and do not obey it.

Thomas à Kempis, 15th century:
member of an informal brotherhood in the Netherlands

Grant to us, O Lord,
to know that which is worth knowing,
to love that which is worth loving,
to praise that which pleaseth thee most,
to esteem that which is most precious unto thee,
and to dislike whatsoever is evil in thy eyes.
Grant us with true judgment to distinguish things that
differ,
and above all to search out and do what is well pleasing
unto thee,
through Jesus Christ our Lord. Amen.

Thomas à Kempis

O Holy Spirit of God, who with thy holy breath
doth cleanse the hearts and minds of thy people;
comforting them when they be in sorrow,
leading them when they be out of the way,
kindling them when they be cold,
knitting them together when they be at variance,
and enriching them with manifold gifts;
by whose working all things live:
We beseech Thee to maintain and daily to increase

the gifts which Thou has vouchsafed to us;
that with Thy light before us and within us
we may pass through this world
without stumbling and without straying.

Erasmus of Rotterdam, 1466–1536

God in heaven, we beg you;
bless all who make endeavors for peace and human welfare;
take from us anxiety about the future
and let us contribute to the peace of the world
by the way we ourselves behave.

From Fürbitten und Kanongebete der holländischen Kirche, 1972

Population, language, and government
Belgium: 9.9 million; French, Dutch, German.
Luxembourg: 367,000; French, Letzeburgesch, German.
Netherlands: 14.6 million; Dutch.
All are constitutional monarchies.

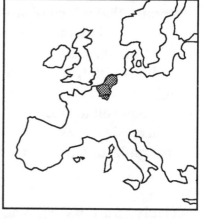

These three countries have been linked together since the Middle Ages. The term "Netherlands" (the Low Countries) was originally used for the whole area, but now applies only to the northernmost country. Highly industrialized, the three have been linked together in the Benelux Economic Union since 1960.

Christianity was brought to the Low Countries during the 6th and 7th centuries by Celtic missionaries, who were the first evangelists and martyrs. Utrecht was one of the earliest centers, and Willibrord and Boniface among the first leaders.

At the end of the Middle Ages this area was a collection of principalities united by the fact that foreign princes inherited them one after another. One of the main causes of the separation between the northern and southern Netherlands was the Reformation, combined with rebellion against the Spanish Hapsburgs who sought to impose Catholicism. The northern area became a refuge for the followers of Luther, Zwingli, and Calvin. After an 80-year war the northern provinces became an independent republic under William of Orange, the southern provinces remaining under the Hapsburgs. The south, including

the southernmost part of the present kingdom of the Netherlands, has remained predominantly Roman Catholic, while Calvinism has been dominant in the north. After Napoleon the Netherlands and Belgium were united into one kingdom, with Luxembourg, a grand-duchy, also under the Oranges. Belgium became independent in 1830, and Luxembourg in 1890.

A number of international and European organizations use the major cities of the Low Countries as their headquarters, thus ensuring the presence of a sizable international community. Immigration, especially from Mediterranean countries, has brought members of other faiths, and there are appreciable Muslim communities in Belgium and the Netherlands. The Jewish community, present in these countries for centuries, was largely decimated in the second world war.

The Christian church is predominantly Roman Catholic in Belgium and Luxembourg (89% and 96% of the population, respectively). In the Netherlands about 40% of the population is Roman Catholic, 30% Protestant, and 26% profess no religion at all. Church people in this area are progressive in their views. Concern within the Protestant churches, many of which have had women priests for years, with issues relating to the role of women in church and society, and changing attitudes in the Roman Catholic church to the question of married priests and to divorce and remarriage, all indicate a readiness for change. Joseph Suenens, one-time Cardinal Archbishop of Malines-Brussels, and active in Vatican II, sees the charismatic movement and a more spontaneous prayer life as a necessary sequel, at a time when observance of the traditional forms of Roman Catholic devotion has greatly declined.

Shared experiences of suffering during the second world war and common challenges facing the churches today have resulted in increasing ecumenical contacts. The United Protestant church has existed in Belgium since 1979, and in the Netherlands the synods of the two Reformed churches have declared themselves to be "in the situation of reuniting." The Council of Churches in the Netherlands incorporates a wide spectrum, including the Roman Catholic church. Increasing secularism has forced the churches to rethink their role and identity in society. All have become more actively involved in political and social issues: peace and justice, nuclear disarmament, north-south dialogue, unemployment and social security, welcoming and accepting immigrants, and the problems of a plural society. Although often polarized and divided within themselves, the churches perform an increasingly important role as watchdogs of government policy, and in championing the cause of the underprivileged.

We thank God

for the missionaries and martyrs who brought the gospel to these lands

for the courageous struggles of the peoples of the Low Countries for freedom of thought, faith, and conscience

for the protection given to Jewish citizens during the second world war and for the life and witness of many courageous Jews

for the ecumenical initiatives of the churches in these countries and especially for the contribution of Willem A. Visser't Hooft, the first general secretary of the World Council of Churches

for the many movements of renewal in both Protestant and Catholic churches.

We pray God

for a greater coming together of the churches in response to the need for a joint Christian witness in a secularized society

that just and compassionate solutions may be found to tensions arising from economic pressures

for the handicapped, the unemployed, and migrant workers; and for their acceptance and integration in local communities

for a change of heart and habit on the part of all who prosper or suffer from the bondage of drugs; and courage for those who seek to break free

for the resolution of friction between the French- and Dutch-speaking communities in Belgium

for the International Court of Justice in the Hague, and Institutions of the European Community in Brussels and Luxembourg; and for the church's responses to them

that initiative taken by these countries for peace and disarmament may be fruitful.

Let us pray to God who calls us in Jesus Christ to unity

for the Christian churches on earth: that they may no longer allow themselves to be separated from each other by questions and problems that have often long since ceased to be ours

for the leaders in our churches: that like the apostles they may be open to the call of the Spirit, put off all fear and may speak in words all Christians can understand

for all theologians and ministers: that they may humble themselves under the mighty hand of God and, setting aside human caution and shrewdness, may trust in the Spirit who comes to the aid of our weakness

for those men and women who can no longer understand the separation of Christians and also for those who equate the church of Jesus Christ only with their own favorite customs: that they all may recognize that it is not the way back but the way into the future that they tread together which alone can give us unity.

Lord, our God,
lead us through the love of your Son
our Lord Jesus Christ
to the unity we long for.

From Fürbitten und Kanongebete der holländischen Kirche

Go now, all of you, in peace
to the place where God has given you responsibility
and he himself will bless you,
the Father, the Son and the Holy Spirit.

Prayers, Poems and Songs, Huub Oosterhuis

Week 12

France • Portugal • Spain

Lord, grant that Christians may again find visible unity, that they may be one that the world may believe.

Our God,
we are one in solidarity with those who live in danger and struggle. Whether near or far, we share their anguish and their hope.

Teach us to extend our lives beyond ourselves and to reach out in sympathy to the frontiers where people are suffering and changing the world.

Make us one in solidarity with the aliens we ignore, the deprived we pretend do not exist, the prisoners we avoid.

God, let solidarity be a new contemporary word for this community into which you are constantly summoning us.

But, God, may our solidarity be genuine, and not a dishonest maneuver.

May our solidarity be effective, and not just consist of wordy declarations.

May our solidarity be grounded in hope, and not in the tragedy of disaster.

May our solidarity be in humility, because we cannot bear all the world's troubles.

God, purify us in our solidarity with others; may it be genuine, fruitful, fervent, and humble.

We ask it in the name of him who was resolutely one in solidarity with abandoned, despised humankind, Jesus Christ, your son, our brother.

Amen.

100 prières possibles, André Dumas

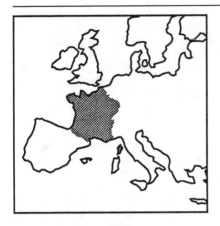

France

Population: 55.2 million.
Languages: French; Breton, Basque, Occitan and Alsatian are also spoken.
Government: Republic.
Religion: Christians about 80% (Roman Catholics 76.4%, Protestants 2.4%, Orthodox 0.8%); Muslims 5%; Jews 1.4%; Buddhists 0.2%.

Christians arrived in France from Italy at an early date, and by the end of the first century groups were meeting for worship in the south. The mass baptism in 496 of the Frankish king Clovis with his warriors was significant in the spread of Christianity in the region. The Middle Ages were marked by the Crusades, the monastic reforms of Benedict of Cluny and Bernard of Clairvaux, and the political intrigue which installed a rival pope in Avignon. At the time of the Reformation the Protestant movement became strong; but, as a result of the Counter-reformation and later persecution, Protestants remained a persecuted minority until the Revolution of 1794. Napoleon's concordat with Rome (1802) recognized Roman Catholicism as the major religion, the Lutheran and Reformed churches being recognized a year later. Since 1905 church and state have been separate except in Alsace-Lorraine.

By far the majority church, but with a dwindling number actively participating, the Roman Catholic church in France relies entirely on its collection boxes. It is, however, active, with a number of lay movements engaged in programs of mission, education, and renewal. The church takes a firm stand against racism. Secours catholique, the largest non-government organization in the country, has thousands of volunteers working with immigrants, single parent families, and others in social need. With half a million members, the Reformed church of France is the largest Protestant body. Although scattered throughout the country, Protestants are strongest in Alsace and in the Rhone Valley. The Protestant Federation, as well as the Roman Catholic church, is concerned to safeguard the rights of refugees and immigrants. The CIMADE is an interdenominational organization working for the welfare of refugees, migrant workers, and other displaced persons. Since War II, the ecumenical communities of Taizé, Pomeyrol, and Reuilly have increasingly become centers of church renewal. There is much joint activity and witness, ranging from the charismatic movement to ecumenical radio stations.

Portugal and Spain

Although today quite separate and independent nations, these two countries of the Iberian peninsula share a common Christian heritage. According to ancient tradition, the apostles James and Paul visited here, and certainly Christianity was firmly established by the end of the 2nd century.

Muslim influence came with the Berbers in the 8th century. During the Mid-

dle Ages the Muslims, Jews, and Christians living in the peninsula held one another in mutual respect. In the Christian north, the veneration of the apostle James, the patron saint of Spain, led to the establishment of an important European center of pilgrimage in Santiago de Compostela. In the Moorish south a special liturgy, the Mozarabic rite, developed, and is still in use today. The Christian "reconquest," which was in the nature of a crusade, took four centuries to complete, and was indirectly responsible for the declaration of Portugal as an independent nation in 1139. The coexistence of the three religious communities was destroyed, the Jewish and Muslim populations being forced to accept baptism or leave.

Reformation influence reached the peninsula through its political links with Germany. However, the rigor of the Counterreformation made progress impossible, and it was not until the 19th century that Protestant missionaries were permitted, and a number of small Protestant congregations established.

The great voyages of discovery by Spanish and Portuguese sailors, which were also viewed as missionary journeys, marked the beginnings of the spread of Western Christianity to many other parts of the world. Regrettably, they also brought the beginning of the colonial era, and the destruction of ancient cultures. The "golden age" of Spain and Portugal, albeit also the time of the Inquisition and the Counterreformation, bequeathed to Christians for all time the diverse spiritual treasures of Saints Teresa of Avila, John of the Cross, Ignatius Loyola, and others.

Portugal

Population: 10.2 million.
Language: Portuguese.
Government: Republic.
Religion: Christians 98% (Roman Catholics 97%, Protestants 0.8%). There are very small Jewish, Muslim, and Bahai communities, and a number of Marranos (whose forebears were compelled to accept baptism, but who nevertheless continued to keep Jewish observances).

Today Portugal is one of the poorest countries in Europe with high levels of inflation and unemployment. The illiteracy rate is also high—one of the legacies of the dictatorship which was overthrown in the 1974 "Revolution of the Carnations." Portugal's recent integration into the European Economic Community has helped to overcome its isolation.

The Roman Catholic church, still very conservative, faces some anticlericalism because of its previous association with the dictators. Vast numbers of the faithful continue to make the pilgrimage to the shrine of Our Lady of Fatima associated with the call to prayer and repentance. The small but vigorous Protestant churches are involved in social work, particularly with children, old people, and refugees. The Portuguese Council of Christian Churches links together the historic Protestant churches.

Spain

Population: 39.4 million.
Languages: Spanish, Catalan, Basque, Galician.
Government: Constitutional monarchy.
Religion: Christians 92.5% (Roman Catholics 92%, Protestants 0.1%). Very small Muslim, Jewish, and Bahai communities, and some Marranos.

Spain, also recovering from a fascist dictatorship and poor by European standards, is troubled by the ongoing problem of the Basque separatist movement.

The Catholic church holds together two overlapping elements: a pious, conservatively traditional section in an increasingly progressive, socially conscious church. Many local Christian communities are socially and politically active. There is some uneasiness among church leaders about the stance of the socialist government toward religion. "It isn't easy for a socialist government to respect liberty. There's a tendency to try and change mentalities: freedom is in danger." The Spanish Evangelical church (Methodists, Presbyterians, Congregationalists), facing the problem of being a small minority, is concerned about the church's mission in the world and active in a number of social fields. It is on record as saying "...we place our confidence and hope in God and in the help given by the ecumenical community."

Let us unite
with Catholic Christians of these wine-producing countries in the words they say in their weekly Mass:

Blessed are you, Lord God of the universe
you are the giver of this wine,
fruit of the vine and of human labor
let it become the wine of the eternal kingdom.

Let us join
also with small groups of Protestants in these same countries in praising God for the freedom of God's word, and for the power of the scriptures to strengthen and refresh them in their daily lives.

Let us rejoice
with all these Christians whenever they together thank
God for all they hold in common.

You are always with us, Lord,
You are water in the desert,
the fruit of life in the garden,
light at evening time.
In that way you are with us, Lord.

You are always with us, Lord,
You are the face reflected in the mirror,
the wine of joy at the celebration meal,
the sharing between friends.
In that way you are with us, Lord.

You are always with us, Lord.
You are the pilot in the boat,
the healer of the injured,
the parent in the home.
In that way you are with us, Lord.

Fr. Pierre-Etienne

We thank God
for the missionary witness of the first Christian communities in these lands
for the spread of the Christian faith from Portugal and Spain to other parts of the world
for the courageous witness of many Protestant believers
for the restoration of democracy and religious freedom in Portugal and Spain
for the church's ministry among children, workers, the sick, and the elderly
for the renewal and inspiration flowing from Taizé and the many other religious communities in France.

We remember before God

Charles de Foucauld, priest and monk, shot in his hermitage in the Sahara by raiding tribesmen in 1916, but whose work for mission and reconciliation still goes on through the little Brothers and Sisters of Jesus.

St. James, whose shrine at Santiago de Compostela has been described as "one of the most ecumenical places in Europe." With it is associated the pilgrimage emblem of the shell. Here contemporary pilgrims unite in prayer for a reconciled Europe.

Lord God,
You accepted the sacrifice of St. James,
patron of Spain and the first of the apostles,
to give his life for your sake.
May your church today find strength in his martyrdom
and support in the constant prayers of all the saints,
through Jesus Christ our Lord.

From the Roman Liturgy

O heavenly Father, we bend the knee before Thee on behalf of all kings and rulers of this world, beseeching Thee to grant unto them by thy inspiration to rule in righteousness, to rejoice in peace, to shine in goodness, and to labor for the well-being of the people committed unto them, so that, by the rectitude of the government, all faithful people may live without disturbance in the knowledge of Thee, and labor without hindrance to thy glory. Amen.

Mozarabic liturgy, 600 C.E.

We pray

that God will heal the many deep wounds which Christians have inflicted on one another in the past

for Christians in France, exposed to the ever-present influences of secularization and consumerism

for Portuguese and Spanish migrant workers, that they may be treated with respect and hospitality in their host countries

for stability in public life, and continuing development of justice and peace in Portugal and Spain

that local churches may be strengthened and encouraged in their common ministry to the needs of the community

that the diverse peoples of France may live together in harmony and interdependence.

You are my family, an African
you gave me a piece of bread.
You are my friend, an Algerian,
you gave me your hand.
You are my brother, a Jew,
you helped me when trouble came my way.
And, you, a Chinese, you showed me the way.

Let's stand by one another, my friends,
because you, the African,
don't have a lot of bread;
to you, the Algerian,
people don't give their hand;
people make trouble for you, the Jew;
and stand in the way of you, the Chinese.

But, this bread,
    this hand,
    this help in trouble,
    this way,
will lead us to peace.

Affirmation of Patrice, a young Frenchman

All Africa Conference of Churches (AACC)

O God, you who are from generation to generation the Creator of the ends of the earth and all that it contains, we of the continent of Africa bow our heads to you in humble thanks for the work that you have wrought in our lands and communities over the years.

We remember with joy the refuge which your only begotten Son our Savior and his earthly parents took in Africa. We rejoice when we remember the journey of the Ethiopian eunuch, and his Christian fellowship with your disciple Philip in the Gaza desert.

It is a wonderful tribute to Africa that Simon of Cyrene helped to bear the heavy wooden cross upon which you hung and suffered for us sinners here in Africa and all over the world.

We can never forget the countless men and women of other lands who spread throughout Africa the gospel news of the saving grace of Christ, and now that same call comes to us to do the same.

When we think of these things our gratitude knows no bounds.

Francis Akanu Ibiam, Nigerian Christian
one-time president of the All Africa Conference of Churches

Founded in 1963, the All Africa Conference of Churches is made up of 138 member churches and associated councils in 33 countries. It represents over 50 million African Christians, i.e., more than one-third of the total Christian population of Africa. Taking legitimate pride in the manner in which God's purpose has been so richly fulfilled using the people of Africa, the AACC seeks to keep before its members matters relating to the life and mission of the church in the continent, and to promote consultation and action.

African women these days identify with their Old Testament counterparts and give thanks for the Cushite wife of Moses (Nb 12) and for those Egyptian midwives, Shiphrah and Puah (Ex 1) "who feared God" and by whose compassion the children of the Israelites were saved.

Almighty and eternal God,
we fervently lift up our eyes to you,
searching for help and guidance in the midst of very many problems.
Come and show us how to serve the refugees and the oppressed;
how to stand alongside those who struggle for social justice
and for the human rights of women and young people.
Come, liberate us from captivity to confessionalism,
and make us agents of reconciliation and unity.
Give us a will to love and serve you
through loving and serving others.
Keep us from insisting upon our own way.
Show us your way.
Enable us to grow in the knowledge of your truth.
Make us bearers of hope, and instruments of peace.
May we be living witnesses of that unity
which binds Divine Parent, Son, and Holy Spirit
into one forgiving and redeeming God.

Prepared by women students
in the Pan-African leadership course, Kitwe, Zambia

Week 13

Djibouti • Ethiopia • Somalia

And in a random scorching flame of wind
that parches the painful throat and sears the flesh,
may God, in compassion, let you find
the great-boughed tree that will protect and shade.

From a Somali prayer

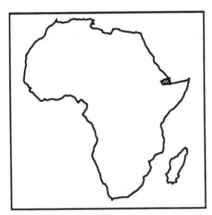

Djibouti

Population: 430,000 (including refugees and resident foreigners).
Languages: French, Arabic, Somali, Saho-Afar.
Government: Single-party republic.
Religion: Muslims 94%; Christians approximately 5%. There is a small Indian Hindu community.

Formerly the French territory of the Afars and the Issas, Djibouti gained its independence in 1977.

Two ethnic groups, the Issa of Somali origin, and the Afar of Ethiopian, make up the majority of the population, which has been greatly swollen in recent years by the influx of refugees from Ethiopia and Somalia. Djibouti has attempted to mediate in the conflict between its neighbors.

A volcanic desert, the inhospitable terrain provides little arable land, and about half the population are pastoral nomads herding goats, sheep, and cattle. The other half live in the capital and mostly work in the thriving free port, which is a major source of revenue for the country. Djibouti is almost entirely dependent on its trade services and on foreign aid.

The majority of Christians in the country are Roman Catholic and nearly all French expatriates. There are small French Reformed, Greek Orthodox, and Coptic congregations, and a handful of local Christians. Although the church ministers mainly to expatriates, a small Christian bookshop makes the Scriptures and Christian literature available to any who are interested.

Lord, I am not worthy that you should
come under my roof, but speak the word only
and my soul shall be healed.

Prayer before communion, Western rite

Used in the eucharist of many different traditions, and therefore probably said by Roman Catholic Christians in Djibouti, this prayer reflects the first instance in the New Testament of faith surmounting barriers of culture, race, and religion.

In its spirit we pray
for the busy port of Djibouti; and for all seafarers from this part of Africa, that they may be helped in overcoming difficulties of custom, language, and race as they travel around the world
for refugees
for local Christians, that they may be sustained by the words of Jesus.

In its spirit we give thanks
for all peacemaking efforts made by the government of Djibouti
for the hospitality and peacefulness of its nomadic people.

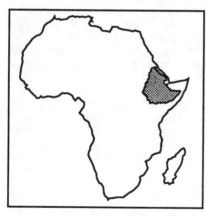

Ethiopia

Population: 42.2 million.
Languages: Amharic, English, Italian, Arabic, and about 90 local languages.

Government: Single-party socialist state, currently under military rule.
Religion: Christians 52% (41% Ethiopian Orthodox, 10% Protestant, 1% Roman Catholic); Muslims 35%; followers of traditional African religions 10%. There are also small Hindu, Sikh, and Jewish communities.

According to local tradition, the gospel was first brought to Ethiopia by St. Matthew. It was brought again in the 4th century by two shipwrecked young men from Syria, one of whom was subsequently consecrated bishop by the Patriarch of Alexandria. Thus began the link with the Coptic church of Egypt which lasted until the Ethiopian church was granted autonomy in the present century. The church was weakened in the 16th century by the Muslim invasion. Jesuit missionaries also came into the country, and conflict be-

tween the two churches led to much bitterness and bloodshed. Protestant missions began work in the 19th century and there are now some 28 different denominations.

Christianity became the official religion of Ethiopia in the 4th century, and the Orthodox church became a symbol of unity binding together a diverse people and helping to maintain the country's independence over the centuries. Although one of the oldest and most conservative churches in the world, it was a founding member of the WCC. Something of this long and rich history is reflected in the church's ancient prayer over the sacrament:

O Lord our good and life-giving God
who stretched forth your holy hands on the tree of the cross,
lay your holy hand upon this paten which is full of goodness,
and on which food of a thousand years is prepared
by those who love your holy name.

Ethiopia became a socialist state in 1974 following the military revolution which deposed Emperor Haile Selassie. The revolution was followed by considerable unrest, leading to many deaths and the detention of a large number of people. In addition, numerous independence movements have been active, especially in the Ogaden (claimed by Somalia) and in Eritrea; and there has been heavy fighting. The new constitution has granted a measure of autonomy to several regions. During 1984–1985, the rains failed for the third consecutive crop season, resulting in severe drought and famine in which an estimated one million people died and hundreds of thousands fled in search of food. Recurrent drought continues to be a serious problem, and the average daily calorie intake is still well below the FAO minimum level. With an economy based mainly on agriculture and herding, the country is at the mercy of climatic conditions.

There has been pressure on all religions since the socialist revolution, and the Ethiopian Orthodox Church especially, losing its status as state religion, was thrown into some turmoil. Nearly all foreign missionaries were withdrawn between 1975–1978, and many church properties and institutions were nationalized. The importation and publication of Scriptures are severely restricted. Nevertheless, both Orthodox and Protestant churches are experiencing a deepening of faith and revitalization.

Yes, Lord, you are the God of all.
Yes, Lord, you are the King of all.
Yes, Lord, you are the Almighty.
Yes, Lord, you are the Governor of all.
Yes, Lord, you are the Savior of all.
Yes, Lord, you are the Judge of all.
Yes, Lord, you are the Life-giver of all.

Yes, Lord, you are the Keeper of all.

Yes, Lord, you are the Nourisher of all.

Acclamation, Anaphora of St. Dioscorus,
25th Patriarch of Antioch, 451

Taking strength from such an acclamation, let us pray

that Christians may remain steadfast in the face of every kind of political pressure

that churches may have freedom to proceed with the training of the priests and pastors of the future

for Christian groups meeting in homes, and their leaders

for Christian education and work among young people

for orphanages providing homes for children whose parents perished in time of famine; and for the many homeless children who roam the streets of Addis Ababa and other major cities in the region.

Remember, Lord, the sick among your people: visit them in your mercy, and heal them in your compassion. Remember, Lord, our fathers and our brothers who have traveled and who have sojourned to trade; bring them back to their dwelling places in safety and peace.

Remember, Lord, the dew of the air and the fruits of the earth, bless them, and keep them without loss.

Remember, Lord, the down-coming of the rains and the waters and the rivers, and bless them.

Remember, Lord, the plants and the seeds and the fruits of the fields of every year, bless them and make them abundant.

Remember, Lord, the safety of your own holy church and all the cities and countries of our Orthodox fathers, the apostles.

Remember, Lord, the safety of humankind and of beasts and of me, your sinful servant.

Remember, Lord, our fathers and our brothers and our sisters who have fallen asleep and gone to their rest in the Orthodox faith.

Remember, Lord, the captives of your people, and bring them again in peace to their dwelling place.

Remember, Lord, the afflicted and distressed.

Remember, Lord, your servants, the poor who are under oppression, have pity upon them and establish in them the right faith and make them a dwelling place of the Holy Spirit, through our spiritual joy and the love of humankind.

Evening prayer of the Covenant, Ethiopian Orthodox liturgy

Somalia

Give comfort, O Lord, to all who are torn away from their homes and their loved ones by war, famine, or the cruelty of their fellows; grant that we who dwell secure in this insecure world may be generous in caring for our displaced sisters and brothers.

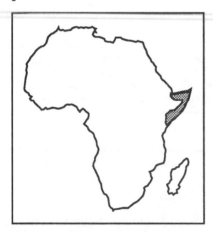

Population. 4.7 million. Mostly pastoral nomads.
Languages: Somali, Arabic, Italian, English.

Government: Single-party socialist republic.
Religion: Muslims 99.8%. Miniscule Christian minority.

One of the poorest countries in the world, Somalia is a generally dry and barren land with few natural resources. Sporadic fighting in the Ogaden and recurrent drought in the region have created a major refugee problem.

The independent Somali republic came into being in 1960 with the agreed merger of British Somaliland and Italian Somaliland, at the same time as these territories obtained their independence. Both were committed to the unification of all Somali territories including those in French Somaliland (now Djibouti), Ethiopia

(Ogaden), and Kenya. This aim led the country into continuing conflict with Ethiopia, and tension with Kenya which has largely been resolved. Following a military coup in 1969, the country was declared a socialist state.

After the revolution the state regarded all religion unfavorably, but the attitude to Islam has changed; this is now the state religion. The Christian church is tolerated, but is not free to evangelize. Although Roman Catholic institutions of education and social work were nationalized in 1972 the church continues to serve the local community in various ways. Following the revolution Protestant activity was also curtailed, though some workers have now been allowed to return. The majority of Christians in the country are expatriates. Most are Roman Catholics, but there are Episcopalian and Lutheran congregations. There are also small groups of indigenous believers.

"Somalis were quite stunned at the thought that Christians around the world might pray for the welfare of Muslims," writes a correspondent. Specifically they asked for prayer for rain. "Natural forces...have a direct impact on their daily lives.... When rain does not come, they are forced to move or prepare for dire consequences. This gives them a special view of God's power that most Christians have never experienced."

O God, give us rain,
we are in misery, we suffer with our children.
Send us the clouds that bring the rain.
We pray thee, O Lord, our Father,
to send us the rain.

In keeping with nomadic tradition, Somali people greet each other asking about peace. The resolution of border tension between their country and Ethiopia would indeed be good news to share. Given that they are not currently involved in fighting, the peace they long for embraces all of life, not least, the peaceful transition from one government to the next.

O God, give us peace,
give us tranquility,
and let good fortune come to us.

Invocation for peace, rain, and health:
The Prayers of African Religion, John Mbiti

Lord God,
there are places in this world some of us will never visit,

and people we have hardly ever thought of until we are reminded that
they are there, and that you know about them.
Such a place is Somalia;
the Somalis are such a people.
Bless the church there, negligibly small in this world's terms.
Give it an appropriate witness,
a lively experience of worship,
and a lifestyle which commends the gospel. Amen.

Week 14

Sudan • Uganda

O Thou, who art the Lion of Judah,
be thou also the Lion of Africa,
and burst all the chains
that still bind our African brothers and sisters
and deliver them from all fear.

A prayer for Africa

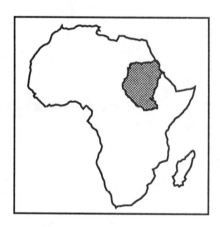

Sudan

Population: approximately 21 million.
Languages: Arabic, English, and over a hundred other languages.
Government: Multi-party republic.
Religion: Muslims 74%; followers of traditional African religions approximately 15%; Christians 9.8% (Roman Catholics 5.2%, Protestants 3.1%, Orthodox 0.8%).

The Democratic Republic of Sudan is today the largest country in Africa. Formerly known as The Sudan, it achieved independence in 1956.

The territory of present-day Sudan was the site of ancient Sudanese civilizations, notably the kingdom of Nubia which persisted for almost a thousand years in the millennium that saw the life of Christ on earth. Indeed the Ethiopian eunuch of Acts 8 was the servant of the Candace of Merowe which is now in northern Sudan. This, presumably, is how Christianity first reached the area. Certainly by the 4th century it had spread up the Nile from Egypt, and a Coptic church became established. With the spread of Islam this church became isolated and finally disintegrated. Roman Catholic missionaries came in the mid-19th century, followed by those of other denominations. Direct evangelism was not permitted in the Muslim north, but educational and medical work was established. In the south there were no such limitations and the church grew.

The people of Sudan belong to many ethnic groups with a major division between north and south. In 1955, shortly before Sudan achieved independence, the southern provinces began to rebel against rule from the Muslim north. Successive governments, both civil and military, were unable to deal with this problem and fighting continued for 17

years. Mass killings occurred and many people fled. The church came under intense pressure. After a period of uneasy peace, fighting broke out again.

Internal rebellion, economic crisis, drought and famine, and the influx of refugees from Ethiopia, Chad, and Uganda have created massive problems, and resulted in a prolonged emergency situation. The Sudan Council of Churches (Roman Catholic, Protestant, and Orthodox) is coordinating the church's relief effort.

"In the troubled regions of the Southern Sudan the steadfast faith of Shadrach, Meshach, and Abednego, and indeed the entire book of Daniel, has taken on new meaning in recent years."

Pray
for church leaders and all Christian people in Sudan, that they may continue to be aware of the presence of God as they walk through the fire.

O God, make speed to save us;
O Lord, make haste to help us.

Versicle and Response:
Prayer Book of the Church of the Province of the Sudan

Numbed by war, struggling on amid near starvation, pastors and people try with paltry resources to be faithful to their calling; and yet, in that very situation they contrive a new hymnody. "These are the new songs of worship, the ones that rise from the struggling Christian groups...So perfectly do some of these songs meld together the sorrow and trauma of these years, with the rhythm and the words. As we sing 'Father of our Lord in heaven' it is the last, hard-beating line of each verse that leaves a chill as I see the solemn, lost faces of my Dinka brethren round the fire."

The Father of our Lord in Heaven,
Visit us for we are worried in our hearts.
We are without faith, O Lord; try to visit us all.
We are all worried; the hardships of this world are upon us.

The sin of the world has cut us away from your path.
We are left alone, we are left, we are left, we are left.

"All the problems of the rest of Africa focused on this one country with its impossible geography, impossible mixture of people...its refugee population the biggest in Africa...."

O Lord Christ,
who as a boy lived with his parents by the banks of the Nile,
have compassion on all the refugees in Sudan,
the land of the Niles;
help and encourage all those who work to relieve their distress
for your name's sake. Amen.

Pray
for political stability in Sudan; and for the leaders of the government and the Sudan Peoples' Liberation Army, the will and wisdom to negotiate peace. The universal plea from Sudan is "above everything else pray for peace."

O God,
our Creator, Redeemer,
sustain the people of the Sudan,
give food to those who hunger,
strength to those who suffer,
and peace and security to all.

Prayer of Sudanese Christian woman

God bless Sudan;
Guide her rulers;
Guard her peoples;
And grant her peace based on justice and freedom.

Help the church to be again a means of reconciliation, and bless all who are peacemakers.

From the Sudan Council of Churches with an appeal for prayer and fasting

Uganda

Population: approximately 13 million.
Languages: English, many ethnic languages.
Government: Parliamentary system, interim government.
Religion: Christians 65–80% (Roman Catholic and Anglican churches by far the largest); Muslims, approximately 10%, especially in the northwest; adherents of traditional beliefs about 12%, especially in the northeast.

Long known as "the Pearl of Africa," the Republic of Uganda has suffered untold devastation in recent years. Of the three major ethnic groups, the Bantu are mostly in south and west, and the Nilotic and Sudanic people in the north and east. Normally about 90% of the population is engaged in agriculture in this naturally fertile land.

Christian missionaries first came to this area in 1877, and some of the first converts to Christianity were young men being trained for future leadership at the court of the Kabaka of Buganda. They were regarded as a threat, and many were martyred. Christianity spread rapidly around the turn of the century, and some thirty years later the revival movement spread from neighboring Rwanda. The church pioneered educational work, and continued to play a very significant part until the government took over all schools in 1964. In the same year a joint Christian council (Roman Catholic and Anglican) was established.

Formerly a British Protectorate, Uganda became independent in 1962. In the following year, attempts were made to balance political power between the various groups, but since 1966 ethnic rivalries have come to the surface. The country has suffered several coups, a disastrous dictatorship, and civil war. Anarchy and devastation have prevailed. Christians suffered especially under President Amin. The number of people massacred is unknown, and many others fled the country. People were unable to plant their crops, and drought and famine increased the hardship. The interim government formed in 1986 offers a new hope of change and betterment. In this situation the Christian message of reconciliation is vital, and the church, supporting government policies of reform and renewal, continues to offer this alternative way of life to the nation. Serious evangelism, and patient involvement in education, medical services, and community development continue. Most of all, the church in Uganda is known for its prayerfulness.

Praise the Lord

Martyrs gave birth to that great dynamic family of Christ in the heart of Africa 100 years ago. It is the blood of *this* martyr that will give birth to a new burst of faith and loving sacrifice that will shape the church of Uganda in the next 100 years.

Canon Samuel Van Culin, secretary general
of the Anglican Consultative Council,
speaking of Archbishop Janani Luwum

O God, by your providence the blood of the martyrs is the seed of the church: Grant that we who remember before you the blessed martyrs of Uganda may, like them, be steadfast in our faith in Jesus Christ, to whom they gave obedience, even to death, and by their sacrifice brought forth a plentiful harvest...

Collect for the martyrs of Uganda

Tukutendereza, Yesu
Yesu mwana gwendiga
Omusaayi gwo gunaazizza;
Nkwebasza, Yesu Mulokozi.

Glory, glory, Hallelujah
Glory, glory to the Lamb
Oh, the cleansing blood has reached me
Glory, glory to the Lamb.

Chorus of the East African Revival movement
sung on every conceivable occasion, on hearing
the call of God, at a funeral, before making a journey,
on joining the fellowship

Martyrdom and revival are two notable themes of contemporary Ugandan spirituality.

Pray God
for the healing of Uganda; that the bitter ethnic hatreds
may be resolved;
the spirit of revenge disappear; and love flow forth
for the government; and for the national reconstruction
of agriculture, industry, and the entire economy
for the church in Uganda, that Christians may lead the
way in forgiveness, reconciliation, and in promoting fresh
trust among those in the different communities
for the inner strengthening of all God's children in Uganda against all the forces that corrupt, atrophy, undermine,
and weaken the human spirit.

O Father God,
I cannot fight this darkness by beating it with my hands.
Help me to take the light of Christ right into it.

For all in trouble, a prayer from Africa

In common with many other countries there is concern
and anxiety in Uganda about the spread of AIDS.

Keep us, Sovereign Lord
from panic when crisis and panics arise.
Help us to know that though you do
not always remove troubles from us
you always accompany us through them.

A prayer from Uganda

O Lord
establish, strengthen, and settle all Christians in Uganda
and encourage in them and in us
an awareness of our common bond as members of your
body.

Week 15

Kenya • Tanzania

Grant that the peoples of East Africa
may love mercy,
deal justly,
and walk humbly with their God,
and with each other. Amen.

A litany based on a traditional Kikuyu form

Leader: Let us pray to the God of our fathers, through Jesus Christ his Son, in the power of the Holy Spirit.
May the bishops and leaders of our churches have wisdom and speak with one voice.

People: Praise the Lord: peace be with us.

Leader: May the leaders of our country rule with maturity and justice.

People: Praise the Lord: peace be with us.

Leader: May the country have tranquility and the people be blessed.

People: Praise the Lord: peace be with us.

Leader: May the people and the flocks and the herds prosper and be free from illness.

People: Praise the Lord: peace be with us.

Leader: May the fields bear much fruit and the land be fertile.

People: Praise the Lord: peace be with us.

Leader: May the face of our enemies be turned toward peace.

People: Praise the Lord: peace be with us.

Leader: May the path of the world be swept of all danger.

People: Hallelujah! The Prince of Peace is with us.

Eucharistic liturgy, Church of the Province of Kenya

Heavenly Father,
thank you for the peace you have given us in Tanzania;
grant our leaders wisdom and honesty
to seek the welfare of all our people.
Give us strength to plant our fields
and joy in using the land you have given us.
Teach us to care for the sick and poor,
that all may know your love. Amen.

Prayer from Tanzania

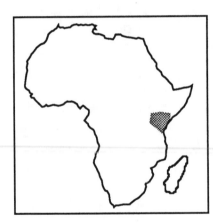

Kenya

Population: 20.4 million.
Languages: Swahili, English, and over 15 others.
Government: Unitary single-party republic.
Religion: Christians 75% (approximately equal numbers of Roman Catholics and mainline Protestants; slightly fewer members of African indigenous groups); adherents of tribal religions 16%; Muslims 6%.
Christianity was first brought to the coastal regions of these countries by Portuguese mariners in the 15th and 16th centuries, but failed to survive when the Arabs reconquered the area in 1730. Both Roman Catholic and Protestant missionaries came in the colonial era. Some began work on the island of Zanzibar before crossing to the mainland, and some worked initially in settlements for freed slaves. In Kenya especially there were soon flourishing Christian communities.

When Africa was carved up by the colonial powers in the latter half of the 19th century, Kenya became a British colony. Independence was gained in 1963, and apart from brief periods of unrest, stability has been maintained. Some 85% of the population is engaged in agriculture and the dairy industry. The high rate of population growth together with the effects of drought has largely offset economic successes. There are many different African ethnic groups, including the Kalenjin, Kamba, Kikuyu, Kisii, Masai, Meru, Miji Kenda, Luo, Luyia, and Somali, as well as appreciable Asian and European communities.

The number of Christians in all denominations has grown rapidly in this century, and the East African revival resulted in a deepening of spiritual life. Arising out of an essentially African appropriation of the gospel, indigenous churches have emerged, and there are now over 200 such "independent" churches. The years 1952–1956 saw the Mau Mau crisis, in which a resurgence of African traditional oathing combined with rising nationalism was directed against the British and those associated with them. Many Kikuyu Christians refused to take the Mau Mau oath and were martyred. The church subsequently tended to remain aloof from civil affairs, but is now playing a more active part, and has voiced concern on a number of issues.

Nairobi is a key communications center in East Africa, and is the headquarters of the All Africa Conference of Churches and of the Association of Evangelicals of Africa and of Madagascar, representing conservative evangelical Christians.

Bwana Asifiwe! Translated "Praise the Lord!" this is a common greeting among Kenyan Christians as they meet, shake hands, and discuss the happenings of the day. Moreover, *Bwana Asifiwe* also speaks of a God continually watching over the activities, needs, relationships, and thoughts of all in Kenya, and is therefore an ascription which passes naturally from praise into prayer.

Pray therefore
that peaceful development may continue in Kenya, and that all people may share in the material welfare of the country.

We beg you, O God
to rule over this and every town and city.
Increase our blessings,
and bring us prosperity.

Prayer from Kenya

for those living in areas of famine, and for parents who must watch their children suffer
for the continued numerical growth of the church, and for unity, devotion, and compassion surmounting all barriers of tribe and denomination
for all priests, pastors, and teachers, that they may be

given gifts to meet the spiritual needs of people; and that many may come to know Christ as Savior and follow him along African paths

that Christians in Kenya may enter more deeply into their biblical and sacramental heritage, and rejoice in its present-day relevance:

From a wandering nomad, you created your family;
for a burdened people, you raised up a leader;
for a confused nation, you chose a king;
for a rebellious crowd, you sent your prophets.
In these last days, you have sent us your Son,
your perfect image, bringing your kingdom,
revealing your will, dying, rising, reigning,
remaking your people for yourself.

Eucharistic liturgy, Church of the Province of Kenya

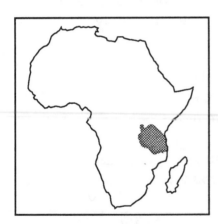

Tanzania

Population: 21.8 million.
Languages: Swahili, English, and over a hundred others.
Government: Unitary, single-party republic.
Religion: Christians 45% (Roman Catholic, Lutheran, and Anglican denominations are the largest); adherents of traditional African beliefs 22%; Muslims 33%, notably in Zanzibar and along the coast.

Tanzania came into being in 1964 by the merger of Tanganyika, a former German colony that gained independence in 1961, and the Sultanate of Zanzibar, a former British protectorate. Zanzibar retains a degree of autonomy. The Tanzanian people belong to very many different ethnic groups, but this has not caused significant divisions. Some 90% are farmers often at subsistence level. The socialist government implemented a new village system, Ujamaa (familyhood), which is a cooperative for farmers in which decisions are made communally and products shared according to need. Lack of technical knowledge and experienced leadership are continuing problems. Drought and adverse terms of trade have led to severe economic problems, and the country, one of the world's poorest, is dependent on foreign aid.

The Christian church is growing

rapidly in Tanzania, but is not yet Africanized, and there is a relative absence of indigenous churches. There is, however, considerable vitality, with the renewed discovery of healing and other spiritual gifts, and a lively response from young people. Churches are required to become more involved in the formation and organization of Ujamaa, and many Christians have responded willingly. The church continues to minister in a number of social and development projects.

We pray

for all in authority in the land, from the ten-cell leader in the village to the president in Government House, that they may display courage, honesty, and integrity

for wisdom and skill for those who manage the economy; and for a fair distribution of food, fuel, soap, and whatever basics are obtainable

for responsible use of the land and the forests; and for all those combating insects and other pests that eat away growing crops and stored grain

for local Christian congregations; for pastors, lay leaders and people; and their witness in the community.

Good Lord:
Just as you were pleased to relax,
in the home of Martha and Mary,
abide also, we pray, in our homes.

Bestow upon them an atmosphere of Christian love
where your presence can be found,
your word made known,
your will accepted and your purpose worked out.

Prayers for Today, for African congregations

"Here in Tanzania neighboring churches of different areas—Roman Catholic, Anglican, Lutheran—observe the Week of Prayer for Christian Unity moving from one church to another on successive days. In this way they all share messages and experience fellowship outside their own church."

O God, forgive us for bringing this stumbling block of disunity to a people who want to belong to one family. The church for which our Savior died is broken, and people can scarcely believe that we hold one faith and follow one Lord. O Lord, bring about the unity which you have promised, not tomorrow or the next day, but today.

A prayer from Africa

Week 16

Madagascar • Malawi • Zambia

Let your love be like a steady, gentle rain,
not a cloudburst...

A Malagasy petition

Gracious Lord,
in this season of fullness and completion,
we praise you for all living and all dying.
We thank you for that great circle
in which we are united with all who have gone before us.
Bring us all, good Lord, to the day
when you will free our eyes from tears,
our feet from stumbling,
when we shall walk before you in the land of the living.

The greater family: a prayer by Gabe Huck

God of goodness and love, in whom we human beings
may trust in every hour of need: have mercy on all who are
faced with fear and distress by cyclone. We ask that help
may be given wisely and speedily, and this need turned
into an opportunity to strengthen the bonds of love and
service which bind human beings and nations together,
through Jesus Christ our Lord.

*Christian Aid. May be adapted
for those suffering any other disaster*

Evening in Africa
At last, O God, the sun's heat has given way to the cool
evening.
Take, we pray, the heat out of our desires and our tempers,
and in this evening hour calm us,

that we may experience the peace and serenity which come from you.

At last, O God, the sun's brightness has given way to the rich colors of the evening.

Prevent us, we pray, from being blinded by the apparent brilliance of human achievement.

And, in this evening hour,
help us to rediscover the varied beauty of your creation,
and appreciate afresh, in the stillness,
the value of your abiding presence.

For the sake of Jesus Christ our Lord. Amen.

Prayers for Today, for African congregations

Madagascar

Population: 10 million, and rising rapidly.
Languages: Malagasy, French. English, Swahili, Hindi, Arabic, and Chinese are also spoken.
Government: Single-party republic.
Religion: Christians 46% (of whom about half are Roman Catholics); adherents of traditional religions approximately 45%; Muslims 1.7%.

"Daunting, enchanting, and almost overwhelming" is how a recent visitor described Madagascar. The country is poor, and suffers annual devastation from cyclone. The people came originally from Indonesia and the South Pacific, but others have migrated from Africa and Arabia.

Madagascar was a monarchy from the 16th century onward, but became a French colony in 1896 and independent in 1960. The first Christian contacts in 1500 were Portuguese sailors, but missionary activity was spasmodic with no lasting results until the early 19th century. In the reign of Queen Ranavalona I (1835–1861) Christians were persecuted and many put to death for their faith. However, in 1869, Queen Ranavalona II accepted Christianity, and a mass movement followed.

Poverty, poor communication in a difficult terrain, and fear of change in a strongly traditional society all contribute to the problems of people and church; and, according to the Christian Council, "corruption also is still known everywhere." There are signs of a renewal of traditional culture; and also a lapsing into traditional religions in which an excessive preoccupation with the dead is a feature. The churches have been officially recognized by the socialist state, and a relationship established between the local Christian Council and the

government in the sphere of education. There is growing support for the CCCM in which the Roman Catholic church of Jesus Christ in Madagascar (union of Congregationalists, French Reformed, and Quakers), Lutheran, and Episcopal churches participate. The Council is much concerned with human rights and social problems.

For the early martyrs of Madagascar, and for all those who in successive waves of bitter persecution have remained faithful—Thanks be to God

For the present-day growing together of Christians of very varied traditions—Thanks be to God

For the ecumenical commemoration of All Souls Day (November 2, coinciding with Ancestors' Day); and the opportunity this gives to Christians to share with others the teaching of Jesus about life after death—Thanks be to God.

O God, who calls us to your service, may we be faithful witnesses to Jesus Christ through our words and through our works.

Prayer of a Malagasy Christian woman

Heavenly Father, you who taught your Son all he knew, in a situation where everything was in a state of transition:

we pray for today's young population of Madagascar, and for all who look to the church for guidance and inspiration in a situation of rapid change.

Lord Jesus Christ, you who were born poor, and lived and moved among the poor, the sick, and the needy:

we pray for all those in Madagascar who until this day keep their faith in you alive in the face of hardship and chronic illness.

Holy Spirit of God, you who inspired the early church to witness with great boldness before kings and rulers:

we pray that your church in Madagascar today may be an inspiration and challenge to the people of this Marxist-socialist island.

Church of Jesus Christ in Madagascar, adapted

Malawi, Zambia

The area of these two adjoining countries was originally inhabited by bushmen until the Bantu came around 500 C.E. European travelers came in the early 19th century, although the Portuguese had been around Lake Malawi earlier. Arab and Yao slave raiders were also active in what is now Malawi, and slavery did not end in this part of Africa until this century. Both these countries were British protectorates (Nyasaland and Northern Rhodesia), both became independent in 1964, and both have since become single-party republics. English is the official language.

The first Christian missionaries to the area met with failure, largely as a result of illness and natural disasters, but from about 1875 onward, first in Malawi and later in Zambia, many Protestant denominations, as well as the Roman Catholic church, became established. As a result of evangelism the church has grown steadily, and has pioneered educational and medical services throughout the area.

Malawi

Population: 7.3 million.
Religion: Christians 65%; Muslims 16.3%; adherents of traditional beliefs 15%.

This densely populated country, predominantly agricultural and with few natural resources, is host to some 300,000 refugees from Mozambique. A proportion of Malawian men seek work in the mines of Zimbabwe or South Africa. The majority of Christians belong to either the Roman Catholic church or the Church of Central Africa, Presbyterian, although other Protestant denominations are present. There are a number of African indigenous churches, but a relative absence of Pentecostalists. Although church and state remain separate, they are partners in development, and the church is heavily involved in education, medical, and social service. The Christian Council of Malawi incorporates a wide spectrum of traditions, and the church's relationship with the Muslim community is notably cordial.

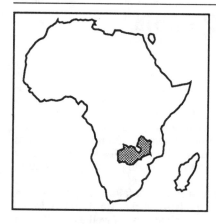

Zambia

Population: 6.7 million.
Religion: Christians about 75%; adherents of traditional beliefs about 25%. Small Muslim, Bahai, and Hindu communities.

The largest industrial concentration in Black Africa is along the copper belt of Zambia, and the country has other mineral resources. The earlier closure of the border with Rhodesia in compliance with United Nations sanctions had a crippling effect on the economy from which it has not yet recovered. The church is concerned with the problem of refugees (of whom there are about 135,000), mostly from Angola, Zaïre, Mozambique, Namibia, and South Africa. The Roman Catholic Church and the United Church of Zambia (the largest of the 45 Protestant bodies) are the two largest denominations. Of the significant number of African indigenous churches, many have come in from other countries. The Jehovah's Witnesses have had an extraordinary influence in the country, and it is estimated that over 25% of the population has been involved at some stage in their lives, although many of these now belong to mainstream churches. The government has restricted the sect at various times. The Zambian Christian Commission for Development incorporates thirty member churches, including the Roman Catholic Church and indigenous bodies.

At the concluding meditation of a recent ecumenical meeting in Lusaka, of leaders of movements fighting white minority domination in Southern Africa, somebody said: "We must see ourselves as a connected people. We are connected to those who have come before us, and those who will come after us. In this meeting, connections have been made in powerful and moving ways." The making and retaining of connections is the object of our prayer for Christians in this part of the world.

May Africa praise you, you the true God
from the south even to the north,
from east to west, from sea to sea.
May the mighty wind bear your name
through cities and hamlets,
by quiet valleys and silent mountains,
over moving waters and sounding falls,
across the sunlit desert,
over the quivering savannah,
through the mysterious forest.

Across the immense African land, overflowing with your
praise,
   imprint all with your splendor which words cannot express.
May your name be known and loved all over the land.

Jerome Bala

We praise God
   for the harmony existing between the different religious
communities in Malawi
   for the rich mineral resources of Zambia, and the opportunities for employment which these provide
   for the steady growth of the Christian church in both
these countries, and its partnership with government in
working for the development of all God-given resources.

We pray for Malawi
   for the growing Christian church, for the development of
African styles of worship, and for a deepening faith among
Malawian Christians
   for a spirit of discernment among the people in response
to the presence of many foreign missionaries and evangelists
   for the church's involvement in education, and in medical and agricultural work
   for those men who have to work far from their homes
and families, and for their wives and children left behind.

We pray for Zambia

Your people tremble, wonder and are perplexed
   as they see their nation grappling with creeping materialism,
   atheism and gnawing corruption in high and low places.
Grant your church strength, wisdom, and courage

to confront the people of Zambia,
and announce the good news of eternal life through Jesus Christ.

John Banda

Dear God in heaven,
We pray for the tens of thousands of refugees living in Zambia.
May they find some measure of comfort and peace and healing in their exile.
May peaceful solutions be found to the problems and unrest which plague their home countries.

From Zambia, a prayer for refugees, adapted

Merciful God,
from the sky you send the rain on the hills to fill the earth
with your blessing,
you make the grass grow for your cattle,
and plants grow as food for your people;
may it please you to send your abundant gifts of goodness
to spread into the homes of all your people in Zambia,
so that their hunger may be satisfied,
and none may be in want.

A prayer for drought-prone Zambia

Week 17

Brazil

O God of all youth, we pray to you:
We are young people, and we want to celebrate life!
We cry out against all that kills life:
    hunger, poverty, unemployment, sickness,
    repression, individualism, injustice.
We want to announce fullness of life:
    work, education, health, housing,
    bread for all.
We want communion, a world renewed.
We hope against hope.
With the Lord of history we want to make all things new.

A group of Brazilian young people
with a visiting peace and justice volunteer

You know, O God,
    how hard it is to survive captivity without any hope of
the Holy City.
    Sing to us, God, the songs of the promised land.
    Serve us your manna in the desert,
    and give us grace to enjoy our day of rest
    as an expression of our trust.

Let there be, in some place,
    a community of men, women, elderly, children, and new-
born babies
    as a first fruit, as our appetizer,
    and an embrace of the future. Amen.

Rubem A. Alves, who teaches in the Department of Philosophy,
University of Campinas, São Paulo

Population: 135.7 million.
Language: Portuguese.
Government: Multi-party federal republic.
Religion: Christians approximately 92% (Roman Catholics 82%, Protestants 10%, Orthodox 0.1%). Most of the remainder practice various forms of spiritism. There are small Buddhist, Jewish, and Muslim communities.

The fifth largest country in the world, with staggering physical attributes—magnificent coastline, plateau, jungle, and the great Amazon River—Brazil covers almost half the continent of South America.

Originally occupied solely by South American Indians, Brazil became a Portuguese colony in 1500. The Indians, gradually retreating further into the interior, declined drastically in numbers, largely as a result of malnutrition and disease. In the three centuries of colonization, some three and a half million Africans, mostly from western Sudan and Angola, were brought over as slaves. The mixing of these three racial groups has resulted in the great variety of physical attributes seen in Brazilians today. Since the 1880s, considerable numbers of immigrants have come from various European countries, the Middle East, and Japan.

It was a member of the Portuguese royal family who proclaimed Brazilian independence in 1822, becoming himself the first emperor. The country became a republic in 1889. Military leaders have been influential in political life, and there have been periods of military rule.

Roman Catholic missionaries accompanied the first explorers and settlers. The Jesuits in particular worked among the Indians as well as among the settlers. In addition to churches and schools they established cooperative Indian villages. Opposition from colonists and government resulted in their expulsion in 1750. In the 19th century the first sustained Protestant work began, and the present century has seen a tremendous growth of the Pentecostal movement.

Potentially a rich country, with vast mineral and agricultural resources as well as modern industrialization, Brazil today suffers from inflation, unemployment, and a massive foreign debt. Rural people remain desperately poor, and every city has its favelas (shanty towns). All over the country people are coming together to pray, to worship, and to share their problems in basic Christian communities. When they read the Bible together they are able to accept for themselves the good news for the poor in a very concrete way. Writing of his experience with fellow Christians in the favelas of São Paulo, a European visitor recently confessed: "I have never before realized what the Christian gospel meant until I saw it being lived out and practiced in Brazil."

Within the Roman Catholic church there are many bishops, clergy, and laity who identify with the poor, and suffer as a consequence, often being branded as communists for their support of the underprivileged. A large part of the church, however, remains neutral in the face of the problem confronting Brazilian socie-

ty; that of the tremendous disparity between rich and poor. Protestants play an important part in social work and education, and most denominations are growing. The Pentecostals, the largest of the Protestant bodies, are also active in the favelas.

The rubbish dump outside one city in Brazil supports 4–5,000 people. For many the only source of income is garbage picking. "But their potential is shown on the dump itself, where an area has been fenced off as a garden. There people have planted seeds found in the garbage. Corn, beans, pumpkins grow there; to feed their families and as a sign of hope."

Thank God

for all signs of hope in Brazil today

that new hope in Christ has been brought within reach of ordinary men, women, and children through basic Christian communities

for the country's return to democracy after a long period of military rule.

Pray God

for Brazil's truly apostolic men and women of God who in all walks of life are committed to the quest for the Holy City in the midst of much that is unholy

for Christians working among the poor, often labeled communist

for cities like São Paulo, set to become the world's second largest agglomeration; and for all who seek to find an appropriate response to its needs

that the country's bountiful resources may be more effectively used for the benefit of all

that the anger and frustration felt by many Brazilians at unfair economic systems may be met by understanding and assistance from the international community

for the Christian Council of Brazil, and for closer ties between those of different confessions

that standing firm beside Brazilian Christians we also may live by creeds which make costly demands upon us.

Lord, no matter what we Christians get called, let the service of the poor and the asking of awkward questions continue together in Brazil and everywhere else.

I truly believe in the new humanity.

I believe in a different humankind, of brothers and sisters—politically I would call it "socialized." The world needs to breathe in harmony and be human. We human beings must come to acknowledge one another as all members of the human race, as brothers and sisters—what I would describe as the utopia of faith.

I do not believe in racial or class segregation: because the image of God in humankind is one and one only.

I do not believe in development for minorities, nor in "developmentalist" development for the majority: because that sort of development does not bear the new name of peace.

I do not believe in progress at any price: because the human race was bought for a price with the blood of Christ.

I do not believe in the automated technology of those who say to the computer, "You are our father": because our only Father is the living God.

I do not believe in the consumer society bent on consumption: because only those who hunger and thirst after justice are blessed.

I do not believe in the heavenly city at the expense of the earthly city: because the earth is the only path which can lead us to heaven.

I do not believe in the earthly city at the expense of the heavenly city: "for here we have no lasting city, but we seek the city which is to come."

I do not believe in the old humanity: because I believe in the new humanity.

I believe in the new humanity, which is Jesus Christ risen from the dead, the firstborn of the whole new human family.
Amen. Alleluia!

Well known for his commitment to the cause of the downtrodden and his readiness to bear the consequences of his political witness to Christ, this confession of an all-embracing hope by Dom Pedro Casaldaliga, bishop of São Felix, Mato Grosso, is the kind of affirmation by which many Christians stand or fall in Brazil today.

Week 18

Argentina • Paraguay • Uruguay

O God, to those who have hunger give bread,
and to us who have bread give the hunger for justice.

Prayer from Latin America

True evangelical faith
  cannot lie dormant
  it clothes the naked
  it feeds the hungry
  it comforts the sorrowful
  it shelters the destitute
  it serves those that harm it
  it binds up that which is wounded
  it has become all things to all creatures.

Menno Simons, 16th-century founder of the Mennonites

The original inhabitants of this area were the semi-nomadic Guarani Indians. Spanish conquistadores came in the first half of the 16th century, and for three centuries the area was governed and exploited by Spain, although the ownership of what is now Uruguay was for a time disputed between Spain and Portugal. The first missionary work among Indians was begun in 1539 by Franciscans. Jesuits soon followed, and worked to both protect and Christianize the Indians. They established cooperative village communities until they were expelled in 1767. Today there are few Indians left in Argentina, and none in Uruguay.

In the early part of the 19th century independence movements developed all over South America, and rule from Spain disintegrated. Argentina became independent in 1816, Paraguay in 1811, and Uruguay in 1825. Following independence Protestant work became possible, the first contact being made in Argentina by James Thomson of the Bible Society, who was the first Protestant missionary in several Latin American countries. In the following decades waves of immigrants as well as other missionaries brought many denominations to the area.

Argentina

Population: 31.1 million.
Language: Spanish.
Government: Federal republic.
Religion: Christians 95.6% (Roman Catholics 91.6%, Protestants 2.8%, Argentinian indigenous 0.7%, Orthodox 0.4%); Jews 2%; Muslims 0.2%.

With a predominantly white population, Europeanized and increasingly secular, Argentina is more fully developed than most South American countries, but currently faces huge economic problems. In this century long periods of military rule have alternated with times of civilian government.

During the years of the last military dictatorship (1976–1983), tens of thousands of people, mostly young, "disappeared." Many bodies, tortured and mutilated, have been found, but some 15,000 people still remain unaccounted for. Grief and anger about the fate of the "disappeared," and strong feelings about the course of justice for the perpetrators of atrocities dominate the thinking and feeling of many people. The Roman Catholic church has been accused of failing to confront the regime, but many individual bishops, priests, and laypeople stood up for

justice and human rights, and some of them also "disappeared." Mainline Protestant church leaders were actively involved in organizations for the defense of human rights.

The Roman Catholic church enjoys a privileged but difficult position in relation to the state. Considerable renewal followed Vatican II with increased lay participation and concern for social issues. Of the numerous Protestant bodies, the Argentina Baptist Convention is one of the largest. The Evangelical church of the River Plate incorporates people of largely Lutheran and Reformed traditions in all three countries. Pentecostal groups are active, and at least nine different Orthodox churches, both Eastern and Oriental, are present. A union theological seminary in Buenos Aires serves eight Protestant confessions in Argentina and Uruguay as well as receiving students from other countries. The Argentine Federation of Evangelical Churches has thirty member churches.

Paraguay

Population: 3.3 million.
Languages: Spanish, Guarani.
Government: Multi-party republic, currently under military dictatorship.
Religion: Christians 98.5% (Roman

Catholics 96%, Protestants 2%, Orthodox 0.2%, Anglicans 0.2%, Latin American indigenous 0.1%). A diminishing number follow tribal religions.

Most Paraguayans are of Indian, or at least part Indian, origin. The majority live in the fertile area east of the River Paraguay, the Grand Chaco region to the west being occupied by nomadic Indian tribes and cattle ranchers. Since 1814 Paraguay has experienced a succession of dictators, and some devastating wars. In the Triple Alliance War (1865–1870) against Brazil, Argentina, and Uruguay, more than half the population died, and losses were heavy in the 1933–1935 war against Bolivia. As a result of these wars and the emigration of men to neighboring countries in search of work, the male to female ratio today is approximately 1 to 2, a fact that contributes to considerable family instability.

A military coup in 1954 brought the present administration to power, and a state of siege was declared in 1955 which has continued, except for a short break, until the present time. It is the longest military dictatorship in South America. Political opponents and members of labor groups are harassed, and human rights violated. It is estimated that 60% of all Paraguayans live outside the country.

The Roman Catholic church, subservient to the government for centuries until the patronage system was abolished in 1967, was profoundly influenced by Vatican II, and since then has increasingly come into conflict with the government. Against a background of increasing unrest, the church consistently protests against human rights violations and abuse of power by the government. Mennonite refugees from Russia at the time of the revolution began work among the Chaco Indians, and sought help from Mennonites in the USA. This is now the largest non-Roman Catholic

Christian community in the country. Since 1889 Anglicans have also been working in the Chaco region, and were the first to live among the Lengua Indians. Several other Protestant denominations are present. Since Vatican II there has been increasing cooperation between Roman Catholics and Protestants.

Uruguay

Population: 3 million.
Language: Spanish.
Government: Multi-party republic.
Religion: Christians 63% (Roman Catholics 59.5%, Protestants 2%, Orthodox 0.7%, Catholics of other rites 0.7%); atheists and nonreligious 35%; Jews 1.7%.

After an initial period of political strife following independence, a time of stability ensued in which progressive social policies were implemented, and Uruguay became the first welfare state in South America. However, increasing military intervention in civil affairs led ultimately to 11 years of military rule from which the country struggles to recover. The present civilian government faces a severe economic crisis and the question of trial or amnesty for

those accused of civil rights violations has been a major issue.

Many European immigrants to Uruguay were opposed to a state-related Roman Catholic church, and by 1900 there was a substantial group of free-thinkers. The proportion of atheists and nonreligious is now higher in Uruguay than in any other South American nation. Church and state were separated in 1918. In the Roman Catholic church the earlier emphasis on evangelism has shifted more recently to social concerns, especially in relation to development problems in urban ghettos. Concern for the poor is also an issue for the Protestant churches, of whom the Pentecostals and Waldensians are numerically the largest groups. The Methodists, the first Protestant group to enter Uruguay, are active in the national ecumenical movement, and seek to deepen relationships, especially with the Pentecostals and Roman Catholics.

Thank God

for all who share their faith in such practical ways

that in recent years Argentina and Uruguay have emerged from bitter experiences of military dictatorship, repression, and violation of human rights

for all new experiences of freedom and the restoration of civil liberties, particularly on the part of the young

for the concern of the Latin American Council of Churches to promote peace in the region.

Pray God

for all countries struggling under massive burdens of debt to the international community, while close at hand their own poor perish of hunger and poverty

for countries whose people have much cause to be unforgiving of each other; that for them the gospel may be about freedom, dignity, and a new look in the eye. (Asked what impact the gospel had made upon them as an indigenous people, one Indian Christian said: "It enables us to look Spaniards straight in the eye.")

for the church in Paraguay, and especially its presence among Indians in the more remote areas

for those families who continue to hope that long disappeared family members will reappear.

It must be the hardest thing, not to know what has happened,

or what wounds have been inflicted,
or what cell or grave marks the spot,
or whether there will ever be a homecoming.

Heavenly Father, the whole family of humanity is yours
and in your care,
So we remember in your presence
those who have been torn from their families,
those who have taken them away,
and those who are left...
Help us today to be signs of your care for them

If you had a hundred sheep and lost one of them,
which of you would not leave the ninety-nine and go
looking for the lost one until it is found?

Lord, be shepherd, healing stream, and guard,
that lost ones may find peace with you.
From Prayers for the Disappeared, Latin American Federation of Relatives
of Disappeared Persons

For the people of Uruguay

After 11 years of military government our small country
has returned to democracy. So, dear Lord, we pray that you
will bless especially all under 30, who, for the first time in
their lives, were able to vote to elect their new leaders.
Bless all those who were elected—the new president facing
a daunting task; the senators and deputies; the city and regional mayors. Give to all of us the tenacity to build a new
nation and take from us feelings of bitterness and revenge.

for the Christian Council in its task of keeping over a
hundred different Protestant churches and organizations in
touch with each other and with the needs around them;
and particularly for their concern to renew ecumenical vi-

sion and leadership in each new generation of young people.

Seek the good of the city
We pray to you, O Lord, our God and Father,
because we are encouraged by Jesus Christ,
your Son and our Brother to do so.
You have said through the mouth of the prophet:
"Seek the good of the city and pray for it to the Lord":
we therefore pray you today for our cities and villages
and for the whole land,
for justice and righteousness, for peace and good order there.
—Have mercy, Lord, we pray.

We pray for those who govern.
Teach them that you are the ruler of all
and that they are only your instruments.
Grant them wisdom for their difficult decisions,
a sharp eye for what is essential,
and courage to obey your commandment.
—Have mercy, Lord, we pray.

We pray for all who, by your ordaining,
are responsible for justice and peace.
Hold back members of the police and armed forces
from practicing torture.
Help them not to regard every suspect as a criminal
and not to treat every criminal as an object.
—Have mercy, Lord, we pray.

We pray for all who continue to seek salvation in violence.
Show terrorists that no blessing rests in violence.
Take the young among them especially into your care

and bring order into their confused thoughts.
Bring murder and kidnapping to an end.
—Have mercy, Lord, we pray.

We pray for all who are no longer able to sleep in peace
because they fear for their own life
and for that of those near and dear to them;
we pray for all who no longer hope in your kingdom;
for all who are tormented by anxiety or despair.
Grant that they may be blessed
with faithful friends and counselors alongside them
to comfort them with your strengthening gospel and sacrament.
—Have mercy, Lord, we pray.

Lord, you have the whole wide world in your hands;
You are able to turn human hearts as seems best to you;
grant your grace therefore to the bonds of peace and
love,
and in all lands join together whatever has been torn
asunder.

From an intercessory prayer for use on Rogation Sunday
by the Evangelical Church of the River Plate, Argentina

Week 19

Bolivia • Chile • Peru

Why on earth had the Spaniards dragged enormous mirrors
and pipe organs from Europe across the Atlantic
through Panama and over the Andes to this valley?
And at what human cost to the peasants?

With such a history
is it any wonder South American Christians
now speak of God
who frees the oppressed
and loves the poor.
Not in the next life
But now.

Like a Mighty River, Lois Wilson

O Lord, in times of weariness and discouragement continue, we pray, to nudge people along in the ways of justice
and peace.

L'Amérique latine en prière, compiled by Charles Antoine

Drawn up especially for use at the Faith and Order Commission meeting in Lima, Peru, in January 1982, the so-
called Lima liturgy provides an opportunity for Christians
of different traditions to go as far as possible together in a
eucharistic liturgy:

Lord God, gracious and merciful,
you anointed your beloved Son with the Holy Spirit
at his baptism in the Jordan,
and you consecrated him prophet, priest, and king:

pour out your Spirit on us again

that we may be faithful to our baptismal calling,

ardently desire the communion of Christ's body and blood,

and serve the poor of your people and all who need your love,

through Jesus Christ, your Son, our Lord,

who lives and reigns with you in the unity of the Holy Spirit,

ever one God, world without end. Amen.

Common to these three countries are the great range of Andes mountains, and conquest by Spain in the 16th century. As a result of war, disease, and expropriation of land, the indigenous Indian population was drastically reduced during the early years of Spanish rule.

American Indians are a profoundly religious and mystical people and accepted the Roman Catholic faith brought by the conquistadores without too much difficulty, although many traditional Indian practices also persisted.

Bolivia

Population: 6.5 million.
Languages: Spanish, Quechua, Aymara.
Government: Multi-party republic.
Religion: Christians 94.5% (Roman Catholics 92%, Protestants 2.5%); Bahais 2.6%.

In spite of many revolts against Spanish rule, Bolivia did not gain independence until 1825. Since then political instability with innumerable coups and changes of government has seriously impeded progress. Badly hit by the collapse of the tin market, and lacking investment to develop other natural resources, Bolivia is the poorest of the South American countries. Over half the population today are Indian, and about a quarter of mixed race. The remainder are mostly of Spanish descent. About two-thirds of the people live on the high plateau. At 15,000 feet, La Paz is the highest capital in the world. In recent years, the cultivation of coca (from which cocaine is obtained) has increased alarmingly, and it has been estimated that 75% of cultivated land is used for this purpose. Illicit drug trafficking is a major problem.

Although the Roman Catholic church has not experienced vigorous renewal to the same extent as in neighboring countries, and suffers from a shortage of priests, its recent support of the rights of land workers and small farmers has brought it into

conflict with vested interests and led to harassment. Christian education, the righting of social injustices, and discovering ways and means of using indigenous Indian elements creatively in worship are major concerns. The first Protestants to come to Bolivia, in 1827, were itinerant Bible Society colporteurs who preceded resident missionaries by about 70 years. Methodists and Baptists placed considerable emphasis on schools and agricultural projects, and the Methodists opened medical centers. Evangelical Protestant churches are both growing and multiplying; and all churches and religions are required to register with the state. Many sects and cults are entering the country which is facing what one bishop calls "a barbarous syncretism" bearing little relation to the real needs of the people.

Chile

Population: 12.3 million.
Language: Spanish.
Government: Republic. Military junta since 1973.
Religions: Christians 90% (Roman Catholics 75%, Protestants 15%).

Gaining independence in 1818, Chile was relatively quick to develop a sense of nationhood in spite of tremendous regional differences. In spite of the present long-running military regime, democracy is deep-rooted, and for most of its life since independence, Chile has been ruled by elected parliaments. Long-standing economic problems have dogged the country, and attempts to reform the social order and meet the basic needs of the people have met with resistance from privileged landowners and industrialists. Since the present "National Security" regime, dedicated to the elimination of Marxism, gained power, innumerable people have been the victims of political execution, have disappeared, been tortured, or forced to leave the country.

The first Protestant missionary, a Bible Society agent, came in 1821 at the invitation of the president, and established schools. Later, Presbyterians, Lutherans, Methodists, and others came. Anglicans engaged in evangelistic work with the Araucanian Indians. In 1909 the Pentecostal movement arose, initially within the Methodist church, but soon split from this and subsequently divided again within itself. These two Pentecostal churches have grown rapidly, and are now the largest non-Roman Catholic churches in the country.

Renewal in the Roman Catholic Church in Chile began before Vatican II, and this was the first country in the world to hold synods after that event. Liturgical reform, priority for evangelism, and concern and involvement in social problems are hallmarks of that renewal. Since the coup, concern for human rights and criticism of the regime have resulted for some priests in torture and death, and many foreign priests have been expelled. In response to the human emergency, the churches (Methodist, Lutheran, Orthodox, Pentecostal, Roman Catholic) as well as the Jews, united to set up an ecumenical Peace Committee, which was the only

place to which victims of repression could turn for help. The committee provided legal and humanitarian aid on a large scale throughout the country. In 1975 it was closed by the government, its German Lutheran director refused entry, and personnel arrested. Much of the work has continued in other ways. However, within the churches themselves there is a polarization between those who have aligned themselves with the poor and exploited, and those who continue to opt for the status quo. The Christian Confraternity of Churches, formed in 1985, with member churches from a wide spectrum, plays a prophetic role in keeping the goal of unity before its members.

Peru

Population: 20.3 million.
Languages: Spanish, Quechua, Aymara, and other Indian languages.
Government: Multi-party republic.
Religion: Christian 98% (Roman Catholics 95%, Protestants 3%).

A land of stark contrasts, Peru's cultural history goes back at least 20,000 years. The last indigenous civilization, the Inca empire, which extended beyond the bounds of present-day Peru, ended with the Spanish conquest. Independence was gained in 1826.

The major changes which have taken place in the Roman Catholic Church in Latin America did not leave Peru aside. In response to the call to a new commitment to the poor, the church has spoken out against social injustices. A network of basic Christian communities developed in the 1970s, and remains a strong force today especially in rural areas and shanty towns. Protestants, who were forced to worship in private until 1915, came with a wave of immigrants from northern Europe. Denominations from North America came later, and a number of independent churches have sprung up. Pentecostal and Adventist groups together comprise the majority of the Protestant population, the traditional confessions remaining small. Protestants have become increasingly involved in social action programs and several missions are working among Indians in the jungle areas.

The vast majority of people are extremely poor. Many from the rural areas have migrated to the cities where they live in sprawling shanty towns. Since 1980 a Maoist guerrilla organization, Sendero Luminoso (Shining Path), has drawn considerable support. The violence of the organization has been matched by the response from government and military, and both sides are implicated in the massacres which have taken place. Of six Peruvian bishops who have eloquently championed the poor, four have been "mysteriously" killed in recent years—it is not known by whom. The present government, elected in 1985, faces a daunting task in attempting to tackle the country's many problems.

A recent visitor to Latin America tells of how he learned to say *gracias* ("thanks"), and how the familiar expression "demos gracias" became something more than a prayer said before eating, but a whole way of life lifted to God in an all-pervading atmosphere of gratitude.

For the sense of deep gratitude that pervades the life of Christian churches in South America—Demos gracias

For every sign of the church's identification with the poor and marginalized—Demos gracias

For the incredible courage and faithfulness of so many fellow Christians in these countries—Demos gracias

That for many in Latin America, hardships, suspicion, vilification, attacks, imprisonment, torture, and exile are signs that they are in line with the gospel—Demos gracias

For the witnesses of hope, and the sense of communion and solidarity felt by Christians with martyrs of all lands, past and present—Demos gracias.

Marking the frontier between Argentina and Chile, the monument, Christ of the Andes, pledges peace between the two countries.

The Christ of the Andes is no longer a statue, but is taking flesh and blood in the tormented struggles of the peoples of Latin America. He comes striding out of the Gulag Archipelagos...

I Believe in the Great Commission, Max Warren

Amen, even so, come, Lord Jesus.

The following meditation is from ten people while detained in the central police station, Santiago.

Our Father...here and now.

Our Father who art in heaven
(and here in the police headquarters, among us, the detained.
We who meet in your name day by day)
Hallowed be your Name
(despite the jeers and roughness with which they treat
us when we name you)
Your kingdom come
(where there is no degrading treatment, nor privations
of liberty,
nor roving salesmen dressed in rags, nor humiliated
prostitutes,
nor police obeying unjust laws)
Your will be done on earth
(and on this part of the earth in particular)
As it is in heaven
Give us this day our daily bread
(the bread which takes away hunger, and the bread
which
maintains within us the hunger and thirst for justice)
And forgive us our sins
(those that we have done to the police when we refuse
to treat
them as brothers, or when we refuse to accept that
they live
under great tensions and contradictions)
As we forgive those that sin against us
(or rather, as we try with all our being to forgive those
that
sin against us, even the commissioner of police)
Don't allow us to fall into temptation
(by responding to a curse with a curse
to hatred with hatred, to maltreatment with maltreatment)
Free us from evil

(from groveling and fawning, from humiliation, from despair and

desperation, and from our sense of loneliness and isolation)

Amen.

By your presence, Lord

transcend the limitations of our solidarity with your suffering children in Latin America

calm and comfort those who live in any kind of fear

deal compassionately with families suffering from unemployment and hunger

touch the consciences of all who hope to gain by the growth, trade, and use of cocaine

strengthen the true faith; and grant that men and women may put their confidence in that which is enduring

draw Christians together around one table and in one service of the poor and needy.

Lord of mystery, let us feel your presence at the very heart of life, and seek and find you in the depths of everyday things.

Prayer of Louis Espinal, Jesuit priest murdered in Bolivia

Latin American Council of Churches (CLAI)

Solidarity is another name for love.

Solidarity is another name for the kind of love
that moves feet, hands, hearts,
material goods, assistance, and sacrifice
toward the pain, danger, misfortune, disaster,
repression, or death
of other persons or a whole people.
The aim is to share with them
and help them rise up, become free,
claim justice, rebuild.

In the pain, misfortune, oppression,
and death of the people,
God is silent.
God is silent on the cross,
in the crucified.
And this silence is God's word,
God's cry.

In solidarity God speaks the language of love.
God makes a statement,
utters a self-revelation,
and takes up a presence in solidarity.

God is love,
God stands in solidarity,
God is solidarity.
Where there is solidarity,
there is God, making an efficacious statement.

And everything God says—
in speech, in silence, in stridency—
is to seek solidarity, greater solidarity.

Jon Sobrino, Salvadoran Jesuit

Established as recently as 1982 and therefore one of the newest ecumenical organizations, the *Consejo Latinoamericano de Iglesias* represents a vigorous attempt to forge a unity of witness and service among Christians in Latin America. With its officers drawn from a number of different Latin American countries, its headquarters are presently based in Quito, Ecuador. The Council relates to more than a hundred Protestant churches and organizations throughout Latin America.

Functioning as "an attentive, objective and prophetic voice in enabling divine truths to be expressed in a timely way," the attention of CLAI is currently directed to a wide range of very practical issues including the widespread unrest felt on account of the burden of foreign debts; peace; the defense of human rights and the return of exiles; the unequal distribution of land, and the welfare of indigenous peoples.

CLAI publishes a newsletter, *Rapidas,* and a broadsheet, *Pastoral Solidaria,* designed to promote solidarity with the poor and to help churches in their pastoral work. In addition to its concern to promote ecumenical leadership, the Council of Churches also seeks to respond to requests from member churches for help with new patterns of worship more related to today's needs.

They speak of the unchanging need to make use of "the rhythms which our people love" and of "the simple and direct words of the psalms and gospel" in expressing their solidarity with one another, and their assurance of the Lord's presence in what they describe as "a time of pain, but also a time of song for Latin American believers."

Almighty God, we come to your presence with the awareness of your gracious love. You have given us a continent full of the glory of your creation. You have blessed us with people who have developed cultural beauties that even today enrich our lives. You have given us the glory of your gospel—promise and reality of our liberation. We thank you, Lord!

We confess that we have not been faithful stewards of so many blessings. The brutal conquest, the division of classes, the dictatorial oppression, the premature death of so many, are realities of yesterday and today which cause us pain and of which we are ashamed. Have mercy, Lord!

For the indigenous people of Latin America we give thanks to you and ask for the manifestation of your liberating power.

For the marginal inhabitants of our big cities, for the abandoned children on the streets, we ask your blessing.

Open our eyes to the reality of the resurrection of Jesus Christ as an anticipation and promise of a new day of love and justice which you are preparing for your people. Send your Holy Spirit, the power which gives testimony of your liberating action in our lives and the life of our people.

We pray for the coming of justice and the realization of peace. We pray for your church so that she may live and announce freedom in Jesus Christ.

O Lord, we give thanks to you and ask forgiveness. Come to liberate your people, in Jesus' name.

Emilio Castro

Week 20

Czechoslovakia • Poland

To you, Creator of nature and humanity,
of truth and beauty, I pray:
Hear my voice, for it is the voice of the victims of all wars
and violence among individuals and nations.
Hear my voice, for it is the voice of all children
who suffer
and will suffer when people put their faith
in weapons and war.
Hear my voice when I beg you to instill into the hearts
of all human beings the wisdom of peace,
the strength of justice,
and the joy of fellowship.
O God, hear my voice, and grant unto the world your everlasting peace.

From a prayer of Pope John Paul II

When I'm down and helpless
When lies are reigning
When fear and indifference are growing
—May your kingdom come.

When joy is missing
When love is missing
and unbelief is growing
—May your kingdom come.

To the sick and lonely
To the imprisoned and tortured

—May your kingdom come.
Into the churches
Into our praying, into our singing
—May your kingdom come.

Into our hearts
Into our hands, into our eyes
—May your kingdom come. Soon!

A Czech litany

The concentration camp number of Blessed Father Maximilian Kolbe of Poland focuses attention and prayer on all victims of conscience, past and present, including those many persons without a "number" who have "disappeared" in so many countries.

16670

May the Lord accept our prayers
and grant that we may see substantial progress
in ecumenical understanding and in the will of God.

Karol Wojtyla (Pope John Paul II)

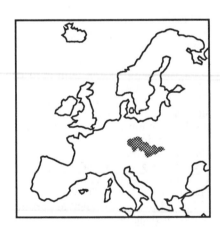

Czechoslovakia

Population: 15.5 million.
Languages: Czech, Slovak. Hungarian, Polish, and Ukranian are also spoken.
Government: Federal republic.

Religion: Christians 80%; Jews about 0.1%. Almost a quarter of the population is atheist or nonreligious.

Situated in Central Europe, Czechoslovakia has been exposed to Franco-Teutonic influences from one direction, and Magyar and Slavic influences from the other. Early German missionaries brought the Roman Catholic faith into the area, Bohemia (northern Czechoslovakia) becoming Roman Catholic under King Wenceslas in the 10th century. In the 9th century, in response to a request from the king of Moravia (central Czechoslovakia) for missionaries who would teach his people in their own language, the Byzantine patriarch sent the brothers Cyril and Methodius. They encountered opposition as a result of the growing rift between Rome and Constantinople, but nevertheless received support from the pope. Reformation influenc-

es were strong in the 15th and 16th centuries, with the movement begun by the Protestant martyr Jan Hus, the founding of the Moravian Brethren, and the influence of Luther. In 1621 the Catholic Hapsburgs gained control, and although Counterreformation pressures eased with the Edict of Tolerance, it was not until 1848 that Protestants gained equal rights with Roman Catholics. The dissolution of the Austro-Hungarian empire had political implications for the area, and since 1948 communist control has affected all the churches.

Although the constitution guarantees freedom of religion, all churches and religious communities require official recognition by the government. The majority Roman Catholic church has experienced considerable restriction, and tension continues. There have been particular difficulties regarding ecclesiastical appointments, and many positions have remained vacant for years.

The Czechoslovak Hussite church, born out of a Roman Catholic modernist movement, influenced by the spiritual tradition of Hus, and incorporating a strong biblical theology, is the second largest confessional body. The Evangelical church of Czech Brethren is a union of the Brethren and the fruits of the Hussite movement in which women played a prominent role. Various Lutheran and Reformed bodies are present.

The Orthodox church, autocephalous since 1951, is strongest in eastern Slovakia. All Christians face the problems of maintaining a faithful witness in a socialist state, and are concerned about issues of human rights and of peace.

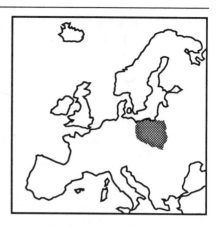

Poland

Population: 37.4 million.
Language: Polish.
Government: Republic.
Religion: Christians 90%. There are very small Muslim and Jewish communities, and a proportion of atheists and nonreligious.

Poland became officially Christian in 966 with the baptism of the ruler, who was converted to Christianity through his Roman Catholic wife. Over the centuries the faith spread and deepened under the influence of Christian rulers, and German missionaries and settlers, and Poland produced many saints and scholars. Protestant influences spread in the 16th century, but the Roman Catholic church was given official recognition and the Protestant faith restricted. The 18th-century political partition of Poland played an essential part in reinforcing the religious and cultural sense of identity that led to the founding in 1918 of an independent republic. During the Second World War something like 6 million Polish citizens, half of whom were Jews, were killed. A further 1.7 million were deported to Russia. The Jewish pediatrician Janusz Korczak, the Roman Catholic priest Maximilian

Kolbe, and the Lutheran bishop Juliusz Bursche are representative of the countless martyrs.

The Roman Catholic church in Poland has traditionally served as a national and social focus, and the election of a Polish pope and his subsequent visits to his homeland have inspired and encouraged the people. Tolerated by the communist regime, the church continues to hold great significance in the daily lives of most people, and the proportion of Roman Catholics practicing their faith is much higher than in Western European countries. The Solidarity movement, both in terms of the now banned trade union, and the wider movement toward democratization, has been both tempered and supported by the church. The younger Freedom and Peace movement seeks to hold together issues of international peace, individual freedom and justice, and ecology, as well as to increase understanding across the East-West line. The Orthodox church, autocephalous since 1924, was greatly reduced in numbers when a large area of land with a considerable Orthodox population became Russian territory in 1945. Of the various Protestant bodies, only about a third are recognized by the government as churches. Although tensions remain, the Roman Catholic church is slowly drawing closer to the other churches in Poland. One of the main tasks of all the churches is the education of children and young people in a communist society.

Let us thank God

for all such affirmations of faith and hope arising out of situations of restraint and hostility

for the early missionary activity of Cyril and Methodius, apostles to the Slavs

for a history of martyrdom, and solidarity between church and suffering people which has characterized life in Poland through the centuries.

In the words of the Sunday eucharist prayer of the Czechoslovak Hussite church,

let us pray

for the continuing everyday needs of the people of Czechoslovakia:

Bless, O God, the diligent work of all people who try to earn their daily bread for themselves and their families. Good Lord, help the miserable, comfort the sad, give rest to the tired and weary; give courage to those who suffer, freedom to the oppressed, protection and shelter to orphans, and strength to the weak in their struggle against all temptations of violence and danger....

Let us also pray

for Poland; for the movements of Solidarity, and Freedom and Peace; and for a recognition of the dignity and the right to self-determination of the Polish people

for the Christian education of children and young people; for increased practice of Bible reading and prayer in homes; for perseverance in confessing the faith in a socialist environment

for those things which concern women in Poland: "There are so many social problems which bother women as mothers, wives and sisters, and lead to a breakdown of family life—problems of alcoholism, drugs, and lack of means to live"

that the churches may grow together in a deeper ecumenical fellowship; that minority churches be saved from becoming inward-looking; and majority churches look to the needs of their brothers and sisters

that in the uncertain circumstances of life in communist countries Christians may be conscious of the prayers of others.

We are two hands: but belong to one body.
We differ: we are right hand and left,

one stretched joyfully to heaven, one rejoicing in victory,
and one hanging sadly down incapable of grasping anything again;

one hand full of strength and power,
clenched in the desire for freedom,
and the other tight with desperation;

one hand that can throttle and beat and wound
and one that bleeds—

We differ; but belong to one body.

Help us, O Lord, we who are your hands,
that we may not be raised against each other,
but together repeatedly show that we are one in prayer
for your rule,
and that we may remain united,
because to you we pray together:
May your kingdom come!

From Poland

Week 21

Albania • Bulgaria • Yugoslavia

As the bread which we break
was scattered over the mountains
and when brought together became one,
so let your church be brought together
from the ends of the earth into your kingdom;
for yours is the glory and the power
through Jesus Christ for evermore.

Didache, 2nd century

You, O God, have made us human beings for yourself,
and our hearts are restless until they find their rest in you.
Grant unto your sons and daughters in Albania a renewed
awareness of their creation at your hands, and an irrepressible longing to find their rest in you.

After the words of St. Augustine

O Lord, in you have I trusted:
let me never be confounded.

From Te Deum Laudamus: 5th century, Yugoslavia

Remember, Lord, the city in which we dwell,
and every city and region, and the faithful that inhabit it.

Remember, Lord, them that voyage, that travel, that are
sick,
that are laboring, that are in prison, and their safety.

Remember Lord, them that bear fruit, and do good deeds
in your holy churches, and that remember the poor.

And send forth on us all the riches of your compassion, and grant us with one mouth and one heart to glorify and celebrate

your glorious and majestic name, Father, Son, and Holy Spirit,

now and ever, and to ages of ages.

And the mercies of the great God and our Savior Jesus Christ shall be with us all.

The Divine Liturgy of St. Chrysostom,
commemoration of the diptychs of the living

Small Christian communities reportedly existed at least in the coastal areas of this region at about the time of the end of St. Paul's ministry. They may have been largely composed of converted Jews of the diaspora. Later, organized Christianity came from both Rome and Constantinople, the Byzantine influence being considerable in the 9th century. By 927 Bulgaria was an independent Christian nation with its own autonomous church ranking as a patriarchate. The Serbian Orthodox Church first became independent in the 13th century. The whole area, however, was subjected to endless waves of invasion, and changes of rulers. Independence was gained and lost; patriarchates were suppressed and reestablished. Protestant influences penetrated Yugoslavia in the 16th century, and newer Protestant denominations arrived in the 19th. Following centuries of control by the Ottoman Turks and consequent suffering of Christians, the area again experienced turbulence in this century, until the emergence of socialist republics after the second world war.

Albania

Population: 3 million.
Language: Albanian.

Government: Single-party socialist republic.

Before the Peoples' Republic was established in 1946, two-thirds of the population was Muslim and the remaining third Christian (20% Greek Orthodox, 10% Roman Catholic, and very small Protestant groups). Antireligious pressure soon began to build up in this atheistic state, and in 1967 all religious institutions were closed. Churches and mosques alike were either destroyed or converted to secular use; a very few being preserved as "cultural monuments." Officially, religion does not exist, and Albanians have been denied contact with the rest of the world. Recently, however, the country has begun to emerge a little from this isolation. Al-

though the poorest country in Europe, it is self-sufficient in fuel and grain, and people are well clothed and apparently well nourished. All agriculture and industry is state-run—efficiently enough to provide for free education and a social welfare system without the necessity of income tax.

Bulgaria

Population: 9 million.
Languages: Bulgarian. Turkish and Macedonian spoken in some areas.
Government: Republic.
Religions: Christians approximately 80%, Muslims about 10%.

Formerly a monarchy, Bulgaria became a socialist republic in 1946. Approximately 80% of people belong to the Bulgarian Orthodox Church which "is the traditional faith of the Bulgarian people. It is bound up with their history and as such, by its structure, its nature, and its spirit can be considered a church of the popular democracy" (Article 3 of the Law concerning Religious Faiths). This church, recognized again as auto-cephalous in 1945 and a patriarchate in 1953, was separated from the state in 1947. Armenians have been in this area since the 5th century, and today there is a small community (less than 0.25%) belonging to the Armenian Apostolic Church. Roman Catholics (about 0.7%) are mostly of the Western Rite, but some are of the Byzantine. There are about 16,000 Protestants—Congregationalists, Methodists, Baptists, Pentecostals, and Adventists.

Legally, there is freedom to practice religious rites—and also to engage in anti-religious propaganda. Although the churches operate within certain restrictions, their witness is bearing encouraging fruit. There have been some indications recently of a greater degree of tolerance toward the Christian church by the state. They find common ground in loyalty to the country and in contributing to the building of a new society, and participating in the movement for peace, unity, and mutual understanding.

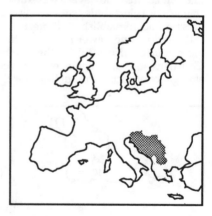

Yugoslavia

Population: 23.2 million.
Languages: Serbo-Croat, Macedonian, Slovenian.
Government: Single-party federal republic.
Religion: Christians 73%; Muslims 11%; a small Jewish community.

Born of the movement to unite the southern Slav peoples, the country of Yugoslavia was formed on the dissolution of the Austro-Hungarian empire at the end of the first world war. Invaded by German and Italian forces in 1941, and torn by civil war between rival resistance movements, it emerged as a communist republic in 1945. It practices a decentralized form of communism, and travel in both directions is freely permitted across its frontiers. Economic difficulties, with rising unemployment and inflation, have led to some unrest.

Considerable religious liberty is allowed in Yugoslavia, and it is possible to hold dialogue between Christians and Marxists. Senior jobs, however, tend to go to party members who are not allowed to belong to any religious body. Many churches are full, and young people, not necessarily from Christian families, form a significant part of the congregations.

Orthodox Christians number about 40% of the population, and are to be found especially in the east and center of the country. Over the centuries, the Patriarchate of the Serbian Orthodox Church has twice been suppressed. When the new nation emerged, the patriarchate was reestablished and recognized by the Ecumenical Patriarchate of Constantinople. Although not a state church, it is the traditional church of the people, and exerts considerable influence. It produces a large variety of Christian newspapers and journals. There are sizable communities of other churches of the Orthodox family, notably Albanian and Bulgarian. The Roman Catholic community, concentrated in the republics of Slovenia and Croatia to the west, accounts for about a third of the population. A proportion are Albanian, and there are a number of Byzantine Rite Catholics. Old Catholic communities also exist. Members of the Lutheran and Reformed churches are largely of German and Hungarian background, and there are congregations of newer Protestant denominations.

"And a vision appeared to Paul in the night: a man of Macedonia was standing beseeching him and saying, 'Come over to Macedonia and help us.'"

In company with the people of those lands which gave rise to that plea, let us thank God

for those who from the earliest times to the present day have sought to share the Christian faith in the Balkans

for Cyril and Methodius, the apostles to the Slavs, who spread Christianity in southeastern Europe

for the endurance of the church in its witness to the faith throughout the ages, and especially at the time of the Ottoman domination and in this century

that God is not only where religion is permitted, but has a way of infiltrating even the most restrictive circumstances.

Let us seek the forgiveness of God and of each other for the divisions that have hindered Christian witness:

Lord, we have sinned against you and against each other.

—Lord, have mercy.

O Christ, our divisions are contrary to your will, and have impeded our common witness to you.

—Christ, have mercy.

Lord, we have not loved you enough in our sisters and brothers, created in your image, but different from us.

—Lord, have mercy.

Creator God, stop us wandering in alienation from one another. Satisfy the longings of our hearts, grant our rightful requests, and unite us soon in one holy church through your Son Jesus Christ who with you in the communion of the Holy Spirit lives and reigns eternally.

Prayer of an ecumenical group consisting of members
of the Roman Catholic, Lutheran, Orthodox,
and Pentecostal churches in Yugoslavia

Let us pray

for the churches and monasteries of Bulgaria, their metropolitans, bishops, priests, monks, and people

that icons honored by the people may continue to speak to them of a divine realm and the communion of saints

for all in these countries who humbly and quietly seek to be obedient to their Christian vocation while maintaining the vision of a wider whole.

Grant, O Lord, that with your love I may be big enough to reach the world; and small enough to be one with you.

Mother Teresa of Skopje and Calcutta

for hidden Christians in Albania, that God will continually strengthen their faith, and give them an awareness of belonging with us to a worldwide family

for growing harmony between various population groups;

and for God's blessing on all efforts to facilitate local ecumenical cooperation and good will.

Lord, you sent your Son Jesus Christ into the world to reconcile us to yourself and to one another. Help us to know how to work together with Christ toward the achievement of universal reconciliation. Amen.

Prepared by an ecumenical group from Slovenia, Yugoslavia,
for the Week of Prayer for Christian Unity, 1986

Week 22

Hungary • Romania

O Heavenly King, Comforter, Spirit of truth,
present in all places and filling all things;
Treasury of blessings and Giver of life:
Come and dwell in us, cleanse us from every impurity,
and of your goodness save our souls.

Orthodox invocation of the Holy Spirit

O Christ, our God, who for us and for our salvation came down from heaven, and stretched out your loving arms upon the cross that all might be gathered into one body: deliver us from all forms of separation and disunity.

O Lord, who gives unto each nation its place and time and mission: grant us the gift of unity of the Spirit in the bond of peace, that the ancient church, and all Christians of this land, each loyal to their confession, culture, and nationality, may discover new forms of common Christian witness, and stand before the divided world as a united and humble fellowship.

O Lord, who commanded your disciples to pray both for their neighbors and their enemies: give us such love for one another, that with one voice and honest heart we may glorify your name, the Father, the Son, and the Holy Spirit. Amen.

Prayer for unity: Ion Bria

O Lord our God,
we thank you for the peace of our country and our homes.

We pray that the fruits of work well done may give joy to every worker.

Give your blessing to our congregation and church.

May we truly praise you and serve all your people.

We pray for our homeland, for the leaders of our nation, and for all who have power and bear responsibility.

We pray for our loved ones, and for those who have lived and died in the faith.

May we follow their example, and with them have a share in your kingdom of peace and light,

through our Lord Jesus Christ. Amen.

Prayer from the Reformed Church of Hungary, adapted

Hungary

Population: 10.7 million.
Language: Hungarian.
Government: Republic.
Religion: Christians 84% (Roman Catholics 55–60%, Protestants 25%, Orthodox 0.5%); Jews 1%; atheists and nonreligious 15%.

Christianity can be traced from the 3rd century in this land where at first both Roman and Orthodox missionaries were active. The Magyars (Hungarians), coming into the area from the east, had strong ties with the Byzantine church, but the Western tradition was adopted in 1001. The Reformation brought Lutheran and Calvinistic influences, and by the end of the 16th century Protestants were in a majority, most belonging to the Reformed church. This situation was reversed when the Austrian Hapsburgs expelled the Ottoman Turks, Roman Catholic settlers moved into the region, and a harsh Counterreformation began. Hungary did not really gain independence from the Hapsburgs until after the first world war, and then only at the expense of much loss of life and a large area of territory. Becoming a republic after the second world war, Hungary is now a socialist state. From the pattern of a feudal agricultural society it has become an industrialized nation—with an efficient agricultural sector also—in which all can participate.

Contacts between the churches and the state are dealt with through the state office for ecclesiastical affairs, which also give some financial support. The Roman Catholic church, which had previously enjoyed special preference, found it harder than some Protestants to adapt to life in a communist country. At first resisting the changes, it has felt threatened by increasing secularization and the official atheism of the government. But religious life remains active, and peace is a major concern. Of the Protestant denominations, the Hungarian Reformed

church is by far the largest, with smaller Lutheran, Baptist, and Methodist churches. The theology of service, developed after the war, has given added impetus to the church's ministry among children with disability, old people, and the sick. A unique venture in Eastern Europe is Christian-Marxist dialogue, in which the Reformed church is active. The churches are particularly concerned by the effect of increasing secularism—alcoholism, divorce, and the break-up of family life. In this context Christian education is especially important. Most churches belong to the Ecumenical Council of Churches, and mission is an ecumenical priority.

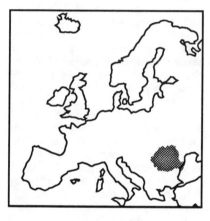

Romania

Population: 22.9 million.
Languages: Romanian, Hungarian, German, and others.
Government: Republic.
Religion: Christians 86% (Orthodox 75%, Protestants 6%, Roman Catholics 5%); Muslims 1.2%, mostly ethnic Turks; Jews 0.5%; atheists 7%.

Its people an amalgam of the local Dacian population and their rulers, Romania emerged out of one of the Roman provinces. For a long time it remained a wedge of Latin culture between Slavs and Mongols. After being an autonomous national unit within the Ottoman empire for three and half centuries, its people were buffeted between the armies of Austria, Hungary, and Russia. Transylvania, formerly part of the Austrian Hapsburg empire, was incorporated into Romania in 1918.

Traditionally, Christianity was brought by the apostle Andrew, and by the 3rd century existed in strength on the shores of the Black Sea. There were many local martyrs under the emperor Diocletian. Orthodoxy has been the main tradition for centuries and remains so today. Hungarian and Polish immigrants spread the Roman Catholic faith in Transylvania. Reformation influences reached the Hungarian and German people living in Transylvania early in the 16th century, and Reformed and Lutheran churches were established. The first Baptist community emerged among Germans in 1856. Following independence from Ottoman rule, the Romanian Orthodox church became autocephalous. It became a patriarchate in 1925.

Services of worship in most churches are lively and well attended. Industrialization and rural depopulation, together with spreading secularism, pose new pastoral and missionary problems and opportunities. Ecumenical witness in the country depends very much on efforts to bring all churches, historical or new, together with all cultures and nationalities into a community serving and struggling with all people. In this connection the "social apostolate," a summons to pastoral care and service toward the whole of society, initiated by the late Patriarch Justinian (1948–1977), is a major influence. Peace and disarmament are vital concerns. The Romanian Orthodox church has launched three appeals for peace in recent years.

We give thanks

for the centuries of Orthodox tradition which gave Christianity its roots in Romania

for the renewal of Christian faith and life prompted by the Reformation, especially in Hungary and Transylvania

for the faithfulness with which many held to their Christian faith through centuries of suffering, persecution, and oppression

for the spiritual strength which radiates from the Romanian monasteries

for the witness of service offered by the church in Hungary.

We pray to God

for the members of different confessions, that they may grow together into a deeper ecumenical fellowship, sharing the richness of their Christian heritage, and strengthening one another in faith, hope, and love

for the Christian education of young people

for the training of future generations of theologians

for a fruitful outcome of dialogue between Christians and Marxists

for the churches as God's instruments, that they may contribute to peaceful development in the process of reconciliation between neighboring countries, and in the world.

Almighty God, in your majesty and nearness I look into my soul and examine myself with regard to this great profession to which you have called me. I want to teach children and young people in a manner worthy of our homeland, of humanity, and of your heavenly kingdom. I sense the importance of the task and I feel my own weakness. God of strength, support me by your grace. Help me so to do my

work that I am worthy of my calling. Grant me respect and love for young people, joy in my work, enthusiasm, and commitment, that I may be a worthy worker for the future of your kingdom. Amen.

A Hungarian teacher's prayer

Week 23

Mongolia •
Union of Soviet Socialist Republics

Khristos voskress!
Voistinu voskrese
Christ is risen!
He is risen indeed!

Christ is risen from the dead: trampling down death by
death; and upon those in the tombs bestowing life. Though
you descended into the grave, O Immortal One, yet you
put down the power of Hades, and rose as conqueror, O
Christ our God: you spoke clearly to the myrrh-bearing
women, Rejoice: you bestowed peace upon your apostles,
and to the fallen you brought resurrection.

Russian Orthodox

O God,
    that we may receive your blessing
    touch our brows, touch our heads,
    and do not look upon us in anger.

In a hard year be thou mercy;
    in a year of affliction, be thou kindness;
    dark spirits banish from us,
    bright spirits bring close to us;
    gray spirits put away from us,
    good spirits draw near to us.

When I am afraid, be thou my courage;
When I am ashamed, be thou my true face;

Be thou over me like a blanket,
Be thou under me like a bed of furs.

Prayer from Mongolia

Lord, through the shedding of the blood of your saints,
gather in joy all the scattered children of your church,
and all who weep bitterly at the sadness of disunity,
you who give grace for our salvation.

Armenian Orthodox

When my soul sheds its tears,
When my heart languishes in longing,
When my whole being shivers in fatigue,
Come, O Jesus, I beg you to come.
Draw near, Reviver and Consoler!
What is it you wish to tell me
by means of these people,
by these circumstances,
by this span of time?
Jesus, I implore you to shorten
the time of trial for us
for my dear ones, for my exhausted nation.
Jesus, I ask you—help those who laid down their lives
for our welfare;
assist them for whom you wish me to pray.

Prayer of Lithuanian prisoners

O Lord, I do not know what to ask of you. You alone know my true needs. You love me more than I myself know how to love. Help me to see my real needs which are concealed from me. I dare not ask either a cross or consolation. I can only wait on you. My heart is open to you. Visit and help me, for your great mercy's sake. Strike me and heal me, cast me down and raise me up. I worship in silence your holy will and your inscrutable ways. I offer my-

self as a sacrifice to you. I put all my trust in you. I have no other desire than to fulfill your will. Teach me how to pray. Pray yourself in me.

Prayer of the well-known hierarch and theologian,
Metropolitan Philaret of Moscow (1553–1633),
and described as "a prayer which has been used
by millions of believers for many centuries"

Christianity made little lasting progress in this area. To the extent that anything is known about religious life in Mongolia today, it seems likely that there are no more than a few thousand Orthodox Christians in the state. Expatriate diplomats and technicians, and possibly some Orthodox and Evangelical believers among Soviet troops stationed in Mongolia, constitute a constantly changing Christian presence.

Mongolia

The Mongols made their mark on world history when, in the 13th and 14th centuries under Genghis Khan, they conquered an empire which included the territories of present-day Turkey, Iran, Russia, and the whole of China. Since 1924, Mongolia has been an independent communist state in the sphere of influence of the Soviet Union. It has a population of approximately two million people and a landscape of grasslands and desert. Its traditional religion is Shamanism, with Buddhist Lamaism as a later addition. Together they claim the allegiance of about a third of the population. Although there was some Nestorian activity in this area in the 6th and 7th centuries, and later missionary effort on the part of Roman Catholic religious orders, and eventually in the 19th century by Protestants, there were also many persecutions and setbacks, and

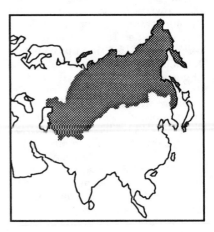

USSR

Population: 278.8 million.
Languages: Russian. Each republic also has its own language.
Government: Federal republic.
Religion: Christians number over 96 million, or 36% of the population, of whom 60 million are Orthodox, 4 million Protestant, 3 million Roman Catholic. There are some 30 million

Muslims, and 3 million Jews. A quarter of the population are active and militant atheists, and a third are agnostic or nonreligious.

Christianity began in the very early centuries slowly to penetrate in the southern parts of this territory, and gave birth to the Georgian Apostolic Church, believed to be one of the most ancient churches of Christendom. In more recent centuries Georgian Christians have experienced many vicissitudes under Arab, Mongol, and Russian rule. Today the Georgian church, with its main center in Tiflis, and an official membership of 5 million, is said to be enjoying a period of renewed church attendance with many young people in the congregations.

Also ancient is the Armenian Apostolic Church, Christianity becoming the state religion in Armenia in the 4th century. Armenians suffered severely under Turkish rule, and as recently as 1915–1916 approximately 1.5 million Armenians were victims of genocide. Today, more than 3 million Armenians live in the Soviet Republic of Armenia, 1.5 million in other parts of the Soviet Union, and the remaining 2 million are scattered around the world. The monastery of Etchmiadzin near Yerevan is the present administrative center of the Armenian Apostolic church, increasingly noted for the fervor of its Christian spirituality and practice.

It is the baptism in 988 of Vladimar, Grand Prince of Kievan Russia, which is accepted as the beginning of the Russian Orthodox church as an organized, recognized, and historical church of all tribes and nations of Early Russia. The year 1988 marked the millennium of the life of this church, an event celebrated by the whole of Christendom. The center of church and political life shifted from Kiev to Moscow in the 13th century, and in 1589 the Russian church became a patriarchate. Attempts by the patriarch to implement reforms in the 17th century resulted in schism, and various groups of Old Believers broke away. After having been abolished in the 17th century, the See was restored again following the Revolution, thus laying the foundation for the renewal of the order and inner life of the church. A difficult transitional period followed as the church adjusted itself to the radically changed conditions of church-state relationships in the new socialist society. The Second World War was a decisive period, during which the church gained the respect of the government and of society by the patriotism shown by its members. Emerging from the war united and inwardly consolidated, the church through its members became actively involved in the process of post-war restoration and the building of a new socialist society. The Russian Orthodox church has been a member of the WCC since 1961 and participates fully in the life of the ecumenical movement. With a membership of at least 50 million, it is by far the largest church in Russia, and is widely involved in peacemaking activities.

The 4.5 million Catholics in Russia are concentrated primarily in Lithuania, western Ukraine, and Byelorussia. They face considerable antireligious pressure, many bishops and priests have been imprisoned and some executed, and the church is subjected to severe restrictions. They include members of various Uniate churches, which makes relationships between Catholic and Orthodox more difficult. There is no central leadership and not much contact with the Vatican. In this and in other areas of Russia there are many unregistered, illegal, and clandestine denominations—some estimates put their membership as high as 10% of the population—known to the Western world as the "underground" church. They are of all confessional backgrounds, and are mostly highly

critical of the Soviet regime.

Fruit of the Reformation, Lutheran churches exist today in Estonia and Latvia; and there are congregations in Siberia and Kazkhstan, which maintain ecumenical connections through the Lutheran World Federation. Baptists came in the 18th century, and the Pentecostal movement spread during the 1920s. In 1944 Baptists, Mennonites, Adventists, and Pentecostals joined to form the Union of Evangelical Christian Baptists of the USSR. There are about 80 other Protestant denominations, humbly and quietly maintaining faith in difficult days, and in this sense a challenge to us all. "Russian believers," it has been said, "can resist without stridency, persevere without the image of world victory that sometimes tempts us Christian activists in our political and religious struggle. In their long suffering they can humble and teach us."

Good Jesus, patient as a lamb in the presence of your captors, keep us silent and still with love for you.

In peace let us pray to the Lord
for the peace of the whole world, let us pray to the Lord—Kyrie eleison

Orthodox liturgy, USSR

for those who hold power and carry responsibility that they may consistently pursue policies that lead to peace, understanding, and justice, let us pray to the Lord—Kyrie eleison

for the people of Mongolia about whom we know so little, let us pray to the Lord—Kyrie eleison

for the ordinary people of the Soviet Union, going about their daily tasks and experiencing the joys and sorrows common to all humanity, let us pray to the Lord—Kyrie eleison

for all who suffer for their faith, let us pray to the Lord—Kyrie eleison

for greater mutual understanding between Christians, let us pray to the Lord—Kyrie eleison

for the celebration of a thousand years of Christianity in the Russian Orthodox Church; for the Armenian Church's thanksgiving for the gift of the holy chrism, and for God's blessing on all the meeting together which these events will bring, let us pray to the Lord—Kyrie eleison.

Help us, save us, have mercy on us, and keep us, O God, by your grace.

Introduction to Weeks 24–27

More than anything else I shall remember the visit to the old English fort at Cape Coast where the African slaves were kept chained in a dark dungeon at water-level till the boats took them to the slave ships, while in the chapel immediately above, the English garrison conducted worship, keeping watch through a hole in the floor on the inmates of the dungeon below. I am always amazed that these crimes can be so easily forgotten. Ever since that visit I have wished that some representative Englishman—an archbishop or a prime minister—might come to Ghana and go down in that dungeon, kneel down on the floor, and offer a prayer of contrition. I still hope it may happen.

Lesslie Newbigin, writing of his visit to Ghana, Unfinished Agenda

Lord, have mercy upon us.
Christ, have mercy upon us.
Lord, have mercy upon us.

Not only Ghana, but all the countries to be prayed for in these next four weeks are situated on what used to be known as the Slave Coast, from which millions of Africans were transported by traders of many nationalities to work as slave labor on the plantations of the New World. There are a great many places where such acts of penitence are appropriate, but few as poignant as here on the coast of West Africa.

Today, with the exception of Nigeria, and to a lesser extent Ivory Coast, these countries are all poor. Most are sparsely populated and predominantly agricultural, often at subsistence level. Their principal means of livelihood make them very vulnerable to weather conditions and to the fluctuations of world market prices, and many remain in debt. However, many countries are developing a tourist industry. Good beaches, fine scenery up-country, game reserves, and fishing are tourist attractions.

Present-day boundary lines stem from the countries' colonial history; but of course the area in general has a history extending back for very many centuries before that, when ancient African kingdoms traded across the Sahara. A good deal of the quest for African authenticity looks back to those earlier days.

Christianity first reached these West African countries in the 15th century when Portuguese mariners and traders came to the coastal areas. Roman Catholic priests came with them, but contact tended to be intermittent, and in many places the church slowly died out. There was no Christian activity in the hinterland; and on the whole, the gospel message was received more readily on the offshore islands than on the mainland. The missionary movement of the 19th century led to the establishment of more permanent churches.

Week 24

Liberia • Sierra Leone

May God give you a long life, a well body, and a cool heart (peace).

A Krio blessing

Liberia

There are literally two Liberias. In one Liberia, children have clothing and shelter for their bodies, education for their minds, and freedom and human dignity for their spirits. In the other Liberia, life is so drastically different that its daily ugliness transforms the buoyancy of hope into the fatigue of despair. *Come, Lord Jesus, and rescue the perishing. Amen.*

Anglican bishop of Liberia

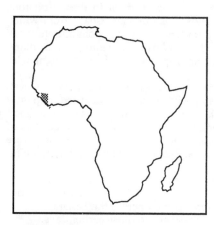

Population: 2.2 million.
Languages: English and many local languages.
Government: Republic.
Religion: Officially a Christian state, though about one quarter of the population is Muslim, and many hold traditional beliefs. Most Christians are Protestant; 2% of the population is Roman Catholic.

Founded by the American Colonization Society for liberated slaves repatriated from the Southern USA, Liberia became an independent republic in 1847. Widely regarded as one of the more stable African independent states, the country has experienced a period of military rule. It was freed slaves who welcomed the arrival of both Protestant and Roman Catholic missionaries in the 19th century, and also set up churches including the oldest indigenous Baptist church in Africa. Educational work was begun at this time.

Although the Christian church in Liberia has remained small, it has made a significant contribution to national life, and its influence is out of

all proportion to its numbers. In response to the social upheavals following from the 1980 coup, the churches have been active in championing the peoples' rights, and forthright in speaking out on matters of social justice.

Sierra Leone

"If Mary and Joseph had arrived at an African village [almost any village in Sierra Leone] they would have found a place. Someone would have given Mary a mat by the cooking fire, and there would have been grannies and aunties to help her with the birth. The men would have made room around the rice bowl for Joseph to dip his hand in while he told his story. Angel visitations, dreams, and signs in the sky would have called forth awe and wonder but no surprise, for here the spirit world is fully as real as the physical one."

Dorothy R. Gilbert

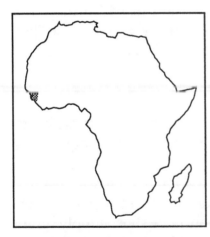

Population: 3.8 million.
Languages: English, Krio (i.e., Creole), and numerous local languages.
Government: Unitary single-party republic.
Religion: Most people are Muslims (40%), or follow traditional African beliefs (50%). The Christian community is small.

Freetown, the capital, was originally founded as a settlement for ex-slaves, many of whom had been introduced to Christianity during slavery and now brought their faith with them. The settlement became a British colony in 1808, and was used as a reception center for the large numbers of Africans being freed from ships which continued to trade illicitly after the slave trade was abolished. Many of the descendants of these slaves, the Creoles, eventually rose to positions of relative wealth and influence. Independence was gained in 1961.

The country remains poor, with very little industrial development, 80% illiteracy, and one of the highest infant mortality rates in the world. The government is trying to tackle the economic crisis and deep-rooted problems of corruption, but "few people can afford the luxury of being incorruptible when their salaries are

far too small to feed their families." Islam is actively promoting medical and educational work. Numerically speaking, the Creoles of Freetown have continued to constitute the bulk of the church in Sierra Leone, and the vast majority of people living up-country remain untouched by Christianity, although some churches are now active in these areas. Christian leaders who maintain a vision for outreach are able to point to areas of growth and renewal. The United Christian Council, formed in 1924, has twelve member denominations and one of the independent churches is also affiliated to it.

We give thanks

for Liberia's significant Christian community, and for those who despite hardships and temptations remain cheerful and retain faith

for the rich human resources of Sierra Leone, and for the generosity and ancient wisdom of her people

that out of the adverse climatic, economic, and historical circumstances of this part of Africa so many remarkable men and women of God have emerged. "We have seen God at work in the lives and homes of many people, who, under much suffering and in great need, have learned to accept with contentment the situation in which they find themselves, and still give thanks for the goodness of God. 'All things work together for good...' has come alive for us in Africa!"

We pray

for the recovery of the national economy in these countries, and for honest and responsible stewardship on the part of national leaders

for the poor and needy. "The approaching season July–September is the 'hungry season' for those in the country areas of Sierra Leone; when food is in short supply, grain stocks exhausted, and people do and sell whatever they can to make a little money."

for boldness to preach the gospel of peace in the face of political instability in Liberia.

We pray

that the story of Jesus may be effectively told and find a

welcome in the hearts of country people in this part of Africa.

Lord, we pray that in all the contacts
and conversations between people
your story may be enthusiastically told
and your living presence acknowledged. Amen.

Week 25

Cape Verde • Guinea • Guinea Bissau • Senegal • The Gambia

May the word of God
reach all nations
and may He be recognized
as the only one true God.

A prayer from Guinea

O God our Heavenly Father,
you will that all should be saved
and come to the knowledge of the truth;
We pray for the children of Islam in Senegal and The
Gambia.
Grant that they unto whom your unity is made known
may learn the richness of your love,
as it is revealed in your Son, our Prophet, Priest, and
King,
even Jesus Christ our Lord.

Prayer for use in the Muslim world

Lord, you want everybody to live in your Truth,
increase our faith in your Son Jesus Christ.

Prayer of a Senegalese Christian

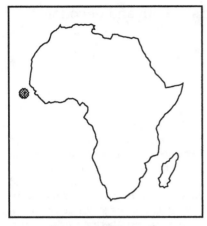

Cape Verde

The Republic of Cape Verde is an archipelago of 15 islands lying about 300 miles west of Senegal. It was colonized by the Portuguese in the 15th century, and Roman Catholic missionary orders met with considerable response in the islands. The population today is Christian, although secularization is increasing. The majority are Roman Catholics but there are also small Protestant churches on most of the islands. The official language is Portuguese, a local Creole form being widely spoken, as well as a number of ethnic languages. The resident population is approximately 300,000.

The impetus for independence was originally linked with that of Portuguese Guinea (now Guinea Bissau), although Cape Verde pursued a slightly separate course. Independence was granted in 1975. The link with Guinea Bissau was severed in 1981, but diplomatic relations have since been restored.

The country has suffered greatly from recurrent drought and consequently tends to import a high proportion of food requirements, and foreign aid is essential. About one million Cape Verdeans live outside the country, and the money they send home helps to alleviate the economic problems. The government is actively grappling with these problems and seeking to improve health and educational facilities; but the difficulties are enormous.

Give thanks

for the continuing receptivity of the islanders of Cape Verde to the Christian faith

for the efforts of the government to improve the economy and to develop health services and education in the country.

Pray

for the many Cape Verdeans living and working abroad, and for those who face economic difficulties and the effects of drought at home

for all places, like Cape Verde, of which we know little; yet where the Lord's Prayer is prayed, the Creed is recited, the Gloria Patri is sung and the good news of the Annunciation to Mary is commemorated; that each of us in our own very different circumstances may be united with our fellow

Christians in the use of such acts of faith and devotion.

Glory be to the Father,
and to the Son,
and to the Holy Spirit. Amen.

Guinea

The Republic of Guinea has a population of 6.1 million. French is the official language, but a number of African languages are widely spoken. The majority of people are Muslims (69%), although some (29.5%) adhere to tribal religions. Christians are a tiny minority (1.3%), of whom the majority are Roman Catholics. Guinea is one of the world's poorest countries.

In earlier times, Guinea was part of the great African kingdom of Ghana. Islam was introduced by the Ru-lani in the 18th century and gained a considerable following. The country became part of French West Africa in the 19th century, and declared independence in 1958. A difficult period followed, during which relationships with neighboring states deteriorated, and the country became virtually isolated. Tensions have since eased, especially since the military coup in 1984.

Roman Catholic missionaries came to Guinea in 1877; Protestants in 1918. The total Protestant community including Anglicans numbers less than 3,000, and there are no African indigenous churches. Following independence, the government was very pro-Marxist, and at this stage the church was persecuted. In 1967 all foreign missionaries, including priests, were expelled as part of an indigenization program. This ultimately resulted in a strengthening of the local church as it responded to increased responsibility. The churches are especially active on the off-shore islands where there are signs of renewal. The present government, though Muslim, is sympathetic and welcomes their cooperation in the work of development.

Let us give thanks

for the opportunity open to the church in Guinea to cooperate with the government in the development of the country

for all signs of renewed vigor in the Christian community.

Let us pray

for the poor and hungry of Guinea

for all who, in whatever small way, can begin to bring about change in the national policies and international economic systems that reinforce their poverty.

I saw a child today, Lord, who will not die tonight, harried into hunger's grave. He was bright and full of life because his father had a job and feeds him, but somewhere, everywhere, 10,000 life-lamps will go out, and not be lit again tomorrow. Lord, teach me my sin. Amen.

Prayer of an African Christian

Grant, O God, to your children in Guinea that in all their times of testing they may know your presence and obey your will, through the grace of Christ our Lord. Amen.

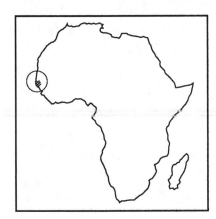

Guinea Bissau

The Republic of Guinea Bissau has a population of approximately 850,000. Portuguese is the official language, but Crioulo and a number of dialects are widely spoken. About 60% of the people follow traditional beliefs, and 35% are Muslim. The Christian minority of 5% is predominantly Roman Catholic, of whom a number are foreigners.

Guinea Bissau was settled by the Portuguese in the 15th century and the Roman Catholic Church here dates from then. Liberation movements began to develop in the 1960s, and the Partido Africano da Independência da Guiné e Cabo Verde (PAIGC) was formed. Fighting broke out between the PAIGC and the Portuguese in 1962, and in 1973 the PAIGC proclaimed independence which was recognized by the Portuguese a year later. The link with Cape Verde was maintained until 1980, when the latter withdrew as a direct result of a coup in Guinea Bissau.

Protestants arrived in 1939. The Igreja Evangélica da Guiné (founded by an evangelical group) is the only sizable Protestant church in the country. There is a tiny Anglican community.

Let us thank God

that using whatever imperfect means—whether soldier, trader, traveler, colonialist, missionary, or the humblest of local Christians—he has allowed the gospel to be planted in many lands, and has provided for its reformation and renewal.

Let us pray

for those people who find it hard to change and who continue to cling to old beliefs

that the churches today may be faithful to our Lord's command to preach the gospel and make disciples of all people.

Bless, O Lord, the independent nations of Africa as they emerge into the modern world and come into contact with the secular materialism of the West. May they ever value the spiritual awareness of their ancestors, and find its fulfillment in the face of your Son, Jesus Christ.

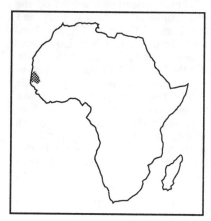

Senegal

Converted to Islam in 1040, the vast majority of Senegal's people remain firmly Muslim, owing strong allegiance to three Sufi brotherhoods.

Most Christians (about 3.5% of the total population) are Roman Catholics, with a small Protestant community springing from the work of missionaries of the Lutheran church, Assemblies of God, and the Evangelical Church of West Africa. Over the years, Christians have made a significant contribution to the country through their institutions, particularly schools, even though the number of church members has remained small.

The population is 6.4 million. French is the official language, with Arabic widely spoken, along with many local languages. Senegal became independent from France in 1960, and in 1982 entered into a confederation with its close neighbor Gambia. In spite of some prolonged contact with Christianity, most of the people remain either untouched or unresponsive to the Christian faith.

Local Christian leaders are few, and ways of sharing the Christian faith in a meaningful and compassionate way remain largely unexplored.

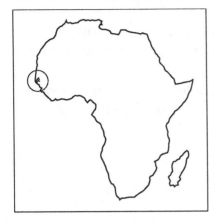

The Gambia

A narrow strip of country along the banks of the river, The Gambia extends like a finger into Senegal. Of necessity, links between the two countries are close. An attempted coup in 1981 was quelled with the aid of Senegalese forces, and this led to the formation of the Senegambian Confederation which is already making progress in the integrating of common services and policies. Formerly a British colony, The Gambia gained its independence in 1965. English remains the official language. Like Senegal it is a parliamentary republic, with freedom of religion guaranteed to its people. Some 87% of the population (750,000) re-main firmly Muslim. About 10% continue to adhere to African traditional religions, though many are being gradually Islamicized. Christians total about 3%, of whom the great majority are Roman Catholics, with Protestants numbering but a few thousand.

In 1821 the first Christian church south of the Sahara was established in The Gambia by the Rev. John Morgan, a Methodist minister among African repatriates in Georgetown, MacCarthy Island Division. The liberated Africans later became known as the Creoles/Akus of Banjul. The Methodists were followed by the Roman Catholics and Anglicans, and work among the Akus and the Wollofs of Banjul seemed more successful than in the province.

This situation has changed since the second world war. There are today many Christian groups among the Manjargos and the Karoninkas, the majority of whom are Roman Catholics and Methodists. The bulk of Manjargos are in the Casamance and in Guinea Bissau. The Gambia Methodists have pioneered among the Konyagies and have built the most recent church in the MacCarthy Island Division at Bani for this once migrant group. The Anglicans have now a full-time pastor at Basse and so have the Roman Catholics. Work continues to develop in the provinces with priests, pastors, and evangelists stationed in the main centers at Georgetown, Basse, and Farafenni. The Roman Catholics form the majority among the Christian population.

We thank you, Lord, for the Senegambian Confederation and its progress in the sharing of resources and services and for signs of cooperation between the churches of the region. Amen.

We pray
with the people of Senegambia and other countries in the
area that their lands may be spared the effects of drought.

O God, in whom we live and move and have our being,
grant us the rain we need, so that your answer to our
present earthly needs
may give us greater confidence to ask for eternal benefits.

Prayer from the Roman liturgy

Week 26

Benin • Ghana • Ivory Coast • Togo

Years ago our Elders said,
"It is God who drives away flies from the tail-less animal."

The same God touches each of us with the Spirit of power
to cope and overcome,
to drive away fears and anxieties,
to help us to walk through life in the fire of faith.

Moderator of the Evangelical Presbyterian Church in Ghana

19 Aug 07

Lord our God,
we pray for the holy church.
That it be deeply rooted
in faith and in your love.

Prayer from Benin

Let us pray for those who foster violence,
those who do not forgive others.
May the Lord change their hearts
that they seek peace and love their brothers and sisters.

Prayer from the Ivory Coast

Bite not one another.

Adinkra symbol of unity

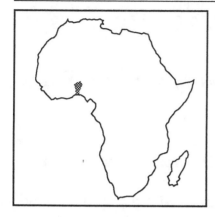

Benin

Benin's population of almost 4 million is almost entirely African. French is the official language, but each ethnic group has its own language. The country is a single-party republic and the present Marxist-oriented government has established stability after a very unstable period following independence. The majority of people (approximately 64%) follow traditional beliefs. About 14% are Muslims, and 21% are Christians, of whom the majority are Roman Catholics. The Methodist church is the largest Protestant body. There are a number of African Independent churches.

Benin is constitutionally a secular state with equal rights given to all religions, but since 1975 religious and spiritual cults have been discouraged. Just over a decade ago, all schools were nationalized, and the Roman Catholic church in particular suffered pressure from the government, but this has eased in recent years. Although many ethnic groups remain untouched by the Christian faith, there have recently been some migrations to coastal cities, and a number of small congregations have been established. In 1965 the Methodist church initiated Action aposto-lique commune, an evangelistic thrust among the Fon people serviced by an international, interracial, and interecclesial team, in which Roman Catholics assist in the production of the Scriptures in Fon. The Methodist church plays an active role in the socioeconomic life of the country, and is involved in dialogue with Muslims, as is the Roman Catholic church.

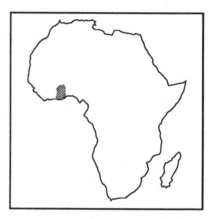

Ghana

Population: 14 million.
Languages: English, four national languages recognized, among others.
Government: Republic. Currently under military rule.
Religion: Christians 54%; Muslims 12%. The rest follow traditional beliefs.

Formerly a British colony known as the Gold Coast, Ghana was joined by the British-administered part of Togoland to become an independent nation in 1957. Since then its search for an appropriate form of government has been painful, frustrating, and elusive, with alternating civilian and military rule. The search for an authentic and effective form of self-government, reflecting indigenous values and statesmanship, is rooted

in a crisis of identity being experienced throughout Africa.

The first Christian preaching was undertaken by early chaplains in the fort settlements on the Slave Coast. Later, various missions began more sustained work outside the fort areas moving gradually up-country. The growth of this work was largely due to ordinary church members moving about the country as traders and government officials. The church made a very significant impact on the community in the sphere of Christian education.

Today schools and colleges continue to serve the people of Ghana, offering education based on the Christian faith. Nowadays the management of such institutions is community-based, and the influence of the church is experienced more through individuals whose faith is held as an integral part of their professional lives. In recent years Ghana has been facing problems in the economic, political, cultural, and social spheres, some resulting from external factors, e.g., the arrival of some one million homeless and unemployed Ghanaians expelled from Nigeria. "Whatever the external and internal factors acting on individuals as well as on the nation," says a representative of the Christian Council, "none of them can mold or determine the future more than the attitudinal response of the peoples to these pressures."

In the midst of many shortages and much religious tension, human dignity, hope, and faith abound in Ghana— *Thanks be to God.*

Our heavenly Father, we in Ghana heartily thank you for the manner in which you have been helping us in our struggle for survival and our fight against ignorance, disease, and sorrow. We acknowledge your loving kindness to us in our efforts to establish your kingdom here, where we hope to rule ourselves in truth, love, and justice. Let our land prosper in your might, as we pray in Jesus' name.

General secretary of the Christian Council of Ghana

Let us pray

for a stable and efficient government and administration, that armed interventions may give way to peaceful transition through the ballot box

for the responsible use of ecology; for honest financial management and appropriate economic policies

for the guidance of the Holy Spirit in the search for genuine expressions of life and living as well as the promotion of growth and responsibility.

O God, we implore you,
bless the people of this land,
this beautiful land,
this green land,
this yellow land
under your wonderful sun.
You know what we need:
food for body, soul, and spirit...

Prayer of a young Ghanaian

"Hold Ghana in your minds for just one second," comes the plea from Christians in Ghana. "Whatever you would pray for yourselves on your busiest or most lethargic, your most joyous and even your saddest day, pray for us. All prayers count."

God of all nations,
we thank you for creating us with love in your own image.
You are united with your Son in the Holy Spirit in perfect unity.
We ask you to unite also all peoples and churches
in order to bring about your kingdom in this world.

Prayer from Ghana

Hallelujah

in Ewe Ghana
as taught by Alexander Gondo

Hal-le - lu- jah, Hal - le - lu - jah. Hal-le-lu - jah.

Hal-le - lu-jah, Hal - le- lu - jah. Hal-le-lu - jah.

Ivory Coast

With an economy based on an astute development of its agricultural potential, and with a record of stable government (single-party republic) since independence from France in 1960, the Ivory Coast is today the most prosperous state in Francophone Africa. Until recently there was a large foreign population (over 1 million), mostly French and Levantine, employed in state enterprises. The Ivorean population is growing rapidly and now stands at around 10 million.

Although about 50% of the population still adhere to traditional African religions, and some 24% are Muslims, there is also a sizable (32%) Christian community, mostly Roman Catholic, but including significant African indigenous and Protestant communities. The first Roman Catholic mission arrived in 1687, and over the years the church has made a deep impact through education. The years 1913–1915 were marked by the presence of Prophet William Wade Harris of Liberia, whose preaching led to a remarkable mass movement of coastal people to Christianity. Many subsequently joined the Roman Catholic and Methodist churches; others founded an independent church of their own. The Methodists arrived in 1924 and remain the largest Protestant denomination.

Today there are a number of concerns common to other countries with a similar background of prosperity: the growth of materialism, a lack of concern for outreach on the part of Christians, and an easygoing lapse into syncretistic ways. More local worries revolve around the uncertain political future of the country, growing tribalism, rising unemployment, and unfulfilled expectations among educated young people. Most Protestant bodies belong to the Evangelical Federation of the Ivory Coast. The Taizé community is attempting to promote conversations between Protestants and Roman Catholics.

We pray

for all African Independent churches

for young people unemployed, and for the support and understanding of church and nation

for new initiatives to share the good news of Jesus with others

for Christ's gifts of unity and love among Christians in the Ivory Coast.

O God, most mighty among the heavens, forgive us our sins—Amen

For private and secret sins, O God forgive us—Amen
For not walking uprightly, O God forgive us—Amen
Forgive our young people—Amen
Forgive our adults—Amen
Forgive our men—Amen
Forgive our women—Amen
Visit not the sins of our fathers on us—Amen
If you should visit their iniquities on us who worship
here,
we shall be hurt—Yes, Lord
Therefore blot out all their sins this day, O Lord—Amen
Forgive us individually—Amen
Forgive us corporately—Amen
Grant forgiveness to all who worship you and do your
will on earth—Amen.

*An excerpt from a prayer of confession
recorded in an African Independent Church*

Togo

The Togolese Republic was formerly a part of Togoland, at one time a German colony and subsequently divided between the British and French. French Togoland (Togo) became independent in 1960. A period of political instability followed. The present government, however, has become a focus of national unity and stability, with equal participation between different ethnic groups in the country's sole political party.

It is estimated that about 60% of the population of almost 33 million follow traditional beliefs, some 25% are Christians, and about 7.5% Muslims. The majority of Christians are Roman Catholics. The first Protestants to enter the country were those (either immigrant or local) trained in Christian schools of the Gold Coast. The educational role of religious institutions today is recognized, and almost half the large school-age population is educated in Christian schools. The expulsion of all German missionaries at the beginning of the first world war resulted in greater self-reliance among indigenous Christians, and the Eglise évangélique du Togo is now an autonomous body. This, the Methodist Church, and Assemblies of God are the major Protestant denominations; and there

are some African indigenous churches. A number of Protestant churches have been participating together in a Christian council since 1983; and Roman Catholics and Protestants cooperate in the South Togo cultural and religious research group which is currently engaged in cultural and ecumenical research.

Let us pray

for the many people in Togo who suffer desperate poverty, and for all attempts to alleviate it consistent with the peoples' dignity

for the large young population; for schools and for job opportunities

for the emergence of a strong Togolese Christian leadership

for the development of forms of evangelism appropriate to the country

for tourists, that they may be enriched by contact with local Christians.

We pray

that in the bond of prayer and worship Christians in Togo may feel their solidarity with Christians elsewhere

Lord, you told the apostles that they should all be one.
Let all Christians show and bear witness to this unity
through their loving kindness.

Prayer for unity from Togo

Week 27

Nigeria

O Almighty God, we humbly ask you
to make us like trees planted by the waterside,
that we may bear fruits of good living in due season.
Forgive our past offenses,
sanctify us now,
and direct all that we should be in the future;
for Christ's sake. Amen.

Prayer from Nigeria

Musing with a Nigerian Christian
Lord, we were brought up together, we and our Muslim neighbors; their mothers were our mothers, their children were our children.

If they resented our church going, our identification with Western forms of religion, the privileges we enjoyed in mission structures, they didn't show it.

But suddenly, suspicion has entered between us, solidarity with fellow Muslims across the world, new ideas, new feelings, new stirrings, a new self-consciousness and identity on their part has plunged our easygoing and taken-for-granted relationships into disarray.

Now we imagine all sorts of things about each other, impute to each other all sorts of unworthy motives, read all sorts of things into each others' words and actions.

Lord, there is no way back.

In our bewilderment please show us the way forward.

A prayer for freedom from fear
O Lord, we beseech thee to deliver us from the fear of the

unknown future; from fear of failure; from fear of poverty; from fear of bereavement; from fear of loneliness; from fear of sickness and pain; from fear of age; and from fear of death.

Help us, O Father, by thy grace to love and fear thee only, fill our hearts with cheerful courage and loving trust in thee; through our Lord and Master Jesus Christ.

Francis Akanu Ibiam

A chorus of farewell

At the end of some special service or meeting it is customary for the usual silence after the blessing to be broken by someone quietly but clearly lilting the words of an Ibo chorus:

Ezigbo hwannem, nyem aka gi—Ezigbo hwannem, nyem obi gi,

a refrain taken up powerfully by all present:

My good brother/sister, give me your hand,
My good brother/sister, give me your heart.

And, shaking hands with each other as they sing, all move leisurely and lovingly out of the church until the compound re-echoes with

My good brother/sister, give me your hand,
My good brother/sister, give me your heart.

Likewise let us offer our hands and hearts to our Christian brothers and sisters in Nigeria in gratitude and in solidarity.

Population: 95.2 million.
Languages: English, Hausa, Ibo, Yoruba, and over 500 other ethnic languages.
Government: Military administration.
Religion: Overall numbers of Christians and Muslims are believed to be approximately even. Of the many denominations the Roman Catholic, Anglican, and Fellowship of Churches in Christ in Nigeria are the largest. Muslims predominate in the north and are numerous in the west. Traditional religions have their main strength in the central plateau.

The area now known as Nigeria is home to over 500 ethnic groups of which the Yoruba, Hausa, Fulani, and Ibo are the largest. It is the richest and most populous country in Black Africa. The oil boom affected Nigeria, and cities, roads, population, and the church have all expanded rapidly in recent years.

The unity of Nigeria as a nation was imposed upon it by colonization, but the region itself has a long and rich cultural history. The main trade routes were to the north and east across the Sahara; and from this direction came Islam, which was established in the north by the 11th century, and spread more widely through the populace in the 19th, at the same time as Christianity was being introduced in the south. The slave trade brought Europeans to the coastal area and a gradual process of exploration and colonization followed. Independence was achieved in 1960. A period of turbulence followed which included a civil war, from which Nigeria has emerged as a much more united nation.

The first Christian missionaries came in response to requests from returning freed slaves who were themselves Christians. Methodists, Anglicans, Presbyterians, and Baptists arrived in quick succession, followed by Roman Catholics and Lutherans. Some of the early missionaries were themselves African. Cooperation was well developed from an early date. In 1926, a Christian Council for Northern Nigeria was formed, and the NCC for the whole of Nigeria in 1950.

The resurgence of Islamic fundamentalism in other parts of the world, and the move to take Nigeria into the Organization of Islamic Countries are sources of considerable disquiet among Christians; and Christian-Muslim relationships have become extremely sensitive and sometimes inflammatory. Fear and suspicion have grown. Some look back to the destruction of the church in North Africa in early centuries, and wonder if that could happen in Nigeria.

In the face of all this the churches are becoming increasingly united and are taking evangelism more seriously. They are expanding steadily. The indigenous African Independent churches are not only growing but proliferating, and there are now over 900 different denominations, although many are linked in one association or another. One of the larger groups, the Nigerian Association of Aladura Churches, incorporates 95 member churches. There are three ecumenical institutes which work closely with each other, as well as several interdenominational organizations promoting medical work, Christian education, and interreligious dialogue.

Creator of Heaven and earth accept our thanks and accept our praises—Amen

Messiah, accept our thanks and accept our praises—Amen

As young people and adults, accept our thanks and accept our praises—Amen

As male and female, accept our thanks and accept our praises—Amen

On this holy day accept our thanks and accept our praises—Amen

On all days accept our thanks and accept our praises—Amen

Let not the mouths with which we thank thee become sour—Amen

Let us not give thanks in sorrow—Amen

Let us not give thanks in tears—Amen

Let us not give thanks in regret—Amen

Let us not be thankful half-heartedly—Amen

Accept out thanks and our praises, O Lord,

Make us useful to thee—Amen

Hear, O Ruler of Heaven, through Jesus Christ our Lord—Amen.

Part of a prayer of thanksgiving
recorded in an African Independent Church

Christian Conference of Asia (CCA)

Inaugurated in 1959 as the East Asia Christian Conference, and today known simply as CCA, the Christian Conference of Asia contains in its fellowship some 113 churches and national councils from 16 Asian countries including Australia and New Zealand, comprising over 40 million Christian people.

The CCA functions "as an organ of continuing cooperation among its member churches and national Christian bodies." Among other things, it sponsors development, justice, and human rights programs; encourages ecumenical leadership development and many other ecumenical ventures; focuses attention on the problems of tourism in the area; and promotes interest in Asian Christian hymns, art, and architecture.

Leader: We pray for the churches where many suffer for the sake of freedom and justice. *(Silence)*

People: Servant Lord, lead us to be the willing servants of all.

Leader: We pray for the churches where there is success in terms of wealth, prestige, and influence. *(Silence)*

People: Servant Lord, lead us to be the willing servants of all.

Leader: We pray for the churches working closely with peoples' movements for peace for the good of all. *(Silence)*

People: Servant Lord, lead us to be willing servants of all.

O God, our Creator,
who gave us all that we are and have;
release us from self-love
to be able to share

what we are
what we know
what we have
with one another
and in the world which you love.
In the name of Christ who makes this a possibility.
Amen.

Sisters and brothers, let us claim the freedom Christ gives.
May he empower us to serve together in faith, hope, and love.
Go in peace to love and serve the Lord.

Prayers used at the 8th Assembly
of the Christian Conference of Asia, Seoul, Korea

Fellowship of the Least Coin

God of peace,
  help us to be committed as Christians to be peacemakers.
Give us the courage to speak up for truth and justice.
Empower us to be Christians not only in word but in action.
May your peace be achieved
  by the power of love, tolerance, and justice.
In the name of Jesus, the Prince of Peace. Amen.

Our Father, we thank you that in Jesus Christ there are no rich or poor, but we are all one in you. As we present our "least coins," we remember the women of every land, rich and poor, educated and illiterate, in isolated villages and teeming cities, who share in this Fellowship. May we be rich in the things of the spirit by your grace and to your glory.

Prayers by two members of the Fellowship

Conceived in 1956 as the brainchild of the Asian Christian Women's Conference, the Fellowship of the Least Coin continues to catch the imagination and to draw a response from women all over the world. Whatever their backgrounds and circumstances, women are invited to set aside regularly the smallest coin of their country's currency, offering it with the prayer that women may become instrumental in bringing peace and reconciliation in the world.

Although the fellowship retains a strong link with its countries of origin, it is now organized on an international basis, with its fund handled by WCC, Geneva. In spite of the fact that gifts to its fund have increased greatly over the years and are now very widely applied, the main emphasis of the Fellowship continues to be on the prayer and solidarity of Christian women worldwide.

Introduction to Weeks 28 and 29

With all my heart I take refuge in God,
the Lord of all things,
the Creator of the universe,
the merciful Father and Source of all good.

With all my heart I take refuge in Christ,
the Remover of all sin,
the One who reestablishes our pure nature within us,
the perfect revelation of the eternal Word of God.

With all my heart I take refuge in the One who embraces the whole
universe and has myriad ways and means of influencing souls,
the pure and tranquil Holy Spirit.

From the Norwegian of Karl Ludvig Reichelt,
Buddhist/Christian Center, Tao Fong Shan, Hong Kong

The Theravada Buddhism of Kampuchea, Laos, Burma, and Thailand, and the broader and more accommodating Mahayana Buddhism of Vietnam both trace their history back to the birth in approximately 560 B.C.E. of an Indian prince, Gautama, later to be universally known as the Buddha. At the age of 30 he renounced family life in order to seek after the truth, and after much rigorous searching came upon what he sought in an experience of a growing awareness of emancipation from self, known as his Enlightenment.

According to the teaching of the Buddha, those who desire enlightenment must follow the eight-fold path of right knowledge, resolve, speech, behavior, livelihood, effort, mindfulness, and meditation. This kind of self-discipline, with the very gentle lifestyle which accompanied it, moulded early Buddhist practice, and continues to make it a very attractive option to many people today.

Following the death of the Buddha the teaching of Buddhism developed in two main directions. Mahayana, or the Great Vehicle, broad enough to include all, spread to China, Tibet, Korea, Japan, and Vietnam. The concept of the compassionate Buddha, who foregoes nirvana to devote himself to saving others, developed in Mahayana Buddhism. Theravada Buddhism, sometimes referred to as the Lesser Vehicle, emphasized that each person must work out his or her own salvation. "Make an island unto yourself" reads one of the sayings of the

Buddha according to Theravada Buddhism. This rather rigorous and austere Buddhism experienced a revival in the 12th century C.E. and, starting in Sri Lanka, spread through Burma into Thailand, Cambodia, and Laos. With its well-known Triple Gem:

I take refuge in the Buddha
I take refuge in the Dhamma (the teaching)
I take refuge in the Sangha (the community)

Theravada Buddhism has continued in recent years to experience renewal of its vitality and missionary impulse, not least in the countries prayed for during these weeks. In this connection, some Christians engaged in dialogue with Buddhists have seen the possibility of an adaptation of the Triple Gem, but all would echo the words of another scholar to the effect that "the relationship between Jesus Christ, believed in as 'the light of the world,' and the Buddha called 'the light of Asia' continues to be one of the persistent challenges to the Christian mission."

Week 28

Kampuchea • Laos • Vietnam

God came down to us like the sun at morning
wounded to the heart by our helplessness.
Let us proceed in his strength
to love and serve one another.

Asia Youth Assembly

Look with mercy, O Lord,
on the suffering people of Indo-China;
give respite and rest to those who have never known
peace. Protect the weak from oppression.
Grant that those who are enlightened by the Buddha
may see the light that is in Christ.

Dear God, we thank you for your love shown to us
through Jesus Christ. Our hearts are heavy with sorrow for
the people of Kampuchea who are suffering so much at this
time. We pray that their load of suffering may be eased. We
pray that you will give strength and courage to the people
in that place, and help them to find their refuge in you.
Amen.

Prayer of Cambodian Christian refugee woman

We remember, O Lord,
those who suffer from any kind of discrimination;
your children, and our brothers and sisters,
who are humiliated and oppressed;
we pray for those who

are denied fundamental human rights,
for those who are imprisoned,
and especially those who are tortured.
Our thoughts rest a few moments with them...
and we pray that your love and compassion
may sustain them always.

Week of Prayer for World Peace

We pray
for the governments of these countries, and all who seek
to help in the work of reconstruction
for all refugees from Kampuchea, Laos, and Vietnam, especially those who are not accepted by any country
for those living in areas of continuing warfare, where life
is very insecure and uncertain
for priests and pastors still held in prisons and re-
education camps in Laos and Vietnam.

for scattered Christian groups in Laos and Kampuchea,
and the catechists, lay leaders, and young people who minister to them
for those in the Golden Triangle, forced by economic circumstances to cultivate too much opium and for all efforts
being made to control its growth and to substitute other
means of livelihood.

We pray for the peoples of Asia as they struggle for justice, peace, and an end to wars in the face of situations of
desperate poverty and yet with great hopes for a new society in which human rights are carefully respected, looking
for adequate ways of development, seeking to preserve
their ancient and noble cultures as the context of human existence, and as a gift to the whole human family....

Christian Prayer for Peace,
Pope John Paul II, Assisi, 1986

As we are together, praying for peace, let us be truly with each other *(Silence)*

Let us be aware of the source of being common to us all and to all living things *(Silence)*

Evoking the presence of the Great Compassion, let us fill our hearts with our own compassion—toward ourselves and all living beings *(Silence)*

Let us pray that all living beings realize that they are all brothers and sisters, all nourished from the same source of life *(Silence)*

Let us pray that we ourselves cease to be the cause of suffering to each other *(Silence)*

Let us plead with ourselves to live in a way which will not deprive other living beings of air, water, food, shelter, or the chance to live. *(Silence)*

With humility, with awareness of the existence of life, and of the sufferings that are going on around us, let us pray for the establishment of peace in our hearts and on earth. Amen.

Thich Nhat Hanh: Vietnamese scholar, monk, poet, and contemplative, nominated by Martin Luther King, Jr., for the Nobel Peace Prize in recognition of his work for reconciliation in Vietnam. This litany was led by him at an interfaith gathering in Canterbury in 1976.

May the grace of our Lord Jesus Christ
protect us from killing one another;
and may God's love fill our lives
with a peace that extends its hand to others
in true reconciliation and friendship.

Benediction, Christian Conference of Asia

Kampuchea

Population: 7.3 million approximately.
Language: Khmer.
Government: Single-party republic.
Religion: Buddhists 85%, atheists 9%, adherants of tribal religions 3%, Muslims 3%, a tiny Christian minority.

Cambodia (Kampuchea) obtained independence in 1953 and enjoyed a period of relative stability, but was increasingly affected by the war in Vietnam and a communist insurgency movement (Khmer Rouge). A coup in 1970 ushered in a right-wing anti-Vietnamese government and thousands of resident Vietnamese were massacred. Others escaped across the border. The Roman Catholic church, primarily a church of the Vietnamese and Europeans, suffered considerably. The ensuing civil war resulted in much loss of life and large-scale destruction.

In 1975 the Khmer Rouge gained control of the whole country, and put into operation a drastic program of social change. Whole populations were moved out of the towns to work in the fields under forced labor conditions where many died. Profes-
sional and educated people were exterminated; 75% of all teaching staff and 96% of university students were killed. The Khmer Rouge attempted to eradicate all religion, and some 90% of Buddhist priests and an unknown number of Christians perished. It is estimated that at least 3 million people died during the four years of the regime.

In 1978 Vietnam, supported by a Kampuchean opposition group, invaded the country, and since January 1979 a Vietnamese-supported government has ruled in Kampuchea while the Khmer Rouge, in alliance with Prince Sihanouk, constitute a government in exile. As a result of the war and the social policies of the Khmer Rouge the country's economy, infrastructure, and industry have been completely disrupted. As the then secretary general of the United Nations said: "The Kampuchean tragedy may have no parallel in history." Now, after years of relative stability and considerable outside aid, food shortages have been largely overcome, and recovery is beginning, but there is a serious lack of skilled and trained people. The government is not widely recognized internationally, and war continues between the various factions.

Little is known about the present situation of the Christian church. The number of Christians is small, and they are scattered. Christian gatherings were made illegal in 1983.

ary enthusiasm, socialist policies are being implemented gradually. The government allows religious freedom, and Christians collaborate with civil authorities in development programs. The number of Christians is not known, but the small church, severely tried, "is being renewed and is growing." Christians "are now more convinced of their faith, more faithful, and more courageous."

Laos

Population: 3.6 million
Languages: Lao, French, numerous tribal languages.
Government: Unitary single-party republic.
Religion: Buddhists 58%, adherents of tribal religions 33% mainly among non-Lao ethnic minorities, atheists 6%, small Muslim and Christian minorities.

Laos, then a constitutional monarchy, obtained independence in 1953, but communist opposition had already begun. By 1965 the Pathet Lao (communist forces) had gained control of the northeast of the country, and a de facto partition existed, with guerilla warfare continuing. Laos was closely involved with the war in Vietnam and the 1973 peace agreements provided for a cease-fire in Laos. A new government was set up involving both sides, but by 1975 the communists had won control.

In the year following, all foreign missionaries were forced to leave the country. A number of Roman Catholic priests and Protestant pastors were imprisoned in forced labor or "re-education" camps. Most have since been released.

After the first wave of revolution-

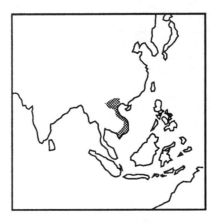

Vietnam

Population: 57.1 million.
Language: Vietnamese.
Government: Unitary single-party republic.
Religion: Buddhists 55%, atheists 22%, syncretistic new religions 11%, Christians 7.5% predominantly Roman Catholics. The main Protestant church is the Evangelical Church of Vietnam.

In Vietnam, nationalist groups operated from an early stage, and following Japan's surrender in 1945 proclaimed the Independent Democratic Republic without French agreement. Hostilities ensued, eventually leading to division of the country into North and South. But trouble did not cease, and in 1961

USA entered the war which was to continue for another 12 years. Two years after the cease-fire the communist North Vietnamese gained control in the south. Since then, despite many difficulties, considerable progress has been made toward reconstruction. After 1954 many Christians moved to the South to avoid living under a Marxist government. More people moved south to escape American bombings and since 1975 many, especially ethnic Chinese, have fled the country. However, a number of Christians stayed on in the North, and continued to relate to the communist government. It seems likely that arising out of continuous church activity during the long years of war, and after, a new interpretation of the Christian faith has been emerging in the North which may one day be shared with the rest of the world church.

The church in the South, both Catholic and Protestant, is now seeking to adjust to life under a Marxist government. The government has constituted a committee for Solidarity of Patriotic Vietnamese Catholics, and it is through this body that the Roman Catholic church ordinarily relates to the government. All open evangelism ceased in 1975, seminaries were closed, and many priests were interned. About a hundred still remain in "re-education" camps. The church is able to function, but with restrictions, and is carefully watched by the government which nevertheless seems anxious to avoid confrontation.

Week 29

Burma • Thailand

Dear Lord, you wanted all people to live in unity and to love each other. Help us to break down the walls of separation. Break down the walls of race, color, creed, and languages. Make us one so that our unity and love for each other may win many to your fold. Amen.

Prayer of Burmese Christian woman

O God, our Father,
the fountain of love, power, and justice,
the God who cares, particularly for the least,
the most suffering and the poorest among us.

O God, Lord of creation,
grant us today your guidance and wisdom
so that we may see the human predicament for what it is.

Give us courage and obedience
so that we may follow you completely.
Help us, Lord, to bear witness
to the cross of your son, our Lord Jesus Christ,
who alone is the reason for hope,
and in whose name we pray. Amen.

Koson Srisang, Thailand

Lord, we take refuge in your compassionate name,
we take refuge in your gospel of forgiveness,
we take refuge in the fellowship of your universal
Church
on behalf of all Christians in Buddhist lands. Amen.

Burma

Population: 38 million.
Languages: Burmese, 125 other languages and dialects.
Government: Single-party republic.
Religion: Buddhists 87%; Christians 6% (of whom the Baptists are the largest single denomination); Muslims 4%; and adherents of tribal religions.

Sometimes described as a country "shaped like a kite with a long tail," and with an early history of numerous small kingdoms struggling for ascendancy, Burma was annexed by the British in 1886, occupied by the Japanese during the second world war, and became independent in 1948. Considerable turmoil followed, but a coup in 1962 led to the eventual emergence of a socialist state. In an attempt to unite the nation, Burma broke off its ties with the outside world in 1966. It resumed contact in 1978.

The earliest Christians in Burma were the Nestorians in the 10th century. Roman Catholics came in 1544, and Protestant missions may be said to have begun with the coming of Adoniram and Ann Judson, America's first missionaries to Asia, in 1813. Others followed, and the church became firmly established, particularly among the tribal peoples. The extensive program of lay training, undertaken prior to 1966, stood the church in good stead for the period of isolation, which many Christians regarded as an opportunity for the church to become indigenized.

Today there is a reality, a resourcefulness, and a vitality about the church in Burma which is catching to those who visit. Considerable freedom is allowed, and relationships with the state are good. Holding the view that "Christian unity and national unity cannot be separated," the churches work together to a high degree, and support national unity through their activities. Lay theological education continues to be an important ecumenical activity. They live daily with the question of what it means to be a Christian "in the land of the strongest, most true-to-the-original type of Buddhism."

One of Adoniram Judson's most famous sayings, "the future is as bright as the promises of God," still characterizes the church in Burma.

Give thanks

for the Burmese peoples' determination to achieve selfhood, resist foreign influence, and to work for unity and equality

for the church's presence and growth in some of the remotest parts of the country.

Pray

that the "Burmese way of socialism" may lead to the unity and development of the nation

for an end to ethnic conflict, and for greater understanding and fellow feeling between those of different ethnic groups

for those who, in a situation of restricted freedom, are dedicated to the task of discovering and implementing ways of authentic Christian witness to the gospel of the kingdom of God in this land

for pastoral care and sensitive evangelism among the tribal people of Burma.

Good Shepherd, we ask that you will seek the lost, heal the sick, bring back those that wander off, and let your people graze in safety in the mountains and valleys of Burma today.

Council for World Mission

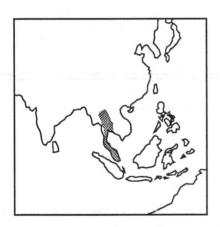

Thailand

Population: 52.7 million.
Languages: Thai, English, Chinese.
Government: Constitutional monarchy.
Religion: Buddhists 92%; Muslims 4%; adherents of Chinese folk religions 2%; Christians 1%. The king is protector of religions, and there is a high degree of religious liberty.

Staying in Bangkok briefly it was of course obligatory to visit the fabulous palaces built by the king made famous in the book and film, *The King and I*. Pillars and roofs covered in gold leaf, a huge statue of the Buddha in solid gold, and another of jade. But the place that remains in the memory is a whole roomful of figures showing the Buddha in different acts of meditating, blessing, and peacemaking. But one of them was different. It showed the Buddha before his enlightenment, as an ascetic, emaciated, with his ribs sticking out and a look of intense suffering on his face. Only in front of this statue did I see a small heap of flowers. The calm faces of the other figures had drawn no such oblation. I even wonder whether people in their own ago-

ny and suffering do not sometimes want to hit out at that serene passivity. Sublimely inspiring at times, it could also infuriate. Especially in times of flood, famine, and the ever-present possibility of war, the belief that God has shared our suffering makes a deep appeal, and draws out love.

A tourist

With ethnic roots traceable back 2000 years to China, Thailand emerged as a nation in the 13th century. Formerly known as Siam, the country took its present name in 1939. Thailand today recognizes the Kampuchean government in exile; a situation that breeds antagonism with Vietnam, and unrest and uncertainty in the refugee communities along its borders. Refugees from Burma, Kampuchea, Laos, and Vietnam continue to seek entrance.

As in the case of Burma, the Christian presence in Thailand can be traced to the arrival of the Nestorians in the 10th century. French Roman Catholic priests arrived in 1662, but from 1688 onward they were persecuted. Today, however, the Roman Catholic Church is the largest in the country. The Church of Christ in Thailand owes its origins to the arrival of Baptist, Congregational, and Presbyterian missions in the mid-19th century, and to their eventual demise in 1934 in order that an indigenous united Protestant church may come to birth. According to its department of ecumenical relations, this continues to be "a body struggling to be an indigenous church, with strong influences from the charismatic and pentecostal movements." These influences are strongest in Bangkok, whereas the church's membership is predominantly in the rural areas, where "the fundamental social reality of patron-peasant relationship is not challenged by the gospel." Human rights, and other community action groups, however, are emerging. Members of this and other churches, along with Buddhists, Muslims, and Sikhs, are involved in a program of continuing dialogue.

In addition to being an important center of Theravada Buddhism, Thailand is noted for its temples, palaces, and pagodas. Tourism is the country's largest source of foreign exchange. The Christian Conference of Asia, together with sub-units of the WCC, has for some time been much concerned with the problem of prostitution linked with tourism in southeast Asia—sometimes called sex tourism—and has been active in promoting a Christian response to this problem.

Pray

for the members of the small minority Christian community in Thailand

for compassion and integrity for the rulers of the country, that resources and opportunities for improvement may be more equitably shared

for all who are abused and debased by prostitution tourism, and for those who exploit them

for refugees in Thailand, that the pain and agony of warfare and exile may be overcome.

O God, be with us in this new day. Heal the wounds made by war. Ease the suspicions that lurk in the back of the mind about people we cannot see and do not know. Prepare us for a life as full of unexpected joys as it is of unexpected sorrows. All this we ask in Jesus' name—who is always the same—yesterday, today, and tomorrow.

Prayer of Thai Christian woman

Week 30

Indonesia

Bhinneka Tunggal Ika—Diversity in Unity

Motto of the Republic of Indonesia

I believe in God, who is love and who has given the earth to all people.

I believe in Jesus Christ, who came to heal us, and to free us from all forms of oppression.

I believe in the Spirit of God who works in and through all who have turned toward the truth.

I believe in the community of faith which is called to be at the service of all people.

I believe in God's promise to finally destroy the power of sin in us all, and to establish the kingdom of justice and peace to all humankind.

An Indonesian creed, Christian Conference of Asia

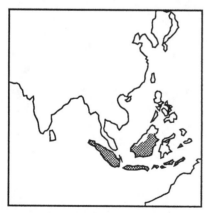

Religion: Muslims 82%; Christians 14%; Hindus 2%; Buddhists 2%.

Referred to by its people as "water land," Indonesia is an archipelago of 13,677 islands, of which 6,044 are inhabited. A chain of active volcanos increases soil fertility even as it causes destruction.

Most Indonesians are of Malayan racial origin. Their forebears probably came to the archipelago in two waves, the first arriving about 3000 B.C.E. and the second about 300–200 B.C.E. Because of the geographical features of the islands, they developed in isolated groups, and now there are over 300 distinct ethnic communities. Indian influences penetrated from about 100 C.E., bringing Hinduism and Buddhism. Bali is predominantly Hindu today. Islam

Population: 165.2 million and growing rapidly. The fifth most populous country in the world.
Languages: Bahasa Indonesia, over 200 other languages and dialects.
Government: Unitary republic.

came first in the 13th century and its spread continued. There are now more Muslims in Indonesia than in any other country.

The Portuguese came in the 1520s, bringing Roman Catholic Christianity, and Francis Xavier laid the foundations of a church which suffered heavy losses through anti-Portuguese reaction. Dutch occupation, begun in 1605, brought Protestant pastors, and Roman Catholic missionaries were expelled. Church growth among Indonesians was slow until the 19th century when missionary activity increased and Roman Catholic work was again permitted. Christians suffered during the Japanese occupation (1942–1945), but at the same time the churches began to experience independence. The country itself had been striving for independence for some time, and proclaimed it three days after the Japanese surrender. The Netherlands granted legal independence in 1949.

In view of the religious diversity of the people, it was decided to create neither a religious nor a secular state. Instead, it is based on the Pancasila (Five Pillars): belief in One Supreme God; just and civilized humanity; national unity; democracy; social justice. Five religious groups (Islam, Catholic Christianity, Protestant Christianity, Hinduism, and Buddhism) are recognized, and all have equal rights and status. Recently all organizations, including religious groups, have adopted the Pancasila as their only foundation in the life of society, nation, and state. The church, although strongly committed to the Pancasila, affirms that Jesus Christ is its Lord and Head.

The distribution of Indonesia's population is extremely uneven, with nearly two-thirds living on the islands of Java, Bali, and Lombok. This has led the government to embark on an extensive transmigration policy involving moving millions of people. One effect of this is to spread the influence of Islam more widely, although others are also moving.

While Christianity is represented throughout the country, some areas are predominantly Christian, and the church continues to grow. About a quarter of Christians are Roman Catholic. Some of the numerous Protestant bodies are regional and some indigenous; by far the largest tradition is the Reformed. The churches have an extensive ministry in education, somewhat less in health, and a little in social work. Internally, many have a range of programs for women that reflect a widening of the status and activities of women in society generally. Youth organizations are considered important both on account of the large percentage of young people in the churches, and the rapid social changes taking place in society.

The Communion of Churches in Indonesia was founded in 1950 and now has 58 member churches, some of them Pentecostal. It is unique in that its stated purpose is to become one Christian church in Indonesia. Relationships with the Roman Catholic church have steadily improved since Vatican II, and there are now many areas of cooperation.

Give thanks

for the richness of diverse races, cultures, and religious communities of the Indonesian archipelago

for the faith and witness of the church in Indonesia; and

for the contribution of Christians to nation-building and national unity

for the ministry of the church among the poor and under-privileged.

Give us strength, give us courage
in joyful willingness and humble readiness
to be thrown into the struggle of humanity
to be with the people,
those crawling in the gully of misery
moaning, stabbed by sorrow, squirming in agony,
isolated from everything that could alleviate their distress;
that they may see the brightness of solidarity
and feel the never-ceasing love of fellowship in Christ.

Fridolin Ukur

Pray
for all efforts to live together in harmony, and to promote justice and well-being for the whole people of Indonesia

that Christians may continue to uphold integrity and truth, and help the nation succeed in its struggle against corruption

that Christians may truly be a community for the people, faithful and imaginative in their ministries, and sensitive and generous in their relations with people of other faiths and persuasions

for the many people who continue to live in poverty, who are unemployed, or who live in overcrowded circumstances

for a just and humane implementation of the transmigration scheme; for all families who are moving, and for those already living in the area, that the necessary adjustments may be made peacefully

for young people growing up in a rapidly changing social environment

for the Communion of Churches in Indonesia, that its ef-

forts to foster Christian education and renewal, and to promote greater union among the churches may become a blessing to all.

O God,
who sent the Holy Spirit on the first disciples of Jesus
who were waiting in Jerusalem for this promised gift,
we beseech you to pour this same inspiration
on Christians in Indonesia and all over the world.

Prayer of an Indonesian Christian woman

Week 31

United States of America

O God, who has bound us together in this bundle of life, give us grace to understand how our lives depend upon the courage, the industry, the honesty, and the integrity of our fellow human beings; that we may be mindful of their needs, grateful for their faithfulness, and faithful in our responsibilities to them; through Jesus Christ our Lord.

Reinhold Niebuhr

Grandfather, Great Spirit,
you have always been, and before you nothing has been.
There is no one to pray to but you.
The star nations all over the heaven are yours,
and yours are the grasses of the earth.
You are older than all need, older than all pain and
prayer.

Grandfather, Great Spirit,
fill us with light.
Give us strength to understand and eyes to see.
Teach us to walk the soft earth
as relatives to all that live.
Help us, for without you we are nothing.

From an American Indian prayer, Dakota

God of our weary years, God of our silent tears,
Thou who hast brought us thus far on the way;
Thou who hast by thy might, led us into the light,
Keep us forever in the path, we pray.

James Weldon Johnson
This prayer, taken from what is called the Negro national anthem,
lifts up the unique pain and suffering of black people in the USA.

208

We pray that our neighborhoods, cities, and nation
become places where justice and peace are honored and
celebrated
and humanity revered and dignified.
And show us how and where to make a start.

Bishop Lyman Ogilby

O God, you are like a weaver-woman in our lives. Out of
the energy of the universe you have spun each one of us
into a unique, colorful strand with our own special hue and
texture, and have woven us together into your human family that blankets the globe. We admit that our own choices
have severed us from your loom of life and created rents in
the whole of our human fabric.

We have allowed ourselves to be bound by the narrow
contexts into which we were born and now live our daily
lives. To insulate ourselves from fatigue and isolation and
to insure our own survival, we have often refused to ask
the hard questions that need to be asked for the sake of the
well-being of all people.

O weaver-woman God, open our eyes to the mystery and
power of your Spirit. Refresh us with the light of your vision so that we may once again recognize the beauty and
wonder of the specially spun thread that we are, the splendor of the one colorful cloth of humanity. Reattach us to
your loom so that your vision may be made plain through
us.

In the name of the Christ, the One who was at one with
all of life. Amen.

Prayer from the USA, exact source unknown

Population: 238.8 million.
Languages: English, Spanish, indigenous Indian and immigrant languages.
Government: Federal republic.
Religion: Christians 88% (Protestants 59%, Roman Catholics 27%, Orthodox 2%, Episcopalians 2%); Jews 3.2%; Muslims 1%. Small communities of other faiths.

It is no accident that one of the first modern devotional acknowledgments of our human interdependence should come out of a nation rich in human potential, material resources, and political significance. This theme of interdependence was later reinforced by Martin Luther King in his now famous speech pleading with the American people for "a revolution of values," in which loyalties might become ecumenical rather than sectional. "Every nation," he urged, "must now develop an overriding loyalty to humankind as a whole in order to preserve the best in their individual societies."

Prior to the arrival of settlers in the "new world," the country was inhabited by Indian tribes who lived by farming and hunting. Their tribal culture included a deeply spiritual faith that rooted itself in the integrity of God's creation. Through the years the land that was first theirs has been taken away, and much of the popula-tion forced to live on reservations or required to become acculturated into society at large. Although the American Indian population has decreased dramatically, Indian spirituality, tribal identity, and culture have been kept alive, and today there are strong movements to restore land rights and to preserve the rich Indian heritage.

The Spanish conquistadores first brought Christianity to the country in the early 16th century. Waves of immigrant settlers followed, mostly from Europe, but there were also sizable immigrations from Asia and Latin America. Many of the European settlers came because of religious persecution at home, so from early days freedom of religion has been a hallmark of the country, although there was a time of intense discrimination against Roman Catholics. Though in the earliest years of settlement most states recognized a state church, that pattern was abolished by the constitution of 1789 which legally separated church and state. This has meant that each church depends on its own religious vitality and faithfulness for growth, and has made it possible for each entity to preserve its own tradition and style of life. The preservation of religious freedom continues to be a challenge in an increasingly diverse society.

For more than two centuries Africans were brought over to work as slaves. Although the Civil War (1861–1865) ended slavery, the nation was left with a deep scar on its vision of equality—a scar which remains even today. Discrimination against Black people in both church and society led to the birth, in 1787, of the first historical Black church, the African Methodist Episcopal church. Today there are seven large historic Black churches. They are a strong force in the Black community, and wield considerable political influence in society at large. All but one are members of the World Coun-

cil of Churches and the NCC, and their relationship to these bodies remains one of challenge to the ecumenical movement.

The complexity of the religious landscape in the USA can hardly be overstated, the plethora of denominations being largely a result of earlier patterns of immigration. However, within the major confessions a number of mergers have taken place in recent decades, and others are in process. Ecumenical life has been enriched since Vatican II with increased cooperation with the Roman Catholic church. The strong presence of the Jewish community (which, although small in proportion to the total population, represents the largest number of Jews in any country of the world), and growing numbers of Muslims, Bahais, Buddhists, Hindus, and others have created an increased awareness of the need for interfaith dialogue and action.

Today the National Council of the Churches of Christ in the USA has 32 member communions. In addition, there are approximately 400 regional and local councils of churches. Of these, many have Roman Catholic members, and some are interfaith. Church Women United brings together women from Roman Catholic, Protestant, and Orthodox traditions. Many conservative Protestant denominations are joined together in the National Association of Evangelicals which gives ecumenical expression to the concerns of many not engaged in the National Council. The issues, however, are common, and include matters like economic justice in a world of limited resources, ecology, nuclear disarmament, peace, women's rights, racial justice, and renewal of congregational life.

The richness and diversity, the size and complexity, the power and the promise of the USA make it a major influence in the world. Let us pray with Christians and those of all living faiths who fast and work and pray in this nation, that its people might live up to their vision of equality and justice and peace.

We pray

for God's grace to heal the festering divisions between peoples and histories

for ecumenical encouragement for Black church leaders concerned about family breakdown, growing illiteracy, drug abuse, violence, and all other social ills traceable to the fundamental problem of deprivation

for the 40 million poverty-stricken people living on the edges of US society, and for those who work to alleviate their situation

for all immigrants, and those who serve God's fugitive people through the Sanctuary Movement

that the measure of freedom given to the churches may inspire them to seek a new unity, as bold and radical now as was the notion of religious liberty two hundred years ago.

Almighty God, we offer our prayers
for the National Council of Churches of Christ in the USA,
earthen vessel, fragile, flawed, incomplete…
yet with a vision of unity.
We struggle to become all we could be.
We pray for the gift of love
that we may trust and care for one another.
We pray for the gift of patience
that we may hear and respond to each other.
We pray for the gift of courage
that we may be bold in our work and witness.
We pray for the gift of humility
that we may accept what cannot be changed.
We pray for the gift of grace
that we may rejoice in our shared humanity.
We pray for the gift of faith
that we might believe we will be one.
We pray that you will hold the ecumenical movement in
your care,
and make us wholly yours. Amen.

Joan Campbell

Short prayers for big needs
Adolescents
Lord, I could use some help.

AIDS
God, help everyone living with AIDS
Guard their lives and their loved ones
Guide their healers and their helpers
Give us all new wholeness and new hope.

Homelessness
Let those who have no home to go to in the evening, Impartial Provider, who have no place to rest their bones, no

place to lay their head, no place but the street, an alley, a niche, have the best of your company.

The urban poor
Lord, we know that you'll be coming through the line to-day,
so, Lord, help us to treat you well, help us to treat you well.

Prayer of a poor Black helping woman
before the weekly foodline a mile and a half from the White House

Statistics in this book
Thank you, Lord, for counting me one of your sheep.
Teach me, Lord, to count better, like you. Amen.

A personal God
Lord, one of the problems I have with praying is that you always get too personal. I keep praying because your being so personal is one of the joys. Amen.

Jesus
You are the healing, the loving, the touching.
You are the laughing, you are the dancing,
Jesus, Verb of God—you are the moving—move in me.

Prayers by: Grant M. Gallup, John Fandel,
Mary Glover, Albert S. Newton, Marilee Zdenek

Prayer for Peace
Let us pray for the world that is immeasurable,
a society of millions of people and newspapers full of news.

Let us pray for the smaller world around us:
for the people who belong to us, for the members of our families,
our friends and those who share our worries,
and those who depend on us.

Let us pray for the leaders of governments
and those whose words and actions
will influence the situation in the world—
that they may not tolerate injustice, seek refuge in violence
or make rash and ill-considered decisions
about the future of other people.

Let us also pray for all who live in the shadow of world
events,
for those who are seldom noticed:
the hungry, the poor, the broken, and unloved.

We beseech you, O God, send your Holy Spirit
to help us give a new face to this earth that is dear to us.
may we help create peace wherever people live.

Give us the wisdom to see where we can make a difference
in the great nuclear debate that goes on around us,
and grant us the courage to form our conscience
in the image of Christ.

Let your Spirit have power over us
and put us on the path that leads to peace. Amen.

Pax Christi, USA

Week 32

Canada

Lord, in your creation you have revealed your awesome power,
and in redemption you reveal your relentless love.
Through your vigilance by night and by day,
teach us more intimately of your power and your love.
Amen.

From Ecumenical Prayers,
compiled by churches in Canada and the USA

Welcome
You have come from afar
and waited long and are wearied:
Let us sit side by side
sharing the same bread drawn from the same source
to quiet the same hunger that makes us weak.
Then standing together
let us share the same spirit, the same thoughts
that once again draw us together in friendship and unity
and peace.

Prières d'Ozawamick, Canadian Indian liturgical text

Thanksgiving
For human contact, for courage and vision that bring people together for loving embrace—we give thanks.

For those around the world who stand together and work together for justice and peace—we give thanks.

In the knowledge that death and terror, bombs and hunger, do not have the last word—we give thanks.

For the promise that justice and peace will embrace, that love and fidelity will come together—we give thanks.

For Justice and Peace, Alyson Huntly, United Church, Toronto

Linked with the words of 1 Peter 2:24, "By his wounds you have been healed," the figure in a Toronto church of a woman, arms outstretched as if crucified, provides the inspiration for the following prayer:

O God,
through the image of a woman crucified on the cross
I understand at last.

For over half of my life I have been ashamed of the scars I bear.
These scars tell an ugly story, a common story, about a girl who is the victim when a man acts out his fantasies.

In the warmth, peace, and sunlight of your presence
I was able to uncurl the tightly clenched fists.
For the first time
I felt your suffering presence with me in that event.
I have known you as a vulnerable baby,
as a brother, and as a father.
Now I know you as a woman.
You were there with me
as the violated girl caught in helpless suffering.

The chains of shame and fear no longer bind my heart and body.
A slow fire of compassion and forgiveness is kindled.
My tears fall now for man as well as woman...

You were not ashamed of your wounds.
You showed them to Thomas as marks of your ordeal and death.
I will no longer hide these wounds of mine.
I will bear them gracefully.
They tell a resurrection story.

Anonymous

Jesus, make our hearts ever gentler and more humble,
so that we may be present to those you have confided to
our care,
and in this way make us instruments of your love
which gives life and joy and real freedom.

*Jean Vanier, Canadian founder of L'Arche Community
for people with mental handicaps and their families*

The blessing of the God of Sarah and Hagar, as of Abraham,
the blessing of the Son, born of Mary,
the blessing of the Holy Spirit who broods over us
as a mother over her children,
be with you all. Amen.

Lois Wilson, Toronto

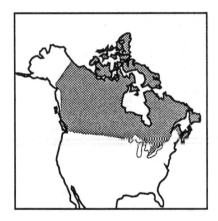

Population: 25.4 million.
Languages: English, French, various indigenous, European and Asian languages.
Government: Federal parliamentary state.
Religion: Christians 90% (Roman Catholics 47.3%; Protestants 41.2%; Orthodox 1.5%); Jews 1.2%. Members of other faiths increasing in number largely due to immigration.

Undefended since it was first drawn, the border between Canada and the USA is the longest in the world, and today three-quarters of the population of Canada live within 200 miles of it, in irregularly spaced areas separated from each other by vast distances. Many nations of native peoples had inhabited this continent for thousands of years by the time Europeans began to arrive in the early 16th century. In what is now Canada, they were scattered throughout the whole country, and were very much prepared to share with these newcomers the resources the Creator had given them. It was they who taught the settlers how to "live the land." As Europeans discovered the natural resources, and Britain assumed government in the early 19th century, treaties were drawn up under which the Indians lost their land rights, and eventually also their culture and traditions. The Christian church participated in the process of assimilating the native peoples into the European way of life; and it was not until 1986 that an apology was made, by the United Church of Canada, for this denigration of dignity, culture, and spirituality.

The Roman Catholic church is the longest established and most wide-

spread confession in the country, owing its origins to 16th- and 17th-century French immigrants. It is strongest in Quebec, the predominantly French-speaking province in the east. In the 18th century, British Anglican, Methodist, Presbyterian, and other immigrants introduced their denominations into the Atlantic provinces and Ontario. Later, other European immigrants established Orthodox, Lutheran, Reformed, Baptist, and Mennonite congregations. In 1925, Congregationalists, Methodists, and the majority of Presbyterians joined to form the United Church of Canada, which is now the largest Protestant denomination in the country. The Canadian Conference of Catholic Bishops is an associate member of the Canadian Council of Churches, established in 1944.

Ethnic and religious pluralism contribute to the rich variety of life in Canada, as well as to some tensions. Difficulties between French- and English-speaking Canadians are now gradually decreasing. Most of the churches, separately and together, are strongly committed to the struggles for justice of the native peoples of Canada. Ecumenical concerns include worldwide peace initiatives, the status of refugees, human rights, and pressure for disinvestment in South Africa. Theological and ethical questions are acquiring increasing importance in relation to ecumenical growth. Future programs will take account of the country's wide variety of churches and other faiths.

We pray

that ecumenical initiatives within and outside Canada toward disarmament, justice, and peace may be strengthened

that there may be respect for the heritage, culture, and rights of the native peoples of Canada

for a better understanding between English- and French-speaking people

for a more responsible stewardship of natural and mineral resources

for all who by force of circumstances must live very isolated lives

for all recent immigrants as they settle down and seek to make a new life for themselves and their families; and for harmony between the various racial and ethnic groups.

You, O God, have spoken to us through the story of Ruth the sojourner and were yourself present among us in Jesus to gather and welcome all those who were cast out or adrift from their societies; stir us and speak to us afresh through the migrant people of our time.

United Church of Canada, adapted

Week 33

Australia • New Zealand

O God, you are my God: early will I seek you,
My soul thirsts for you, my flesh longs for you.
As the eagle belongs in the air,
and the dolphin belongs to the sea,
so we belong to you, O God, my God.

Australian Prayers, Bruce D. Prewer

Give wisdom to those in authority in this and every land,
and guide all peoples in the way of righteousness and
peace,
so that they may share with justice the resources of the
earth,
work together in trust, and seek the common good.
Father, hear our prayer, through Jesus Christ our Lord.

From the Service of Holy Communion, Second Order
An Australian Prayer Book, 1978

Lord God of all Peoples,
We have settled in this land, Aotearoa.
We bring to you an offering from our abundance.

Here we acknowledge that many of our ancestors
came from other lands,
to escape tyranny and oppression
to discover freedom and space
and to appreciate your good earth.

We praise you for clear unpolluted skies and comet-filled
heavens,

for tree-filled suburb, and flowers of street and garden.

We acknowledge that for all of this land's beauty of people and places,

there are also shadows where we have spoilt or broken your world.

We pray that this offering may be used here in Aotearoa to mend the brokenness,

challenge destructive attitudes,

and build trusting relationships.

Hear our prayer in the name of Jesus. Amen.

From an offertory prayer, New Zealand

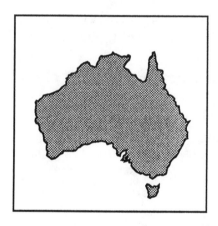

Australia

Population: 15.8 million.
Languages: English and many others.
Government: Federal parliamentary state.
Religion: Christians 85%. Small minorities of Muslims, Jews, and Buddhists, and some of no religion at all.

Australia has been home to its Aboriginal people for more than 40,000 years. British occupation began in 1778, using the country at first as a penal colony. More recent immigrants have come from many countries. The Aborigines were gradually crushed as their land was taken, and by the end of the 19th century their numbers had been greatly reduced to perhaps one hundred thousand people. Chaplains accompanied the first convicts and until 1936 the Church of England enjoyed privileges not granted to others. The foundations of many Protestant churches were laid by early pioneers. More recent immigration has increased the number of Roman Catholics and strengthened the various Orthodox churches.

At present the largest denominations are Roman Catholic, Anglican, and Uniting Church in Australia. This church, formed in 1977 by a union of Congregationalists, Methodists, and Presbyterians, uses liturgies drawn from many traditions, and seeks to affirm and practice diversity in unity. In the Orthodox family the Greek Orthodox is the largest body. The Christian church is increasingly multicultural, concerned to care for new immigrants. Support for the Aborigines, now increasing in number again, in their plea for justice with particular reference to land rights, is a major concern. Another

aspect of the church's life is ministry to those in remote areas, at the mercy of climatic extremes, and separated by vast distances. In this generally affluent country the Australian Council of Churches is involved in issues of justice for the poor and for women.

You must think me silly, God.
I just wanted to take your hand and walk with you
and show you things you'd seen a million times before.

Australian Images, Aubrey Podlich, a Queensland pastor

and thank you
for the awesome beauty of this wide red land
for the rich diversity of its peoples
for your Aboriginal sons and daughters, and their ancient longing for you

and ask you
for inspiration and administrative skills for churches conducting ecumenical assemblies
that interchurch relationships at local levels may be deepened, and cooperation extended to neglected sections of the community

that the rights and identity of Aboriginal peoples may be respected:

God of our ancient people, Lord of all tribes, show those of us who are more recent arrivals in this great south land how best we can acknowledge the dignity of Aborigines and allow them to make their rich contribution to the well-being of our growing nation.

Australian Prayers: from a prayer by Bruce D. Prewer

for forgiveness and reconciliation between different ethnic groups

Dear God, you have forgiven us our sins;

please enable us to forgive each other.
Lord Jesus, bring healing and reconciliation to this nation,
and make us people who will walk and live together
in lasting acceptance and respect for each other.
In Jesus' name and for his sake. Amen.

Prayer offered in St. Andrew's Cathedral, Sydney,
by Bishop Arthur Malcolm, himself an Aboriginal,
in response to an apology made by the Anglican Church for
its part in the suffering inflicted on the Aboriginal peopless

New Zealand

Population: 3.3 million, of whom 12% are of Maori descent.
Languages: English, Maori.
Government: Parliamentary state.
Religion: Predominantly Christian, the largest denominations being Anglican (25% of the population), Roman Catholic (15%), and Presbyterian (12%).

The Maori, of Polynesian origin, are the indigenous people of Aotearoa-New Zealand. Christian missionaries from Britain successfully urged the British Queen to enter into the Treaty of Waitangi (1840), which guaranteed to the Maori the full enjoyment in perpetuity of their possessions. The Treaty's promises were broken in the rush of Pakeha (white) settlement. A period of forced "assimilation" failed to integrate the Maori, who have never ceased the struggle to preserve what they hold dear. A number of different denominations accompanied the rapidly increasing number of settlers.

New Zealand-Aotearoa is conspicuous for its humane social welfare legislation, opposition to apartheid, and its anti-nuclear commitment. In all these areas the churches are active as single denominations and together through the Conference of Churches in Aotearoa-New Zealand, which has replaced the NCC with a wider membership, including the Roman Catholic Church. The NCC Maori section had previously reconstituted itself as Te Runanga Whakawhanaunga i Nga Hahi o Aotearoa, the Maori Ecumenical Council, which also includes Roman Catholics. "We have grasped Christianity with an unshakable grip," claimed a Maori elder recently, "because it makes sense to everything that is noble and good in being Maori." Many churches have been suffering a decline in numbers and commitment, but with the emergence of indigenous demands arising out of the Maori membership, the church may now be experiencing a renewal in depth as a century and a half of history is reviewed, redressed, and redirected in paths closer to the gospel of justice and peace.

One in Christ

The heart at the center represents the love of God. The two curls surrounding the heart are the two peoples, Maori and Pakeha (whites), joined together under the umbrella of Christ (the large curl at the top).

The two sets of curls of waves at either side of the base represent the troubles we have to face in the world, but as long as we have faith in Christ we can overcome these troubles.

Using this symbol we pray with Christians in Aotearoa-New Zealand

for the government, in its firm stand for peace, and efforts to maintain freedom from nuclear pollution;

for young people tempted by materialism, alcohol, and drugs;

for the unemployed;

for the Conference of Churches in Aotearoa-New Zealand, and the Maori Ecumenical Council Te Runanga Whakawhanaunga i Hga Hahi o Aotearoa;

for growing unity and understanding between all the churches;

that the partnership within the churches of women with men, Maori with Pakeha, may mirror the unity sought for the whole nation.

Gracious God,
we pray for the peoples of
New Zealand-Aotearoa.

Help them to discover what allegiance
to Christ means in their land.

Free them from the colonial mentality
to shape a church which challenges the forces of death

and celebrates the promise of their present reality.

May there be an authentic encounter
between the people of the land, the Maori,
and those who have come from afar.

By your spirit, keep the churches open
to listen and respond to the yearnings for justice
of Maori and women, youth and unemployed.

Through repentance and conversion
guide your church into a unity
that serves Christ's vision for your new creation,
through Jesus Christ, Amen.

T.W., a prayer from the Conference of Churches
in Aotearoa-New Zealand

Pacific Conference of Churches (PCC)

O Jesus,
Be the canoe that holds me up in the sea of life;
Be the rudder that keeps me in the straight road;
Be the outrigger that supports me in times of temptation.
Let your Spirit be my sail that carries me through each
day.
Keep my body strong, so I can paddle steadfastly on
in the voyage of life. Amen.

An islander's prayer from Melanesia

"Much water has gone under the canoes since 1961," says the long-time chairman of the National Council of Churches in Tonga, himself involved in the very first regional gathering of churches held in 1961, which led to the inauguration of the Pacific Conference of Churches in 1966.

In the face of the vast distances, the isolation, and the enormous cultural and linguistic disparities of the Pacific, the Christian church has acted as a powerful center and uniting force in Pacific society, though it has itself been greatly hampered by its own denominational insularity. Embracing many national councils of churches, some thirty different Protestant denominations, and the Roman Catholic Episcopal Conference of the Pacific (including ten Roman Catholic dioceses) the Pacific Conference of Churches has gone a long way toward overcoming that insularity.

Promoting ecumenism, and a theology of the Pacific sometimes called "coconut palm theology," the Conference's emphasis on the riches which those of different cultures and traditions have to share with each other has been facilitated by the holding of workshops, and the promotion of Pacific research and scholarship. Unhappily, not only fertile coconut seeds in the shape of good ideas and experiences have circulated in the Pacific, but other less welcome elements. All kinds of sects have proliferated in recent years, secularism threatens to erode the traditional values of the island people, while the testing of nuclear devices and the dumping of nuclear waste by foreign powers continue to be matters of grave concern.

Other concerns include cooperation between the island nations, and the question of self-determination for those still under colonial rule; dialogue with other faiths, unemployment; the creative involvement of women and young people; and the search for a Pacific identity.

Week 34

The Pacific Islands

Almighty God, your word of creation caused the water to be filled with many kinds of living beings and the air to be filled with birds. With those who live in this world's small islands we rejoice in the richness of your creation, and we pray for your wisdom for all who live on this earth, that we may wisely manage and not destroy what you have made for us and for our descendants. In Jesus' name we pray. Amen.

Prayer from Samoa

Keep the ocean clean
Keep Palau clean
Keep the air clean
Keep your air.
Leave us alone so we can stay alive and happy.
Leave the ocean so the fish can survive and we people can survive.
Keep the nuclear waste out of the ocean.

From the West Caroline island of Palau, a fifth-grader's cry of protest

We believe that Creation is a gift of God, an expression of our Creator's goodness.

We believe that as human beings we are part of this creation and that we share in a special way in the creative power of God.

We believe that the resources of our lands and waters and air are precious gifts from our Creator, to be used and looked after with loving care.

We believe that there is a rhythm to God's creation, like a

drumbeat; when we lose the beat, or the drum is damaged, the music is out of tune.

We believe that in order to be good stewards of creation, we have the responsibility to seek information on important concerns of our people and our region, and to share information in our communities.

We believe that like flowers we can bloom fully only when we are planted in God's love.

We believe that as Christians we are called to be peacemakers, in the true peace which God promises us.

We believe that this may sometimes mean "disturbing the peace" as Jesus did, for a purpose—to restore the purpose of God.

We believe that our Pacific ways are also a gift from God; we are invited to use the values of our Pacific culture to build societies of justice and peace.

We express these beliefs, reminded of the love of God, the grace of Christ, and the fellowship of the Holy Spirit. Amen.

Taken from a creed. Women of the Pacific: Worship Workshop

Lord, in your mercy
help all the peoples of the vast Pacific Ocean
to be good stewards of the sea and its resources.
help all people everywhere
to acknowledge that you alone have spread out the heavens
and rule over the seas,
and that the waters are a gift from you.

Lord, in your mercy, hear our prayer.

Lord, in your mercy
help the scientists and technicians of the world
to use their knowledge and skills for the good of all,

and not for destructive purposes.
May the countries which produce nuclear energy
channel such bounty for the good of humankind.

Lord, in your mercy, hear our prayer.

From a litany by Jabez L. Bryce, Anglican bishop in Polynesia

We pray for the peoples of Oceania in their concern to
preserve their cultures, and to keep their lands and their
seas free from war and the effects of war technology; may
they be strengthened as they strive to keep true values
alive, and as they seek in a happy and peaceful spirit, opportunities and justice for all.

Christian prayer for peace, Pope John Paul II, Assisi, 1986

O God our Father,
save our shores from the weapons of death,
our lands from what may deny our young ones love and
freedom.
Let the seas of the Pacific Ocean
carry messages of peace and goodwill.
Turn away from our midst any unkind and brutal practices.
Let each child swim, and breathe the fresh air
that is filled by the Holy Spirit.

O Lord Jesus, bless all that are makers of that inner peace
that breaks down the barriers of hatred;
and unite us with the open arms of your cross,
that all the peoples of the world may live happily together. Amen.

Sione Amanaki Havea, Tonga

This area, sometimes known as Oceania, includes over 2000 islands in more
than 30 major groupings. Culturally and geographically, they fall into three
main areas, although there is some overlap. In general terms *Polynesia* lies to
the east. Extending from Hawaii to New Zealand, it includes Tonga, Samoa, the
Cook Islands, Niue, Tuvalu, Tokelau, and others. *Melanesia,* the largest of the

areas, is also the most diverse, with small social groupings and very many languages. It lies to the west and includes New Guinea, the Solomon Islands, Vanuatu, New Caledonia, and Fiji. *Micronesia* lies on and north of the Equator, and includes the Marshall Islands, Kiribati, Nauru, the Caroline Islands, Guam, the Mariana Islands, and others.

Political groupings are more complex, and although in many cases a small group of islands comprises one nation, this is not always so because of the way in which they have been colonized and sometimes changed hands. Many are now independent, but France, the United States, and Indonesia remain colonial powers. However, the small size of the independent nations often renders them economically and technically dependent on some foreign power.

Until about 50,000 years ago, these islands were uninhabited. People then began to arrive in small numbers from Asia, and over thousands of years groups of diverse people spread eastward, gradually establishing new human communities. The first Europeans to penetrate the region were Spanish explorers and missionaries in the 16th century. Sustained Christian missionary activity began in 1797 when members of the London Missionary Society landed in Tahiti. From then on, many denominations and nationalities were involved, and soon islanders themselves began to spread the good news to other island groups.

Early missionaries faced many difficulties. Warfare was endemic; and cannibalism and infanticide were practiced as part of traditional belief systems. Many Europeans lost their lives, and there were many martyrs among the islanders. However, the faith spread from Tahiti to Papua New Guinea. In the 1939–1945 war some islands became battlegrounds, and some were occupied; most remaining missionaries either perished or were interned. The churches themselves not only survived but became more independent, and local grassroots forms of worship and spirituality emerged.

Today the population of these islands is about 6 million, of whom about

80% are Christians. Roman Catholics are strong in Papua and New Caledonia, Methodists in Tonga and Fiji, Congregationalists in Samoa and the Cook Islands, Anglicans in the Solomon Islands, Presbyterians in the New Hebrides, and Lutherans in Papua. As in other respects, diversity is a keynote of the region. A gradual lessening of tensions between the denominations has been evident throughout this century, and ecumenical cooperation has developed much more rapidly in recent decades.

In the coconut palm—the tree of life which provides food and drink, clothing and shelter—people see many aspects of God's provision and the workings of the spirit in their lives. "Coconut palm theology" instances the way seeds are carried from island to island, and take root; likening this to their own growing awareness of their interdependence across denominational boundaries and island allegiances.

There has always been, and continues to be, movement of people in all directions in the Pacific. Current trends are toward the larger cities, larger islands, border countries, and greater employment possibilities. Many find a higher material standard of living, but at some cost to their dignity and traditional way of life. Tourism is a growing industry in some parts of the region, and some islands have rich mineral deposits. Others are used by foreign powers for strategic and military purposes. Since the first testing of a nuclear weapon at Bikini Atoll in 1946, the area has continued to be used for this purpose, as well as for the dumping of nuclear waste. Often precautions for the local population, and arrangements for their rehabilitation, have been grossly inadequate, and many continue to suffer the effects of radiation.

The environment of the small but vivacious communities of the islands is the nourishing, at times threatening, sea. Pacific Islander Christians have a special way of comprehending the world. Most human beings look outward on solid earth. Islanders live on small pieces of earth surrounded by the wealth—and menace—of the sea. Travel and arrival, life and death, the Good News...have distinctive meanings for church and people. Christ is the Pacific Prince, chief of chiefs come from afar.

To Live Among the Stars, John Garrett

Together with the people of the Pacific we give thanks
for the coming of the Christian faith

for those many Islanders who hazarded their lives in spreading the good news; and in keeping the faith through the years of war and occupation

for community and celebration, and the wholeness of life lived in the region.

We pray

for the national councils of churches, and the Pacific Conference of Churches with its many regional concerns

for theological education, carried out on an ecumenical basis

for those who are suffering the effects of radioactive fallout, and those who fear for the future

for schools (46% of the population is under 15), trying to provide a modern education while preserving a rich cultural heritage

for young people leaving the rural areas in search of "better" jobs, experiencing difficulties and frustrations, and sometimes resorting to drink or drugs, which often lead to violence

for families bewildered by the changes and pressures brought by the tourist industry and an increasing consumer economy.

We ask you, dear God,

that just as the great Southern Cross

guides our people as they sail over the Pacific at night,

so may the cross of Jesus Christ

be our sure and certain guide to lead us day by day.

The Bible Society of Papua New Guinea

The coconut, marked with a cross, and kicked, rolled, and finally hacked with a knife, is used as a moving commentary on Isaiah 53 and 55 in a service which concludes with the water and meat of the coconut being used to celebrate the Lord's supper. It is perhaps the incorporation of this rather more painful aspect in the symbolism of the coconut palm which is to the fore in the minds of Christians in the Pacific in these troubled days.

O Lord, our palm trees can no longer hide us from the world.

Strengthen our hearts that we may look with confidence to the future.

Prayer of Tahitian pastor

Week 35

The Islands of the Indian Ocean

O God, we pray that you will give us enough wisdom and faith to realize the depth and richness of our human dignity; and the necessary courage to defend our own dignity and that of others, against all that would distort and devalue it.

Prayer from Seychelles

By far the largest islands in this vast ocean are Madagascar (Week 16) and Sri Lanka (Week 49). The other main groups are the Comoros, Maldives, Mauritius, and Seychelles, which all have a history of colonial rule. Various countries hold other island territories in the region.

The Comoros

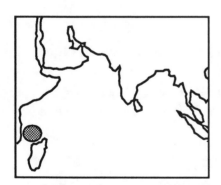

The archipelago of the Comoros, situated between Madagascar and the coast of mainland Africa, consists of four volcanic islands and numerous small islets. The country declared independence in 1975, except for the island of Mayotte which elected to retain links with France. The islands are poor and severely underdeveloped, exporting perfume oils and vanilla. The population (about 400,000) of the Federal Islamic Republic of the Comoros is of mixed Arab, African, and Malagasy descent. Arabic and French are the official languages, but most people speak Comoran. The vast majority are Muslims. There are very small Christian and Bahai communities, mostly made up of Malagasy and other expatriates, many of them seasonal workers. The country was totally unevangelized until 1973, and open evangelism continues to be unwelcome.

Maldives

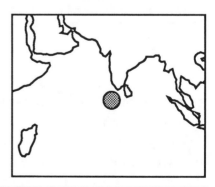

232

The Republic of Maldives embraces over a thousand small islands southwest of Sri Lanka, of which only 202 are inhabited. The Maldivian population of 181,500 are of Sinhalese origin, and speak Dhivehi, a language related to Sinhala. Their forebears were Buddhists but were converted to Islam in 1153. Living on the small coral islands most subsist by fishing and collecting coconuts. A tourist industry has been developed in recent years and contributes greatly to the economy. Islam is the only officially recognized religion. Christianity is represented by Sri Lankan and Indian workers and visiting tourists.

Mauritius

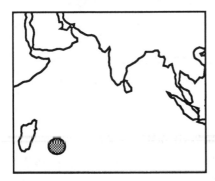

Consisting of the larger island from which the country takes its name and several smaller ones, Mauritius has been independent within the British Commonwealth since 1968. The official language is English, but Creole and a number of Indian languages are widely spoken. With no indigenous inhabitants, the islands were settled mainly from India and East Africa, and colonized by the French and then the British.

The present population of 1.1. million is composed of Indians (about two-thirds), Creoles (about a quarter), and small European and Chinese minorities. Reflecting the ethnic balance, Hindus make up 52% of the population. There are significant Christian (27%, of whom the majority are Roman Catholics) and Muslim (18%) communities; and smaller numbers of Buddhists, Jews, Sikhs, Bahais, and adherents of traditional religions. The main priority of the Roman Catholic Church is the transformation of institutional parishes into warm, caring basic Christian communities, sharing the good news of the gospel in villages and city wards. Drug abuse is an acute problem in Mauritius, and the church is expanding its work in the rehabilitation of addicts. Contact between members of the different faiths, and a recently held interfaith conference, have given an added dimension to the ecumenical scene.

Seychelles

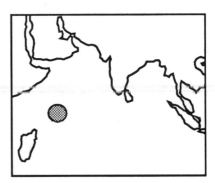

A group of more than a hundred widely scattered islands, and originally uninhabited, Seychelles was annexed by France in the 18th century and later ceded to Britain. Independence as a republic was gained in 1976, and the country now has a socialist single-party system of government. Very few of the islands are inhabited, and 98% of the population (about 66,000) live on the three which are most developed. Tourism,

agriculture, and fishing are the major industries.

The people are of mixed African, European, Polynesian, Chinese, and Indian origin; Creole is the official language. Almost all are Christians, about 90% being Roman Catholics, and 8% Anglicans. The creation of a peace zone in the Indian Ocean, with particular reference to the absence of nuclear weapons, and protection of the environment are special concerns of Seychelles.

Let us give thanks

for the beauty of the islands of the Indian Ocean and the blending of different races and peoples

for the way in which Christianity has been faithfully practiced and served by pastors and people over many years, and for the facility for renewal in the face of new needs and opportunities

for the growing cooperation of the different churches and for many enterprises undertaken together

for the warmth of welcome and hospitality experienced by Christian visitors to churches in the region.

O God of all the people and all the nations of the earth,

we praise you for the loveliness and diversity of your creatures.

This day we thank you for Mauritius,

where you have gathered the people of Africa and Asia and Europe

into one island nation, surrounded them with great beauty, and

blessed them with a spirit of tolerance and with growing prosperity.

Defeat, O God, the forces of evil

which exploit human weaknesses and prejudices

for the selfish interests of the few.

Confirm the Christian churches in their struggle to be faithful to the gospel, and also open and loving in their relations with the people and institutions of other faiths.

Strengthen, O God, all those who work for true justice and peace among the people of Mauritius; that tolerance may grow into understanding, and that prosperity may benefit all.

Prayer from the Presbyterian community in Mauritius

Let us pray
for continuing peace in the region; and for all efforts to protect the environment
for small communities of people, eking out a basic living from the natural resources around them
for drug addicts and those who work for their rehabilitation
that those who visit the islands as tourists may do so with sensitivity, that local people may benefit, and the understanding of all be enhanced
for isolated Christians in the Comoros and Maldives, that their sense of belonging to the worldwide church may be strengthened

Lord Jesus, we claim your promise
for all small groups of Christians;
that where two or three are gathered together in your name
you will be present in the midst of them;
present to inspire, present to encourage, present to bless.
Risen Lord, we claim your promise.

for God's blessing on an ecumenical project to translate the Bible into Mauritian Creole; and for Roman Catholics, Anglicans, and Presbyterians cooperating in theological education by extension

for God's gift of unity between people of different races and religions

Almighty God,
always you have wished for the unity of all humanity.
Distrust and division are none of your doing!

Grant to all humanity, and especially the people here,
unity in diversity, and peace in mutual respect.
Grant us the joy of living together in your friendship,
and of working for the good of our nation
under your watchful care.

This we ask of you through Jesus Christ our Lord,
who lives and reigns with you and the Holy Spirit,
in perfect unity forever and ever. Amen.

Part of a prayer, dear to Hindus and Buddhists as well as to Christians,
which is used on the feast day of blessed Fr. Jacques-Désiré Laval,
a French missionary priest, revered in Mauritius
as an apostle of unity and a founder of the church

Week 36

The Caribbean Islands
• French Guiana • Guyana
• Suriname

Red eyes, batons,
red fire, red blood,
black oppressed, fearful white
uncertain and ambivalent mulatto—help us to serve thee,
O God.

Black power, racial harmony
socialism, democracy
law and order
subversion, oppression,
Imperialism, rule by the masses—help us to know thy
will, O God.

Which road to follow?
leave the country?
Vigilante protection?
Fight for the peasants?
arbitrary legislation?—help us to know thy will, O God.

Help us to know thy will, O God.
How can we pray this?
Such a prayer
Cast against the background
of our unconcern, our apathy,
our denial of our heritage
of racial harmony
of our sufferers,

such a prayer, O God,
shall be our judgment—help us to do thy will, O God.

Intercession on Caribbean Choices, E. Anthony Allen, Kingston, Jamaica

We are weary
of the years of sowing and reaping;
of planting the good, new seed with hope,
and harvesting nothing.

We are weary
of the days of fruitless toiling;
of lending our strength to an alien's gain
and profiting nothing.

We are weary
of hypocrisy, falsehood, corruption,
of slogans fashioned to allay the fear of the disinherited.

We are weary
of the voices shrouded in shadows of war, crying out for
peace,
    yet knowing no peace.

Lord, we are weary.

From a litany of justice, hope, and peace, Caribbean Conference of Churches

O Lord, lead us not into imitation!

Prayer of the East Asia Youth Assembly

We believe in you, O God,
    for you have made the suffering of humanity your suffer-
ing.
    You have come to establish a kingdom of the poor and
humble.
    Today we sing to you, because you are alive,
    you have saved us, you have made us free.

Affirmation from Cuba

Lord, how glad we are that we don't hold you,
but that you hold us.

Prayer from Haiti

Throughout the immensely varied and bewildering collage of nations and races, creeds, and cultures, political systems and languages of the Caribbean, one thing remains common: the history of colonial domination from which the present situation derives.

The region, which includes Guyana, Suriname, and French Guiana on the South American mainland, and Belize (Week 37), as well as the islands, was originally inhabited by the peaceful Arawaks and rather less peaceful Caribs. The Amerindian population was largely decimated by the early colonizers is now reduced to small minority groups living in Trinidad, St. Vincent, Dominica, Belize, Guyana, and Suriname. The first colonizers, the Spanish, were soon followed by the Dutch, British, and French, and for more than 300 years the conflicts of Europe were partially played out in the Caribbean. By the end of the colonial era Spain had lost out to Britain and the United States.

"The region was historically not meant to be a society," says Dr. Dale Bisnauth, associate general secretary of the Caribbean Conference of Churches, "it was meant to be a plantation, owned and operated by European capitalists. The colonies were perceived as sources of primary agricultural products which could be made into manufactured goods for the European market. Economically, then, the region's history has been one of the metropolitan plunder and exploitation from which it will take years to recover."

Plantations necessitate a sizable labor force, and this had to be imported. Thousands of West African slaves were brought annually, so that the population became predominantly African. In addition, Indians, Chinese, Indonesians, and Europeans were brought as indentured labor.

Most Caribbean countries are now politically independent, but a number are still under British, French, Dutch, and US sovereignty. Some, for example, Puerto Rico and the Netherlands' Antilles, have varying degrees of associated

status. Spanish, English, French, or Dutch is the official language in most places; and more than one of these or a local patois is often the norm. In addition, various Asian and Amerindian languages are widely spoken in some areas.

Economic domination, however, remains and the region "caught in a trade bind forged in colonial times" is a region of poverty. "The problem of the external debt hangs around the region's collective neck like an albatross, adding to the misery of its impoverishment and underdevelopment. The problems—unemployment, inadequate health and housing facilities, drug abuse, etc.—which derive from the economic deprivation of the region are many. Add to them the fact of cultural alienation and the picture is not encouraging." (Dale Bisnauth)

In the past, in addition to the loss of identity resulting from the conditions of slavery, European cultural and value systems were imposed on the Caribbean peoples; and the historic churches contributed to this process. Now there is a new identity problem. "Situated as it is between the poor South and the rich North, the region shares the poverty of the South, but its peoples aspire to life-styles of the North whose consumer patterns bombard them from media programs. The fracture in the psyche that this creates is not helped by the region's vulnerability to other pressures from the North." (Dale Bisnauth)

Cuba, the largest of the Caribbean islands, threw off cultural and economic domination in its Revolution of 1959, which toppled the previous repressive dictatorship. Since then the country has been developing its own brand of socialism, and restructuring its basically agricultural economy. An Ecumenical Council is active in developing a corporate Christian response to the new social and political realities of the Revolution.

Christianity first came to the Caribbean with the colonizers, who brought all their own separate denominational churches with them. Some of the first slaves were also Christians. Roman Catholics or Protestants dominated according to who ruled, and the churches have sometimes been criticized for furthering the interests of their parent nations.

Today in most Caribbean territories over 90% of the people are Christians. This figure drops to about 50–75% in Trinidad and Tobago, Suriname, and Guyana, where there are significant numbers of Hindus and Muslims; and to 42% in Cuba, where 55% of the population are either atheists or nonreligious. There are small Bahai communities throughout the region. Traditional African and Amerindian religions are still followed, and Voodoo, a syncretism of Christianity and African rites, is strong in Haiti.

History has left the Caribbean with a very broad religious spectrum, complicated by loyalties to the country of origin and the practicalities of language. In recent years there has been an influx of new and largely fundamentalist sects from North America, aided and abetted by the tremendous influence of the electronic church. Current concerns are many, and individual churches vary in their emphases, but theological reflection related to the region, peace with justice, the problem of drug abuse, unemployment, the deepening of spiritual life, and growing ecumenism are recurring themes. In many national councils of churches the Roman Catholic church is a full member.

Give thanks

for the growth of the Christian faith in the Caribbean
for the growing unity of churches as expressed in the

Caribbean Conference of Churches and in the national councils of churches of the region

for growing tolerance between Christians and peoples of other faiths and beliefs

Thank you, O Lord our God, for all that you have done to sustain us.

Here in the Caribbean there are so many things that give us pleasure:

beaches, mountains, valleys, trees, fruits, and flowers.

Indeed, all nature celebrates you in this part of your creation.

Thank you for the people who dwell in our territories,

that in them we see a reflection of all the races of the world.

Thank you for your beloved Son Jesus Christ;

for his life, his mission, his teaching, his sufferings,

his death and resurrection;

And that this Jesus who is our Savior, lives today.

Caribbean Conference of Churches, 4th Assembly

Pray

for peace in the region, and particularly in strife-torn Haiti, and in Suriname now returned to parliamentary rule

for justice and the observance of human rights

for the poor and disadvantaged that they may have hope

for the eradication of poverty and a fairer distribution of resources in all countries

for the Caribbean Conference of Churches, and for individual churches that they may be instruments of peace, justice, and development

for all Christian families in the region.

O God, in baptism you have called us by name and made us members of your people, the church.

Raise up good and holy families, loving husbands, wives and parents.

Raise up from among our families and friends, dedicated and generous leaders who will serve as sisters, priests, brothers, deacons, and lay ministers.

Give your Spirit to guide and strengthen us, that we may serve your people following the example of your Son, Jesus Christ, in whose name we offer this prayer.

A prayer for family life and for vocation suggested for use by members of congregations in the Roman Catholic Archdiocese of Kingston, Jamaica

We pray that thou wilt watch over us in St. Lucia,
for there are so many things happening on this small island of ours.

Schoolgirl's prayer from St. Lucia

For this and other areas of the world where life has been grossly disturbed by the advent of tourists, we pray:

Loving Creator,
may those who visit the Caribbean
enjoy its natural beauty and the rich variety of its people
not as things to be paid for by money
but as your gifts to be loved and handled with care.

With those who, long after our prayers have ended, continue to serve the church in the Caribbean we pray:

O God, we pray that you will keep together those you have united.
Look kindly on all who follow Jesus your Son,
and who are consecrated to you in a common baptism.
Make us one in the fullness of faith,
and keep us in the fellowship of justice, peace, and love.
Amen.

Caribbean Conference of Churches, opening service of the Fourth Assembly

Caribbean Conference of Churches (CCC)

Loving God, we are concerned about the spread of hatred in our time.
Some of it has led to crime, violence of all sorts, marital breakdown,
tribal conflicts and tensions among peoples and nations.
Strike out, O God, the root causes of all hatred,
that justice, peace, and love might prevail.

Lord, in your mercy,
Hear our prayer.

We commit to God the work of all who strive to create a more healthy society in these Caribbean lands: who work among the poor, the unemployed; who try to point our youth to a life away from drugs, alcohol, licentious behavior, and to point them rather to the paths of true human dignity and responsibility. Grant them the encouragement to continue their noble aims.

Lord, in your mercy
Hear our prayer.

Caribbean Conference of Churches, 4th Assembly

"We, as Christian people in the Caribbean, separated from each other by barriers of history, language, culture, class, and distance, desire because of our common calling in Christ to join together in a regional fellowship of churches for inspiration, consultation, and cooperative action"—so read the opening words of the constitution of the Caribbean Conference of Churches.

Inaugurated in 1973, the CCC now has 33 member churches from a wide variety of traditions, including the Roman Catholic Church and a number of evangelical bodies. With its headquarters in Barbados, and with area offices in Trinidad, Jamaica, and Antigua, the CCC extends its regional ecumenical umbrella to such mainland countries as Belize, Panama, Costa Rica, Guyana, and Suriname.

"Promoting ecumenism and social change in obedience to Jesus Christ and in solidarity with the poor" is the current mandate. Ongoing concerns include

regional integration, Caribbean identity, third-world tourism, the region as a zone of peace, human rights, racism, the well-being of migrants and refugees, as well as concern about the avenues for self-destruction being made increasingly available, especially to the young.

In this context "the thrust of the CCC is declaredly developmental." Working for the benefit of those at the bottom of the economic ladder, whether those in rural communities or the great number of unemployed or underemployed in the cities, it "is convinced that developmental programs must be integrative, participatory, community-based and oriented, facilitative of reflection, renewal, change, and human liberation. Above all, they must be with the poor, by the poor, and for the poor" (Dale Bisnauth).

Many Caribbean Christians would feel more at home *singing* the prayer cycle! This prayer by Patrick Prescod is best sung to the accompaniment of steel band, piano, flute, and guitar, but any lively accompaniment will serve.

The right hand of God is pointing in our land,
Pointing the way we must go.
So clouded is the way, so easily we stray,
But we're guided by the right hand of God.

The right hand of God is striking in our land,
Striking out at envy, hate, and greed.
Our selfishness and lust, our pride and deeds unjust
Are destroyed by the right hand of God.

The right hand of God is healing in our land,
healing broken bodies, minds, and souls.
So wondrous is its touch with love that means so much,
When we're healed by the right hand of God.

The right hand of God is planting in our land,
Planting seeds of freedom, hope, and love.
In these Caribbean lands, let God's people all join hands,
And be one with the right hand of God.

Patrick Prescod

Week 37

Belize • Guatemala • Honduras • Mexico

Give us, Señor, a little sun, a little happiness and some work.
Give us a heart to comfort those in pain.
Give us the ability to be good, strong, wise, and free
so that we may be generous with others as we are with ourselves.
Finally, Señor, let us all live in your own, one family.

Prayer on a church wall in Mexico

But let justice roll down like waters,
and righteousness like an overflowing stream.

Amos 5

The message that the poor Christians from Latin America hear comes straight from the Bible. Isaiah 65, Amos 5, and Psalm 146 are, among many others, passages that Latin American Christians are reading as promises God holds out to them, both now and when Christ returns.

A testimony given before the US House of Representatives Subcommittee on Human Rights and International Organizations, Committee on Foreign Affairs

Captivate me, Lord.
Till the last of my days,
wring out my heart
with your hands
of a wise old Indian
so that I will not forget your justice

nor cease proclaiming
the urgent need
for humankind to live in harmony.

Prayer/poem of Julia Esquivel, self-exiled Guatemalan resistance poet

Lord,
if this day you have to correct us
put us right not out of anger
but with a mother and father's love.
So may we your children
be kept free of falseness and foolishness.

Prayer from Mexico

Belize

Formerly known as British Honduras, Belize was under Spanish sovereignty before it was under British. It became fully independent within the Commonwealth in 1981, and has a parliamentary form of government, and close links with the Caribbean. The official language is English, but Spanish and some American Indian languages are also spoken. Guatema-

la has laid claim to Belizean territory since the mid-19th century, and successive attempts at a settlement have so far failed. In spite of the fact that over half the population (166,300) lives in the capital, the economy depends mainly on agriculture. Floods and hurricanes are natural hazards. In recent years considerable immigration from neighboring Latin American countries, especially El Salvador, has approximately balanced movement out of Belize to the United States, from whence people send much-needed money home.

About 95% of the people are Christians, approximately 60% being Roman Catholics and 40% Protestants, of whom half are Anglicans. There are small Bahai and Jewish communities. The Belize Christian Council seeks to provide "a comprehensive service program under ecumenical leadership for the benefit of the people of Belize." With a wide range of membership including the Roman Catholic church and the Salvation Army, as well as various associate bodies, it relates to the Caribbean Conference of Churches.

Let us pray
for Belize, that its people may live in harmony with each

other and with those of neighboring lands

that its young people may make the fullest use of their energies and opportunities; and their elders give them ground for hope in a worthwhile future for their country

for the Belize Christian Council and its social action programs, particularly those among women and preschool children

for the concern of the churches to encourage local leadership and for their involvement in education and primary health care

for the unemployed and the homeless; those caught up in the sale and use of drugs; for families split by migration.

Grant, O Lord, that the people of Belize may have peace and prosperity, and be a stabilizing influence in the turmoil of Central America. Prosper the educational work of the Christian church, and give unity where there is discord, for Jesus Christ's sake. Amen.

Guatemala

Population: 8.5 million.
Languages: Spanish and more than 20 indigenous languages.
Government: Multi-party republic.
Religion: Christians 99% (Roman Catholics 94%, Protestants 5%).

The indigenous inhabitants of Central America, the Mayan Indians, were more than halved in number by the effects of the Spanish conquest in the 16th century. Most of those who survived lived in the highlands of what is now Guatemala. This country enjoyed a period of democratic government earlier this century. But fears of communist infiltration prompted the US government to support the military coup which ended it. Since then there has been considerable instability and increasing violence.

The root causes—poverty and landlessness—remain unresolved. There have been reports of violations of human rights, and many deaths for political reasons. The country has been described as "a nation of widows and orphans," and many of these children now roam the streets. Up to 500,000 Indians have been displaced by the fighting, many of whom have sought refuge in camps

in Mexico. At the same time, Guatemala is host to many Salvadorean refugees. A new government has now been elected and faces a massive task.

Christianity was first brought by the Spanish, later by other Europeans, and then North Americans. The Roman Catholic Church, formerly closely allied with the ruling power, experienced a considerable reawakening in the 1950s, and many bishops, priests, and lay people took up the option to identify with the poor. As a consequence they have been harassed and branded as communists, and some have been tortured or lost their lives. Protestant churches, which have grown steadily since 1940, have also been involved in human rights issues. The first Protestants to enter the country were the American Presbyterians in 1882. It was they who developed the system of theological education by extension which has been taken up worldwide. Education and health have been major concerns of the mainstream Protestant churches. In recent years numerous fundamentalist sects have entered the country and attracted many converts. Unfortunately, their message of salvation often includes anti-communist propaganda, and they are regarded with suspicion by traditional Protestants and Roman Catholics alike. The experience of being poor and the struggle for justice have drawn together many Christians from both Roman Catholic and Protestant backgrounds.

Pray for

all current Guatemalan initiatives for peace with neighboring countries, and for a positive response

all who seek to bring about constructive land reform and a more just distribution of the country's resources

the thousands of families in unabated distress, still hoping for news of "disappeared" family members

the large numbers of Indian people who have fled, or been displaced by army activity

Guatemala's unemployed and poor people, and the many young children who have lost one or both parents in political violence

Christian communities and all other means by which the good news of the resurrection is mediated in Guatemala today.

Jesus, we believe that you are living.

The steps that you took before, we are taking now.

Your resurrection is present in each sister and brother who rises up.

250

Help us so that all people may be resurrected in a new
Guatemala
where peace, justice, and equality will reign,
so that nobody is hungry.

Prayer of an Indian woman member
of the Guatemalan Committee for Justice and Peace

Honduras

Population: 3.9 million.
Language: Spanish.
Government: Multi-party republic.
Religion: Christians 98% (Roman
Catholics 95%, Protestants 3%).

A major center of ancient Mayan culture before the 10th century, Honduras today is one of the poorest countries of Latin America. Largely dependent on agriculture, and at the mercy of hurricanes, floods, and drought, the country is reliant on economic aid. Landowners have never been as rich and powerful as in neighboring countries, and perhaps for this reason, Honduras has not experienced the same degree of violence as its neighbors. Nevertheless, in recent years political unrest has been increasing. The presence of about 47,000 refugees from El Salvador and Nicaragua and some Contras, as well as heavy US military involvement in the country, add to the tensions.

In the 1960s, the Roman Catholic church pioneered the training of lay people from remote areas as rural "delegates of the word." This grassroots evangelism went hand in hand with concern for social issues, and the concrete problems affecting people. Rural education programs and pressure for land reform provoked antagonism, and there were arrests, deaths, and confiscation of property. A number of Protestant confessions are present. Although numerically small, they have made significant contributions in areas of social concern, notably education and health, in addition to their evangelistic work.

We pray
for Honduras, one of the poorest nations in the hemisphere, with massive malnutrition among its rural population, and constantly threatened by floods, drought, and crop failures
for the Christian church's response to the potentially volatile situation existing in the country

for church-run schools, clinics, nutrition centers, and agricultural projects

for the massive influx of refugees from El Salvador, Guatemala, and Nicaragua.

To Guatemalan refugees in Mexico, from Salvadoran refugees in Honduras:

We still pray, we still sing
We still dream of the day
when the birds will return
and the flowers
and our lost loved ones.

We still live with the belief
that love and gentleness and faith
will blossom forth one day
like roses in winter.

We still believe that God
will be born again in our land
as we prepare the stable of our hearts
for the birth of a new people.

By his coming to the world in the form of a stranger seeking welcome,

and as an exile looking for the promise of refuge and hope,

may the God of Ruth and Moses bless the people of Honduras.

Mexico

Population: 79.6 million.
Languages: Spanish and indigenous Indian languages.
Government: Federal republic.
Religion: Christians 98% (Roman Catholics about 94%, Protestants 3.7%).

The revolution of 1910, which began largely as a movement to free the country from prolonged dictatorship, continued as a revolt against large landowners, and marked the beginning of social change in Mexico. Despite this there are still large numbers of landless people, and poverty and malnutrition in rural areas is extensive. A growing population, together with Mexico's remarkable industrial expansion, has encouraged migration to the cities, and Mexico City, one site of the ancient Aztec capital, is now the largest urban concentration in the world. New cities have grown up along the border with the United States, where foreign-owned factories employ large numbers of people. Poverty and lack of work encourage further migration, both legal and illegal, across the border into the United States. There have been times when this source of cheap labor was more or less welcomed, but now the situation is different and these migrants are very vulnerable to both exploitation and deportation. In spite of its own population explosion—half the population is under 16 years—Mexico is host to some 46,000 refugees, mostly from Guatemala.

The 1910 revolution profoundly affected the Roman Catholic church which was one of the largest landowners, and for a time the church was persecuted. Now there is a kind of *modus vivendi* between church and state, and although the ruling party is officially atheist, many of its leaders are Roman Catholics. While the hierarchy tends to be conservative and the majority of people traditional Catholics, there are those who are attempting to relate their theology and liturgical practice to social issues and to local culture. Some prestigious Jesuit schools have closed, and transferred their resources to educational work in slum areas. Some bishops have protested publicly against violations of human rights, for although Mexico has the reputation of being one of the least oppressive countries in the region, there have been reported violations. The first Protestants to come to Mexico came as individuals during Spanish rule, and faced the Inquisition. Protestant missionaries came later. Now there are a considerable number of Protestant groups and sects. The flourishing Pentecostal churches constitute about two-thirds of all Protestants in the country.

The violent earthquake of 1985 killed thousands of people and affected maybe 100,000 families. The work of reconstruction and rehabilitation will continue for years. In various church-sponsored organizations the people themselves have been mobilized to help build their own homes, thereby reducing costs as well as giving them a sense of purpose and community organization.

We pray

for the "damnificados" or earthquake victims of Mexico, and for the ecumenical committee offering help to them

for those many poor people who are nevertheless heirs to a rich life in Christ; and for all who seek to help them to enter into more of the material promises of the kingdom

for countless children on the streets, and for all who work to give them some kind of dignity and future

for young women tempted away from their own communities by the prospect of work in border factories, with all the problems inherent in such a situation

for all who furtively cross borders in search of work and refuge

for those who have to administer the law in border areas, theat they may afford human dignity to all

for the work of the church on the border, offering hospitality, advice, and practical help,

for Mexico City, with its population growing by at least a million a year.

God of our daily lives,
we pray for the people of the cities of this world
working and without work;
homeless or well housed;
fulfilled or frustrated;
confused and cluttered with material goods
or scraping a living from others' leavings;
angrily scrawling on walls, or reading the writing on the wall;
lonely or living in community;
finding their own space and respecting the space of others.
We pray for our sisters and brothers,
mourning and celebrating—
may we share their sufferings and hope.

Jan Pickard, Methodist Church Overseas Division

Week 38

Costa Rica • El Salvador • Nicaragua • Panama

Señor,
sálvanos de caer en el pecado
de creer que la esclavitud en Egiptoes
es mejor que la lucha aquí en el desierto.

Lord,
free us from falling into the sin
of believing that the slavery in Egypt
is better than the struggle here in the desert.

Tómas Téllez, Nicaragua

We live in a world of division, where over $1 million a minute is spent on military expenses, and the gifts that God gave to the human family are used for division and domination. Trusting in God's mercy, we say—Lord, have mercy.

We live in a world where half the members of the human family do not have safe drinking water, thus failing to complete the creation task which a loving God has left us. And so we pray—Christ, have mercy.

We live in a world whose land and wealth is so poorly divided that while many are obese and go on diets, 700 million people are malnourished. And so we pray—Lord, have mercy.

Lord God, we ask you to forgive us our sins, to enlighten our imagination, so that we can share more equally the gifts you have left for all of your children, so that creation may join us in praising your name. Amen.

Oscar Romero, Archbishop of San Salvador, martyred in 1980

I believe in you, companion,
human Christ, worker Christ,
who conquered death.
With your immense sacrifice
you begat the new person for liberation.
You are resurrecting
each time we raise an arm
to defend the people from the dominating exploiter:
because you are alive in the ranch,
in the factory, in the school,
I believe in your struggle without truce
I believe in the resurrection.

from the Creed, Nicaraguan Campesino Mass

Blessed be God,
who is always renewing the church by his Holy Spirit,
making young again what had grown old.

Act of praise following Vatican II

Loving Lord, you will the health and wholeness of all
your people,
    we pray for all those who suffer in Central America
    those who suffer anxiety and terror
    those who suffer deprivation of food and shelter
    Lord, please hear us—Mercifully hear us.

We pray for refugees, for the homeless and those who
are fleeing from violence
    for the sick, the unsettled, and for widows and orphans
    for those who identify with the poor and oppressed, and
as a consequence suffer
    Lord, please hear us—Mercifully hear us.

We pray for those who are working for peace, and for the
healing of human bodies and communities
    for doctors and nurses and teachers

for members of basic Christian communities

for those who strive for the peaceful and fruitful use of the earth

for all in the region who seek to bring about justice and lasting peace

Lord, please hear us—Mercifully hear us.

Christian Aid: adapted

Our Father, who are in this our land,
may your name be blessed
in our incessant search for justice and peace.
May our kingdom come for those
 who have for centuries awaited a life with dignity.
May your will be done on earth and in heaven
and in the church of Central America,
a church on the side of the poor.
Give us today our daily bread to build a new society.
Forgive us our trespasses,
do not let us fall into the temptation
of believing ourselves already new men and women.
And deliver us from the evil of war
and from the evil of forgetting that our lives
and the life of this country are in your hands.

The Lord's Prayer as used by Christian communities in Nicaragua

Population, religion, government, and language
Costa Rica: 2.4 million, Christians 98%.
El Salvador: 4.9 million, Christians 99.2%.
Nicaragua: 2.9 million, Christians 99.3%.
Panama: 2.2 million, Christians 92%.
Traditional Indian religions still exist, and in Panama there are adherents of many different world faiths.
All these countries are multi-party republics.
The official language is Spanish, but in-

digenous Indian languages are spoken throughout the region, as well as English in parts of Nicaragua.

Columbus reached this part of Central America in 1502, and the settlers who followed were accompanied by priests who were ardent evangelists toward the indigenous Indians. Many took up their cause, and opposed the harsh and repressive measures adopted by the authorities; but for the most part the Catholic church, firmly allied to Spain, greatly increased its wealth and power. Some 90–95% of people are Roman Catholics except in Panama where the proportion is slightly lower. Following the second world war, and largely in response to a wave of anti-communism, the rural areas of Central America were singled out for attention by an influx of foreign clergy and religious orders. For the first time priests and nuns came face to face with the severe poverty and exploitation of rural people. Through this experience the church underwent a reawakening, and began to contribute to a slow process of building among its people an awareness of their rights and dignity as children of God.

Methodist immigrants from the Caribbean arrived in Panama in 1815. German Moravians began work in Nicaragua in 1849, and by involvement in agriculture and literacy, as well as wider educational and medical work, provided a social and pastoral ministry to various ethnic groups. In Costa Rica expatriate traders initiated Protestant services in private homes, and the first church to be built was nondenominational. The traditional Protestant churches, mostly founded by North American missionaries, have been active in the fields of education and health, notably the Baptists in Nicaragua who have established medical training programs. Pentecostal churches have grown rapidly since the second world war. Today Protestants number between 3% and 8%, and there are also a number of indigenous groups. Some, but not all, Protestant Christians have increasingly spoken out against repression and identified with the poor, working closely with Roman Catholics at this grassroots level.

In *Costa Rica*, which has one of the most advanced social welfare systems in the world, the church has had an important role in implementing social reform. The Roman Catholic diocesan center concerned with social teaching, besides offering courses for clergy, provides them also for community workers and trade union officials. A Protestant center for the region is engaged in pastoral and ecumenical training programs.

Torn by strife, *El Salvador* has been the scene of political murders and human rights violations; and suffering continues. Exactly who—government, armed forces, or the death squads of the landed aristocracy—carries out the atrocities has varied from time to time. "I have frequently been threatened with death," said Archbishop Oscar Romero shortly before his death. "I should tell you that as a Christian I do not believe in death without resurrection....My death will be for the liberation of my people and as a testimony of hope for the future." Christian people, gathering together in small basic communities to celebrate the eucharist, study the Bible, share their sorrows and strengthen each other, draw inspiration from those who have died in the struggle, and live in that same spirit of resurrection hope.

According to one description, *Nicaragua* "is as weak and fragile as a newborn. It desires peace and the freedom to live and grow as it chooses. The Herods of the world have a disproportionate fear of this tiny country..." Initially embarking on wide-ranging reforms, the government, under the Sandinistas until 1990, at first had the support of many Christian leaders who have, however, been critical of more recent government restrictiveness. Baptist and Moravians—both active ecumenically—were initiating members of the Evangelical

Committee for the Development Aid which has played a vital part in social development work.

Panama's geographical situation brings it the benefits derived from the canal and its international banking system, but also the problems and external pressures which accompany these. The Christian church has been challenged and inspired by the example and witness of Latin American Christians. A member of one denomination speaks of a "spring of the church" which is blowing across the continent, crossing denominational and geographical boundaries, issuing in a fluorescence of faith and theology unknown perhaps since the early days of the church.

With Christians in Central America, let us recall that great company of Christian martyrs, known and unknown, who have stood firmly by their faith in the time of testing.

In their company, let us pray

for peace in Central America; for the efforts of the Contadora group of nations, and all peace initiatives

for the displaced people of El Salvador, and all who are helping them to settle in new places

for ecumenical cooperation in Nicaragua in all matters concerning the welfare of the wider human family

for congregations in Panama and Costa Rica; for their work and worship together, and their joint concern for the community, particularly the young and unemployed, the destitute, and the elderly

for perseverance and an awareness of Christ's living presence for all Christians in Central America.

And now
when I fall down
under the burden of my cross,
Lord Jesus,
be my Cyreneo.

Jerjes Ruiz, Nicaragua

Week 39

Colombia • Ecuador • Venezuela

Blessed be God.
Blessed be our Father in heaven.
Blessed be the God and Father of our Lord Jesus Christ.
Blessed be his holy name.
Blessed be Jesus Christ, true God and true man,
the Savior of the world.
Blessed be the life-giving, the liberating Spirit, the Holy Ghost,
the Counselor, the Comforter.
Blessed be God in the splendor of his angels,
in the glories of his saints.

The Divine Praises, a devotion in the Roman Catholic church,
appropriately said with the majority of Christians
in the countries prayed for this week

O Christ,
as the spear opened a passage to your heart
we pray that you would ever keep a way open
to the hearts of your people everywhere....

from Ecuador

O God, we bring before you the people of Latin America whose suffering seems to have no end, tearing our hearts apart and challenging our faith in the God of justice. In spite of the suffering, we want to be instruments of reconciliation, not allowing hate to be the motivation behind our struggles to eradicate injustice. Listen to the pleas of your people. Amen.

Felipe Adolf, general secretary, Latin American Council of Churches

We believe in a loving God,
whose Word sustains our lives
and the work of our hands in the universe—God is life.

We believe in his Son among us
who brought the seed of life's renewal.
He lived with the poor to show the meaning of love—He
is the Lord.

We believe in the Spirit of Life,
who makes us one with God;
whose strength and energy renews our fight—The Spirit
is Love.

We believe in the church of God
at the service of all the people
so that we may see the truth on earth—She bears God's
word.

We believe in this new life
which bread and wine give to us
to work for God in unity—this is our glory.

We believe in everlasting life and the future of a new
world
where the word of God will be the truth to all
in Christ our Lord.

Creed of Camilo Torres, Colombia

Stop! ferocious animal.
God was here first,
Then you.

Ecuador, prayer to stop a dog biting
Psalm 59:14, 15

Population, language, and government
Colombia: 27.9 million and rising rapidly.
Ecuador: 9.7 million (excluding nomadic Indian tribes). Increasing rapidly.
Venezuela: 17.8 million (excluding Indian jungle inhabitants).
The language is Spanish, but Quechua and other indigenous languages are widely spoken.
Colombia and Ecuador are unitary multi-party republics. Venezuela is a federal republic.

The coast of this area, originally inhabited by American Indians, was sighted by Columbus in 1498. The Spanish conquest quickly followed, and African slaves were subsequently brought in to work on the plantations. The area of what is now Colombia was liberated in 1819 and the remainder of the territory soon after. Initially the whole of this area, together with Panama, constituted Gran Colombia. Ecuador and Venezuela seceded as independent republics in 1830, and Panama separated in 1903. The area is subject to natural disasters: earthquakes, floods, landslides, and the eruption of volcanos.

Roman Catholic missionaries came with the Spanish, and as in other parts of the continent the Roman Catholic church became the state religion, closely aligned with the ruling power. However, diversity of language, difficult terrain, and in some areas the hostility of the Indians made for difficulties in evangelization, and the acceptance of Christianity was of varying depth and completeness. Independence created difficulties for the church, and the number of priests fell drastically. Although Roman Catholicism is the religion of the vast majority of people—more than 95%—there is no state religion in any of these countries. The first Protestant witness was that of Bible Society agents traveling in the region shortly after independence. Sustained work began in Colombia in 1856 when Presbyterian missionaries from the Untied States established schools and medical centers. Christian Brethren organized a permanent congregation in Venezuela in 1883, and the Gospel Missionary Union began work in Ecuador in 1896. Other groups followed, and work often expanded from one country to the next.

Colombia

Potentially a rich country, and in some respects relatively well developed, Colombia has suffered an extraordinary amount of politically motivated violence since independence. As if that were not enough, thousands lost their lives in a volcanic eruption in 1985. Successive governments have faced the problems of violence, illicit drug cultivation and trafficking, and severe poverty among the people. The gap between the "haves" and the "have-nots" remains wide, and Colombia has one of the highest infant mortality rates in the world.

It was at Medellín in Colombia that the Conference of Latin American bishops took place, which was to have such a profound effect on the life of the Roman Catholic church in

the region. Recognizing the widespread social ills, and the church's apparent alliance with the rich and powerful, the bishops made a commitment to become "the church of the poor." The church became committed to "liberación,"—liberation from oppression of all kinds. Despite this, the church in Colombia remains one of the most conservative in Latin America, and small, more radical groups arising within it have often faced opposition from the bishops. Some priests and lay people (notably Camilo Torres, killed in 1966) frustrated in their efforts to bring about social change by peaceful and political means, joined revolutionary groups. At the grassroots level there has been a resurgence of traditional Catholic practice in spite of a severe shortage of priests.

Given government recognition in 1930, Protestants are a small minority, and at times have been regarded with suspicion. On the whole, the Protestant churches are conservative. A number of independent churches, mostly Pentecostal, have developed. Protestants in Colombia now enjoy considerable freedom.

Ecuador

In days gone by, the Spaniards solemnly dedicated Ecuador to the Sacred Heart of Jesus. With or without such dedication, Christians believe all people and places to be firmly held in the heart of God, even though today's Christians in Ecuador have widely differing understandings of its implications for them.

With a long history of oppression of the people, generally at the hands of wealthy landowners, Ecuador continues to suffer under a massive debt, and an ever-widening disparity between rich and poor. Cuts in social services, wage freezes, and unemployment have led to unrest, and precipitated displays of force by those in authority. Normally a peaceful people, current outbreaks of violence are a new and disturbing feature of Ecuadorian life.

The Roman Catholic church, while offering the traditional comforts and consolations of religion, has by and large been content to maintain the status quo. Protestant churches, invited into the country during a more liberal period of government, contributed educational facilities. The many later Protestant arrivals have been very conservative, emphasizing personal evangelism, and wary of social involvement. There have, however, been significant exceptions in both Catholic and Protestant communities. Inspired by Vatican II and the Medellín conference, some Roman Catholic bishops, priests, and lay people have dedicated themselves to the service of the poor, and to agitation for land reform and the observance of human rights, attempting to develop forms of piety more related to the real circumstances in which people live. They have been regarded with suspicion by the authorities of church and state. In the Protestant churches—a small community of some 20,000 persons—an early lead in ecumenical and social work was given by the United Evangelical church of Ecuador. Much of its work was later tak-

en on by the United Andean Christian Foundation, involving a number of different confessions in the running of schools and clinics, in agricultural work and the giving of scholarships. Individual members of a number of Protestant churches have been influenced by the wider ecumenical movement, and the Christian Council of Latin America seeks to build bridges of understanding between different religious communities. An earthquake in 1987 affecting some 90,000 people, prompted the reactivation of a seven-organization Ecumenical Committee for Earthquakes. By and large, however, Christians in Ecuador, like people the world over, pray about domestic matters like forthcoming elections, jobs, youth, and for peace of mind and peace of life. It is along these lines that they would have us pray with them.

unrest, with strikes, riots, and guerrilla activities. The country has become a major trade route for illicit drugs, grown and processed elsewhere; and it is feared that illegal cultivation in the country is increasing.

The Roman Catholic church faces a shortage of priests, of whom a small proportion are indigenous, whereas a much higher proportion of sisters are Venezuelan. A system of "parish curates" (sisters with special training who carry out pastoral work in cooperation with priests and directly under the bishop) was tried as an experiment in the slum areas of Caracas. It subsequently spread and is especially appropriate in rural areas. The largest of the Protestant confessions is the Assemblies of God who are engaged in evangelistic work among the Guajiro Indians, among other things. Other Pentecostal groups are also present, and there is a significant number of indigenous churches. An evangelical newspaper, published in Venezuela, circulates in every Latin American country. A number of Orthodox churches are present, all related to bodies in the USA. The Venezuela Council of Churches unites most Protestant churches and missions, but has no outside affiliations.

Venezuela

Until recently, oil exports made Venezuela relatively wealthy, and with the wealth came increasing materialism. Recently, however, the economic situation has deteriorated, and Venezuela now faces a large foreign debt. Stringent economy measures, always unpopular, have resulted in

We give thanks

for those who, drawing their strength and courage from the presence of lively Christian communities, speak out boldly against injustices

for common ecumenical action born of necessity, and yet going beyond it

for the mountain and forest scenery of this region; for tropical jungles, lakes and waterfalls, and beautiful beaches attracting many visitors and much-needed foreign currency

O Lord, I don't want to be a spectator
A tour passenger looking out upon the real world,
An audience to poverty and want and homelessness.

Lord, involve me—call me—
implicate me—commit me—
And Lord—help me to step off the bus.

A tourist's prayer, Freda Rejotte

We pray

for those who live in places where law and order are difficult to maintain, and where life is insecure and uncertain

for family members disappeared; and for those without hope

for those caught up in the awful net of dependency, and for those who cultivate and trade in illicit drugs

for schools and health centers, and for those who do not have access to adequate health care or education.

In Ecuador repayments on international loans cost millions of dollars a year while every half hour a child dies from malnutrition:

I hunger and I eat, three times a day—or more;
They hunger and they do not eat,

They hunger and they do not eat,
They hunger and they do not eat;
Help me to help them.

A North American prays for the hungry: John Fandel

With an estimated annual average of more than a hundred natural and human-caused disasters occurring each year, we pray for the emergency desks of United Nations, of CICARWS (the interchurch aid commission of the WCC), and all who seek to coordinate international aid in time of need.

O God, we find ourselves dealing in death and deprivation where we know your will is fullness of life for all. Forgive us and stir us to new life in the service of your kingdom of truth and justice, that the whole world may be made new and drawn into unity in him who is the life of the world, Jesus Christ, our Lord. Amen.

Week of Prayer for Christian Unity, 1983, John Poulton

Week 40

Burkina Faso • Chad • Mali • Mauritania • Niger

O Lord, grant us to love you.
May the love of you be dearer to us
than ourselves and our families;
than wealth, and even than cool water.

Prayer attributed to the prophet Muhammad

We must have patience: patience with others; patience with thirst while traveling; patience with weariness; patience with children. We must accept everything in patience, both happiness and suffering.

A woman of the Peulhs, a Fulani nomadic group from Niger

Life is made up of happiness and suffering. Do you know what happiness is like? Little drops of milk which splash up over your body while you are milking. And do you know what suffering is like? Sparks of fire that burn you as you sit round the fire. The suffering of fire and the happiness of milk. You know that they are nothing like each other. And in the life of each of us there is fire and milk.

A Fulani woman

O God, who comes to us in our great joys, our crushing sorrows, and in our day-to-day lives; be with us now as we share ourselves with our Sahelian sisters and brothers in this time of prayer. In Jesus' name. Amen.

Vancouver Worship Book, adapted

Together with Cape Verde, Senegal, and The Gambia, these countries constitute the Sahel, which literally means "edge of the desert." Once a lush fertile
area, thousands of years ago, it is increasingly being invaded by the desert.
From approximately the 8th to the 16th century, great African kingdoms
thrived in what was then a savannah region, and their cities were centers of
trade for the caravan routes crossing the Sahara to the Mediterranean. Now
these are some of the least developed and poorest countries in the world. Rainfall is erratic, and between 1968–1974 the whole area suffered devastating
drought. This has recurred in more recent years and is now extending into
some areas hitherto unaffected.

Formerly French colonies, all these countries obtained independence in
1960. All are republics, but Burkina Faso, Mauritania, and Niger are currently
under military rule, and the military play a significant part in the government
of Mali. The people belong to a considerable number of ethno-linguistic
groups, often culturally very different. French is the official language (plus Arabic in Mauritania), and numerous local languages are widely spoken. The multiple health problems are mostly those of poverty and lack of water. Only a
small proportion of adults are literate.

Islam was first introduced into the area in about the 10th century. Today the
majority of people overall are Muslims, although the proportion varies from
country to country. Traditional African religions remain a significant force.
Some Berber Christians, driven out of North Africa, were in what is now Niger
in the 7th century, but they were isolated and disappeared. A sustained Christian presence dates from 1895 when the White Fathers entered Mali from Senegal. Gradually over this century work has proceeded throughout the area, but
in general the church is not well established and many Christians are expatriate. Most are Roman Catholics. Protestants are few, mostly belonging to pentecostal or fundamentalist groups. The Assemblies of God is the largest Protestant group in the region.

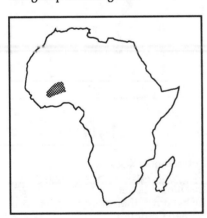

Burkina Faso

Population: 8 million.
Religion: Adherents of traditional religions 42%; Muslims 41%; Christians
11.8% (Roman Catholics 7.6%, Protestants 4.2%).

Known as Upper Volta until 1984,
Burkina Faso has the highest population density in the area and is exceptionally poor. More than 80% of the
people are farmers or nomadic herders. Both groups have been severely
affected by the drought, and loss of
livestock has forced many nomads to
attempt more settled farming. About
a quarter of the population has left
the area to seek work in the cities of
Ivory Coast and elsewhere.

In such a setting the churches
have previously been largely involved in work in rural areas; and today the Roman Catholic church and
the Fédération des Eglises des missions évangeliques are actively engaged in simple practical schemes to
help subsistence farmers to increase
productivity. During the drought of
the 1970s, a joint Christian-Muslim
lay organization was formed to work
together for the provision of basic

needs and education under the slogan "Where two people agree to walk along part of a road together, God is the third." Recent migration to the cities means that now there are new opportunities for the church there also. The Roman Catholic church in Burkina Faso organizes and promotes the Week of Prayer for Christian Unity for the region.

Chad

Population: 5.1 million.
Religion: Muslims 44%; Christians 33% (of whom the majority are Roman Catholics); adherents of traditional beliefs 23%.

With a great many ethnolinguistic groups, predominantly Arab and Muslim in the north, and Black African (mostly Christian or adherents of traditional beliefs) in the south, Chad has suffered intermittent but prolonged civil war. In recent years thousands have fled to neighboring Sudan, Central African Republic, and Cameroon to escape the fighting. Since 1980 the drought has been increasingly severe and widespread, and the cause of further refugee migration.

The Christian church grew relatively quickly in the 1960s and 1970s,

but 1973 brought a period of persecution when at least 130 African pastors were put to death because they refused to submit to initiation rites decreed by the president of the time. Since the coup of 1975, however, religious freedom has been officially upheld, although in a situation of war there have been local incidents. The Roman Catholic church patiently continues its pastoral and evangelistic ministry in the villages, many of which have small Christian communities with a chapel or a place in the open air with benches made of branches where the congregation gathers on Sundays to pray. For all the churches the training, disrupted by the fighting, of priests, pastors, and evangelists is a major concern.

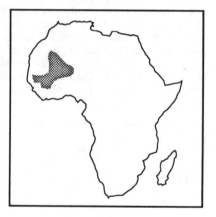

Mali

Population: 8.3 million.
Religion: Muslims 80%; adherents of traditional beliefs 18%; Christians 2% (of whom rather more than half are Roman Catholics).

A large part of Mali is in the Sahara, and most of the people live in the more fertile south. About 90% of them are engaged in subsistence farming and herding, but the extending drought continues to reduce the

area of suitable land. In spite of food shortages, the desperately poor farmers sell some of their crops in the more lucrative markets of neighboring countries, and crop smuggling is a longstanding problem.

The Roman Catholic church and a number of Protestant groups are working in the country. The administration by Christians of famine relief supplies has strengthened relationships between Christians and Muslims.

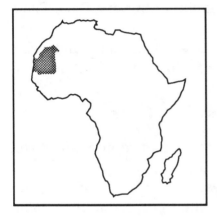

Mauritania

Population: Approximately 2 million (no recent official estimates available).
Religion: Muslims 99.4%; Christians 0.4%.

Mauritania is an Islamic republic with an Arab-speaking Moorish majority. Before the drought, 80% of the population were nomadic pastoralists; by the 1980s, 80% of their pasture land had become desert. The Negro population in the Senegal valley to the south is engaged in settled agriculture.

The ceding of the southern part of western Sahara to Mauritania in 1976 (see Week 4), and the subsequent fighting, brought the country almost to bankruptcy. Fish and iron-ore are the main natural resources. The church is entirely expatriate and mostly Roman Catholic, with a handful of Protestants.

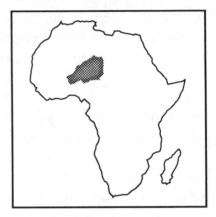

Niger

Population: 5.7 million and rising.
Religion: Muslims 88%; adherents of traditional beliefs 11.6%; Christians 0.4%, of whom most are Roman Catholics.

In the years following independence the government of Niger seemed to be one of the most stable in Africa. But the effects of the drought, which affected Niger more than any other Sahel country, led to widespread civil disorder, and an army coup followed in 1974.

Some 95% of Roman Catholics in Niger are expatriates, but the church has recently renewed evangelistic effort in the villages and is meeting with some positive response. The Protestant evangelical churches make a significant contribution through educational and medical work which is much appreciated. Relationships between the church and the government and Muslim community are good.

Joining our joys and sorrows with those of the people of the Sahel let us thank God

for their faith and fortitude

for every opportunity we have to share in the fire and milk of the human condition

for new cooperative ventures, enabling people to work together for a better and more secure life.

Let us pray

for the governments and peoples of Burkina Faso, Chad, Mali, Mauritania, and Niger

for all missionaries, expatriate technicians, and relief workers, local pastors and religious, working in areas where conditions are very harsh

for refugees from war and drought

for the rural poor

for those many people who have moved into towns and cities in search of food and livelihood

for those affected by health problems linked with drought; eye diseases, intestinal and other infections; and all workers and agencies which bring relief

for the WCC Program of Solidarity for Development in Sahel, and its many small-scale projects; irrigation schemes, market gardening, well-digging, village grain banks, tree-planting, and women's education

for responsible and sensitive use of outside aid

for the traditional "naam" or "power" groups being re-discovered and adapted to today's needs.

We pray, O Lord, for the nomads and peasants who strive to make a living on the edge of the Sahara Desert, and especially those driven by hunger into the refugee camps and city slums. Give wisdom to those who plan the long-term rehabilitation of these lands: this we ask in the name of Jesus who hungered in the wilderness. Amen.

Lord God, spring of living water,
give to those who live in dry and barren lands,
the vision to see them as they might be,
the skill and resources needed to make them fertile again,
and more than these, the spiritual insight needed to recognize
that in you alone the human spirit finds its true satisfaction.
For Jesus' sake. Amen.

Michael Saward, adapted

Let us pray also
for peace throughout the region
for all Christian congregations in town and countryside
for healing of divisions in the Protestant communities,
and the promotion of deeper understanding and sympathy
between Catholics and Protestants.

Lord, help us to accept the gift of peace
that Jesus came to bring.

In Chad and in other places we are invited to imagine
small local Christian communities meeting together to pray
on Sundays; while statistics in Mauritania and Niger
present a picture of a small, largely expatriate Christian
presence. With all of them we pray:

Almighty God, you have given us grace at this time with
one accord to make our common supplications to you; and
you have promised that when two or three are gathered together in your name you will grant their requests. Fulfill
now, O Lord, the desires and petitions of your servants, as
may be most expedient for them, granting us in this world
knowledge of your truth, and in the world to come, life everlasting.

Prayer of the Third Antiphon, Liturgy of St. John Chrysostom, 5th century

Week 41

Cameroon • Central African Republic

Lord Jesus, print on us your likeness,
Your divine likeness,
For it is your face,
Your divine face that we long for.

At the Sixth Station of the Cross, Engelbert Mveng, S.J., Cameroon

Lord God,
grant that we might sleep in peace in this hut;
and that at the break of day we may find ourselves in
safety.

A night prayer from Cameroon

My God, I praise you, I thank you for my mother.
For all that she could give me,
for all that she gave of herself,
a true, living school of love and humility.
She reveals to me your mystery—
thank you for her revelation of your truth.
Now, O God, I pray for all the children
of Africa, of Asia,
of America and Europe.
For all the children of the world.
Give me a heart like that of a mother
the heart of a black woman for her children.

Le tronc béni de la prière, Mamia Woungly-Massaga

We pray you, Lord our God and Father,
remember all those who are deprived of their country;
who groan under the burden of anguish and sorrow

enduring the burning heat of the sun and the freezing
cold of the sea,
   or live in in the humid heat of the forest,
   searching for a place of refuge.
   A refuge which they will find nowhere,
   for you alone are our true refuge.

   Lord, cause this storm to cease.
   Move the hearts of those in power
   that they may respect human beings
   whom you have created in your own image;
   That the grief of these refugees may be turned into joy,
   as when you led your people Israel out of captivity.

From a prayer for refugees, Pedro Tunga

Almighty God, Lord of heaven and earth, we humbly
pray that your gracious care may give and preserve the
seeds which we plant in our farms that they may bring
forth fruit in good measure; that we who constantly receive
from your goodness may always give thanks to you, the
giver of all good things; through Jesus Christ, your Son our
Lord.

Prayer often used in the Cameroon
during the planting season, March/April

   God of love, God of mercy, God of all power!
   Why do you let your people die
   —your people whom you have redeemed?
   Why do you let the earth suffer
   —the earth you have created in your sovereign power?
   Lord, look and see the misery of the famine
   that is ravaging your people;
   Look and see these children, these women and men, who
are dying of
   hunger and who cry to you in their need.

Give them, we pray, according to your grace and according to their need, to the glory of your name.
Lord God, our Father and God of all power,
you who hold the universe in your hand;
Give your people bread we pray;
Cause the rain to fall
and make the soil fertile in the fields of your people.
Give them an abundant harvest
and protect it from the ravages of climate and pests,
that your people may rejoice in the fruits of their labors,
according to your promise.

Grant the prayer of your people, Lord to the glory of your name.
May your name be magnified in Jesus Christ,
our Lord and Savior. Amen.

From a prayer for harvest in a time of drought, Pedro Tunga

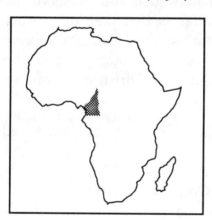

Cameroon

Population: 9.6 million.
Languages: French, English, and many local languages.
Government: Single-party republic.
Religion: Christians about 50% (Roman Catholics 32%, Protestants 17%); adherents of traditional beliefs about 25%; Muslims 22%.

When I think of my mother, I see not only the woman who gave me birth, but all those rural African women, hardly visible to the modern eye, who wake up early each morning to produce, process, and store 80% of the food we eat in Africa. I see those rural women who, unfortunately, are progressively being deprived of access to arable land and of control of modern agriculture. I see the effects and its consequential link with Africa's grave food shortage.

I continue to see this "invisible" African woman in her condition and potential. Although the most silent and unrecognized, she remains the hardest worker in the entire world; she is also among the finest and strongest Christians in any land. With less than US $25 as the only annual monetary income, she performs wonders; she builds churches, pays and feeds pastors, sends her children to good Christian schools, and teaches them daily to pray and trust God.

Ruth Engi-Tjeca, Cameroon
Fellowship of the Least Coin

The impetus to bring the gospel to Cameroon came originally from Jamaica when slaves obtained their freedom, and some of the first missionaries were Jamaicans. The subsequent history of the country resulted in the work being taken over by different missions, thus sowing the seeds of separate churches. Today Baptists and Presbyterians make up the largest Protestant bodies. There are smaller Lutheran groups and a number of indigenous churches. Roman Catholics arrived in 1890 during the period of German occupation, and a mass movement began in 1934, particularly among young people. All the churches continue to make significant contributions to the country, especially in the fields of health, education, and agricultural development, which are major concerns of the government at the present time. The church is actively engaged in evangelism in rural areas, and is growing, while an ecumenical body is concerned with spiritual, social, and economic issues in the capital.

Central African Republic

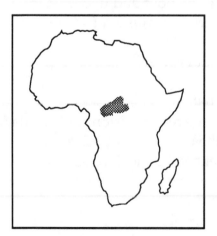

Population: 2.7 million.
Languages: French, Sango.
Government: Single-party republic.
Religion: Christians 84.5% (Protestants 50%, Roman Catholics 33%, African Indigenous 1.5%); adherents of tribal beliefs 12%; Muslims 3%.

Situated in the heart of Africa, the Central African Republic had been ruled and administered by tribal chiefs, a Sultan, colonial traders, and the French government before gaining independence in 1960. Since then it has experienced both civil and military government. In recent years thousands of refugees from Chad have entered the country, which has made land available for them. The refugees have built homes and begun to establish traditional patterns of village life while they wait to return.

The first Roman Catholic mission was established decades before Protestants arrived after the First World War. There have been some schisms from churches founded by North American and European missions to form independent indigenous churches. Numerically the Christian church grew dramatically after independence. There are now some ten Protestant denominations, predominantly Baptist and Brethren. Many were established largely on an ethnic basis, and today, sadly, there is little cooperation among them. According to a senior pastor, the present authorities "are conscious that true peace and justice come from God." They recently set aside a fast day when all churches, as well as those of other faiths, prayed for peace and justice in the country. The need, at the local level, is for pastors more suitably equipped to meet the needs of the more educated members of their congregations and, at the national level, to address the conscience of the government on matters of peace and justice.

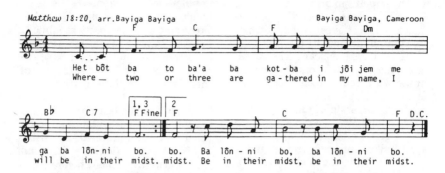

Matthew 18:20, arr.Bayiga Bayiga

Bayiga Bayiga, Cameroon

Het bõt ba to ba'a ba kot-ba i jõi jem me
Where _ two or three are ga-thered in my name, I

ga ba lõn-ni bo. bo. Ba lõn-ni bo, ba lõn-ni bo.
will be in their midst. midst. Be in their midst, be in their midst.

Christians in both these countries, accustomed largely to the practice of extempore prayer, welcome fellowship with Christians throughout the world, and invite us to "engage in free prayers of intercession before Almighty God" for:

In Cameroon
the peace and security of the country
efforts to promote the green belt through the training of men and women in appropriate methods of farming, tree-planting, and conservation
the "Health for all by the year 2000" program
young people in an increasingly secular and materialistic environment
women in their day-to-day life and work
the church's ministry among the poor and deprived, and all efforts to combat the underlying causes of alcoholism and juvenile delinquency
all programs of evangelism and revival.

In the Central African Republic
God's continuing blessing on every decision and action taken by the government for the well-being of the people
resolution of ethnic differences in the interests of the common good
the development of the country in such a way as will serve the best interests of local people

the refugees of Africa and of the world
resources to train church leaders
a new unity of spirit and action among members of different church bodies.

Commemorating their autonomy, and at the same time aware of their shortcomings, Presbyterian Christians in Cameroon use this form of confession in which we are invited to join:

O Lord, with sorrow and dismay we confess before you our failure to live up to the trust committed to us. For so many years your word has been preached among us, but has yielded so little fruit. We have not given the example of redeemed lives. Because of our lack of love and joy and devotion there are still those, even among our friends and in our families, who have not yet accepted you as Savior and Lord. The power of worship of ancestral spirits is yet unbroken in our country. Even many who were once baptized and have grown up in our midst have become cold and have turned away from you. O Lord, we humble ourselves before you in shame, and plead with you, through Jesus Christ, your Son, our Lord. Amen.

Week 42

Congo • Equatorial Guinea • Gabon • São Tomé and Príncipe

He comes to us as one unknown, without a name, as of old by the lakeside he came to those men who knew him not. He speaks to us the same word: "Follow thou me" and sets us to the tasks which he has to fulfill for our time. He commands. And to those who obey him, whether they be wise or simple, he will reveal himself in the toils, the conflicts, the sufferings which they shall pass through in his fellowship, and as an ineffable mystery they shall learn in their own experience who he is.

Albert Schweitzer, one-time missionary in Gabon

I will follow you, Jesus
And I will give you all
For by your strength
I will follow you in everything.

Congolese hymn, sung with mounting excitement on the way to baptism

Leader: Jesus, we want to grow in knowledge.
All: Help us to grow in body, mind, and spirit.

Leader: Jesus, we want to grow in faith,
All: We thank you for the people of faith in Bible times and in our times whose lives are an example to us.

Leader: Jesus, we want to grow in hope.
All: We pray for all who are helping to bring freedom, peace, and justice in our world.

Leader: Jesus, we want to grow in love.

All: Help us to love one another as you have loved us and given yourself for us. We pray for those who today are giving their lives for others.

Children's prayer: prepared by women of Africa

O God:

Enlarge my heart

that it may be big enough to receive the greatness of your love.

Stretch my heart

that it may take into it all those who with me around the world

believe in Jesus Christ.

Stretch it

that it may take into it all those who do not know him,

but who are my responsibility because I know him.

And stretch it

that it may take in all those who are not lovely in my eyes,

and whose hands I do not want to touch;

through Jesus Christ, my Savior. Amen.

Prayer of an African Christian

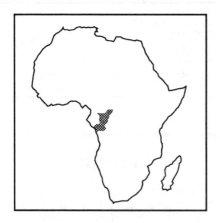

Congo

Once part of the African Kingdom

of the Congo, and touched by early Portuguese explorers and missionaries, this area came under French influence in the 18th century and obtained independence in 1960. It is now a single-party socialist republic with a population of 2 million. Industrialization—it is one of the most industrialized countries in Africa—has resulted in migration to the cities where unemployment is rising.

Christians number about 93% (54% Roman Catholics, 25% Protestants, 14% African indigenous) of the population. Sustained Christian activity began in 1883 when Roman Catholic priests arrived at the coast, and subsequently sent missionaries inland along the Congo river. The Roman Catholic church has grown

steadily since the beginning. Protestants arrived early in this century. The autonomous Evangelical church of the Congo, with its charismatic lifestyle and emphasis on evangelism, is the largest Protestant body and is growing. Baptists began work in the sparsely populated north in 1921. Of the indigenous churches, the Kimbanguist (see Week 43) has the largest following. In 1978, the government banned over thirty religious bodies, not all of them Christian. Seven religions, the Roman Catholic church, the Evangelical church of the Congo, the Salvation Army, the Kimbanguist church, the church of Zepherin Lassy, Islam (0.5%), and Tenrikyo (one of the Japanese new religions), remain legally permitted. All church schools were nationalized in 1965, but the churches are allowed to maintain training institutions for evangelists, pastors, and religious communities. They remain involved in medical and development projects.

Equatorial Guinea

Consisting of the mainland territory of Rio Muni, the island of Bioko (Fernando Póo), and three small groups of islands, this country experienced colonization, first Portuguese and then Spanish, from the 15th century onward, before becoming independent as a republic in 1968. For almost eleven years it was ruled by a president who assumed dictatorial powers. There was much suffering and many fled. Since a coup in 1979, it has been under military rule. The economy was in ruins at that time, and the country continues to rely on international aid. The official language is Spanish, but Fang and others are widely spoken.

89% of the population of 300,000 are Christian, the vast majority Roman Catholic; less than 5% adhere to traditional beliefs. The earlier regime was militantly atheistic, and atheists and nonreligious account for about 6%. The Roman Catholic church came with the colonial powers. Baptist missionaries from the West Indies came to Fernando Póo in 1841, but were later expelled by the Spanish. In 1870 the British Methodist church responded to an appeal from local Protestants sent via a ship's captain, and a Methodist community grew on the island. Presbyterians came to Corisco in 1850 and thence to the mainland. The resulting Evangelical church of Equatorial Guinea became the major Protestant body. This church, together with Methodist congregations and members of Crusade, recently joined together to form the Reformed church of Equatorial Guinea. Sadly there is now strife within this body over issues of lay participation and responsibility.

Gabon

This single-party republic, formerly part of French Equatorial Africa, obtained independence in 1960. A relatively small population (1.2 million), together with abundant mineral resources and forests help to make

it the richest country in sub-Saharan Africa in terms of average income. Nevertheless, more than half the population is engaged in subsistence agriculture, unaffected by modern economy. French is the official language. Fang and Bantu are widely spoken.

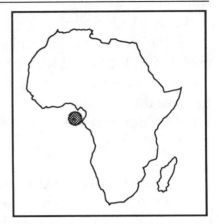

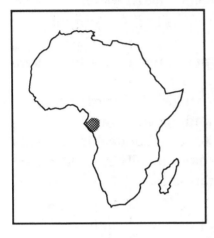

Christian missionaries, both Roman Catholic and Protestant, came in the 1840s. At first they faced considerable resistance and met with many difficulties; and only slowly did they penetrate inland from the coast. However, since the end of the 19th century the church has grown steadily. Now about 95% of people profess Christianity: 65% Roman Catholics, 19% Protestants, and 12% members of African indigenous churches.

There are three Protestant groups: the Evangelical church of Gabon, which is much the largest numerically, the Evangelical church of South Gabon, and the smaller Evangelical Pentecostal church. Traditionally, the churches have been involved in education and health services. Now increasingly urbanization and the associated secular tendencies of corruption and indifference present additional concerns and challenges.

São Tomé and Príncipe

Consisting of two main islands and four rocky islets, the single-party republic of São Tomé and Príncipe has a population of 108,000, almost all Christians. The practice of traditional religions prevalent at the turn of the century, has now almost disappeared due largely to Catholic evangelistic activity. The country has a long association with Portugal. More recently, São Tomé was the penal colony for Angola for many years. Independence was negotiated in 1975. The use of agricultural land for export crops, on which the country depends economically, means that 90% of food requirements have to be imported.

Of the Christian population, the vast majority are Roman Catholics. Although administratively centered elsewhere, a diocese was established for the territory in 1534. Protestants and members of indigenous churches total about 5%. The Evangelical church owes its existence entirely to indigenous efforts. It was planted by an Angolan Christian exiled to São Tomé for penal servitude, and originally the Scriptures and hymn book were written down from memory.

We thank God
for the power of the Bible to speak to the present-day
needs of children and women and men everywhere
that God so often uses unlikely people and circumstances
to serve the kingdom
for all local missionary movement and outreach
for the large Christian communities in these countries.

The eucharist or Lord's supper plays a very important
part in the lives of Congolese Christians. Having carefully
prepared themselves, local Christians, Catholics and Protestants alike, including the old and the sick, travel long distances to attend such a service. As an act of imaginative solidarity, let us join with Christians in all these lands in
saying the Sanctus in their African setting:

Holy, holy, holy Lord, God of power and might,
heaven and earth are full of your glory.
Hosanna in the highest.
Blessed is he who comes in the name of the Lord.
Hosanna in the highest.

Let us pray
for the cities of these countries, their growing populations, and the response of Christian congregations to their
needs and opportunities
for the work of the church in mining areas and in growing townships
for Christian witness against corruption and indifference
for new ways of sharing the good news with those who
succumb to superstition and sorcery

for vocations among young people to full-time service in the church

for the Christian formation of pastors and priests, evangelists, teachers, and youth workers

for the fluctuating economies of these countries, and for those most affected, the poor and lowest paid, including many pastors

for unity within and between the different churches.

Lord Jesus Christ, you said to your apostles:
I leave you peace, my peace I give you.
Look not on our sins,
but on the faith of your church,
and grant us the peace and unity of your kingdom
where you live for ever and ever. Amen.

The Roman Mass

Week 43

Burundi • Rwanda • Zaïre

The cross is the hope of Christians
the cross is the resurrection of the dead
the cross is the way of the lost
the cross is the savior of the lost
the cross is the staff of the lame
the cross is the guide of the blind
the cross is the strength of the weak
the cross is the doctor of the sick
the cross is the aim of the priests
the cross is the hope of the hopeless
the cross is the freedom of the slaves
the cross is the power of the kings
the cross is the water of the seeds
the cross is the consolation of the bondmen
the cross is the source of those who seek water
the cross is the cloth of the naked.
We thank you, Father, for the cross.

A 10th-century African hymn

We bless you for sending your Spirit into the heart of
the men, women, and children of Burundi,
so that they recognize Jesus as Son of God and Savior,
and are brought together in the church.

Through the fraternal charity which overcomes divisions,
through baptism and confirmation which plunges them
into Christ
and makes them witnesses of the faith,

and through the grace of ordination which gives them their

own bishops and priests,
confirm your children in their faith through all trials
and persecutions.

Prayer for Burundi Christians: Louis Lochet of the Foyers de Charité

The 15th-century Kingdom of the Congo covered a wider area than present-day Zaïre when Portuguese explorers and missionaries first made contact with its people. One of their kings, Afonso I, became a major Christian figure in African history. In his reign churches were built, and schools established to provide Christian education for children. His son Henrique became the first Black African bishop, serving in the region until his death in 1534. However, Portugal's primary interest was trade, and it failed to nurture the new Christian community in this kingdom which, together with its church, eventually disintegrated. When Roman Catholic priests and Baptist missionaries came to the area over three centuries later, they found little remaining of that earlier church.

Of the three ethnic groups in Rwanda and Burundi, the Twa pygmies, now by far the smallest numerically, were earliest here. Tutsis, the last to arrive, migrated from the north and established supremacy over the majority Hutu people. The Tutsi kingdoms continued, almost until independence in the case of Rwanda, and a little after in the case of Burundi. Tension between the Hutu and Tutsi has continued, and there has been a major episode of violence in each of these countries since independence.

In the 19th century, European explorers opened the way for missionaries to come into the region; and also for colonization. Zaïre (Belgian Congo) was colonized by Belgium; Rwanda and Burundi by Germany. The latter was evicted in the first world war, and the area administered under mandate by Belgium. Zaïre became independent in 1960, Rwanda and Burundi in 1962.

Roman Catholic missionaries began to penetrate into these areas in the latter half of the 19th century, and this church enjoyed a privileged status under Belgian rule. In Rwanda and Burundi, a mass movement began in the 1930s, and at its height there were a thousand baptisms a week in Burundi. Baptists and Presbyterians soon followed the Roman Catholics into the Congo region, and were themselves followed by many others. The first Protestants to enter Rwanda and Burundi were German Lutherans from Tanzania, but they were forced to leave during the first world war. Their work was subsequently taken over and expanded by various Protestant bodies. The Anglican church entered from Uganda, and it was in the mission stations of this church in Rwanda that the revival movement first began.

In 1921 Simon Kimbangu, a Baptist catechist in the Congo, began a ministry of preaching and healing, and rapidly gained a large following. The authorities became alarmed, and he was imprisoned as a dissident for the rest of his life. His followers were severely persecuted and many were exiled; but the movement continued to grow, and in 1959 the Church of Jesus Christ on Earth by the Prophet Simon Kimbangu was officially recognized. It is the largest indigenous church in Africa, and is active in a number of countries.

Burundi

Population: 4.8 million.
Languages: French, Kirundi, Swahili.
Government: Single-party republic. Under military rule since 1987.
Religion: Christians 85%; adherents of traditional beliefs 13.5%; Muslims 1%.

The vast majority of people in Burundi live in rural areas, where poverty and unemployment, though enormous problems, are not easy to quantify. A rapidly increasing population adds to the difficulties, but the extended family system ensures that all are cared for, and no one goes without food and shelter. The traditional sense of solidarity leads those who have resources to share with those who have not.

With 78% of the population Roman Catholic, this is one of the most Catholic countries in Africa. Protestants including Anglicans number about 7%, of whom the largest body is Pentecostal. The East African revival spread through Burundi in the 1950s and had its greatest impact in the Anglican church. Prior to the 1987 coup, the regime was antagonistic toward the church, Christians suffered, and expatriate priests were expelled. All the churches are involved in educational, medical, and social work, but are crippled by poverty. One of the major concerns is for reconciliation and the healing of the deep and longstanding ethnic divisions.

We give thanks

for the Roman Catholic contribution to this land; for the devotion and fortitude of early missionaries; for schools and Christian education, and for courageous outspokenness in times of need

for the message of the cross at the heart of the East African revival, and for its continued power to speak to a new generation of African Christians.

We pray

for all in need in this country; for widows and orphans, refugees, and those displaced

for those who suffered in past conflicts, and those who inflicted suffering on others; for forgiveness and healing

for church leaders and catechists, and all engaged in

town and countryside in nurturing Christian congregations.

Let us identify with Christians in this region in repeating the words of a well-known devotion, *Salvator mundi*:

O Savior of the world,
who by your cross and precious blood
has redeemed us;
Save us and help us,
we humbly beseech you, O Lord.

Of this prayer it has been observed that sometimes an element of superiority enters our prayers for others, "but when we ask a third person to help us both, that element is eliminated, and we see ourselves at the same level of dependence and need as the ones for whom we pray."

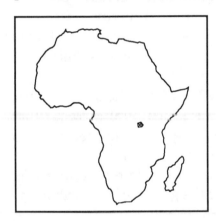

Rwanda

Population: 5.8 million.
Languages: French, Kinyarwanda.
Government: Single-party republic.
Religion: Christians 73% (Roman Catholics 55.5%, Protestants 11.5%, Anglicans 6%), adherents of traditional beliefs 18%; Muslims 8.6%.

This landlocked country faces many problems. It is the most densely populated country in Africa, with 95% of people living in rural areas where there is not enough agricultural land. In October 1982, 44,000 refugees together with 50,000 head of cattle streamed across the border from Uganda. Although all of the same ethnic group, many of these were Ugandan citizens; others were Rwandans who had fled from earlier strife in their country. The problems of refugees, overpopulation, and poverty continue. "As the credibility of the church's message depends on its response to situations of misery, poverty, hunger, illness, ignorance, and illiteracy, it" (in this case referring to the Presbyterian church of Rwanda, but applicable to others also) "tries to maintain a balance between social engagement and the teaching of the biblical message." The churches provide much-needed services to the country in hospitals, primary health care, education, and vocational and agricultural training; but the churches also are poor in material terms.

The experience of the psalmist of having a new song put upon his lips, and that of St. John that "if we walk in the light as he is in the light, we have fellowship with one another, and the blood of Christ cleanseth us from all sin" continue to be central themes of the East African revival. Beginning in Rwanda in 1929, this movement spread into eastern Africa, parts of Zaïre, and beyond. For the most part remaining within the mainline churches it has had a profound influence. The movement's greatest challenge today lies in relating faith to matters of social justice. In Rwanda itself some of the fire has died down in the older generation, but there are signs of a fresh response among younger people.

We pray

for the spiritual, social, and economic well-being of Rwanda

for refugees in this country—those in camps, and those integrated into the community yet denied citizenship; and for Rwandan refugees in Burundi and elsewhere

for the Twa pygmy people, and all who seek to proclaim the gospel among them

and for the fruitful and harmonious contact between Christians and the growing Muslim community

for those preparing for the ministry in different centers in Africa and elsewhere, and for the congregations which will eventually receive and support them

for the Christian community life of hospitals and clinics, vocational training schools, and agricultural projects; that all such communities may be adaptable and sensitive to changing needs and circumstances

that in this nation which has been torn by ethnic strife, Christians may continually live the gospel of reconciliation.

May the brokenness of our Lord Jesus Christ
and the Calvary love of God
and the fellowship of the Holy Spirit
be with us all. Amen.

Revival grace

Zaïre

Population: 30.4 million.
Languages: French and over 400 Sudanese and Bantu languages.
Government: Single-party republic.
Religion: Christians 94% (Roman Catholics 48%, Protestants 29%, African indigenous 17%); adherents of traditional beliefs 3.5%; Muslims 1.5%.

With considerable agricultural, mineral, and energy resources, Zaïre is potentially a rich country; but poor roads, corruption and smuggling, inflation, and foreign debt have impeded development. The many refugees in the country are mostly from Angola. The Christian church, which has grown from 1% to 90% of the popula-

tion within a century, continues to play a very significant role in schools, hospitals, development work, and social service.

As in many other countries in Africa, the Roman Catholic pastoral plan for small Christian communities is operating in Zaïre. This represents a shift from effort concentrated in large institutions to the nurture of small communities of lay people working out their faith in daily life. The training and support of lay leaders and catechists is a high priority.

Formed in 1970 at the Assembly of the Congo Protestant Council, and without referring back to participating churches, the Church of Christ in Zaïre is the only Protestant church recognized by government and other bodies in a national rural health project.

Financially self-supporting from the beginning, the Kimbanguist church, also recognized by government, has built churches, schools, clinics, workshops, and agricultural colonies. These provide jobs for the unemployed, and young offenders are accepted in some. Kimbanguists are active in counseling those who suffer from AIDS and their families. The voluntary pastoral support system and sense of togetherness within this church are replacing the traditional family community in situations where this is disrupted by social change.

We give thanks
for the courage and devotion of the many who have given their lives in the service of the gospel
for the rapid growth of the church in this century
for all who sing the praises of God in this African setting
for the positive gains and enrichments enjoyed by the Protestant denominations united in L'Eglise du Christ au Zaïre

for all who combine a strong faith in the unique relevance of Christ for Africa with a wider ecumenical vision.

I thank you, Almighty God,
maker of heaven and earth,
that heaven is your throne and the earth your footstool,
and that your will is done in earth as it is in heaven.
Bless all the peoples of the earth,
great and small, men and women, whites and blacks.
May the blessing of heaven fall on the whole world
so that we all may enter heaven.
We pray to you, trusting that you will receive us,
in the name of Jesus Christ our Savior.

A prayer said to have been used daily by Simon Kimbangu

We pray
for the unity of this vast country
for all small Christian communities, and the women and men who provide the leadership
for growing urban areas, and their need of churches sensitive to their situation
for seminaries and colleges training people for the ordained ministry; and for all local Bible schools and lay training programs
for the church's expanding ministries of evangelism, education, health, and development.

"In Zaïre, evangelism and social action are one. The life of the spirit is fully as real as physical life. In a situation of extreme poverty and injustice 'courageous Christians build churches, clinics, schools, libraries, water wells, fish ponds, dormitories, roads, and bridges.'"

Bless, O Lord,
all such courageous Christians,

and all work undertaken in your name and in your spirit in Zaïre today. Amen.

God, bless Africa
Guard her children
Guide her leaders
And give her peace.

Conference of European Churches

Grant us prudence in proportion to our power,
wisdom in proportion to our science,
humaneness in proportion to our wealth and might.
And bless our earnest will to help all races and peoples
to travel, in friendship with us,
along the road to justice, liberty, and lasting peace:
but grant us above all to see that our ways
are not necessarily your ways,
that we cannot fully penetrate the mystery of your designs,
and that the very storm of power now raging on this earth
reveals your hidden will and your inscrutable decision.
Grant us to see your face in the lightning of this cosmic storm,
O God of holiness, merciful to your creatures.
Grant us to seek peace where it is truly found
In your will, O God, in our peace. Amen.

Prayer for Peace, Conference of European Churches,
Gloria Deo Worship Book, 9th Assembly, 1986

The Geneva-based Conference of European Churches (CEC) is a fellowship of non-Roman Catholic churches whose 118 members are from every European country, both East and West, except Albania. The Roman Catholic church, although not a member, cooperates closely. In an area of immense cultural, political, and religious diversity, CEC provides a forum for the churches to reach across the barriers which divide them, and enables them to work out together their place in the Europe of today and in the future. Its main thrusts, therefore, are ecumenism in Europe, peace with justice, and concern for human rights.

Week 44

Federal Republic of Germany • German Democratic Republic

Graciously comfort and tend all who are imprisoned, hungry, thirsty, naked, and miserable; also all widows, orphans, sick, and sorrowing. In brief, give us our daily bread, so that Christ may abide in us and we in him for ever, and that with him we may worthily bear the name Christian. Amen.

Martin Luther

God, our Father, we thank you for putting new life into your people, so that they never die. Prevent us from being paralyzed with wrong worries. Let us enjoy all new things, which show us that you are still at work in our world. Amen.

Prayer of East German woman

I believe
that God both can and will bring good out of evil
For that purpose God needs men and women
who will make the best use of everything.

I believe
that God is willing to provide us in any emergency
with all the powers of resilience that will be necessary for us.
But he does not give in advance
lest we should rely upon ourselves and not on him alone.
It is such a faith that will overcome all anxiety and fear of the future.

I believe
that God is not a timeless fate,
but that he is attending and responding
to sincere prayers as well as to responsible action.

Letters and Papers from Prison, Dietrich Bonhoeffer

Population, language, government, and religion
FRG: 61 million. German. Federal republic. Christians 86.6% (Roman Catholics 43.5%, Protestants 42.4%, Orthodox 0.7%); Muslims 2.8%; a very small Jewish community
GDR: 16.1 million. German. Socialist republic. Christians 53.6% (Protestants 46.1%, Roman Catholics 7.2%); substantial numbers of atheists and those of no religion.

Lying in the center of Europe, and with few natural frontiers, Germany has always been exposed to a variety of cultural and political influences. Christianity spread gradually into this area, from south and west to north and east, between about the 3rd and 12th centuries. Martin Luther's Reformation, beginning at Wittenberg in 1517, has had a profound influence both within Germany and throughout the world. The name of Germany is associated with great achievements in music, literature, philosophy, and science; but also with the memory of two dreadful wars. In the present century immense suffering has been inflicted, particularly to European Jewry, but also to others. Christians of the Confessing Church, who resisted the fascist regime, were persecuted. Germany itself lost vast territories and was divided. Since World War II there have been two German states: the Federal Republic of Germany, and the German Democratic Republic. The FRG a federal republic; the GDR a socialist republic. They were aligned with the two great power blocs which were constituted in Europe after the war, and have been distanced from each other by sociopolitical and military barriers. The demarcation line has run through the middle of a once united Germany, a painful reminder of the unhappy past. They may be reunited soon again.

Both German republics have made remarkable recoveries, after the second world war, partly as a result of foreign aid, but also because of their own achievements in reconstruction. The FRG is one of the wealthiest countries in the world, but like other densely populated and highly industrialized countries it faces various difficulties: increasing unemployment, many migrant workers, and problems of environmental protection. In the GDR, a communist political and economic system has operated. It has the most successful economy in eastern Europe.

The churches in the FRG share many of the same concerns, and work in friendly partnership with the state, but are legally separate. The Roman Catho-

lic church, once in the minority, has increased numerically in recent decades largely because of an influx of migrant workers from southern Europe. The 27 Landeskirchen (regional churches), Lutheran, Reformed, and United, have since 1948 constituted the Evangelical church in Germany. They are heavily involved in social service both at home and overseas. Various free church bodies (Baptist, Methodist, Free Evangelical, Moravian, Pentecostal, and others), as well as the Old Catholic church and Orthodox churches, are small but vigorous. Most are full or associate members of the Federation of Christian churches of which the Roman Catholic church is a full member. In recent decades there has been greater contact between Roman Catholics and Protestants.

As the GDR is a socialist society, the situation for the various churches is different, and limits have been set with regard to the work they do publicly. The eight regional churches have come together to form the Federation of Evangelical Churches in the GDR, and this body has expressed its readiness to look upon itself as "the church in a socialist society." Important conversations between church (both Protestant and Roman Catholic) and state have resulted in opportunities for freer contacts with the wider church.

The great gatherings of laity, the Kirchentag (Protestant) and Katholikentag (Catholic), which take place every two years in both parts of Germany and attract many thousands of participants, are an important feature of church life in both states.

We thank God

for the awakening of the church at the time of the Reformation, and for all movements of renewal in more recent times

for all men and women who have worked to enlarge the kingdom of God over the centuries

for the interpretation of the biblical story offered by poets, musicians, painters, and theologians.

We pray

for increasing understanding and better relations between the two states

for the Christians of Berlin, and for the continuing process of prayer, reflection, and action directed toward overcoming the city's divisions

for the churches in the two states, that they may bear witness to the hope of the gospel, give support and encouragement to each other, and be a channel for reconciliation and peace in Europe

for all members of minority groups, immigrants and migrant workers, that they may experience tolerance and consideration

for all those involved in programs to combat racism, to promote peace with justice, and to provide bread for a hungry world.

Almighty and eternal God
we pray for the unity of your church on earth:
We have all resigned ourselves too long
to the division of the church.
　Let us pray
　that our eyes may see the offense we thus give
　as Christians in the world. *(Silence)*

We are still not free from pettiness and prejudice.
　Let us pray
　that God will give us the Spirit of his love,
　a love that knows no bounds. *(Silence)*

We talk of "separated brethren"
heedless of the contradiction lying in these words.
　Let us pray
　that love and fellowship be not mere words
　but that we act to seek togetherness
　in word and work. *(Silence)*

We have all burdened ourselves with guilt
and given in too easily to difficulties.
　Let us pray
　that we do not passively sit and wait,
　as if unity would be bestowed upon us from outside,
　but rather we become friends and trust each other
　so that in us unity may grow and mature.

from a Roman Catholic Agape Celebration

Week 45

Austria • Liechtenstein • Switzerland

Lord, save us from being self-centered in our prayers,
and teach us to remember to pray for others.
May we be so bound up in love with those for whom we
pray
that we may feel their needs as acutely as our own,
and intercede for them with sensitiveness,
with understanding, and with imagination.
This we ask in Christ's name. Amen.

Prayer based on words of John Calvin

O God, the giver of life,
we pray for the church throughout the world:
sanctify its life; renew its worship;
empower its witness; restore its unity.
Remove from your people all pride
and every prejudice that dulls their will for unity.
Strengthen the work of all those who strive to seek
that common obedience that will bind us together.
Heal the divisions which separate your children from
one another,
that they may keep the unity of the spirit in the bond of
peace.

Prayer used in the Ecumenical Center, Geneva,
on the occasion of the visit of Pope John Paul II

Let our chief end, O God, be to glorify thee,
and to enjoy thee for ever,
and let our second endeavor be to share with others
what we so richly enjoy.

After Calvin's Catechism

Dear heavenly Father,

Send your Holy Spirit on us all, we pray, now and ever anew, that the Spirit may awaken us, illumine us, encourage and give us the strength to dare to take the small yet gigantic step, to leave behind the comfort with which we can comfort ourselves and to step forward into the hope that is in you. Turn us to yourself. Do not let us hide ourselves from you. Do not accept it when we try to do everything without you. Show us how magnificent you are, and how wonderful it is that we may trust and obey you. This we ask also for all people:

That nations and their governments may submit to your Word and be willing to strive for justice and peace on earth

That, through word and deed, your Word may be rightly told to all who are poor, all who are sick, all prisoners, all who are in distress, all those who are oppressed, all who do not believe; that they may hear it and understand it and heed it as your answer to their groans and cries

That all Christians of all churches and confessions may understand your Word with new eyes and learn to serve it with renewed faithfulness

That its truth may shine forth here and now and stand firm amid all human confusion and chaos until at last it illumines all people and all things.

Praise be to you who in your Son, Jesus Christ, set us free to confess and affirm always that our hope is in you.

Prayer at Pentecost, Karl Barth

These three Alpine countries, whose geographical situation makes them an important link between Eastern and Western Europe, all pursue a policy of active neutrality, and are thus well placed to facilitate international consultation. A number of well known international organizations have their headquarters in Austria and Switzerland.

The region came under Roman rule very early in the Christian era, and Christianity was slowly introduced, first into what is now Austria and later into Switzerland. The mountainous terrain which prevented the rapid spread of Christianity also helped isolated groups of believers to maintain their faith during the repeated invasions of the next thousand years. In the Middle Ages the monasteries were important centers of scholarship and mission.

Austria

Population: 7.6 million.
Languages: German. Various minority languages are also spoken.
Government: Federal republic.
Religion: Christians 96% (Roman Catholics 89%, Protestants 6%, Orthodox 1%); Muslims 1%; Jews 0.1%

The origins of Christianity in Austria date from before the time of Constantine. A sermon preached by Paul Speratus in St. Stephen's Cathedral in Vienna on 12 January 1522 was influential in the Reformation. For some 150 years the systematically conducted Counterreformation of the 17th and 18th centuries forced Protestant Christians to go underground as secret communities. The decree of tolerance issued by Emperor Josef II in 1781 allowed the reestablishment of small Lutheran and Reformed congregations with limited religious freedom. Similar provisions were also made for Orthodox Christians and for Jews. Both these religious communities had been present in Austria for centuries. It was not until after the second world war that the motto of a "free church in a free state" became a reality for all the minority churches.

Ecumenical cooperation has also increased. The federal capital Vienna, in particular, has become a center of ecumenical relations. The two Protestant churches, the Old Catholic, Methodist, Anglican, five Eastern Orthodox, and four Oriental Orthodox churches work together ecumenically. Although the Roman Catholic church officially has observer status only in the Ecumenical Council of Churches in Austria, it plays a full part in the Council's work. The Pro Oriente Foundation is a forum for encounters between Eastern and Western churches. Austrian radio broadcasts a regular ecumenical Sunday morning service.

Liechtenstein

Population: 27.1 thousand, including resident foreigners.
Language: German.
Government: Constitutional principality.

Religion: Christians 98.5% (Roman Catholics 88%, Protestants 10.5%).

The Principality of Liechtenstein has been an independent state since 1719. Rapid industrialization since the second world war has created a demand for labor and there is virtually no unemployment. Nowadays about a third of the resident population is foreign and many more cross each day from Austria and Switzerland to work in the Principality. The Roman Catholic church is the state church, and administratively is part of the Swiss diocese of Chur. The inter-denominational Evangelical church was formed in 1881 by skilled textile workers, mostly members of the Lutheran or Reformed churches, immigrating from neighboring countries, and was broadened by those who came more recently to meet the needs of industrial expansion. In 1954 a separate Lutheran congregation was formed. Lively ecumenical cooperation exists in many fields.

Switzerland

Population: 6.5 million.
Languages: German, French, Italian. Romansch in some areas.
Government: Federal republic.
Religion: Christians 96%; Jews 0.3%; Muslims 0.3%.

Reformation influences were strong in Switzerland, especially in Zurich through Zwingli and Bullinger, and in Geneva where Calvin and Farel were notable figures. Some cantons became strongly Protestant; others remained strongly Catholic. Rivalry between the two persisted for centuries, but more recently migration patterns have altered the balance and furthered closer cooperation. Overall, among Swiss citizens, Protestants are in the majority (approximately 50.5% Protestants, 43.5% Roman Catholics), but if resident foreigners are included, the balance is reversed.

The Protestant churches are cantonal churches, each being autonomous. Their legal status varies from canton to canton, and there is diversity in liturgy and constitution. Together with the Free Evangelical churches and the Methodist church they join in the Federation of Protestant Churches of Switzerland, through which a number of activities and issues are dealt with jointly. The Federation is concerned about human rights, religious liberty, peace and disarmament, social justice, and development in the third world. Nearer home there is concern about alcoholism and drug abuse, and work among ethnic minorities.

More than 3 million Roman Catholics are spread throughout the country in 6 dioceses. Bridging the linguistic and cultural characteristics particular to each canton is a problem for some of the larger dioceses, and local feelings arising out of the historical rivalries between Protestants and Catholics make reorganization difficult. As in most western countries this church is concerned to find ways and means of presenting the gospel in a way which touches people in their daily lives. The Conference of Swiss Bishops and the congregations are active in the continuous search for ways toward Christian unity.

We thank God

for the long centuries of Christian tradition in Austria, Liechtenstein, and Switzerland

for the Catholic tradition of devotion, pilgrimage, and scholarship, and for all contemporary manifestations of an ecumenical spirit

for the faith of the Reformation emanating from Zurich and Geneva

for the faithfulness of Christian minorities in Austria in hard and oppressive times

for the saints, scholars, ecumenists, and ordinary Christians of these countries

for the stand taken by these countries in defense of human rights and in upholding the dignity of human life

for all places of great natural beauty

We thank you, gracious God, for the beauty of the earth and of its continents and oceans; for the abundance of mountains and plains; for the song of birds and the loveliness of flowers.

For all these good gifts we praise you. Help us, we beseech you, to protect and conserve them for those who follow us. Help us to grow in gratitude for the riches of your creation, and increase our joy in you, to your glory and the praise of your name.

from the Liturgy of the German-speaking Evangelical Reformed Church of Switzerland, 1986

We pray

that Christians will be open to one another and that trust may grow among the churches

that the churches in East and West may derive mutual enrichment and fulfillment from their contacts

that new ecumenical initiatives may be taken and sustained

for the World Council of Churches and other international Christian organizations with their headquarters in Geneva, for their members and concerns in every part of the world

for priests and missionaries from Austria and Switzerland, sacrificially at work in many parts of the world

that migrants and asylum seekers may find a refuge and a welcome in these lands

for the Red Cross, sections of the United Nations based in Geneva, and other international organizations concerned with the rights and welfare of people

that the natural environment of these parts of Europe may be conserved and continue to be a source of refreshment, recreation, and renewal for many people.

Upheld by the prayers of St. Nicholas von Flüe,
we humbly beseech you, O Lord,
that you will constantly protect us;
and to those who lead us give the light of your grace.

Prayer for the Feast Day of the 15th-century soldier-saint
Brother Nicholas von Flüe,
revered in Switzerland as a figure of reconciliation and unity

Week 46

Italy • Malta

All-powerful and ever-living God,
today we rejoice in the holy men and women
of every time and place.
May their prayers bring us your forgiveness and love.

Solemnity of All Saints: The Roman Missal

O God, Creator, Redeemer, and Sanctifier,
we thank you that we may be together
to hear your word of life and hope.
We are all equal before you.
You know our life in in its deepest recesses.
You have not forgotten us;
you love us, and again and again you fill the empty
hands
which we stretch out toward you.
Through the suffering and death of your Son Jesus
Christ,
you took our darkness and fear upon yourself
in order that we might know light and joy.

Prayer of the Waldensian Church

O Lord, you have said to us "Peace I leave with you."
This peace that you give is not that of the world:
it is not the peace of order, when order oppresses;
it is not the peace of silence, when silence is born of suppression;
it is not the peace of resignation, when such resignation
is unworthy.
Your peace is love for all people

is justice for all people, is truth for all people,
the truth that liberates and stimulates growth.

Lord, it is this peace we believe in because of your promise.

Grant us peace, and we will give this peace to others.

From the Waldensian Liturgy

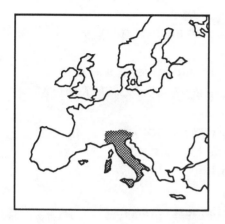

Italy

Population: 57.3 million.
Language: Italian.
Government: Multi-party republic.
Religion: Christians 84% (Roman
Catholics 83.4%, Protestants 0.5%,
Orthodox 0.1%). Atheists and nonre-
ligious 16%. Small communities of
Jews and Muslims, and some Bud-
dhists.

Well known for its historic association with the apostles Peter and
Paul, it was the presence and witness
of faithful members of the Christian
church in Italy in the early centuries
that gave the universal church its
first taste of being "a church of the
catacombs." In later years, and with
a growing desire to express the inter-
communion of the living and the
dead in the Body of Christ, Roman
Christians were led to commemorate
all those who had professed faith in
the living Christ in days past, and to
observe a Feast of All Saints. Significant early saints from this region
were Ambrose of Milan, and Benedict, regarded as the founder of
Western monasticism. The great
medieval movements of renewal
gave rise to the mendicant orders,
such as the Franciscans, and also to
the Waldensian movement, which
originated in France in the 13th century and spread into the valleys of
the Pinerolo region of Italy. Identifying with the Reformation, Waldensians were severely persecuted in the
Counterreformation.

The country was finally unified in
1870, with the Holy See remaining a
separate state. Since the second
world war, there has been rapid economic development and industrialization, especially in the north which
is relatively well off, while the south
remains poor and underdeveloped.

Since the Concordat of 1984, Roman Catholicism is no longer the
state religion, but the Roman Catholic church continues to have a strong
influence in the daily lives of very
many Italians. Communism is growing, especially in the north, and an
increasing number of people are
largely ignoring the church. Within
the church, however, there are movements of renewal and a growing concern about social problems. The
mainstream Protestant churches, like
the Waldensians, are also heavily involved in social action. Since Vatican
II the ecumenical climate has been
changing, leading to a much greater
openness and understanding. In the
Waldensian valleys, where Roman
Catholics and Waldensians have
been living together for centuries, local ecumenism is growing.

Malta

Population: 341,200, excluding foreign residents.
Languages: Maltese, English, Italian.
Government: Multi-party republic.
Religion: Christians 99%. There is a small Jewish community and some atheists.

St. Paul's shipwreck on the island of Malta marks the coming of Christianity, and it is no exaggeration to say that his arrival was the greatest event in Maltese history. The country was later occupied by the Arabs before being captured by the Normans. It was subsequently given to the Knights of St. John of Jerusalem. It became a British Crown Colony in 1814 and gained independence in 1964.

"The faith brought by Paul, preserved, protected, and propagated down the centuries, is very much alive in Malta today. It is reflected in the elaborate architecture of heavily ornate churches studded in profusion all over the island, as well as in the rhythmic tolling of bells calling the faithful to prayer at regular intervals." Virtually all Maltese nationals are baptized Roman Catholics, and this church has exercised significant institutional power. Through the Missionary Society of St. Paul, a considerable number of Maltese priests and religious are working outside the islands. A number of other denominations serve the expatriate community.

We thank God

for the witness of many Christians, known and unknown, who through the ages have risked their lives for their faith

for the rich spirituality and the missionary contribution of the Roman Catholic church

for the faithful witness of the Protestant churches, and their work of Christian service

for all signs of renewal in the Body of Christ in these countries

for two thousand years of art, architecture, thought, devotion, and common life inspired by the Christian faith:

Blessed are you, O Lord our God, King of the universe,

Who has given the wisdom of your hands to flesh and
blood
that beautiful cities might rise to your glory.

Rabbi Moshe Hakotun: said to have been written in Venice

We pray
for a joint Christian witness for justice, peace, and the integrity of creation in the face of increasing militarization of
the Mediterranean
for growing trust between members of all churches, and
wisdom for their leaders in furthering the process of reconciliation and common action
for the Bishop of Rome and members of the Curia
for leaders of the Protestant and Orthodox churches
for the people of Italy and Malta, at their work and in
their worship, seeking to live out their faith in daily life.

Lord
may I ever speak
as though it were the last word that I can speak.
May I ever act
as though it were the last action that I can perform.
May I ever suffer
as though it were the last pain that I can offer.
May I ever pray
as though it were for me on earth
the last chance to speak to you.

Prayer of Chiara Lubich, founder of the Focolare Movement

Week 47

Bangladesh • Bhutan • Nepal

Dear Jesus,
as a hen covers her chicks with her wings
to keep them safe,
protect us this dark night
under your golden wings.

Prayer from the region

The village women of Bangladesh frequently embroider pillows with Bengali words meaning *an end of tiredness*. Whether on behalf of its very many poor people who wearily go to sleep under constant threat of cyclone, flood, or famine, or of minority groups in endemic fear of violence and robbery by night, it is a country which stands in special need of the night prayers of Christians everywhere:

Save us, O Lord, waking; guard us, sleeping;
That awake we may watch with Christ,
and asleep we may rest in peace.

from Compline, and used as a night prayer
by the religious communities of Bangladesh

O Lord, hear our petitions,
Open the door of salvation for the Gorkhalis.
Father, Son, Holy Spirit, hear our petition,
Show us the way by a cloudy fiery pillar.
Peoples of different regions are to the east, west, and south;
Tibet is north, and Nepal our home in the middle.
There are cities: Thapathali, Bhatgaon, Patan, Kathmandu:
Our desire is to make them your devotees.

Up! We must go, ignoring hate and shame,
Leaving wealth, people, comfort, to do the holy task.

Prayer-hymn originally sung on the borders of Nepal,
and now a favorite among Nepali Christians

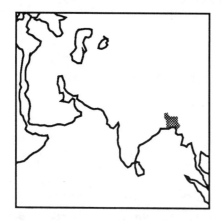

Bangladesh

Population: 98.7 million, 80% of it below the poverty line.
Languages: Bengali, English. Santali, Garo, Bawm, Khashia, and many others are spoken in some areas.
Government: Presidential form of government.
Religion: Muslims 86.6%; Hindus 12.1%; Buddhists 0.6%; Christians 0.3%.

Situated on the Ganges delta and very low-lying, Bangladesh is subjected annually to devastation from natural disaster—cyclone, flood, drought, and tidal wave. At the same time the climate and fertility of the land are such that it is extraordinarily green and lush and abounding with life of all kinds.

Before 1947 Bangladesh was part of India. With the partition of that country and the creation of Pakistan, the state of Bengal was divided; the predominantly Muslim east becoming East Pakistan, and the predominantly Hindu west remaining part of India. Subsequent unrest between East and West Pakistan developed into a war of liberation and Bangladesh declared itself an independent country in 1971. The first sustained Christian communities date from the late 15th century.

At present there is liberty to practice any religion, but not the freedom to evangelize. About three-fifths of Christians are Roman Catholics, and Baptists form the largest Protestant group. Anglicans, Presbyterians, Methodists, and Lutherans united in 1970 to form one of the dioceses of the church of Pakistan, but were cut off when Bangladesh became independent, and now form the United Church of Bangladesh. The Roman Catholic and Protestant churches are meeting together on matters of common witness and service. Christians come mainly from poor Bengali communities and minority tribes, and the church is therefore a church of the poor.

"People generally can only see Bangladesh in material terms. They are prepared to think of it as an impoverished society. To feel sorry for it, and do what they can to help. But they aren't prepared to see its beauty and respect its strength."

Therefore let us give thanks for

the teeming burgeoning life of Bangladesh

the strength of family life, and a lifestyle which encourages conversation and friendship

the hospitality of the people, with their seemingly infinite capacity for suffering, survival—and song.

About prayer—what people commonly do whenever any of the household is seriously ill is to invite a whole lot of friends for a prayer meeting. If the evening is fine and warm we sit in the courtyard on rush mats, the men on one side and the women on the other. The host will say what he has called the meeting for, and while he is about it he will add a number of supplementary biddings—Mary is taking an important examination, Peter is away catching turtle, Uncle is going for a journey, and so on. We start with a hymn, a lilting ragtime sung to drum and cymbal. There follows the Bible reading with a brief (or not so brief) sermon attached. Then begin the prayers, the president first and then others, often repeating each other, and the good Lord is informed of a lot of things that he knows very well already. Then sometimes we go on far into the night with hymn after hymn. Usually at about 1 or 2 a.m. the final prayer is said, some light refreshments are served, and everyone trails off across the fields to their own homes.

A former bishop of Dacca

Therefore let us pray

for ordinary folk preoccupied with keeping body and soul together

for Christian leaders facing immense need with few resources

that opportunities may be given to local people to exercise leadership, so that the church may be strengthened

for the search for deeper unity of thought and action

among members of the different churches

for those who seek to alleviate poverty, illiteracy, and injustice

for wisdom and compassion for those in authority in Bangladesh, and for the maintenance of peace.

Grant, O Lord, that we may expect great things of thee, and attempt great things for thee.

William Carey of Serampore, Bible translator
and founder of the Baptist Church in Bengal

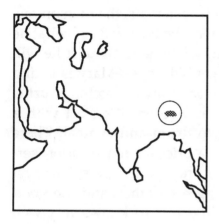

Bhutan

Population: 1.3 million, scattered and consisting mainly of Bhotias but also a considerable number of Tibetan refugees and some Nepalis.
Languages: Dzongkha, Nepali, English.
Government: Monarchy with elected National Assembly.
Religion: Buddhists 70%; Hindus 24.8%; Muslims 5%.

Bhutan is a small independent country in the Eastern Himalayas. The mountainous north borders on Tibet with which the country has cultural and trade links. In the south, the land sweeps down to plains adjoining India.

Bhutan was impenetrable to foreigners until 1965, but has recently been developing links with other countries, and became a full member of the United Nations in 1971. It has had agreements first with the British and then with India, in matters of foreign affairs. Since 1966 certain Christian agencies have been permitted to enter the country to engage in medical and educational work.

The government of Bhutan is concerned that the Buddhist religion should be maintained, not least for the sake of cultural stability at a time when significant social change is taking place through development. There are Christians among the many Indians working for the government, and several groups among the Nepali minority in southern Bhutan. There are very few Bhotia Christians. All these groups are independent. Christians are free to worship, but not to preach or evangelize.

We pray

for the king and government, and all who work for the development and welfare of this kingdom

for Christians who celebrate the Lord's presence here, and work hand in hand with all who fight illiteracy and disease.

One of the Christian agencies of the country describes its role as "simply loving and serving the people, just as Christ loves and serves both us and them."

O Servant Lord,
teach us how to serve.

Nepal

Population: 16.7 million.
Languages: Nepali, Gorkhali and other tribal languages, English.
Government: Constitutional monarchy.
Religion: Hindus 90%; Buddhists 7%; Muslims 2%; others 1%.

This small mountainous landlocked country in the Himalayas is the only Hindu kingdom in the world, and is incredibly beautiful. Most people live on subsistence farms, and 23% are literate. They are not starving, but they are continuously undernourished.

Nepal was closed to the rest of the world until 1951, when the first Westerners were invited to enter the country and establish medical ministries. However, over the years, Nepalis themselves have crossed the borders in search of work, thus encountering Christian congregations, and some have returned as Christians. For many years, there have been small groups of Christians in border areas praying for the country.

The church is indigenous and self-supporting, and scattered over the country. The preoccupation of Christians in the villages is with health and general well being, and the need to claim the power of Christ for deliverance from the main uncontrollable influences in life; and in the towns, with the need to resist the temptations that come with Western influences. Christians are frequently harassed by police action against any who are baptized or who dare to witness to their faith. This can lead to jail sentences, as conversion is not allowed by the constitution.

Traditional missionary work is not permitted, but at the invitation of the Nepalese government, and for specified periods of time, a number of Christian agencies are carrying out projects in areas of education, health, and land, water, and electrical development.

God is here
God is present in Nepal
God has called us to be his servants here
We respond in faith, willing to accept our vulnerability.

So affirms one such agency, involving Christians of many different denominations and nationalities.

We pray
for the king, and the government, and councils of Nepal
that the country may be saved from corruption and the abuse of power
that religious freedom may come
for support and strength for Christian pastors under persecution
that God will confirm and strengthen all that is for the good of the nation and the welfare of its most needy people.

Using the words of Nepali Christians, sometimes out of tune with each other, and often facing strong local opposition, we pray:

Lord give us the strength that comes from your living presence
to remain true to you, to honor you,
and to witness to you in our land of Nepal. Amen.

"Nepal has often been described as the picture-postcard paradise of clear streams, alpine hiking trails, and snowy peaks"—for this we give thanks and praise.
"But the country is also traversed by barefooted people trudging miles every day with heavy loads supported by slings across their foreheads. They lead a hard life which lasts on average only about 40 years"—for them we pray.

If the carrying of enormous loads is a common feature of life in the mountains of Nepal so also is the provision of burden benches on which heavy loads may be rested. Used in one church as the design for its Lord's Table, the "chautara" stands as a very local reminder for Christians of the promise of Jesus:

Come to me, all who labor and are heavy laden, and I will give you rest.—Amen. So be it Lord.

Week 48

Afghanistan • Pakistan

Almighty God, whose dominion is in the hearts of people and nations, set, we beseech you, in our Christian hearts a care for our Muslim brothers and sisters, and so foster love that understanding follows. And if, as understanding deepens, a need of penitence appears, then, Lord, do not withhold it.

Prayer for Christian/Muslim understanding

O heavenly Father,
open wide the sluice gate into my heart
that I may receive your living water and be fruitful.

Prayer of Punjabi Christian

Look graciously, O Lord, upon this land.
Where it is in pride, subdue it
Where it is in need, supply it
Where it is in error, rectify it
Where it is in default, restore it
And where it holds to that which is just
and compassionate, support it.

Based on the words "O Lord, be gracious to our land"
from Morning and Evening Prayer, Church of Pakistan

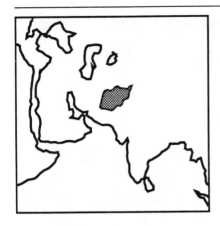

Afghanistan

Population: 18.2 million.
Languages: Pushtu, Dari, and many others, both tribal and European.
Government: Marxist republic.
Religion: Almost all are Muslims; Hindus 0.6%; very few Christians.

In this high, landlocked country, about 6% of the land is cultivable, the remainder being mountain or desert. The vigorous tribal people are mostly farmers or herders, and some are entirely nomadic.

Before sea routes were developed, this territory was at the center of Asian trade, and a Christian bishop from Herat was at the Council of Selucia in 424. There is mention of the Nestorians in the Middle Ages, but the Christian presence was terminated in the 14th century. A tribal confederation, with the beginnings of a monarchy, emerged in 1747, but subsequently broke up. Unity was eventually restored and the monarchy strengthened. This ended in 1973 with increasing unrest, and the entry of forces from the Soviet Union in 1979.

Afghan freedom fighters resisted Soviet domination and there was a long period of strife. A quarter of the population fled the country or was killed, and famine resulted in some areas. With the withdrawal of Soviet troops and negotiations for the return of refugees, there are signs of hope for the future. Expatriate Christians working with the government in aid agencies and in embassies have remained in the country. As well as service to the people of Afghanistan, they see their role as a token representative presence for Christ in the land. Afghan Christians are few and scattered.

We pray
for the land and people of Afghanistan
for those who suffer the horrors and hardships of war, and all who are refugees
for all efforts to bring about a just and lasting peace.

"In the absence of Afghan Christians able to come together publicly to give thanks to God for their own country, should there be no thanksgiving for its mountains, its streams, its antiquity, its history, its poetry, and music?" asks a frequent traveler in Afghanistan.

O Creator God,

we rejoice that the ruggedness of this land
has produced a people
of great resourcefulness and tenacity,
of hospitality and diversity;
and we ask for them
a share in your new creation.

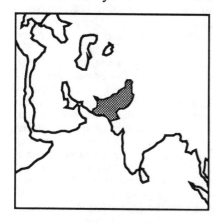

Pakistan

Population: 97.7 million and growing rapidly
Languages: Urdu, regional languages, English.
Government: Islamic republic.
Religion: Muslims 96%; Christians 1.8%; Hindus 1.3%.

Conceived as a land for the Muslims of the subcontinent, Pakistan came into being in 1947 when British rule in India ended. It originally included Bangladesh, which later became an independent state. History in the area can be traced back to the Indus civilization of about 2000 B.C.E. Traceable Christianity dates from the 8th century, but owes its more recent growth to the work of 19th-century missionaries. A small but significant flow of Christian converts from the major religions of the area, and the great mass movement among landless laborers formed the beginnings of today's church. Christian schools, colleges, and hospitals have made a widely acknowledged contribution to the life of the country.

Of today's Christians approximately half are Roman Catholics. The Church of Pakistan, formed in 1970 by a union of Anglicans, Lutherans, Methodists, and some Presbyterians, is the largest Protestant body. Among a number of other denominations the United Presbyterian is the most significant. Current government policy favors a program of Islamization which particularly affects education, banking, the position of women, and courts of law. This has implications for the Christian community, and has resulted in the nationalization of schools and colleges. The church promotes Christian-Muslim dialogue and is involved in a range of social and developmental projects, and theological education. Some Christians face problems of identity and discrimination. Many are very poor, doing menial jobs in the cities and laboring work in rural areas. The church struggles with internal factions, but can also rise to heights of great vitality, and simple, sincere faith.

Many Pakistanis, both Christian and Muslim, work overseas and their earnings constitute the second main source of foreign exchange. Some 3 million Afghans in the country, almost three-quarters of them women and children, constitute the largest refugee population in the world.

Discovered locally, and adopted as the symbol of the Church of Pakistan, the ancient Taxila cross serves as a reminder of a very early Christian presence in this area. Present-day Christians, using the refrain of a well-known convention hymn, pray that they may remain firm in this long and sometimes very costly tradition:

Yisu ke pichhe main chalne laga, na lautunga, na lautunga...

I have begun to follow Jesus, no turning back, no turning back...

With them we pray

for faithful following of Jesus in situations of great hardship and difficulty

for alertness to the possibilities of Christian service and self-giving (renewal, lay training, and development are among the stated priorities of the church)

for village people, whose livelihood is dependent on the availability of water and on the goodwill of landowners and government officials

for the church in rural areas and semi-literate communities, relying much on the local catechist or teacher and the occasional visit of a priest

for the Christian women of Pakistan, often the backbone of families and of new ventures of one kind or another

for refugees from Afghanistan, the Pakistani communities who accommodate them, and the international agencies that support them

for all meeting between Muslims and Christians at the neighborhood level, and for study centers and seminars

that facilitate specialized discussion and understanding
  for wise, compassionate, and stable leadership in church
and in state.

  O Creator and Mighty God,
  you have promised
      strength for the weak
      rest for the laborers
      light for the way
      grace for the trials
      help from above
      unfailing sympathy
      undying love.
  O Creator and Mighty God,
  help us to continue in your promise. Amen.

Prayer from Pakistan

Week 49

India • Sri Lanka

 Holy Apostle Thomas,
your memory is exalted here.

Almighty God, who to your holy apostle St. Thomas our patron, revealed your incarnate Son in his risen glory; draw, we beseech you, the peoples of our lands to know and confess him as their Lord and God, that coming to you by him they may believe and have life in his name. Amen.

Collect for the commemoration of St. Thomas

O God, we would pray at this time for all those who suffer, for all who are in want, for those who have no home, for widows and orphans, for refugees, for prisoners, for those who are in despair and on the verge of madness or violence, for those who are tortured or persecuted, for the aged, the sick, for those about to undergo operations, for the hungry and the poor, for those who are discriminated against on account of race or of caste, and for all who have need of our prayers.

Daily prayer suggested for members
of the Syrian Orthodox Church, dispersed abroad

Remembering St. Thomas, we invoke the blessing promised to those who have not seen the nailmarks of your hands, and the spear thrust in your heart, and yet believe; that leading others to confess you as their Lord and God, they may together find life in you. Amen.

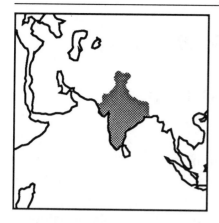

India

Population: Nearly 800 million.
Languages: Hindi, English, and 13 others officially recognized. Over 1500 others are "mother tongue" for various groups of people.
Government: Parliamentary federal republic.
Religion: Hindus 79%; Muslims 12%; Christians 3%; Sikhs 2%; adherents of tribal religions 1.5%; Buddhists 0.8%.

At heart this vast country, with widely varying terrain and climate, is an agricultural nation, with about two-thirds of the people living in villages. Industrial development in the cities is advanced.

India's diverse population is largely the result of a succession of invasions which have occurred in the long history of the subcontinent. Early invaders came from the northwest. Europeans came later by sea, and the subcontinent eventually became part of the British empire. Independence was gained in 1947, with partition of the country.

Tradition holds that the apostle Thomas came to India in 52 C.E., and preached the gospel in the south of the country. Certainly a church was established in the south by the year 200. The Mar Thoma Church, the Malankara Orthodox Syrian Church, and the Syrian Orthodox Church all trace their origins to this ancient church. Together they have over two million members, the Syrian Orthodox Church having more members in India than anywhere else. Roman Catholics came with the Portuguese, and Anglicans with the East India Company, but it was not until the 18th and 9th centuries that Protestant work really began. The formation of the Church of South India in 1947, uniting Anglicans and British Methodists with an already united body of Congregationalists and Presbyterians, was the first such union in the world. The Church of North India, incorporating a slightly wider grouping, came into existence in 1970.

In today's secular state, increasing religious rivalries have resulted in communal conflicts which continue to erupt in violence and loss of life. Caste discriminations, though legally banned, continue to cause hardship for many.

Following rapid growth in the last century, the church continues to grow in some areas. Catholics join with others in promoting interfaith dialogue. The CSI, CNI, and Mar Thoma church have entered into a conciliar union, bringing together the Eastern and Western traditions for the first time. The Methodist church in India is also seeking to join. Having undertaken a stringent self-examination, the CSI and CNI have gained a new determination to fight against social evils and to serve the real needs of those around. Christians are a small minority in the north, and consequently the CNI has tended to be somewhat inward-looking, but the moderator has recently launched a comprehensive program of renewal and outreach. He says: "Because the church is poor, its wealth is people.... Our sense of insecurity, of being a minority, and our financial weakness are our greatest assets."

O Lord, let me rest the ladder of gratitude against your cross, and mounting, kiss your feet.

Prayer of an Indian Christian

Gratitude

for the CSI and CNI, and for continuing efforts to bring about greater and more fruitful unity of the churches

for the freedom enjoyed by the church in its life and activities, and for recent movements of renewal and outreach

for the faithfulness in poverty of pastors and congregations in hundreds of villages and towns

for progress achieved in the fields of food production, medical care, literacy, and social welfare

for the women of India, their contribution in many spheres of care and development, and their participation in movements for peace, environmental protection, and economic justice.

Intercession

for peace and communal harmony, and for all victims of conflict

for the building up of awareness in the church and in society of justice, peace, and the integrity of creation in the Indian context

for the National Council of Churches in India, and for the ongoing negotiations toward a broader union of churches

for interfaith ventures between Christians and Hindus, Muslims, Sikhs, and others

for ashrams, religious communities, church institutions, and all Christian households

for the growing cities of India.

Cities are springing up like mushrooms
Cities which have come in the wake of industry
Cities that portray vivid and striking contrasts.

Lord, look at those young men and women
standing in line from morning till evening
in front of the army office for recruiting
waiting to get a patient hearing.
Look at those beggars sitting
with bowls in hands, complaining.
Look at the mansions of those moneylenders;
guarded by watchers to keep out
street dogs and job-hunting callers.
The motorists come and go in pomp and splendor;
the hotels are crowded, six-course dinners served.
The church bells toll, and the pews are filled.
But Christ is sitting at the gate with the beggars,
a bowl in hand, complaining.
Why, Lord? Why must there be this difference?
Why must there be this gap
this gap that is widening instead of narrowing;
this gap that has no bridge?
And still they come from village to city,
from farming to industry.
Lord, do you have a message for the city?

M.A. Thomas, Bangalore

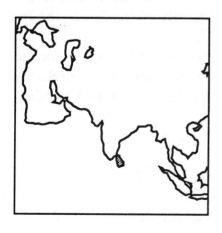

Sri Lanka

Population: 16.2 million, made up of Sinhalese (74%), Sri Lankan Tamils (13%), Indian Tamils (5.1%), and other minority groups.
Languages: Sinhalese, Tamil, English, and others.
Government: Democratic socialist republic with an executive president.
Religion: Buddhists 69.3%; Hindus 15.5%; Muslims 7.6%; Christians 7.5%.

In the tropical island of Sri Lanka, 70% of people work on the land and are poor, but they are relatively well nourished and educated. Unemployment is high in towns.

Sri Lanka, the oldest center of Theravada Buddhism, flourished as

one of the small but important ancient civilizations of Asia. From the 16th century it came into trading relationships with European nations, and was a British colony from 1802 until independence in 1948. The Roman Catholic church dates from the Portuguese period and most Protestant churches from the Dutch and British periods. There is archaeological evidence of an early Nestorian church, and a tradition that St. Thomas visited the island's sacred mountain, a center of pilgrimage for the four religions.

Each ethnic group maintains its own belief and customs. Differences and inequalities between the Sinhalese and Tamil communities have led to armed conflict, with the worst violence in the north where groups of Tamils fight for a separate state. Transport and trade between north and south are disrupted, and there is an acute refugee problem. The churches, embracing all areas and ethnic communities, work for reconciliation and peace with justice.

The vast majority of Christians are Roman Catholics. Conversations are taking place between the Roman Catholic and Anglican churches to promote greater cooperation. Taking the view that if Sri Lanka was to have a united church it must work out its own scheme, the Anglican church did not join in the union scheme with South India. However, the Congregational church in the north, which owes its origins to the work of the American Board and is predominantly Sri Lankan Tamil in membership, became the Jaffna diocese of the CSI. The other major Protestant body is the Methodist Church. There are efforts to reactivate the scheme for church union thwarted earlier by legal opposition. The Ecumenical Institute for Study and Dialogue in Colombo brings Buddhists and Christians together for interfaith programs, and a similar institute in Jaffna seeks to work among Christians and Hindus.

We give thanks

for the deep capacity for worship and devotion of the people of Sri Lanka

for all who work lovingly and courageously for reconciliation and peace, and the just ordering of community life.

What we need, Lord, is mercy from all, and forgiveness wherever there has been wrong, and the infusion of intrinsically Christian attitudes in all who have anything whatever to do with Sri Lanka.

Petition of Sri Lankan church leader

We pray

for those affected by ethnic conflict, that mutual respect, justice, and peace may prevail

that Christians may be given a new spirit of prayer and praise, and ever fresh inspiration, vision, and vitality

for the National Christian council of Sri Lanka, and all efforts to promote unity

for all in any community who set their faces against exploitation, violence, and corruption in business and public life, and seek to build up trust.

Lord Jesus, you were awakened by the cry of your disciples on a storm-tossed sea. Hear also our cry for help. There is no justice in our land for the weak and the powerless, because the powerful and the strong have decided what is and what is not right and just. We, the minority of the humble and weak, are tired of crying for justice and peace. How much longer must the strong dominate and the weak suffer? Bring your justice and grant us your peace. Let your kingdom become a reality on this earth.

A prayer from Sri Lanka

Week 50

Angola • Mozambique

We pray for Africa with all its richness of spirit, that its peoples may be strengthened as they build their own nations and work for peace and justice: that they may be delivered from the terrors of famine and drought, of disease, of conflict, and of discouragement.

Christian prayer for peace, Pope John Paul II, Assisi, 1986

I wonder if we are aware of the deep implication, in matters of faith, of belonging to the Christian era...in all these years since Christ's birth, a new, not just style, but essence of life, a life which cannot be crushed down by pressures, physical or spiritual, has begun...We are in 19-- of the Era *of* Christ, not after Christ as if Christ is overdue, outdated. We are in Christ and "the disciple is not above his teacher"...Christ's Era means that we are to be ready to face what Christ had to face.

Dinis Sengulane, Bishop of Lemombo, Mozambique

These two countries, on opposite sides of Africa, each experienced nearly 500 years of Portuguese rule before becoming independent in 1975, after a prolonged armed struggle. In Angola a period of civil strife followed; and Mozambique suffered as a result of the war in neighboring Rhodesia. Continuing unrest in the south of Angola, together with incursions of South African forces, and persistent guerrilla activity throughout Mozambique, supported by various outside governments and agencies, place heavy burdens on the respective governments.

Population, religion, language, and government
Angola: 8.6 million. Christians about 80% (Roman Catholics 61%, Protestants 18%), African indigenous 1.5%), adherents of tribal religions 15%.
Mozambique: 13.5 million. Adherents of tribal religions 47%; Christians 39% (Roman Catholics 31.5%, Protestants 6.8%, Anglicans 0.7%); Muslims 13%.
In both countries Portuguese is the official language, although numerous African languages are also spoken.
Both are single-party republics.

Angola

The Roman Catholic church has been continuously present since 1560 when Jesuits accompanied the first Portuguese to the Ndongo Kingdom. Early progress was seriously reversed by the ravages of the slave trade, and it was not until 1940 onward that the church began to grow rapidly. Baptists came in 1878, followed by Congregationalists, Methodists, and others; each working among different ethnic groups. Protestants were prominent in the independence movements, and the church was under suspicion from the Portuguese authorities.

Now strong throughout the country, the Roman Catholic church is frequently in conflict with the Marxist government, and has itself a problem of living down its early association with the colonial regime. However, wherever it is active in social work it has the approval of the government. The main Protestant churches continue for the most part to work in different areas. Though its membership is divided in political allegiance, the Christian church worships and acts as one in serving the spiritual and human needs of the Angolan people. In a situation of continuing conflict and uncertainty about the future, it ministers to a growing Christian community, meeting often in the simplest of buildings and shelters, praying and working for unity and reconciliation.

We pray

for the work of the Christian Council of Angola in coordinating evangelism and social service projects; and for growing contact and good will between the Roman Catholic and Protestant churches

for the training of leaders, educators, and pastors

for all those who help scattered groups and congregations in their Christian life and witness

for refugees from Namibia, South Africa, and Zaïre, and all displaced Angolans harassed by the ongoing war

for peace in this huge and troubled land.

We sincerely thank you, O God, for your powerful gift of hope in the face of seemingly hopeless situations. We thank you for your peace in the hearts and minds of men and

women in this part of Africa who believe you are the living God, quick to save in time of danger. You reign above all, directing the course and destiny of the universe.

João Makondekwa, Bible Society of Angola

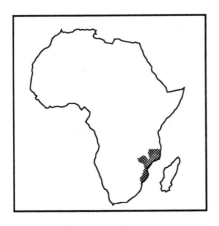

Mozambique

Roman Catholic missionary orders came with the first Portuguese, and worked in the areas of the southern coast and the Zambesi river. Not until the late 19th century did work begin further north. At about this time Protestant missionaries began to arrive and many more came after the first world war. Prior to independence the Roman Catholic church was closely identified with the state, although some individuals protested. Protestants were under suspicion and suffered considerable persecution.

Coordinating the work of some two dozen churches, the Christian Council of Mozambique has done much to break down the hostility between the Marxist government and the church. Beginning with aid given to Zimbabwean refugees, the church has gone on to build health centers and schools in the villages, to establish agricultural projects, and to make available emergency food aid in times of drought. Most church buildings are now reopened, and the church continues to grow. Many Mozambican men go to neighboring countries to find work; and poverty and family breakdown cause enormous hardship. Poor communication and terrorist attacks make pastoral care extremely difficult. In remote areas of the north, practical ecumenism finds Anglican and Roman Catholic priests ministering to the same congregations, in which members of both denominations are baptized, confirmed, and receive communion together.

We pray

for reconciliation and peace

for Christians seeking to prove their loyalty to the socialist state while remaining true to their faith

for pastors making frequent, hazardous, and exhausting journeys from village to village to minister and encourage

for the women of Mozambique, that they may be able to sustain a Christian family life amid the strains imposed by the migratory labor system

for those who serve others through medicine, education, and social service.

O Lord, we pray for justice, peace, and stability through-out Southern Africa,
    for the end of apartheid and racial intolerance,
    of tribalism and all exclusive nationalism
    We pray that in Africa and in each and every country
    men and women may honor and respect
    their fellow beings of every race and color.
    We pray that those who abuse power may be humbled,
    and the meek inherit the earth.

Prayer for Mozambique

Week 51

Botswana • Zimbabwe

Almighty God,
as your Son our Savior
was born of a Hebrew mother,
but rejoiced in the faith of a Syrian woman
and of a Roman soldier,
welcomed the Greeks who sought him,
and suffered a man from Africa to carry his cross;
so teach us to regard the members of all races
as fellow heirs of the kingdom of Jesus Christ our Lord.

Amen.

O God of all nations and people, we come before you remembering and interceding for the people of Africa. You know the struggles and predicaments of our continent and the hopes of its people. We pray for justice, peace, and reconciliation in Africa. We remember the All Africa Conference of Churches, the member churches, the Christian councils, and the Organization of African Unity, as they struggle to bring peace, reconciliation, and unity in Africa.

African bidding

Botswana

Population: 1.2 million.
Languages: English, Setswana.
Government: Multi-party republic.
Religion: Christians approximately 50% (Protestants 26.5%, African indigenous 12%, Roman Catholics 9.5%, Anglicans 2%); adherents of traditional beliefs 50%.

The people of Botswana mostly belong to a group of Bantu who migrated

here in the early centuries of the Christian era. Bushmen, who also live here, may have been in southern Africa since the Middle Stone Age. As Bechuanaland, the country became a British protectorate in 1885, and obtained independence in 1966. Largely savannah and desert, the land is increasingly afflicted by drought. Most of the people live along the eastern border, which is both more fertile and close to the main railway line. Social and economic patterns are changing as a result of the discovery of minerals.

The United Congregational church is the traditional church of Botswana, although other Protestant bodies have been present since the early 19th century. The first Roman Catholic mission was established in 1895. Today the Botswana Christian Council coordinates the work of over 20 member churches, including the Roman Catholic, and an increasing number of African independent churches. In this large, thinly populated country, pastoral work is not easy to sustain. Through a program of theological education by extension, Christians of many professions—teachers, nurses, government servants, and others—are undertaking courses. The growing mining townships constitute a challenge to provide welcoming Christian communities especially for the many young people who, in the absence of jobs and social structures, are subject to new temptations and sometimes drift into delinquency. Drought has decimated the country's cattle, and the churches are involved with the government in projects aimed at more long-term solutions as well as divine immediate aid.

In response to the plight of Hambukushu refugees from Angola, the Christian Council embarked on one of its most imaginative projects, which led to the emergence among these people of a lively church, ecumenical from the beginning. A visitor writes:

"To those brought up in the ordered life of the traditional church, the life of a Christian community devoid of accumulated traditions presents the faith in Christ both vividly and starkly...For the Hambukushu Christians the god of their exodus from Angola has been rediscovered in the Christ whose presence they celebrate at the eucharist, whose gospel they walk miles to hear, and whose spirit now dwells exuberantly among them."

Sadly, even here dissensions have occurred, and the prayer of our Lord that *they all may be one* needs to be said for this community also.

Let us pray

for local catechists and members of the ecumenical team who live and work in the New Testament ambience of the Hambukushu Christian community

for the Christian Council of Botswana with its diverse membership tackling new problems in the country

for priests and pastors ministering to congregations in villages and in growing townships

for young people drifting into towns, and the church's response to their needs

for the success of projects to combat drought, and for the many who suffer from its effects. "There are children in Botswana who have never seen rain."

O God,
we pray for those places in the world
made awful by climatic conditions;
places of intense cold and heat and drought,
places of great hardship and privation,
where man, woman, and beast are constantly endangered
by the elements and environment.
We give thanks for all that sustains and helps them,
and pray that such may be multiplied
in the hands of Jesus Christ and those who serve in his name. Amen.

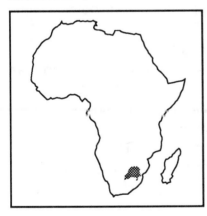

Zimbabwe

Population: 8.2 million.
Languages: English, Shona, Sidebele.
Government: Multi-party republic.
Religion: Christians 58% (Protestants 21%, Roman Catholics 16%, African indigenous 16%, Anglicans 5%); adherents of traditional beliefs 41%; Muslims 1%; a small Hindu community.

Occupied by a Shona-speaking peoples, who have probably been in this area for over a thousand years, and the Ndebele, who came from the south, Zimbabwe achieved legal independence in 1980. Both Shona and Ndebele were at the mercy of the manipulations of the British South Africa Company, which took control of their land. Colonization followed (the country was then known as Southern Rhodesia), and then an influx of white settlers mainly from Britain and South Africa. This minority white community exerted political and economic control, while African political organizations were successively banned, and their leaders exiled or imprisoned. The long struggle for a just independence with majority rule involved warfare and immense suffering.

Although Portuguese Jesuits had contact with the Shona in the 16th century, a sustained Christian presence dates from the work of 19th-century missionaries, who initially worked in close cooperation with the

white regime. In this century many Christian leaders, both Roman Catholic and Protestant, protested against government repression and segregation, and some missionaries were expelled. Now church and state are seeking to work out their relationship with each other; for although the majority political party is committed to the eventual creation of a Marxist-Leninist one-party system, religious freedom is respected and many members of government are practicing Christians. Tensions and unrest within the country have persisted, and are the subject of Christian prayer and concern.

During the years of military struggle church membership declined greatly, but many, especially young people, are now returning. The largest single body is the Roman Catholic church. Within the Protestant community there is no one predominant denomination. The African Apostolic church, the first indigenous to the country, was established in 1906, and there are now many others, some with a large membership. Through its Department of Christian Care, the Zimbabwe Christian Council provides technical assistance to farming cooperatives and small farmers, and an emergency committee responds to the needs of refugees. Individual churches are involved in medical, educational, social, and development work, and a united theological college trains candidates for the ministry. Pastoral care and the nurture of new Christians are priorities.

We pray
for those in government facing the many problems common to developing countries
for peace and stability in the region
for reconciliation, love, unity, and peace where there has been violence and enmity between those of different communities and political allegiances
for the young people of Zimbabwe
for those who train pastors, priests, and lay leaders
for God's blessing on all efforts on the part of the Zimbabwe Christian Council and individual churches to bring help to the poor and needy.

O God, friend of the poor,
help us to be their friends as well...

A pastor's prayer

Open my eyes that they may see
the deepest needs of people;

Move my hands that they may feed the hungry

Touch my heart that it may bring warmth to the despair-
ing;
Teach me the generosity that welcomes strangers;
Let me share my possessions to clothe the naked;
Give me the care that strengthens the sick
Make me share in the quest to set the prisoner free;

In sharing our anxieties and our love,
our poverty and our prosperity,
we partake of your divine presence.

Reverend Canaan Banana
First President of Zimbabwe

Week 52

Lesotho • Namibia • South Africa • Swaziland

Lord Jesus Christ,
you are the truth and rule over all the nations of the
earth:
give us wisdom to discern the truth
among all the conflicting voices that claim to be true.
Protect us from the violence
of words, fire, bullet, stone, and quirt*.
Make us agents of your truth, righteousness, and peace,
and give us boldness to be ambassadors for you.
For you reign supreme
with the Father and the Holy Spirit forever.

Prayer from South Africa

In word and deed,
in loving and caring, in sharing and compassion,
in participation and confrontation;
Lord, speak your word to us all,
give us ears to listen
and willingness to be involved with and for one another
and a spirit of obedience.

A multi-racial group in Johannesburg

A litany of rejoicing
Leader: For rebirth and resilience,
People: Blessed be God.
Leader: For the spiritually humble,
People: Glory to God, Hallelujah.

---

* The quirt is a short-handled whip with a braided leather sash.

Leader: For all who are hungry and thirsty for justice,

People: Praise him and magnify him forever.

Leader: For all who are banned for speaking the truth,

People: Blessed be God.

Leader: For all who triumph over their bitter circumstances;

People: Glory to God, Hallelujah!

Leader: For all who risk reputation, livelihood, and life itself for Christ's sake and the gospel,

People: All praise and all glory; this is God's kingdom; praise him and love him forever.

A service of celebration, Cape Town

Lesotho

Population: 1.6 million.
Languages: Sosotho, English.
Government: Hereditary monarchy.
Religion: Christians 92% (Roman Catholics 43%, Protestants 30%, Anglicans 11%, African indigenous 8%). The remainder are mostly adherents of traditional beliefs.

Formerly known as Basutoland,

Lesotho became a British protectorate in 1868 and, following a gradual process of increasing self-government, obtained independence in 1966. The country is completely surrounded by, and economically dependent on, South Africa. In 1984, approximately half the adult male labor force was working in South African mines.

By arrangement with King Moshoeshoe I of the Basuto, the Paris Mission sent missionaries to Lesotho in 1833. The Lesotho Evangelical Church, now the second largest Christian denomination in the country, emerged out of this work. Roman Catholic missionaries followed in 1862, and then Anglicans. The Roman Catholic church is a full member of the Christian Council of Lesotho, which is concerned with refugees and matters of peace and justice, and maintains an ecumenical agricultural school. The Christian church is greatly involved in educational and medical work, and there are a number of ecumenical ventures in these fields.

We pray

for the church in Lesotho, asking—at the request of the Christian Council—that the Spirit of forgiveness may

"blow through the churches in this country, that Christians may work together for unity, justice, and peace"

for religious communities, maintaining a chain of prayer for the needs of the world, and South Africa in particular, while providing centers of refreshment in an often parched and needy environment

for Christian congregations in the lowland towns, where a steady inflow of people is exacerbating the problems of loneliness, crime, alcoholism, and violence

for those who grow food in the mountain areas, where crops may fail because of drought or be destroyed by flood.

Lord, we think you know our land, it is so like the country you once lived in—mountains and sometimes snow contrasting with the thirsty lowlands.

You, who often went alone upon hillsides, know the mysterious peace and beauty to be found there. You know also the clamoring crowds waiting down below.

We wait for you today. We pray that you will have compassion on the poor—those who have no chance of school, no work, no place to belong. Give strength to those in exile and the thousands who work in mines far from home. We remember those who live in fear, and any who have been threatened or attacked.

Give courage to your people. Enable our Christian leaders to inspire hope and unity. Help all who are striving for justice. And let your peace descend again and wash over the land.

Prayer prepared by staff and students
of Roma Theological Seminary

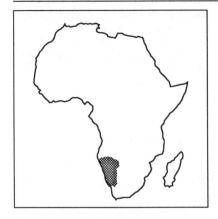

Namibia

Population: 1.2 million.
Languages: Afrikaans, English, Oshiwambo, Herero, Damara, and other African languages, German.
Government: Illegally occupied by South Africa, which holds administrative power.
Religion: Christians over 90% (Protestants 60%, Roman Catholics 20%, Anglicans 11%). Others adhere to traditional beliefs.

Formerly known as South West Africa, this land, much of it now desert but with rich mineral resources in some areas, became a German colony in 1884. South African forces entered the country in the first world war, and in 1920 it was entrusted to Britain under a League of Nations Mandate, which then passed to South Africa. After the second world war, when other mandated territories became United Nations Trust Territories, South Africa refused such an agreement for Namibia, and a prolonged dispute with repeated recourse to the International Court of Justice began. The UN General Assembly voted to terminate the Mandate in 1966, and in 1971 the ICJ ruled that South Africa's presence in the territory was illegal.

From the beginning of white occupation, the indigenous peoples of Namibia have been made to suffer. Under German rule unscrupulous cattle trading deals and appropriation of land resulted in an uprising which was brutally crushed. The Herero-Nama communities, with a combined population of 120,000, were reduced to less than 40,000 in just four years. During the Mandate period, a rush of white South Africans took possession of the best land and all of the mines. Dispossessed of their land, Africans were increasingly forced to sell their labor under the contract labor system, in which men have to work on a migrant basis for prolonged periods. In 1966 the South African security and apartheid laws were formally extended to Namibia. Meanwhile, nationalist movements campaigning to end racial discrimination and secure independence had been formed. In 1966 the South West African Peoples' Organization (Swapo), disappointed by the failure of the international community to secure any progress, and feeling that peaceful means had been exhausted, decided that there was no alternative to armed struggle. In 1973 Swapo was recognized by the UN General Assembly as "the sole and authentic representative of the Namibian people."

The Christian church in Namibia owes its origins to 19th-century missionaries, and initially the only education available for Africans was that undertaken by the churches. Under South African rule the church, like everything else, has been segregated, and the government has imposed its own system of Bantu education. Today Lutherans make up more than half the population, followed by Roman Catholics, Anglicans, Methodists, and others, all active in their support for independence. Among the white population, the Dutch Reformed church is strong. The Council of Churches in Namibia, of which

the Roman Catholic church is a member, was formed in 1978.

The suffering of the Namibian people has escalated in recent years, and the north is virtually a war zone. Under the pretext of curbing Swapo "terrorism," the military and security forces seemingly stop at nothing. Beatings, torture, rape, and killings occur, and the local population lives in constant fear and dread. Some 75,000 Namibians are refugees in Angola, Zambia, and Botswana. The struggle for liberation continues, the churches being actively involved in it.

We wail and cry, not in self-pity or in despair, but in hope and hard labor of preparing for a new nation with a constitution based on the love of God and respect for a human person. We cry to God because the road to that new Namibia and just society is full of pains, trials, detentions, and deaths. We refuse to be consoled until we finally reach there as a nation of black, white, and brown, of all Namibians.

Abisai Shejavali, general secretary of the CCN

Let us thank God
that in the midst of incredible difficulties and suffering, courage, determination, and resurrection, life still burst through

and let us affirm our solidarity
with Christians in all such situations as we declare our common faith that "the third day he rose again from the dead," and all that that belief implies for life now.

To you, O God, we lift our outstretched hands.
Give us your justice and peace in Namibia.

We pray
for those many people who suffer harshly at the hands of the South African security forces, or who are in prison for their vision of a new Namibia

O God, I am oppressed: undertake for me.

Ascribed to Hezekiah, King of Judah in 707 B.C.E.

for bereaved families; that God will comfort the widows, protect the orphans, and provide company for the lonely

for those who live in constant fear of being picked up or killed

O Christ, who hast known fear,
be with all who are afraid today.

for all who have fled from Namibia, and for those who are uprooted in their own land

O Lord, help us who roam about. Help us who have been placed in Africa and have no dwelling place of our own. Give us back our dwelling place, O God, all power is yours in heaven and earth.

Chief Hosea Kutako of the Hereros

for thousands of Black pupils and students whose education discriminates against them, and who see few prospects for the future

for the Council of Churches in Namibia, and for all who unite to stand together against forces of division and destruction

Lord Jesus Christ, voice of the voiceless and comforter of the oppressed; bless and strengthen the people of Namibia in their trials and quest for justice and peace. Grant to all the people of Namibia and their Christian leaders a sense of your presence; and lead them, Prince of Peace, to the reality of your eternal love.

from Kulimukweni, adapted

South Africa

Population: Over 32 million.
Languages: Afrikaans, English, Xhosa, Zulu, Sosotho, and others.
Government: Republic.
Religion: Christians 79% (Protestants 39%, African Independent 22%, Roman Catholics 11%, Anglicans 7%); adherents of traditional religions 16%; Hindus 2%; Muslims 1.5%; Jews 0.6%.

The time has come. The moment of truth has arrived. South Africa has been plunged into a crisis that is shaking the foundations and there is every indication that the crisis has only just begun and that it will depend and become even more threatening in the months to come. It is the kairos or moment of truth not only for apartheid but also for the church.
Kairos Document, Braamfontein, 1985

The chain of historical events which led up to this crisis began in 1652 when the first European settlers arrived in South Africa. These first settlers were Dutch, but nearly a century and a half later, Great Britain gained control of the Cape. Dissatisfied with British rule, Dutch settlers trekked northward and fought the Bantu states of the region to occupy the Orange Free State, Natal, and Transvaal. Later, Britain gained control of these territories also. The four states merged in 1910 to form the Union of South Africa, which became independent in 1934 but under exclusively white rule. The present ruling party gained control of government in 1948 and began to legalize the policy of apartheid.

One of the most painful aspects of this policy is the forced removal of African people into so-called homelands (Bantustans). Between 1960 and 1984 an estimated 3.5 million people were forcibly resettled, and the process continues. It involved concentrating 75% of the population on 13% of the land. It means that the migrant labor system is reinforced; and the granting of "independence" to the Bantustans means that those who live there are technically foreigners in South Africa. Some 50% of children in the Bantustans die before they are 5, and thousands suffer from malnutrition. Government expenditure on education for Black children is minimal. Stringent security laws have resulted in detention without trial and a very large prison population, including increasing numbers of children; and there are many instances of torture. The main African political organizations have been banned since 1960. Increasing unrest has resulted in violence and deaths, and strongly repressive measures.

Proponents of apartheid claim to be "upholding Christian civilization," and for some, change is unthinkable. For a few, even the 1984 constitution, which provided for parliamentary representation for Colored and Indian people, but not for Africans, was going too far. On the other hand, the president, without giving specific details, has announced proposed legislation to allow two of the three black races to have some limited representation in parliament. However, the govern-

ment attitude to more progressive groups remains unchanged, and the banning of 17 organizations simultaneously prompted the historic march to parliament by church leaders. Black Africans do not gain from South Africa's considerable mineral and agricultural resources which continue to provide wealth for those who are economically powerful, but hardship and misery for those exploited by unjust economic systems.

"The moment of truth has arrived...not only for apartheid but also for the church." The oldest and largest group of churches in South Africa is the Dutch Reformed. Organized on racial lines and with a large membership among Afrikaaners, this church did much to promote and support the concept of apartheid. This stance led to its withdrawal from the WCC in 1961, and the severance of relations with the Netherlands Reformed church in 1978. There have been notable dissenting voices for some time, and now the church has acknowledged that there is no scriptural justification for apartheid. Other churches, united in their opposition to apartheid, are committed to working for peaceful change. They are increasingly outspoken and active, and thus come into critical confrontation with the government.

There are over 3,000 African independent churches, with a combined membership of some 5 million, representing the second largest group of Christians in the country. African in their expression of Christianity, these bodies have always been independent of financial support from abroad. Of the mainstream Protestant churches the Methodist church is the largest, but there are significant Presbyterian, Lutheran, and Congregational bodies, and a smaller Moravian community. At this time of crisis social justice and an end to apartheid are overriding concerns. Within the Christian church there are a growing number of examples of the coming together of those of different races and social backgrounds.

We pray

for the Republic of South Africa, that it may experience freedom, justice, and the peace of God's kingdom soon

for the South African Council of Churches and all church leaders, that God will give them wisdom, courage, and protection as they witness for justice and the dignity of all people

for local congregations struggling to break free from the assumptions of apartheid

for those forced to live in the Bantustans—described by a recent visitor as "a sea of shacks reaching to the horizon, aluminum latrines, no electricity or proper roads, and only scattered single water taps—in short, organized poverty"; "Martin Luther King had a dream," said another; "well, what we saw was a nightmare."

for those in detention or prison, and those banned and si-
lenced as a consequence of their struggle to see right prevail

Now, God, will you please open all prison doors.

Arrow prayers of Archbishop Desmond Tutu

for all who have been wounded, tortured, bereaved, or
made homeless in South Africa
for all who are refugees from South Africa, elsewhere in
Africa, or in the world

Almighty God,
you whose own son had to flee the evil plans of King
Herod
and seek refuge in a strange land,
we bring before you the needs of the many refugees
throughout the world, particularly those in Africa.
We pray for those known personally to us
whom we now name before you…
We pray for them in their need for the necessities of life—
for shelter and food.
Grant that they may have the skills and equipment
to build better shelters and to grow food.

South African Council of Churches

for Black young people, involved in the struggle, deprived of a decent education

Loving Father, your young and lovable Son was found
amid the teachers of the law listening and enquiring of
them;
Have pity on South African young people who,
in quest of freedom and a better future,
have been shot at, maimed, and killed
and have fled from home and country.

Sustain them in all danger; give them your wisdom and protection,
and let their every sacrifice
yield peace, justice, and freedom in their day.
Through Jesus Christ, our Lord.

Simeon Nkoane CR, Bishop Suffragan of Johannesburg East
for those in authority

O God, whose righteous wisdom governs the heavens and controls also the destinies of men and women; teach the rulers of this and other nations the things that belong to peace.

Save, Lord, by love, by prudence and by fear, for Jesus Christ's sake. Amen.

From a service called by the Christian Council
to pray for families in the Crossroads Camp

Swaziland

Population: 706,200, excluding absentee workers.
Languages: siSwati, English.
Government: Absolute monarchy.
Religion: Christians 75% (Protestants 33%, African Independent 28%, Roman Catholics 10.5%, Anglicans 3.5%); adherents of tribal religions 23%; Bahais 2%.

The Swazi people migrated into what is now Swaziland in the late 18th century. Many of the scattered groups of people already there were of the same ancestry, and all were formed into a nation. At one time a British protectorate, it became independent again in 1968. Two-thirds of the land is held in trust by the king as Nation Land, and used for subsistence farming. The remainder is privately owned by Europeans or commercial companies. Underemployment forces many men into South Africa's migrant labor system, and the tourist industry at home brings the usual problems. This small country is also host to some 26,000 refugees, most of them from Mozambique.

Methodist missionaries came into the country in 1825 at the invitation of King Sobhuza I, and today the African Methodist Episcopal Church is the largest Protestant body. There are some forty African independent churches. Roman Catholics began work in 1913 and the church is a member of the Council of Swaziland

Churches. Incorporating nine member churches the CSC is concerned with development and educational projects, and involved in assisting refugees, providing water to rural people and initiating a legal aid education program.

Let us pray

for the king, that he may rule the country with wisdom, justice, and peace, so that love and concern for one another may increase

for this and other countries living in proximity and in close dependence on their powerful neighbor, that they may be enabled to maintain their own integrity and their constant witness to a fellowship of people transcending race and color

for the Council of Swaziland Churches, for its development and education programs, and its particular concern to help families cope with problems of alcoholism and teenage pregnancy

for young people

for the planting of new churches and the renewal of old ones.

O God, may this great, carefully wielded thread of worldwide prayer and concern serve the healing and salvation of our brothers and sisters in Swaziland; through Jesus Christ our Lord. Amen.

As the earth keeps turning, hurtling through space;
and night falls and day breaks from land to land;
Let us remember people—waking, sleeping, being born,
and dying—of one world and of one humanity.
Let us go from here in peace. Amen.

Closing prayer, WCC Assembly, Vancouver

Calendar 1990-1996

In order that all may use the same material each week we offer here a calendar for 1990-1996.

It will be noted that the prayer cycle starts each week on a Sunday, and that Week 1 always includes 1 January. Because the calendar year does not divide into 52 weeks exactly, there is at intervals an extra week. In the span covered by this calendar this occurs once; at the turn of the year 1994-95. It is suggested that Jerusalem be prayed for during this week, as well as at other appropriate times and seasons.

	1990	**1991**	**1992**
Week 1	31 Dec. (89)	30 Dec. (90)	29 Dec. (91)
Week 2	7 Jan.	6 Jan.	5 Jan.
Week 3	14 Jan.	13 Jan.	12 Jan.
Week 4	21 Jan.	20 Jan.	19 Jan.
Week 5	28 Jan.	27 Jan.	26 Jan.
Week 6	4 Feb.	3 Feb.	2 Feb.
Week 7	11 Feb.	10 Feb.	9 Feb.
Week 8	18 Feb.	17 Feb.	16 Feb.
Week 9	25 Feb.	24 Feb.	23 Feb.
Week 10	4 March	3 March	1 March
Week 11	11 March	10 March	8 March
Week 12	18 March	17 March	15 March
Week 13	25 March	24 March	22 March
Week 14	1 April	31 March	29 March
Week 15	8 April	7 April	5 April
Week 16	15 April	14 April	12 April
Week 17	22 April	21 April	19 April
Week 18	29 April	28 April	26 April
Week 19	6 May	5 May	3 May
Week 20	13 May	12 May	10 May
Week 21	20 May	19 May	17 May
Week 22	27 May	26 May	24 May
Week 23	3 June	2 June	31 May
Week 24	10 June	9 June	7 June
Week 25	17 June	16 June	14 June
Week 26	24 June	23 June	21 June
Week 27	1 July	30 June	28 June
Week 28	8 July	7 July	5 July

	1990	1991	1992
Week 29	15 July	14 July	12 July
Week 30	22 July	21 July	19 July
Week 31	29 July	28 July	26 July
Week 32	5 Aug.	4 Aug.	2 Aug.
Week 33	12 Aug.	11 Aug.	9 Aug.
Week 34	19 Aug.	18 Aug.	16 Aug.
Week 35	26 Aug.	25 Aug.	23 Aug.
Week 36	2 Sept.	1 Sept.	30 Aug.
Week 37	9 Sept.	8 Sept.	6 Sept.
Week 38	16 Sept.	15 Sept.	13 Sept.
Week 39	23 Sept.	22 Sept.	20 Sept.
Week 40	30 Sept.	29 Sept.	27 Sept.
Week 41	7 Oct.	6 Oct.	4 Oct.
Week 42	14 Oct.	13 Oct.	11 Oct.
Week 43	21 Oct.	20 Oct.	18 Oct.
Week 44	28 Oct.	27 Oct.	25 Oct.
Week 45	7 Nov.	3 Nov.	1 Nov.
Week 46	11 Nov.	1 Nov.	8 Nov.
Week 47	18 Nov.	17 Nov.	15 Nov.
Week 48	25 Nov.	24 Nov.	22 Nov.
Week 49	2 Dec.	1 Dec.	29 Nov.
Week 50	9 Dec.	8 Dec.	6 Dec.
Week 51	16 Dec.	15 Dec.	13 Dec.
Week 52	23 Dec.	22 Dec.	20 Dec.

———————— • ————————

	1993	1994	1995	1996
Week 1	27 Dec. (92)	26 Dec. (93)	1 Jan.	31 Dec. (95)
Week 2	3 Jan.	2 Jan.	8 Jan.	7 Jan.
Week 3	10 Jan.	9 Jan.	15 Jan.	14 Jan.
Week 4	17 Jan.	16 Jan.	22 Jan.	21 Jan.
Week 5	24 Jan.	23 Jan.	29 Jan.	28 Jan.
Week 6	31 Jan.	30 Jan.	5 Feb.	4 Feb.
Week 7	7 Feb.	6 Feb	12 Feb.	11 Feb.
Week 8	14 Feb.	13 Feb.	19 Feb.	18 Feb.
	1993	**1994**	**1995**	**1996**

Week 9	21 Feb.	20 Feb.	26 Feb.	25 Feb.
Week 10	28 Feb.	27 Feb.	5 March	3 March
Week 11	7 March	6 March	12 March	10 march
Week 12	14 March	13 March	19 March	17 March
Week 13	21 March	20 March	26 March	24 March
Week 14	28 March	27 March	2 April	31 March
Week 15	4 April	3 April	9 April	7 April
Weekl 16	11 April	10 April	16 April	14 April
Week 17	18 April	17 April	23 April	21 April
Week 18	25 April	24 April	30 April	28 April
Week 19	2 May	1 May	7 May	5 May
Week 20	9 May	8 May	14 May	12 May
Week 21	16 May	15 May	21 May	19 May
Week 22	23 May	22 May	28 May	26 May
Week 23	30 May	29 May	4 June	2 June
Week 24	6 June	5 June	11 June	9 June
Week 25	13 June	12 June	18 June	16 June
Week 26	20 June	19 June	25 June	23 June
Week 27	27 June	26 June	2 July	30 June
Week 28	4 July	3 July	9 July	7 July
Week 29	11 July	10 July	16 July	14 July
Week 30	18 July	17 July	23 July	21 July
Week 31	25 July	24 July	30 July	28 July
Week 32	1 Aug.	31 July	6 Aug.	4 Aug.
Week 33	8 Aug.	7 Aug.	13 Aug	11 Aug.
Week 34	15 Aug.	14 Aug.	20 Aug.	18 Aug.
Week 35	22 Aug.	21 Aug.	27 Aug.	25 Aug.
Week 36	29 Aug.	28 Aug.	3 Sept.	1 Sept.
Week 37	5 Sept.	4 Sept.	10 Sept.	8 Sept.
Week 38	12 Sept.	11 Sept.	17 Sept.	15 Sept.
Week 39	19 Sept.	18 Sept.	24 Sept.	22 Sept.
Week 40	26 Sept.	25 Sept.	1 Oct.	29 Sept.
Week 41	3 Oct.	2 Oct.	8 Oct.	6 Oct.
Week 42	10 Oct.	9 Oct.	15 Oct.	13 Oct.
Week 43	17 Oct.	16 Oct.	22 Oct.	20 Oct.
Week 44	24 Oct.	23 Oct.	29 Oct.	27 Oct.
Week 45	31 Oct.	30 Oct.	5 Nov.	3 Nov.
Week 46	7 Nov.	6 Nov.	12 Nov.	10 Nov.
Week 47	14 Nov.	13 Nov.	19 Nov.	17 Nov.

	1993	1994	1995	1996
Week 48	21 Nov.	20 Nov.	26 Nov.	24 Nov.
Week 49	28 Nov.	27 Nov.	3 Dec.	1 Dec.
Week 50	5 Dec.	4 Dec.	10 Dec.	8 Dec.
Week 51	12 Dec.	11 Dec.	17 Dec.	15 Dec.
Week 52	19 Dec.	18 Dec.	24 Dec.	22 Dec.

Sources and Acknowledgments

Jerusalem

Lord, dear Lord, I long, from *I Sing your Praise all the Day Long: Young Africans at Prayer,* edited by Fritz Pawelzik, © 1966 Friendship Press, New York, USA.

Lord God, then I would see, from *I Sing your Praise all the Day Long: Young Africans at Prayer,* edited by Fritz Pawelzik, © 1966 Friendship Press, New York, USA.

Pelican: from *Seasons and Symbols: a Handbook for the Church Year,* by Robert Wetzler and Helen Huntington, 1962 Augsburg Fortress Publishers, Minneapolis, USA.

Blessed Jesus. Source unknown.

Lord Jesus, we pray for the church, from "Network," winter 1978, USPG, London, UK. Adapted.

Jesus comes to Benares from "Jesus Christ the Life of the World: a Selection from Asia," 1982 Christian Conference of Asia, Hong Kong.

Jesus, ride again, from "Prayers for Peace," New Being Publishers, Palo Alto, California, USA.

Week 1

O God of the ever present crosses, Coptic Orthodox Patriarchate, Cairo, Egypt.

O Master, Lord God, Almighty, the Father of our Lord, Coptic Orthodox Patriarchate, Cairo, Egypt.

Lord, give us such a faith, from *The Wisdom of the Suffis* (p. 88), by Kenneth Cragg, 1976 SPCK, London, UK.

We pray, Lord, for the rising, from *Another Day: Prayers of the Human Family* (p. 12), compiled by John Carden, 1986 Triangle Books/SPCK, London, UK.

Accept, our Lord, from us, Coptic Orthodox Church, Cairo, Egypt. God of grace and providence, by Kenneth Cragg, from "Morning, Noon and Night," compiled by John Carden, 1976 Highway Press/Church Missionary Society, London.

Pray not for Arab or Jew, by a Palestinian Christian. Source untraced.

As Christians, especially do we pray. Christian prayer for peace with representatives of the church and ecclesial communities and of world religions at the invitation of Pope John Paul II, Assisi, October 27, 1986, published jointly by the British Council of Churches and Catholic Truth Society, London, in "Together in Prayer for Peace."

For all peoples, that thy light, Melkite petition translated from the Arabic by Kenneth Cragg.

Lord, after all the talking. Source unknown.

O Lord Jesus, stretch forth, prayer for the unity of the Middle East, from *Morning, Noon and Night,* compiled by John Carden, 1976 Highway Press/Church Missionary Society, London, UK.

We commend to thy fatherly goodness, from the prayer book of the Arab Evangelical Episcopal Church.

O God, send into the hearts, from *The Book of Common Prayer.* Extracts from the Book of Common Prayer 1662, the rights of which are vested in the Crown in perpetuity within the United Kingdom, are reproduced by permission of Eyre & Spottiswoode Publishers, Her Majesty's Printers, London, UK.

Come in peace, Maronite liturgy.

Lord Christ, give me some of your Spirit, by Terry Waite, from *Lent for Busy People,* The Bible Reading Fellowship, Warwick House, 25 Buckingham Palace Road, London SW1W 0PP,

UK. © Shelagh Brown.

Lord God, lover of peace, from *Another Day: Prayers of the Human Family*, compiled by John Carden, 1986 Triangle/SPCK, London, UK.

O glorious apostle Paul, "At the Apistchon" (first tome) from the Melkite Prayer Book, translated from the Arabic by Kenneth Cragg.

To me, who am but black cold charcoal, a prayer after St. John of the Damascus.

In peace let us make, divine liturgy of St. James.

Week 2

O God, I haven't recognized thee, prayer of Mohammed.

O God, who by a star, Epiphany Collect from the Church of South India Prayer Book (adapted). Courtesy Christian Literature Society, Madras, India.

How often it happens, preface to *Christians in the Arab East*, by Robert Brendon Betts, 1978 SPCK, London, UK.

We pray, O Father, for the land that nurtured the prophet Mohammed, from "Quarterly Intercession Paper," No. 318, USPG, London, UK.

God protect this country, ancient prayer of Darius in "Morning, Noon and Night," compiled by John Carden, 1976 Highway Press/Church Missionary Society, London.

Thou who didst spread, Armenian liturgy.

O God, thou hast not endowed, from *City of Wrong*, by Kamil Hussein, translated by Kenneth Cragg, published by Geoffrey Bles, Garnstone Press Ltd, Petworth, West Sussex, UK.

Our condition is very much, quotation from *Bible Lands*, by the Jerusalem and East Church Aid Association, August 20, 1982.

The cross of our Lord protect those who belong to Jesus, a blessing by Bishop Simon of Iran. Source untraced.

Litany for Iraq. Source unknown.

You, Lord of all, we confess, Chaldean liturgy.

O Lord, we beseech you grant. Source unknown.

Week 3

Lord, who through a vision. Source unknown.

O God of peace, good beyond, liturgy of St. Dionysius.

O Barnabas, who art equal, from the service of St. Barnabas the Apostle, founder of the Church of Cyprus.

For the land and people of Greece. Source unknown.

Lord Jesus Christ, Orthodox.

Grant, O God. Source unknown.

Our thoughts rest, Week of Prayer for World Peace, Centre for International Peacebuilding, Wickham House, 10 Cleveland Way, London E1 4TR, UK.

For our Muslim brethren, from the Melkite liturgy in *Byzantine Daily Worship*, The Byzantine Seminary Press, Pittsburgh, Pennsylvania, USA.

To God be the glory, a prayer from the old Syriac.

Week 4

Lord of the lovers, by Kenneth Cragg, from Provisional Calendar, Grace Cup, Quarterly Study Paper, Easter 1981, published by the Central Synod of the Episcopal Church in Jerusalem and the Middle East.

Lord, let me offer you, by St. Augustine of Hippo.

Another day of sand. Source: Meditations on the Sand in *God the Difficult* (p. 75), by A. Pronzato, St. Paul Publications, UK. Origin: "Meditazioni sulla sabbiah" by Alessandro Pronzato, Piero Gribaudi Editore, © 1981.

My brother, bridge the Christian centuries, by Randle Manwaring, in *Another Day: Prayers of the Human Family*, compiled by John Carden, 1986 Triangle/SPCK, London, UK.

Almighty God, whose son our Savior taught us, by Kenneth Cragg, from Provisional Calendar, Grace Cup, Quarterly Study Paper, Easter 1981, published by the Central Synod of the Episcopal Church in Jerusalem and the Middle East.

Islam...takes God, quotation from Hendrik Kraemer. Source untraced.

Almighty God, grant that we may listen, from "Quarterly Intercession Paper," USPG, London, UK.

As the needle naturally turns, prayer to Jesus by Raymond Lull. Source untraced.

Give, O God, peace and harmony. Source unknown.

"The 12 million or so Christians," by David Kerr, from "MECC Perspectives," Geneva, Switzerland.

God bless the countries of the Middle East. Source unknown.

Week 5

Christ look upon us in this city, by Thomas Ashe. Source untraced.

Heavenly Parent, from *World at One in Prayer*, edited by D.J. Fleming, Friendship Press, New York, USA.

Pray for us, brothers and sisters, a plea from Hong Kong, Anglican Diocese of Hong Kong, Bishop R.O. Hall. Source untraced.

O God our Father, by Raymond Fung, World Council of Churches, Geneva, Switzerland.

God the Father, the voice, Mass, Feast of St. John the Baptist, Patron Saint of Macau, Roman Missal.

We reverently worship, ancient Chinese ascription, used in worship by the Nestorian Church.

Help each one of us, prayer from China. Source untraced.

O God, teach us to be, Amity Foundation, Eugene, Oregon, USA.

God, creator of heaven and earth, a contemporary prayer from China. Source untraced.

Now may the God of peace, Hebrews 13:20-21.

If the Lord is in prison, by Hsu T'ien Hsien, from *Testimonies of Faith: Letters and Poems from Prison in Taiwan*, studies from the World Alliance of Reformed Churches, Geneva, Switzerland.

Gracious God, let your will, prayer from Taiwan, from "Calendar of Prayer 1986-87" (p. 77), United Church of Christ Board for World Ministries, New York, USA. Used with permission.

You have shown us, O God, prayer based on Micah. Source untraced.

Week 6

If I had not suffered, by Mizuno Genzo, from "Your Will Be Done," 1985 Christian Conference of Asia Youth, Quezon City, Philippines.

"As a Catholic I feel," by Kim Myong Shik, Japan, CIIR News, November 1986, reprinted in "Now," September 1987, Methodist Church Overseas Division, London. © CIIR News, London.

Eternal God, we say good morning, by Masao Takenaka, from "Your Will Be Done," 1985 Christian Conference of Asia Youth, Quezon City, Philippines.

Lord, touch with your fingers. Source unknown.

O God, we do not protest, by Tohoyiko Kagawa, from "Your Will Be Done," 1985 Christian Conference of Asis Youth, Quezon City, Philippines.

Lord, bless the work. Source unknown.

O God, you have made us glad, thanksgiving for Korean martyrs, from the "Prayer Book" of the Anglican Church of Korea.

Christians in North Korea, by Erich Weingärtner, from "One World," April 1986, © World Council of Churches Publications, Geneva, Switzerland.

Our Father, hallowed be your name, in Korea. Source unknown.

We give thanks, O God, for the rapid growth, from the Quarterly Intercession Paper, No. 317, USPG, London, UK. Paraphrased.

We must not forget, Park Hyung Kyu. Source untraced.

O Christ, whose loving eyes. Source unknown.

The story is told, by Erich Weingärtner, from "One World," November 1986, © World Council of Churches Publications, Geneva, Switzerland.

Lord, with Korean Christians. Source unknown.

Lord, thanks to you. Source unknown.

Lord, break down the walls, chorus of theme song Fifth Assembly, WCC, Nairobi 1975, from "Break Down the Walls," lyrics by Fred Kaan, music Peter Janssens, © Peter Janssens Musik Verlag, Telgte, Federal Republic of Germany.

Week 7

United through grace, offering of the day, prayer used in the Philippines. Prayer to Christ the King, Cursillo in Christianity Prayer Book.

As you anointed kings, prayer from the Philippines.

We pray that we may be, "Prayers for Asia Sunday," Christian Conference of Asia, Hong Kong.

Your death, O Lord, we commemorate, acclamation used by Filipino members, Cursillo in Christianity Prayer Book.

Week 8

May the peaceful nature, prayers of a Malaysian Christian, from *The World at One in Prayer,* Friendship Press, New York, USA.

O God of many names, Christian prayer for peace with representatives of the church and ecclesial communities and of world religions at the invitation of Pope John Paul II, Assisi, October 27, 1986, published jointly by the British Council of Churches and Catholic Truth Society, London, in "Together in Prayer for Peace."

Just call me by my name, "Alone, I am not yet alone," words and music by Samuel Liew, from "New Songs of Asian Cities," No. 18, Christian Conference of Asia/URM, Hong Kong.

Thank you, Father, for your blessing, by Lim Swee Cher, from "The Light of the World," CWM Prayer Handbook, 1981 Council for World Mission, London, UK.

In the brightness of your Son, opening recollection and benediction, from "Your Will Be Done," 1985 Christian Conference of Asia Youth, Quezon City, Philippines.

Week 9

Destroy, O Lord, prayers from Sweden. Source untraced.

O Lord, I have come, from the "Danish Church Service," Church of Denmark, Council on Inter-church Relations, Copenhagen.

Father in heaven, from *The Prayers of Sören Kierkegaard 1813-55,* edited by Percy D. Le Fev-

re, © 1956 University of Chicago. All rights reserved.

Oh God, our Father and Mother, taken from a prayer by Kerstin Lindqvist and Ulla Bardh, Sweden, "Accept Our Deep Longing to Live," from *Women's Prayer Services*, 1983, Twenty-Third Publications, Mystic, Connecticut, USA.

God, grant that in my mother tongue, Hallgrimur Peterson, "Hymns of the Passion," 1674.

Lord our God, who taught wisdom, the blessing of a computer, Finnish Orthodox.

Heavenly Father, we thank you, from "The New Lutheran Manual in Finland." Adapted.

Lord, we bring you thanks for the care, prayer used on the Norwegian Radio, March 6, 1987.

God, our creator, as we join, prayer from Finland. Source untraced.

Week 10

O Holy Spirit, giver of light, slightly adapted after a prayer by Monica Furlong, c/o Movement of the Ordination of Women, London, UK.

Lord Jesus Christ, you are the way, from "Unity," newsletter of the Irish School of Ecumenics, Dublin, Ireland.

Three things are of the Evil One, 15th-century Irish benediction.

We are tired, Lord, by T.A. Patterson, N. Ireland, written for "A World at Prayer: The New Ecumenical Prayer Cycle."

God, our Mother and Father, from "Corrymeela Worship," © 1987 Corrymeela Press, Belfast, N. Ireland. Used with permission.

All-merciful tender God, Janet Berry, South West Manchester Group of Churches, UK.

Lord God, we thank you, prayer for the interchurch process by Jamie Wallace, British Council of Churches, London, UK.

Week 11

O Lord Jesus, let not your word, Thomas à Kempis, from *Prayers for the Future of Mankind* (p. 212), Wolfe Publishing Ltd., London, © Pyramid Communications Inc.

Grant to us, O Lord, Thomas à Kempis, from *Prayers for the Future of Mankind* (p. 56) Wolfe Publishing Ltd., London, © Pyramid Communications Inc.

Let us pray to God who calls us, from "Fürbitten und Kanongebete der holländischen Kirche" (p. 266), edited by A. Schilling, 1972 12th edition, Verlag Hans Driewer, Essen, Federal Republic of Germany.

O Holy Spirit of God, who with thy holy breath, Erasmus of Rotterdam, from *The Oxford Book of Prayer*, No. 506, edited by George Appleton, 1985 Oxford University Press, London.

God in heaven, we beg you, from "Fürbitten und Kanongebete der holländischen Kirche," edited by A. Schilling, 1972, 12th edition, Verlag Hans Driewer, Essen, Federal Republic of Germany.

Go now, all of you, from *Prayers, Poems and Songs*, by Huub Oosterhius, 1975 Sheed & Ward Ltd., London, UK.

Week 12

Lord, grant that Christians, from *Praise in All Our Days: Common Prayers at Taizé*, 1975. Mowbray's & Co. Ltd., © Cassell Plc, London, UK.

Blessed are you, Lord God, prayer from the Roman liturgy.

You are always with us, Lord, by Fr. Pierre-Etienne, French in "Nos coeurs te chantent," 1977 Taizé, 71250 Cluny, France. English source unknown.

Lord God, you accepted the sacrifice, from the Roman liturgy.

O heavenly Father, we bend, prayer from the Mozarabic sacramentary, *Prayers for the Future of Mankind* (p. 18), published by Wolfe Publishing Ltd, London, © Pyramid Communications Inc.

You are my family, affirmation of Patrice, from "Expressions of Faith from the Universal Church" (p. 33), Département évangélique français d'action apostolique.

Our God, we are one, One in Solidarity, from *100 prières possibles*, by Andrè Dumas, 1982 Editions Cana, Paris, France.

O God, you who are from generation, Francis Ibiam, All Africa Conference of Churches, Source untraced.

Almighty and eternal God, we fervently lift, prepared by women students in the Pan-African leadership course, Kitwe, Zambia, from *Journey of Struggle, Journey in Hope: People and their Pilgrimage in Central Africa*, edited by Jane Heaton, Friendship Press, New York, USA.

Week 13

And in a random scorching flame, Somali prayer, by Allen Lane, from *Heart of Prayer: African, Jewish and Biblical Prayers*, by Anthony Gittins CSS (p. 113), Wm. B. Collins, London, UK.

Lord, I am not worthy, prayer before communion, Western rite.

O Lord, our good and life-giving God, prayer from litany of the Ethiopian Orthodox Church, published by the Continental Printery, Kingston, Jamaica. Also the "Liturgy of the Ethiopian Church," translated by Marcos Daoud, The Egyptian Book Press.

Yes, Lord, you are the God, acclamation, Anaphora of St. Dioscorus, prayer from liturgy of the Ethiopian Orthodox church, published by the Continental Printery, Kingston, Jamaica. Also the "Liturgy of the Ethiopian Church," translated by Marcos Daoud, The Egyptian Book Press.

Remember, Lord, the sick, evening prayer at the Covenant, prayer from liturgy of the Ethiopian Orthodox church, published by the Continental Printery, Kingston, Jamaica. Also the "Liturgy of the Ethiopian Church," translated by marcos Daoud, the Egyptian Book Press.

Give comfort, O Lord, to all, from the "Quarterly Intercession Paper," No. 322, USPG, London, UK.

O God, give us rain, from *The Prayers of African Religion*, by John S. Mbiti (p. 162), SPCK, London, UK.

O God, give us peace, from *The Prayers of African Religion*, by John S. Mbiti (p. 162), SPCK, London, UK.

Lord God, there are places. Source unknown.

Week 14

O Thou, who art the Lion of Judah, a prayer for Africa by George Appleton, From *In His Name*, Lutterworth Press and Macmillan Publishers. © George Appleton.

O God, make speed to save us, versicle and response, Prayer Book of the Church of the Providence of Sudan.

These are the new songs, quotation from Christian Missionary Society source.

The Father of our Lord in Heaven, hymn from Christian Missionary Society source.

All the problems of the rest. Source unknown.

O Lord Christ, who as a boy, "Quarterly Intercession Paper," No. 316, USPG, London, UK. Adapted.

O God, our Creator, Redeemer, Fellowship of the Least Coin. Used with permission.

God bless Sudan, "Quarterly Intercession Paper," No. 316, USPG, London, UK.

Martyrs gave birth, Canon Samuel Van Culin, secretary general of the Anglican Consultative Council, speaking of Archbishop Janani Luwum.

O God, by your providence, collect for the martyrs of Uganda, Anglican church of Uganda, Kampala.

Tukutendereza, Yesu—Glory, glory, Hallelujah, from *Breath of Life,* by Patricia St. John, Ruanda Mission CMS, London, UK.

O Father God, I cannot fight, prayer from Africa, from *Light of the World Prayer Book,* Highway Press/Church Missionary Society, London, UK.

Keep us, Sovereign Lord, prayer from Uganda, from July/September 1984 issue of "Yes," Church Missionary Society, London, UK.

O Lord, establish, strengthen and settle. Source unknown.

Week 15

Grant that the peoples of East Africa. Source unknown.

We beg you, O God, to rule, prayer from Kenya, from *The UNICEF Book of Children's Prayers,* by William I. Kaufman, The Stackpole Company, Harrisburg, Pennsylvania, USA. © with the permission of William I. Kaufman.

From a wandering nomad, from the draft eucharistic liturgy, Church of the Province of Kenya.

Let us pray to the God of our fathers, from the draft eucharistic liturgy, Church of the Province of Kenya.

Heavenly Father, thank you for the peace, prayer from Tanzania, by W.F. Darby, from "Network" January 1986, USPG, London, UK. Adapted.

Good Lord: just as you were pleased to relax, Richards & Richardson, "Home Meeting," in *Prayers for Today,* first published 1977 by Uzima Press Ltd, Nairobi, Kenya.

Here in Tanzania, quote from the Christian Council of Tanzania.

O God forgive us for bringing, prayer of an African minister, from *Morning, Noon and Night* (p. 83), compiled by John Carden, 1976 Highway Press/Church Missionary Society, London, UK.

Week 16

Let your love, a Malagasy petition. Source untraced.

Gracious Lord, in this season of fullness, "The Greater Family," from *A Book of Family Prayer,* edited by Gabe Huck, 1979 Seabury/Continuum Publishing Co., New York USA.

O God, who calls us to your service, Fellowship of the Least Coin. Used with permission.

God of goodness and love, Christian Aid, London, UK.

Heavenly Father, you who taught your Son, by Eleri Edwards, *From Proverbs for Today,* CWM Prayer Handbook, 1984 Council for World Mission, London, UK. Adapted.

We must see ourselves, quote from Ecumenical Press Service on Lusaka, 1988 World Council of Churches, Geneva, Switzerland.

May Africa praise you, by Jerome Bala, from *Prayers for Mission* (p. 18), USPG, London, UK, and "Another Day: Prayers of the Human Family," compiled by John Carden, 1986 Triangle/SPCK, London.

We pray for Zambia, by John Banda from *The Light of the World Today,* CWM Prayer Handbook, 1984 Council for World Mission, London, UK.

Dear God in heaven, we pray for, from Zambia, a prayer for refugees. Adapted. Source untraced.

Merciful God, from the sky you send, by Jean Hall, from *Proverbs for Today,* CWM Prayer Handbook, 1984 Council for World Mission, London, UK.

At last, O God, the sun's heat, Richards & Richardson, "Evening," in *Prayers for Today,* first published 1977 by Uzima Press Ltd, Nairobi, Kenya.

Week 17

O God of all youth, from "Calendar of Prayer 1986-1987," United Church of Christ Board

for World Ministries, New York. Used with permission.

But their potential, quote from "Now" (p. 5), February 1987, Methodist Church Overseas Division, London, UK.

You know, O God, how hard it is, Rubem A. Alves. Source untraced.

Lord, no matter what we Christians. Source unknown.

I truly believe in the new humanity, by Dom Pedro Casaldaliga, Rio de Janeiro, 1978, from *Confession Our Faith Around the World IV: South America* (pp. 32/33), 1985 World Council of Churches Publications, Geneva, Switzerland.

Week 18

O God, to those who have hunger, prayer from Latin America. Source untraced.

True evangelical faith, Menno Simons, 16th-century founder of the Mennonites, from "Bible Lands Society Magazine," © The Bible Lands Society, High Wycombe, UK. Used with permission.

It must be the hardest thing, Bernard Thorogood, from "Prayers for the Disappeared," Latin American Federation of Relatives of Disappeared Prisoners, London, UK.

After 11 years of military government, from "Network," January 1985, USPG, London, UK. Adapted.

We pray to you, O Lord, prayer for use on Rogation Sunday, Evangelical Church of the River Plate, Argentina, from "Confession Our Faith Around the World IV: South America" (p. 10), 1985 World Council of Churches Publications, Geneva, Switzerland.

Week 19

Why on earth had the Spaniards, from "Like a Mighty River," by Lois Wilson, 1981 Wood Lake Press, Winfield, Canada.

For the deep sense, by John Carden.

The Christ of the Andes, by Max Warren, from *I Believe in the Great Commission,* © Hodder & Stoughton, London, UK. Wm. B. Eerdmans Publishing Co, Grand Rapids, for USA and Philippines.

Our Father...here and now, quoted from "We Believe," 1986 United Church in Australia, Sydney, Australia.

Lord of mystery, by Louis Espinal, quoted in *We Drink from Our Own Wells* (p. 165), by Gustavo Gutiérrez, 1974 SCM Press Ltd, London, UK, British and Commonwealth rights. For USA and Canada: Orbis Boks, New York, USA.

O Lord, in terms of weariness, excerpted from "L'Amèrique latine en prière," compiled by Charles Antoine, 1981 Editions du Cerf, Paris, France.

Lord God, gracious and merciful, from *The Eucharistic Liturgy of Lima,* Faith and Order 1982, World Council of Churches Publications, Geneva, Switzerland.

Paragraphs 1-4, quotes from *Signs of the Times,* © CLAI (Latin American Council of Churches). Excerpted from Prayer "Manual 1986-1987" (p. 19), Methodist Church Overseas Division, London, UK.

Almighty God, we come to your presence, Emilio Castro, World Council of Churches, Geneva, Switzerland.

Solidarity is another name, by Jon Sobrino, from *Theology of Christian Solidarity,* by Jon Sobrino and Juan Hernandez Pico, © 1985 Orbis Books, Maryknoll, USA.

Week 20

To you, Creator of nature, from a prayer by Pope John Paul II during his visit to Hiroshima 1981, in *Prayers for Peace,* by Robert Runcie and Basicl Hume, 1987 SPCK, London, UK.

When I'm down, Czech litany. Source untraced.

Bless, O God, the diligent work, from the Czech Hussite church, Sunday eucharist.

We are two hands, from Poland, translated from the German "Wir sind zwei Hände." Source untraced.

May the Lord accept our prayers, by Karol Wojtyla (John Paul II), prayer for ecumenical understanding. Source untraced.

Week 21

As the bread which we break, Didache, 2nd century.

You, O God, have made us, after the words of St. Augustine.

O Lord, in you have I trusted, from Te Deum Laudamus, 5th century, Yugoslavia.

Lord, we have sinned against you, from "Week of Prayer for Christian Unity 1986," British Council of Churches, London, UK.

Grant, O Lord, that with your love, Mother Teresa of Skopje and Calcutta. Source untraced.

Lord, you sent your Son Jesus Christ, from "Week of Prayer for Christian Unity 1986," British Council of Churches, London, UK.

Remember, Lord, the city in which we dwell, from the Divine Liturgy of St. Chrysostom commemoration of the diptychs of the living.

Week 22

O Heavenly King, Comforter, Spirit of truth, Orthodox invocation of the Holy Spirit.

O Christ, our God, who for us, prayer for unity by Iona Bria, © World Council of Churches, Geneva, Switzerland.

Almighty God, in your majesty, a Hungarian teacher's prayer from "Die Schönsten Gebete der Erde" (pp. 75-76), © 1964 Südwest Verlag GmbH & Co. KG, Munich, Federal Republic of Germany.

O Lord our God, we thank you for the peace, prayer from the Reformed Church of Hungary. Adapted.

Week 23

Khristos voskress! Christ is risen! Russian Orthodox prayer from *The Oxford Book of Prayer,* No. 658, by George Appleton, 1985 Oxford University Press, London, UK.

O God, that we may receive, prayer from Mongolia, from "Die Schönsten Gebete der Erde," © 1964 Südwest Verlag GmgH & Co. KG, Munich, Federal Republic of Germany.

Lord, through the shedding, Armenian Orthodox liturgy, in "La prière oecumènique," collection of litanies put together by the Faith and Order Commission and published by Taizé, 71250 Cluny, France.

When my soul sheds its tears, prayer by Lithuanian prisoners in Northern Siberia, 1960 Paulist Press, New Jersey, USA, quoted by Cicily Saunders in "Beyond all Pain," SPCK, London, UK.

Russian believers, quote from *Sojourners,* November 1983, Washington, DC, USA.

Good Jesus, patient as a lamb, by E.B. Pusey. Source untraced.

Kyrie eleison, Orthodox liturgy, USSR.

O Lord, I do not know what to ask, by Metropolitan Philaret of Moscow (1553-1633), from the *Russian Orthodox Liturgy.*

More than anything else, from *Unfinished Agenda* by Lesslie Newbigin, 1985 World Council of Churches Publications, Geneva, Switzerland.

Week 24

There are literally two Liberias, Anglican bishop of Liberia.

If Mary and Joseph, by Dorothy R. Gilbert, Bo, Sierra Leone, excerpted from the 1985 Prayer Calendar (p. 18), General Board of Global Ministries, The United Methodist Church, New York, USA. Used by permission.

Lord, we pray that in all the contacts. Source unknown.

May God give you a long life, a Krio blessing, excerpted from the 1985 Prayer Calendar (p. 60), General Board of Global Ministries, The United Methodist Church, New York, USA. Used by permission.

Week 25

May the word of God, a prayer from Guinea. Source untraced.

I saw a child today, Lord, prayer of an African Christian, quoted in "Prayers of Harvest Leaflet 1986," Christian Aid, London, UK.

Grant, O God, to your children. Source unknown.

Bless, O Lord, the independent nations, "Quarterly Intercession Paper," No. 324, USPG, London, UK.

We thank you, Lord. Source unknown.

O God, in whom we live, prayer from the Roman liturgy.

O God, our Heavenly Father, prayer for use in the Muslim world, by Oliver Allison, Diocese of the Sudan, quoted in *New Threshold,* by David Brown, 1976 British Council of Churches, London, UK.

Lord, you want everybody to live, prayer of a Senegalese Christian. Source untraced.

Week 26

Years ago our Elders said, from "Calendar of Prayer 1986-1987," United Church of Christ Board for World Ministries, New York, USA. Used with permission.

Lord our God, prayer from Benin. Source untraced.

Our heavenly Father, we in Ghana, general secretary of the Christian Council of Ghana, from "Calendar of Prayer 1986-1987," United Church of Christ Board for World Ministries, USA. Used with permission.

O God, we implore you, prayer of a young Ghanaian, "Make us your people," from *I Lie on My Mat and Pray* (p. 56), edited by Fiotz Pawelzik, © 1966 Friendship Press, New York, USA.

God of all nations, prayer from Ghana. Source untraced.

Hallelujah, in Ewe Ghana, as taught by Alexander Gondo, in *African Songs of Worship,* edited by I-to Loh, © 1986 Renewal and Congregational Life, World Council of Churches Publications, Geneva, Switzerland.

O God, most mighty among the heavens, excerpt from a prayer of confession recorded in an African Independent Church by Akin Omoyajowo, for a symposium on Christian theology in Nigeria, 1981.

Let us pray for those who foster violence, prayer from the Ivory Coast. Source untraced.

Week 27

Lord, you told the apostles, prayer for unity from Togo. Source untraced.

O Almighty God, we humbly ask you, prayer used in Yoruba parishes in Nigeria, from *Morning, Noon and Night* (p. 87), compiled by John Carden, 1976 Highway Press/Church Missionary Society, London, UK.

Creator of heaven and earth, accept our thanks, excerpt from a prayer of thanksgiving recorded in an African Independent Church by Akin Omoyajowo, for a symposium on Christian theology in Nigeria, 1981.

Lord, we were brought. Source unknown.

O Lord, we beseech thee to deliver us, prayer of Francis Akanu Ibiam. Source untraced.

Ezigbo hwannem, Ibo chorus of farewell, Nigeria. Source untraced.

We pray for the churches, from prayers used at the 8th Assembly of the Christian Conference of Asia in Seoul, Korea, 1985.

God of peace, help us to be committed, Fellowship of the Least Coin. Used with permission.

Our Father, we thank you, prayer by two members of the Fellowship of the Least Coin. Used with permission.

With all my heart I take refuge, from the Norwegian of Karl Ludvig Reichelt, Buddhist/Christian Centre, Hong Kong.

Week 28

God came down to us, from "Your Will Be Done" (p. 156), 1985 Christian Conference of Asia Youth, Quezon City, Philippines.

We cannot go, quoted from "Fides," April 1987.

Look with mercy, O Lord,"Quarterly Intercession Paper," No. 326, USPG, London, UK. Adapted.

Dear God, we thank you for your love, prayer of a Cambodian Christian refugee woman, Fellowship of the Least Coin. Used with permission.

We remember, O Lord, those who suffer, from "Week of Prayers for World Peace," Centre for International Peacebuilding, London, UK.

We pray for the peoples of Asia, Christian prayer for peace with representatives of the church and ecclesial communities and of world religions at the invitation of Pope John Paul II, Assisi, October 27, 1986, published jointly by the British Council of Churches and Catholic Truth Society, London, in "Together in Prayer for Peace."

As we are together, praying for peace, by Thich Nhat Hanh, a Buddhist litany for peace, from *Oxford Book of Prayer,* No. 935, edited by George Appleton, 1985 Oxford University Press, London, UK.

May the grace of our Lord Jesus Christ, benediction, Christian Conference of Asia, Hong Kong.

Week 29

Dear Lord, you wanted all people, prayer of a Burmese Christian woman, Fellowship of the Least Coin. Used with permission.

Good Shepherd, we ask that you will seek, by Gwen Rees Roberts, from *Psalms for Pilgrims,* CWM Prayer Handbook (p. 19), 1983 Council for World Mission, London, UK.

Staying in Bangkok briefly, a tourist, Joyce Peel, Church Missionary Society, London, UK.

O God, our Father, the fountain of love, by Koson Srisang, Thailand, from "Your Will Be Done," 1985 Christian Conference of Asia Youth, Quezon City, Philippines.

O God, be with us, prayer of a Thai Christian woman, Fellowship of the Least Coin. Used with permission.

Lord, we take refuge, by John Carden, prayer prompted by a thought in Bishop Neill's *The Supremacy of Jesus* (p. 52), *The Hodder Book of Christian Prayers* by Tony Castle, Hodder & Stoughton, London, UK.

Week 30

I believe in God, an Indonesian creed, Christian Conference of Asia, Hong Kong.

Give us strength, Fridolin Ukur, Indonesia. Source untraced.

O God, who sent the Holy Spirit, prayer of an Indonesian Christian woman, Fellowship of the Least Coin. Used with permission.

Week 31

O God, who has bound us, by Reinhold Niebuhr, from *Hymns of Worship,* edited by Ursula Niebuhr, 1939 Association Press, New York, USA.

Grandfather, Great Spirit, Dakota Indian prayer, from *The Gift is Rich,* by E. Russell Carter, 1955 and 1968 Friendship Press, New York, USA.

God of our weary years, by James Weldon Johnson, third verse of hymn "Lift Every Voice and Sing," © 1927 Edward B. Marks Music Corporation, USA.

We pray that our neighborhoods, prayer by Lyman Ogilby. Source untraced.

O God, you are like a weaver-woman, "The Weaver Woman," prayer from the USA. Source untraced.

Almighty God, we offer our prayers, by Joan Campbell, used by permission of the National Council of the Churches of Christ in the USA, October 1983.

Lord, I could use some help. Source unknown.

God, help everyone living with AIDS, Grand M. Gallup, Episcopal Diocese of Chicago, Illinois, USA.

Let those who have no home, John Fandel "Am/PM," Forward Movement Publications, Cincinnati, Ohio, USA.

Lord, we know that you'll be coming, Mary Glover, quoted in *Sojurners,* Washington, DC, USA, in Jim Wallace's "The Rise of Christian Conscience."

Thank you, Lord, for counting me, Albert Newton, All Saints Episcopal Church, Montgomery, Alabama, USA.

Lord, one of the problems, Albert Newton, All Saints Episcopal Church, Montgomery, Alabama, USA.

You are the healing, God is a Verb, by Marilee Zdenek, excerpted from 1985 Prayer Calendar (p. 39), General Board of Global Ministries, The United Methodist Church, New York, USA. Used by permission.

Let us pray for the world, Pax Christi, USA. Source untraced.

Week 32

Lord, in creation you have revealed, Ecumenical Prayers, © Paulist Press, Ramsey, New Jersey, USA.

You have come from afar, "Prières d'Ozawamick," Canadian Indian liturgical text. Source untraced.

For human contact, Alyson Huntly, Canada, reprinted with permission from "Faithful Reflections on Our Experience," published by the Women's Inter-Church Council of Canada, 1984.

You, O God, have spoken to us, United Church of Canada, Toronto. Adapted.

O God, through the image of a woman (By His Wounds You Have Been Healed), Canada from *No Longer Strangers: a Resource for Women and Worship* (p. 33), edited by Iben Gjerding and Katherine Kinnamon, 1983 World Council of Churches Publications, and *Ecumenical Decade 1988–1998: Churches in Solidarity with Women—Prayers and Poems—Songs and Stories* (p. 23), 1988 WCC Publications, Geneva, Switzerland.

Jesus, make our hearts, Jean Vanier in *Eruption to Hope* (p.50), 1971 Griffin House Publishers, Toronto, Canada. Used with Permission.

The blessing of the God by Lois Wilson, Toronto, Canada, from *No Longer Strangers: a Resource for Women and Worship* (p. 45), edited by Iben Gjerding and Katherine Kinnamon, 1983 World Council of Churches Publications, Geneva, Switzerland.

Week 33

O God, you are my God, "As Dolphin and Eagle," from *Australian Prayers,* by Bruce D.

Prewer, used by permission of Lutheran Publishing House, Adelaide, South Australia.

You must think me silly, from *Australian Images* by Aubrey Podlich, used by permission of Lutheran Publishing House, Adelaide, South Australia.

God of our ancient people, first stanza of "Our Black People," from *Australian Prayers* (p. 122), by Bruce D. Prewer, slightly modified, used by permission of Lutheran Publishing House, Adelaide, South Australia.

Dear God, you have forgiven us by Arthur Malcolm, Australia.

Give wisdom to those copyright Anglican Church of Australia Trust Corporation, from the text of *An Australian Prayer Book*, published by the Anglican Information Office, reproduced with permission.

Lord God of all Peoples, from an offertory prayer, New Zealand.

Gracious God, we pray for the peoples, T.W., a prayer from the Conference of Churches in Aotearoa-New Zealand, Wellington.

O Jesus, be the canoe, an islander's prayer for Melanesia, from "Melanesia News" and *Morning, Noon and Night* (p. 95), compiled by John Carden, 1976 Highway Press/CMS, London, UK.

Week 34

Almighty God, your word of creation, prayer from Samoa, quoted from "We Believe" (p. 49), Uniting Church in Australia, Sydney, Australia.

Keep the ocean clean, from the West Caroline island of Palau, a fifth-grader's cry of protest, excerpted from the 1985 Prayer Calendar (p. 104), General Board of Global Ministries, The United Methodist Church, New York, USA. Used by permission.

The environment of the small, from *To Live Among the Stars: Christian Origins in Oceania*, by John Garrett, 1982 World Council of Churches, Geneva, Switzerland.

We believe that creation, taken from a creed "Women of the Pacific: Worship Workshop," JPIC women's meeting "Caring for God's Creation," Tonga, September 1987.

We ask you, dear God, "Southern Cross Prayer," © The Bible Society of Papua New Guinea, Port Moresby.

Lord, in your mercy, litany by Jabez L. Bryce, Fiji. Source untraced.

We pray for the peoples of Oceania, Christian prayer for peace with representatives of the church and ecclesial communities and of world religions at the invitation of Pope John Paul II, Assisi, October 27, 1986, published jointly by the British Council of Churches and Catholic Truth Society, London, in "Together in Prayer for Peace."

O God our Father, save our shores by Sione Amanaki Havea, Tonga, excerpted from Prayer Calendar 1986–1987 (p. 43), Methodist Church Overseas Division, London, UK.

O Lord, our palm trees, prayer of Tahitian pastor. Source untraced.

Week 35

O God, we pray that you will give, prayer from Seychelles. Source untraced.

O God of all the people and all the nations, Brian Crosby, Beau Bassin, Mauritius.

Lord Jesus, we claim. Source unknown.

Almighty God, always you have wished, by kindness of Jean Margeot, Bishop of Port-Louis, Mauritius.

Week 36

Redeyes, batons, E. Anthony Allen, Bethel Baptist Healing Centre, Kingston, Jamaica.

We are weary of the years, from a litany of justice, hope, and peace, Caribbean Conference of Churches. Used with permission.

O Lord, lead us not into imitation!, prayer of the East Asia Youth Assembly, 1984.

We believe in you, O God, affirmation from Cuba. Source untraced.

Thank you, O Lord our God, 4th Assembly, Caribbean Conference of Churches, 1986. Used with permission.

Lord, how glad we are, prayer from Haiti, from *God is No Stranger,* by Sandra L. Burdick, Baker Book House, Grand Rapids, Michigan, USA.

O God, in baptism, prayer for family life and vocations, from "Praise Yahweh my Soul: Hymnbook of the Roman Catholic Diocese of Kingston, Jamaica."

We pray that thou wilt watch, schoolgirl's prayer from St. Lucia, from "Network," April 1986, USPG, London, UK. Adapted.

Loving Creator, may those who visit, 4th Assembly, Caribbean Conference of Churches, 1986. Used with permission.

O God, we pray that you will keep, opening service, 4th Assembly, Caribbean Conference of Churches, 1986. Used with permission.

Loving God, we are concerned, 4th Assembly, Caribbean Conference of Churches, 1986. Used with permission.

The right hand of God, words by Patrick Prescod; music by Noel Dexter; from "Sing a New Song," No. 3, edited by Patrick Prescod, Caribbean Conference of Churches, Barbados.

Week 37

Give us, Señor, a little sun, prayer on a church wall in Mexico, from "Calendar of Prayer 1986-1987" (p. 53), United Church of Christ Board for World Ministries, USA. Used with permission.

Grant, O Lord, that the people of Belize, from "Quarterly Intercession Paper," No. 328, USPG, London, UK. Adapted.

The message that the poor Christian, testimony given before the US House of Representatives Subcommittee on Human Rights and International Organizations, Committee on Foreign Affairs. Source: *A Vision of Hope,* by Trevor Beeson, 1984 Fontana/Collins, London, UK.

Captivate me, Lord, from "Confession," in *Threatened with Resurrection,* Julia Esquivel, © 1982 Brethren Press, Elgin, Illinois, USA. Used with permission.

Jesus, we believe that you are living, prayer of an Indian woman member of the Guatemalan Committee for Justice and Peace, in "Prayer Manual 1984/1985" (p. 22), Methodist Church Overseas Division, London, UK.

We still pray, Maryknoll Magazine (p. 22), June 1987, Maryknoll, New York, USA. Used with permission.

By his coming. Source unknown.

God of our daily lives, Jan Pickard, "Prayer Manual 1987-1988," Methodist Church Overseas Division, London, UK.

Lord, if this day, prayer from Mexico. Source untraced.

Week 38

Señor, sálvanos de caer, Tómas H. Téllez, Baptist Convention of Nicaragua, Managua.

We live in a world, Oscar Romero, in "Prayer Manual 1984-1985," Methodist Church Overseas Division, London, UK.

I believe in you, Misa Campesina Nicaraguense de Carlos Mejia Godoy.

Nicaragua is as weak, © Division of World Outreach, United Church of Canada, Toronto, quoted in "United Church Observer."

Blessed be God, who is always renewing, act of praise following Vatican II.

Loving Lord, you will the health, Christian Aid, London, UK. Adapted.

And now, when I fall down, Jerjes Ruiz, Seminario Teologico Bautista de Nicaragua, Managua.

Our Father, who are in this our land, Lord's prayer adapted from Christian communities in Nicaragua. Source untraced.

Week 39

Blessed be God, the Divine Praises, Roman Catholic church.

O Christ, as the spear. Source unknown.

O God, we bring before you, Felipe Adolf, from "Calendar of Prayer 1987-1988" (p. 76), United Church of Christ Board for World Ministries, USA. Used with permission.

We believe in a loving God, creed of Camilo Torres, Colombia, from *The Revolutionary Priest: The Complete Writings and Messages of Camilo Torres,* edited by © John Gerassi, 1969 Penguin Books.

O Lord, I don't want, a tourist's prayer, Freda Rajotte, World Council of churches, Geneva, Switzerland.

I hunger and I eat—or more, John Fandel from "AM/PM," Forward Movement Publications, Cincinnati, Ohio, USA.

O God, we find ourselves, by John Poulton, 1983 "Week of Prayer for Christian Unity," British Council of Churches Publications, London, UK.

Stop! ferocious animal, prayer to stop a dog from biting, from *Unicef Book of Children's Prayers,* by William I Kaufman, The Stackpole Co., Harrisburg, USA. © With the permission of William I. Kaufman.

Week 40

O Lord, grant us to love you, prayer attributed to the prophet Muhammed.

We must have patience, a woman of the Peulhs, a Fulani nomadic group from Niger, from a collection in *Christian Aid Focus on the Sahel,* Christian Aid, London, UK.

Life is made up of happiness, a Fulani woman, from a collection in *Christian Aid Focus on the Sahel,* Christian Aid, London, UK.

O God, who comes to us, No. 42 in *Jesus Christ the Life of the World: a Worship Book,* 1983 World Council of Churches Publications, Geneva, Switzerland. Adapted.

We pray, O Lord, for the nomads, from "Quarterly Intercession Paper," No. 321, USPG, London, UK.

Lord God, spring of living water, Michael Saward, from *Task Unfinished,* Falcon Booklet, London, UK. Adapted.

Lord, help us to accept, from "Day by Day," Forward Movement Publications, 412 Sycamore Street, Cincinnati, Ohio 45202-4195, USA.

Almighty God, you have given us grace, prayer of the Third Antiphon, Liturgy of St. John Chrysostom, 5th century.

Week 41

Lord Jesus, print on us, from *Take up Your Cross: Meditations on the Way to the Cross,* Fr. Engelbert Mveng, SJ, 1963 ©1963 Fr. Engelbert Mveng, SJ. Reprinted by permission of Geoffrey Chapman, a division of Cassell Publishers Ltd., Artillery House, Artillery Row, London SW1P 1RT, UK.

When I think of my mother, Ruth Engi Tjeea, Cameroon, Fellowship of the Least Coin. Used with permission.

Where two or three are gathered, Bayiga Bayiga © music; text, Bassa and English: Bayiga Bayiga, Edéa, Cameroon.

O Lord, with sorrow and dismay, prayer of confession from Presbyterian Church in Cameroon, Buea, Republic of Cameroon. Used with permission.

Lord God, grant that we might sleep, a night prayer from Diola, Cameroon by Cirillo Tescaroli, from *Heart of Prayer: African, Jewish, and Biblical Prayer,* by Antony Gittens, Wm. B. Collins, London, UK.

My God, I praise you, I thank you, Mamia Woungly-Massage, "Le tronc béni de la prière," 1980 Editions du Soc, Lausanne, Switzerland.

We pray you, Lord our God and Father, from a prayer for refugees, Pedro Tunga, Association des Eglises baptistes évangéliques central-africaines, B.P. 1350, Bangui. Permission given.

Almight God, Lord of heaven and earth, prayer of planting, Presbyterian Church in Cameroon. Permission given.

God of love, God of mercy, from a prayer for harvest in a time of drought, Pedro Tunga, Association des Eglises baptistes évangéliques central-africaines, B.P. 1350, Bangui. Permission given.

Week 42

He comes to us, Albert Schweitzer, from *The Quest for the Historical Jesus,* by Albert Schweitzer, 1968 The Macmillan Publisher Co, Inc. © A. & C. Black Ltd., London, UK.

I will follow you, Jesus, Congolese hymn, from *Simon Kimbangu: An African Prophet and His Church,* by Marie-Louise Martin, 1975 Wm. B. Eerdmans Publishing Co., Grand Rapids, Michigan, USA.

Jesus, we want to grow, children's prayer, in *Journey of Struggle, Journey in Hope: People and Their Pilgrimage in Central Africa,* by Jan Heaton, Friendship Press, New York, USA.

Lord Jesus Christ, you said to your apostles, the Roman Mass.

O God: enlarge my heart, prayer of an African Christian. Source untraced.

Week 43

The cross is the hope, 10th-century African hymn, used in the prayer manual of the Methodist Church Overseas Division, London, UK.

We bless you for sending, prayer for Burundi Christians, Louis Lochet, Foyers de Charité.

O Saviour of the world, Salvator mundi.

May the brokenness, revival grace. Source unknown.

I thank you, Almighty God, a prayer said to have been used by Simon Kimbangu, from *Simon Kimbangu: an African Prophet and his Church,* by Marie-Louise Martin, 1975 Wm. B. Eerdmans Publishing Co., Grand Rapids, Michigan, USA.

Bless, O Lord, all such courageous Christians. Source Unknown.

God, Bless Africa, prayer for Africa, Trevor Huddleston.

Grant us prudence, prayer for peace, Conference of European Churches, Gloria Deo Worship Book, 9th Assembly, 1986.

Week 44

Graciously comfort, Martin Luther, reprinted by permission from *Luther's Prayers,* © 1967 Augsburg Publisher House, Minneapolis, USA.

God, our Father, we thank you for putting new life, prayer of East German woman, Fellowship of the Least Coin. Used with permission.

Almighty and eternal God, from a Roman Catholic agape celebration, edited by A. Schilling, "Fürbitten und Kanongebete der Holländischen Kirche," 1972 12th edition, Verlag Hans Driewer, Essen, Federal Republic of Germany.

I believe that God both can and will, an extract from Dietrich Bonhoeffer, *Letters and Papers*

from Prison, enlarged edition, 1971 SCM Press, London, UK. British Commonwealth rights including Canada. For USA: Macmillan Publishing Company, Inc., New York, USA.

Week 45

Lord, save us from being self-centred, prayer based on words of John Calvin, *Contemporary Parish Prayers* (pp. 106–107), by Frank Colquhoun, 1975 Hodder & Stoughton, London, UK.

O God, the giver of life, prayer used in the Ecumenical Centre, Geneva, on the occasion of the visit of Pope John Paul II, 1984.

Let our chief end, O God, after Calvin's catechism.

We thank you, gracious God, for the beauty, from the liturgy of the German-speaking Evangelical Reformed Church of Switzerland, Taschenausgave, p. 16, No. 4, 1986 Zurich. Adapted from a prayer of the Episcopal Church, USA, by H. Bernoulli.

Upheld by the prayers of St. Nicholas, prayer for the feast of Nicholas von Flüe, Swiss Missal.

Dear Heavenly Father, send your Holy Spirit, we pray, Aus: Barth, Karl: Gebete. 4 Aufl. 1974 (München). Rechte: Theologischer Verlag Zürich.

Week 46

All-powerful and ever-living God, Solemnity of All Saints, the Roman Missal.

Blessed are you, O Lord our God, Rabbi Moshe Hakotun, said to have been written in Venice, from "God of a Hundred Names" (p. 115), compiled by Barbara Greene and Victor Gollancz, 1962 Victor Gollancz Ltd, London, UK.

Lord, may I ever speak, prayer of Chiara Lubich, founder of The Focolare Movement, "Spiel mit gottlichen Rollen" (p. 130), Neue Stadt Verlag, Munich, Federal Republic of Germany. © Città Nuova Editrice, Rome, Italy. Used with permission.

O God, Creator, Redeemer, prayer from the Waldensian liturgy.

O Lord, you have said to us, prayer from the Waldensian liturgy.

Week 47

Dear Jesus, as a hen covers, Indian origin. Source unknown.

About prayer, a former bishop of Dacca. Source untraced.

Grant, O Lord, that we may expect, William Carey of Serampore.

Save us, O Lord, waking, from Compline.

O servant Lord, teach us, Episcopal Church of Scotland, Mission Department. Used with permission.

God is here. Source unknown.

Lord, give us the strength. Source unknown.

O Lord, hear our petitions, prayer-hymn originally sung on the borders of Nepal. Source untraced.

Week 48

Almighty God, whose dominion, from "Empty Shoes" (p. 27), Highway Press/Church Missionary Society, London, UK.

In the absence of Afghan Christians, traveler in Afghanistan. Source untraced.

O Creator God, we rejoice. Source unknown.

Yisu ke pichhe main chalne laga. Source unknown.

O Creator and Mighty God, prayer from Pakistan from "Now," December 1987, Methodist Church Overseas Division, London, UK.

O Heavenly Father, prayer of a Punjabi Christian. Source untraced.

Look graciously, O Lord, upon this land, based on the words "O Lord, be gracious to our land," from *Morning and Evening Prayer*, Church of Pakistan.

Week 49

Almighty God, who to your holy apostle, collect from the commemoration of St. Thomas.

O Lord, let me rest, prayer of an Indian Christian. Source untraced.

Cities are springing up, "Message for the City," from *About You and Me* (p. 44), by M.A. Thomas, Courtesy Christian Literature Society, Madras, India, 1975.

O God, we would pray at this time, daily prayer suggested for use by members of the Syrian Orthodox church dispersed abroad, from *Prayer Book for Young People*, Sophia Publications, Orthodox Seminary, Kottayam, Kerala, India.

What we need, Lord, is mercy, petition of Sri Lankan church leader. Source untraced.

Lord Jesus, you were awakened, prayer from Sri Lanka, fellowship of the Least Coin. Used with permission.

Remembering St. Thomas, Olive Hitchcock. Source untraced.

Week 50

We pray for Africa with, Christian prayer for peace with representatives of the church and ecclesial communities and of world religions at the invitation of Pope John Paul II, Assisi, October 27, 1986, published jointly by the British Council of Churches and Catholic Truth Society, London, in "Together in Prayer for Peace."

We sincerely thank you, O God, João Makondekwa, © Bible Society of Angola, used in "Prayer Manual 1984-1985" (p. 13), Methodist Church Overseas Division, London, UK.

O Lord, we pray for justice, prayer for Mozambique, USPG, London, UK.

I wonder if we are aware, by Dinis Sengulane, Bishop of Lebombo, Mozambique, courtesy of "Lebombo Leaves," Spring 1979, chronicle of the Diocese of Lebombo, published by the Lebombo Association, London, UK.

Week 51

Almighty God, as your Son or Saviour, Toc H. quoted from George Appleton's *The Oxford Book of Prayer*, No. 218, 1985 Oxford University Press, London, UK.

To those brought up, Chris Race, a South African priest, reported in "13/Background to Mission, Botswana, Partners in Mission with the Province of Central Africa", USPG, London, UK.

O God, we pray for those places. Source unknown.

O God, friend of the poor, a pastor's prayer, "Prayer Manual 1985-1986," Methodist Church Overseas Division, London, UK.

Open my eyes, Canaan Banana, first president of Zimbabwe, from *The Gospel According to the Ghetto* (p. 21), 1981 Mambo Press, Gweru, Zimbabwe.

O God of all nations and people, African bidding. Source untraced.

Week 52

Lord Jesus Christ, you are, prayer from South Africa. Source untraced.

Lord, we think you know, prayer prepared by staff and students of Roma Theological Seminary, from "Network," April 1986, USPG, London. Adapted.

We wail and cry, Abisai Shejavili, Council of Churches in Mamibia.

To you, O God, we lift, Source unknown.

O God, I am oppressed: ascribed to Hezekiah, King of Judah in 707 BC, "An Anthology of Prayers," A.S.T. Fisher, Longman, Green & Co., London, UK.

O Christ, who hast known fear, "Network," USPG, London, UK.

O Lord, help us who roam about, prayer used in 1947 by the late chief of the Hereros, Hosea Kutako, in entrusting Michael Scott with the mission of persuading the UN to take up Namibia's case. Source untraced.

Lord Jesus Christ, voice of the voiceless, from "Kulimukweni. © Council of Churches in Namibia. Adapted.

The time has come, Kairos Document, Braamfontein, 1985.

In word and deed, prayer of a multi-racial group in Johannesburg. Source untraced.

Thank you God, that you care, by Desmond Tutu, South Africa.

Now, God, will you please open, by Desmond Tutu, South Africa.

Almighty God, you whose own son, South African Council of Churches, Refugee Sunday liturgy.

Loving Father, your young and lovable Son, Simeon Nkoane CR, "Spirituality in a Violent Society," Eric Symes Abbot Memorial Lecture, Kings College, London, May 1987.

O God, whose righteous wisdom, Crossroads Camp prayer, in *Cry Justice*, by John de Gruchy, © 1986 Orbis Books, Maryknoll, USA. UK: Wm. B. Collins, London, UK.

A litany of rejoicing, a service of celebration, Cape Town, in *Cry Justice* (pp. 212-213), by John de Gruchy, © 1986 Orbis Books, Maryknoll, USA. UK: Wm. B. Collins, London, UK.

O God, may this great, Source unknown.

As the earth keeps turning, closing prayer, WCC Assembly, Vancouver 1983, from *Let's Worship* (p. 25), Risk Book Vol. II, No. 2-3, 1975 World Council of Churches Publications, Geneva, Switzerland.

A World at Prayer
The New Ecumenical Prayer Cycle

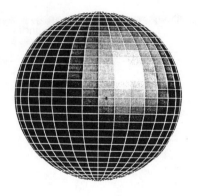